THE PUZZLE POST

PUZZLE FUN!

The Ultimate Brainbending Workout

1 MINUTE NUMBER CRUNCH

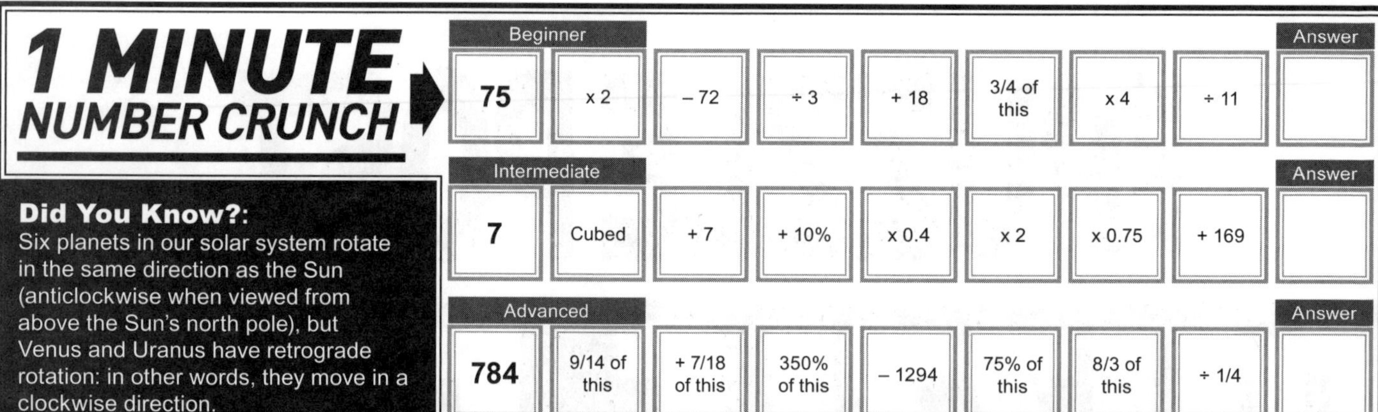

Beginner								Answer
75	x 2	– 72	÷ 3	+ 18	3/4 of this	x 4	÷ 11	

Intermediate								Answer
7	Cubed	+ 7	+ 10%	x 0.4	x 2	x 0.75	+ 169	

Advanced								Answer
784	9/14 of this	+ 7/18 of this	350% of this	– 1294	75% of this	8/3 of this	÷ 1/4	

Did You Know?:
Six planets in our solar system rotate in the same direction as the Sun (anticlockwise when viewed from above the Sun's north pole), but Venus and Uranus have retrograde rotation: in other words, they move in a clockwise direction.

HIGH-SPEED CROSSWORD

Across

1 Went beyond (8)
7 Rationality (6)
8 Start, commencement (6)
10 Metallic cylinder used for storage (8)
11 Look at intently (5)
13 Rumour (7)
16 Atomic (7)
17 Having a sharp inclination (5)
20 Belonging to the past (8)
22 Take into custody (6)
24 Delivered a blow to (6)
25 In no specific place (8)

Down

1 Runs off with fiancé (6)
2 Animal kept as a domestic pet (3)
3 Drainage channel (5)
4 Showing signs of having had too much alcohol (7)
5 Metal food containers (4)
6 Produced by oneself, not mass manufactured (4-4)
9 Whorl (6)
12 Holidaymakers (8)
14 Somewhat (6)
15 Capsicum spice (7)
18 Tool used with a mortar (6)
19 Very frightening (5)
21 Tightly drawn (4)
23 Centre of a storm (3)

IQ WORKOUT

What comes next in this sequence?

CODEWORD CONUNDRUM

DOUBLE FUN SUDOKU

TASTY TEASER

	6				3		1	
		9		6	4	5		
1	7	4				6	2	3
		3			5		7	
7			9		1			2
	4		6			8		
4	8	2				7	9	1
		7	2	8		3		
	9		4				5	

BRAIN BUSTER

		4	9					7
3		6					1	
	5		1			4	8	
		8			2			
2								4
			7			9		
	8	9			7		6	
	6					5		3
1					6	7		

SPIDOKU

Each of the eight segments of the spider's web should be filled with a different number from 1 to 8, in such a way that every ring also contains a different number from 1 to 8.

LOGI-SIX

Every row and column of this grid should contain one each of the letters A, B, C, D, E and F. Each of the six shapes (marked by thicker lines) should also contain one each of the letters A, B, C, D, E and F. Can you complete the grid?

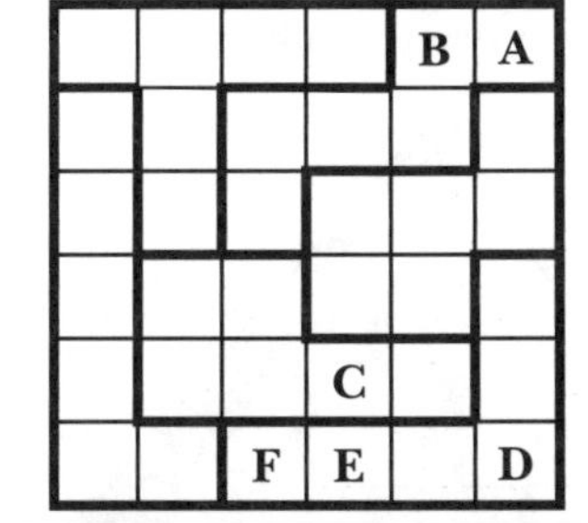

HIGH-SPEED CROSSWORD

Across
1 Job (6)
5 Beetle considered divine by ancient Egyptians (6)
8 Man-eating giant (4)
9 Quantity (6)
10 Judge tentatively (5)
11 Follow instruction (4)
12 Not in action (4)
13 To the opposite side (6)
15 Methods (4)
17 Noise made by a snake (4)
19 Plant similar to the rhododendron (6)
20 Part of a lock (4)
21 Fête (4)
22 First letter of the Greek alphabet (5)
24 Direction leading to the centre (6)
25 Waterside plant (4)
26 Overabundance (6)
27 Marriage partner (6)

Down
2 Branch of mathematics (7)
3 Mournful poem (5)
4 Contest of speed (4)
5 Coast (8)
6 Do away with (7)
7 Swimmers (7)
14 Acting game, popular at Christmas (8)
15 Location of a series of pages on the internet (7)
16 Fill to satisfaction (7)
18 Vendors (7)
21 Greta ___, film star (1905-1990) (5)
23 Succeed in an examination (4)

WORDSEARCH WORKOUT

S	T	A	Y	O	S	X	Y	E	J	M	A	D
D	L	J	I	Y	C	L	T	H	Z	W	J	F
N	A	X	R	S	J	A	O	G	V	I	K	N
A	C	I	D	E	I	U	N	V	B	R	L	O
L	A	E	A	L	V	N	A	O	A	O	Q	B
R	N	I	I	A	I	G	U	M	M	K	K	A
E	A	R	N	W	P	T	N	T	D	J	I	G
H	D	E	A	O	I	E	A	N	G	O	L	A
T	A	L	U	U	D	L	I	B	A	J	Q	W
E	E	A	H	A	B	E	A	H	I	A	A	V
N	V	N	T	E	J	J	C	P	T	R	H	D
N	P	D	I	T	A	L	Y	A	E	B	I	Z
V	B	S	L	F	N	G	R	W	M	N	G	K
L	N	Q	H	E	C	C	Y	K	X	V	X	U
A	I	V	T	A	L	E	U	Z	E	N	E	V

COUNTRIES OF THE WORLD

ANGOLA
CANADA
DENMARK
DJIBOUTI
GABON
IRELAND
ITALY
KIRIBATI
LATVIA
LITHUANIA
MACEDONIA
MONACO
NEPAL
NETHERLANDS
QATAR
SLOVAKIA
SYRIA
TUNISIA
VENEZUELA
WALES

DOUBLE FUN SUDOKU

TASTY TEASER

			5	6	9			
	5					1		3
4	8			3		6	2	
8			3			9	1	2
		5	6		2	3		
7	3	2			8			4
	4	6		8			5	9
1		3					8	
			2	7	6			

BRAIN BUSTER

		8	6		1	3		
1								6
9		7		4		2		8
			2		4			
6								9
			3		9			
5		9		3		1		4
2								5
		4	9		5	8		

MATCHSTICK MAGIC

Move two matchsticks to make two squares.

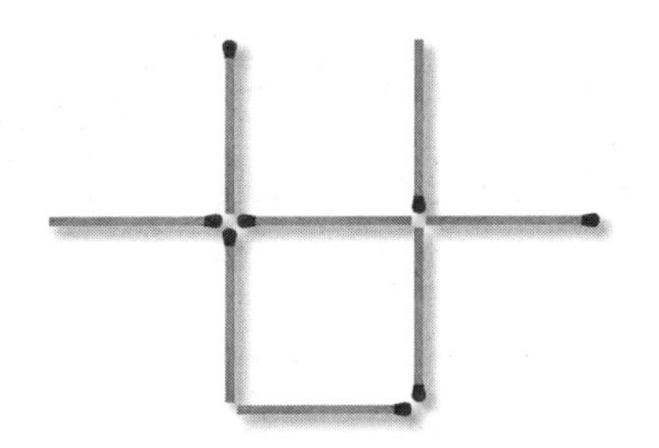

BRAIN TEASER

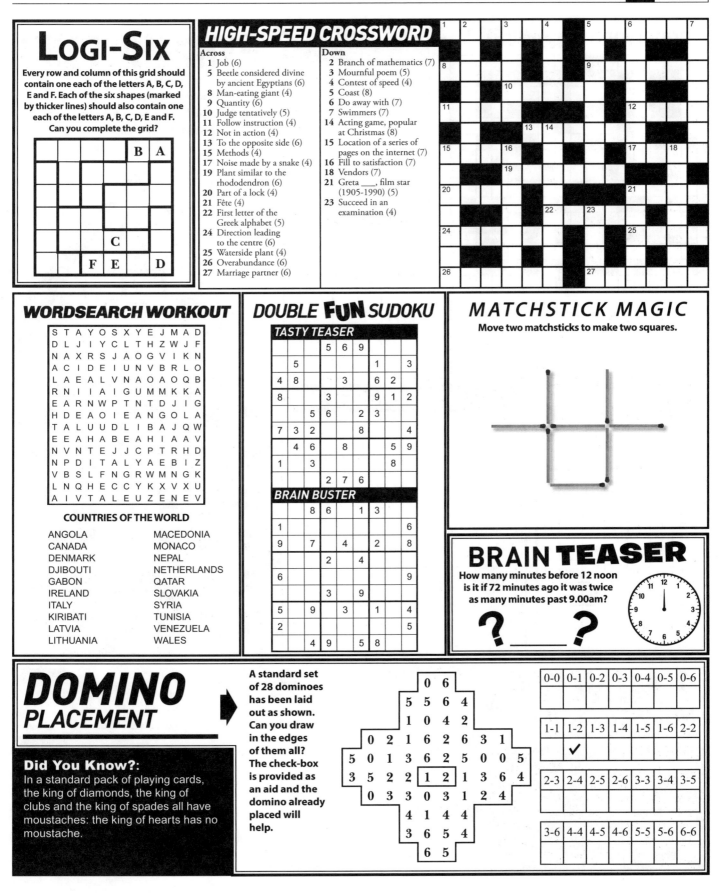

How many minutes before 12 noon is it if 72 minutes ago it was twice as many minutes past 9.00am?

______

DOMINO PLACEMENT

A standard set of 28 dominoes has been laid out as shown. Can you draw in the edges of them all? The check-box is provided as an aid and the domino already placed will help.

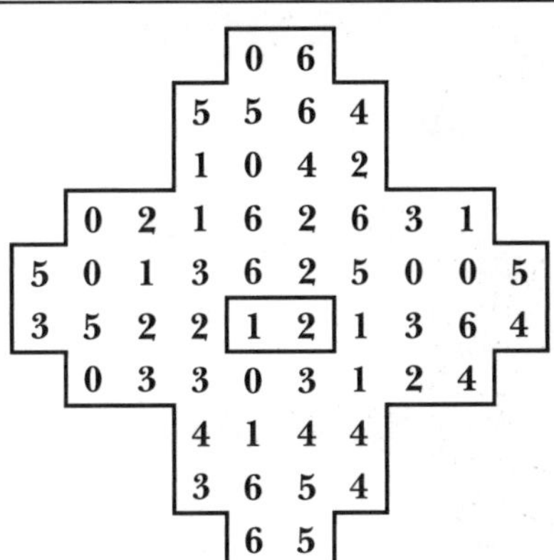

0-0	0-1	0-2	0-3	0-4	0-5	0-6

1-1	1-2	1-3	1-4	1-5	1-6	2-2
	✓					

2-3	2-4	2-5	2-6	3-3	3-4	3-5

3-6	4-4	4-5	4-6	5-5	5-6	6-6

Did You Know?:

In a standard pack of playing cards, the king of diamonds, the king of clubs and the king of spades all have moustaches: the king of hearts has no moustache.

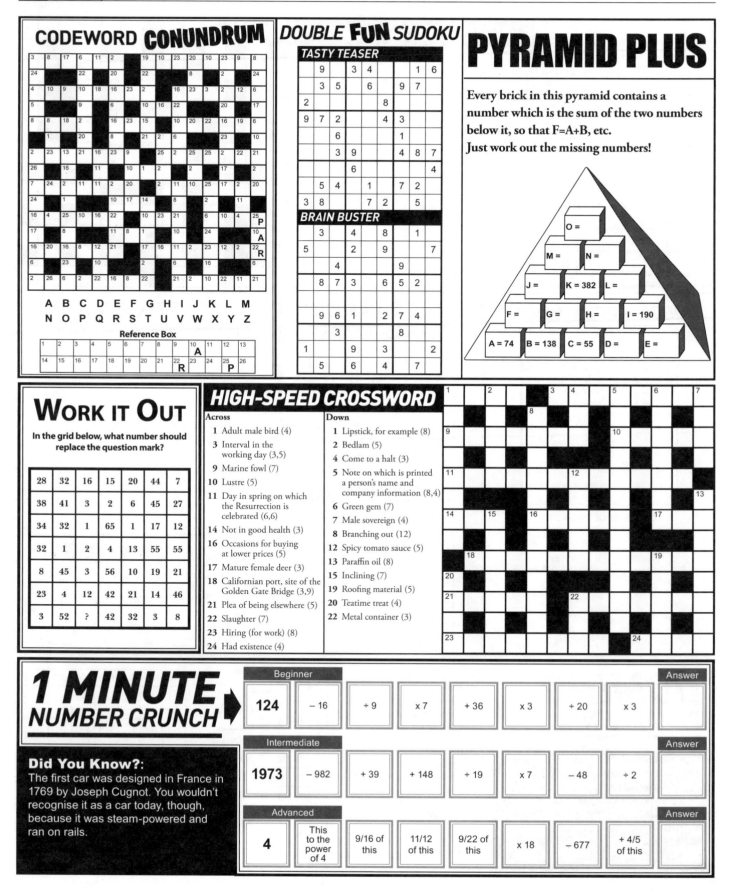

CODEWORD CONUNDRUM

A B C D E F G H I J K L M

N O P Q R S T U V W X Y Z

Reference Box

1	2	3	4	5	6	7	8	9	10 A	11	12	13
14	15	16	17	18	19	20	21	22 R	23	24	25 P	26

DOUBLE FUN SUDOKU

TASTY TEASER

	9		3	4			1	6
	3	5		6		9	7	
2					8			
9	7	2			4	3		
		6				1		
		3	9			4	8	7
			6					4
	5	4		1		7	2	
3	8			7	2		5	

BRAIN BUSTER

	3		4		8		1	
5			2		9			7
		4				9		
	8	7	3		6	5	2	
	9	6	1		2	7	4	
		3				8		
1			9		3			2
	5		6		4		7	

PYRAMID PLUS

Every brick in this pyramid contains a number which is the sum of the two numbers below it, so that F=A+B, etc.
Just work out the missing numbers!

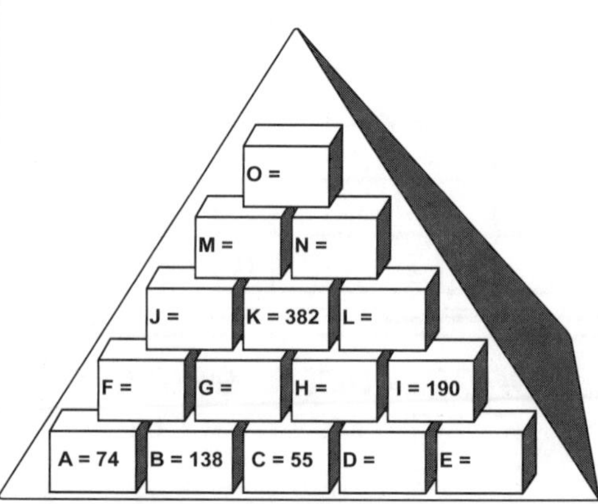

WORK IT OUT

In the grid below, what number should replace the question mark?

28	32	16	15	20	44	7
38	41	3	2	6	45	27
34	32	1	65	1	17	12
32	1	2	4	13	55	55
8	45	3	56	10	19	21
23	4	12	42	21	14	46
3	52	?	42	32	3	8

HIGH-SPEED CROSSWORD

Across

1 Adult male bird (4)
3 Interval in the working day (3,5)
9 Marine fowl (7)
10 Lustre (5)
11 Day in spring on which the Resurrection is celebrated (6,6)
14 Not in good health (3)
16 Occasions for buying at lower prices (5)
17 Mature female deer (3)
18 Californian port, site of the Golden Gate Bridge (3,9)
21 Plea of being elsewhere (5)
22 Slaughter (7)
23 Hiring (for work) (8)
24 Had existence (4)

Down

1 Lipstick, for example (8)
2 Bedlam (5)
4 Come to a halt (3)
5 Note on which is printed a person's name and company information (8,4)
6 Green gem (7)
7 Male sovereign (4)
8 Branching out (12)
12 Spicy tomato sauce (5)
13 Paraffin oil (8)
15 Inclining (7)
19 Roofing material (5)
20 Teatime treat (4)
22 Metal container (3)

1 MINUTE NUMBER CRUNCH

Beginner								Answer
124	– 16	÷ 9	x 7	+ 36	x 3	÷ 20	x 3	

Intermediate								Answer
1973	– 982	+ 39	+ 148	÷ 19	x 7	– 48	÷ 2	

Advanced								Answer
4	This to the power of 4	9/16 of this	11/12 of this	9/22 of this	x 18	– 677	+ 4/5 of this	

Did You Know?:
The first car was designed in France in 1769 by Joseph Cugnot. You wouldn't recognise it as a car today, though, because it was steam-powered and ran on rails.

HIGH-SPEED CROSSWORD

Across

1 Snag (5)
4 Drop sharply (7)
8 Egg cells (3)
9 Has in mind (5)
10 Sharp part of a knife (5)
11 In a cheerful manner (10)
13 Slip away (6)
15 Clothes cupboard (6)
18 Warning given in error (5,5)
22 Deport from a country (5)
23 Make a thrusting forward movement (5)
24 Grow older (3)
25 Emanating from stars (7)
26 Holds fast (5)

Down

1 Writer of music (8)
2 Disreputable wanderer (5)
3 Woman who invites guests to a social event (7)
4 Local church community (6)
5 Characteristic of a city (5)
6 Childhood disease (7)
7 Swarm (4)
12 First courses (8)
14 Greed (7)
16 Brochure (7)
17 Salted roe of a sturgeon (6)
19 Alloy of iron and carbon (5)
20 Mood disorder (5)
21 Professional charges (4)

IQ WORKOUT

Draw in the hands on the final clock.

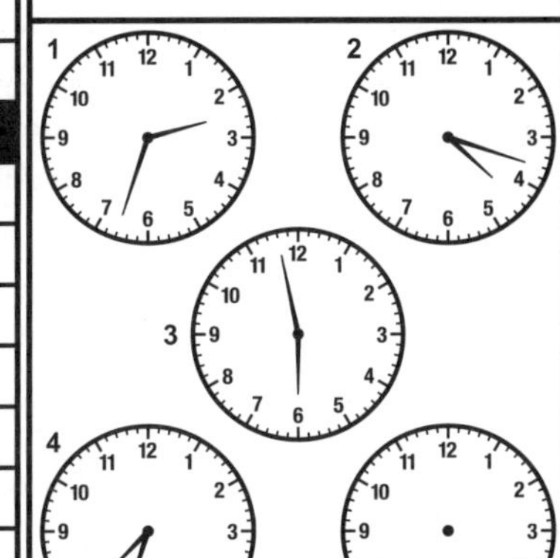

1 MINUTE NUMBER CRUNCH

Beginner								Answer
9	x 8	Plus half of this	– 56	÷ 4	+ 94	– 11	÷ 6	

Intermediate								Answer
87	+ 56	x 3	Double it	– 669	4/9 of this	5/7 of this	220% of this	

Advanced								Answer
20	Cubed	99% of this	3/5 of this	+ 3/16 of this	– 3979	9/32 of this	x 7	

Did You Know?:
The coconut crab lives on land and will drown if submerged in water. It lives on islands in the Indian Ocean and can grow to one metre across.

WORDSEARCH WORKOUT

W T U N I B B Y D A Z F E
Z E S U G E C C P B M N H
C V R O F O G I L I A N J
H C I U R G V O S C D N G
I H V S T I C T I G N E Y
L A T Y I A A R N E L A G
L Z C Y L B R F W E T C O
F Y R L P U I E E I T Y L
A D Y P H H Z L P E E R O
C C H A R T O G I M M E R
T W L D T A C O Z T E P O
O G I O H T C O N M Y T E
R A I N U D C J M L D H T
S S T D D D R Q W V O F E
R T Z K R P G B F T V H M

WEATHER

CHART
CHILL FACTOR
CLOUD
DRY
FAIR
FOG
GALE
HAZY
HOT
HURRICANE
ICY
LOCALLY
METEOROLOGY
MIST
RAIN
TEMPERATURE
TYPHOON
VISIBILITY
WET
WIND

DOUBLE FUN SUDOKU

TASTY TEASER

	1			8			7	
4			1		7			2
	7	2		5		8	9	
	4	5	3		8	7	6	
7			5		4			8
	3	8	7		9	4	1	
	2	4		3		9	8	
9			8		1			6
	6			4			5	

BRAIN BUSTER

		3			2		9	7
	9			3				5
1		6				8		
			4			9	8	
	2	1			9			
		7				6		8
5				4			1	
8	3		6			2		

WHATEVER NEXT?

In the diagram below, which letter should replace the question mark?

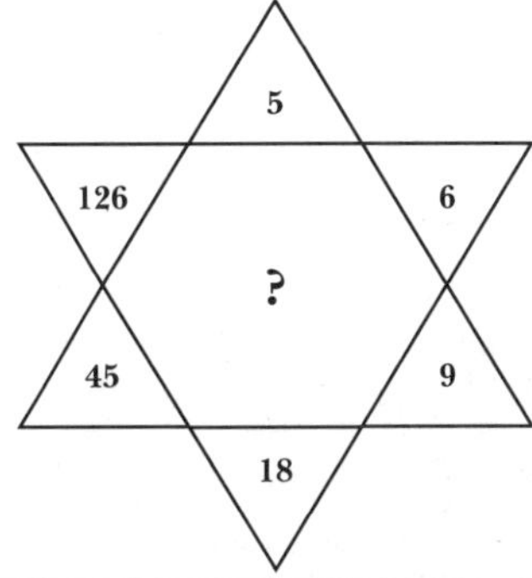

BRAIN TEASER

What number should replace the question mark?

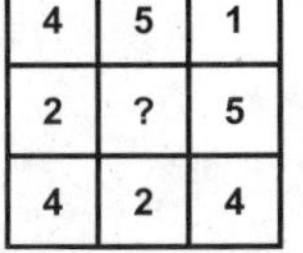

4	5	1
2	?	5
4	2	4

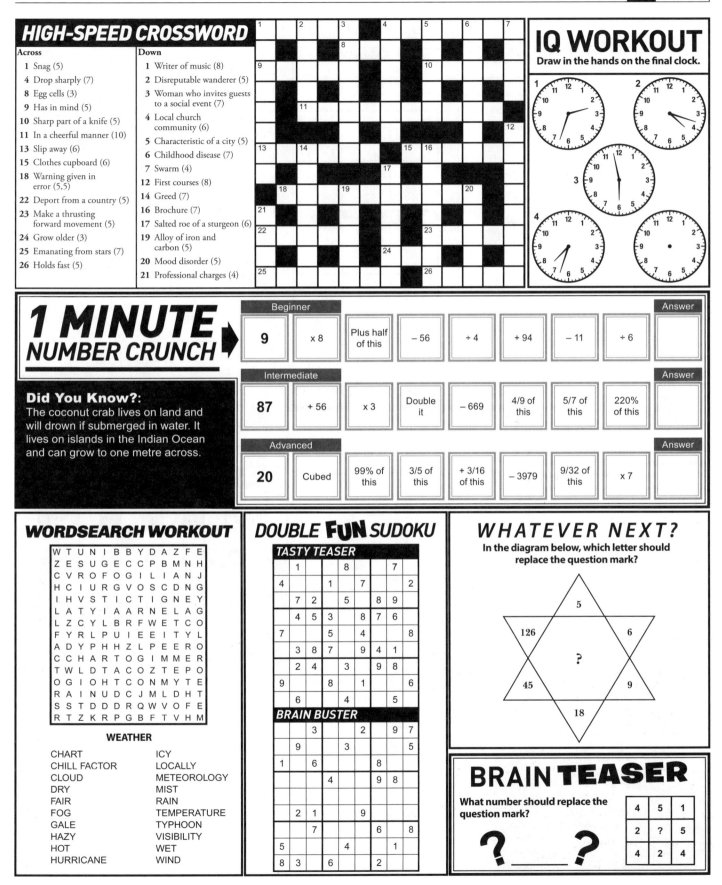

? ______ ?

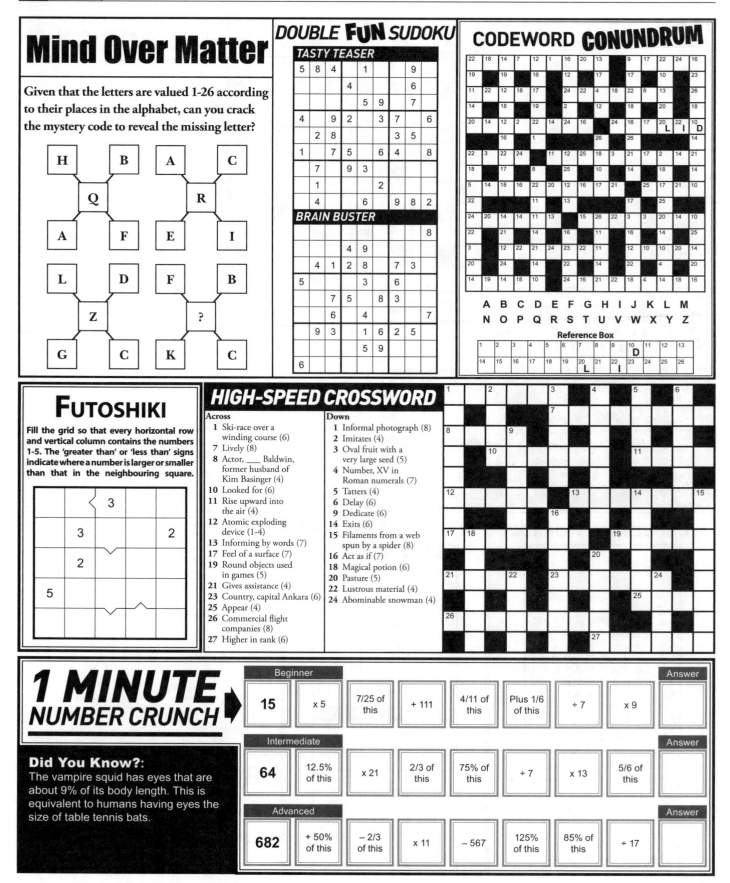

Mind Over Matter

Given that the letters are valued 1-26 according to their places in the alphabet, can you crack the mystery code to reveal the missing letter?

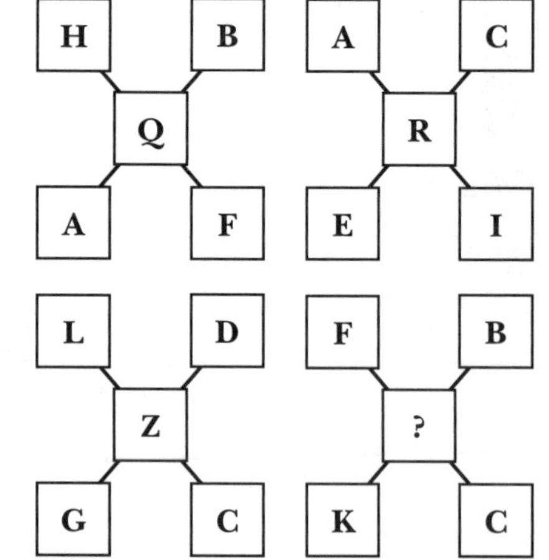

DOUBLE FUN SUDOKU

TASTY TEASER

5	8	4		1			9	
			4				6	
				5	9		7	
4		9	2		3	7		6
	2	8				3	5	
1		7	5		6	4		8
	7		9	3				
	1				2			
	4			6		9	8	2

BRAIN BUSTER

								8
			4	9				
	4	1	2	8		7	3	
5				3		6		
		7	5		8	3		
		6		4				7
	9	3		1	6	2	5	
				5	9			
6								

CODEWORD CONUNDRUM

Fill the grid so that every horizontal row and vertical column contains the numbers 1-5. The 'greater than' or 'less than' signs indicate where a number is larger or smaller than that in the neighbouring square.

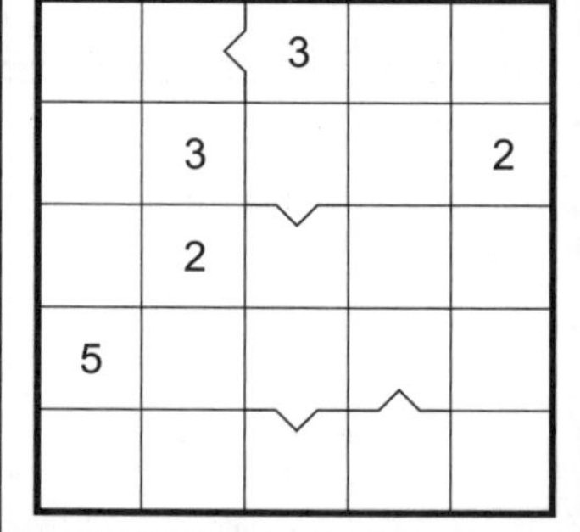

HIGH-SPEED CROSSWORD

Across

1 Ski-race over a winding course (6)
7 Lively (8)
8 Actor, ___ Baldwin, former husband of Kim Basinger (4)
10 Looked for (6)
11 Rise upward into the air (4)
12 Atomic exploding device (1-4)
13 Informing by words (7)
17 Feel of a surface (7)
19 Round objects used in games (5)
21 Gives assistance (4)
23 Country, capital Ankara (6)
25 Appear (4)
26 Commercial flight companies (8)
27 Higher in rank (6)

Down

1 Informal photograph (8)
2 Imitates (4)
3 Oval fruit with a very large seed (5)
4 Number, XV in Roman numerals (7)
5 Tatters (4)
6 Delay (6)
9 Dedicate (6)
14 Exits (6)
15 Filaments from a web spun by a spider (8)
16 Act as if (7)
18 Magical potion (6)
20 Pasture (5)
22 Lustrous material (4)
24 Abominable snowman (4)

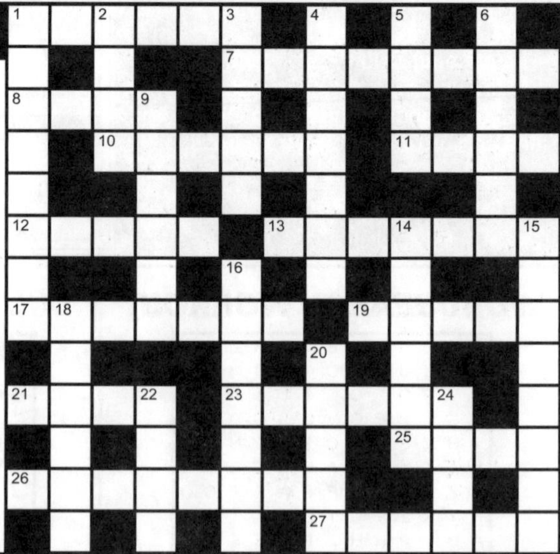

1 MINUTE NUMBER CRUNCH

Beginner

15	x 5	7/25 of this	+ 111	4/11 of this	Plus 1/6 of this	÷ 7	x 9	Answer

Intermediate

64	12.5% of this	x 21	2/3 of this	75% of this	÷ 7	x 13	5/6 of this	Answer

Advanced

682	+ 50% of this	– 2/3 of this	x 11	– 567	125% of this	85% of this	÷ 17	Answer

Did You Know?:
The vampire squid has eyes that are about 9% of its body length. This is equivalent to humans having eyes the size of table tennis bats.

BATTLESHIP BOUT

Can you place the vessels into the diagram? Some parts of vessels or sea squares have already been filled in. A number to the right or below a row or column refers to the number of occupied squares in that row or column.
Any vessel may be positioned horizontally or vertically, but no part of a vessel touches part of any other vessel, either horizontally, vertically or diagonally.

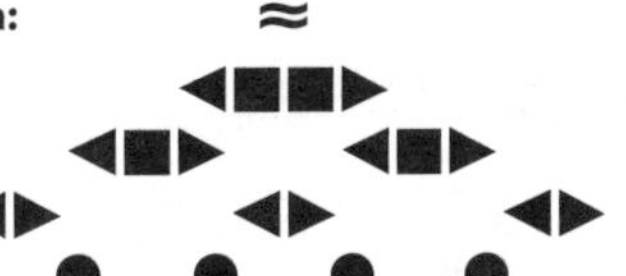

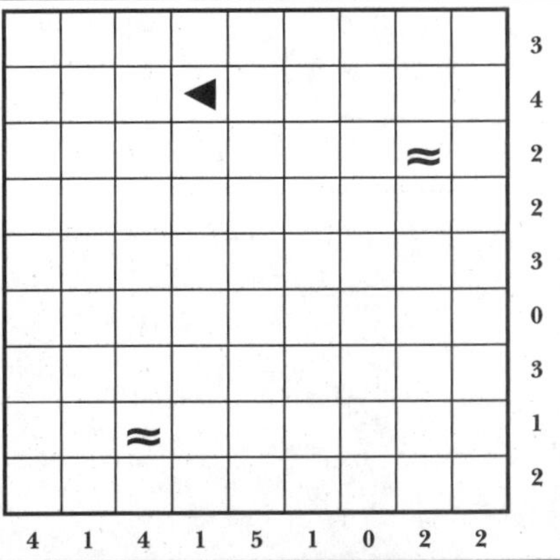

Did You Know?:
The planet Mars has two moons, Phobos and Deimos (Fear and Terror). Unlike Earth's moon, Luna, they are not spherical, and have the appearance of giant potatoes.

HIGH-SPEED CROSSWORD

Across

1 Receptacles for business documents (7,5)
9 Cowboy contest (5)
10 Primitive plant forms (5)
11 Speck (3)
12 Narrow backstreet (5)
13 Put into words (7)
14 Bunch of cords fastened at one end (6)
16 Relative position (6)
20 Sleeping room (7)
22 Largest artery of the body (5)
24 Adult male person (3)
25 Beauty parlour (5)
26 Figure out (5)
27 Meeting requirements (12)

Down

2 Relating to sea waves (5)
3 Analgesic (7)
4 Hurry (6)
5 Car wheel immobilising device (5)
6 Portion (7)
7 Stalks of a plant (5)
8 Bosom (6)
15 Blood-red (7)
17 Passage (7)
18 Formed (6)
19 Fleet of warships (6)
20 Prices (5)
21 Component parts of a skeleton (5)
23 Measuring stick (5)

IQ WORKOUT

What comes next in this sequence?

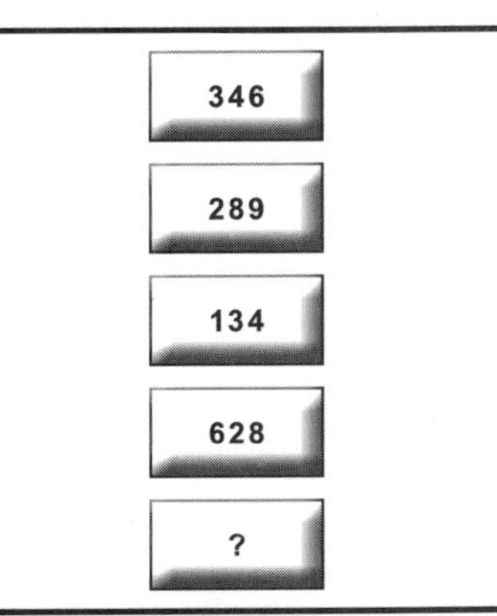

WORDWHEEL

Using only the letters in the Wordwheel, you have ten minutes to find as many words as possible, none of which may be plurals, foreign words or proper nouns. Each word must be of three letters or more, all must contain the central letter and letters can only be used once in every word. There is at least one nine-letter word in the wheel.

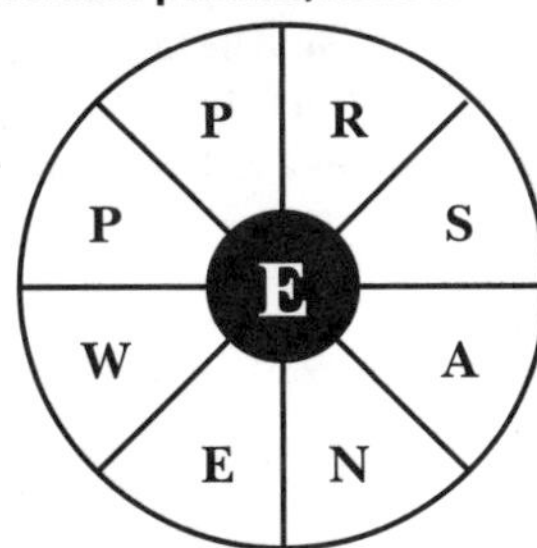

Nine-letter word(s): ______________________

SUM CIRCLE

Fill the three empty circles with the symbols +, – and x in some order, to make a sum which totals the number in the centre. Each symbol must be used once and calculations are made in the direction of travel (clockwise).

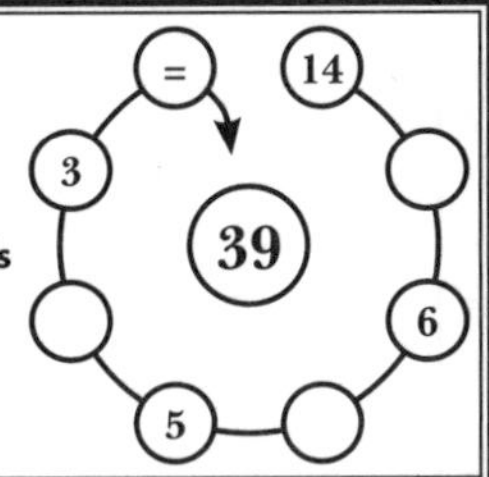

WORDSEARCH WORKOUT

```
S Y T T L R G F T V D L B
C Y F S O E N K R E X A A
A O I B S T I C T O T I A
L D O X S R L A R X B R G
E R D T Y A L J S K V E F
P W E H C U O H B I Z A K
V R V G C Q R G O T L O Z
N E N I U O A B C C O L E
O J T A P D M Z A H V G I
F R L R M N Q P J E Q N U
A O M T I K A O A N E I R
Q Z O S V E A F M N L D Y
O B T R X K R O P E I L V
R E W E R B N A T H T O U
P L Z Y Z E R I H Y S F N
```

LADDERS

AERIAL
ARTICULATED
COMPANION
ETRIER
FOLDING
HOOK
JACK
JACOB'S
KITCHEN
LOFT
QUARTER
ROLLING
ROOF
ROPE
SCALE
SIDE
STEP
STERN
STILE
STRAIGHT

DOUBLE FUN SUDOKU

TASTY TEASER

	8		9		5		7	
6		2		3		9		8
		7		6		4		
9		3	1		8	5		6
	1		4		6		9	
4		6	3		9	7		1
		5		9		1		
2		1		4		8		9
	6		5		1		2	

BRAIN BUSTER

			8					1
				9	2			5
5	8	4		3				9
		2					5	
6		7				1		8
	3					2		
9				1		4	6	2
2			5	7				
3					6			

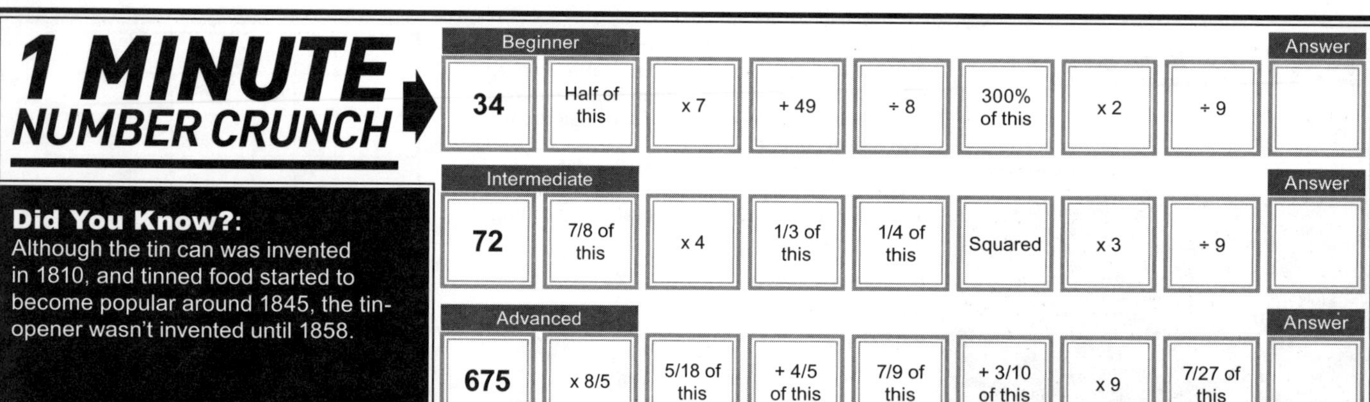

1 MINUTE NUMBER CRUNCH
Beginner
34
Half of this
x 7
+ 49
÷ 8
300% of this
x 2
÷ 9
Answer
Intermediate
72
7/8 of this
x 4
1/3 of this
1/4 of this
Squared
x 3
÷ 9
Answer
Advanced
675
x 8/5
5/18 of this
+ 4/5 of this
7/9 of this
+ 3/10 of this
x 9
7/27 of this
Answer

Did You Know?:
Although the tin can was invented in 1810, and tinned food started to become popular around 1845, the tin-opener wasn't invented until 1858.

HIGH-SPEED CROSSWORD

Across

1 Pitch dangerously to one side (6)
4 Marked by practical hard-headed intelligence (6)
7 Water tanker (6)
9 In a direction towards the Orient (8)
11 Bitter sweet (4)
14 Learned person (7)
15 Computer memory unit (4)
16 Hoax (4)
17 Flat area in a series of slopes (7)
18 One who works during a strike (4)
21 Contagious infection of the skin (8)
22 Fix up (6)
24 Forest gods (6)
25 Caused to stop (6)

Down

1 Ancient unit of length (5)
2 Oarsman (5)
3 Biblical first woman (3)
4 Central American capital city (3,8)
5 Practises before an event (9)
6 Declare to be untrue (4)
8 False or misleading clues in a mystery (3,8)
10 Capital of Zambia (6)
12 Psychiatric hospital (6)
13 Winged creature that transmits sleeping sickness (6,3)
19 Move effortlessly (5)
20 Tired of the world (5)
21 Wading bird (4)
23 Epoch, age (3)

IQ WORKOUT

What comes next in this sequence?

CODEWORD CONUNDRUM

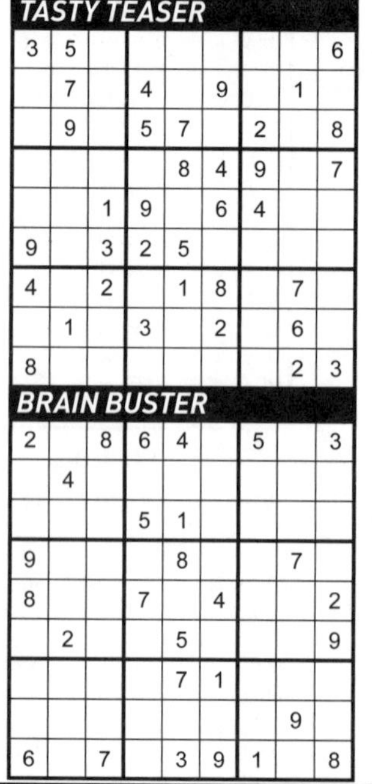

DOUBLE FUN SUDOKU

SPIDOKU

Each of the eight segments of the spider's web should be filled with a different number from 1 to 8, in such a way that every ring also contains a different number from 1 to 8.

LOGI-SIX

Every row and column of this grid should contain one each of the letters A, B, C, D, E and F. Each of the six shapes (marked by thicker lines) should also contain one each of the letters A, B, C, D, E and F. Can you complete the grid?

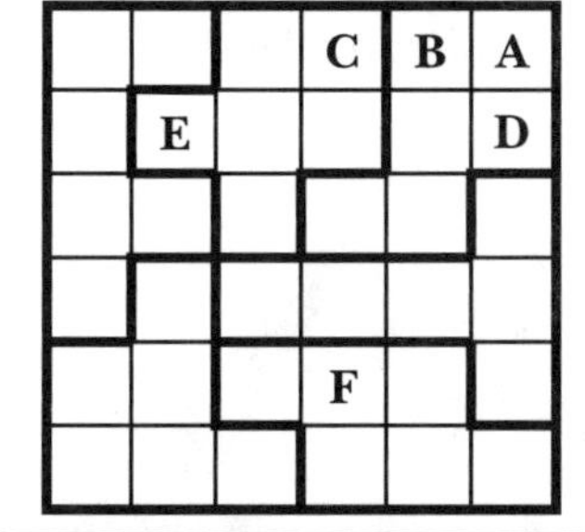

HIGH-SPEED CROSSWORD

Across

1 What you see is what you get – in computing terms! (7)
8 Pear-shaped fruit (7)
9 Pals (7)
10 Women (6)
12 Victim of ridicule or pranks (6)
13 Relating to the land (11)
17 Level a charge against (6)
20 Sickness (6)
23 Cloth used when washing-up (7)
24 Raised in rank (7)
25 Slim or small (7)

Down

1 Pancake batter baked in an iron implement (6)
2 Rotating shaft (7)
3 Cringe (5)
4 Short intake of breath (4)
5 Brag (5)
6 *Key* ___, 1948 film (5)
7 Hat tied under the chin (6)
11 Leather with a napped surface (5)
12 Glossy fabric (5)
14 Certain of (7)
15 Sponsor, investor (6)
16 Carnivorous burrowing mammal (6)
18 Durable aromatic wood (5)
19 Saline (5)
21 Church passage (5)
22 ___ and ends (4)

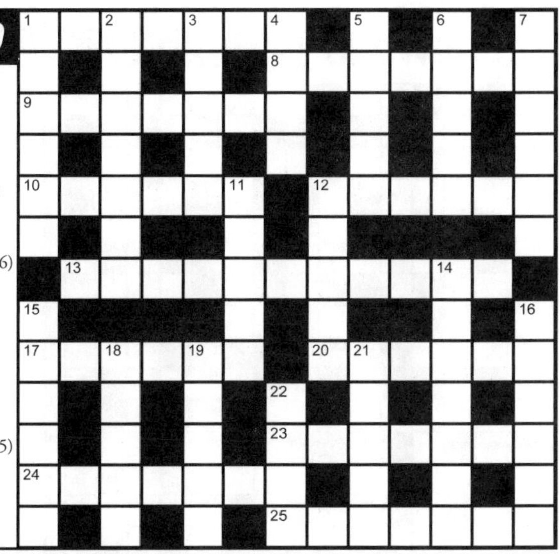

WORDSEARCH WORKOUT

E	M	P	Y	U	G	Y	W	F	S	R	W	B
N	Y	A	W	D	E	M	J	R	I	E	L	T
Y	D	X	O	Y	N	Q	E	B	L	A	O	N
T	B	I	T	O	T	Z	B	L	C	C	S	D
P	D	I	V	E	B	L	A	K	P	E	N	K
S	E	A	I	W	E	N	W	A	M	K	P	M
G	L	F	R	P	D	A	R	A	I	O	X	D
R	I	E	Z	T	T	R	H	S	X	R	O	Q
E	V	Q	N	E	E	T	N	P	K	V	E	Q
A	U	W	R	T	T	E	R	E	E	T	V	R
T	M	E	T	R	N	J	H	Y	N	C	E	E
O	J	N	Y	E	T	Y	Y	F	N	I	Y	B
U	I	S	W	A	Y	A	V	G	E	D	L	M
S	P	U	V	T	R	Z	E	L	T	A	E	U
E	M	M	J	Q	H	E	C	C	C	H	E	H

RIVERS OF BRITAIN

AIRE
AVON
BLACKWATER
DART
DOVEY
GREAT OUSE
HUMBER
KENNET
MEDWAY
NENE
PARRETT
RIBBLE
SPEY
TEIFI
THAMES
TOWY
TYNE
WELLAND
WENSUM
YARE

DOUBLE FUN SUDOKU

TASTY TEASER

	9	7		6		3	4	
4			5		3			1
		3		9		5		
	3	8	2		9	1	6	
9			6		1			3
	1	5	3		7	2	9	
		6		1		8		
8			9		5			7
	7	9		2		4	1	

BRAIN BUSTER

		1	8			5		
9	3			1				
8	7							
					6	2	7	
	1			7			4	
	2	8	5					
							3	8
				4			1	7
		6			9	4		

MATCHSTICK MAGIC

Remove three matchsticks to leave three squares.

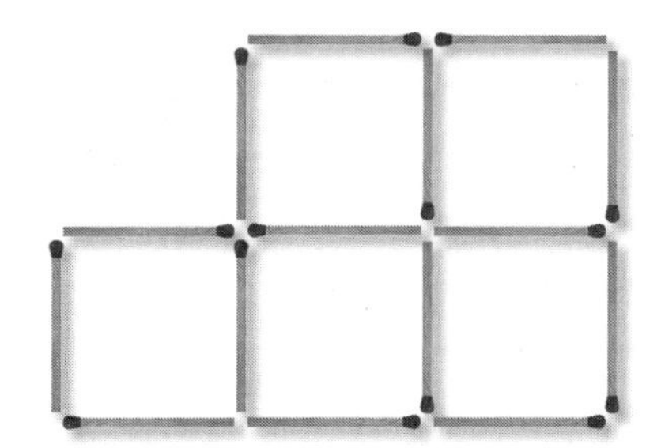

BRAIN TEASER

Frank has half as many again as Sally who has half as many again as Mary. Altogether they have 209.

How many has each?

? ______ ?

Beginner								Answer
99	Plus the sum of its two digits	÷ 3	+ 1/3 of this	Half of this	+ 58	÷ 12	x 5	

Intermediate								Answer
829	– 555	1/2 of this	+ 85	÷ 37	This cubed	3/9 of this	3/8 of this	

Advanced								Answer
94	x 11	÷ 0.5	+ 3/4 of this	– 2917	+ 8/9 of this	Plus half of this	14/9 of this	

Did You Know?:
The horn of a rhinoceros, though as solid as bone, is actually made of keratin – the same substance that forms the hair and nails of humans.

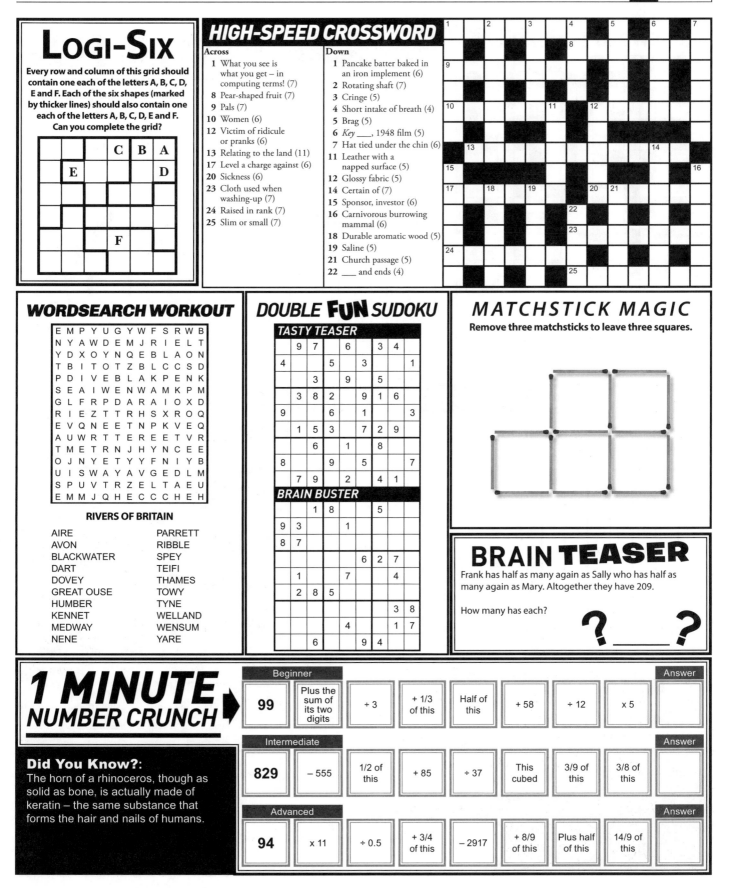

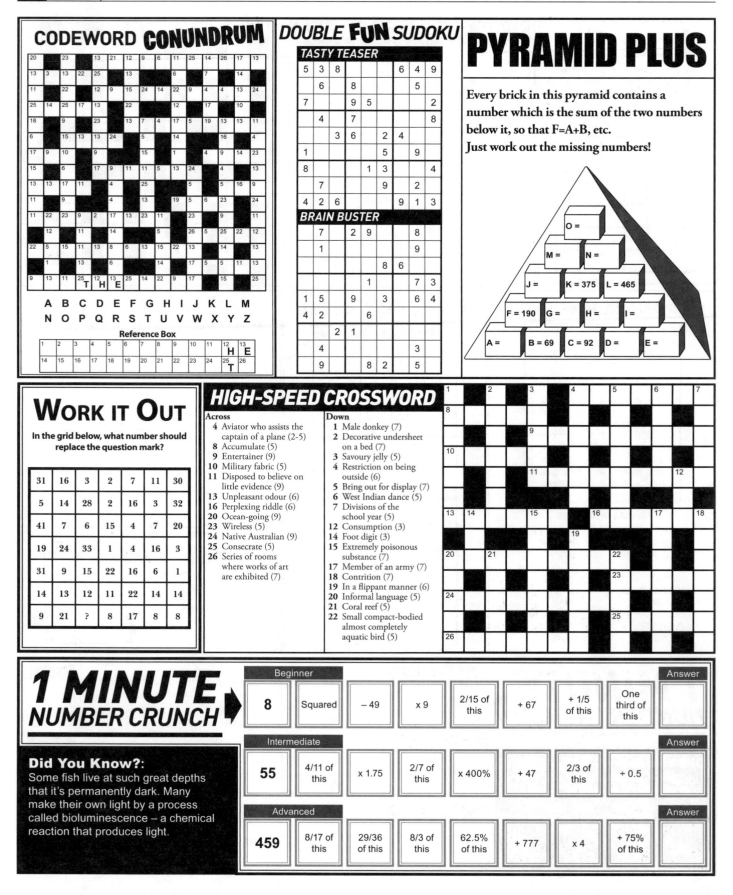

CODEWORD CONUNDRUM

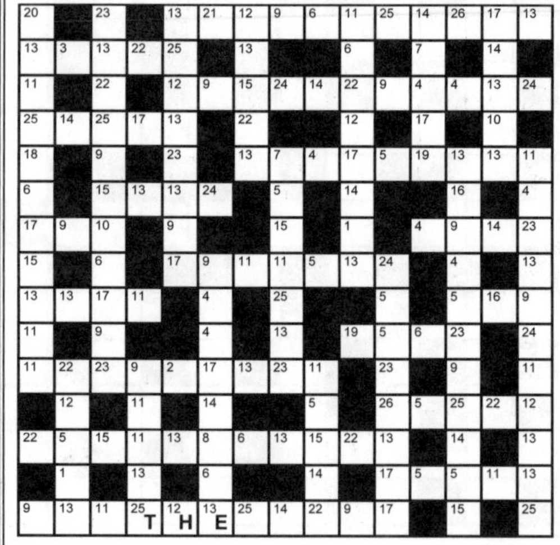

A B C D E F G H I J K L M

N O P Q R S T U V W X Y Z

Reference Box

1	2	3	4	5	6	7	8	9	10	11	12	13
											H	E
14	15	16	17	18	19	20	21	22	23	24	25	26
											T	

DOUBLE FUN SUDOKU

TASTY TEASER

5	3	8				6	4	9
	6		8				5	
7			9	5				2
	4		7					8
		3	6		2	4		
1					5		9	
8				1	3			4
	7				9		2	
4	2	6				9	1	3

BRAIN BUSTER

	7		2	9			8	
	1						9	
					8	6		
				1			7	3
1	5		9		3		6	4
4	2			6				
		2	1					
	4						3	
	9			8	2		5	

PYRAMID PLUS

Every brick in this pyramid contains a number which is the sum of the two numbers below it, so that F=A+B, etc.
Just work out the missing numbers!

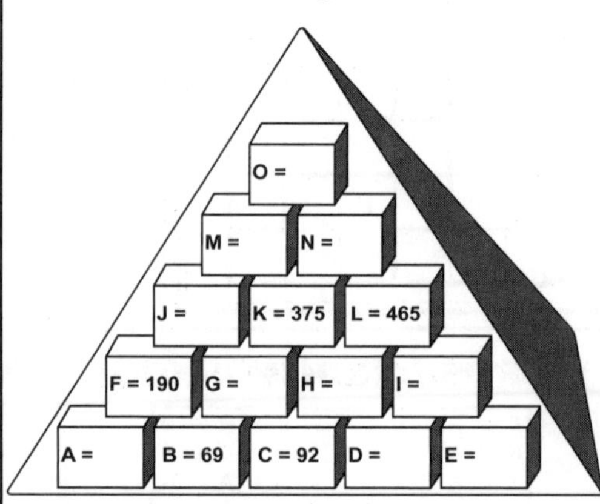

WORK IT OUT

In the grid below, what number should replace the question mark?

31	16	3	2	7	11	30
5	14	28	2	16	3	32
41	7	6	15	4	7	20
19	24	33	1	4	16	3
31	9	15	22	16	6	1
14	13	12	11	22	14	14
9	21	?	8	17	8	8

HIGH-SPEED CROSSWORD

Across

4 Aviator who assists the captain of a plane (2-5)
8 Accumulate (5)
9 Entertainer (9)
10 Military fabric (5)
11 Disposed to believe on little evidence (9)
13 Unpleasant odour (6)
16 Perplexing riddle (6)
20 Ocean-going (9)
23 Wireless (5)
24 Native Australian (9)
25 Consecrate (5)
26 Series of rooms where works of art are exhibited (7)

Down

1 Male donkey (7)
2 Decorative undersheet on a bed (7)
3 Savoury jelly (5)
4 Restriction on being outside (6)
5 Bring out for display (7)
6 West Indian dance (5)
7 Divisions of the school year (5)
12 Consumption (3)
14 Foot digit (3)
15 Extremely poisonous substance (7)
17 Member of an army (7)
18 Contrition (7)
19 In a flippant manner (6)
20 Informal language (5)
21 Coral reef (5)
22 Small compact-bodied almost completely aquatic bird (5)

1 MINUTE NUMBER CRUNCH

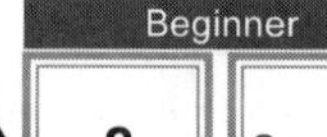

Beginner								Answer
8	Squared	– 49	x 9	2/15 of this	+ 67	+ 1/5 of this	One third of this	

Intermediate								Answer
55	4/11 of this	x 1.75	2/7 of this	x 400%	+ 47	2/3 of this	÷ 0.5	

Advanced								Answer
459	8/17 of this	29/36 of this	8/3 of this	62.5% of this	+ 777	x 4	+ 75% of this	

Did You Know?:
Some fish live at such great depths that it's permanently dark. Many make their own light by a process called bioluminescence – a chemical reaction that produces light.

HIGH-SPEED CROSSWORD

Across
1 Tightly curled and unopened flower (7)
5 Perform without preparation (2-3)
8 To stretch out (3)
9 Course of appetisers in an Italian meal (9)
10 Empower (5)
12 Long fishes (4)
14 Destroy the peace of (7)
16 Not this! (4)
18 Soap froth (4)
20 Ability to walk steadily on the deck of a pitching ship (3,4)
22 Location (4)
23 Bohemian dance (5)
25 More favourable position (9)
26 Deciduous tree (3)
27 Develop fully (5)
28 Add sugar to (7)

Down
1 Vote back into office (2-5)
2 Unwavering (9)
3 Favouring one person or side over another (6)
4 Go out with (4)
6 Boxlike containers in a piece of furniture (7)
7 Footwear that covers the lower legs (5)
11 Adult male deer (4)
13 High-spirited (9)
15 Offshore territory (4)
17 Adolescent (7)
19 Itinerant Australian labourer (7)
21 Globe (6)
22 Step (5)
24 Flexible containers (4)

SUMMING UP

In the square below, change the positions of six numbers, one per horizontal row, vertical column and long diagonal line of six smaller squares, in such a way that the numbers in each row, column and long diagonal line total exactly 137. Any number may appear more than once in a row, column or line.

31	6	11	31	47	8
22	22	35	31	27	23
23	13	22	24	14	23
26	39	27	20	9	24
21	26	16	34	18	27
22	13	11	20	27	29

DOMINO PLACEMENT

A standard set of 28 dominoes has been laid out as shown. Can you draw in the edges of them all? The check-box is provided as an aid and the domino already placed will help.

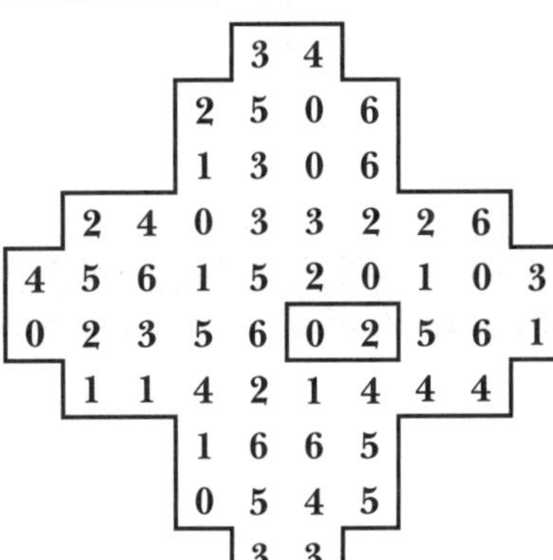

0-0	0-1	0-2	0-3	0-4	0-5	0-6
		✓				

1-1	1-2	1-3	1-4	1-5	1-6	2-2

2-3	2-4	2-5	2-6	3-3	3-4	3-5

3-6	4-4	4-5	4-6	5-5	5-6	6-6

Did You Know?:
Neptune can't be seen with the unaided eye. It was the first planet to have been located by mathematical observation as opposed to being actually seen.

WORDSEARCH WORKOUT

E C N A D S S Y E L L U P
Q S P E T S P I N N I N G
F E J R O T C U R T S N I
S H N O U L Q E S I G N G
L R O I G U L P J S G C Y
L E S R L G L L P G E G E
E W W R S O I L E Z D R T
B O I S S E P N E B M K P
B H M X T X R M G Y R P Z
M S M W H E E G A S S A M
U I I C G R B T K R A N B
D Y N T I C S S E N T I F
X E G M E I G G U A G O Y
B M O R W S Q A N T F O T
O C I F O E S U B V G I U

GYM WORK OUT

BAR-BELL
BENCH
DANCE
DUMBBELLS
EXERCISE
FITNESS
HORSE
INSTRUCTOR
JOGGING
MASSAGE
PRESS-UPS
PULLEYS
SAUNA
SHOWER
SPINNING
STEPS
SWIMMING
TRAMPOLINE
WEIGHTS
YOGA

DOUBLE FUN SUDOKU

TASTY TEASER

7			9		6			1
	8			1			2	
1		5	8		4	9		7
	4		1	6	7		9	
3		6				1		5
	1		3	5	9		4	
2		8	6		3	4		9
	7			9			6	
6			5		1			2

BRAIN BUSTER

	3	1			2		8	
				6	1	7		
	8	7					6	
			2			8		
8		3				5		6
		9			6			
	6					2	1	
		4	7	1				
	9		6			3	5	

WHATEVER NEXT?

In the diagram below, which letter should replace the question mark?

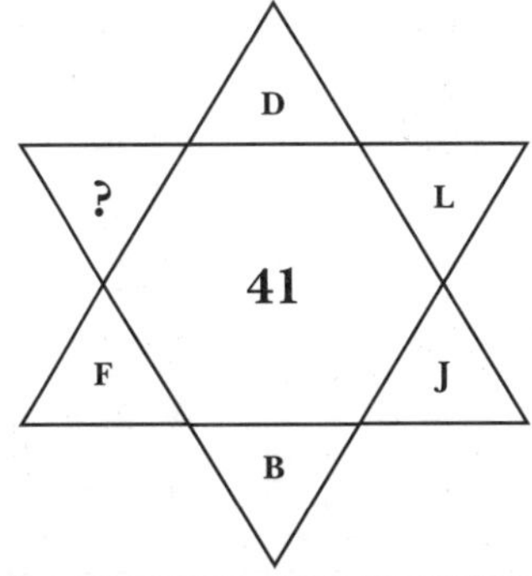

How many circles appear here?

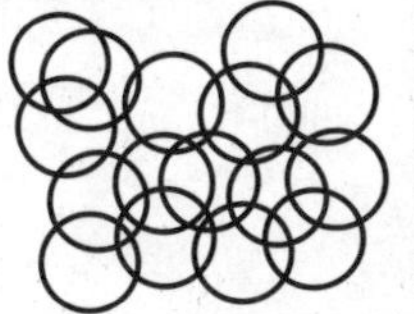

? ______ ?

Mind Over Matter

Given that the letters are valued 1-26 according to their places in the alphabet, can you crack the mystery code to reveal the missing letter?

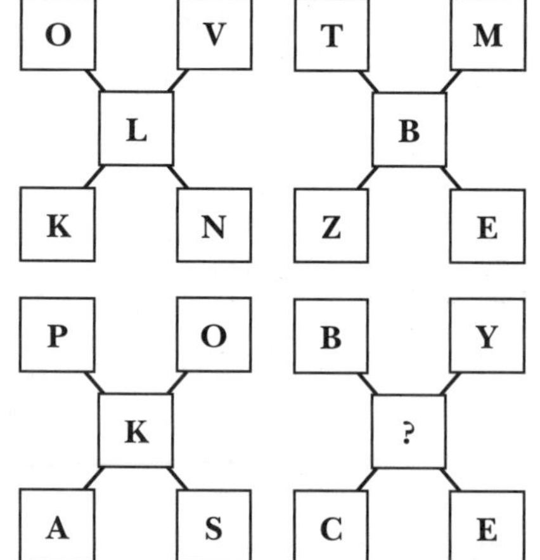

DOUBLE FUN SUDOKU

TASTY TEASER

4		9			2			
		3		1	8		5	9
	8				5	4	2	
7		4			6		9	
2			5		4			3
	1		3			6		7
	6	5	8				7	
8	7		2	9		5		
			6			3		1

BRAIN BUSTER

4				3		9	6	8
5			9					
1				6	4			
		9					3	
6		2				8		7
	5					4		
			4	2				1
					7			3
8	7	4		5				9

CODEWORD CONUNDRUM

20	4	7	9	■	17	2	20	8	16	■	14	18	9	9
2	■	■	15	20	25	■	18	■	20	■	■	14	■	20
9	18	1	25	■	20	17	25	18	9	9	■	18	13	2
18	■	■	11	■	3	■	5	■	■	19	2	15	20	5
■	■	9	18	3	5	■	20	16	1	15	■	■	2	■
19	7	15	■	7	■	21	■	25	■	13	12	15	2	19
7	■	8	■	9	2	18	16	20	8	■	■	4	■	20
6	1	7	2	5	■	9	■	11	■	26	18	1	8	16
1	■	18	■	■	16	20	22	15	14	18	■	23	■	15
15	16	25	15	5	■	7	■	2	■	10	■	15	8	23
■	15	■	■	20	25	17	12	■	14 B	15	8	23	■	■
20	8	5	7	17	■	■	26	■	20 A	■	1	■	■	14
14	15	15	■	18	14	24	15	17	5 T	■	5	20	21	15
15	■	20	■	■	7	■	8	■	12	1	5	■	■	2
5	20	10	15	■	16	25	20	22	15	■	26	20	13	2

A B C D E F G H I J K L M

N O P Q R S T U V W X Y Z

Reference Box

1	2	3	4	5	6	7	8	9	10	11	12	13
				T								

14	15	16	17	18	19	20	21	22	23	24	25	26
B						A						

FUTOSHIKI

Fill the grid so that every horizontal row and vertical column contains the numbers 1-5. The 'greater than' or 'less than' signs indicate where a number is larger or smaller than that in the neighbouring square.

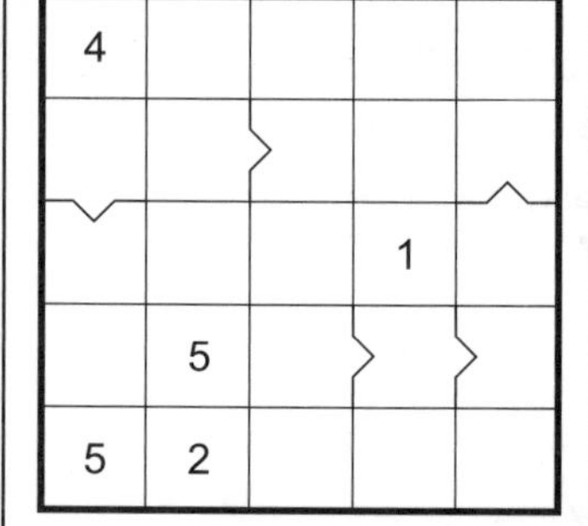

HIGH-SPEED CROSSWORD

Across

1 Maltreater (6)
3 Prickly desert plant (6)
7 Happening again and again, tediously (11)
10 Kept apart (8)
11 Egg on (4)
13 Portable light (5)
14 Public announcement of a proposed marriage (5)
18 Curved gateway (4)
19 Crystalline rock that can be cut for jewellery (8)
21 Ill-fated (4-7)
22 Craftsman who makes cloth (6)
23 In one's place of residence (2,4)

Down

1 Cowardly (6)
2 Way in (8)
4 Highly excited (4)
5 Small pouch for shampoo, etc (6)
6 Give tongue to (5)
8 Long flexible snout (9)
9 Taxing of one's energy (9)
12 Official travel permit (8)
15 Capital of Poland (6)
16 Heave, regurgitate (5)
17 Former minor parish official (6)
20 Cassette (4)

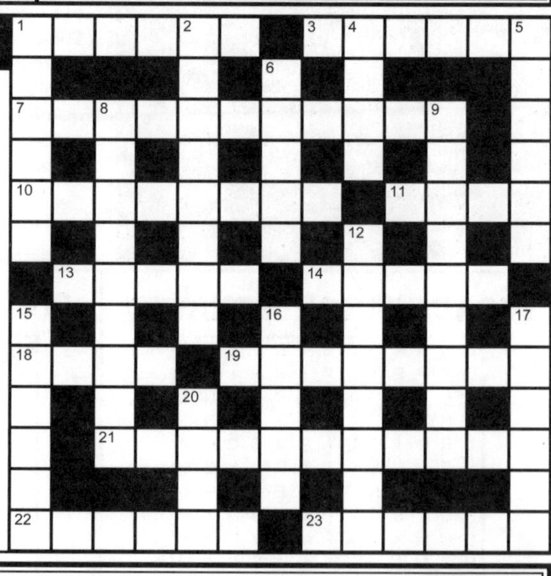

Beginner

								Answer
22	x 7	Half of this	4/11 of this	+ 50% of this	– 9	x 4	7/11 of this	

Intermediate

								Answer
27	x 3	– 56	80% of this	850% of this	7/10 of this	Double it	+ 823	

Advanced

								Answer
96	x 14	+ 3/4 of this	5/6 of this	35% of this	+ 155	Square root of this	x 13	

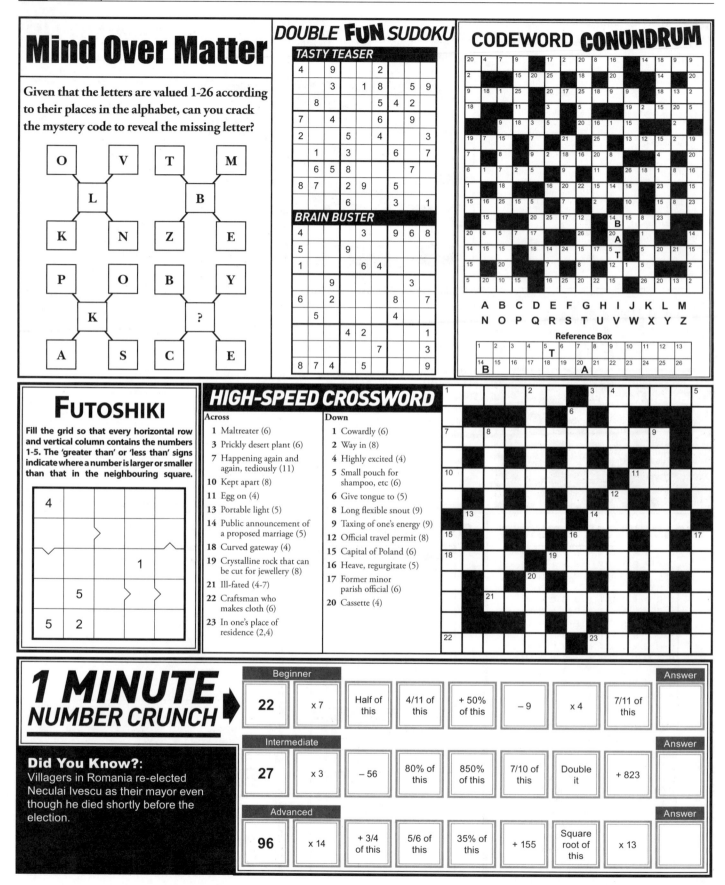

Did You Know?:
Villagers in Romania re-elected Neculai Ivescu as their mayor even though he died shortly before the election.

1 MINUTE NUMBER CRUNCH

Beginner								Answer
1234	x 2	– 999	+ 31	90% of this	÷ 5	1/5 of this	x 3	

Intermediate								Answer
99	5/9 of this	5/11 of this	Square root of this	+ 20%	+ 5	Squared	x 3	

Advanced								Answer
96	x 4	+ 3/16 of this	5/6 of this	– 90% of this	+ 795	x 7	– 2978	

Did You Know?:
It's against the law to sail over Niagara Falls. Nevertheless, over the years several people have drowned trying to do so.

HIGH-SPEED CROSSWORD

Across
1 Native of La Paz, for example (8)
5 Supplication (4)
8 Fits of rage (8)
10 Church tower (7)
11 Daughter of a sibling (5)
12 Roman slave who led an uprising against Roman legions (9)
15 Doubt about someone's honesty (9)
18 Lost (2,3)
19 Move by degrees in one direction only (7)
22 Car exhaust (8)
23 Kill (4)
24 Moral excellence (8)

Down
1 Study of plants (6)
2 Portable lamps (8)
3 Subdivisions of a poem (6)
4 Weapons (4)
6 Spring up (4)
7 Admission (6)
9 Designating sound transmission from two sources (6)
13 Small padded envelope (6)
14 Engage in plotting (8)
15 Similar things placed in order (6)
16 Pinned down (6)
17 Animals used in desert regions (6)
20 Roman cloak (4)
21 Filled tortilla (4)

1		2		3		4		■	5	6		7
	■		■		■		■	■	■		■	
8							9	■	■		■	
	■		■		■	10						
11					■	■		■	■	■	■	
	■		■	12	13					14		
■	■		■	■		■		■	■		■	■
15								16	■		■	17
	■	■	■	■		■	■	18				
19		20				21	■		■		■	
	■		■	■	22							
	■		■	■	■		■		■		■	
23				■	24							

PARTITIONS

Draw walls to partition the grid into areas (some are already drawn in). Each area must contain two circles, area sizes must match those numbers shown next to the grid and each '+' must be linked to at least two walls.

3, 4, 5, 6, 7

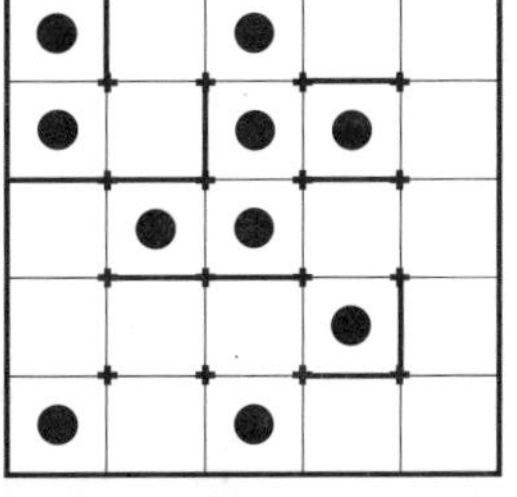

WORDWHEEL

Using only the letters in the Wordwheel, you have ten minutes to find as many words as possible, none of which may be plurals, foreign words or proper nouns. Each word must be of three letters or more, all must contain the central letter and letters can only be used once in every word. There is at least one nine-letter word in the wheel.

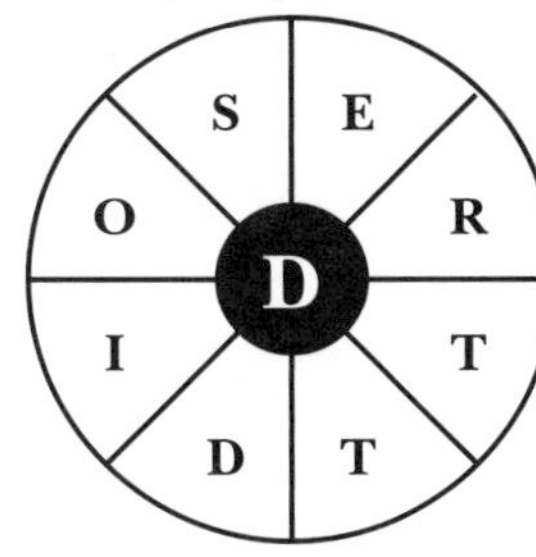

Nine-letter word(s): ____________________

SUM CIRCLE

Fill the three empty circles with the symbols +, – and x in some order, to make a sum which totals the number in the centre. Each symbol must be used once and calculations are made in the direction of travel (clockwise).

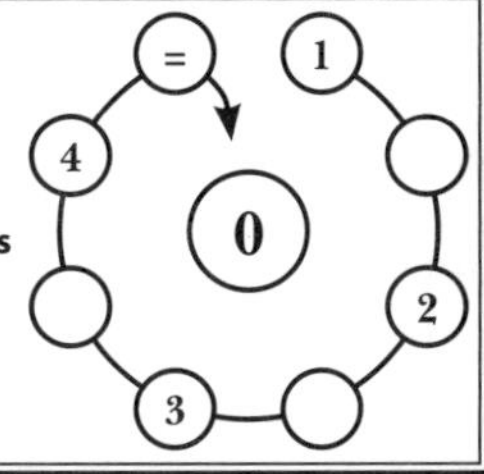

WORDSEARCH WORKOUT

T	E	S	P	S	E	R	U	T	A	E	F	A
O	O	L	G	X	S	L	P	H	C	S	D	L
G	S	L	S	D	C	L	Q	D	E	T	L	D
P	P	R	S	R	M	H	L	Y	N	I	E	O
P	A	A	M	P	E	S	E	E	I	U	C	R
B	I	Y	N	D	W	P	T	R	B	R	N	A
K	X	N	O	O	N	Q	E	I	R	F	A	N
C	U	N	D	U	P	U	A	A	D	I	C	G
B	R	N	P	E	T	P	D	R	T	E	E	E
L	I	S	T	A	R	T	L	G	C	S	R	S
W	I	N	N	I	N	G	E	U	E	A	J	C
J	X	O	F	F	H	P	V	D	M	I	D	E
G	P	M	C	O	L	L	E	C	T	S	L	E
Y	X	E	Q	N	S	F	R	B	P	E	C	U
A	V	L	Y	I	O	I	M	O	I	B	A	Y

FRUIT MACHINE

ARCADE
BARS
BELLS
CANCEL
CHERRIES
COLLECT
CREDITS
FEATURES
FRUITS
LEMONS
LEVER
NUDGE
ORANGE
PAYOUT
PLUMS
REPEAT
SLOT
START
WINDOW
WINNING

DOUBLE FUN SUDOKU

TASTY TEASER

1	6				3	8		
8			4	9			7	3
		7			8			
5	1				7		8	2
		3		5		9		
2	9		6				4	5
			2			6		
6	7			8	5			9
		4	1				2	7

BRAIN BUSTER

	6		3		2		1	
7			4		9			6
		1		7		2		
2		4				5		3
	8						2	
1		6				8		4
		2		4		7		
3			5		7			1
	5		1		8		9	

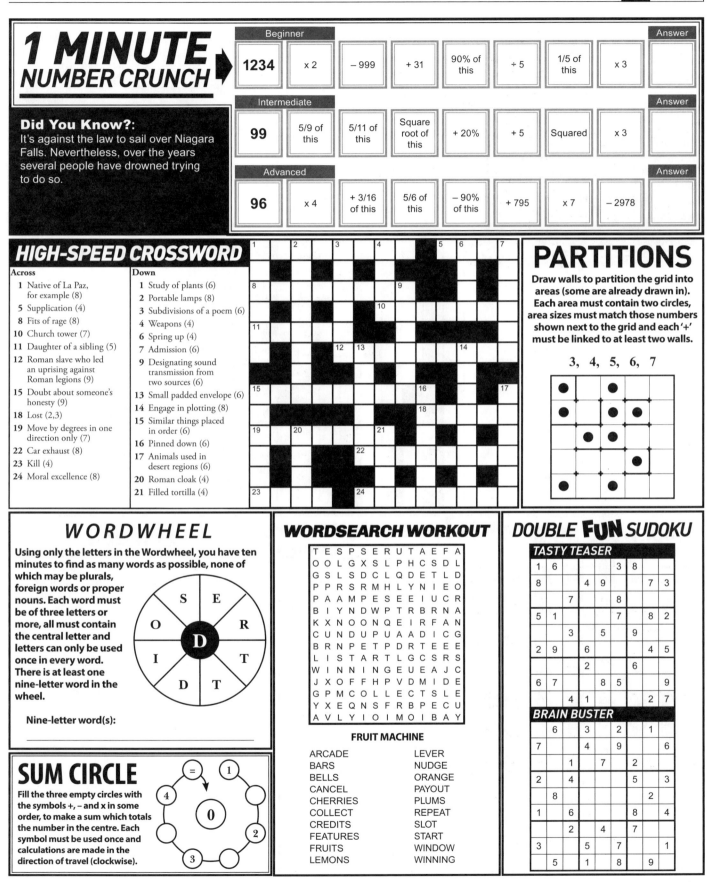

1 MINUTE NUMBER CRUNCH

Did You Know?:
New York City had a bedbug epidemic in 2007. Nearly seven thousand calls were made to pest control companies when the parasites infested hotels, hospitals, schools and homes.

									Answer
Beginner	14	x 6	Half of this	÷ 7	x 2.5	500% of this	x 3	÷ 15	
Intermediate	424	– 128	1/2 of this	÷ 4	x 7	+ 955	x 2	– 1957	
Advanced	558	+ 2/3 of this	7/10 of this	+ 5/7 of this	– 2/9 of this	– 277	8/3 of this	+ 3/8 of this	

HIGH-SPEED CROSSWORD

Across

1 Maybe (7)
7 Ship's kitchen (6)
9 Money (7)
10 Left over, superfluous (5)
11 Hard outer layer of a fruit (4)
12 Frogman (5)
16 Afterwards (5)
17 Withered (4)
21 Colloquial term for one's ancestry (5)
22 Cup, goblet (7)
23 Country, capital Stockholm (6)
24 Lacking freshness (atmosphere) (7)

Down

1 Popular snack made from maize (7)
2 Beaming (7)
3 Lay out in a line (5)
4 Herb with aromatic finely cut leaves (7)
5 Communion table (5)
6 Keyed into a machine (5)
8 Somewhere to live (9)
13 Pet rodent (7)
14 Act as a go-between (7)
15 First book of the Old Testament (7)
18 Alloy of copper and zinc (5)
19 One stroke over par in golf (5)
20 Frolic, cavort (5)

IQ WORKOUT

Fill the grid with the letters ABCDE so that the same letter does not appear in the same horizontal, vertical or diagonal line of two or more squares.

A				
				B
			C	
		D		
	E			C

CODEWORD CONUNDRUM

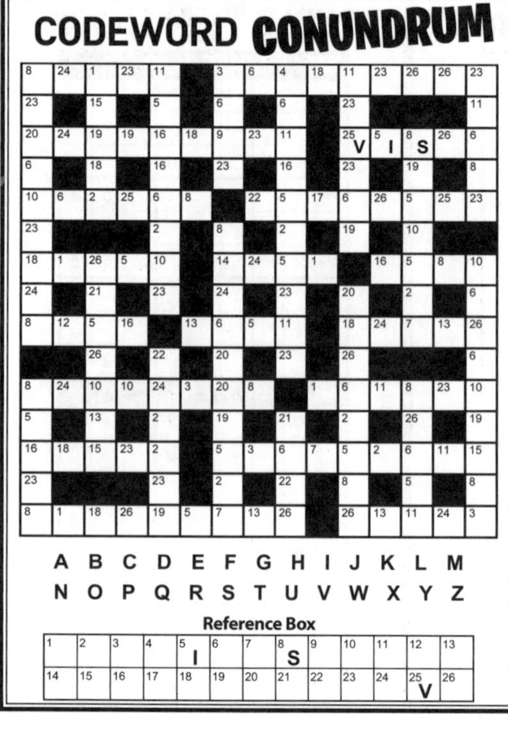

DOUBLE FUN SUDOKU

TASTY TEASER

8	7		5					4
			8			3	2	
4		5	9	1			7	
3			2			4	8	
		9	7		6	2		
	6	4			8			1
	2			3	5	1		7
	1	6			9			
5					7		6	9

BRAIN BUSTER

2		8	1		4	5		9
5								4
			5	2	9			
7		9	2		5	3		6
		3				2		
6		2	7		8	9		5
			3	8	6			
8								1
3		5	4		2	6		8

SPIDOKU

Each of the eight segments of the spider's web should be filled with a different number from 1 to 8, in such a way that every ring also contains a different number from 1 to 8.

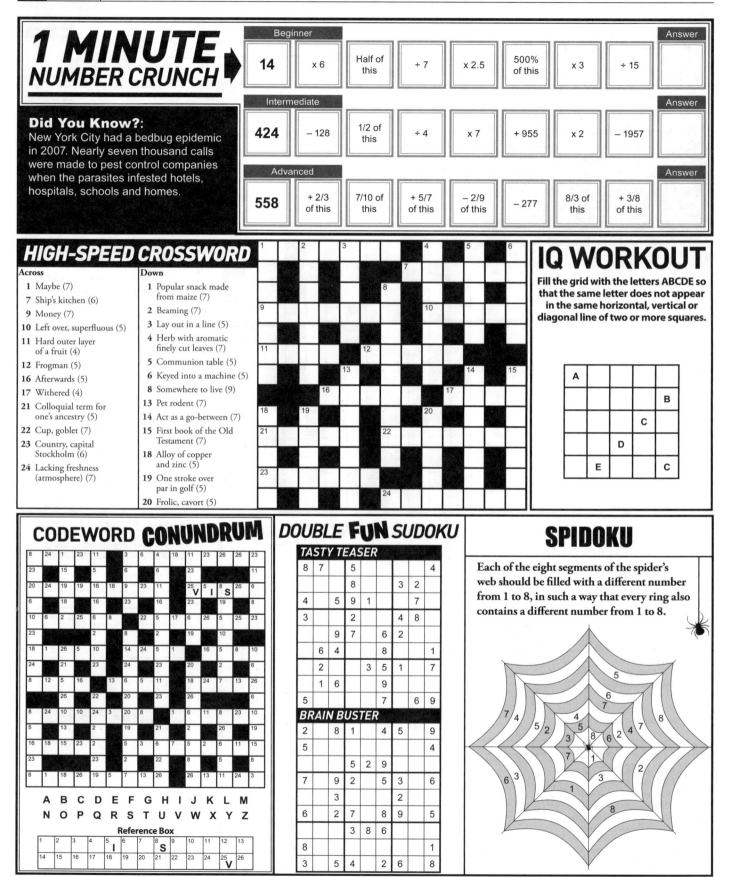

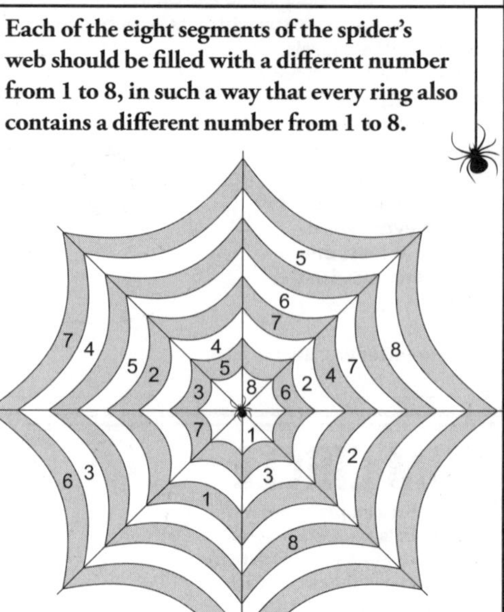

LOGI-SIX

Every row and column of this grid should contain one each of the letters A, B, C, D, E and F. Each of the six shapes (marked by thicker lines) should also contain one each of the letters A, B, C, D, E and F. Can you complete the grid?

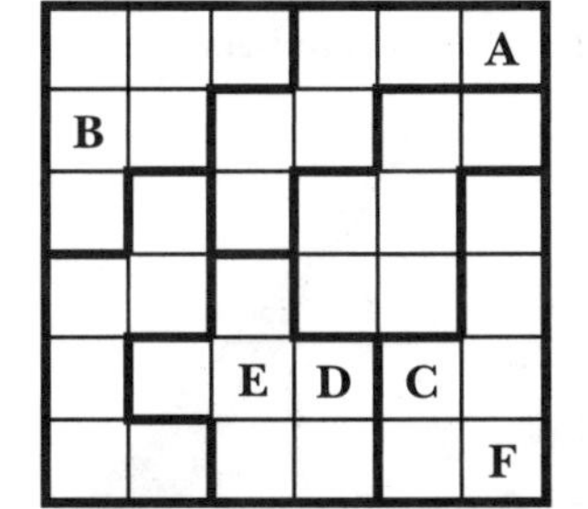

HIGH-SPEED CROSSWORD

Across
1 Stroke lovingly (6)
4 Bordering (6)
9 Lean back (7)
10 Endeavour (7)
11 Surgeon's pincers (7)
12 Compass point (5)
14 Lofty proud gait (5)
15 Jovial (5)
17 Canadian policeman, usually on horseback (7)
19 Abatement (7)
21 Constructing or forming a web, as if by weaving (7)
22 Thoroughfare (6)
23 Baby's plaything (6)

Down
1 Decanter (6)
2 Tubular wind instrument with eight finger holes (8)
3 County (5)
5 Afar (7)
6 Mosque official (4)
7 Sudden, usually temporary malfunction of equipment (6)
8 Act of ascertaining an amount (11)
13 Curtail (8)
14 Medical instrument used to inject (7)
15 Quagmire (6)
16 Association of sports teams (6)
18 Far beyond the norm (5)
20 Disparaging remark (4)

1		2		3		■	4	5		6		7
	■		■		■	8	■		■		■	
9							■		■		■	
	■		■		■	10						
11							■		■	■	■	
	■		■	■	■		■	12		13		
■	■		■	14					■		■	■
15					■		■	■	■		■	16
	■	■	■		■	17		18				
19		20					■		■		■	
	■		■		■	21						
	■		■		■		■		■		■	
22						■	23					

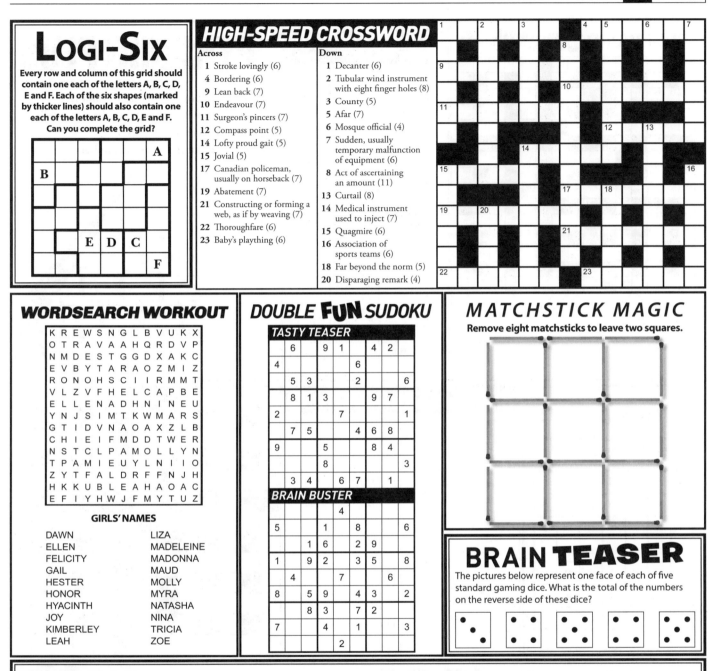

WORDSEARCH WORKOUT

K	R	E	W	S	N	G	L	B	V	U	K	X
O	T	R	A	V	A	A	H	Q	R	D	V	P
N	M	D	E	S	T	G	G	D	X	A	K	C
E	V	B	Y	T	A	R	A	O	Z	M	I	Z
R	O	N	O	H	S	C	I	I	R	M	M	T
V	L	Z	V	F	H	E	L	C	A	P	B	E
E	L	L	E	N	A	D	H	N	I	N	E	U
Y	N	J	S	I	M	T	K	W	M	A	R	S
G	T	I	D	V	N	A	O	A	X	Z	L	B
C	H	I	E	I	F	M	D	D	T	W	E	R
N	S	T	C	L	P	A	M	O	L	L	Y	N
T	P	A	M	I	E	U	Y	L	N	I	I	O
Z	Y	T	F	A	L	D	R	F	F	N	J	H
H	K	K	U	B	L	E	A	H	A	O	A	C
E	F	I	Y	H	W	J	F	M	Y	T	U	Z

GIRLS' NAMES

DAWN
ELLEN
FELICITY
GAIL
HESTER
HONOR
HYACINTH
JOY
KIMBERLEY
LEAH
LIZA
MADELEINE
MADONNA
MAUD
MOLLY
MYRA
NATASHA
NINA
TRICIA
ZOE

DOUBLE FUN SUDOKU

TASTY TEASER

	6		9	1		4	2	
4					6			
	5	3			2			6
	8	1	3			9	7	
2				7				1
	7	5			4	6	8	
9			5			8	4	
			8					3
	3	4		6	7		1	

BRAIN BUSTER

				4				
5			1		8			6
		1	6		2	9		
1		9	2		3	5		8
	4			7			6	
8		5	9		4	3		2
		8	3		7	2		
7			4		1			3
				2				

MATCHSTICK MAGIC

Remove eight matchsticks to leave two squares.

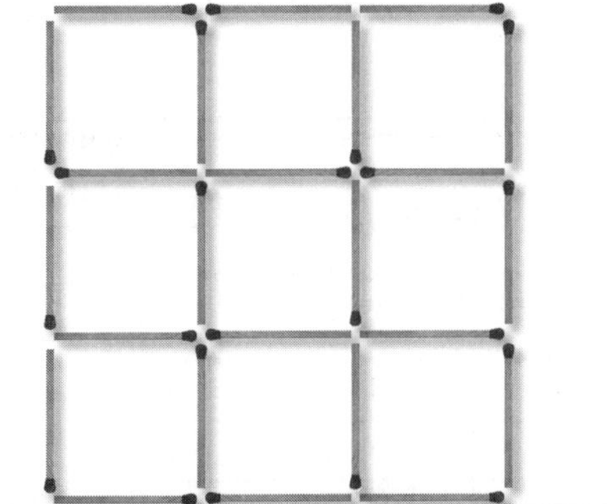

BRAIN TEASER

The pictures below represent one face of each of five standard gaming dice. What is the total of the numbers on the reverse side of these dice?

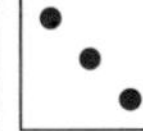 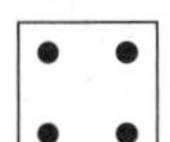 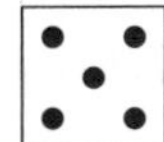 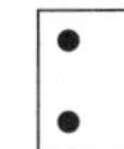 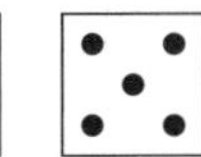

SIMPLE AS A, B, C ?

Each of the small squares in the grid below contains either A, B or C. Each row, column, and diagonal line of six squares has exactly two of each letter. Can you tell the letter in each square?

Across
1 No two letters the same are directly next to each other
2 The Cs are further right than the Bs
3 The Bs are next to each other
4 The Bs are next to each other
5 The Bs are further right than the Cs
6 No two letters the same are directly next to each other

Down
1 Each C is directly next to and below an A
2 No two letters the same are directly next to each other
3 No two letters the same are directly next to each other
4 No two letters the same are directly next to each other
5 The As are next to each other
6 Each C is directly next to and below a B

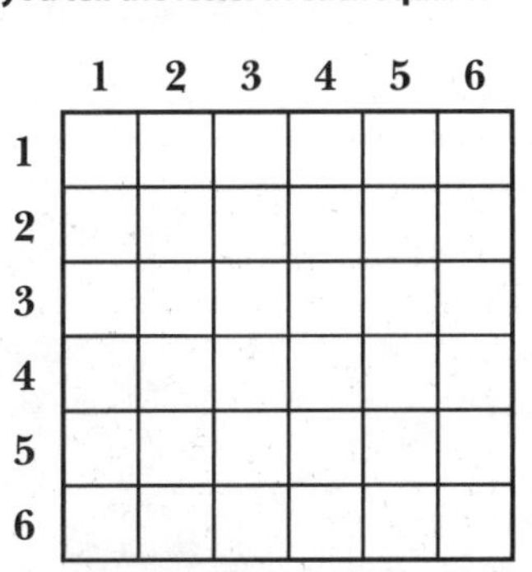

Did You Know?:
The star-nosed mole has six times as many nerves running from its nose to its brain than a human has going from each hand to the brain.

CODEWORD CONUNDRUM

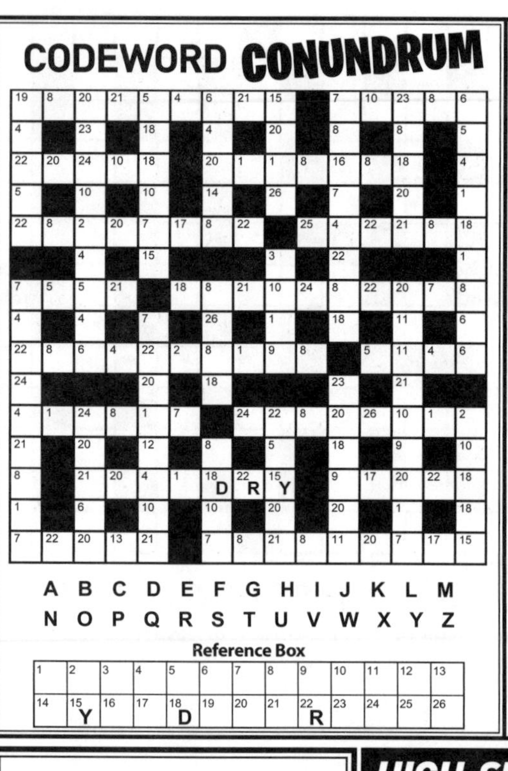

DOUBLE FUN SUDOKU

TASTY TEASER

2					4		3	
9	7				5	4		
4		5	1	2		6		
	1	4		7				9
	8		3		9		7	
6				8		3	5	
		9		1	3	8		5
		6	9				2	3
	5		7					1

BRAIN BUSTER

5	8						9	3
	1						4	
9			7		3			6
		6	5	1	7	3		
		1	2	8	4	9		
2			9		6			8
	6						3	
3	5						2	4

PYRAMID PLUS

Every brick in this pyramid contains a number which is the sum of the two numbers below it, so that F=A+B, etc.
Just work out the missing numbers!

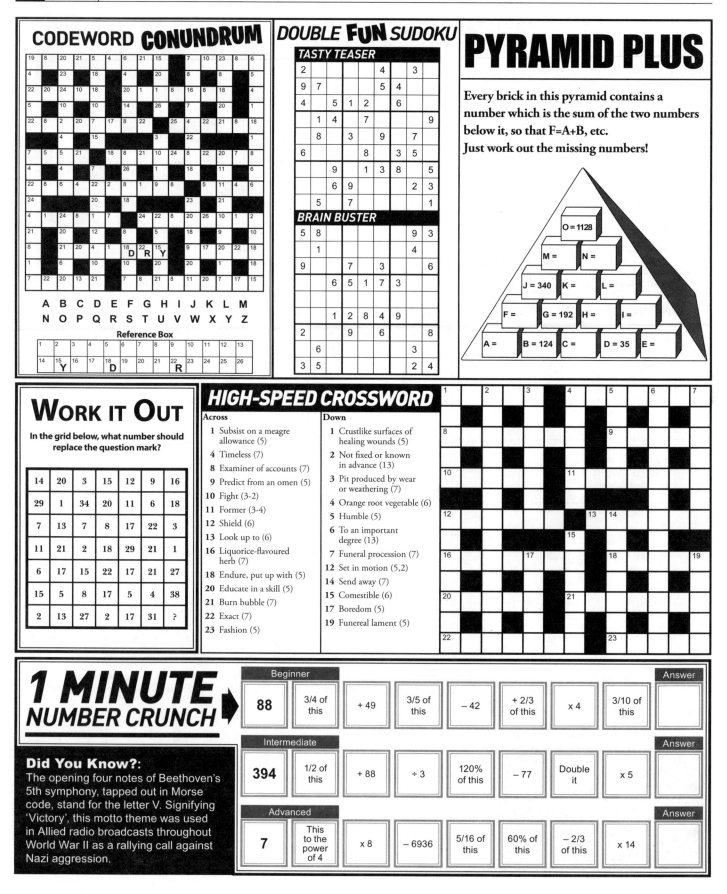

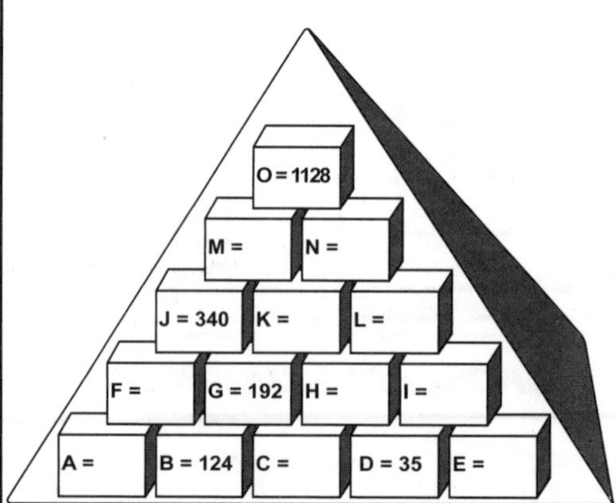

WORK IT OUT

In the grid below, what number should replace the question mark?

14	20	3	15	12	9	16
29	1	34	20	11	6	18
7	13	7	8	17	22	3
11	21	2	18	29	21	1
6	17	15	22	17	21	27
15	5	8	17	5	4	38
2	13	27	2	17	31	?

HIGH-SPEED CROSSWORD

Across

1 Subsist on a meagre allowance (5)
4 Timeless (7)
8 Examiner of accounts (7)
9 Predict from an omen (5)
10 Fight (3-2)
11 Former (3-4)
12 Shield (6)
13 Look up to (6)
16 Liquorice-flavoured herb (7)
18 Endure, put up with (5)
20 Educate in a skill (5)
21 Burn bubble (7)
22 Exact (7)
23 Fashion (5)

Down

1 Crustlike surfaces of healing wounds (5)
2 Not fixed or known in advance (13)
3 Pit produced by wear or weathering (7)
4 Orange root vegetable (6)
5 Humble (5)
6 To an important degree (13)
7 Funeral procession (7)
12 Set in motion (5,2)
14 Send away (7)
15 Comestible (6)
17 Boredom (5)
19 Funereal lament (5)

1 MINUTE NUMBER CRUNCH

Beginner								Answer
88	3/4 of this	+ 49	3/5 of this	– 42	+ 2/3 of this	x 4	3/10 of this	

Intermediate								Answer
394	1/2 of this	+ 88	÷ 3	120% of this	– 77	Double it	x 5	

Advanced								Answer
7	This to the power of 4	x 8	– 6936	5/16 of this	60% of this	– 2/3 of this	x 14	

Did You Know?:
The opening four notes of Beethoven's 5th symphony, tapped out in Morse code, stand for the letter V. Signifying 'Victory', this motto theme was used in Allied radio broadcasts throughout World War II as a rallying call against Nazi aggression.

HIGH-SPEED CROSSWORD

Across

1 Adequate quantity or supply (11)
9 Discontinue (5)
10 Alcoholic brew (3)
11 Workmanship (5)
12 Rolls (5)
13 Clapping (8)
16 Disagreement (8)
18 Radiance (5)
21 Country, capital Madrid (5)
22 Acquired (3)
23 Mother-of-pearl (5)
24 Substance that stimulates love or desire (11)

Down

2 Miserable (7)
3 Relating to reality (7)
4 Makes sore by rubbing (6)
5 Perpendicular (5)
6 Seat (5)
7 Study of ancient people through their material remains (11)
8 Doggedness, perseverance (11)
14 Edible black marine bivalves (7)
15 Meeting for boat races (7)
17 Off, sour (6)
19 Arise (3,2)
20 Adult male singing voice (5)

SUMMING UP

In the square below, change the positions of six numbers, one per horizontal row, vertical column and long diagonal line of six smaller squares, in such a way that the numbers in each row, column and long diagonal line total exactly 146. Any number may appear more than once in a row, column or line.

27	13	14	29	36	37
28	24	12	12	26	21
38	39	24	3	10	23
15	34	26	36	15	35
25	32	13	38	20	24
14	14	34	19	45	21

1 MINUTE NUMBER CRUNCH

Beginner								**Answer**
78	+ 15	1/3 of this	x 4	+ 20	1/12 of this	x 8	1/2 of this	
Intermediate								**Answer**
291	+ 49	20% of this	1/4 of this	x 7	Double it	– 190	+ 32	
Advanced								**Answer**
342	5/19 of this	170% of this	+ 7/9 of this	x 0.625	5/34 of this	Cubed	4/5 of this	

Did You Know?:
British author Barbara Cartland wrote 723 novels. More than a billion copies of her books, in 36 languages, have been sold worldwide.

WORDSEARCH WORKOUT

K	C	L	A	R	E	N	U	F	A	W	F	M
C	O	M	M	I	T	T	A	L	E	B	S	F
P	N	C	V	O	J	C	L	D	P	I	R	H
N	F	R	M	D	H	Q	D	R	T	E	A	A
I	I	G	U	Z	O	I	U	P	C	P	I	W
P	R	N	N	I	N	S	A	Q	P	Y	N	Y
T	M	I	V	G	R	B	E	U	N	D	I	J
E	A	N	E	E	Z	U	H	H	I	N	T	N
R	T	E	I	G	S	C	S	G	G	U	I	U
R	I	P	L	U	A	T	Y	T	N	A	A	P
A	O	O	I	R	T	I	I	U	A	M	T	T
M	N	C	N	D	L	H	R	T	T	M	I	I
R	Q	V	G	R	W	T	S	R	U	N	O	A
I	U	Y	O	N	A	H	C	R	A	R	N	L
T	Y	N	O	M	I	R	T	A	M	M	E	S

CEREMONIES

AMRIT
BAPTISM
CHANOYU
CHUPPAH
COMMITTAL
CONFIRMATION
DOSEH
FUNERAL
INITIATION
INVESTITURE
MARRIAGE
MATRIMONY
MATSURI
MAUNDY
NIPTER
NUPTIALS
OPENING
TANGI
UNVEILING
WEDDING

DOUBLE FUN SUDOKU

TASTY TEASER

	7		6		1			
	2			8		1	6	9
	6		3	2	9			
3			4		5	8		
7	1						5	4
		6	8		7			3
			9	4	6		3	
9	3	5		7			2	
			5		2		8	

BRAIN BUSTER

				7				
	5		4		3		6	
9			1		5			3
2	1		7		9		4	6
		5		8		7		
6	4		2		1		3	9
1			8		2			4
	2		3		7		8	
				1				

WHATEVER NEXT?

In the diagram below, which whole number should replace the question mark?

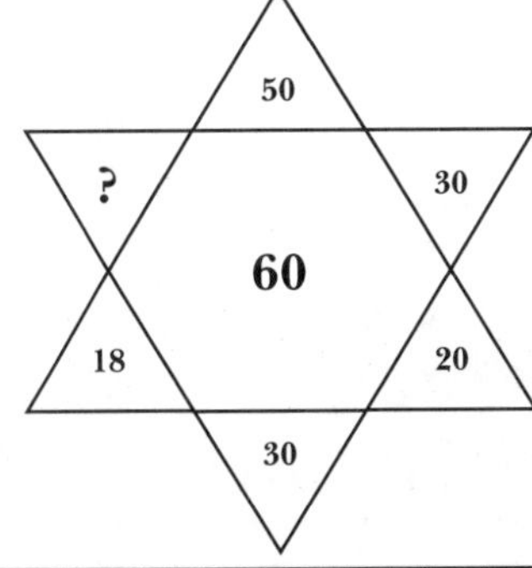

BRAIN TEASER

You have a range of weights available from 1-10 units. They are all single weights. Which one should you use to balance the scale and where should you place it?

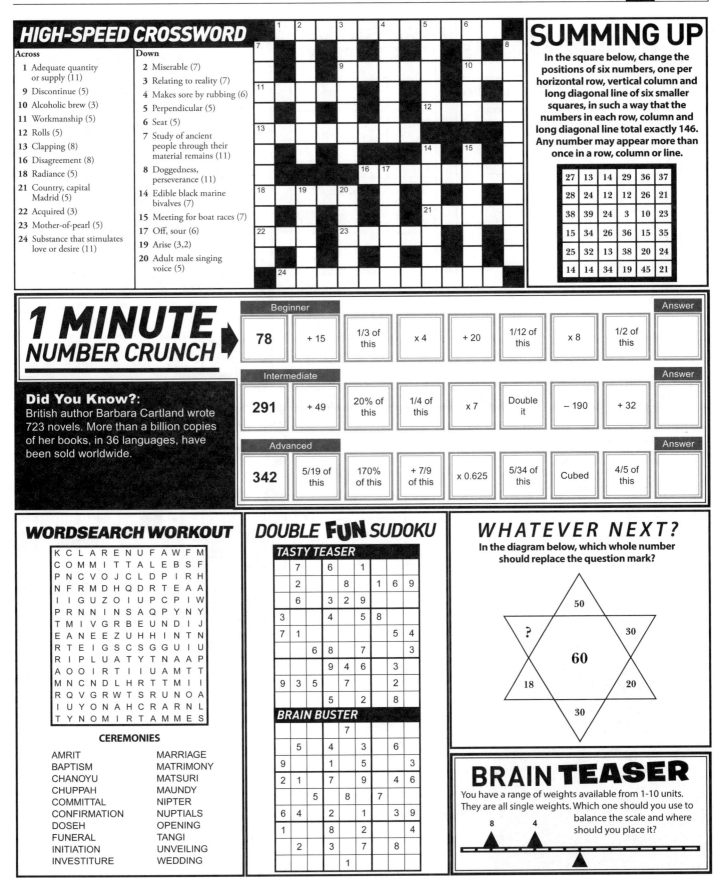

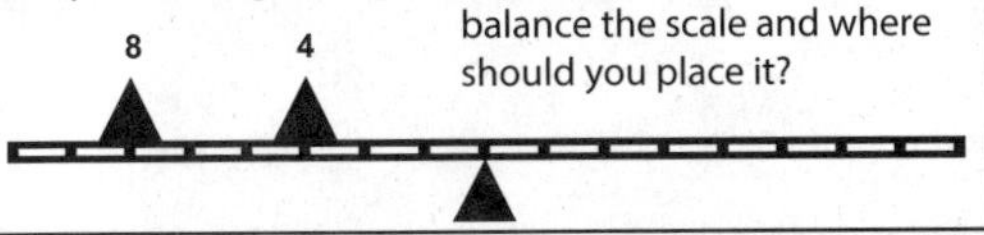

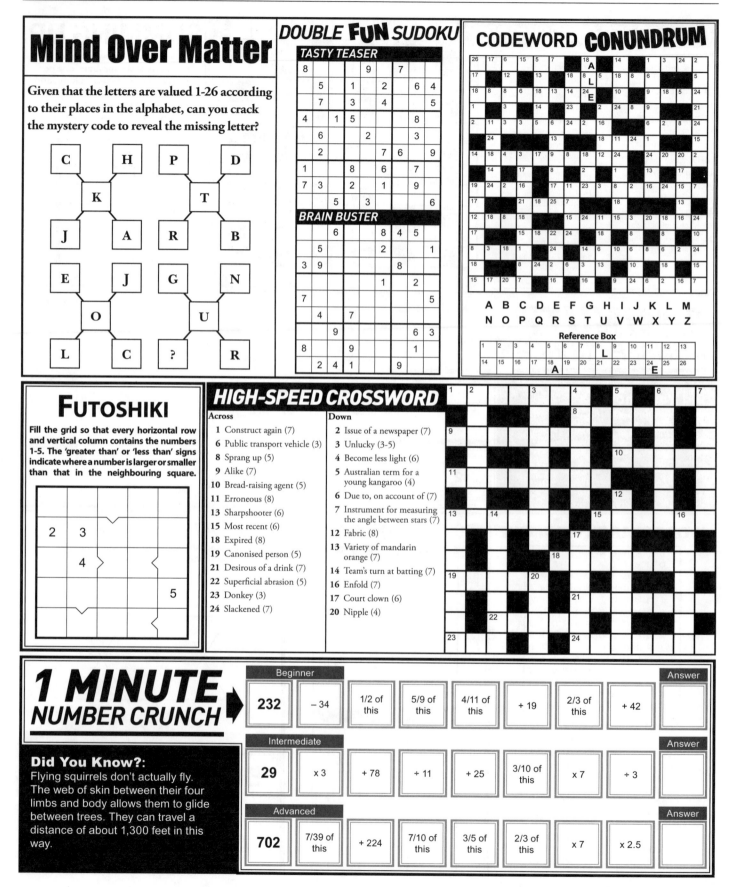

Mind Over Matter

Given that the letters are valued 1-26 according to their places in the alphabet, can you crack the mystery code to reveal the missing letter?

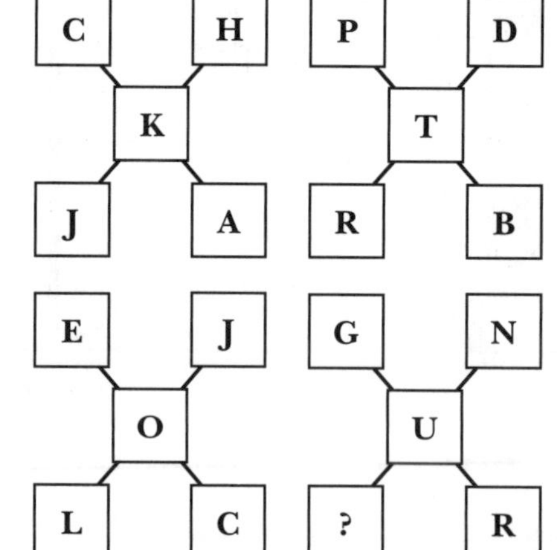

DOUBLE FUN SUDOKU

TASTY TEASER

8				9		7		
	5		1		2		6	4
	7		3		4			5
4		1	5				8	
	6			2			3	
	2				7	6		9
1			8		6		7	
7	3		2		1		9	
		5		3				6

BRAIN BUSTER

		6			8	4	5	
	5				2			1
3	9					8		
					1		2	
7								5
	4		7					
		9					6	3
8			9				1	
	2	4	1			9		

CODEWORD CONUNDRUM

26	17	6	15	5	7	■	18 A	■	14	■	1	3	24	2
17	■	12	■	13	■	18	8 L	5	18	8	6	■	■	5
18	8	8	6	18	13	14	24 E	■	10	■	9	18	5	24
1	■	3	■	14	■	23	■	2	24	8	9	■	■	21
2	11	3	3	5	6	24	2	16	■	■	6	2	8	24
■	24	■	■	■	13	■	■	18	11	24	1	■	■	15
14	18	4	3	17	9	8	18	12	24	■	24	20	20	2
■	14	■	17	■	8	■	2	■	1	■	13	■	17	■
19	24	2	16	■	17	11	23	3	8	2	16	24	15	7
17	■	■	21	18	25	7	■	■	18	■	■	■	13	■
12	18	8	18	■	■	15	24	11	15	3	20	18	16	24
17	■	■	15	18	22	24	■	18	■	8	■	8	■	10
8	3	18	1	■	24	■	14	6	10	6	8	6	2	24
18	■	■	8	24	2	6	3	13	■	10	■	18	■	15
15	17	20	7	■	16	■	16	■	9	24	6	2	16	7

A B C D E F G H I J K L M

N O P Q R S T U V W X Y Z

Reference Box

1	2	3	4	5	6	7	8	9	10	11	12	13
							L					

14	15	16	17	18	19	20	21	22	23	24	25	26
				A						E		

FUTOSHIKI

Fill the grid so that every horizontal row and vertical column contains the numbers 1-5. The 'greater than' or 'less than' signs indicate where a number is larger or smaller than that in the neighbouring square.

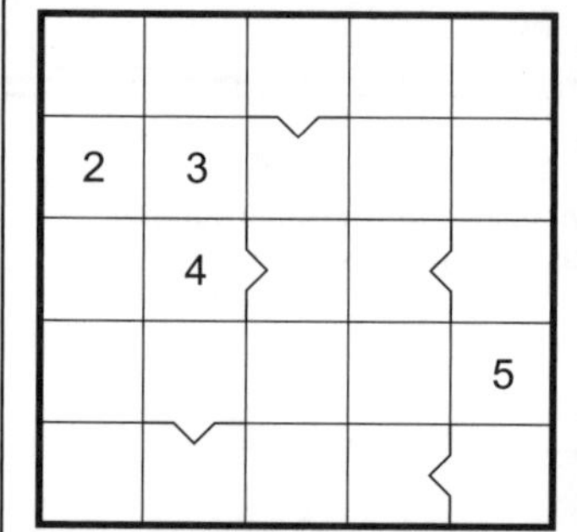

HIGH-SPEED CROSSWORD

Across

1 Construct again (7)
6 Public transport vehicle (3)
8 Sprang up (5)
9 Alike (7)
10 Bread-raising agent (5)
11 Erroneous (8)
13 Sharpshooter (6)
15 Most recent (6)
18 Expired (8)
19 Canonised person (5)
21 Desirous of a drink (7)
22 Superficial abrasion (5)
23 Donkey (3)
24 Slackened (7)

Down

2 Issue of a newspaper (7)
3 Unlucky (3-5)
4 Become less light (6)
5 Australian term for a young kangaroo (4)
6 Due to, on account of (7)
7 Instrument for measuring the angle between stars (7)
12 Fabric (8)
13 Variety of mandarin orange (7)
14 Team's turn at batting (7)
16 Enfold (7)
17 Court clown (6)
20 Nipple (4)

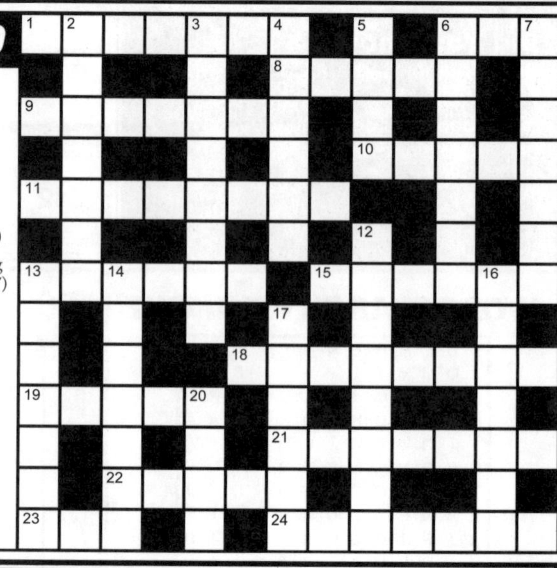

1 MINUTE NUMBER CRUNCH

Beginner								Answer
232	– 34	1/2 of this	5/9 of this	4/11 of this	+ 19	2/3 of this	+ 42	

Intermediate								Answer
29	x 3	+ 78	÷ 11	+ 25	3/10 of this	x 7	÷ 3	

Advanced								Answer
702	7/39 of this	+ 224	7/10 of this	3/5 of this	2/3 of this	x 7	x 2.5	

Did You Know?:

Flying squirrels don't actually fly. The web of skin between their four limbs and body allows them to glide between trees. They can travel a distance of about 1,300 feet in this way.

DOMINO PLACEMENT

A standard set of 28 dominoes has been laid out as shown. Can you draw in the edges of them all? The check-box is provided as an aid and the domino already placed will help.

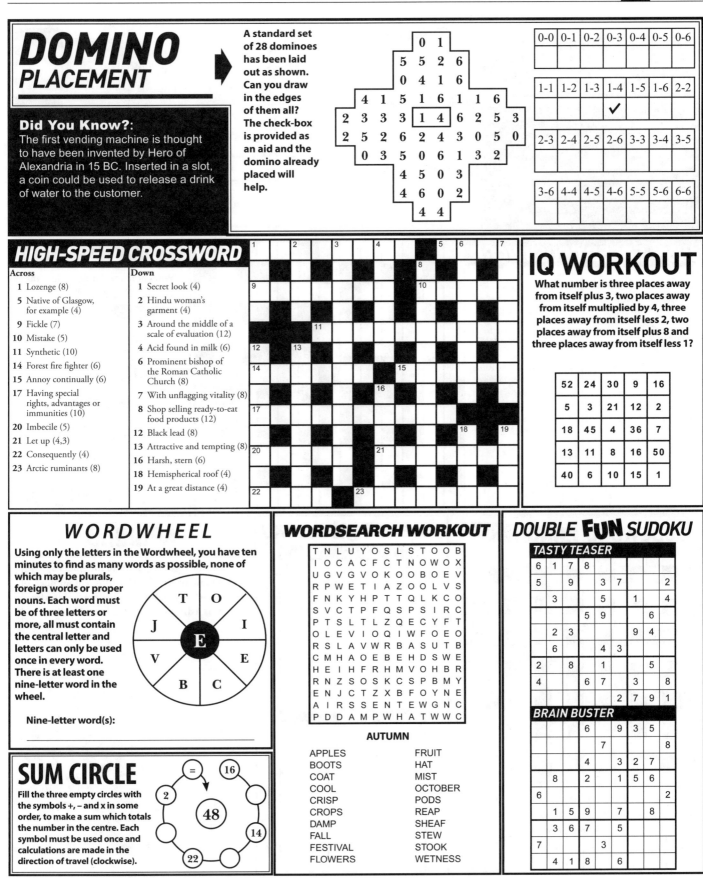

				0	1				
			5	5	2	6			
			0	4	1	6			
	4	1	5	1	6	1	1	6	
2	3	3	3	[1	4]	6	2	5	3
2	5	2	6	2	4	3	0	5	0
	0	3	5	0	6	1	3	2	
			4	5	0	3			
			4	6	0	2			
				4	4				

0-0	0-1	0-2	0-3	0-4	0-5	0-6
1-1	**1-2**	**1-3**	**1-4**	**1-5**	**1-6**	**2-2**
			✓			
2-3	**2-4**	**2-5**	**2-6**	**3-3**	**3-4**	**3-5**
3-6	**4-4**	**4-5**	**4-6**	**5-5**	**5-6**	**6-6**

Did You Know?:

The first vending machine is thought to have been invented by Hero of Alexandria in 15 BC. Inserted in a slot, a coin could be used to release a drink of water to the customer.

HIGH-SPEED CROSSWORD

Across

1 Lozenge (8)
5 Native of Glasgow, for example (4)
9 Fickle (7)
10 Mistake (5)
11 Synthetic (10)
14 Forest fire fighter (6)
15 Annoy continually (6)
17 Having special rights, advantages or immunities (10)
20 Imbecile (5)
21 Let up (4,3)
22 Consequently (4)
23 Arctic ruminants (8)

Down

1 Secret look (4)
2 Hindu woman's garment (4)
3 Around the middle of a scale of evaluation (12)
4 Acid found in milk (6)
6 Prominent bishop of the Roman Catholic Church (8)
7 With unflagging vitality (8)
8 Shop selling ready-to-eat food products (12)
12 Black lead (8)
13 Attractive and tempting (8)
16 Harsh, stern (6)
18 Hemispherical roof (4)
19 At a great distance (4)

1		2		3		4		■	5	6		7
	■		■		■		■	8	■		■	
9							■	10				
	■		■		■		■		■		■	
■	■	■	11									
12	■	13	■		■		■		■		■	
14						■	15					
	■		■		■	16	■		■		■	
17										■	■	■
	■		■		■		■		■	18	■	19
20					■	21						
	■		■		■		■		■		■	
22				■	23							

IQ WORKOUT

What number is three places away from itself plus 3, two places away from itself multiplied by 4, three places away from itself less 2, two places away from itself plus 8 and three places away from itself less 1?

52	24	30	9	16
5	3	21	12	2
18	45	4	36	7
13	11	8	16	50
40	6	10	15	1

WORDWHEEL

Using only the letters in the Wordwheel, you have ten minutes to find as many words as possible, none of which may be plurals, foreign words or proper nouns. Each word must be of three letters or more, all must contain the central letter and letters can only be used once in every word. There is at least one nine-letter word in the wheel.

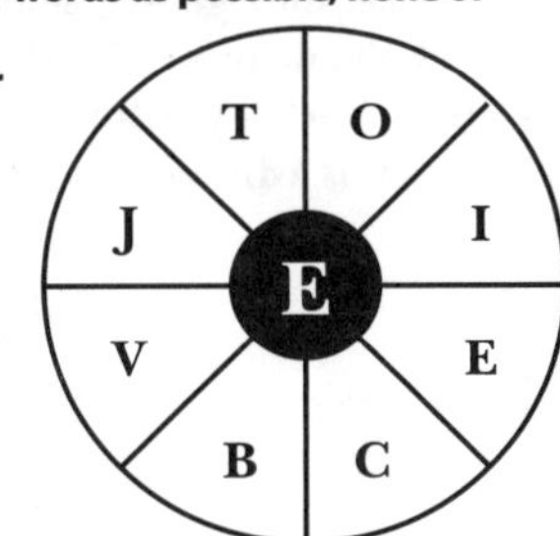

Nine-letter word(s): ____________________

SUM CIRCLE

Fill the three empty circles with the symbols +, – and x in some order, to make a sum which totals the number in the centre. Each symbol must be used once and calculations are made in the direction of travel (clockwise).

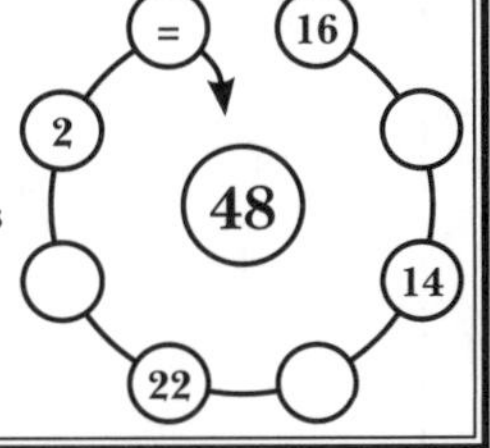

WORDSEARCH WORKOUT

T	N	L	U	Y	O	S	L	S	T	O	O	B
I	O	C	A	C	F	C	T	N	O	W	O	X
U	G	V	G	V	O	K	O	O	B	O	E	V
R	P	W	E	T	I	A	Z	O	O	L	V	S
F	N	K	Y	H	P	T	T	Q	L	K	C	O
S	V	C	T	P	F	Q	S	P	S	I	R	C
P	T	S	L	T	L	Z	Q	E	C	Y	F	T
O	L	E	V	I	O	Q	I	W	F	O	E	O
R	S	L	A	V	W	R	B	A	S	U	T	B
C	M	H	A	O	E	B	E	H	D	S	W	E
H	E	I	H	F	R	H	M	V	O	H	B	R
R	N	Z	S	O	S	K	C	S	P	B	M	Y
E	N	J	C	T	Z	X	B	F	O	Y	N	E
A	I	R	S	S	E	N	T	E	W	G	N	C
P	D	D	A	M	P	W	H	A	T	W	W	C

AUTUMN

APPLES
BOOTS
COAT
COOL
CRISP
CROPS
DAMP
FALL
FESTIVAL
FLOWERS
FRUIT
HAT
MIST
OCTOBER
PODS
REAP
SHEAF
STEW
STOOK
WETNESS

DOUBLE FUN SUDOKU

TASTY TEASER

6	1	7	8					
5		9		3	7			2
	3			5		1		4
			5	9			6	
	2	3				9	4	
	6			4	3			
2		8		1			5	
4			6	7		3		8
					2	7	9	1

BRAIN BUSTER

			6		9	3	5	
				7				8
			4		3	2	7	
	8		2		1	5	6	
6								2
	1	5	9		7		8	
	3	6	7		5			
7				3				
	4	1	8		6			

1 MINUTE NUMBER CRUNCH

Beginner								Answer
29	– 15	÷ 2	+ 86	1/3 of this	x 5	– 122	1/11 of this	

Intermediate								Answer
700	9% of this	– 28	x 4	+ 3/10 of this	÷ 2	– 17	+ 123	

Advanced								Answer
22	Squared	x 4	5/16 of this	÷ 0.25	– 987	Double it	+ 777	

Did You Know?:
In 1912, Leonardo da Vinci's *Mona Lisa* was stolen from the Louvre in Paris. Six fakes subsequently turned up and were each sold for huge sums before the original re-emerged in 1915.

HIGH-SPEED CROSSWORD

Across
- 1 Vehicles in motion (7)
- 5 Heavy wooden pole tossed as a test of strength (5)
- 7 Biting flies (5)
- 8 Become looser (7)
- 9 Interlace (7)
- 10 The first light of day (3-2)
- 11 Calm, with no emotional agitation (6)
- 13 In a slumber (6)
- 18 Kill by submerging in water (5)
- 20 Cut of meat (7)
- 21 Engage in a contest (7)
- 22 Bore a hole (5)
- 23 Birds' bills (5)
- 24 Brickwork (7)

Down
- 1 Female member of the cat family (7)
- 2 Item which enables something to be used in a way different from that for which it was intended (7)
- 3 Mode (7)
- 4 Kidney-shaped nut edible only when roasted (6)
- 5 Covers the surface of (5)
- 6 Put to death (7)
- 12 Fleshy pendulous part of the hearing organ (7)
- 14 Long steps (7)
- 15 Strong feeling (7)
- 16 Forfeit (7)
- 17 Hold in high regard (6)
- 19 Requires (5)

IQ WORKOUT

What number should replace the question mark?

16
21
16 ⅞
20 ¼
17 ¾
19 ½
?

CODEWORD CONUNDRUM

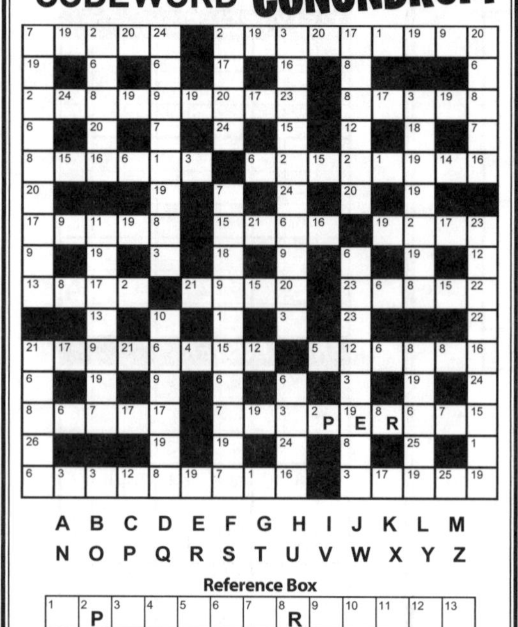

A B C D E F G H I J K L M
N O P Q R S T U V W X Y Z

Reference Box

1	2 P	3	4	5	6	7	8 R	9	10	11	12	13
14	15	16	17	18	19 E	20	21	22	23	24	25	26

DOUBLE FUN SUDOKU

TASTY TEASER

			9	5	1			4
			3		6			7
4	3	9		2				6
		4	5		3		7	
8		2				5		3
	1		7		2	4		
6				7		9	8	1
2			1		8			
1			4	6	9			

BRAIN BUSTER

9			4		1			2
	1		7		6		4	
		6		8		3		
5		4				8		9
	9						7	
7		2				1		3
		1		4		5		
	4		3		8		9	
6			2		7			1

SPIDOKU

Each of the eight segments of the spider's web should be filled with a different number from 1 to 8, in such a way that every ring also contains a different number from 1 to 8.

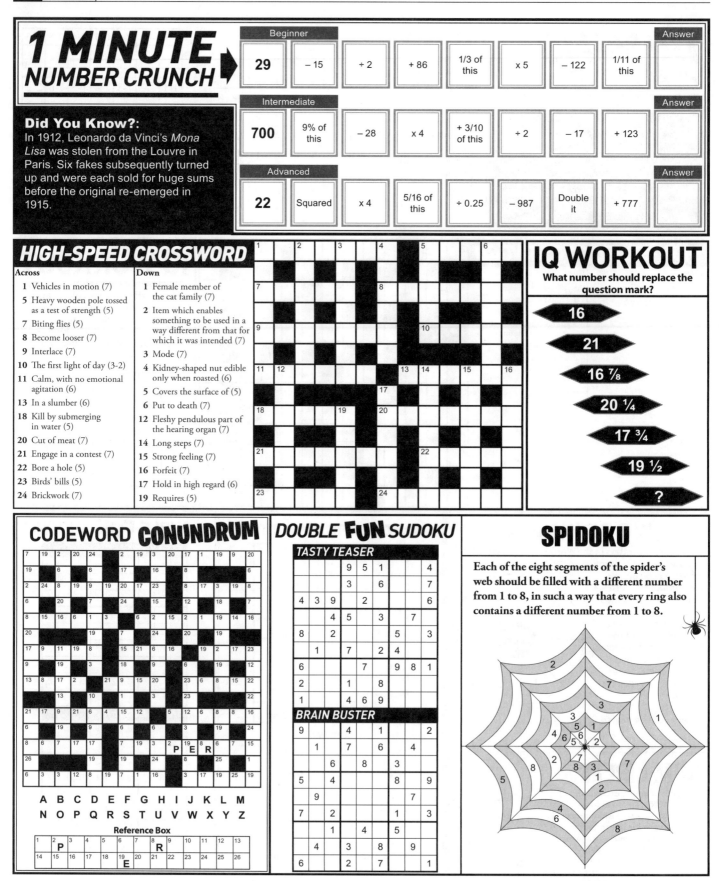

Logi-Six

Every row and column of this grid should contain one each of the letters A, B, C, D, E and F. Each of the six shapes (marked by thicker lines) should also contain one each of the letters A, B, C, D, E and F. Can you complete the grid?

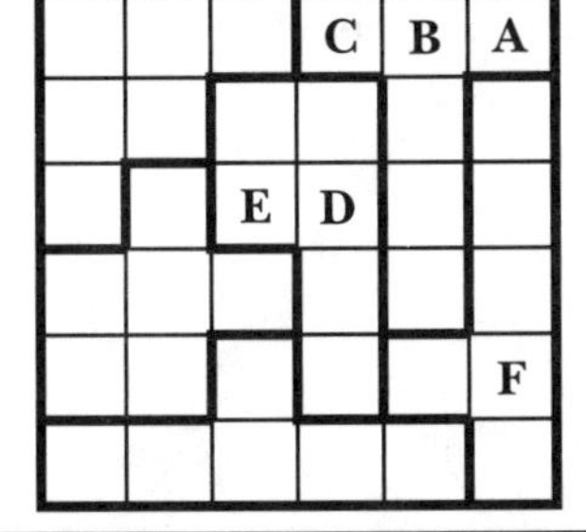

HIGH-SPEED CROSSWORD

Across

1 Shouts of approval (6)
4 Thin sliver of wood (6)
7 Mother superior (6)
8 Formal exposition (8)
12 Steps consisting of two parallel members connected by rungs (6)
14 Money chest (6)
15 Edna ___, Irish writer (born in 1932) (6)
16 Talk like a baby (6)
18 Slaughterhouse (8)
22 Mark of infamy (6)
23 Flamboyantly elaborate, showy (6)
24 Bone of the forearm (6)

Down

1 Partially burn (4)
2 Protective fold of skin (6)
3 Female sibling (6)
4 Free from danger (4)
5 Cobbler's stand (4)
6 Subdue (4)
9 Hawaiian greeting (5)
10 Stinking (6)
11 Gigantic African and Australian tree with edible fruits (6)
13 Bring into play (5)
16 Treasurer at a college or university (6)
17 In arrears (6)
18 Zealous (4)
19 Bathroom fixtures (4)
20 Wild gathering involving excessive drinking and promiscuity (4)
21 Agitates the air (4)

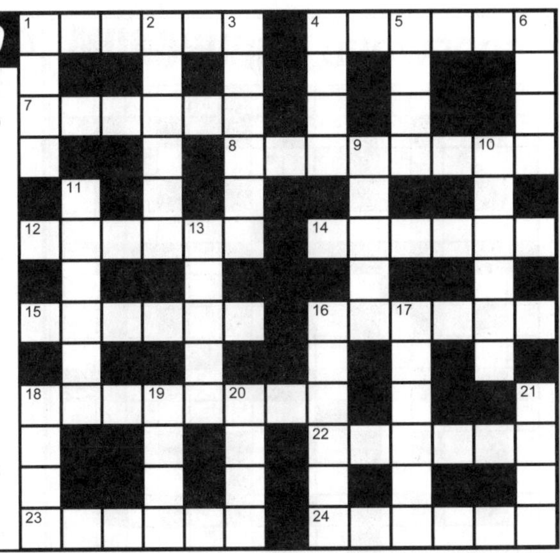

WORDSEARCH WORKOUT

A	R	S	N	K	R	N	A	R	A	H	A	S
I	S	Z	F	U	A	R	A	H	A	N	O	F
R	I	C	H	I	B	R	G	I	B	S	O	N
O	M	F	R	O	K	I	A	U	U	O	Z	D
T	P	Y	H	E	A	H	A	K	T	N	N	E
C	S	D	Q	Y	L	M	W	N	U	U	A	A
I	O	A	A	R	A	B	I	A	N	M	U	T
V	N	S	A	C	H	I	B	O	G	W	H	H
T	Y	H	A	N	A	R	O	N	O	S	A	V
A	T	T	L	O	R	V	E	J	Q	Y	U	A
E	A	E	I	G	I	G	R	W	P	A	H	L
R	K	L	B	B	E	V	A	J	O	M	I	L
G	U	U	Y	V	Y	D	P	O	U	D	H	E
A	C	T	A	D	U	F	A	N	N	A	C	Y
W	Q	U	N	P	E	H	Y	H	D	R	P	U

DESERTS

AN NAFUD
ARABIAN
ATACAMA
CHIHUAHUAN
DASHT E LUT
DEATH VALLEY
GIBSON
GOBI
GREAT VICTORIA
KALAHARI
KARA KUM
LIBYAN
MOJAVE
NEGEV
NUBIAN
SAHARA
SIMPSON
SONORAN
SYRIAN
THAR

DOUBLE FUN SUDOKU

TASTY TEASER

6			5	8		1	2	
2	3		7					
		5	1			7		3
		8			6		9	4
	7		3		1		6	
3	9		4			2		
1		4			5	9		
					4		8	6
	5	9		2	7			1

BRAIN BUSTER

9			2		8			6
		5				1		
	6		4		3		5	
	3	4	7		2	6	9	
	9	7	1		6	4	2	
	1		9		7		8	
		8				7		
4			8		5			3

MATCHSTICK MAGIC

Here is an arrangement showing a diamond shape and a square shape. Move three matches to show a diamond, a square, and two equilateral triangles (an equilateral triangle has three angles of equal degrees and three sides of equal length).

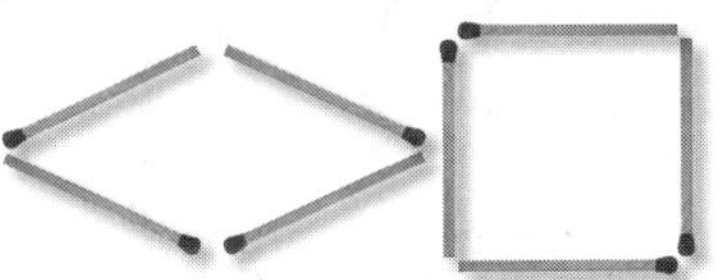

BRAIN TEASER

What replaces the question mark?

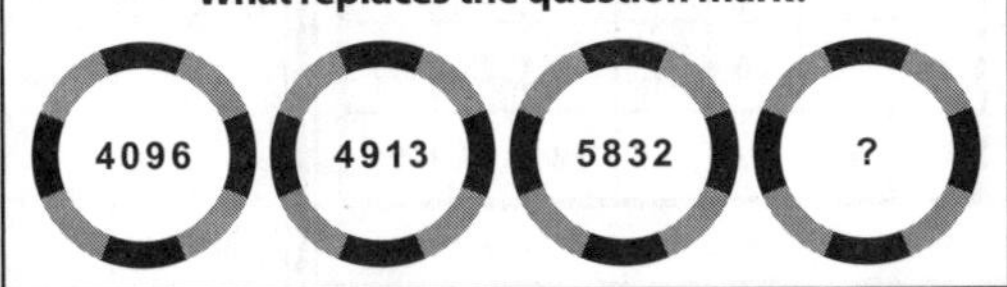

DOMINO PLACEMENT

A standard set of 28 dominoes has been laid out as shown. Can you draw in the edges of them all? The check-box is provided as an aid and the domino already placed will help.

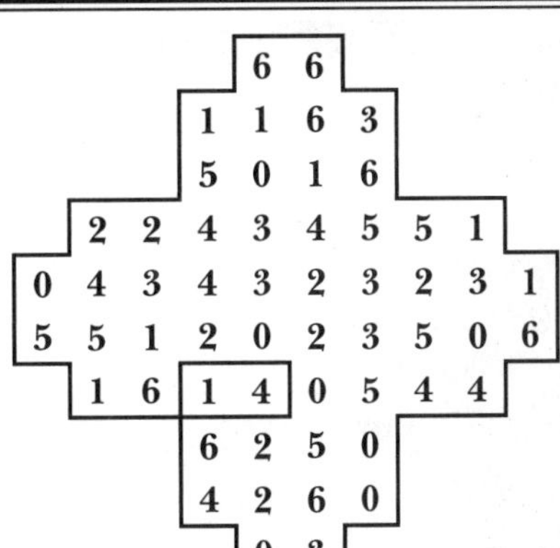

0-0	0-1	0-2	0-3	0-4	0-5	0-6
1-1	**1-2**	**1-3**	**1-4**	**1-5**	**1-6**	**2-2**
			✓			
2-3	**2-4**	**2-5**	**2-6**	**3-3**	**3-4**	**3-5**
3-6	**4-4**	**4-5**	**4-6**	**5-5**	**5-6**	**6-6**

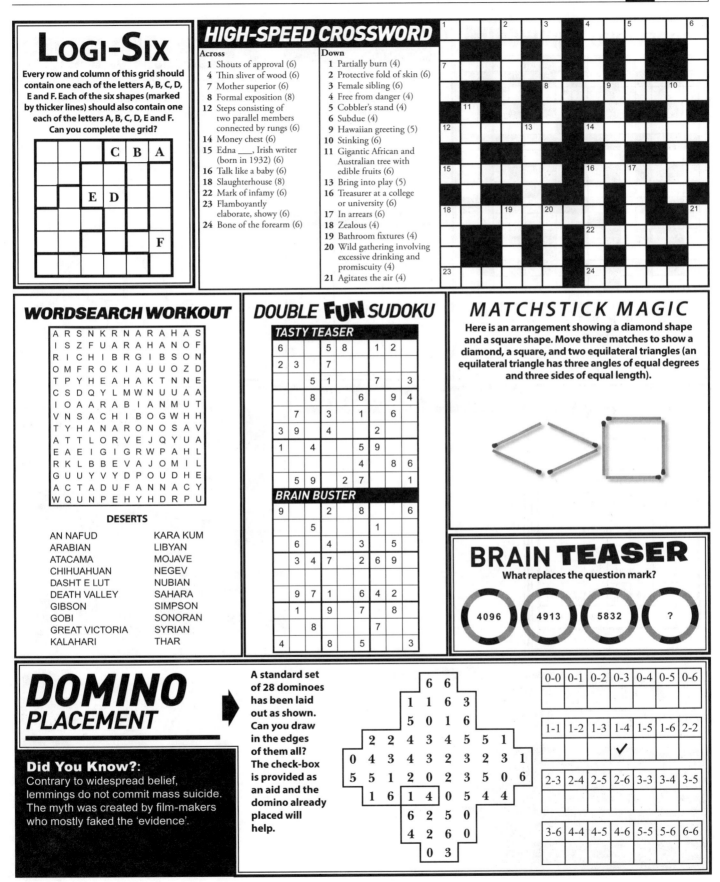

Did You Know?:
Contrary to widespread belief, lemmings do not commit mass suicide. The myth was created by film-makers who mostly faked the 'evidence'.

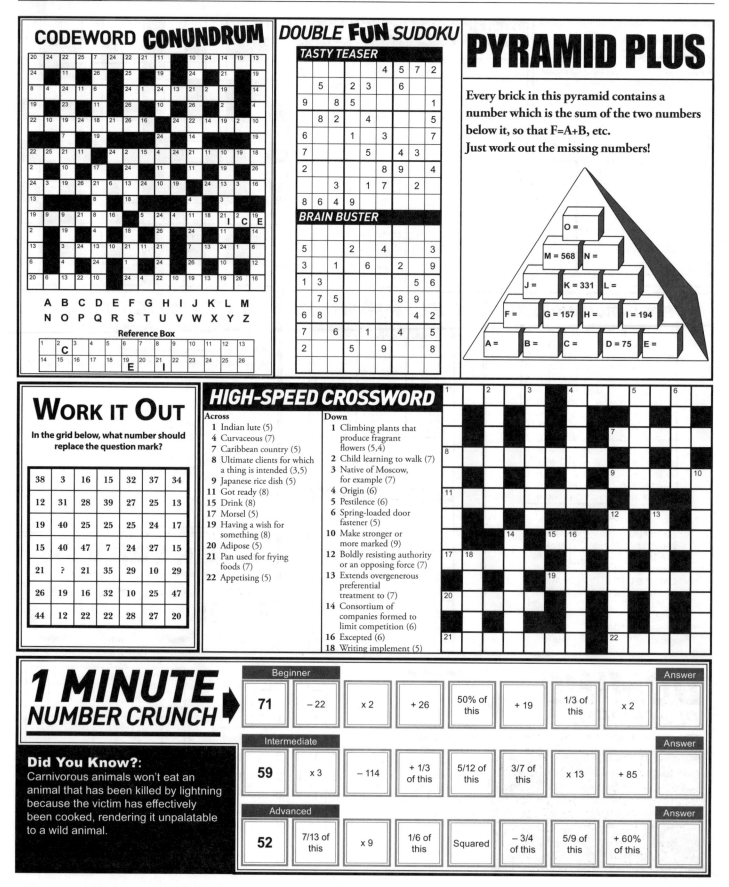

CODEWORD CONUNDRUM

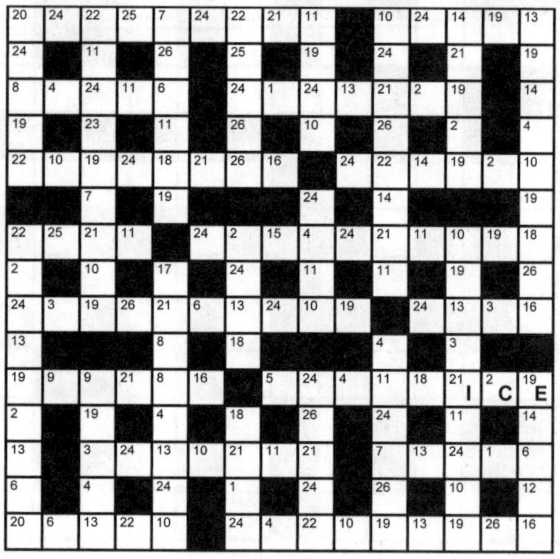

A B C D E F G H I J K L M
N O P Q R S T U V W X Y Z

Reference Box

1	2 C	3	4	5	6	7	8	9	10	11	12	13
14	15	16	17	18	19 E	20	21 I	22	23	24	25	26

DOUBLE FUN SUDOKU

TASTY TEASER

					4	5	7	2
	5		2	3		6		
9		8	5					1
	8	2		4				5
6			1		3			7
7				5		4	3	
2					8	9		4
		3		1	7		2	
8	6	4	9					

BRAIN BUSTER

5			2		4			3
3		1		6		2		9
1	3						5	6
	7	5				8	9	
6	8						4	2
7		6		1		4		5
2			5		9			8

PYRAMID PLUS

Every brick in this pyramid contains a number which is the sum of the two numbers below it, so that F=A+B, etc.
Just work out the missing numbers!

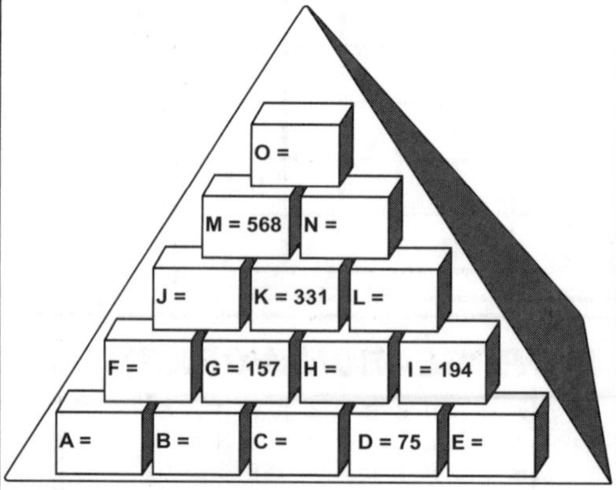

WORK IT OUT

In the grid below, what number should replace the question mark?

38	3	16	15	32	37	34
12	31	28	39	27	25	13
19	40	25	25	25	24	17
15	40	47	7	24	27	15
21	?	21	35	29	10	29
26	19	16	32	10	25	47
44	12	22	22	28	27	20

HIGH-SPEED CROSSWORD

Across
1 Indian lute (5)
4 Curvaceous (7)
7 Caribbean country (5)
8 Ultimate clients for which a thing is intended (3,5)
9 Japanese rice dish (5)
11 Got ready (8)
15 Drink (8)
17 Morsel (5)
19 Having a wish for something (8)
20 Adipose (5)
21 Pan used for frying foods (7)
22 Appetising (5)

Down
1 Climbing plants that produce fragrant flowers (5,4)
2 Child learning to walk (7)
3 Native of Moscow, for example (7)
4 Origin (6)
5 Pestilence (6)
6 Spring-loaded door fastener (5)
10 Make stronger or more marked (9)
12 Boldly resisting authority or an opposing force (7)
13 Extends overgenerous preferential treatment to (7)
14 Consortium of companies formed to limit competition (6)
16 Excepted (6)
18 Writing implement (5)

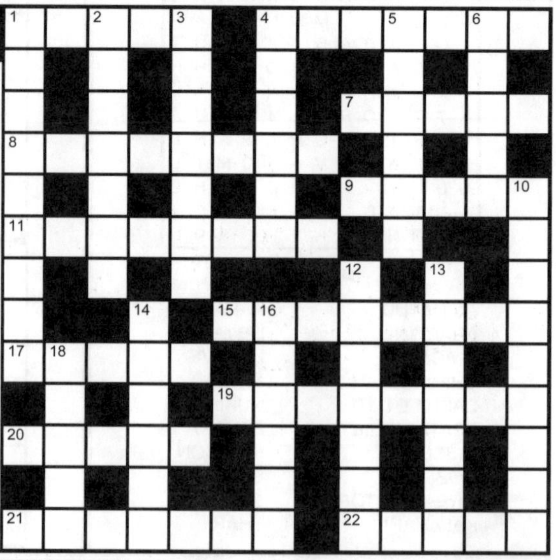

1 MINUTE NUMBER CRUNCH

Level	Start								Answer
Beginner	71	– 22	x 2	+ 26	50% of this	+ 19	1/3 of this	x 2	
Intermediate	59	x 3	– 114	+ 1/3 of this	5/12 of this	3/7 of this	x 13	+ 85	
Advanced	52	7/13 of this	x 9	1/6 of this	Squared	– 3/4 of this	5/9 of this	+ 60% of this	

Did You Know?:
Carnivorous animals won't eat an animal that has been killed by lightning because the victim has effectively been cooked, rendering it unpalatable to a wild animal.

HIGH-SPEED CROSSWORD

Across

1 Rich, buttery sponge with a close texture (7,4)
7 Dots in a text showing suppression of words (8)
8 Tibetan or Mongolian priest (4)
9 Hearty and lusty, crude (6)
11 Arm covering (6)
13 Emblem (5)
14 Corrode (5)
17 Design made of small pieces of coloured stone or glass (6)
20 Blasphemed (6)
22 Star which ejects material (4)
23 Situation, set-up (8)
24 Impoverished, destitute (11)

Down

1 More modest (6)
2 Have actual being (5)
3 Arrange into a different shape or layout (7)
4 Abnormal swellings on the body (5)
5 Ms Minogue (5)
6 Astonished (6)
10 Wanders about (5)
12 Chris ___, ex-husband of Billie Piper (5)
14 Wife of a duke (7)
15 Rectifies (6)
16 Abominable (6)
18 Semi-precious stone (5)
19 Hindu social class (5)
21 Respond (5)

IQ WORKOUT

Draw in the hands on the final clock.

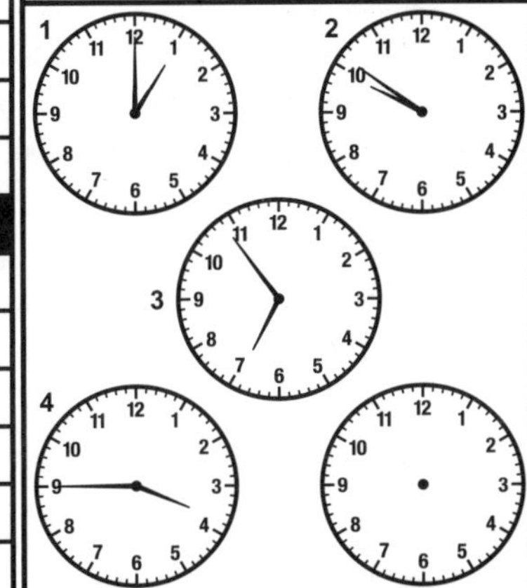

1 MINUTE NUMBER CRUNCH

									Answer
Beginner	36	1/12 of this	x 20	+ 3	÷ 21	x 19	+ 18	1/3 of this	
Intermediate	13	x 9	+ 414	5/9 of this	÷ 5	+ 63	x 5	9/10 of this	
Advanced	26	Cubed	3/8 of this	+ 2/3 of this	60% of this	– 4607	5/16 of this	3/5 of this	

Did You Know?:
A once-common way to lose weight was to swallow live tapeworms. Once inside the stomach the worms would consume a proportion of the host's food.

WORDSEARCH WORKOUT

V Y N P T U A S N I C X O
Z I Z W I B O A Y A O Q J
U O D Z U N K P R R R D E
Z N I A M C O E T U A G D
U I L O L A P T R I I H R
T R N X N B L M N N M V E
O A C F F A L V O O E A V
L B E P A R G A A Q I R R
R L B F H N I E N S O R S
E A L S I H D E T C I Y M
M A A J Z A N E S R L A P
T E M P R A N I L L O O B
H Z L S B E F O N Y I V E
E H R E N F E L S E R N P
Z T P I N O T B L A N C G

GRAPE VARIETIES

ALBARINO
BUAL
CINSAUT
EHRENFELSER
FIANO
KERNER
MALBEC
MALVASIA
MERLOT
OPTIMA
ORTEGA
PINOT BLANC
PINOT NOIR
RIESLING
SYRAH
TEMPRANILLO
VERDEJO
VIDAL BLANC
VIURA
ZINFANDEL

DOUBLE FUN SUDOKU

TASTY TEASER

		1					9	6
3		4		6		5	8	
			1	8	2			
7	5	6			4			3
	1		8		5		6	
4			6			9	2	5
			5	7	8			
	8	3		4		1		2
9	6					4		

BRAIN BUSTER

	2	3		4		9	1	
	9		3		2		7	
		6				3		
			9		6			
		8				2		
			2		4			
		1				8		
	7		1		8		4	
	5	2		9		7	6	

WHATEVER NEXT?

In the diagram below, which letter should replace the question mark?

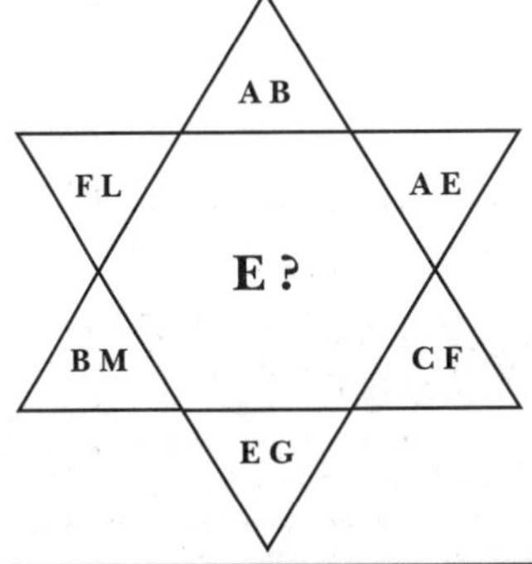

BRAIN TEASER

The average of two numbers is 41½; the average of three numbers is 72; what is the third number?

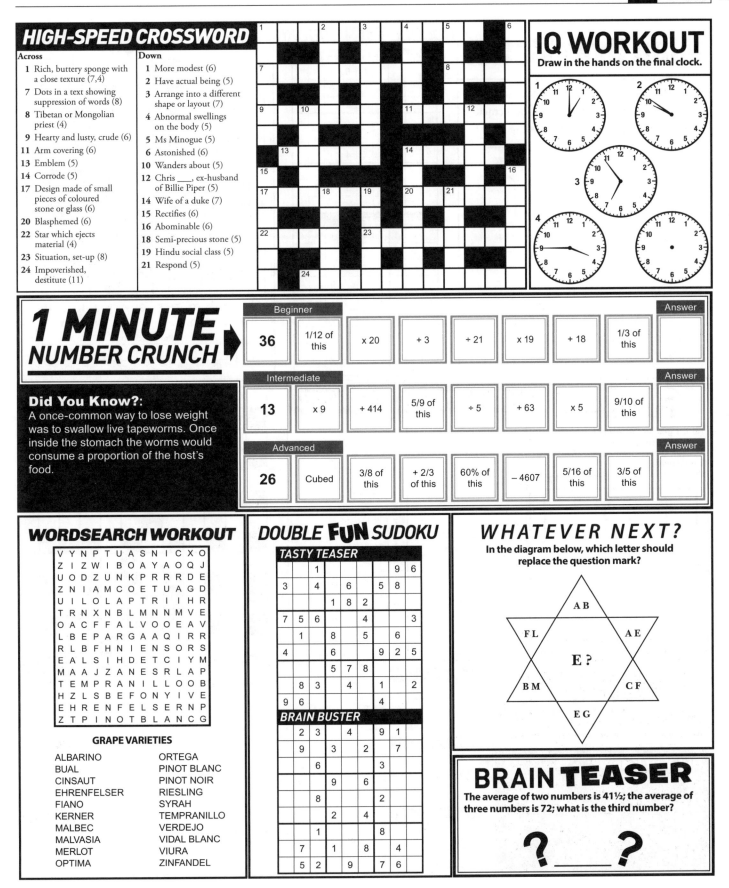

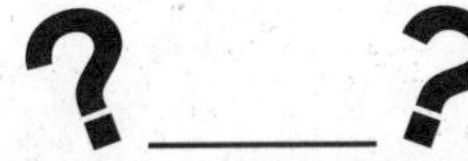

Mind Over Matter

Given that the letters are valued 1-26 according to their places in the alphabet, can you crack the mystery code to reveal the missing letter?

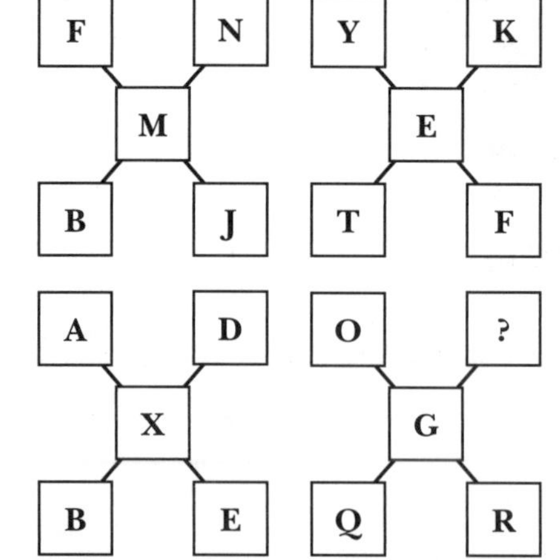

DOUBLE FUN SUDOKU

TASTY TEASER

				6	5	1	7	
	3		4		8	9		
	4	6			1		3	
6			1	7				5
7	1						4	8
2				5	4			7
	5		9			4	6	
		1	5		3		2	
	7	9	2	1				

BRAIN BUSTER

	8			9		1	4	5
	3		1					
	6			7	5			
5						9		
4	1						2	7
		3						8
			5	2			6	
					8		9	
8	4	2		3			5	

CODEWORD CONUNDRUM

19	5	17	21	14		22	12	24	5	14	10	12	12	3
11		7		17		17		5		17				16
2	13	24	17	16	4	17	1	17		8	17	14	2	11
8		16		26		10		22		17		17		13
24	16	11	26	17	21		17	8	12	24	17	16	2	4
23				16		21		17		11		25		
11	24	12	22	8		18	6	21	15		20	18	11	1
13		16		17		7		26		1		16		11
1	2	6	8		14	18	16	17		17	22	17	16	15
		11		23		16		8		4				21
11	22	13	2	12	24 T	2 I	4 C		6	17	22	2	13	2
14		9		13		11		19		22		13		6
14	21	11	15	8		13	11	2	21	23	16	18	8	5
21				11		4		24		17		16		24
17	22	14	24	2	13	17	8	8		16	17	17	1	8

A B C D E F G H I J K L M

N O P Q R S T U V W X Y Z

Reference Box

1	2	3	4	5	6	7	8	9	10	11	12	13
	I		C									
14	**15**	**16**	**17**	**18**	**19**	**20**	**21**	**22**	**23**	**24**	**25**	**26**
										T		

FUTOSHIKI

Fill the grid so that every horizontal row and vertical column contains the numbers 1-5. The 'greater than' or 'less than' signs indicate where a number is larger or smaller than that in the neighbouring square.

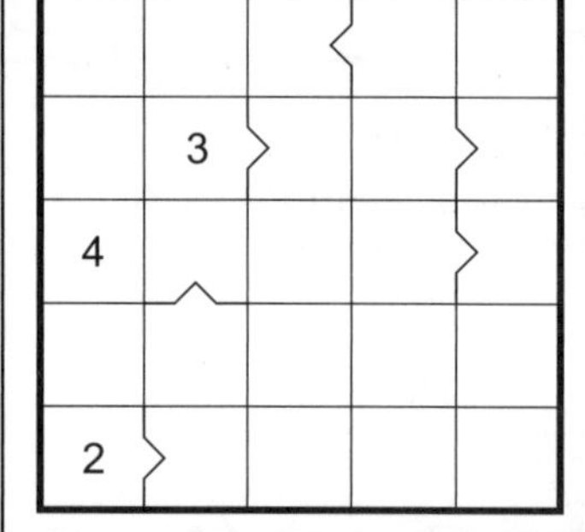

HIGH-SPEED CROSSWORD

Across

1 Travel by foot (4)
3 Completed (8)
9 Plants, often with unusual flowers (7)
10 Copy on thin paper (5)
11 Gather into a ruffle (5)
12 Transports (7)
13 French port city on the Loire (6)
15 Type of firearm (3,3)
17 Direction indicator (7)
18 Entice (5)
20 Distressed (5)
21 Car used as a taxi (7)
22 Inn (8)
23 Live-action film about a piglet (4)

Down

1 Pertussis (8,5)
2 Informal term for money (5)
4 Ant or beetle, for example (6)
5 Sporadic (12)
6 Making warm (7)
7 Item of bedroom furniture (8,5)
8 Gossip (6-6)
14 Goddess of retribution (7)
16 Chemical with the same formula but a different structure (6)
19 Birthplace of Mohammed (5)

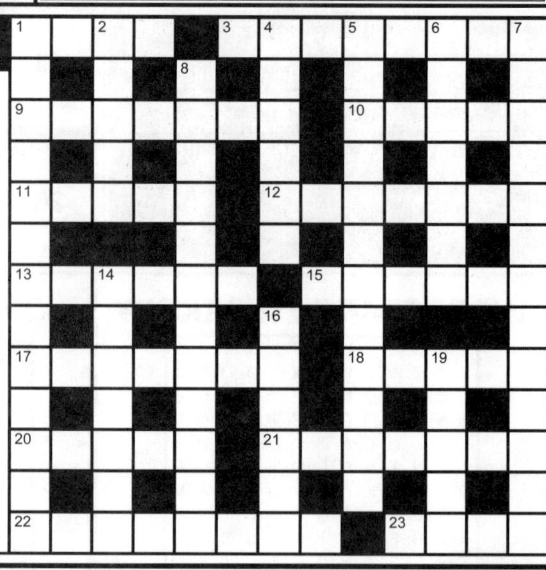

Beginner

36	1/6 of this	x 17	– 86	x 4	5/16 of this	+ 48	Double it	Answer

Intermediate

1215	÷ 5	÷ 27	+ 5/9 of this	3/7 of this	+ 2/3 of this	950% of this	+ 36	Answer

Advanced

13	x 24	5/12 of this	+ 9/10 of this	6/13 of this	+ 2/3 of this	x 4	3/8 of this	Answer

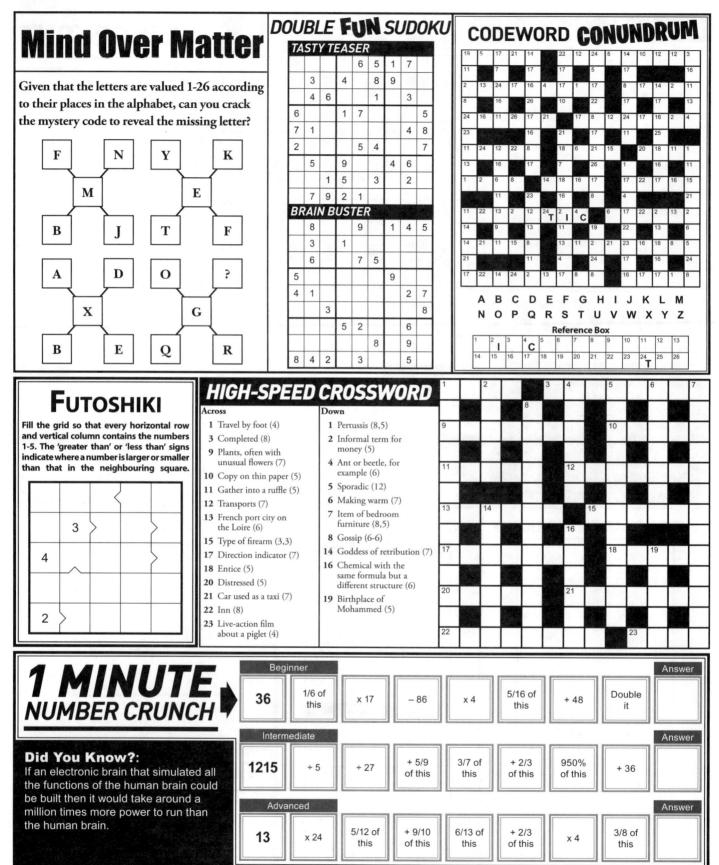

Did You Know?:

If an electronic brain that simulated all the functions of the human brain could be built then it would take around a million times more power to run than the human brain.

BATTLESHIP BOUT

Can you place the vessels into the diagram? Some parts of vessels or sea squares have already been filled in. A number to the right or below a row or column refers to the number of occupied squares in that row or column.
Any vessel may be positioned horizontally or vertically, but no part of a vessel touches part of any other vessel, either horizontally, vertically or diagonally.

Empty Area of Sea: ≈
Aircraft Carrier:
Battleships:
Cruisers:
Submarines:

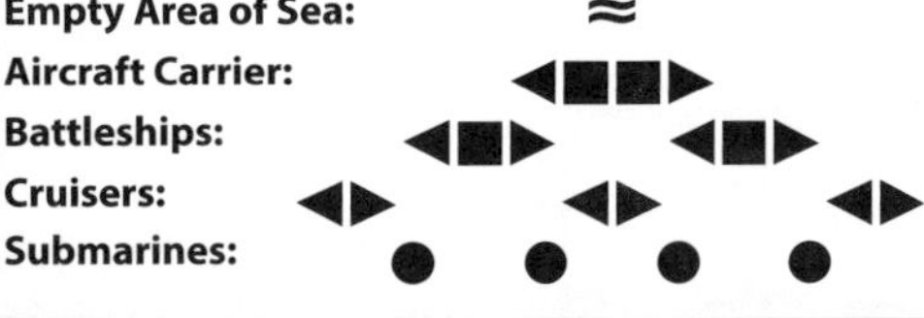

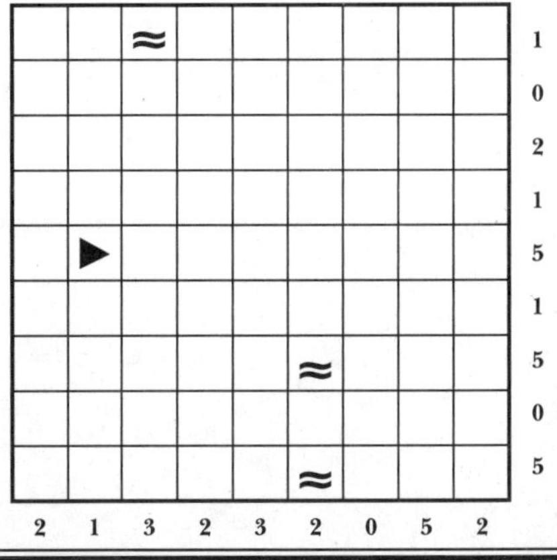

Did You Know?:
The first quantity-produced car was made by the US company, Dureya. In 1896 Dureya produced a first run of 13 cars.

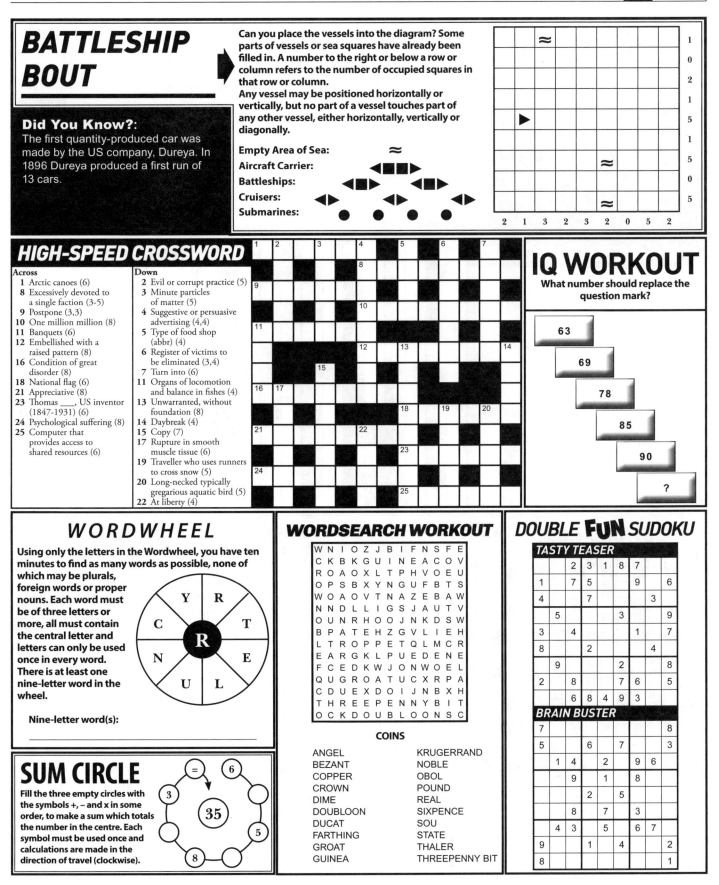

HIGH-SPEED CROSSWORD

Across
1 Arctic canoes (6)
8 Excessively devoted to a single faction (3-5)
9 Postpone (3,3)
10 One million million (8)
11 Banquets (6)
12 Embellished with a raised pattern (8)
16 Condition of great disorder (8)
18 National flag (6)
21 Appreciative (8)
23 Thomas ___, US inventor (1847-1931) (6)
24 Psychological suffering (8)
25 Computer that provides access to shared resources (6)

Down
2 Evil or corrupt practice (5)
3 Minute particles of matter (5)
4 Suggestive or persuasive advertising (4,4)
5 Type of food shop (abbr) (4)
6 Register of victims to be eliminated (3,4)
7 Turn into (6)
11 Organs of locomotion and balance in fishes (4)
13 Unwarranted, without foundation (8)
14 Daybreak (4)
15 Copy (7)
17 Rupture in smooth muscle tissue (6)
19 Traveller who uses runners to cross snow (5)
20 Long-necked typically gregarious aquatic bird (5)
22 At liberty (4)

IQ WORKOUT

What number should replace the question mark?

63
69
78
85
90
?

WORDWHEEL

Using only the letters in the Wordwheel, you have ten minutes to find as many words as possible, none of which may be plurals, foreign words or proper nouns. Each word must be of three letters or more, all must contain the central letter and letters can only be used once in every word. There is at least one nine-letter word in the wheel.

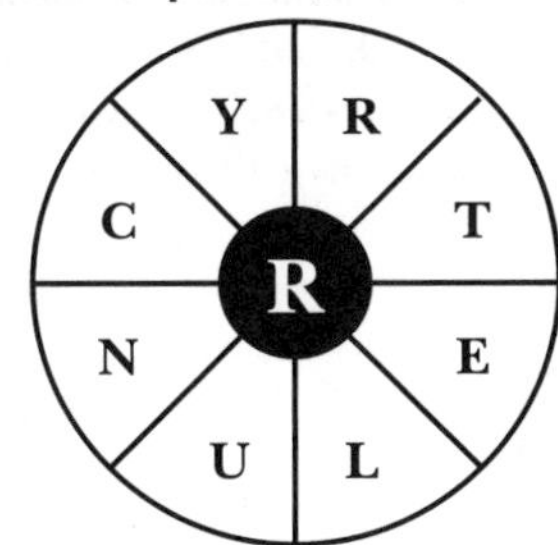

Nine-letter word(s): ____________

SUM CIRCLE

Fill the three empty circles with the symbols +, – and x in some order, to make a sum which totals the number in the centre. Each symbol must be used once and calculations are made in the direction of travel (clockwise).

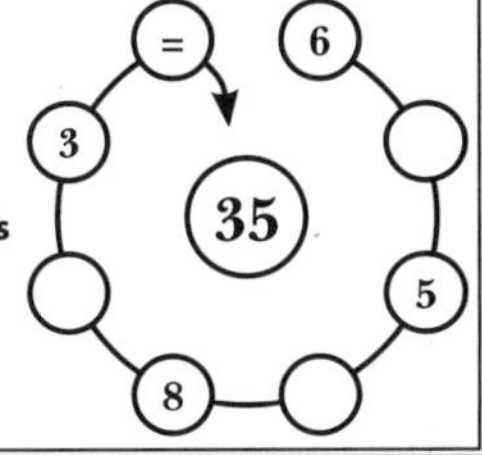

WORDSEARCH WORKOUT

W	N	I	O	Z	J	B	I	F	N	S	F	E
C	K	B	K	G	U	I	N	E	A	C	O	V
R	O	A	O	X	L	T	P	H	V	O	E	U
O	P	S	B	X	Y	N	G	U	F	B	T	S
W	O	A	O	V	T	N	A	Z	E	B	A	W
N	N	D	L	L	I	G	S	J	A	U	T	V
O	U	N	R	H	O	O	J	N	K	D	S	W
B	P	A	T	E	H	Z	G	V	L	I	E	H
L	T	R	O	P	P	E	T	Q	L	M	C	R
E	A	R	G	K	L	P	U	E	D	E	N	E
F	C	E	D	K	W	J	O	N	W	O	E	L
Q	U	G	R	O	A	T	U	C	X	R	P	A
C	D	U	E	X	D	O	I	J	N	B	X	H
T	H	R	E	E	P	E	N	N	Y	B	I	T
O	C	K	D	O	U	B	L	O	O	N	S	C

COINS

ANGEL
BEZANT
COPPER
CROWN
DIME
DOUBLOON
DUCAT
FARTHING
GROAT
GUINEA
KRUGERRAND
NOBLE
OBOL
POUND
REAL
SIXPENCE
SOU
STATE
THALER
THREEPENNY BIT

DOUBLE FUN SUDOKU

TASTY TEASER

		2	3	1	8	7		
1		7	5			9		6
4			7				3	
	5				3			9
3		4				1		7
8			2				4	
	9				2			8
2		8			7	6		5
		6	8	4	9	3		

BRAIN BUSTER

7								8
5			6		7			3
	1	4		2		9	6	
		9		1		8		
			2		5			
		8		7		3		
	4	3		5		6	7	
9			1		4			2
8								1

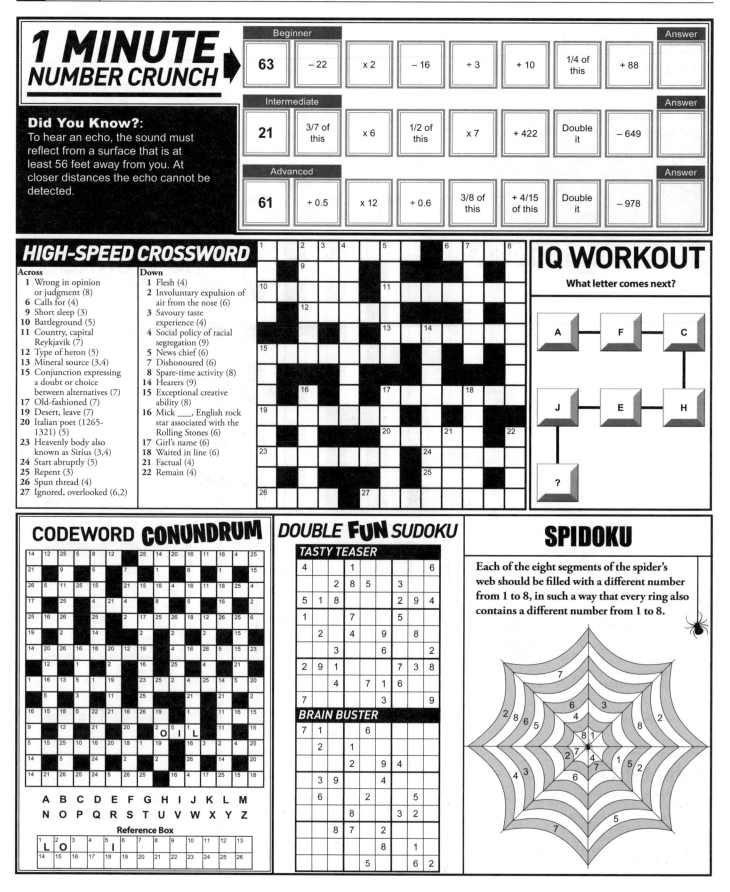

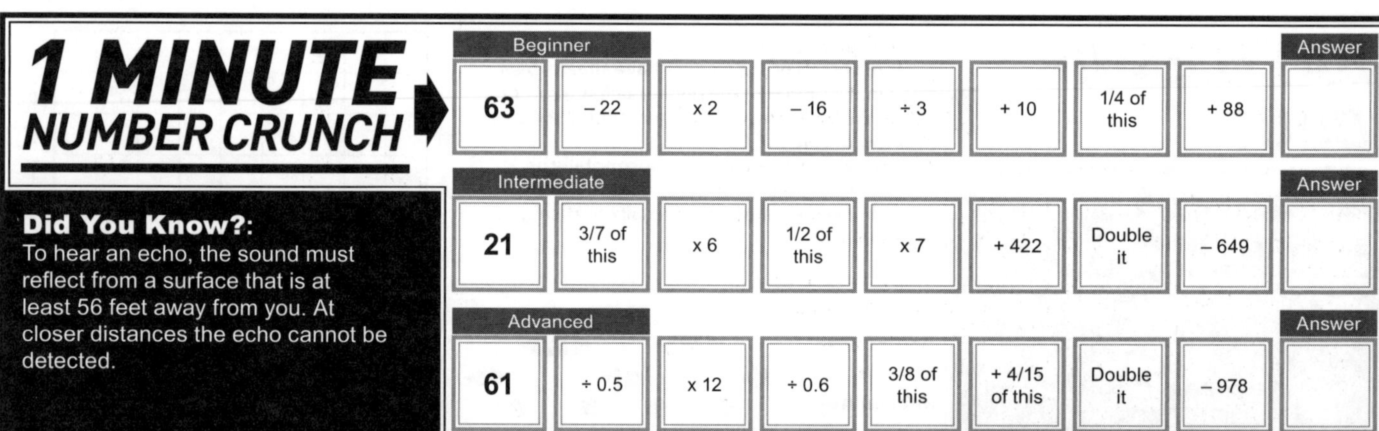

1 MINUTE NUMBER CRUNCH

Beginner								Answer
63	– 22	x 2	– 16	÷ 3	+ 10	1/4 of this	+ 88	

Intermediate								Answer
21	3/7 of this	x 6	1/2 of this	x 7	+ 422	Double it	– 649	

Advanced								Answer
61	÷ 0.5	x 12	÷ 0.6	3/8 of this	+ 4/15 of this	Double it	– 978	

Did You Know?:
To hear an echo, the sound must reflect from a surface that is at least 56 feet away from you. At closer distances the echo cannot be detected.

HIGH-SPEED CROSSWORD

Across
- 1 Wrong in opinion or judgment (8)
- 6 Calls for (4)
- 9 Short sleep (3)
- 10 Battleground (5)
- 11 Country, capital Reykjavik (7)
- 12 Type of heron (5)
- 13 Mineral source (3,4)
- 15 Conjunction expressing a doubt or choice between alternatives (7)
- 17 Old-fashioned (7)
- 19 Desert, leave (7)
- 20 Italian poet (1265-1321) (5)
- 23 Heavenly body also known as Sirius (3,4)
- 24 Start abruptly (5)
- 25 Repent (3)
- 26 Spun thread (4)
- 27 Ignored, overlooked (6,2)

Down
- 1 Flesh (4)
- 2 Involuntary expulsion of air from the nose (6)
- 3 Savoury taste experience (4)
- 4 Social policy of racial segregation (9)
- 5 News chief (6)
- 7 Dishonoured (6)
- 8 Spare-time activity (8)
- 14 Hearers (9)
- 15 Exceptional creative ability (8)
- 16 Mick ___, English rock star associated with the Rolling Stones (6)
- 17 Girl's name (6)
- 18 Waited in line (6)
- 21 Factual (4)
- 22 Remain (4)

IQ WORKOUT

What letter comes next?

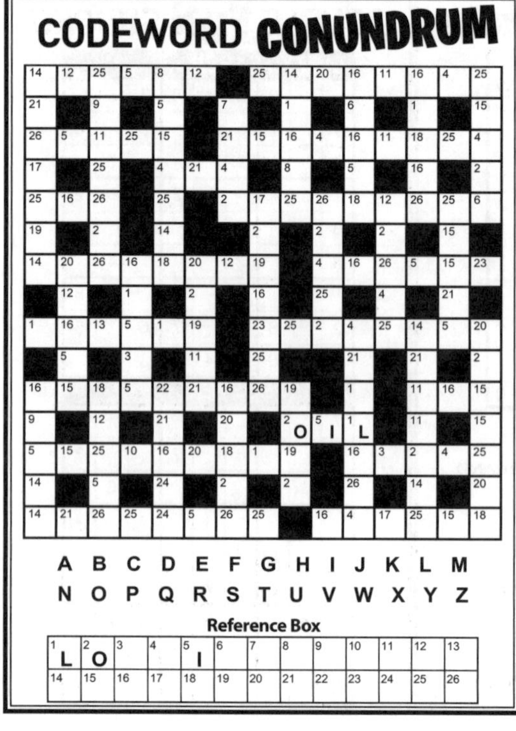

CODEWORD CONUNDRUM

DOUBLE FUN SUDOKU

TASTY TEASER

4			1					6
		2	8	5		3		
5	1	8				2	9	4
1			7			5		
	2		4		9		8	
		3			6			2
2	9	1				7	3	8
		4		7	1	6		
7					3			9

BRAIN BUSTER

7	1			6				
	2		1					
			2		9	4		
	3	9			4			
	6			2			5	
			8			3	2	
		8	7		2			
					8		1	
				5			6	2

SPIDOKU

Each of the eight segments of the spider's web should be filled with a different number from 1 to 8, in such a way that every ring also contains a different number from 1 to 8.

LOGI-SIX

Every row and column of this grid should contain one each of the letters A, B, C, D, E and F. Each of the six shapes (marked by thicker lines) should also contain one each of the letters A, B, C, D, E and F. Can you complete the grid?

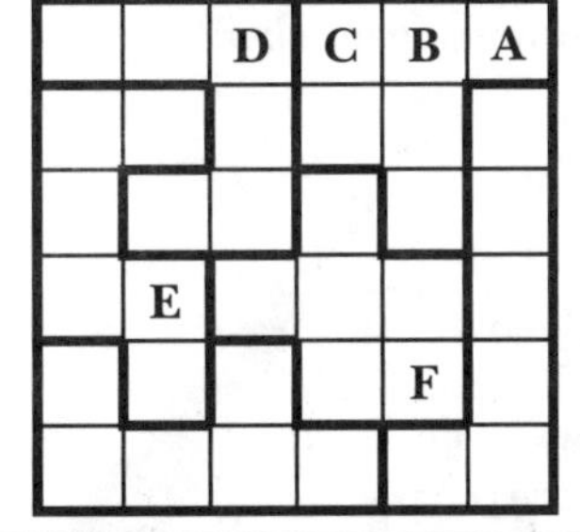

HIGH-SPEED CROSSWORD

Across
- 4 Seed often used on bread rolls (6)
- 6 Italian sponge cake, coffee and brandy dessert (8)
- 7 Desolate (6)
- 8 Release after a security has been paid (4)
- 9 Bounder (3)
- 11 Cold vegetable dish (5)
- 12 Imaginary water nymph (7)
- 15 Climbing plant (7)
- 17 Formal title used when addressing a woman (5)
- 20 Flow back (3)
- 21 Ensnare (4)
- 22 Kitchen appliance, oven (6)
- 23 Duplicitous (3-5)
- 24 Moral principles (6)

Down
- 1 Stout-bodied insect which produces a loud, chirping sound (6)
- 2 Decoration hung in a home (9)
- 3 The letter H written as a word (5)
- 4 Quieted and brought under control (7)
- 5 Breakfast food (6)
- 10 Unprejudiced (9)
- 11 Pouch (3)
- 13 Barrier which contains the flow of water (3)
- 14 Arid regions of the world (7)
- 16 Give an account in words (6)
- 18 Rouse from slumber (6)
- 19 Chief monk (5)

WORDSEARCH WORKOUT

```
S Z S E K I S L L I B Y S
M H D C E P S F N X A K L
I D H L I V T R B G I S R
K F R P U P O Y R M C E B
E A H F R G O E P R V U F
M S F B E Q T I O Y L M R
H I T R N L N O R L X A E
N H C I A I G T S F H G D
T L T W M E S E H G P W T
Y T Z O B I Y I J B S I R
V E O X U E T K D K Y T E
F Y D P M Y M Y S C K C N
T V U A B Q R H N V A H T
L C O D L I N A N I G A F
M A R L E Y N H Y A T I C
```

DICKENS CHARACTERS

BILL SIKES, BULLS EYE, BUMBLE, CODLIN, FAGIN, FRED TRENT, MAGWITCH, MARLEY, NANCY, PIP, POTT, ROGER CLY, SCROOGE, SKIMPIN, SMIKE, STRYVER, TINY TIM, TOOTS, VUFFIN, WALTER GAY

DOUBLE FUN SUDOKU

TASTY TEASER

	6	3				2		
	8		6	5		7		9
	5		4		8		1	
				7	4	5		8
1			8		2			4
3		8	9	6				
	1		3		9		2	
9		4		1	7		5	
		7				3	9	

BRAIN BUSTER

2		1		6		7		8
	3						2	
9			2		8			1
		2		3		4		
			7		5			
		6		4		2		
7			4		2			9
	5						7	
6		3		9		8		4

MATCHSTICK MAGIC

Move four matchsticks to make three squares.

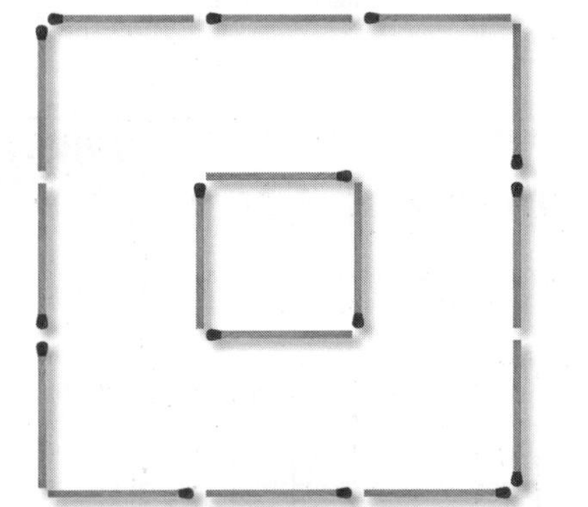

BRAIN TEASER

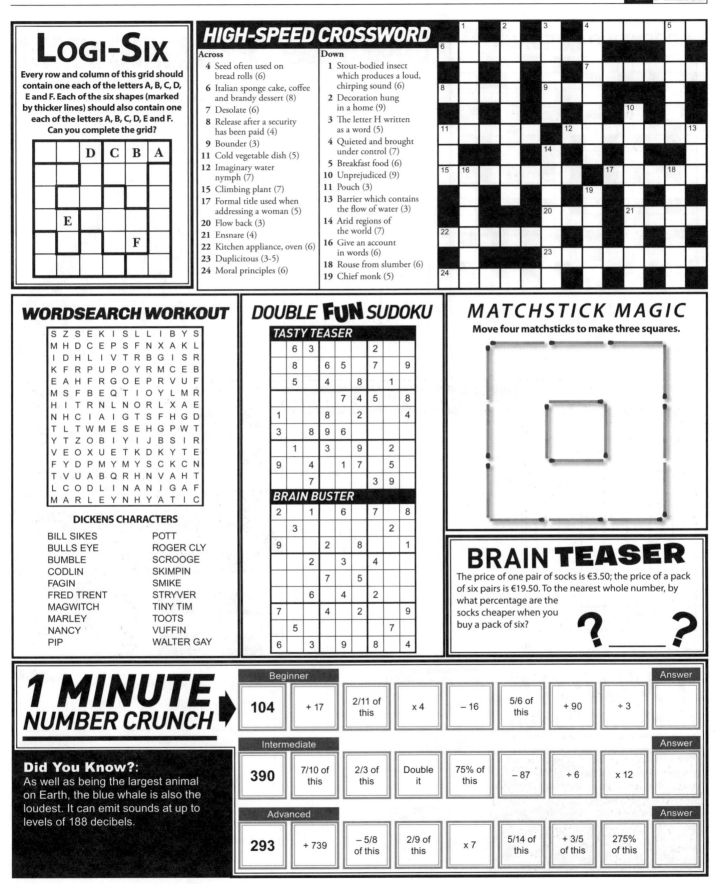

The price of one pair of socks is €3.50; the price of a pack of six pairs is €19.50. To the nearest whole number, by what percentage are the socks cheaper when you buy a pack of six?

? ______ ?

1 MINUTE NUMBER CRUNCH

Beginner

104	+ 17	2/11 of this	x 4	– 16	5/6 of this	+ 90	÷ 3	Answer

Intermediate

390	7/10 of this	2/3 of this	Double it	75% of this	– 87	÷ 6	x 12	Answer

Advanced

293	+ 739	– 5/8 of this	2/9 of this	x 7	5/14 of this	+ 3/5 of this	275% of this	Answer

Did You Know?:
As well as being the largest animal on Earth, the blue whale is also the loudest. It can emit sounds at up to levels of 188 decibels.

CODEWORD CONUNDRUM

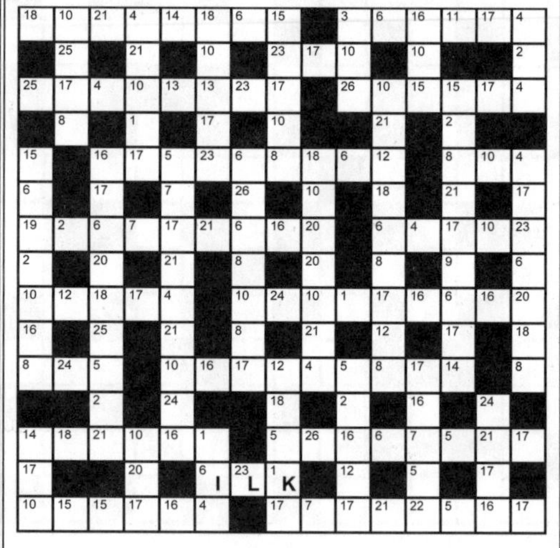

A B C D E F G H I J K L M

N O P Q R S T U V W X Y Z

Reference Box

1	2	3	4	5	6	7	8	9	10	11	12	13
K					I							
14	**15**	**16**	**17**	**18**	**19**	**20**	**21**	**22**	**23**	**24**	**25**	**26**
									L			

DOUBLE FUN SUDOKU

TASTY TEASER

9			1		6			2
	1			7			6	
	6	2		5		7	3	
	9	5	4		7	6	8	
6			5		9			7
	4	7	6		3	9	1	
	2	9		4		3	7	
	8			9			5	
3			7		1			8

BRAIN BUSTER

	5	9		3		8	7	
		6	8		4	2		
2		5				6		7
9	8						2	4
1		3				5		8
		8	6		7	1		
	3	1		5		4	6	

PYRAMID PLUS

Every brick in this pyramid contains a number which is the sum of the two numbers below it, so that F=A+B, etc.
Just work out the missing numbers!

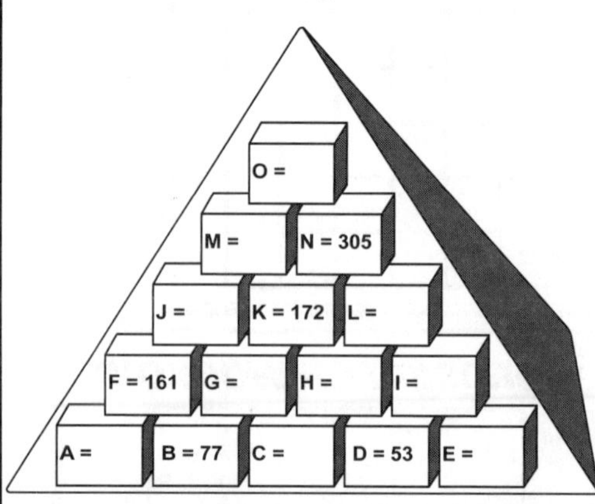

WORK IT OUT

In the grid below, what number should replace the question mark?

4	17	30	43	56	69	82
3	17	31	45	59	73	87
2	17	32	47	62	77	92
5	21	37	53	69	?	101
4	21	38	55	72	89	106
2	20	38	56	74	92	110
1	20	39	58	77	96	115

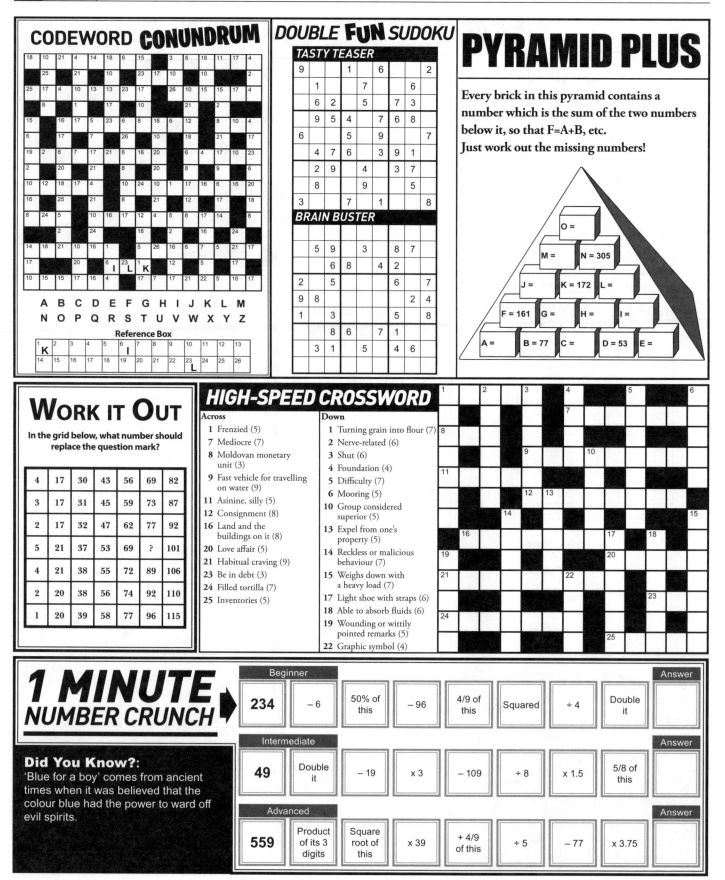

HIGH-SPEED CROSSWORD

Across

1 Frenzied (5)
7 Mediocre (7)
8 Moldovan monetary unit (3)
9 Fast vehicle for travelling on water (9)
11 Asinine, silly (5)
12 Consignment (8)
16 Land and the buildings on it (8)
20 Love affair (5)
21 Habitual craving (9)
23 Be in debt (3)
24 Filled tortilla (7)
25 Inventories (5)

Down

1 Turning grain into flour (7)
2 Nerve-related (6)
3 Shut (6)
4 Foundation (4)
5 Difficulty (7)
6 Mooring (5)
10 Group considered superior (5)
13 Expel from one's property (5)
14 Reckless or malicious behaviour (7)
15 Weighs down with a heavy load (7)
17 Light shoe with straps (6)
18 Able to absorb fluids (6)
19 Wounding or wittily pointed remarks (5)
22 Graphic symbol (4)

1 MINUTE NUMBER CRUNCH

Beginner

234	– 6	50% of this	– 96	4/9 of this	Squared	÷ 4	Double it	Answer

Intermediate

49	Double it	– 19	x 3	– 109	÷ 8	x 1.5	5/8 of this	Answer

Advanced

559	Product of its 3 digits	Square root of this	x 39	+ 4/9 of this	÷ 5	– 77	x 3.75	Answer

Did You Know?:
'Blue for a boy' comes from ancient times when it was believed that the colour blue had the power to ward off evil spirits.

HIGH-SPEED CROSSWORD

Across

1 Gardening scissors (6)
7 Internet site where users communicate in real time (4,4)
8 Go in search of (6)
10 Sliding container in a piece of furniture (6)
11 Short formal piece of writing (5)
13 Becomes angry (coll) (4,3)
16 Combats (7)
17 Gasps for breath (5)
20 Song or hymn of mourning (6)
22 Period of play in cricket (6)
24 Reaction (8)
25 Shade-giving bonnet (3,3)

Down

1 Lithe, limber (6)
2 All the time (4)
3 Fastener with a threaded shank (5)
4 One who trains or exhibits animals (7)
5 Opera song (4)
6 Capable of thinking and expressing oneself clearly (8)
9 Begin (5)
12 Brine (8)
14 Discolour (5)
15 Coming together (7)
18 Small stamp or seal on a ring (6)
19 Exists (5)
21 Catch sight of (4)
23 One twelfth of a foot (4)

SUMMING UP

In the square below, change the positions of six numbers, one per horizontal row, vertical column and long diagonal line of six smaller squares, in such a way that the numbers in each row, column and long diagonal line total exactly 171. Any number may appear more than once in a row, column or line.

44	17	24	30	38	15
32	28	31	18	31	26
45	40	28	50	15	23
35	38	31	6	15	39
26	22	19	42	23	31
19	19	31	20	41	34

DOMINO PLACEMENT

A standard set of 28 dominoes has been laid out as shown. Can you draw in the edges of them all? The check-box is provided as an aid and the domino already placed will help.

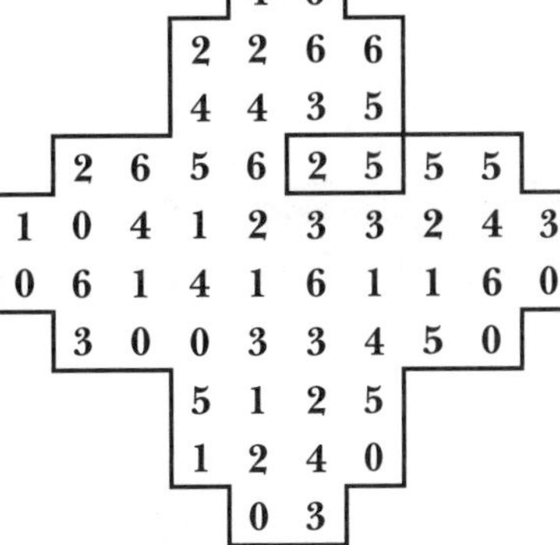

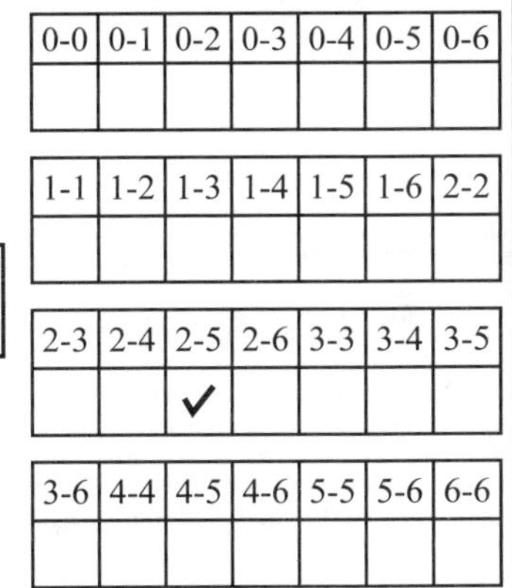

0-0	0-1	0-2	0-3	0-4	0-5	0-6

1-1	1-2	1-3	1-4	1-5	1-6	2-2

2-3	2-4	2-5	2-6	3-3	3-4	3-5
		✓				

3-6	4-4	4-5	4-6	5-5	5-6	6-6

Did You Know?:
The pufferfish is something of a delicacy, but parts of it contain a poison so deadly that a fatal dose weighs just four thousandths of an ounce.

WORDSEARCH WORKOUT

Q	J	M	A	R	I	E	C	U	R	I	E	B
N	O	S	T	R	A	D	A	M	U	S	L	L
N	B	A	R	D	O	T	T	B	A	E	E	Y
Z	A	K	I	C	B	I	E	R	R	F	O	C
D	U	M	A	S	C	R	T	I	F	M	X	A
B	D	A	L	T	L	R	O	I	I	Y	Y	R
E	E	A	E	I	E	T	E	T	M	S	H	E
L	L	E	O	C	L	N	T	N	R	M	D	G
P	A	Z	S	P	R	E	O	O	H	E	C	R
A	I	F	T	S	R	A	L	M	G	H	I	E
S	R	J	R	A	I	E	M	A	I	O	R	B
T	E	S	N	A	D	T	U	R	N	Y	Y	E
E	A	D	Q	T	N	L	A	E	V	P	G	D
U	X	H	R	K	L	C	R	M	G	C	I	X
R	F	R	O	E	H	S	K	K	B	K	J	I

FAMOUS FRENCH PEOPLE

BARDOT
BAUDELAIRE
BERLIOZ
BLERIOT
CHIRAC
DE BERGERAC
DE GAULLE
DELORS
DUMAS
EIFFEL
FRANCK
MARCEAU
MARIE CURIE
MATISSE
MITTERAND
MONET
NOSTRADAMUS
PASTEUR
RENOIR
SARTRE

DOUBLE FUN SUDOKU

TASTY TEASER

		4		1	6	3		
	7				9		2	
8	2	3				6	1	9
	3		7			4		
6			8		2			3
		1			5		9	
4	6	5				9	3	8
	8		4				5	
		7	9	5		2		

BRAIN BUSTER

	6	7		5		8	9	
		2	1		8	3		
4		5				6		8
7	8						3	1
3		6				2		9
		8	9		2	4		
	5	4		6		1	2	

WHATEVER NEXT?

In the diagram below, which letter should replace the question mark?

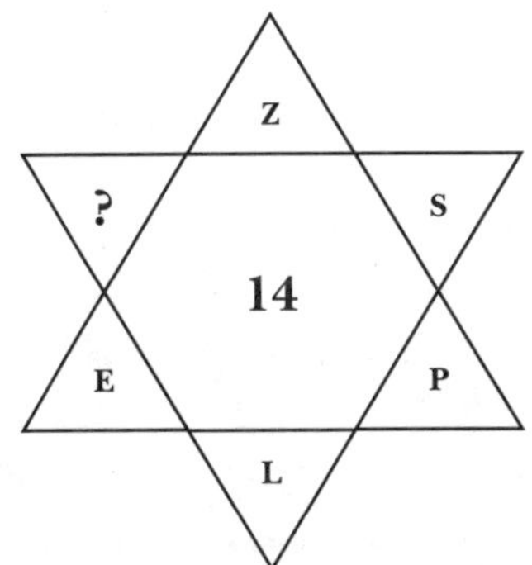

BRAIN TEASER

What day immediately follows the day three days before the day immediately before the day two days after the day immediately before Thursday?

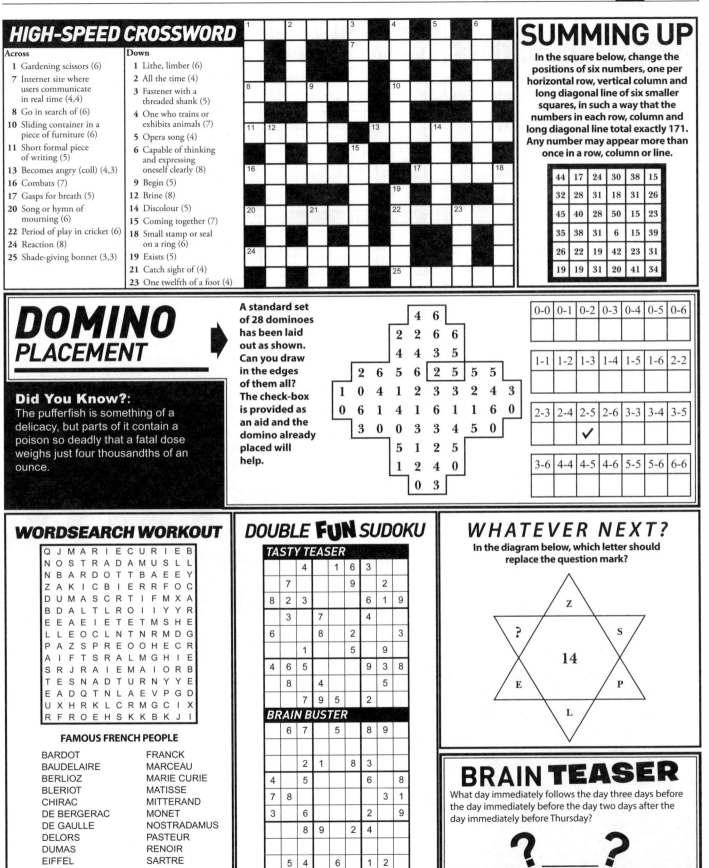

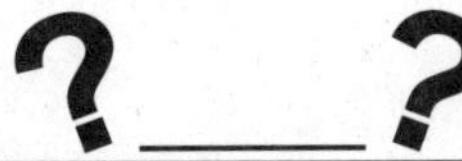

Mind Over Matter

Given that the letters are valued 1-26 according to their places in the alphabet, can you crack the mystery code to reveal the missing letter?

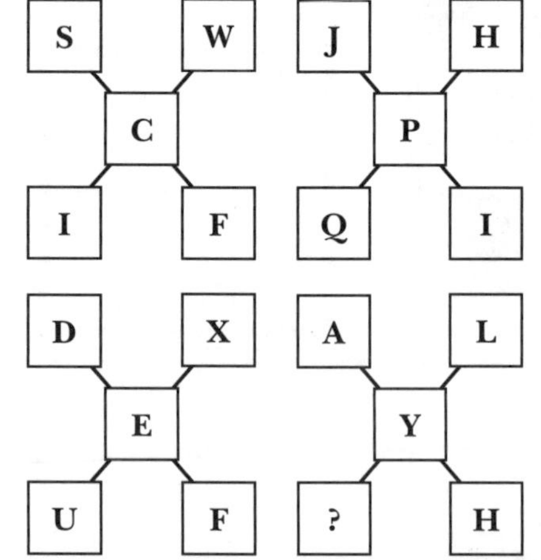

DOUBLE FUN SUDOKU

TASTY TEASER

	6	8		2		7	9	
5			1					
		9		3	8	4		2
	8				9	1	3	7
	2						4	
9	5	7	3				8	
8		1	5	7		6		
					2			3
	3	6		4		5	7	

BRAIN BUSTER

8			4			9	1	
	3			5		6		
4		9						7
2	9		5					
					2		8	3
9						3		4
		6		1			2	
	2	7			8			1

CODEWORD CONUNDRUM

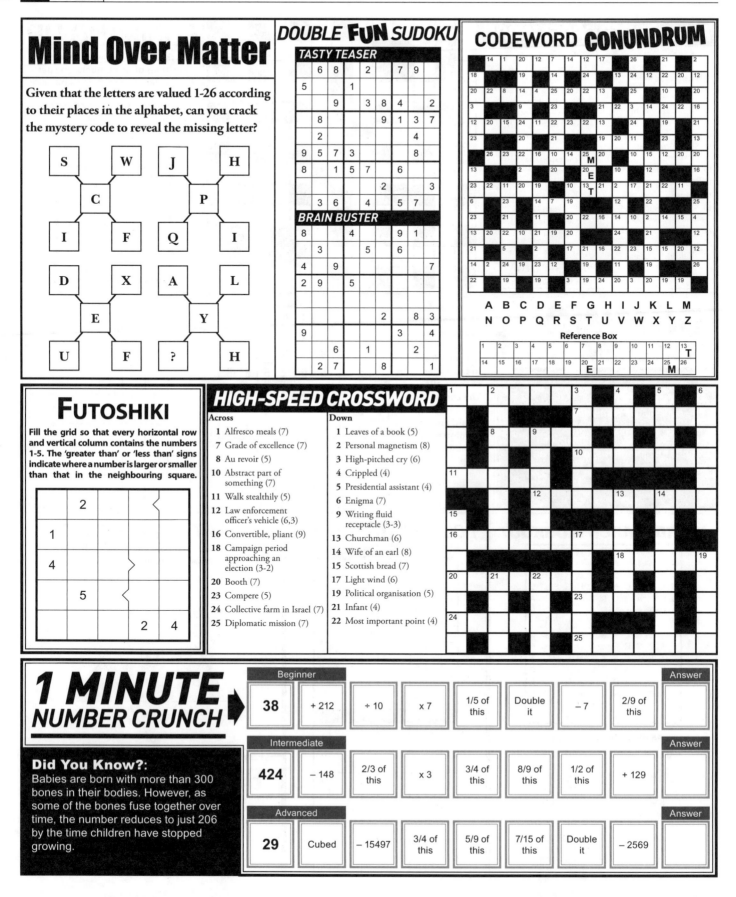

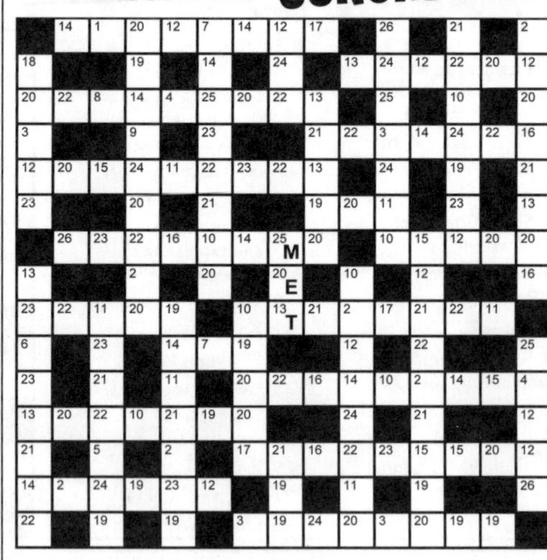

A B C D E F G H I J K L M

N O P Q R S T U V W X Y Z

Reference Box

1	2	3	4	5	6	7	8	9	10	11	12	13 T
14	15	16	17	18	19	20 E	21	22	23	24	25 M	26

FUTOSHIKI

Fill the grid so that every horizontal row and vertical column contains the numbers 1-5. The 'greater than' or 'less than' signs indicate where a number is larger or smaller than that in the neighbouring square.

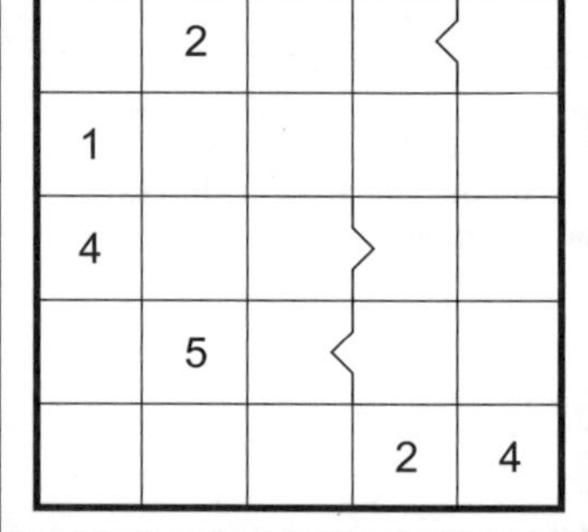

HIGH-SPEED CROSSWORD

Across

1 Alfresco meals (7)
7 Grade of excellence (7)
8 Au revoir (5)
10 Abstract part of something (7)
11 Walk stealthily (5)
12 Law enforcement officer's vehicle (6,3)
16 Convertible, pliant (9)
18 Campaign period approaching an election (3-2)
20 Booth (7)
23 Compere (5)
24 Collective farm in Israel (7)
25 Diplomatic mission (7)

Down

1 Leaves of a book (5)
2 Personal magnetism (8)
3 High-pitched cry (6)
4 Crippled (4)
5 Presidential assistant (4)
6 Enigma (7)
9 Writing fluid receptacle (3-3)
13 Churchman (6)
14 Wife of an earl (8)
15 Scottish bread (7)
17 Light wind (6)
19 Political organisation (5)
21 Infant (4)
22 Most important point (4)

1 MINUTE NUMBER CRUNCH

Beginner								Answer
38	+ 212	÷ 10	x 7	1/5 of this	Double it	– 7	2/9 of this	

Intermediate								Answer
424	– 148	2/3 of this	x 3	3/4 of this	8/9 of this	1/2 of this	+ 129	

Advanced								Answer
29	Cubed	– 15497	3/4 of this	5/9 of this	7/15 of this	Double it	– 2569	

Did You Know?:
Babies are born with more than 300 bones in their bodies. However, as some of the bones fuse together over time, the number reduces to just 206 by the time children have stopped growing.

1 MINUTE NUMBER CRUNCH

Beginner								Answer
104	25% of this	Double it	+ 53	÷ 5	+ 19	1/4 of this	x 39	

Intermediate								Answer
127	+ 43	+ 20% of this	÷ 4	÷ 3	+ 283	31% of this	– 67	

Advanced								Answer
43	x 7	+ 199	69% of this	9/15 of this	17/23 of this	4/9 of this	x 7	

Did You Know?:
In 1977, a strong radio signal with an intensity much higher than the usual background noise was received from the direction of the constellation of Sagittarius. It lasted 72 seconds and may be the first evidence of intelligent life in outer space.

HIGH-SPEED CROSSWORD

Across

1 Evaluate (6)
5 Disperse (6)
8 Consecrate (6)
9 Protestant layman who assists the minister (6)
10 Word of surprise (3)
11 Rate of travel (5)
13 Give or restore confidence in (8)
15 Unconsciousness induced by drugs (8)
16 Cape (5)
19 Pen point (3)
21 Popular drink (6)
22 Type of thorny tree (6)
23 Area set back or indented (6)
24 Ocean floor (6)

Down

2 Accumulation of refuse (9)
3 Circumvent (5)
4 Musical composition with words (4)
5 Obliquely (8)
6 Take in, understand (7)
7 Over, finished (4)
12 Thin syrup made from pomegranate juice (9)
13 Impetuosity (8)
14 Minor skirmish (7)
17 Andean mammal (5)
18 Mark of a wound (4)
20 Lowest adult male singing voice (4)

PARTITIONS

Draw walls to partition the grid into areas (some are already drawn in). Each area must contain two circles, area sizes must match those numbers shown next to the grid and each '+' must be linked to at least two walls.

3, 4, 5, 6, 7

WORDWHEEL

Using only the letters in the Wordwheel, you have ten minutes to find as many words as possible, none of which may be plurals, foreign words or proper nouns. Each word must be of three letters or more, all must contain the central letter and letters can only be used once in every word. There is at least one nine-letter word in the wheel.

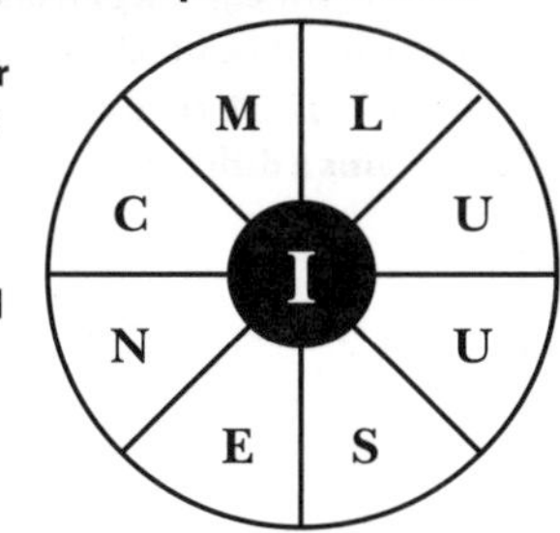

Nine-letter word(s):

SUM CIRCLE

Fill the three empty circles with the symbols +, – and x in some order, to make a sum which totals the number in the centre. Each symbol must be used once and calculations are made in the direction of travel (clockwise).

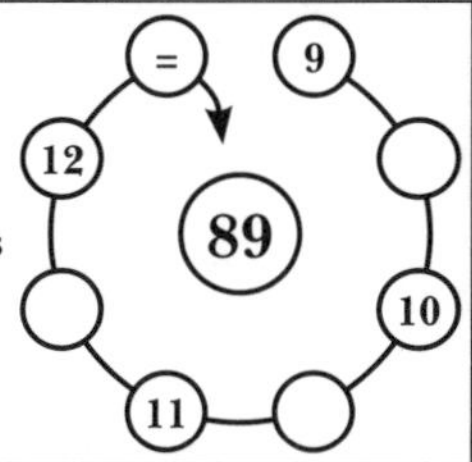

WORDSEARCH WORKOUT

```
E Z J G N I M M I W S S M
I F Y L M V S O X Q T D B
E I O L T R J S O N T S Z
C O L A D E P L E R I I A
P H H D U D Y T U N V L C
O F A M V C E L N O D T L
S B L L N O B E K G I E U
T Q D O E A T U K N V U B
C E U M G T V W Q I I Q H
A H W A P Y C A Z B N I O
R M V E S P Z R R S G T U
D S W R C H L A E A I U S
C A B A R E T M R C C O E
I C E C R E A M L C H B H
X V S N Z G F I M R A E I
```

HOLIDAY CAMP

BINGO
BOUTIQUE
CABARET
CARAVAN
CHALET
CLUBHOUSE
CRAZY GOLF
CRECHE
DIVING
GAMES
ICE CREAM
PEDALO
POOL
POSTCARD
REDCOAT
SQUASH
SWIMMING
TENNIS
TENTS
TV ROOM

DOUBLE FUN SUDOKU

TASTY TEASER

		3		6	7	9	4	
4			2				6	
		1	3				7	8
6		5		2			3	
9			7		3			2
	1			9		7		4
2	3				4	5		
	8				5			7
	5	4	6	8		1		

BRAIN BUSTER

		7	3			9		
1	6			7				
3	5							
	2	3	9					
	7			5			4	
					8	2	5	
							6	3
				4			7	5
		8			1	4		

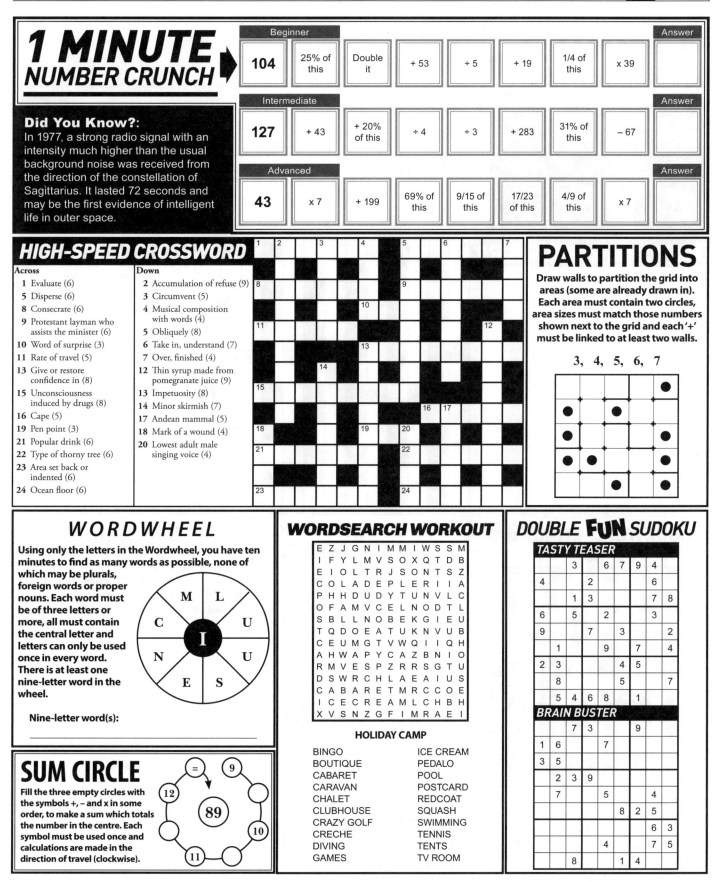

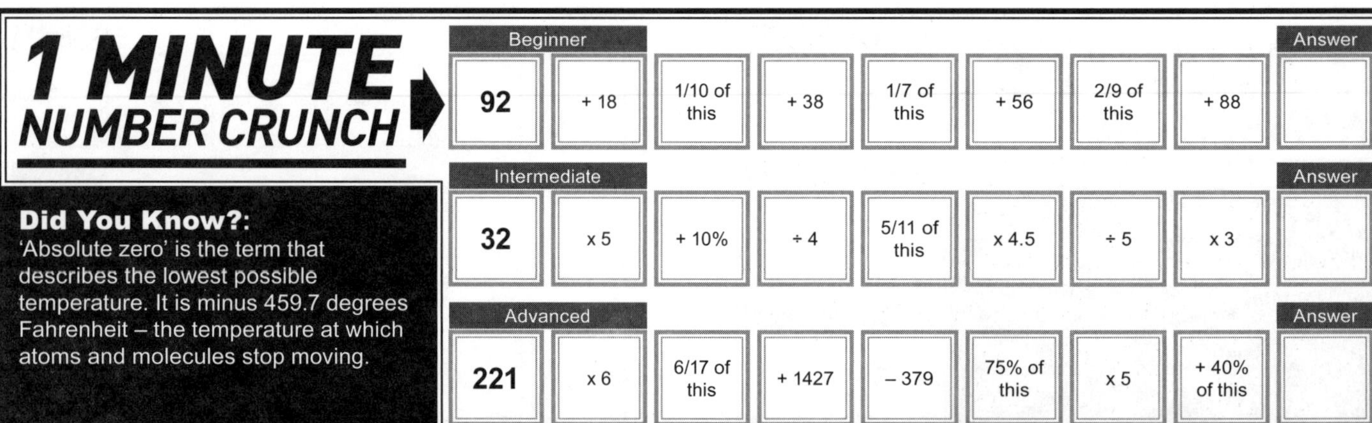

1 MINUTE NUMBER CRUNCH

Beginner								Answer
92	+ 18	1/10 of this	+ 38	1/7 of this	+ 56	2/9 of this	+ 88	

Intermediate								Answer
32	x 5	+ 10%	÷ 4	5/11 of this	x 4.5	÷ 5	x 3	

Advanced								Answer
221	x 6	6/17 of this	+ 1427	– 379	75% of this	x 5	+ 40% of this	

Did You Know?:
'Absolute zero' is the term that describes the lowest possible temperature. It is minus 459.7 degrees Fahrenheit – the temperature at which atoms and molecules stop moving.

HIGH-SPEED CROSSWORD

Across

1 Lawyer who speaks in the higher courts of law (9)
8 Distinctive smell (5)
9 Drinking vessel (5)
10 Bring together (5)
11 Castrated bull (5)
12 Strong, tightly twisted cotton thread (5)
14 Holiday town (6)
16 Population count (6)
20 Attack on all sides (5)
23 Make speeches (5)
25 Carriageways (5)
26 Sugar frosting (5)
27 Panorama (5)
28 Process or result of becoming less or smaller (9)

Down

1 Phoney (5)
2 Literate people (7)
3 Underwriter (7)
4 Removing (6)
5 French composer (1875-1937) (5)
6 Fillip, incentive (5)
7 Receptacles for shopping (7)
13 Hostelry (3)
14 Refuse (7)
15 Lyric poem (3)
17 Wearing away (7)
18 Staying power (7)
19 Pencil mark remover (6)
21 Alarm (5)
22 Attempts (5)
24 Bird of prey (5)

IQ WORKOUT

What number should replace the question mark?

1.5
4.5
13.5
16.5
?

CODEWORD CONUNDRUM

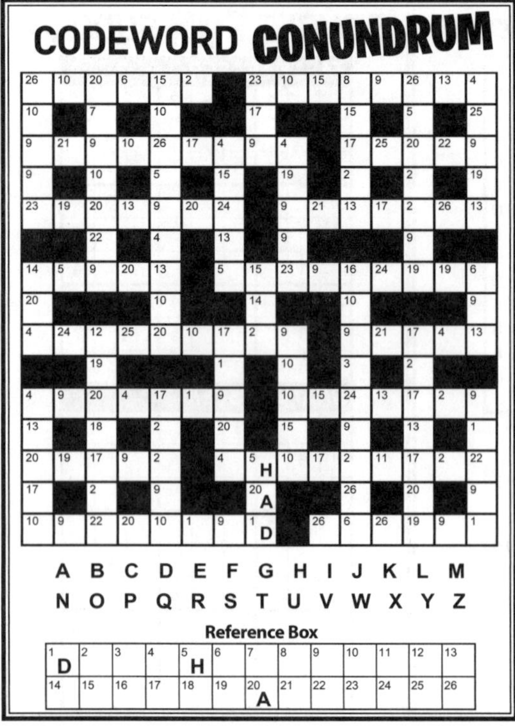

DOUBLE FUN SUDOKU

TASTY TEASER

		5	2		8	1		
6	4			9			8	5
	1			6			7	
7	6		8		9		1	3
		3	6		7	8		
8	9		5		3		2	6
	2			8			3	
4	3			7			5	8
		6	3		2	4		

BRAIN BUSTER

2	5			9			8	7
		1				2		
3			7		2			5
	9			4			2	
			6		8			
	2			1			4	
8			2		4			3
		6				8		
9	1			3			7	4

SPIDOKU

Each of the eight segments of the spider's web should be filled with a different number from 1 to 8, in such a way that every ring also contains a different number from 1 to 8.

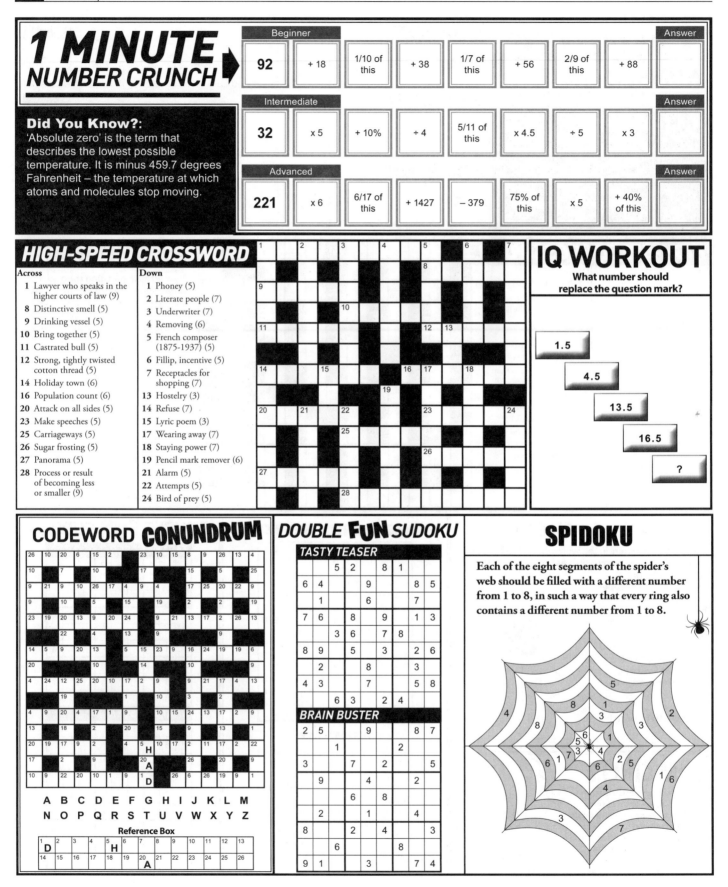

Logi-Six

Every row and column of this grid should contain one each of the letters A, B, C, D, E and F. Each of the six shapes (marked by thicker lines) should also contain one each of the letters A, B, C, D, E and F. Can you complete the grid?

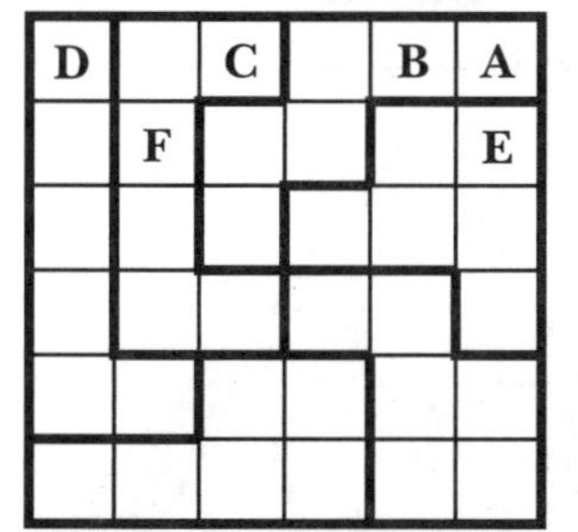

High-Speed Crossword

Across

1 Rascal (5)
7 Enthusiastic approval (7)
9 Oil purification plant (8)
10 Slide unobtrusively (7)
12 Totalling (8)
14 Informal name for a cat (4)
16 Old-fashioned form of the word 'you' (4)
18 Game bird (8)
20 Putting words on paper (7)
23 Precious blue gemstone (8)
24 Brings to a final conclusion (7)
25 Ordered series (5)

Down

1 Military rank (8)
2 Be able to spare (6)
3 Section of glass (4)
4 Prevents (4)
5 Duck-billed creature (8)
6 Muscle that flexes the forearm (6)
8 Chamber within which a piston moves (8)
11 Dole out (medication) (8)
13 Individuality (8)
15 Scenery intended to stand alone (3,5)
17 Become set (6)
19 Heart condition marked by chest pain (6)
21 Strong sweeping cut made with a sharp instrument (4)
22 Musical composition (4)

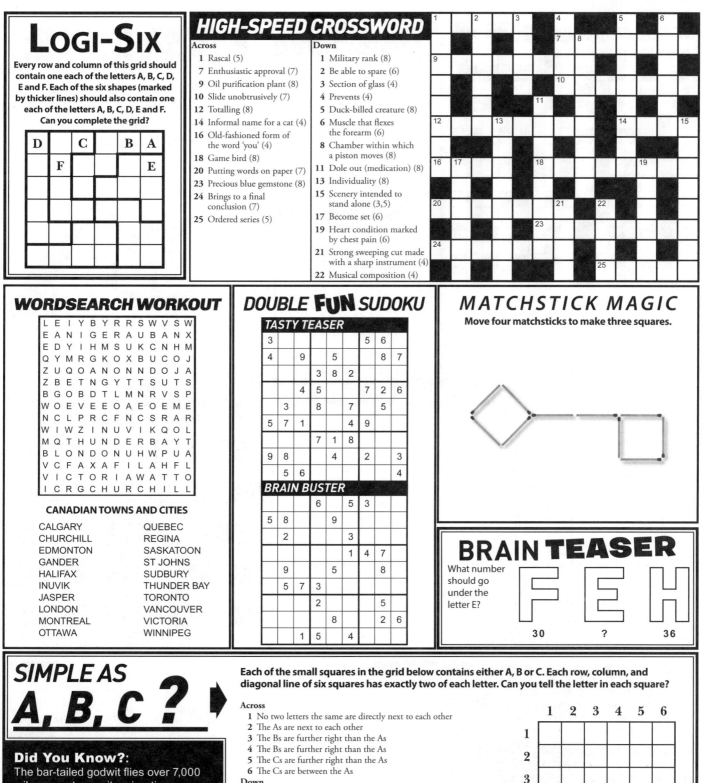

Wordsearch Workout

L	E	I	Y	B	Y	R	R	S	W	V	S	W
E	A	N	I	G	E	R	A	U	B	A	N	X
E	D	Y	I	H	M	S	U	K	C	N	H	M
Q	Y	M	R	G	K	O	X	B	U	C	O	J
Z	U	Q	O	A	N	O	N	N	D	O	J	A
Z	B	E	T	N	G	Y	T	T	S	U	T	S
B	G	O	B	D	T	L	M	N	R	V	S	P
W	O	E	V	E	E	O	A	E	O	E	M	E
N	C	L	P	R	C	F	N	C	S	R	A	R
W	I	W	Z	I	N	U	V	I	K	Q	O	L
M	Q	T	H	U	N	D	E	R	B	A	Y	T
B	L	O	N	D	O	N	U	H	W	P	U	A
V	C	F	A	X	A	F	I	L	A	H	F	L
V	I	C	T	O	R	I	A	W	A	T	T	O
I	C	R	G	C	H	U	R	C	H	I	L	L

CANADIAN TOWNS AND CITIES

CALGARY
CHURCHILL
EDMONTON
GANDER
HALIFAX
INUVIK
JASPER
LONDON
MONTREAL
OTTAWA
QUEBEC
REGINA
SASKATOON
ST JOHNS
SUDBURY
THUNDER BAY
TORONTO
VANCOUVER
VICTORIA
WINNIPEG

Double Fun Sudoku

TASTY TEASER

3						5	6	
4		9		5			8	7
			3	8	2			
		4	5			7	2	6
	3		8		7		5	
5	7	1			4	9		
			7	1	8			
9	8			4		2		3
	5	6						4

BRAIN BUSTER

			6		5	3		
5	8			9				
	2				3			
					1	4	7	
	9			5			8	
	5	7	3					
			2				5	
				8			2	6
		1	5		4			

Matchstick Magic

Move four matchsticks to make three squares.

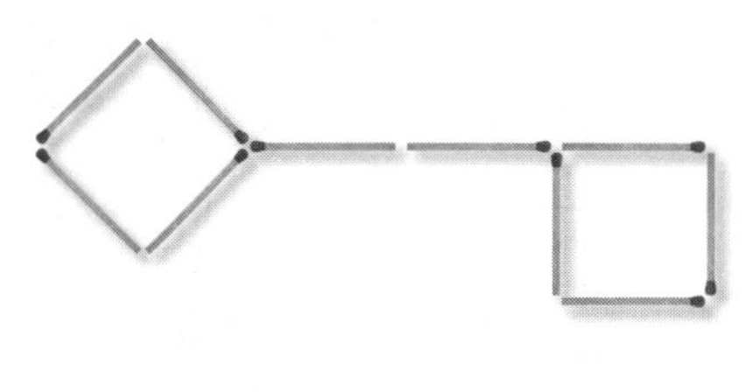

Brain Teaser

What number should go under the letter E?

30 ? 36

Simple as A, B, C?

Each of the small squares in the grid below contains either A, B or C. Each row, column, and diagonal line of six squares has exactly two of each letter. Can you tell the letter in each square?

Across

1 No two letters the same are directly next to each other
2 The As are next to each other
3 The Bs are further right than the As
4 The Bs are further right than the As
5 The Cs are further right than the As
6 The Cs are between the As

Down

1 The As are next to each other
2 No two letters the same are directly next to each other
3 The Cs are lower than the As
4 No two letters the same are directly next to each other
5 The Cs are next to each other
6 The Bs are between the Cs

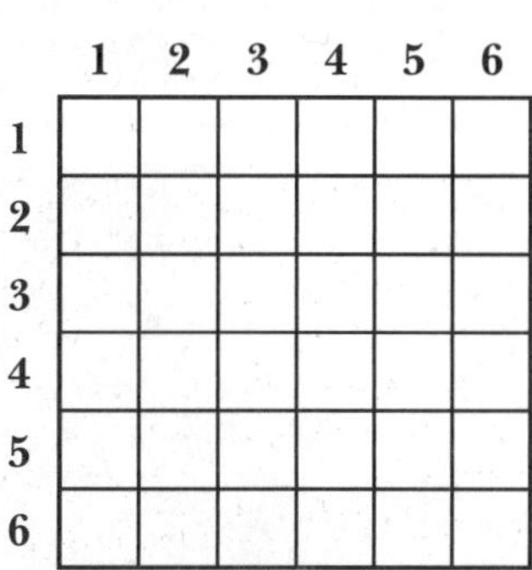

Did You Know?:
The bar-tailed godwit flies over 7,000 miles non-stop on its migration between Alaska and New Zealand, losing more than half its body weight in the process.

CODEWORD CONUNDRUM

DOUBLE FUN SUDOKU

TASTY TEASER

	5	9	2	4				1
3			7		1			4
		8				6		2
	1	4		9	7			
	7		1		8		3	
			5	2		1	6	
5		6				9		
8			6		5			3
4				3	9	7	5	

BRAIN BUSTER

8		2		5	6			
		6						
					1		9	
7	6		9				3	
		5		6		2		
	4				7		6	8
	7		3					
						4		
			1	2		8		6

PYRAMID PLUS

Every brick in this pyramid contains a number which is the sum of the two numbers below it, so that F=A+B, etc.
Just work out the missing numbers!

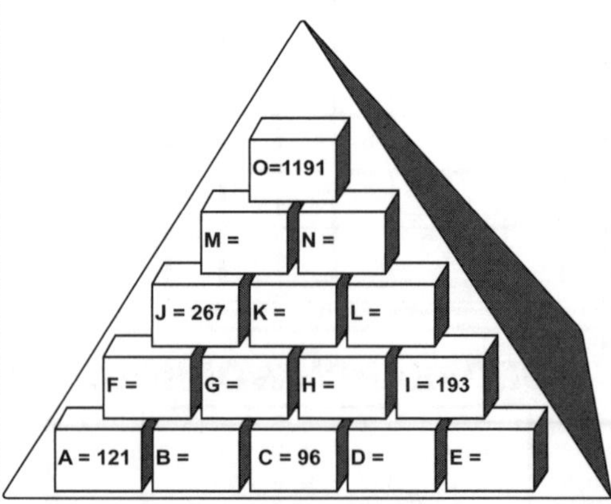

WORK IT OUT

In the grid below, what number should replace the question mark?

12	15	21	13	16	14	19
15	18	24	16	19	17	22
20	23	29	21	24	22	27
27	30	36	?	31	29	34
35	38	44	36	39	37	42
41	44	50	42	45	43	48
45	48	54	46	49	47	52

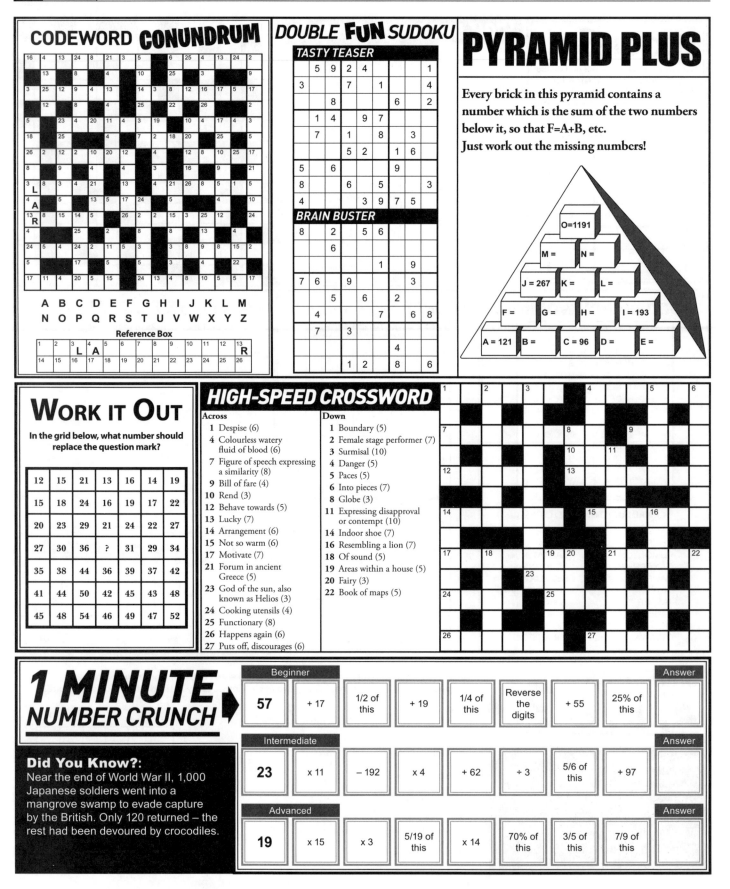

HIGH-SPEED CROSSWORD

Across

1 Despise (6)
4 Colourless watery fluid of blood (6)
7 Figure of speech expressing a similarity (8)
9 Bill of fare (4)
10 Rend (3)
12 Behave towards (5)
13 Lucky (7)
14 Arrangement (6)
15 Not so warm (6)
17 Motivate (7)
21 Forum in ancient Greece (5)
23 God of the sun, also known as Helios (3)
24 Cooking utensils (4)
25 Functionary (8)
26 Happens again (6)
27 Puts off, discourages (6)

Down

1 Boundary (5)
2 Female stage performer (7)
3 Surmisal (10)
4 Danger (5)
5 Paces (5)
6 Into pieces (7)
8 Globe (3)
11 Expressing disapproval or contempt (10)
14 Indoor shoe (7)
16 Resembling a lion (7)
18 Of sound (5)
19 Areas within a house (5)
20 Fairy (3)
22 Book of maps (5)

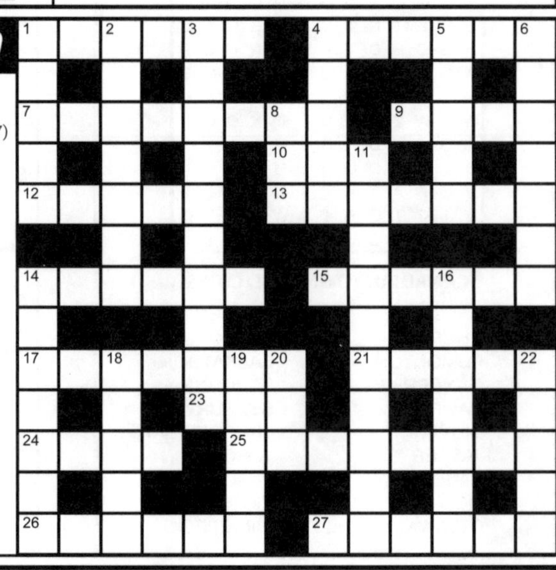

Beginner

57	+ 17	1/2 of this	+ 19	1/4 of this	Reverse the digits	+ 55	25% of this	Answer

Intermediate

23	x 11	– 192	x 4	+ 62	÷ 3	5/6 of this	+ 97	Answer

Advanced

19	x 15	x 3	5/19 of this	x 14	70% of this	3/5 of this	7/9 of this	Answer

Did You Know?:
Near the end of World War II, 1,000 Japanese soldiers went into a mangrove swamp to evade capture by the British. Only 120 returned – the rest had been devoured by crocodiles.

HIGH-SPEED CROSSWORD

Across

1 Adhesive postal tokens (6)
4 Dark-coloured igneous rock (6)
7 Consciousness of one's own identity (3)
8 Becomes older (4)
9 Vigilant (4-4)
11 Extremely and unpleasantly hot (6)
13 Canine film star (6)
15 Service of china or silverware, used at table (3,3)
18 Treat with excessive indulgence (6)
20 Message of protest signed by many people (8)
22 Molten rock (4)
23 Afternoon meal (3)
24 Lethal (6)
25 Fairy (6)

Down

1 Unforeseen obstacle (4)
2 Artist of consummate skill (6)
3 In next to first place (6)
4 Toward or located in the north (6)
5 Emphasis (6)
6 Being of the same dimensions as an original (4-5)
10 Tendency to stick together (9)
12 Decorate with frosting (3)
14 Bustle (3)
16 Hand-held piece of armour (6)
17 One score and ten (6)
18 Fabric for a painting (6)
19 Navy man (6)
21 Walking-stick (4)

SUMMING UP

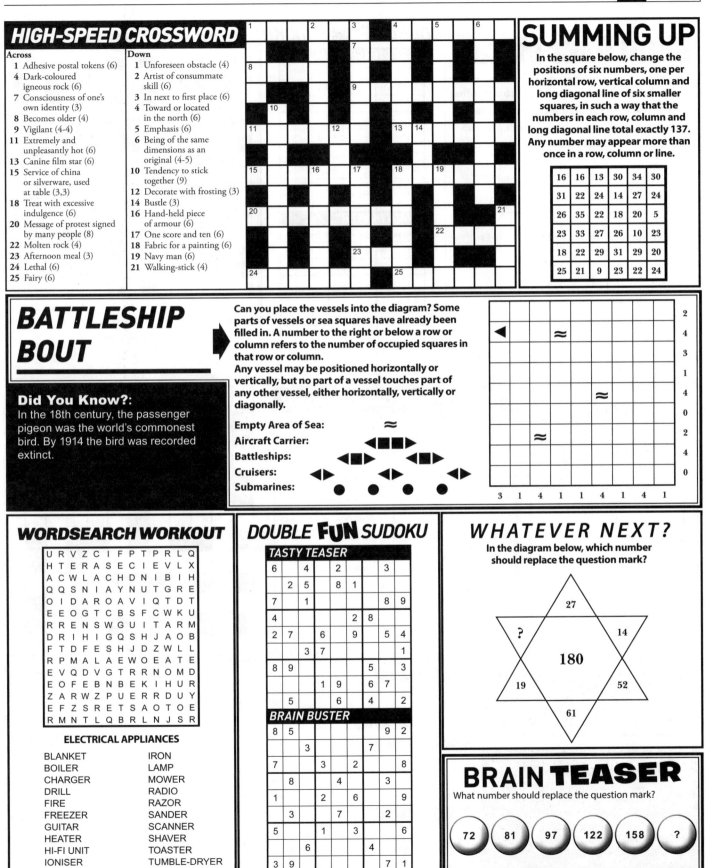

In the square below, change the positions of six numbers, one per horizontal row, vertical column and long diagonal line of six smaller squares, in such a way that the numbers in each row, column and long diagonal line total exactly 137. Any number may appear more than once in a row, column or line.

16	16	13	30	34	30
31	22	24	14	27	24
26	35	22	18	20	5
23	33	27	26	10	23
18	22	29	31	29	20
25	21	9	23	22	24

BATTLESHIP BOUT

Can you place the vessels into the diagram? Some parts of vessels or sea squares have already been filled in. A number to the right or below a row or column refers to the number of occupied squares in that row or column.
Any vessel may be positioned horizontally or vertically, but no part of a vessel touches part of any other vessel, either horizontally, vertically or diagonally.

Empty Area of Sea:
Aircraft Carrier:
Battleships:
Cruisers:
Submarines:

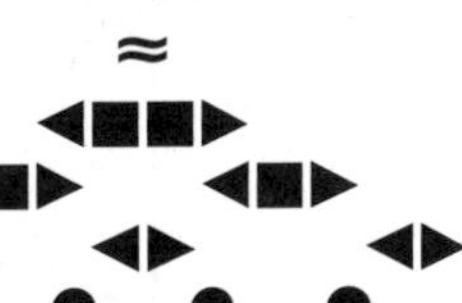

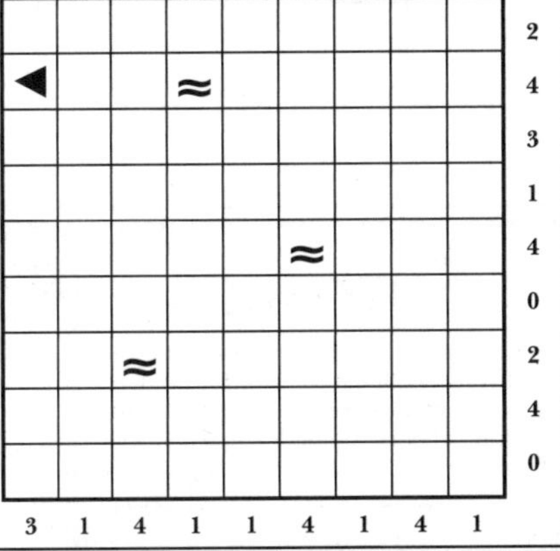

Did You Know?:

In the 18th century, the passenger pigeon was the world's commonest bird. By 1914 the bird was recorded extinct.

WORDSEARCH WORKOUT

U R V Z C I F P T P R L Q
H T E R A S E C I E V L X
A C W L A C H D N I B I H
Q Q S N I A Y N U T G R E
O I D A R O A V I Q T D T
E E O G T C B S F C W K U
R R E N S W G U I T A R M
D R I H I G Q S H J A O B
F T D F E S H J D Z W L L
R P M A L A E W O E A T E
E V Q D V G T R R N O M D
E O F E B N B E K I H U R
Z A R W Z P U E R R D U Y
E F Z S R E T S A O T O E
R M N T L Q B R L N J S R

ELECTRICAL APPLIANCES

BLANKET
BOILER
CHARGER
DRILL
FIRE
FREEZER
GUITAR
HEATER
HI-FI UNIT
IONISER
IRON
LAMP
MOWER
RADIO
RAZOR
SANDER
SCANNER
SHAVER
TOASTER
TUMBLE-DRYER

DOUBLE FUN SUDOKU

TASTY TEASER

6		4		2			3	
	2	5		8	1			
7		1					8	9
4					2	8		
2	7		6		9		5	4
		3	7					1
8	9					5		3
			1	9		6	7	
	5			6		4		2

BRAIN BUSTER

8	5						9	2
		3				7		
7			3		2			8
	8			4			3	
1			2		6			9
	3			7			2	
5			1		3			6
		6				4		
3	9						7	1

WHATEVER NEXT?

In the diagram below, which number should replace the question mark?

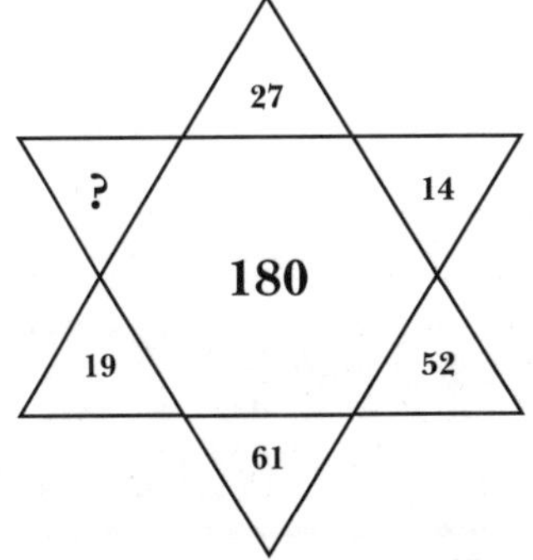

BRAIN TEASER

What number should replace the question mark?

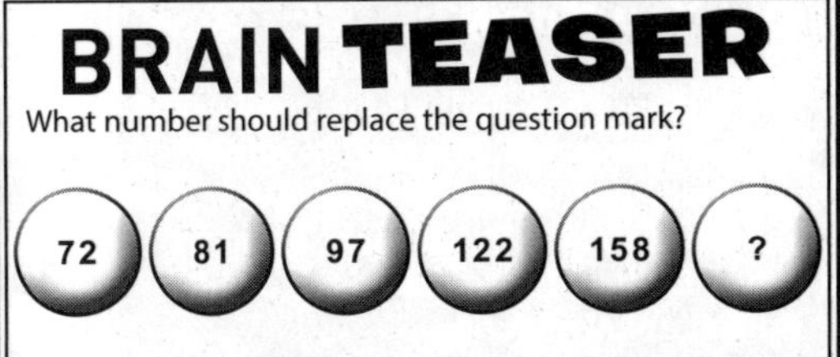

Mind Over Matter

Given that the letters are valued 1-26 according to their places in the alphabet, can you crack the mystery code to reveal the missing letter?

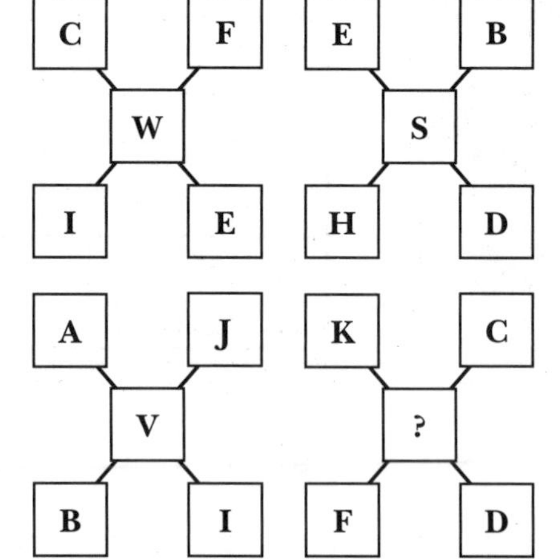

DOUBLE FUN SUDOKU

TASTY TEASER

	6		9				5	
3	2	9				1	6	4
4			3	2				7
7					5		4	
		4	6		1	3		
	9		8					2
6				8	9			5
9	4	1				7	3	8
	8				7		1	

BRAIN BUSTER

7		2		3		4		5
		5	9		8	6		
9								8
			3		4			
8								7
			7		6			
4								1
		3	1		7	5		
1		7		6		9		3

CODEWORD CONUNDRUM

FUTOSHIKI

Fill the grid so that every horizontal row and vertical column contains the numbers 1-5. The 'greater than' or 'less than' signs indicate where a number is larger or smaller than that in the neighbouring square.

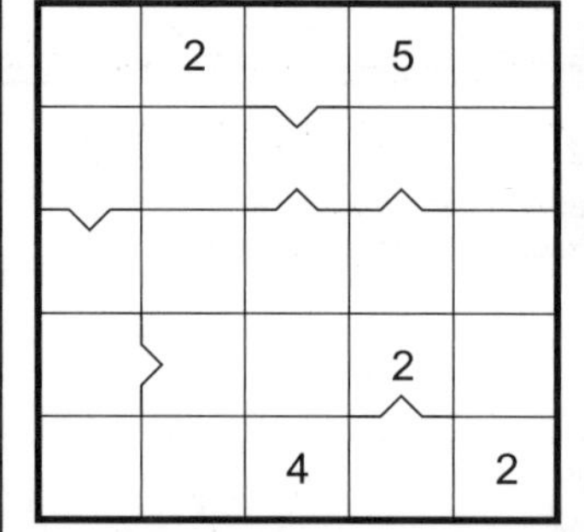

HIGH-SPEED CROSSWORD

Across

1 Snatches (5)
4 Pre-release screening for a select audience (7)
8 In a graceful or stylish manner (9)
9 French river (5)
10 Sepulchral monument (9)
13 Object thrown in athletic competitions (6)
14 Crustacean with seven pairs of legs (6)
16 Expressing ridicule that wounds (9)
19 Helicopter propeller (5)
20 Characteristic (9)
22 One of the three superpowers in *Nineteen Eighty-Four* (7)
23 Church council (5)

Down

1 Unexpected piece of good fortune (7)
2 Manager of a business or school (13)
3 Mixture of rain and snow (5)
4 Food in a pastry shell (3)
5 Exercises evaluating skill or knowledge (5)
6 Observation of one's own mental and emotional processes (13)
7 John ___, film actor who played tough heroes (5)
11 Expels (5)
12 Russian pancake (5)
15 Deprive of by deceit (7)
16 Trap for birds or small mammals (5)
17 Farewell remark (5)
18 Green salad vegetable (5)
21 Large nation (inits) (3)

1 MINUTE NUMBER CRUNCH

Beginner

131	– 28	x 2	+ 39	÷ 5	2/7 of this	x 6	50% of this	Answer

Intermediate

1947	Double it	– 1821	÷ 3	+ 104	÷ 15	x 4	– 79	Answer

Advanced

330	4/15 of this	10/11 of this	5/8 of this	x 5.5	7/25 of this	+ 33	– 7/10 of this	Answer

Did You Know?:
Flatfish, when they are young, look like ordinary fish, with an eye on each side. However, as they mature and gradually become flatter, one eye moves around to lie adjacent to the other. Both eyes are on the top of a flatfish at full maturity.

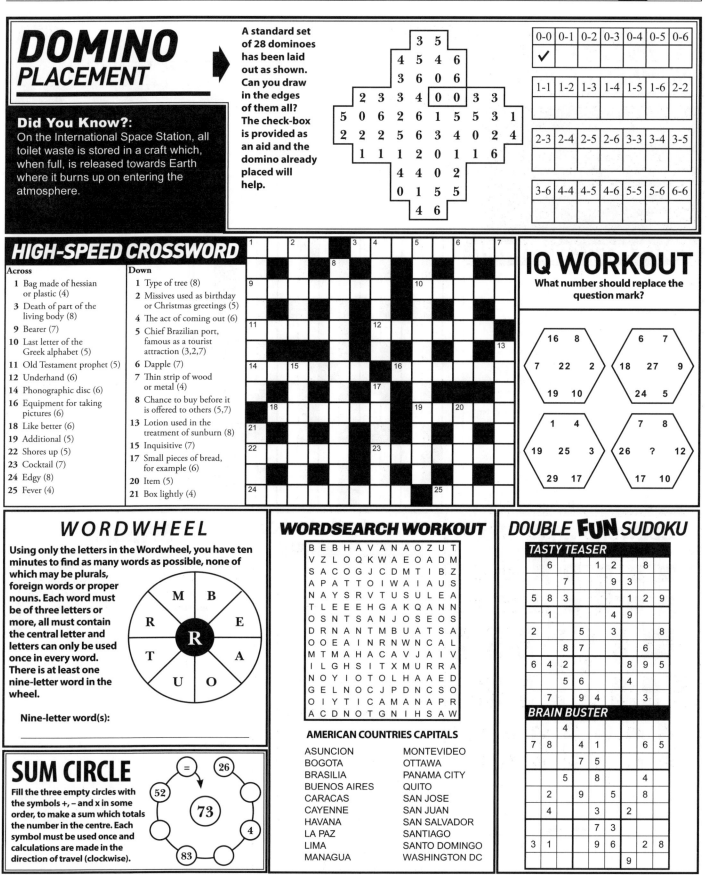

DOMINO PLACEMENT

A standard set of 28 dominoes has been laid out as shown. Can you draw in the edges of them all? The check-box is provided as an aid and the domino already placed will help.

				3	5				
			4	5	4	6			
			3	6	0	6			
	2	3	3	4	0	0	3	3	
5	0	6	2	6	1	5	5	3	1
2	2	2	5	6	3	4	0	2	4
	1	1	1	2	0	1	1	6	
			4	4	0	2			
			0	1	5	5			
				4	6				

0-0	0-1	0-2	0-3	0-4	0-5	0-6
✓						
1-1	1-2	1-3	1-4	1-5	1-6	2-2
2-3	2-4	2-5	2-6	3-3	3-4	3-5
3-6	4-4	4-5	4-6	5-5	5-6	6-6

Did You Know?:
On the International Space Station, all toilet waste is stored in a craft which, when full, is released towards Earth where it burns up on entering the atmosphere.

HIGH-SPEED CROSSWORD

Across

1 Bag made of hessian or plastic (4)
3 Death of part of the living body (8)
9 Bearer (7)
10 Last letter of the Greek alphabet (5)
11 Old Testament prophet (5)
12 Underhand (6)
14 Phonographic disc (6)
16 Equipment for taking pictures (6)
18 Like better (6)
19 Additional (5)
22 Shores up (5)
23 Cocktail (7)
24 Edgy (8)
25 Fever (4)

Down

1 Type of tree (8)
2 Missives used as birthday or Christmas greetings (5)
4 The act of coming out (6)
5 Chief Brazilian port, famous as a tourist attraction (3,2,7)
6 Dapple (7)
7 Thin strip of wood or metal (4)
8 Chance to buy before it is offered to others (5,7)
13 Lotion used in the treatment of sunburn (8)
15 Inquisitive (7)
17 Small pieces of bread, for example (6)
20 Item (5)
21 Box lightly (4)

IQ WORKOUT

What number should replace the question mark?

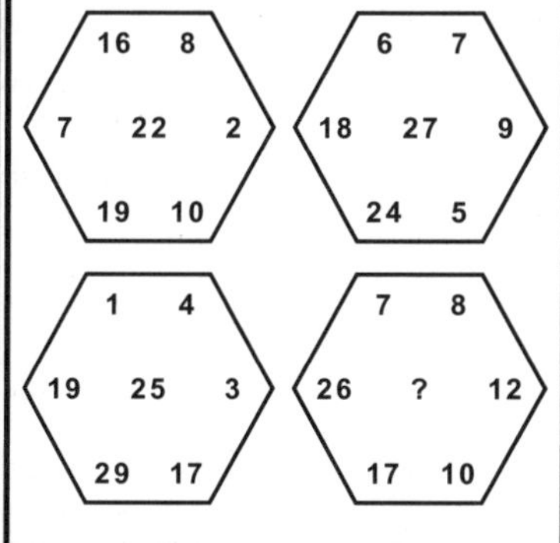

WORDWHEEL

Using only the letters in the Wordwheel, you have ten minutes to find as many words as possible, none of which may be plurals, foreign words or proper nouns. Each word must be of three letters or more, all must contain the central letter and letters can only be used once in every word. There is at least one nine-letter word in the wheel.

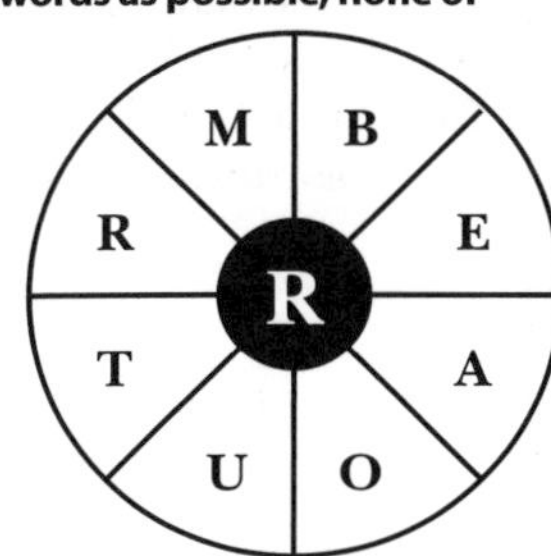

Nine-letter word(s):

SUM CIRCLE

Fill the three empty circles with the symbols +, – and x in some order, to make a sum which totals the number in the centre. Each symbol must be used once and calculations are made in the direction of travel (clockwise).

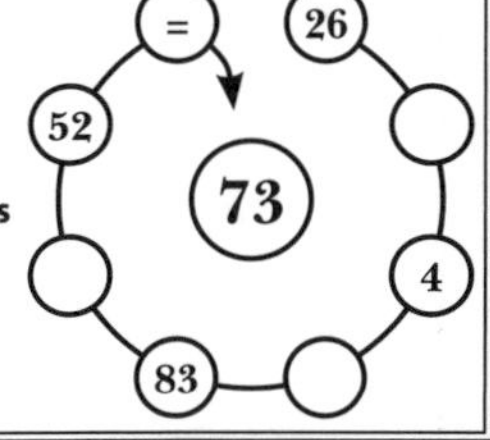

WORDSEARCH WORKOUT

B E B H A V A N A O Z U T
V Z L O Q K W A E O A D M
S A C O G J C D M T I B Z
A P A T T O I W A I A U S
N A Y S R V T U S U L E A
T L E E E H G A K Q A N N
O S N T S A N J O S E O S
D R N A N T M B U A T S A
O O E A I N R N W N C A L
M T M A H A C A V J A I V
I L G H S I T X M U R R A
N O Y I O T O L H A A E D
G E L N O C J P D N C S O
O I Y T I C A M A N A P R
A C D N O T G N I H S A W

AMERICAN COUNTRIES CAPITALS

ASUNCION
BOGOTA
BRASILIA
BUENOS AIRES
CARACAS
CAYENNE
HAVANA
LA PAZ
LIMA
MANAGUA
MONTEVIDEO
OTTAWA
PANAMA CITY
QUITO
SAN JOSE
SAN JUAN
SAN SALVADOR
SANTIAGO
SANTO DOMINGO
WASHINGTON DC

DOUBLE FUN SUDOKU

TASTY TEASER

	6			1	2		8	
		7			9	3		
5	8	3				1	2	9
	1				4	9		
2			5		3			8
		8	7				6	
6	4	2				8	9	5
		5	6			4		
	7		9	4			3	

BRAIN BUSTER

		4						
7	8		4	1			6	5
			7	5				
		5		8			4	
	2		9		5		8	
	4			3		2		
				7	3			
3	1			9	6		2	8
						9		

1 MINUTE NUMBER CRUNCH

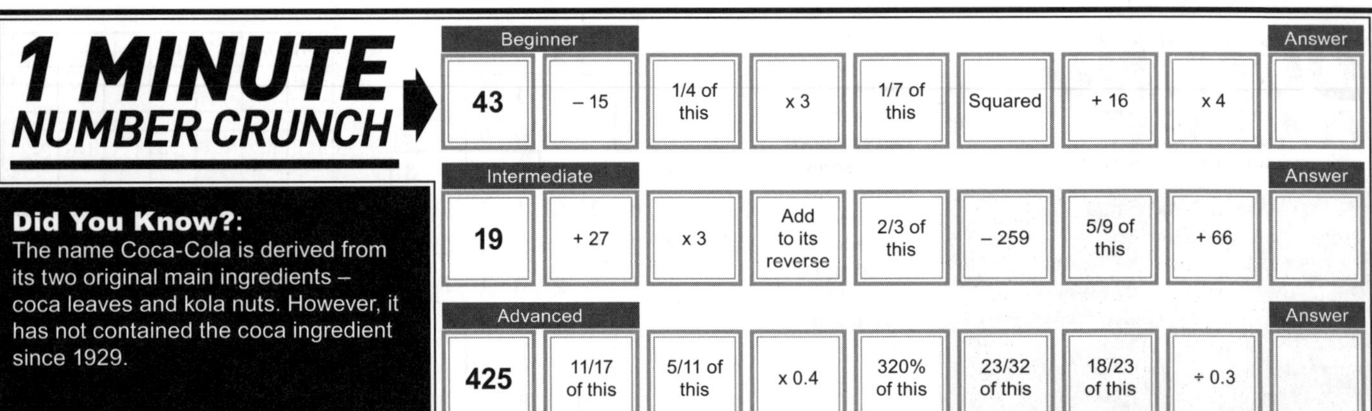

Beginner								Answer
43	– 15	1/4 of this	x 3	1/7 of this	Squared	+ 16	x 4	

Intermediate								Answer
19	+ 27	x 3	Add to its reverse	2/3 of this	– 259	5/9 of this	+ 66	

Advanced								Answer
425	11/17 of this	5/11 of this	x 0.4	320% of this	23/32 of this	18/23 of this	÷ 0.3	

Did You Know?:
The name Coca-Cola is derived from its two original main ingredients – coca leaves and kola nuts. However, it has not contained the coca ingredient since 1929.

HIGH-SPEED CROSSWORD

Across
1 Deep red (7)
5 In the area (5)
8 Remark expressing careful consideration (11)
9 Souvenir (5)
11 Hard to catch (7)
13 Make numb (6)
14 Scribble (6)
17 Pearlescent (7)
18 Irritable, peevish (5)
19 Recklessly wasteful (11)
22 Branchlet (5)
23 Style, flair (7)

Down
1 Coalesced in soft thick lumps (7)
2 ___ and buts, objections (3)
3 Vast plain and National Park in Tanzania (9)
4 Straighten out (6)
5 Garland of flowers (3)
6 Person with whom one shares a secret or private matter (9)
7 Soup-serving spoon (5)
10 Australian arboreal marsupial that feeds on eucalyptus leaves (5,4)
12 Ambiguous (9)
15 Outfit (clothing and accessories) for a new baby (7)
16 Flee (6)
17 Desert watering-hole (5)
20 Duvet warmth rating (3)
21 The alphabet (inits) (3)

IQ WORKOUT

What comes next in this sequence?

CODEWORD CONUNDRUM

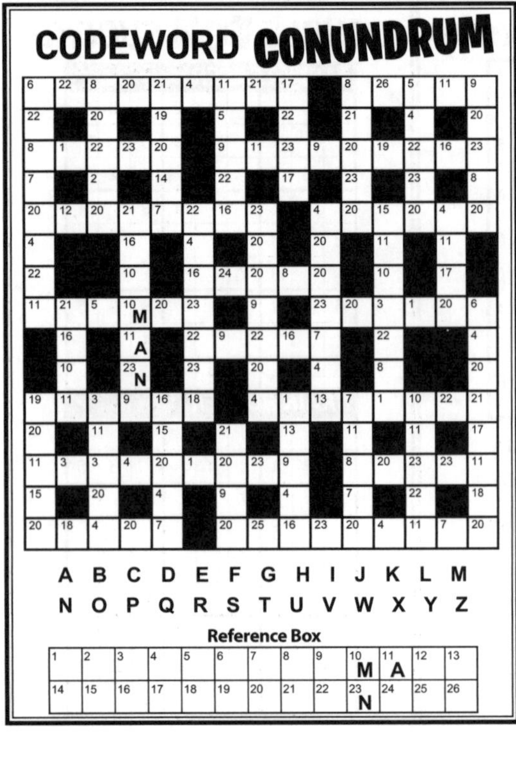

A B C D E F G H I J K L M
N O P Q R S T U V W X Y Z

Reference Box

1	2	3	4	5	6	7	8	9	10 M	11 A	12	13
14	15	16	17	18	19	20	21	22	23 N	24	25	26

DOUBLE FUN SUDOKU

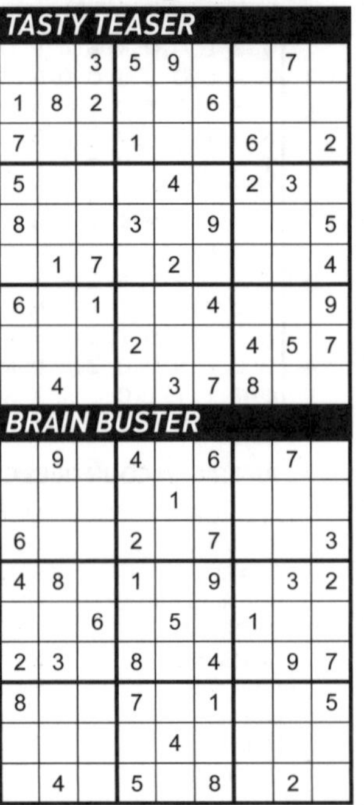

TASTY TEASER

		3	5	9			7	
1	8	2			6			
7			1			6		2
5				4		2	3	
8			3		9			5
	1	7		2				4
6		1			4			9
			2			4	5	7
	4			3	7	8		

BRAIN BUSTER

	9		4		6		7	
				1				
6			2		7			3
4	8		1		9		3	2
		6		5		1		
2	3		8		4		9	7
8			7		1			5
				4				
	4		5		8		2	

SPIDOKU

Each of the eight segments of the spider's web should be filled with a different number from 1 to 8, in such a way that every ring also contains a different number from 1 to 8.

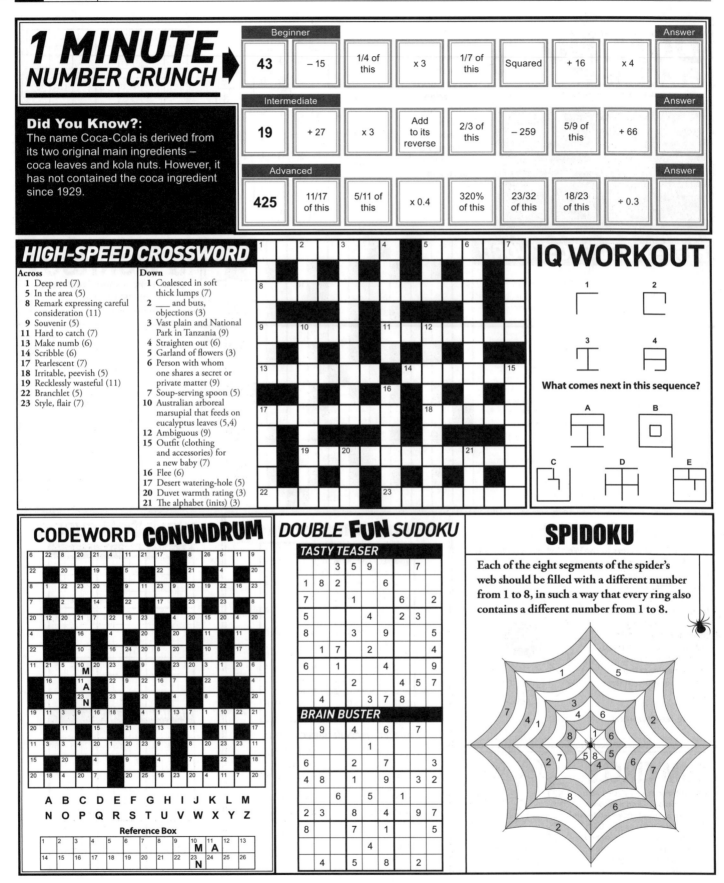

LOGI-SIX

Every row and column of this grid should contain one each of the letters A, B, C, D, E and F. Each of the six shapes (marked by thicker lines) should also contain one each of the letters A, B, C, D, E and F. Can you complete the grid?

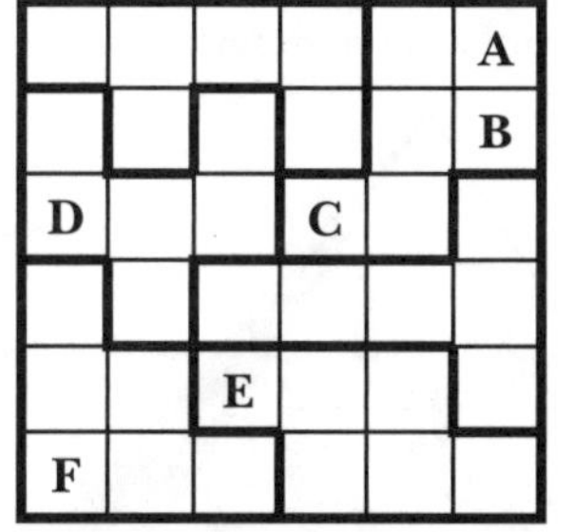

HIGH-SPEED CROSSWORD

Across
1 Woolly-headed (6)
5 Acute (5)
9 Repairs to the highway (9)
10 Chores (5)
11 Serialised TV programme (4,5)
13 Large edible predatory eel (6)
15 Short sleep (6)
19 Contract to do (9)
21 Nigerian monetary unit (5)
22 Disputative (9)
24 Childish word for scrumptious (5)
25 Be undecided (6)

Down
2 Roman goddess of the hunt (5)
3 Depleted (3)
4 Moved rapidly (6)
5 Provide with nourishment (7)
6 Haywire (5)
7 Announcement distributed to the media (5,7)
8 Long race run over open terrain (5,7)
12 Domestic swine (3)
14 To the same degree (7)
16 Choose (3)
17 Revised before printing (6)
18 Musical half-note (5)
20 On your own (5)
23 Bowel (3)

WORDSEARCH WORKOUT

```
X S E K S C T D L L V J I
S N L W A M I I U N I T S
Q O O A T R G E R D J V G
S B C I G H C H A S E U E
Z L K K T V S A N L L T U
G W E N E A E B B P X R V
N J Y E N T L G E L G D Z
I K C V V B I L W A E G D
T E R R N E U U A Y R S O
C U R R E N T L D T V T E
U U T R E W O P B N S S H
D L O H C T I W S P O N B
T U B I N G T X U R U C I
P M X N V F Z R I R V J L
T N N H G Q A Z Y I L B E
```

ELECTRICAL

BULB
CABLES
CHASE
CONDUIT
CURRENT
DUCTING
EARTH
GRID
INSTALLATION
LIGHT
LIVE
PLUG
POWER
ROSE
SLEEVE
SOCKET
SPUR
SWITCH
TUBING
UNITS

DOUBLE FUN SUDOKU

TASTY TEASER

3			6		8	4		1
		7		1			9	
4			2		7	8		
2			9			5	8	
1				6				7
	7	3			4			6
		9	1		5			4
	4			3		2		
7		5	8		6			9

BRAIN BUSTER

	8	2		7				
			3		2			5
	6				5			
4	2		5					
	7			2			8	
					1		4	9
			6				2	
1			2		9			
				8		3	6	

MATCHSTICK MAGIC

Remove nine matches so that no squares with lengths of equal sides will remain.

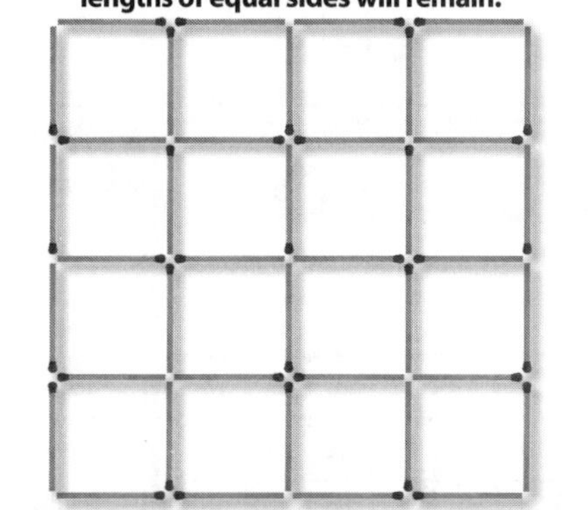

BRAIN TEASER

If the temperature rises 15% from x°C to 103.5°C, what was the previous temperature?

?____?

DOMINO PLACEMENT

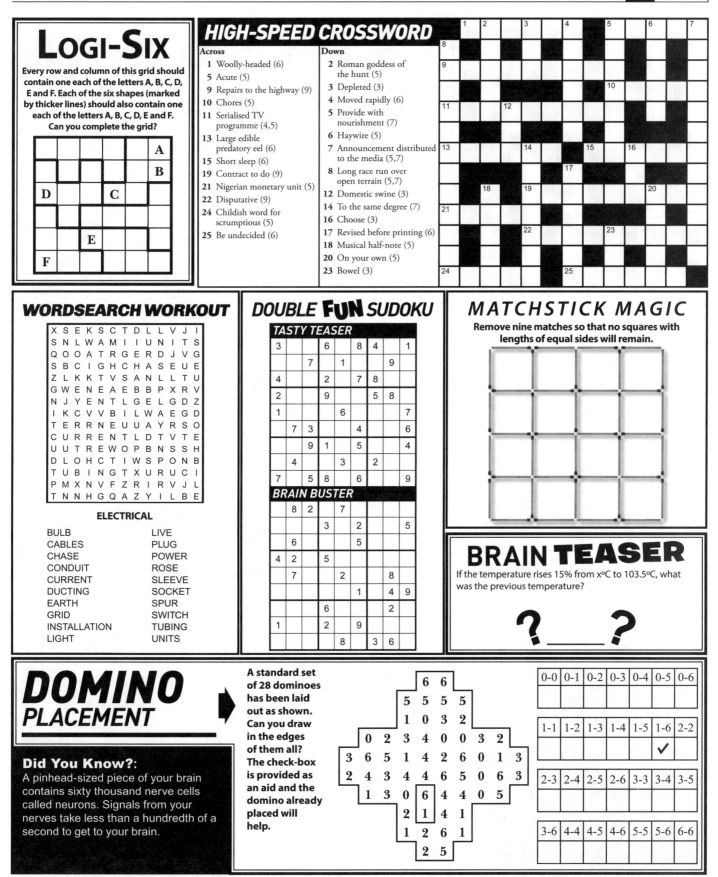

A standard set of 28 dominoes has been laid out as shown. Can you draw in the edges of them all? The check-box is provided as an aid and the domino already placed will help.

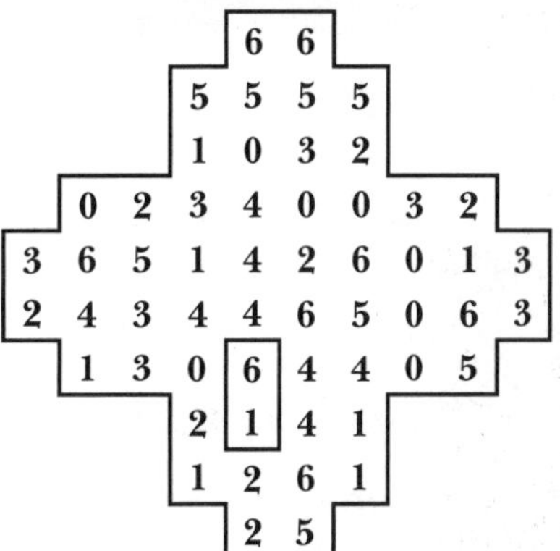

0-0	0-1	0-2	0-3	0-4	0-5	0-6

1-1	1-2	1-3	1-4	1-5	1-6	2-2
					✓	

2-3	2-4	2-5	2-6	3-3	3-4	3-5

3-6	4-4	4-5	4-6	5-5	5-6	6-6

Did You Know?:
A pinhead-sized piece of your brain contains sixty thousand nerve cells called neurons. Signals from your nerves take less than a hundredth of a second to get to your brain.

CODEWORD CONUNDRUM

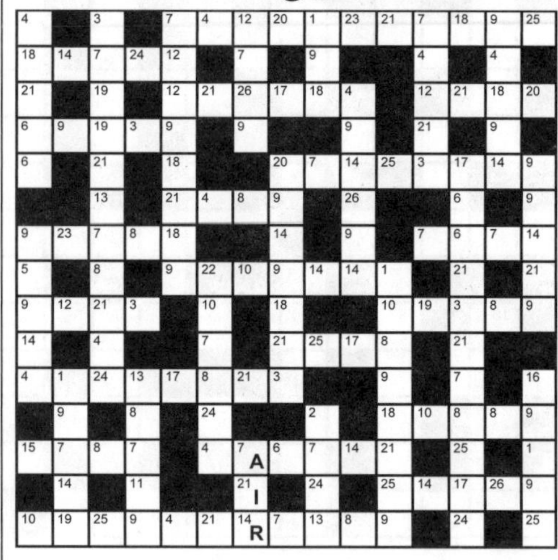

A B C D E F G H I J K L M

N O P Q R S T U V W X Y Z

Reference Box

1	2	3	4	5	6	7	8	9	10	11	12	13
						A						

14	15	16	17	18	19	20	21	22	23	24	25	26
R							I					

DOUBLE FUN SUDOKU

TASTY TEASER

	9			5			2	
	2	6			4	5	3	
1	5		2				8	6
			1	6		3		2
		1				8		
4		2		9	7			
9	3				5		6	7
	1	7	8			4	5	
	4			3			9	

BRAIN BUSTER

			4		9			5
		9			1			
	3	1		7				
					6	9		2
		7		9		8		
4		2	5					
				8		7	9	
			6			1		
6			9		3			

PYRAMID PLUS

Every brick in this pyramid contains a number which is the sum of the two numbers below it, so that F=A+B, etc.
Just work out the missing numbers!

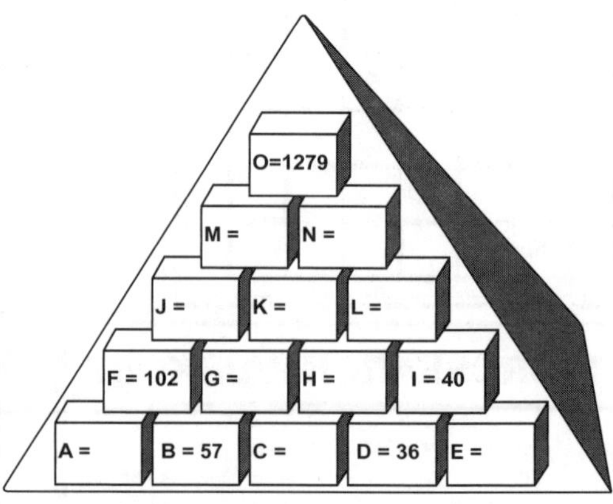

WORK IT OUT

In the grid below, what number should replace the question mark?

19	13	42	77	26	38	16
15	9	38	73	22	34	12
11	5	34	69	18	30	8
7	1	30	65	14	26	4
12	6	35	70	19	31	9
17	11	40	75	24	36	14
22	16	45	80	?	41	19

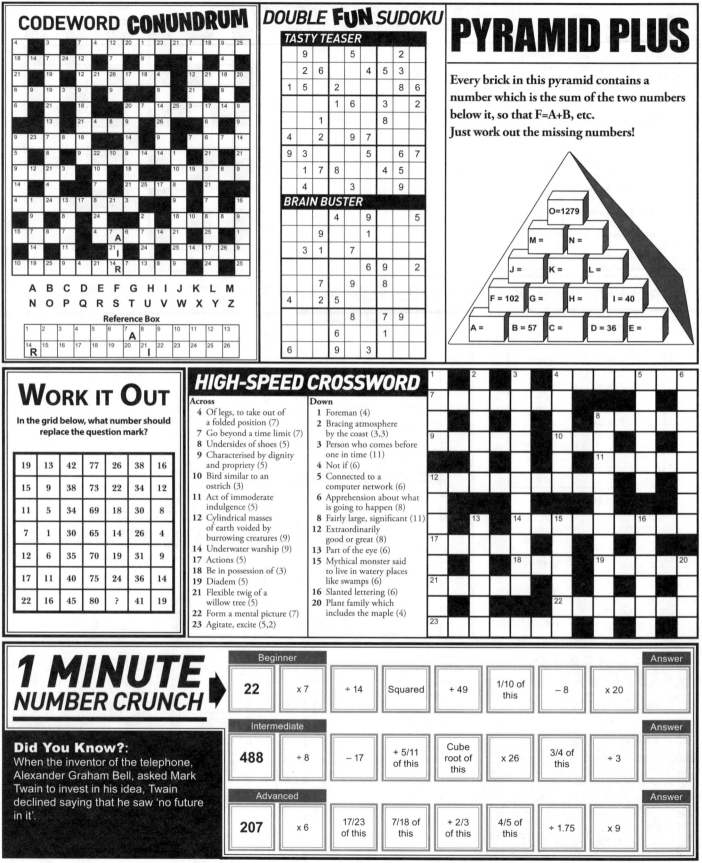

HIGH-SPEED CROSSWORD

Across

4 Of legs, to take out of a folded position (7)
7 Go beyond a time limit (7)
8 Undersides of shoes (5)
9 Characterised by dignity and propriety (5)
10 Bird similar to an ostrich (3)
11 Act of immoderate indulgence (5)
12 Cylindrical masses of earth voided by burrowing creatures (9)
14 Underwater warship (9)
17 Actions (5)
18 Be in possession of (3)
19 Diadem (5)
21 Flexible twig of a willow tree (5)
22 Form a mental picture (7)
23 Agitate, excite (5,2)

Down

1 Foreman (4)
2 Bracing atmosphere by the coast (3,3)
3 Person who comes before one in time (11)
4 Not if (6)
5 Connected to a computer network (6)
6 Apprehension about what is going to happen (8)
8 Fairly large, significant (11)
12 Extraordinarily good or great (8)
13 Part of the eye (6)
15 Mythical monster said to live in watery places like swamps (6)
16 Slanted lettering (6)
20 Plant family which includes the maple (4)

1 MINUTE NUMBER CRUNCH

Beginner

22	x 7	÷ 14	Squared	+ 49	1/10 of this	– 8	x 20	Answer

Intermediate

488	÷ 8	– 17	+ 5/11 of this	Cube root of this	x 26	3/4 of this	÷ 3	Answer

Advanced

207	x 6	17/23 of this	7/18 of this	+ 2/3 of this	4/5 of this	÷ 1.75	x 9	Answer

Did You Know?:
When the inventor of the telephone, Alexander Graham Bell, asked Mark Twain to invest in his idea, Twain declined saying that he saw 'no future in it'.

HIGH-SPEED CROSSWORD

Across
1 Gastrointestinal disorder (4,9)
7 Makes a wager (4)
8 Admirable quality or attribute (6)
9 Thin pancake (5)
10 Major monetary unit (4)
12 Approached (6)
13 Heathen (5)
15 Country of the Arabian Peninsula (5)
18 Encrustation that forms on the teeth and gums (6)
20 Salty Greek cheese (4)
21 Left-hand page (5)
22 Blanket-like cloak (6)
23 Unorthodox or false religion (4)
24 Making a positive impression on someone beforehand (13)

Down
1 Legendary (6)
2 Public dance hall (5)
3 Group of eight (5)
4 Three score and ten (7)
5 Meddle (9)
6 Avaricious (6)
11 Place in a different order (9)
14 Jittery (7)
16 Come to the fore (4,2)
17 Untidy, disorganised (6)
19 Bicker (5)
20 Concentrate (5)

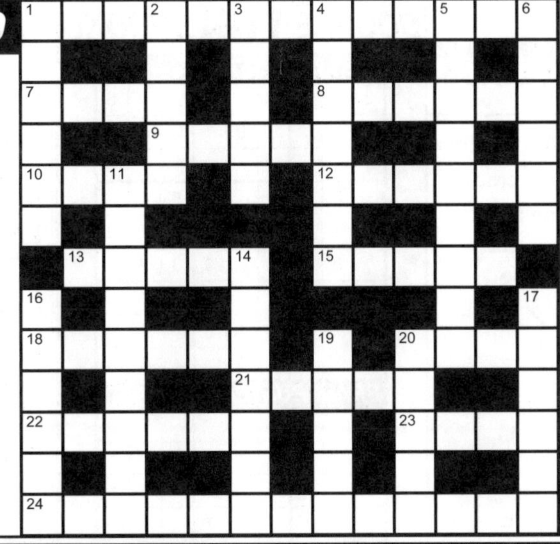

IQ WORKOUT

Draw in the hands on the final clock.

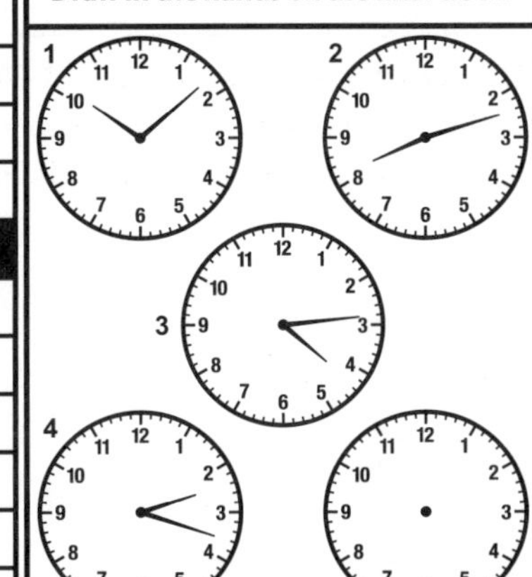

Beginner								Answer
73	+ 17	5/9 of this	+ 8	1/2 of this	Reverse the digits	50% of this	+ 16	

Intermediate								Answer
93	x 3	5/9 of this	– 47	7/12 of this	÷ 7	x 75	+ 97	

Advanced								Answer
104	8/13 of this	Square root of this	x 72	175% of this	5/12 of this	+ 9/10 of this	Add to its reverse	

Did You Know?:
Donated blood is separated into its constituent red and white cells and plasma. This means that each donation can potentially help three different people who each need only one component.

WORDSEARCH WORKOUT

A	V	P	Q	G	B	E	D	T	I	A	K	Z
N	X	V	U	C	H	A	N	G	C	H	U	N
L	H	C	A	Y	A	N	G	Z	H	O	U	N
E	O	U	N	B	K	G	U	K	D	F	X	A
S	P	H	Z	Y	Y	O	A	A	I	O	D	N
H	G	C	H	L	H	Y	T	W	H	S	Q	J
A	N	N	O	Z	U	O	K	I	A	H	I	I
N	A	I	U	G	N	A	H	C	N	A	N	N
K	I	S	S	G	O	N	O	U	G	N	G	G
U	J	H	D	U	F	U	O	G	Z	Z	D	V
N	U	O	E	Q	U	H	E	S	H	J	A	C
M	I	N	H	S	Z	S	G	G	O	L	O	M
I	J	X	L	N	H	N	U	R	U	M	Q	I
N	D	C	A	N	O	A	G	Y	L	P	Q	Y
G	V	L	B	J	U	W	N	M	O	V	Y	X

CHINESE TOWNS AND CITIES

ANSHUN
CHANGCHUN
DATONG
FOSHAN
FUZHOU
HAIKOU
HANGZHOU
HESHAN
HSINCHU
JIUJIANG
KUNMING
LANZHOU
LESHAN
NANCHANG
NANJING
QINGDAO
QUANZHOU
SUZHOU
URUMQI
YANGZHOU

DOUBLE FUN SUDOKU

TASTY TEASER

	3		9		1		4	
6		8		2		3		1
4				8				5
8		5	1		2	7		4
	7		8		5		1	
2		1	3		7	8		9
9				1				7
7		6		5		1		3
	8		7		9		6	

BRAIN BUSTER

6	3						8	9
				9				
		5	3	8			1	7
			6			1	4	
		1				6		
	6	7			4			
4	8			2	9	7		
				6				
1	2						9	6

WHATEVER NEXT?

In the diagram below, which letter should replace the question mark?

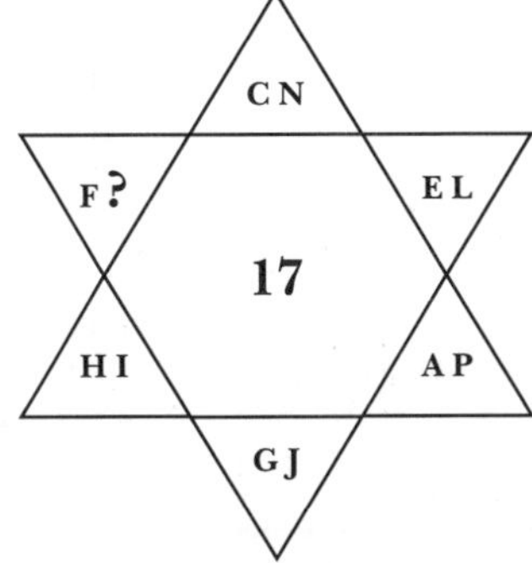

BRAIN TEASER

What weight should be placed at the question mark in order to balance the scales?

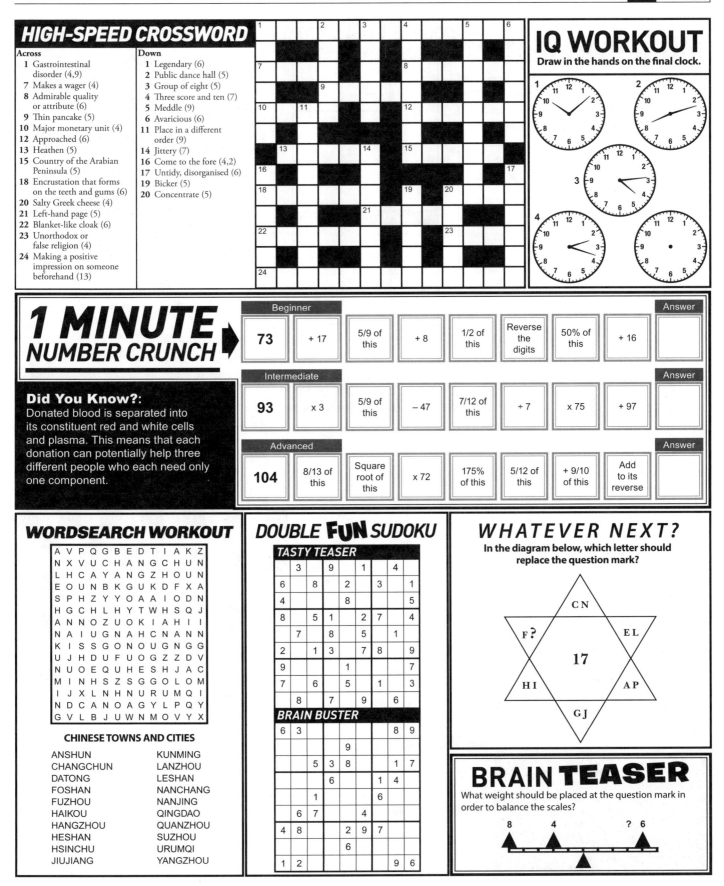

Mind Over Matter

Given that the letters are valued 1-26 according to their places in the alphabet, can you crack the mystery code to reveal the missing letter?

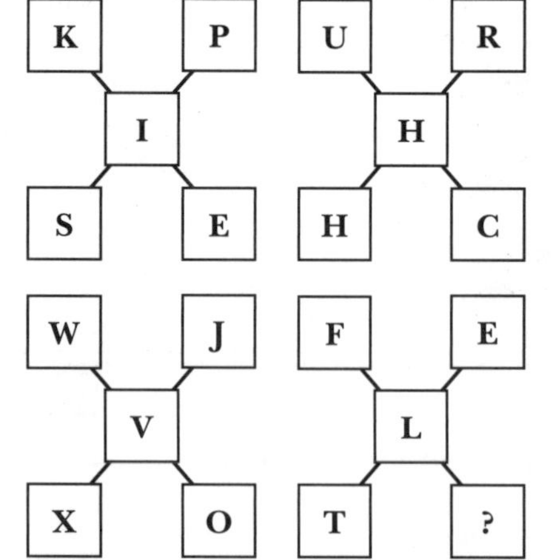

DOUBLE FUN SUDOKU

TASTY TEASER

3	2	9		7				6
			6	9				8
					2			5
	6	2	1		4	5	8	
4	3						1	9
	8	7	5		9	3	2	
7			4					
8				1	6			
2				5		4	6	3

BRAIN BUSTER

9			7				6	8
	5		4	1				
7							3	1
	9				7			
	6	2				7	8	
			3				2	
2	4							7
				7	1		4	
6	1				3			2

CODEWORD CONUNDRUM

A B C D E F G H I J K L M

N O P Q R S T U V W X Y Z

Reference Box

1	2	3	4	5	6	7	8	9	10	11	12	13
								K	N			
14	**15**	**16**	**17**	**18**	**19**	**20**	**21**	**22**	**23**	**24**	**25**	**26**
		I										

FUTOSHIKI

Fill the grid so that every horizontal row and vertical column contains the numbers 1-5. The 'greater than' or 'less than' signs indicate where a number is larger or smaller than that in the neighbouring square.

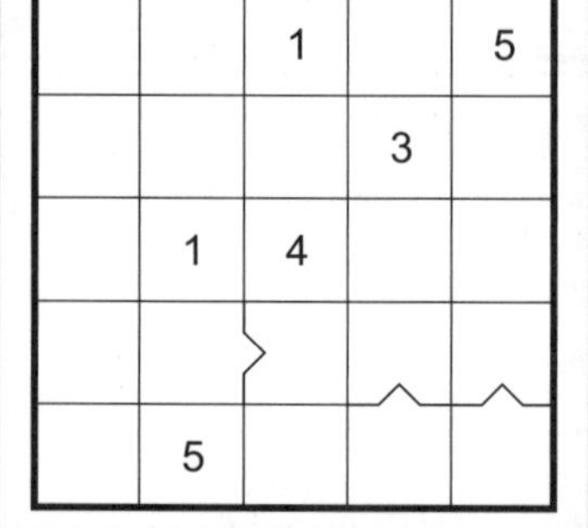

HIGH-SPEED CROSSWORD

Across

1 Not affected by alcohol (5)
5 Girdle (4)
7 Loosened (6)
8 Heals, makes better (5)
9 Celestial body orbiting another (9)
10 Source of metal (3)
11 Cancellation of civil rights (9)
15 Preventative measure (9)
19 Bunkum (3)
20 Merry-go-round (9)
21 Lift (5)
22 Mountain peak on which Noah's ark came to rest (6)
23 Lairs (4)
24 Root vegetable (5)

Down

1 Area, zone (6)
2 Hairdresser (6)
3 Country, capital Moscow (6)
4 Inform (someone) of a possible future danger (8)
5 Material used to form a hard coating on a porous surface (7)
6 More saline (7)
12 Device providing access to a computer (8)
13 Part of a door fastener (7)
14 Lachrymator (4,3)
16 Knit hose covering the body from the waist to the feet (6)
17 Reach a destination (6)
18 Sculpture (6)

1 MINUTE NUMBER CRUNCH

Beginner								Answer
33	– 4	x 5	– 15	x 3	– 90	5/6 of this	+ 14	

Intermediate								Answer
89	+ 57	– 29	5/9 of this	4/5 of this	x 7	x 0.75	÷ 3	

Advanced								Answer
33	x 25	2/3 of this	9/11 of this	28% of this	5/14 of this	+ 89	÷ 0.25	

Did You Know?:
Norwegian soccer player Svein Grondalen once had to miss an international match because of an injury incurred when he crashed into a moose while jogging.

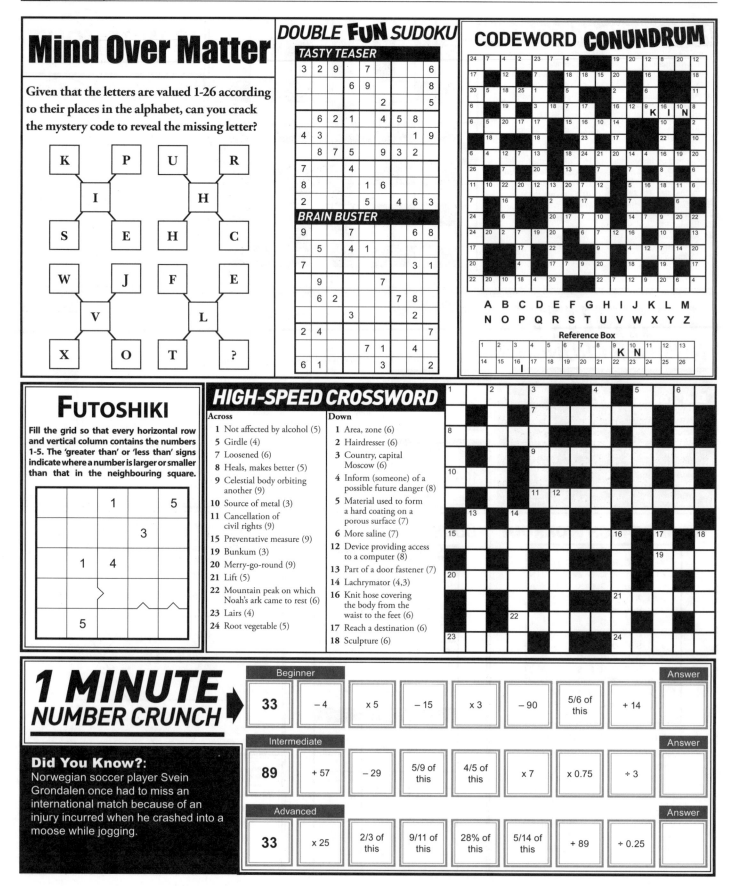

BATTLESHIP BOUT

Did You Know?:
There are more than a million species of animal on the planet, including over 70,000 kinds of spider but only about 4,600 kinds of mammal.

Can you place the vessels into the diagram? Some parts of vessels or sea squares have already been filled in. A number to the right or below a row or column refers to the number of occupied squares in that row or column.
Any vessel may be positioned horizontally or vertically, but no part of a vessel touches part of any other vessel, either horizontally, vertically or diagonally.

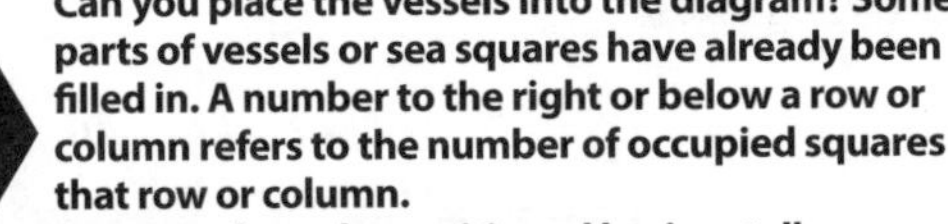

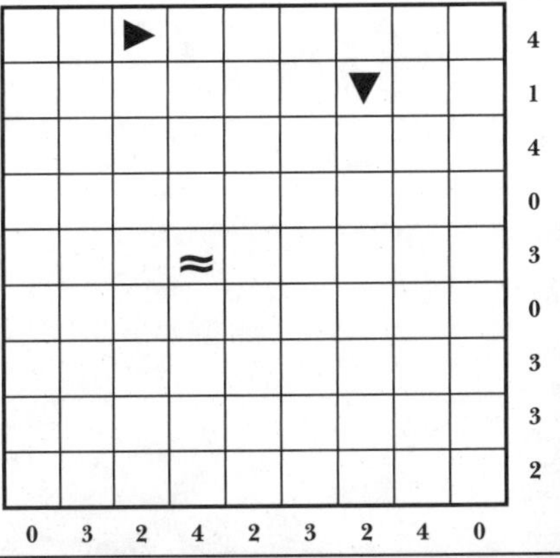

HIGH-SPEED CROSSWORD

Across
1 Australian wild dog (5)
4 Having a high-pitched sound like that of a mouse (7)
8 Grandmother (3)
9 Rose, sweet briar (9)
10 Dame Nellie ___, Australian operatic soprano (5)
11 Clergyman's salary (7)
13 Cultured, appealing to those having worldly knowledge and refinement (13)
15 Everlasting (7)
17 Interprets words (5)
19 Come about, happen (9)
21 Bronze (3)
22 Come down (7)
23 Wears out (5)

Down
1 Jeans fabric (5)
2 Designed to reduce or prevent sliding (3-4)
3 Being in force (9)
4 Marked by excessive complacency (4-9)
5 Container for ashes (3)
6 *A Town like ___*, Nevil Shute novel later made into a film (5)
7 Gave way, relinquished control over (7)
12 Wrong (9)
13 Extracted (metals) by heating (7)
14 Betrayer of one's country (7)
16 Hands out playing-cards (5)
18 Air cavity in the skull (5)
20 Girl's name (3)

IQ WORKOUT

What number comes next?

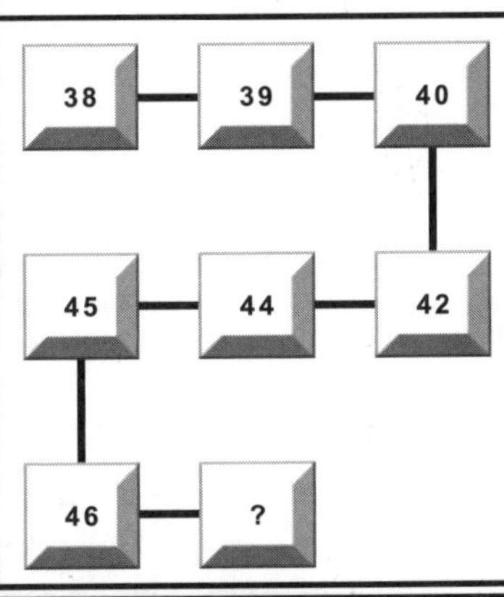

WORDWHEEL

Using only the letters in the Wordwheel, you have ten minutes to find as many words as possible, none of which may be plurals, foreign words or proper nouns. Each word must be of three letters or more, all must contain the central letter and letters can only be used once in every word. There is at least one nine-letter word in the wheel.

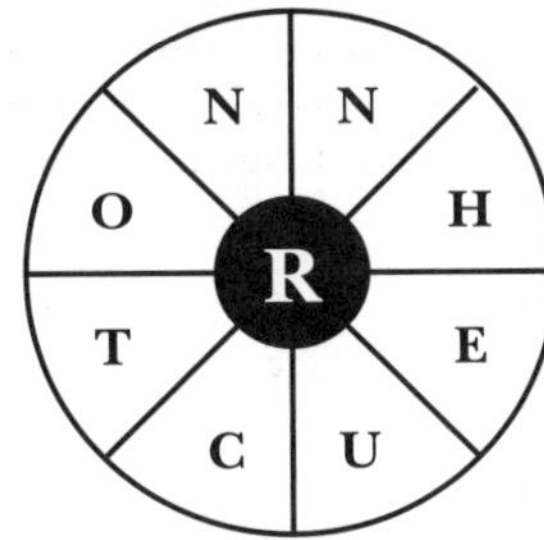

Nine-letter word(s):

SUM CIRCLE

Fill the three empty circles with the symbols +, – and x in some order, to make a sum which totals the number in the centre. Each symbol must be used once and calculations are made in the direction of travel (clockwise).

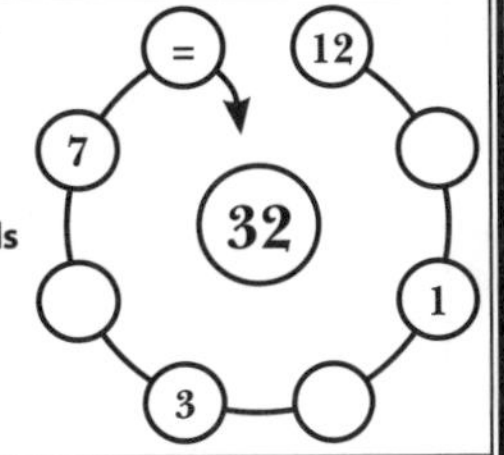

WORDSEARCH WORKOUT

S E J C N H J R I O W P Y
E S C A L E S X A P O U R
H U L P G F E O S P I E H
S O F P P N H E T O N L L
I H N H J O G W E S I L X
F M B R G I Y Z N I M L F
O O E G O T G O A T E I R
P O R E H C R A L I G B J
S N I W T N I E P O S R M
U U H R M U F R A N Z A I
C D A O L J W L P D R V K
R H R S T N H T R A I P E
C Z A X K O E Y B R C N Z
W C X H B C E D G T I J G
G Y W H Q X L O H C G O C

ASTROLOGY

ARCHER
CAPRICORN
CHART
CONJUNCTION
CUSP
FISHES
GEMINI
GOAT
HOUSE
LEO
LIBRA
MOON
OPPOSITION
PLANETS
RAM
READING
SCALES
TWINS
VIRGO
WHEEL

DOUBLE FUN SUDOKU

TASTY TEASER

5			6	9			7	4
		7			5			
1	8				4	5		
2	9		8				6	3
		4		3		9		
3	1				7		5	2
		6	1				2	7
			2			8		
8	7			5	3			9

BRAIN BUSTER

	5		7		4		6	
		2				8		
	4	6				3	1	
6			9	3	2			8
4			1	8	7			5
	2	9				1	4	
		4				5		
	3		6		5		9	

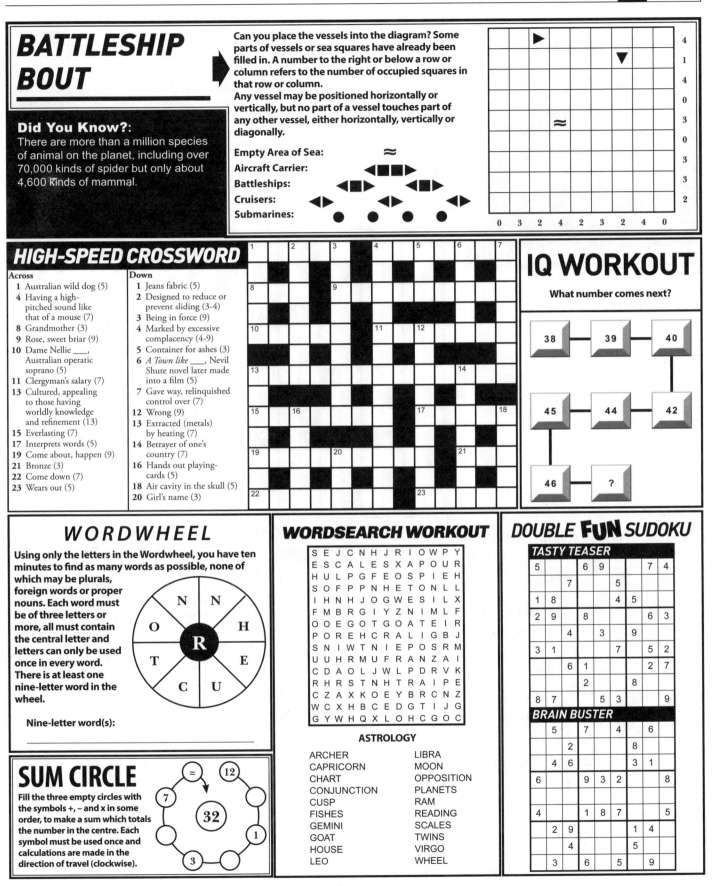

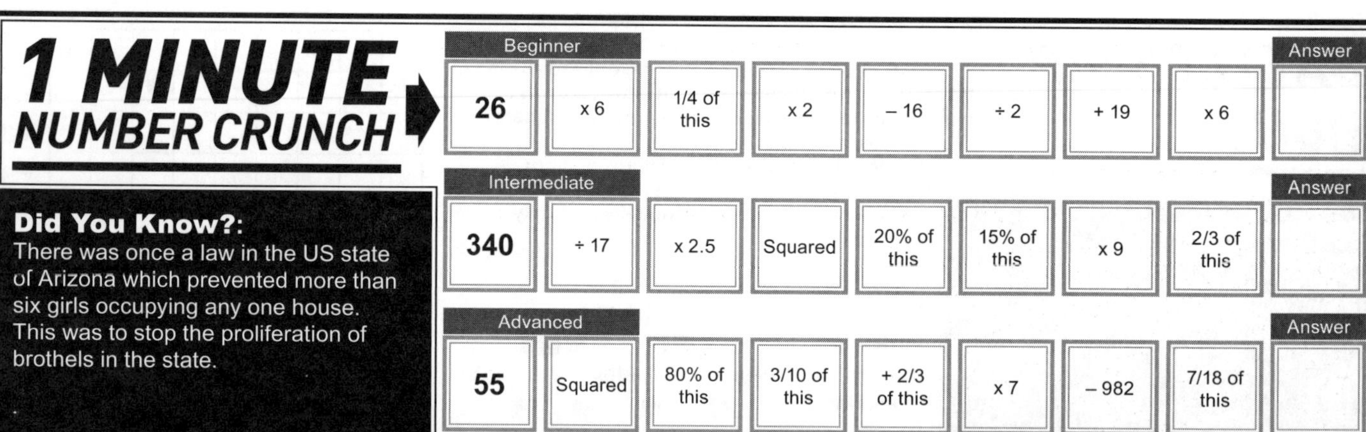

1 MINUTE NUMBER CRUNCH
Beginner
26 | x 6 | 1/4 of this | x 2 | – 16 | ÷ 2 | + 19 | x 6 | Answer
Intermediate
340 | ÷ 17 | x 2.5 | Squared | 20% of this | 15% of this | x 9 | 2/3 of this | Answer
Advanced
55 | Squared | 80% of this | 3/10 of this | + 2/3 of this | x 7 | – 982 | 7/18 of this | Answer
Did You Know?:
There was once a law in the US state of Arizona which prevented more than six girls occupying any one house. This was to stop the proliferation of brothels in the state.

HIGH-SPEED CROSSWORD

Across

1 Acquire for oneself before others can do so (3-4)
5 Tubes (5)
8 Larva of a butterfly or moth (11)
9 Authorises (5)
11 Bloodsucker in folklore (7)
13 Lots and lots (6)
14 Dental decay (6)
17 Drink given to people who are ill (4,3)
18 Breezy (5)
19 Megalithic monument (5,6)
22 Perspiration (5)
23 Burdensome (7)

Down

1 Small flute (7)
2 Consume (3)
3 Confused multitude of things (5-4)
4 Steal something (6)
5 Close friend (3)
6 Vertical structure that divides or separates (9)
7 Arctic marten (5)
10 Person to whom an envelope is written (9)
12 During the intervening time (9)
15 Timidity (7)
16 Small, roofed building affording shade and rest (6)
17 Ecstasy (5)
20 Cereal grass (3)
21 Make the sound of a dove (3)

IQ WORKOUT

What number should replace the question mark?

57
8 6
14 43
2 19
9 8
36 4 17 59 8 ?

CODEWORD CONUNDRUM

26	19	24	11	8	7		21	17	7	4	20	22	7	4
7			8		17		5			23		7		12
19	14	3	20	16	19	24	16		4	10	18	18	8	7
17			16		4		19	9	7			18		7
14	7	6	16		7 E	19 A	16 T		17	7	13	19	24	16
	8		5		17		5	6	6			24		22
19	22	5	24	11	4	16		19	4	16	17	10	14	7
1		21		24		10	24	23		10		24		19
20	24	7	1	20	19	8		7	4	13	25	7	19	16
19		17			8	7	16		25		10		11	
21	7	19	24	20	16		25	5	7		17	25	7	19
8		16			19	2	7		19		4			20
19	16	5	24	7	17		5	26	16	17	20	14	7	14
24		17		15			17		25		16			10
7	19	4	16	7	17	8	2		7	9	7	22	21	16

A B C D E F G H I J K L M
N O P Q R S T U V W X Y Z

Reference Box

1	2	3	4	5	6	7	8	9	10	11	12	13
						E						
14	15	16	17	18	19	20	21	22	23	24	25	26
		T			A							

DOUBLE FUN SUDOKU

TASTY TEASER

5		2			7			1
				2	9	7		4
1			5		8	6		
	3			9	5		4	
7	4						8	5
	2		7	4			9	
		7	9		1			3
4		6	3	7				
9			6			5		2

BRAIN BUSTER

		7				3		
6			5		8			1
	1		2		9		7	
	6	4	1		3	9	8	
	2	9	8		4	1	6	
	3		4		6		5	
9			7		5			2
		5				4		

SPIDOKU

Each of the eight segments of the spider's web should be filled with a different number from 1 to 8, in such a way that every ring also contains a different number from 1 to 8.

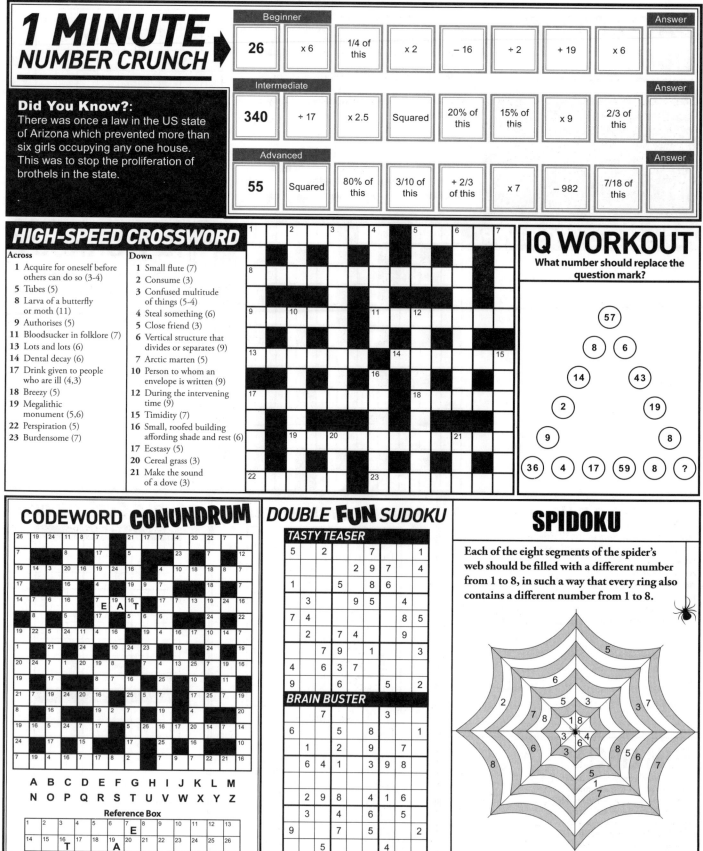

LOGI-SIX

Every row and column of this grid should contain one each of the letters A, B, C, D, E and F. Each of the six shapes (marked by thicker lines) should also contain one each of the letters A, B, C, D, E and F. Can you complete the grid?

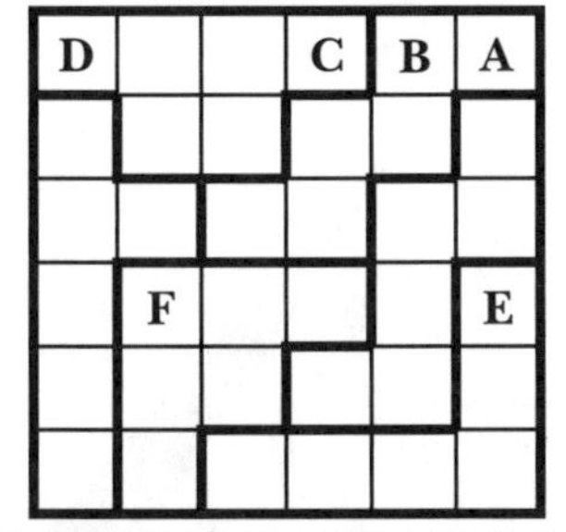

HIGH-SPEED CROSSWORD

Across

1 Clicking pendulum indicating the tempo of a piece of music (9)
5 Catch sight of (3)
7 Performer who moves to music (6)
8 Ceremonial procession (6)
10 Multicoloured (4)
11 Appearance of a place (7)
13 Take away a part from, diminish (7)
17 Male child of your spouse and a former partner (7)
19 Less than average tide (4)
21 Mass of snow which permanently covers the land (6)
22 Laugh at or mock (6)
23 Nitrogen, for example (3)
24 Fastener used on clothing (5,4)

Down

1 Manufactured (4)
2 Game played with racquets (6)
3 Not at the scheduled time (7)
4 Fill with optimism (5)
5 Lines on which musical notes are written (6)
6 All people (8)
9 Minimal wear item (1-6)
12 Going from one side to the other (8)
14 Admit one's guilt (7)
15 Precious stones (6)
16 Lasso (6)
18 Skin covering the top of the head (5)
20 Despatch (4)

WORDSEARCH WORKOUT

H J L Y L A N M Y H K R A
P A V Q H J P H T P Q C P
H A Z I L Y D A T N I M H
H U G E L Y E N O H E I Z
C E I H L L C D P H N U Z
R E P M A H H Y P D A B X
R V V H H I L A R I O U S
E K V T A G N A H H C U J
T A K Q O R N E E D T V Y
N N Z R X C L R D R E L L
U J E O E L B E N D L O I
H I V M O S H H Q I I F F
H O G Q J H X W H U I H F
C I T L S I Y M V H I R U
E V E T A I L I M U H N H

H WORDS

HAMPER
HANDY
HARLEQUIN
HAZEL
HAZILY
HELLO
HEMP
HERBS
HIDDEN
HIEROGLYPHIC
HI-FI
HILARIOUS
HILLY
HINDRANCE
HONEY
HUFFILY
HUGELY
HUMILIATE
HUNTER
HYMNAL

DOUBLE FUN SUDOKU

TASTY TEASER

1	5			8	3			2
4	3	9	7					
		8		1			9	6
			1	5		4		
	8	2				6	5	
		4		6	8			
2	7			9		1		
					2	5	3	9
6			4	3			8	7

BRAIN BUSTER

9				3				2
		2	8		1	4		
	8						1	
4	1		6		8		5	9
			4		3			
8	7		9		5		4	3
	3						7	
		7	1		9	6		
6				5				4

MATCHSTICK MAGIC

Divide this area into five pieces of equal size, using 11 matchsticks.

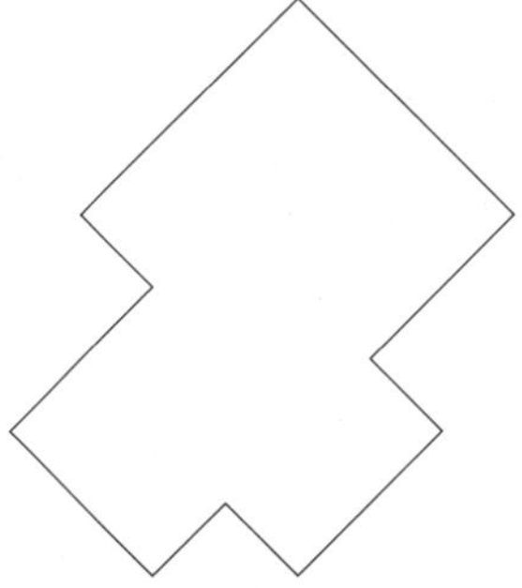

BRAIN TEASER

Divide 600 by one quarter and add 15. What is the answer?

? ______ ?

1 MINUTE NUMBER CRUNCH

Beginner								Answer
52	÷ 4	x 7	+ 17	1/9 of this	+ 142	50% of this	– 38	

Intermediate								Answer
501	– 180	2/3 of this	Double it	+ 3/4 of this	– 627	+ 178	22% of this	

Advanced								Answer
77	7/11 of this	– 4/7 of this	Cubed	1/9 of this	2/3 of this	Double it	x 7	

Did You Know?:
French artist Henri de Toulouse-Lautrec owed his strange shape and gait to breaking his legs in his early teens. His legs subsequently stopped growing, so as an adult he had a fully grown torso but very short legs.

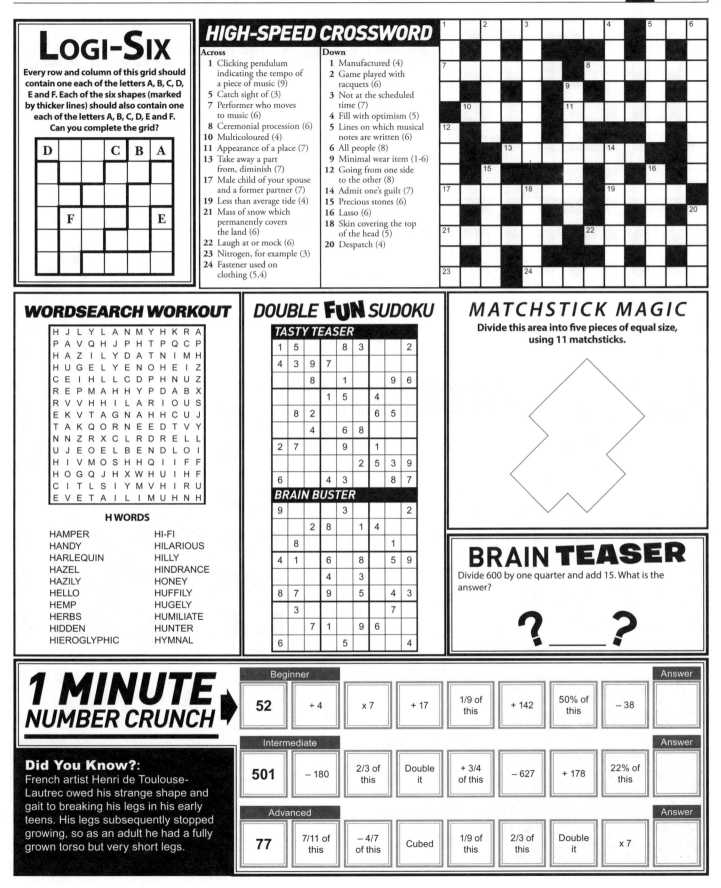

CODEWORD CONUNDRUM

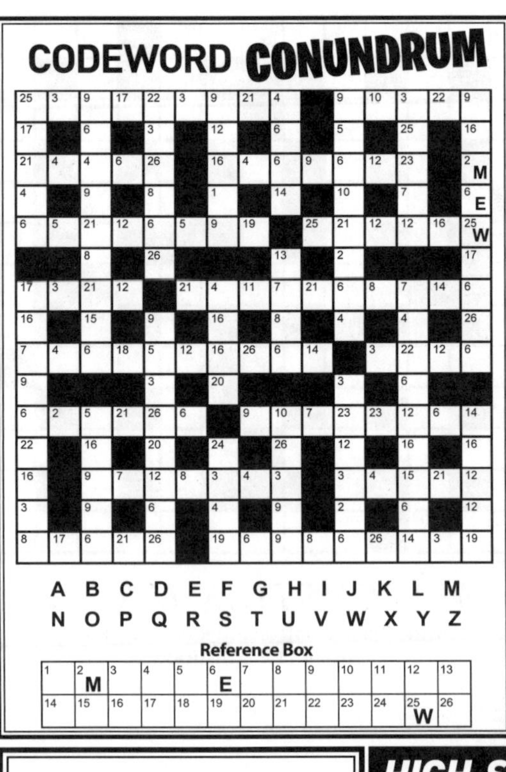

DOUBLE FUN SUDOKU

TASTY TEASER

					8	1		
	6	2	9	5			4	
4	7			2			9	3
5	8	7	4					9
6								2
9					5	4	7	1
7	1			6			3	5
	3			7	1	9	8	
		5	2					

BRAIN BUSTER

	3	4				9	5	
			9		3			
1		5				3		8
8			5		6			3
			1		2			
9			4		7			6
4		3				7		9
			2		8			
	8	7				1	2	

PYRAMID PLUS

Every brick in this pyramid contains a number which is the sum of the two numbers below it, so that F=A+B, etc.
Just work out the missing numbers!

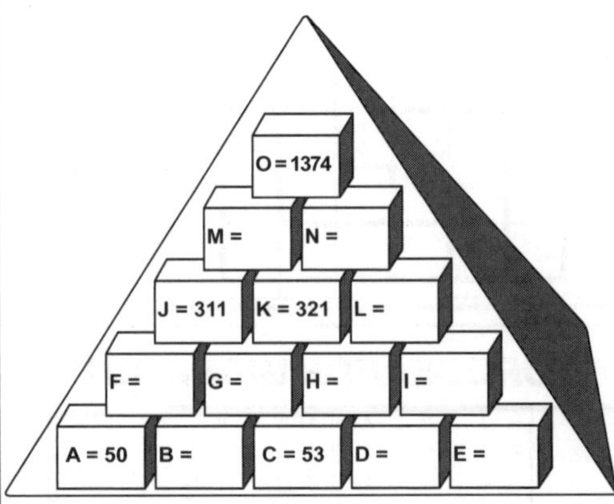

WORK IT OUT

In the grid below, what number should replace the question mark?

15	16	3	9	8	18	11
12	11	7	9	3	10	14
5	8	3	14	2	?	15
7	3	1	13	19	13	6
9	2	22	18	19	6	8
3	20	16	2	7	4	15
12	5	15	4	13	12	6

HIGH-SPEED CROSSWORD

Across

1 Malignant growth or tumour (6)
5 Reaping hook (6)
8 Child's horse (4)
9 Merry-go-round (8)
10 Bathroom fixture (5)
11 Christening (7)
14 Sickness (6)
15 Make certain (6)
17 Animal product used as a furniture polish (7)
19 Breakfast rasher (5)
21 Characteristic of a woman (8)
23 Item used to carry many cups at once (4)
24 Expend in hope of profit (6)
25 English landscape painter (1775-1851) (6)

Down

2 Find repugnant (9)
3 Affectation of being demure in a provocative way (7)
4 Large stone (4)
5 Pennant (8)
6 Be important (5)
7 Side sheltered from the wind (3)
12 Person who takes the place of another (9)
13 One resigned to the inevitable (8)
16 Break into many pieces (7)
18 Skid (5)
20 Adroit (4)
22 Long period of time (3)

1 MINUTE NUMBER CRUNCH

Beginner								Answer
74	+ 47	÷ 11	x 13	+ 9	50% of this	+ 38	50% of this	

Intermediate								Answer
39	x 5	2/3 of this	x 1.6	3/4 of this	+ 92	x 3	+ 146	

Advanced								Answer
23	Squared	+ 633	÷ 0.25	– 3/8 of this	x 3	4/15 of this	1/2 of this	

Did You Know?:
Waterspouts are literally tornadoes at sea, the funnel transferring water droplets from surface to cloud in much the same way that their land-based cousins pick up debris.

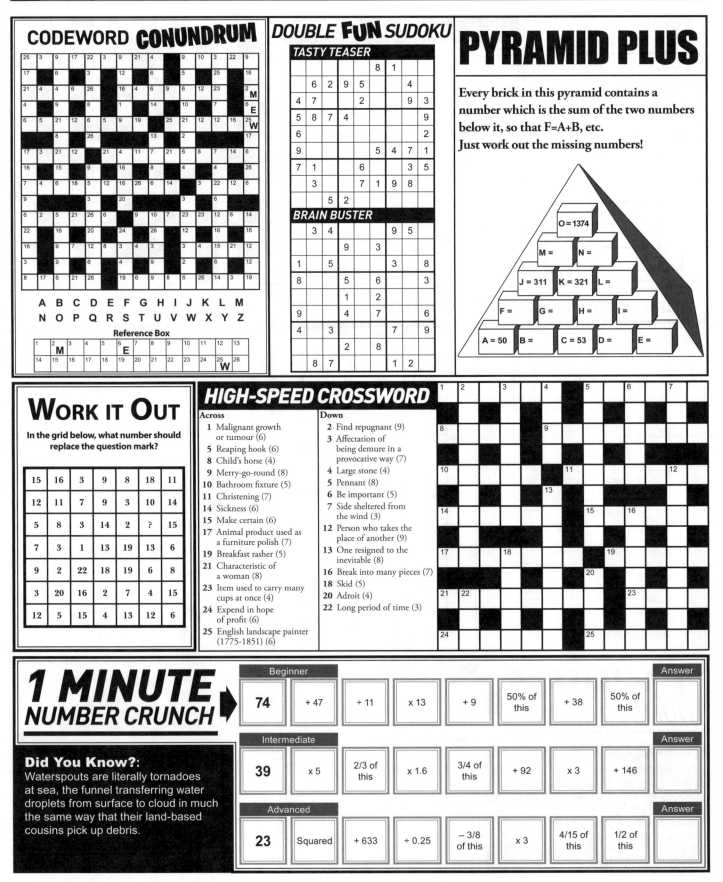

HIGH-SPEED CROSSWORD

Across
1 Fluid circulating through the body (11)
7 Large northern deer (3)
8 Hopeless undertaking (4,5)
10 Beginning of time (4,3)
12 Cause an engine to stop (5)
15 Incumbency (6)
16 Arched (6)
17 Finger next to the thumb (5)
20 Simulated rather than really existing (7)
23 Tearing down so as to make flat with the ground (9)
25 Children's game (3)
26 Proportionate, matching (11)

Down
1 Browbeat (5)
2 Frequently, poetically (3)
3 Followed clandestinely (8)
4 Level betting (5)
5 Means for communicating information (5)
6 Experienced, competent (7)
9 Bathing resort (3)
11 Course (5)
13 Fortune-teller's pack of cards (5)
14 Chance event (8)
15 Accolade (7)
18 Impurities left in the final drops of a liquid (5)
19 Woody part of plants (5)
21 Canton located in the centre of Switzerland, home to William Tell (3)
22 Founded upon law (5)
24 Floral garland (3)

SUMMING UP

In the square below, change the positions of six numbers, one per horizontal row, vertical column and long diagonal line of six smaller squares, in such a way that the numbers in each row, column and long diagonal line total exactly 191. Any number may appear more than once in a row, column or line.

39	17	41	38	59	17
32	31	37	46	36	40
43	35	31	27	14	61
10	28	36	35	19	30
21	29	36	41	15	36
21	18	30	35	35	27

DOMINO PLACEMENT

A standard set of 28 dominoes has been laid out as shown. Can you draw in the edges of them all? The check-box is provided as an aid and the domino already placed will help.

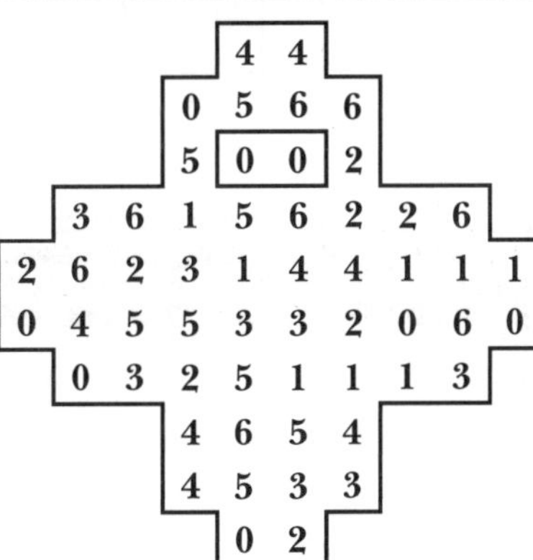

0-0	0-1	0-2	0-3	0-4	0-5	0-6
✓						

1-1	1-2	1-3	1-4	1-5	1-6	2-2

2-3	2-4	2-5	2-6	3-3	3-4	3-5

3-6	4-4	4-5	4-6	5-5	5-6	6-6

Did You Know?:
Mosquitos are attracted to the smell of a person's feet, which is why people are bitten in this area more than other parts of the body. Mosquitos are also attracted to people who have eaten bananas.

WORDSEARCH WORKOUT

I	T	B	M	F	B	C	B	S	H	Y	P	G
A	L	D	A	H	R	H	V	J	U	E	E	I
I	Y	W	J	T	I	A	C	P	J	L	A	L
P	L	P	U	I	T	L	M	O	X	L	R	L
A	T	A	C	K	T	E	J	E	D	A	S	I
D	I	R	M	J	E	L	N	I	T	R	E	E
L	N	K	A	D	N	Z	M	S	W	F	U	S
E	S	C	H	D	I	R	I	B	S	A	R	M
I	L	U	P	N	A	H	T	A	N	J	K	E
F	E	B	U	I	B	W	W	G	C	C	D	E
S	Y	W	D	O	L	E	X	N	K	L	Z	S
N	R	C	W	N	O	S	D	U	H	L	Q	Q
A	A	E	Q	S	N	O	D	R	C	L	X	Q
M	N	Y	D	D	Z	E	X	P	Q	I	V	J
H	D	L	E	I	F	H	C	R	U	B	F	R

FAMOUS NEW ZEALANDERS

ALDA
ALLEY
ATACK
BATTEN
BOWEN
BRITTEN
BUCK
BURCHFIELD
FRAME
GILLIES
HUDSON
MACDIARMID
MANSFIELD
MURDOCH
NATHAN
PARK
PEARSE
TINSLEY
UPHAM
WAKE

DOUBLE FUN SUDOKU

TASTY TEASER

	7			3		6		
8			9		5		1	3
1			4		7		5	
4			6			5	2	
3				9				7
	8	7			1			9
	6		3		2			1
7	2		5		9			6
		1		8			4	

BRAIN BUSTER

	2			5			8	
		8	7		4	6		
6								3
2	3		4		5		9	6
			2		3			
5	4		8		9		2	7
7								9
		2	9		7	1		
	1			3			4	

WHATEVER NEXT?

In the diagram below, which letter should replace the question mark?

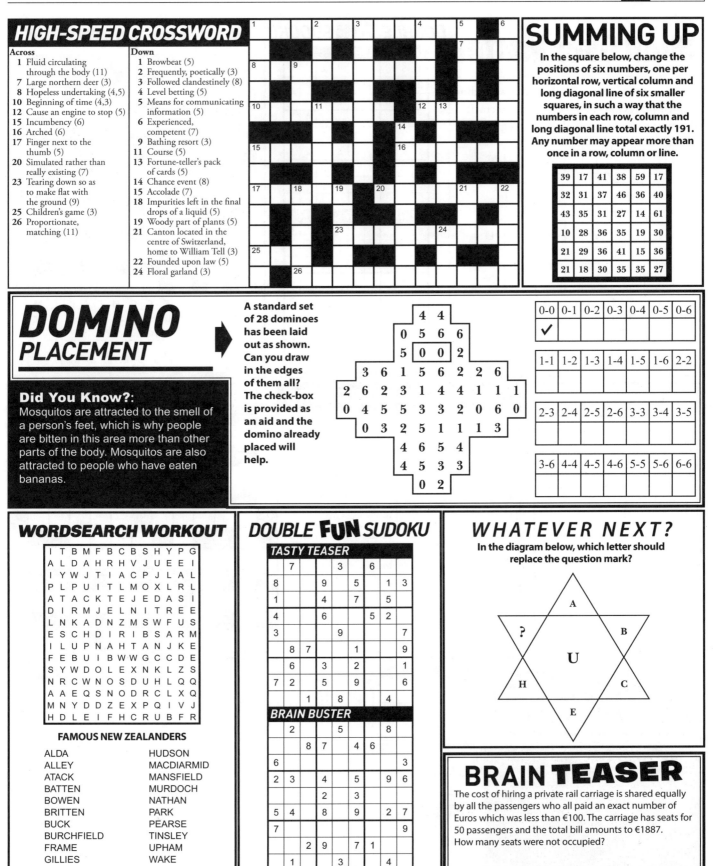

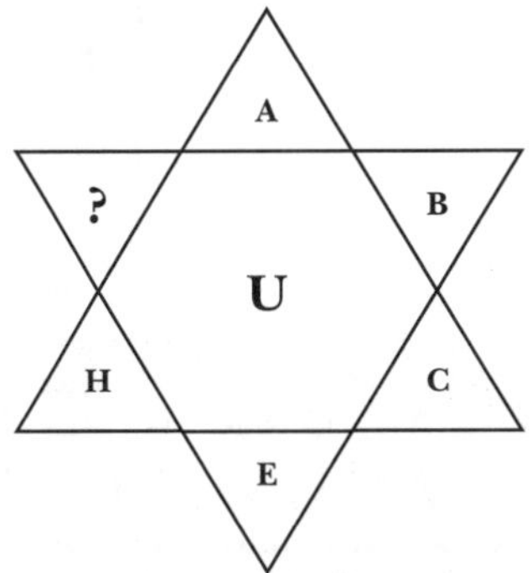

BRAIN TEASER

The cost of hiring a private rail carriage is shared equally by all the passengers who all paid an exact number of Euros which was less than €100. The carriage has seats for 50 passengers and the total bill amounts to €1887. How many seats were not occupied?

Mind Over Matter

Given that the letters are valued 1-26 according to their places in the alphabet, can you crack the mystery code to reveal the missing letter?

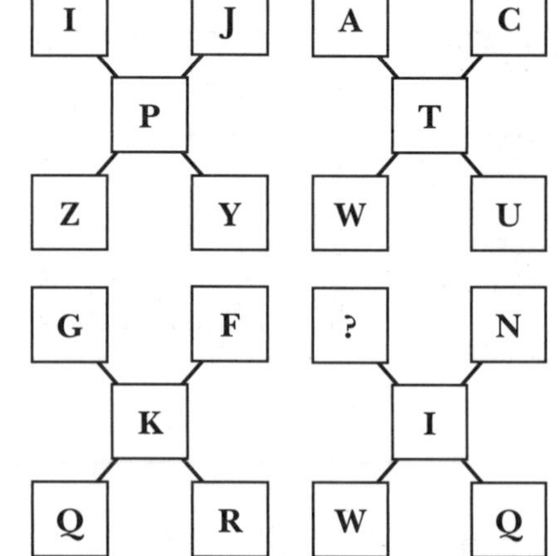

DOUBLE FUN SUDOKU

TASTY TEASER

4	5				3	2		
2			9	7			8	3
		8			2			
6	7		5				9	1
		3		1		7		
1	4				8		2	6
			6			5		
5	8			2	1			7
		9	4				6	8

BRAIN BUSTER

8								9
9			2		6			1
	5	3				6	2	
	3			5			9	
4			8		3			5
	7			4			8	
	1	6				8	4	
2			6		1			7
7								3

CODEWORD CONUNDRUM

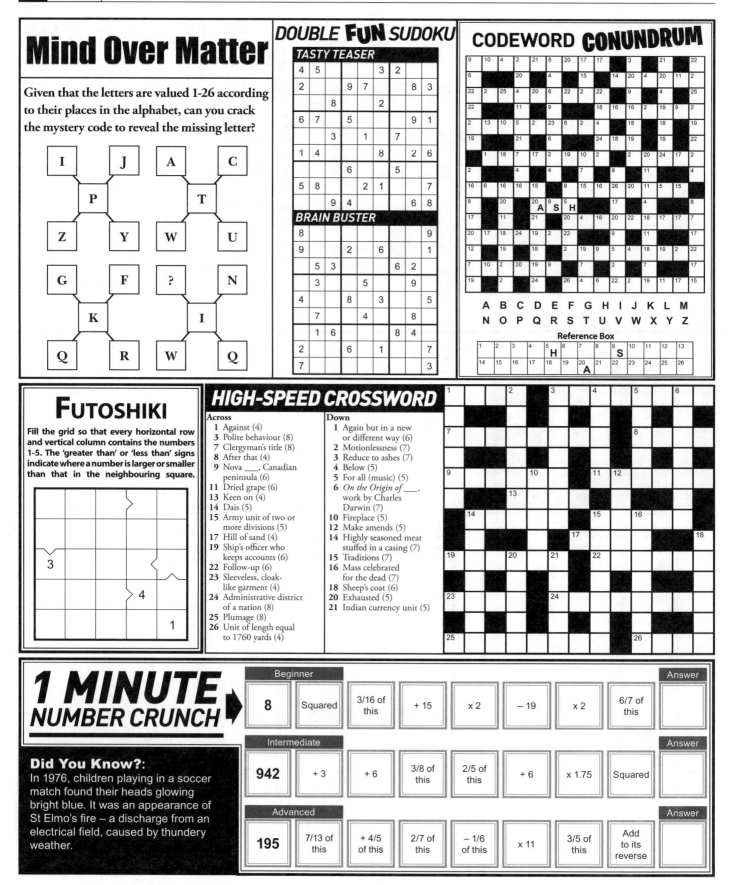

FUTOSHIKI

Fill the grid so that every horizontal row and vertical column contains the numbers 1-5. The 'greater than' or 'less than' signs indicate where a number is larger or smaller than that in the neighbouring square.

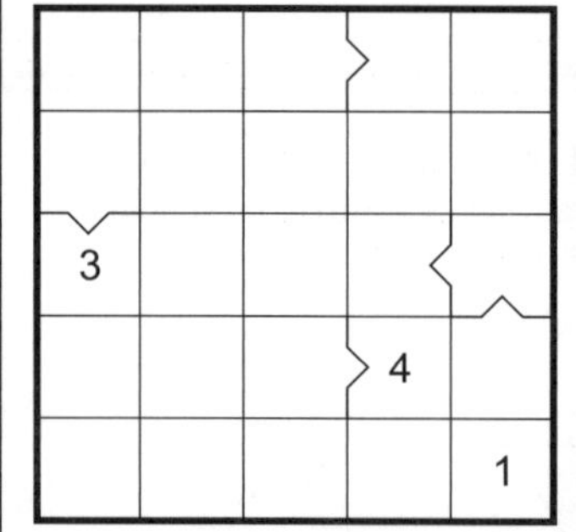

HIGH-SPEED CROSSWORD

Across
- **1** Against (4)
- **3** Polite behaviour (8)
- **7** Clergyman's title (8)
- **8** After that (4)
- **9** Nova ___, Canadian peninsula (6)
- **11** Dried grape (6)
- **13** Keen on (4)
- **14** Dais (5)
- **15** Army unit of two or more divisions (5)
- **17** Hill of sand (4)
- **19** Ship's officer who keeps accounts (6)
- **22** Follow-up (6)
- **23** Sleeveless, cloak-like garment (4)
- **24** Administrative district of a nation (8)
- **25** Plumage (8)
- **26** Unit of length equal to 1760 yards (4)

Down
- **1** Again but in a new or different way (6)
- **2** Motionlessness (7)
- **3** Reduce to ashes (7)
- **4** Below (5)
- **5** For all (music) (5)
- **6** *On the Origin of* ___, work by Charles Darwin (7)
- **10** Fireplace (5)
- **12** Make amends (5)
- **14** Highly seasoned meat stuffed in a casing (7)
- **15** Traditions (7)
- **16** Mass celebrated for the dead (7)
- **18** Sheep's coat (6)
- **20** Exhausted (5)
- **21** Indian currency unit (5)

Beginner								Answer
8	Squared	3/16 of this	+ 15	x 2	– 19	x 2	6/7 of this	

Intermediate								Answer
942	÷ 3	+ 6	3/8 of this	2/5 of this	÷ 6	x 1.75	Squared	

Advanced								Answer
195	7/13 of this	+ 4/5 of this	2/7 of this	– 1/6 of this	x 11	3/5 of this	Add to its reverse	

Did You Know?:
In 1976, children playing in a soccer match found their heads glowing bright blue. It was an appearance of St Elmo's fire – a discharge from an electrical field, caused by thundery weather.

1 MINUTE NUMBER CRUNCH

Beginner								Answer
58	+ 19	4/7 of this	÷ 4	+ 83	50% of this	– 15	1/2 of this	

Intermediate								Answer
18	x 3	1/2 of this	+ 2/9 of this	x 11	Double it	+ 1/3 of this	÷ 8	

Advanced								Answer
64	+ 72	5/8 of this	x 6	4/17 of this	÷ 0.75	9/32 of this	Squared	

Did You Know?:
The Belly Button Festival is held every year in the Japanese city of Shibukawa. It's traditional for revellers to paint faces around their navels and dance in the streets.

HIGH-SPEED CROSSWORD

Across

1 Prison (4)
3 Exaggerated masculinity (8)
9 Dumbfounding (7)
10 Confused scuffle (5)
11 Wasp's defence (5)
12 Be enough (7)
13 Israeli monetary unit (6)
15 Fist fighters (6)
18 Confectionery made from sugar, butter and nuts (7)
19 Japanese verse form (5)
21 Lukewarm (5)
22 Vestige (7)
23 Take too much medication (8)
24 Dull pain (4)

Down

1 Spectacles (7)
2 Animal similar to the giraffe (5)
4 Summer month (6)
5 Place where you are just as comfortable as in your own residence (4,4,4)
6 St Andrew's cross (7)
7 Abnormally fat (5)
8 Determined, resolute (6-6)
14 Instance (7)
16 Travel back and forth between two points (7)
17 Beads produced by oysters (6)
18 Courtyard (5)
20 ___ Asimov, science-fiction writer (5)

PARTITIONS

Draw walls to partition the grid into areas (some are already drawn in). Each area must contain two circles, area sizes must match those numbers shown next to the grid and each '+' must be linked to at least two walls.

4, 5, 5, 5, 6

WORDWHEEL

Using only the letters in the Wordwheel, you have ten minutes to find as many words as possible, none of which may be plurals, foreign words or proper nouns. Each word must be of three letters or more, all must contain the central letter and letters can only be used once in every word. There is at least one nine-letter word in the wheel.

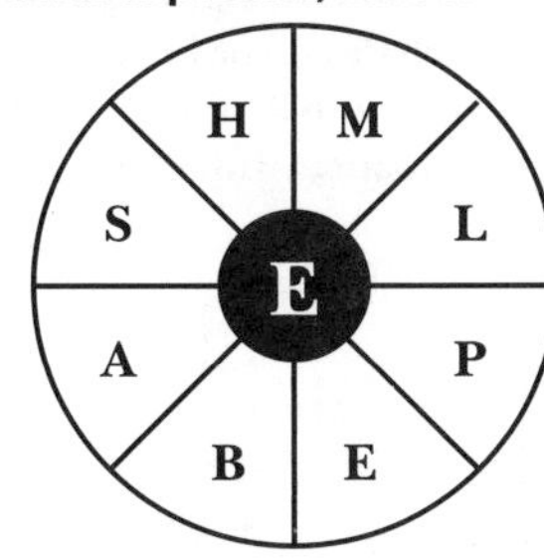

Nine-letter word(s):

SUM CIRCLE

Fill the three empty circles with the symbols +, – and x in some order, to make a sum which totals the number in the centre. Each symbol must be used once and calculations are made in the direction of travel (clockwise).

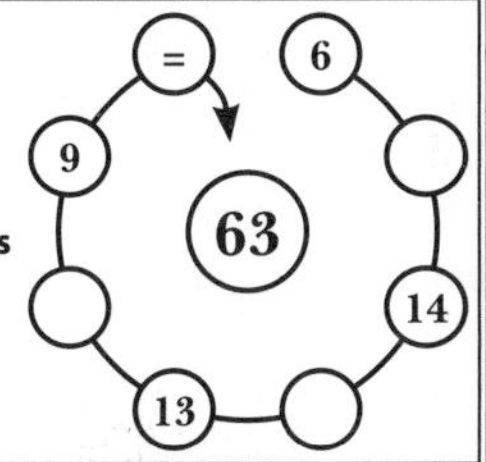

WORDSEARCH WORKOUT

```
Q F O H F O F T H Z V T K
A U C P L E W A Q E L M L
T I Q L G J E Z C L U B J
T K E G X P A A U S U E B
C A R I E C L K A T Z R R
R U S L Y G O N D E T I I
F H A M E J Q J R I A N K
O Y O D A U K H A N L G S
X X R N I N U H B M E D D
H E T N E M A P B Y T C A
M A T F B R X S U B S A L
V I L O V T P M H A C F L
N E L A I D W O Z Y H Q W
B D R F E Z R E T S A P V
T D F R A N Z J O S E F A
```

GLACIERS

ALETSCH
BERING
BRIKSDAL
FEE
FOX
FRANZ JOSEF
FURGG
HARVARD
HORN
HUBBARD
HUMBOLDT
JAMTAL
MER DE GLACE
PASTERZE
RHONE
SAN QUINTIN
STEIN
TASMAN
VATNAJOKULL
YALE

DOUBLE FUN SUDOKU

TASTY TEASER

2		5	1				3	
		4	8	5				6
	8				6		9	2
9	7	1	5	2				
6								4
				3	1	9	2	7
8	1		4				7	
7				9	8	3		
	2				3	6		5

BRAIN BUSTER

		3	8		7	2		
4			6		1			9
	7						5	
8	6		3		2		9	1
5	9		7		6		4	2
	1						8	
7			1		5			3
		4	2		8	9		

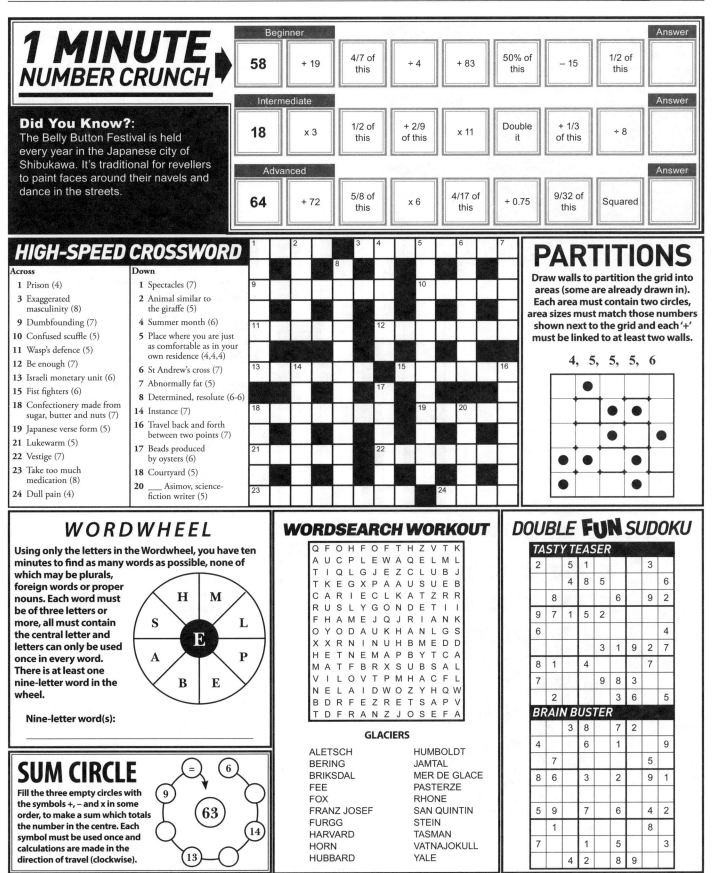

1 MINUTE NUMBER CRUNCH

Beginner								Answer
150	10% of this	x 8	50% of this	3/12 of this	+ 7	÷ 2	x 10	

Intermediate								Answer
269	+ 47	÷ 4	x 3	– 88	+ 27	5/8 of this	+ 10%	

Advanced								Answer
84	5/7 of this	Squared	7/18 of this	– 578	+ 1096	1/2 of this	+ 697	

Did You Know?:
Zeppo Marx, perhaps the least famous of the Marx Brothers, invented a wristwatch that sounded an alarm in the event of the wearer having a heart attack.

HIGH-SPEED CROSSWORD

Across
1 Short underpants (6)
7 Milk pudding ingredient (7)
8 Spiny, insectivore with a long tongue and sharp claws (8)
9 Fail (to) (7)
10 All together, as a group (2,5)
13 Aquatic creature (5)
15 Poems (4)
16 Food used in a trap (4)
17 Extremely angry (5)
19 State of being behind in payments (7)
22 Psychics, supernaturalists (7)
24 Pursuit of pleasure as a matter of ethical principle (8)
25 Disc used in various board games (7)
26 Affirm by oath (6)

Down
2 Angry dispute (3-2)
3 Apartments (5)
4 Naked (4)
5 Very aggressive strain of insect (6,3)
6 Inflammation of the stomach lining (9)
7 Article of faith (5)
10 Branch of social science dealing with finance (9)
11 Helper (9)
12 Drink often mixed with alcohol (4)
14 Level (4)
18 Weapon that delivers a temporarily paralysing electric shock (5)
20 Fowl's perch (5)
21 Utters in an irritated tone (5)
23 Masticate (4)

IQ WORKOUT

Which is the odd one out?

CODEWORD CONUNDRUM

DOUBLE FUN SUDOKU

TASTY TEASER

6			2		9		5	
5			3		8		9	4
	1			7		6		
	9	3	5					1
4				8				2
8					6	4	7	
		5		2			4	
2	6		8		3			7
	3		1		4			6

BRAIN BUSTER

8	5	3		7				4
				6	5			9
			3					2
	4					2		
1	6						8	3
		7					5	
7					4			
9			5	1				
5				2		1	4	8

SPIDOKU

Each of the eight segments of the spider's web should be filled with a different number from 1 to 8, in such a way that every ring also contains a different number from 1 to 8.

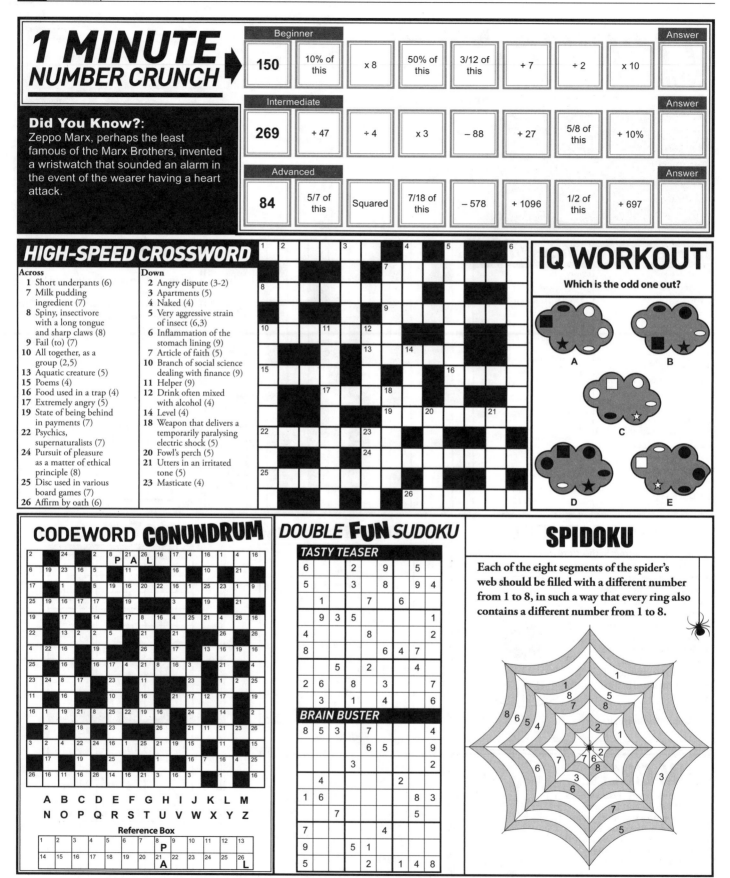

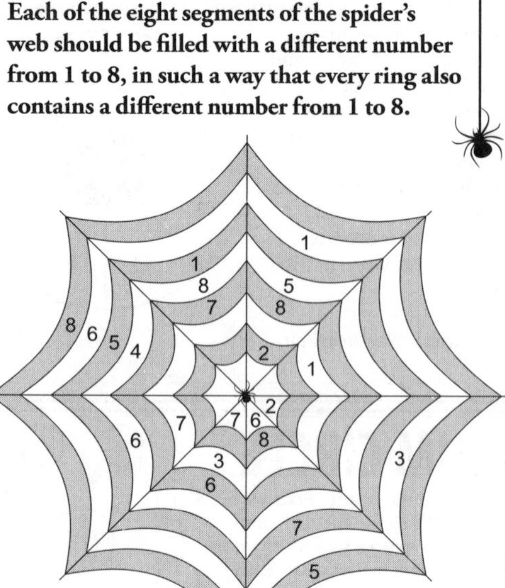

LOGI-SIX

Every row and column of this grid should contain one each of the letters A, B, C, D, E and F. Each of the six shapes (marked by thicker lines) should also contain one each of the letters A, B, C, D, E and F. Can you complete the grid?

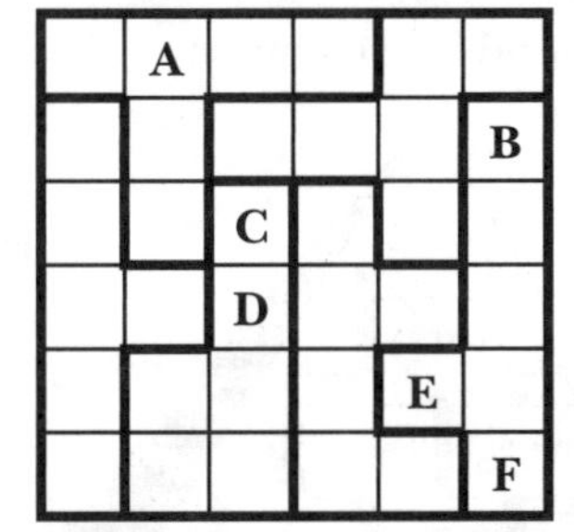

HIGH-SPEED CROSSWORD

Across

1 Meal accompaniment (4,4)
5 Be unsuccessful (4)
7 Registers electronically (7)
8 Underwater missile (7)
9 Grassy plain (7)
11 Depository for displaying objects of historical interest (6)
14 Spherical object (3)
15 Trousers for casual wear (6)
17 Wholly occupy (7)
19 Plunge (7)
22 Jealous (7)
23 Prepares leather (4)
24 Placed very near together (5-3)

Down

1 Condiment, sodium chloride (4)
2 Scattered wreckage (6)
3 Headlong plunge into water (4)
4 Implement used to sharpen razors (5)
5 Fleet of small craft (8)
6 US city famous for entertainment and gambling (3,5)
10 Chest bones (4)
11 Motion (8)
12 Internal organs, collectively (8)
13 Creeping low plant (4)
16 Traditional Christmas songs (6)
18 Fibre used for making rope (5)
20 Crime syndicates (4)
21 Compass point (4)

WORDSEARCH WORKOUT

```
R V Y H I M B Y R R E H S
E S W W Y P P A H W X E T
P I N E M M A N U E L N E
A L W U L E T T C B O X E
P R E C E C S D H E L N W
G F U G J T I S L A D E S
N A G M N N G C I G J X P
I F R C P A O C I A T O I
P R B L N U Y H Q G H W R
P A O E A C N I U Z A Z I
A J T I K N W C C G R H T
R X W R M L D I H G F B J
W R F B K M O N C A R D S
H D S A Z L G G T Q Q G Z
Y T H G I N T N E L I S E
```

CHRISTMAS

ANGEL	NOEL
BAUBLE	OXEN
CARDS	PINE
EMMANUEL	RUM PUNCH
GABRIEL	SHERRY
GARLAND	SILENT NIGHT
HAPPY	SLADE
ICICLE	SPIRIT
ICING	SWEETS
MESSIAH	WRAPPING PAPER

DOUBLE FUN SUDOKU

TASTY TEASER

		7	4	2	5	1		
	8	9	6			7	2	
4			7				3	
	9				4			6
	7	2				3	4	
3			1				5	
	5				1			9
	6	8			7	5	1	
		4	5	3	9	8		

BRAIN BUSTER

		8			7			
								1
				6	5		9	4
	8	9			3	7		
2				9				6
		1	8			9	4	
6	4		9	2				
9								
			5			3		

MATCHSTICK MAGIC

Here are two cocktail glasses. Move six matchsticks and change them into a house.

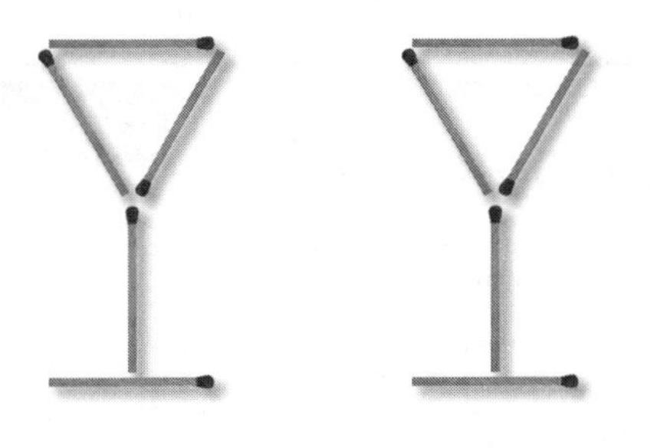

BRAIN TEASER

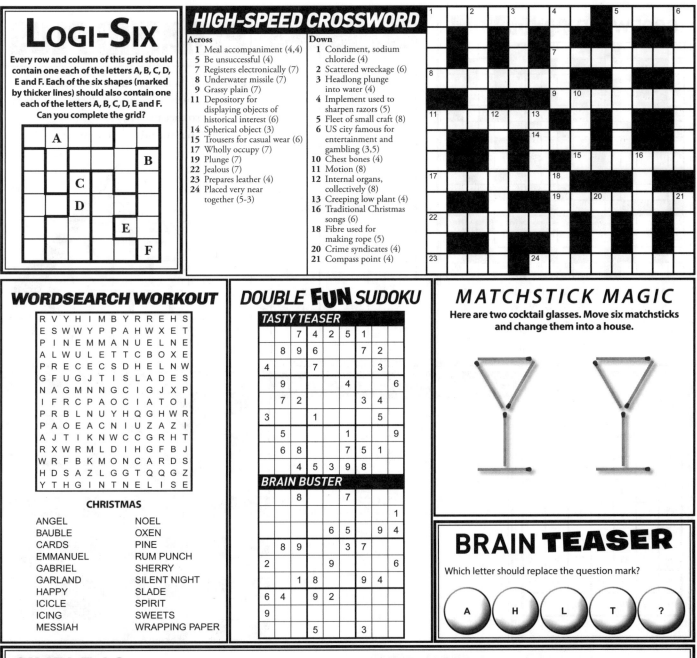

Which letter should replace the question mark?

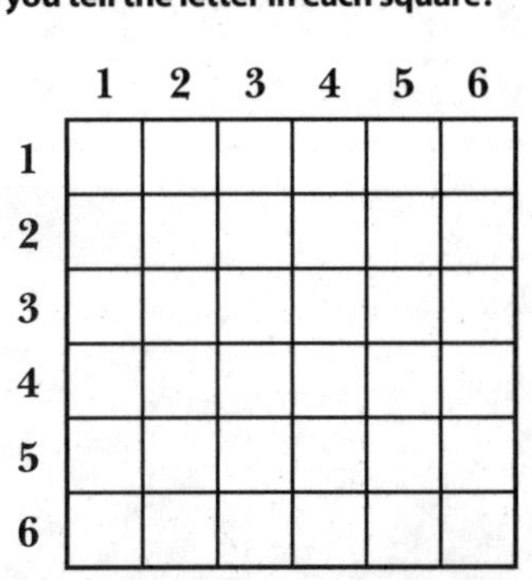

SIMPLE AS A, B, C ?

Each of the small squares in the grid below contains either A, B or C. Each row, column, and diagonal line of six squares has exactly two of each letter. Can you tell the letter in each square?

Across

1 The Bs are next to each other
2 The Cs are next to each other
3 The As are further right than the Bs
4 Each A is directly next to and right of a C
5 The Bs are next to each other
6 The Bs are further right than the Cs

Down

1 No two letters the same are directly next to each other
2 The As are lower than the Bs
3 The Bs are next to each other and lower than the As
4 Each B is directly next to and below a C
5 The As are next to each other
6 Each B is directly next to and below a C

	1	2	3	4	5	6
1						
2						
3						
4						
5						
6						

Did You Know?:

Brazilian priest Adelir de Carli took off in a chair attached to 1,000 helium-filled balloons in 2008. The charity stunt went tragically wrong, however, when he was blown out to sea. The lower half of his body was found in the sea 60 miles away, three months later.

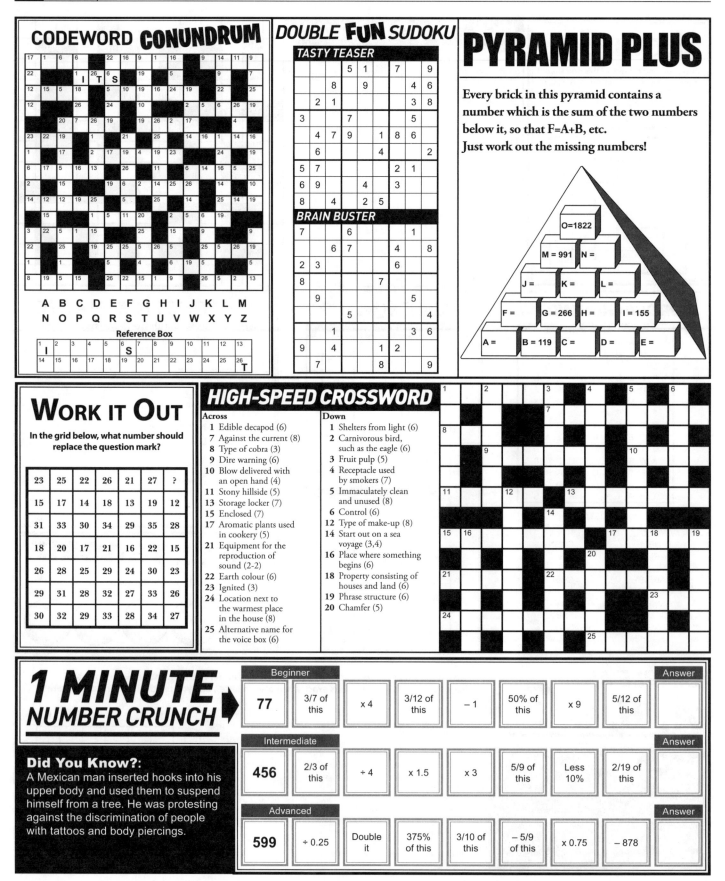

CODEWORD CONUNDRUM

A B C D E F G H I J K L M

N O P Q R S T U V W X Y Z

Reference Box

1	2	3	4	5	6	7	8	9	10	11	12	13
I					S							
14	**15**	**16**	**17**	**18**	**19**	**20**	**21**	**22**	**23**	**24**	**25**	**26**
												T

DOUBLE FUN SUDOKU

TASTY TEASER

			5	1		7		9
		8		9			4	6
	2	1					3	8
3			7				5	
	4	7	9		1	8	6	
	6				4			2
5	7					2	1	
6	9			4		3		
8		4		2	5			

BRAIN BUSTER

7			6				1	
		6	7			4		8
2	3					6		
8					7			
	9						5	
			5					4
		1					3	6
9		4			1	2		
	7				8			9

PYRAMID PLUS

Every brick in this pyramid contains a number which is the sum of the two numbers below it, so that F=A+B, etc. Just work out the missing numbers!

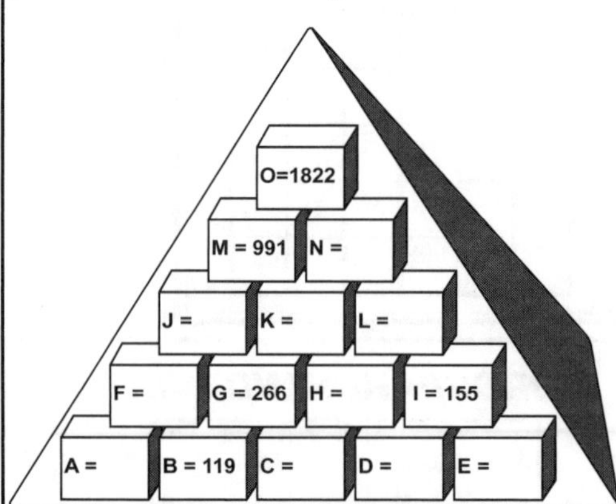

WORK IT OUT

In the grid below, what number should replace the question mark?

23	25	22	26	21	27	?
15	17	14	18	13	19	12
31	33	30	34	29	35	28
18	20	17	21	16	22	15
26	28	25	29	24	30	23
29	31	28	32	27	33	26
30	32	29	33	28	34	27

HIGH-SPEED CROSSWORD

Across

1 Edible decapod (6)
7 Against the current (8)
8 Type of cobra (3)
9 Dire warning (6)
10 Blow delivered with an open hand (4)
11 Stony hillside (5)
13 Storage locker (7)
15 Enclosed (7)
17 Aromatic plants used in cookery (5)
21 Equipment for the reproduction of sound (2-2)
22 Earth colour (6)
23 Ignited (3)
24 Location next to the warmest place in the house (8)
25 Alternative name for the voice box (6)

Down

1 Shelters from light (6)
2 Carnivorous bird, such as the eagle (6)
3 Fruit pulp (5)
4 Receptacle used by smokers (7)
5 Immaculately clean and unused (8)
6 Control (6)
12 Type of make-up (8)
14 Start out on a sea voyage (3,4)
16 Place where something begins (6)
18 Property consisting of houses and land (6)
19 Phrase structure (6)
20 Chamfer (5)

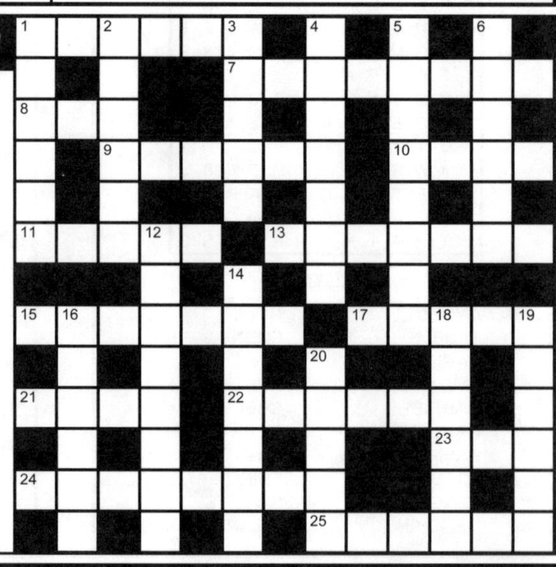

1 MINUTE NUMBER CRUNCH

Beginner								Answer
77	3/7 of this	x 4	3/12 of this	– 1	50% of this	x 9	5/12 of this	

Intermediate								Answer
456	2/3 of this	÷ 4	x 1.5	x 3	5/9 of this	Less 10%	2/19 of this	

Advanced								Answer
599	÷ 0.25	Double it	375% of this	3/10 of this	– 5/9 of this	x 0.75	– 878	

Did You Know?:
A Mexican man inserted hooks into his upper body and used them to suspend himself from a tree. He was protesting against the discrimination of people with tattoos and body piercings.

DOMINO PLACEMENT

A standard set of 28 dominoes has been laid out as shown. Can you draw in the edges of them all? The check-box is provided as an aid and the domino already placed will help.

				2	3				
			2	6	6	6			
			5	5	6	2			
	0	4	2	4	6	0	5	5	
3	5	5	1	2	4	6	1	4	4
0	0	4	6	3	3	0	4	1	4
	1	5	1	3	0	5	2	1	
			2	1	3	6			
			2	3	1	3			
				0	0				

0-0	0-1	0-2	0-3	0-4	0-5	0-6

1-1	1-2	1-3	1-4	1-5	1-6	2-2
	✓					

2-3	2-4	2-5	2-6	3-3	3-4	3-5

3-6	4-4	4-5	4-6	5-5	5-6	6-6

Did You Know?:
Staff at an acupuncture clinic locked up and went home unaware that there was someone in the treatment room. The patient had to remove the needles herself and call for help.

HIGH-SPEED CROSSWORD

Across
1 Hearty enjoyment (5)
4 Avoiding waste (7)
8 Table-tennis racquet (3)
9 Slabs of grass and grass roots (5)
10 Relative by marriage (2-3)
11 Predisposition in favour of something (10)
13 Drew in by a vacuum (6)
15 Implement for cutting grass (6)
18 Physical or mental inability to do something (10)
22 Adult insect (5)
23 Propels with the foot (5)
24 Reverence (3)
25 Large, ocean-dwelling mammal (3,4)
26 African antelope (5)

Down
1 Upright pole on which a hinged barrier is hung (8)
2 Disrobe (5)
3 Lewd (7)
4 Male reproductive organ of a flower (6)
5 Digression (5)
6 Unlawful (7)
7 Robe (4)
12 US state (8)
14 Musical setting for a religious text (7)
16 Common farmyard bird (7)
17 Plaid associated with Scotland (6)
19 Garlic mayonnaise (5)
20 Popular palm-like houseplant (5)
21 Formal offers at an auction (4)

IQ WORKOUT

What weight should be placed at the question mark in order to balance the scales?

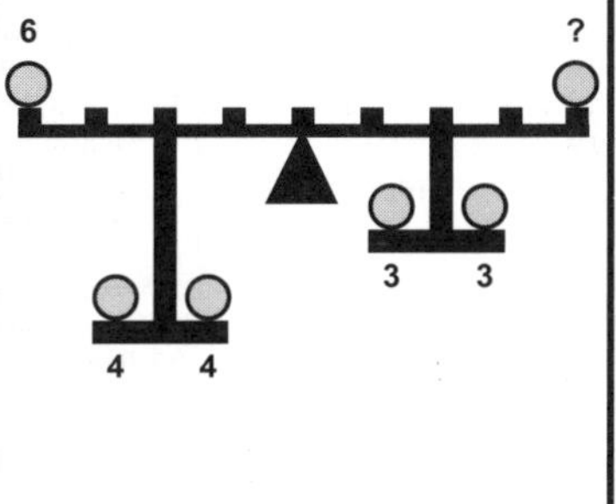

WORDWHEEL

Using only the letters in the Wordwheel, you have ten minutes to find as many words as possible, none of which may be plurals, foreign words or proper nouns. Each word must be of three letters or more, all must contain the central letter and letters can only be used once in every word. There is at least one nine-letter word in the wheel.

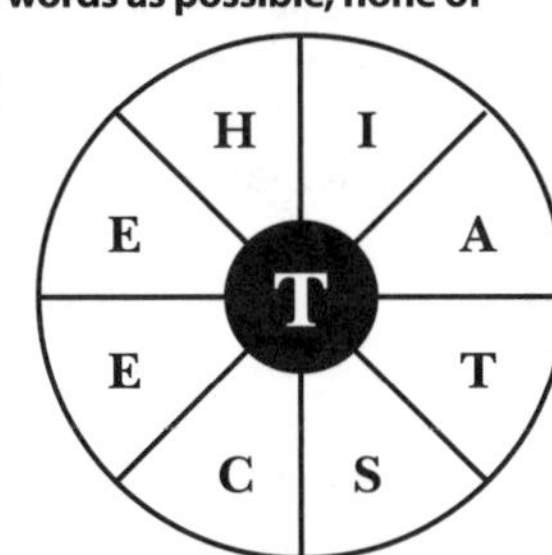

Nine-letter word(s): ____________________

SUM CIRCLE

Fill the three empty circles with the symbols +, – and x in some order, to make a sum which totals the number in the centre. Each symbol must be used once and calculations are made in the direction of travel (clockwise).

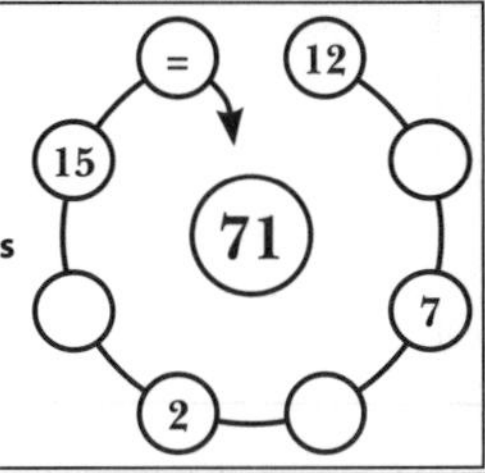

WORDSEARCH WORKOUT

```
N H E F I W R Z E P Y R C
H N O A Z E L H H D B R E
A P A P H R E T H G U A D
N R E T S I S S M M L V R
A C O E L C N U R M A E Z
R M T D G G V Q N R H M R
Y E S X A P R I T T Y I A
N D H D O D W A O M T E E
V O D T N T D R N L F U R
M T S A A A B N L D Y Q N
X X Y P D F B T A K M I F
H E J M E G A S N R S A J
M U M M Y T N C U U G O R
G N I L B I S X O H A Z X
T E L P I R T C Y X F W G
```

FAMILY RELATIONSHIPS

AUNT
BROTHER
COUSIN
DADDY
DAUGHTER
FATHER
GRANDDAD
GRANDMA
HUSBAND
MAMA
MOTHER
MUMMY
PAPA
SIBLING
SISTER
STEPSON
TRIPLET
TWIN
UNCLE
WIFE

DOUBLE FUN SUDOKU

TASTY TEASER

			4	1		9		
6	9	7						3
	2		7			8	6	
2				4	9	5		1
		3	8		5	7		
9		8	1	6				4
	8	1			4		2	
3						4	5	7
		9		3	2			

BRAIN BUSTER

		6	3		7	9		
	2		4		8		5	
4								1
9		1	7		4	5		6
7		8	5		2	3		9
3								8
	6		8		5		9	
		4	1		3	2		

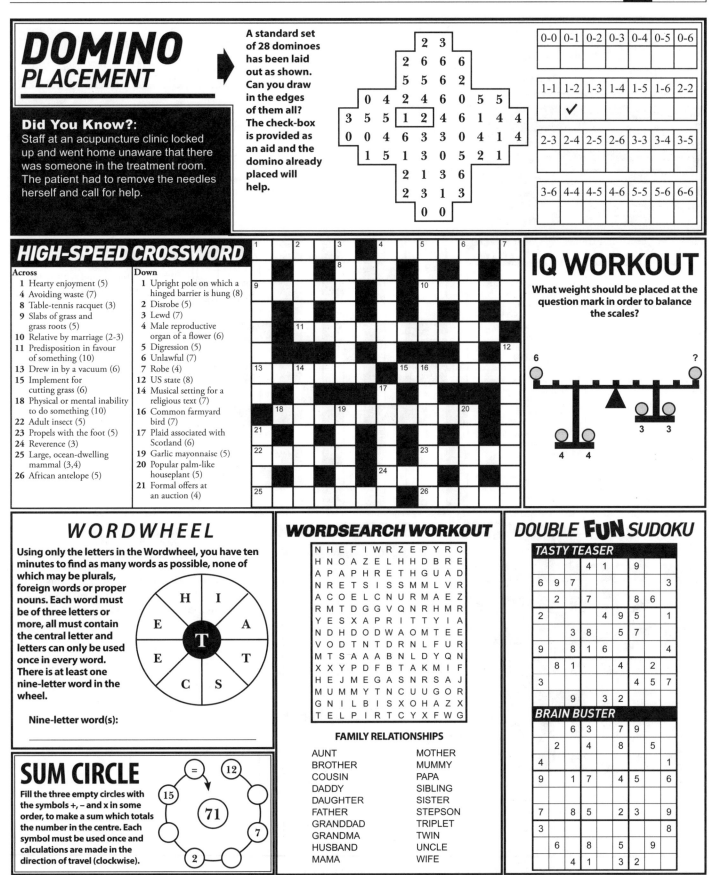

1 MINUTE NUMBER CRUNCH

Beginner								Answer
82	– 39	x 2	– 18	x 2	25% of this	– 14	x 70	

Intermediate								Answer
21	2/7 of this	+ 15	Squared	2/9 of this	+ 4	÷ 17	Cubed	

Advanced								Answer
366	x 5	2/3 of this	– 3/10 of this	– 687	x 3	+ 835	5/8 of this	

Did You Know?:
In 1912, Franz Reichelt designed an overcoat that doubled as a parachute. To demonstrate his invention, he jumped from the Eiffel Tower. You can guess the rest.

HIGH-SPEED CROSSWORD

Across
1 Alter (6)
7 Encircle (8)
8 Academic test (4)
10 Elongated cluster of flowers (6)
11 Parch (4)
12 Linger (5)
13 In a murderous frenzy (7)
16 Flop (3)
17 Perfumed (7)
19 Stonecutter (5)
21 Coloured part of the eye (4)
23 Crown (6)
25 Fury (4)
26 Resistance (8)
27 Tendons (6)

Down
1 Ornamental climbing plant (8)
2 Partly open (4)
3 Organic compound (5)
4 Free from tears (3-4)
5 Flip (a coin, for example) (4)
6 Imbalanced (6)
9 Head nurse (6)
13 Partially opened flower (3)
14 Someone who skims across ice (6)
15 Humanity, sympathy (8)
16 Cul-de-sac (4-3)
18 Point where two lines meet or intersect (6)
20 Projecting edge of a roof (5)
22 Front part of the human leg below the knee (4)
24 Female horse (4)

IQ WORKOUT

What number should replace the question mark?

Hexagon 1: 6, 3, 9, 4, 7, 21 — centre 234
Hexagon 2: 11, 7, 8, 9, 2, 8 — centre 177
Hexagon 3: 8, 6, 14, ?, 31, 5 — centre 312

CODEWORD CONUNDRUM

DOUBLE FUN SUDOKU

TASTY TEASER

	3	7	2					4
	9		6			5		
1	5			9	3			2
3		5		1			4	
		6	3		2	1		
	2			6		9		8
4			9	7			8	5
		3			8		7	
8					5	6	2	

BRAIN BUSTER

		8			3	1	5	
		3				2	7	
	4			2	9			
					7		6	
6	5						1	3
	8		3					
			2	3			9	
	9	6				3		
	2	5	7			6		

SPIDOKU

Each of the eight segments of the spider's web should be filled with a different number from 1 to 8, in such a way that every ring also contains a different number from 1 to 8.

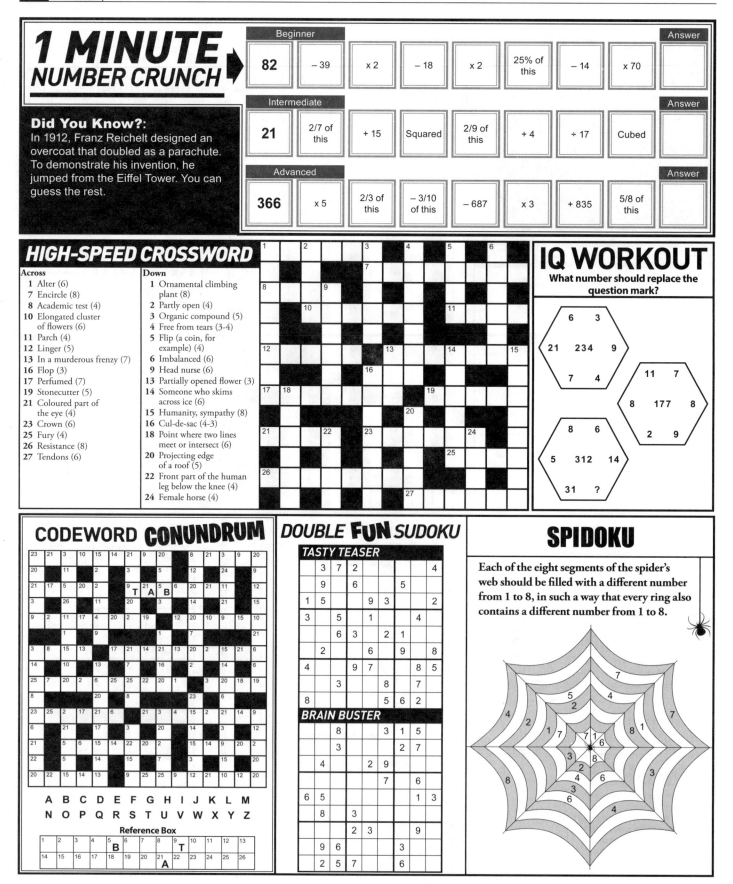

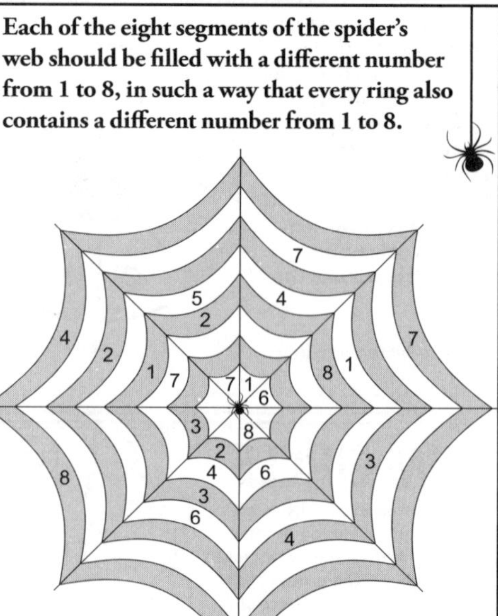

LOGI-SIX

Every row and column of this grid should contain one each of the letters A, B, C, D, E and F. Each of the six shapes (marked by thicker lines) should also contain one each of the letters A, B, C, D, E and F. Can you complete the grid?

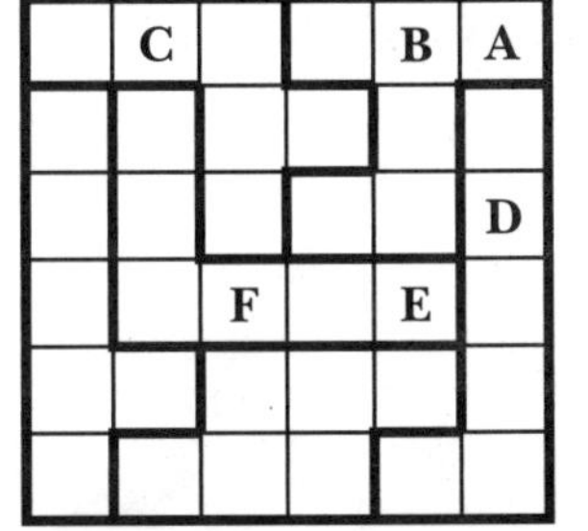

HIGH-SPEED CROSSWORD

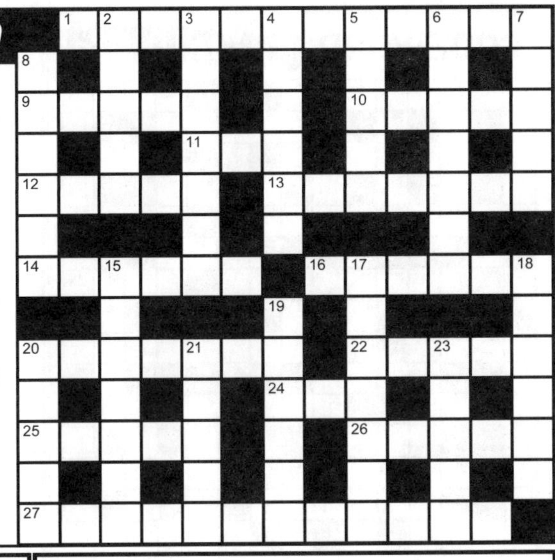

Across

1 Homicide without malice aforethought (12)
9 Toxic form of oxygen (5)
10 Protective garment (5)
11 Fish eggs (3)
12 Civilian clothing (5)
13 Abominate (7)
14 County of southern England (6)
16 Number of lines of verse (6)
20 Family appellation (7)
22 Venomous hooded snake (5)
24 Do something (3)
25 Ball-shaped (5)
26 Likeness (5)
27 Give a false or misleading account of the nature of (12)

Down

2 Detached (5)
3 Aseptic (7)
4 Agree (6)
5 Caprine animals (5)
6 Twisting of shape or position (7)
7 Gamut (5)
8 Universe (6)
15 Austrian composer of waltzes (7)
17 Strategy (7)
18 Proverbs (6)
19 Cup without a handle (6)
20 Firm open-weave fabric used by window-cleaners (5)
21 Mix up or confuse (5)
23 Organ enclosed within the skull (5)

WORDSEARCH WORKOUT

Y	D	D	Q	N	X	A	F	H	G	E	M	V
R	V	I	L	L	A	I	N	V	N	R	R	Q
O	S	V	R	O	T	C	E	V	I	I	T	D
T	O	E	X	C	S	V	L	F	Y	P	S	S
C	E	L	O	U	E	E	A	U	V	M	E	X
I	D	V	N	U	G	R	E	L	V	A	L	R
D	I	E	O	A	L	V	L	D	L	V	I	M
E	V	T	T	G	O	E	Y	D	D	E	V	V
L	V	N	Z	N	U	B	C	T	U	D	Y	O
A	I	V	G	H	V	E	V	I	V	X	N	L
V	E	I	L	V	V	I	S	C	O	U	N	T
W	E	S	Z	Q	V	I	T	R	I	O	L	A
D	S	A	K	T	N	G	O	E	T	K	B	G
V	O	G	W	E	O	N	W	S	Z	J	U	E
Y	N	E	V	A	P	O	U	R	N	V	L	J

V WORDS

VALEDICTORY
VALLEY
VAMPIRE
VAPOUR
VECTOR
VELVET
VENUS
VERVE
VIDEOS
VILEST
VILLAIN
VINTAGE
VIPER
VISAGE
VISCOUNT
VITRIOL
VOGUE
VOLTAGE
VULCAN
VYING

DOUBLE FUN SUDOKU

TASTY TEASER

4					3	2		6
1		3		8	7			
		8	5		4			7
	7		2	4			1	
8	1						9	2
	6			1	8		4	
5			9		2	3		
			4	6		8		1
2		6	8					5

BRAIN BUSTER

	6			8			4	
		8	9		2	3		
3			4		5			6
	3	6				2	7	
7								4
	2	4				5	1	
1			7		6			9
		5	8		1	6		
	4			2			8	

MATCHSTICK MAGIC

How is it possible to remove two matchsticks and leave nine in place?

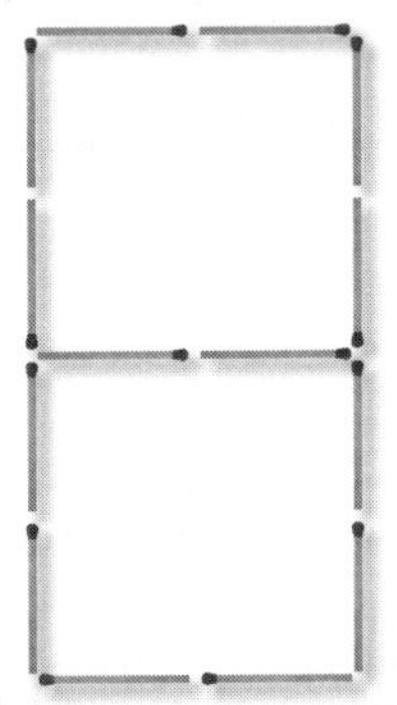

BRAIN TEASER

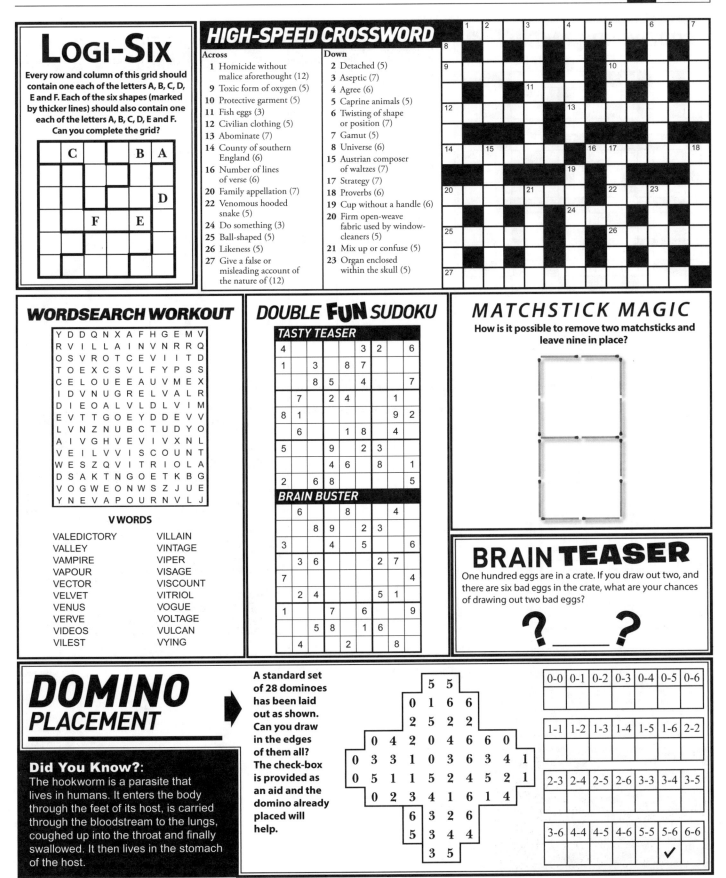

One hundred eggs are in a crate. If you draw out two, and there are six bad eggs in the crate, what are your chances of drawing out two bad eggs?

? ______ ?

DOMINO PLACEMENT

A standard set of 28 dominoes has been laid out as shown. Can you draw in the edges of them all? The check-box is provided as an aid and the domino already placed will help.

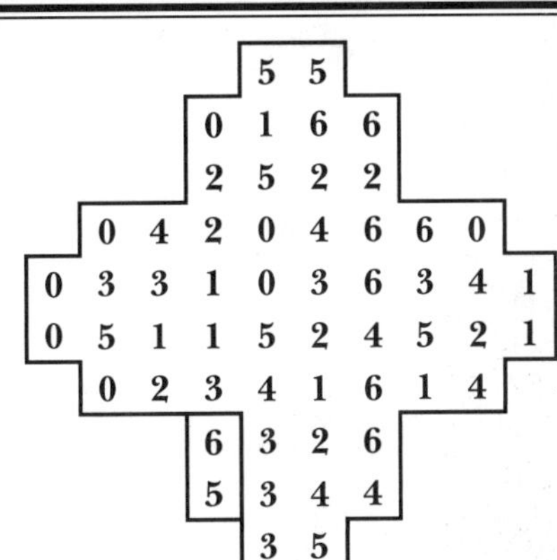

0-0	0-1	0-2	0-3	0-4	0-5	0-6

1-1	1-2	1-3	1-4	1-5	1-6	2-2

2-3	2-4	2-5	2-6	3-3	3-4	3-5

3-6	4-4	4-5	4-6	5-5	5-6	6-6
					✓	

Did You Know?:
The hookworm is a parasite that lives in humans. It enters the body through the feet of its host, is carried through the bloodstream to the lungs, coughed up into the throat and finally swallowed. It then lives in the stomach of the host.

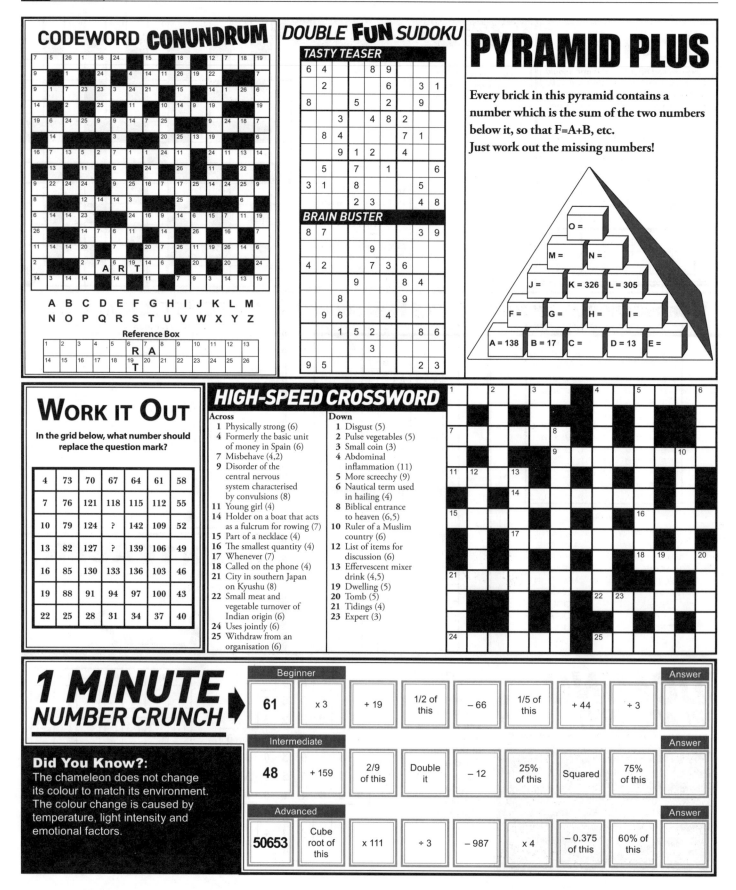

CODEWORD CONUNDRUM

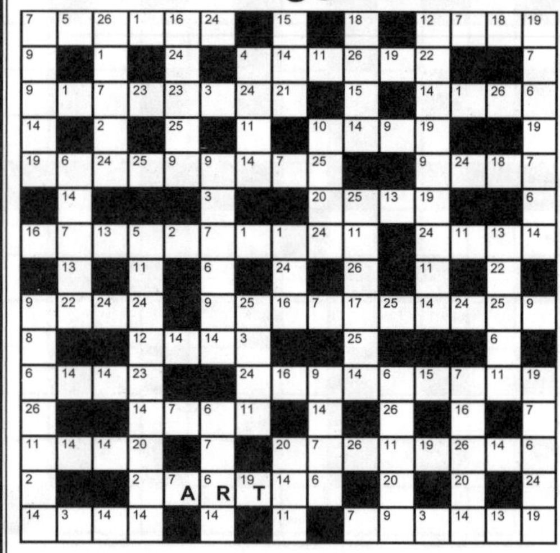

A B C D E F G H I J K L M
N O P Q R S T U V W X Y Z

Reference Box

1	2	3	4	5	6 R	7 A	8	9	10	11	12	13
14	15	16	17	18	19 T	20	21	22	23	24	25	26

DOUBLE FUN SUDOKU

TASTY TEASER

6	4			8	9			
	2				6		3	1
8			5		2		9	
		3		4	8	2		
	8	4				7	1	
		9	1	2		4		
	5		7		1			6
3	1		8				5	
			2	3			4	8

BRAIN BUSTER

8	7						3	9
				9				
4	2			7	3	6		
			9			8	4	
		8				9		
	9	6			4			
		1	5	2			8	6
				3				
9	5						2	3

PYRAMID PLUS

Every brick in this pyramid contains a number which is the sum of the two numbers below it, so that F=A+B, etc.
Just work out the missing numbers!

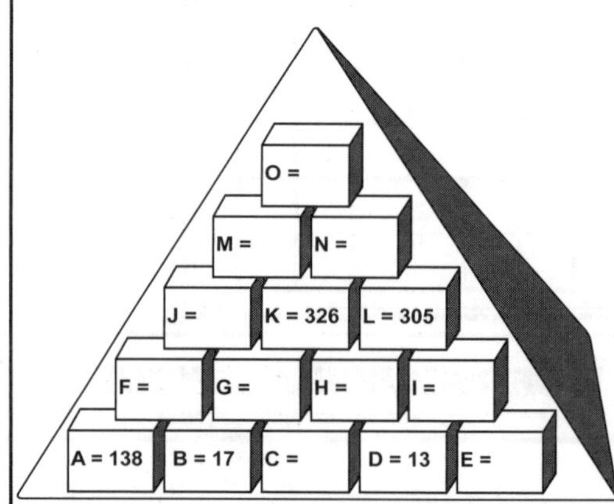

WORK IT OUT

In the grid below, what number should replace the question mark?

4	73	70	67	64	61	58
7	76	121	118	115	112	55
10	79	124	?	142	109	52
13	82	127	?	139	106	49
16	85	130	133	136	103	46
19	88	91	94	97	100	43
22	25	28	31	34	37	40

HIGH-SPEED CROSSWORD

Across

1 Physically strong (6)
4 Formerly the basic unit of money in Spain (6)
7 Misbehave (4,2)
9 Disorder of the central nervous system characterised by convulsions (8)
11 Young girl (4)
14 Holder on a boat that acts as a fulcrum for rowing (7)
15 Part of a necklace (4)
16 The smallest quantity (4)
17 Whenever (7)
18 Called on the phone (4)
21 City in southern Japan on Kyushu (8)
22 Small meat and vegetable turnover of Indian origin (6)
24 Uses jointly (6)
25 Withdraw from an organisation (6)

Down

1 Disgust (5)
2 Pulse vegetables (5)
3 Small coin (3)
4 Abdominal inflammation (11)
5 More screechy (9)
6 Nautical term used in hailing (4)
8 Biblical entrance to heaven (6,5)
10 Ruler of a Muslim country (6)
12 List of items for discussion (6)
13 Effervescent mixer drink (4,5)
19 Dwelling (5)
20 Tomb (5)
21 Tidings (4)
23 Expert (3)

1 MINUTE NUMBER CRUNCH

Beginner

61	x 3	+ 19	1/2 of this	– 66	1/5 of this	+ 44	÷ 3	Answer

Intermediate

48	+ 159	2/9 of this	Double it	– 12	25% of this	Squared	75% of this	Answer

Advanced

50653	Cube root of this	x 111	÷ 3	– 987	x 4	– 0.375 of this	60% of this	Answer

Did You Know?:
The chameleon does not change its colour to match its environment. The colour change is caused by temperature, light intensity and emotional factors.

HIGH-SPEED CROSSWORD

Across
1 Mouldable synthetic substance (7)
8 Italian rice dish (7)
9 Musical toy (7)
10 Loophole (6)
12 Card game (6)
13 Sand, soda and lime compound, pulverised into an abrasive powder (6,5)
17 Stings (6)
20 Fertilised egg (6)
23 Enmity (3,4)
24 Restraining straps (7)
25 Water tank (7)

Down
1 Drive from behind (6)
2 Non-professional (7)
3 Lining of the stomach of a ruminant used as food (5)
4 Pack to capacity (4)
5 ___ Wilde, playwright (5)
6 Valuable violin (informally) (5)
7 Player who delivers the ball to the batsman (6)
11 Hinged lifting tool (5)
12 Brass instrument without valves (5)
14 Work done by a person that benefits another (7)
15 Seat of the faculty of reason (6)
16 Small grotesque supernatural creature (6)
18 Terminate before completion (5)
19 Striped cat (5)
21 Boys, men (5)
22 Flat round object (4)

IQ WORKOUT

Draw in the hands on the final clock.

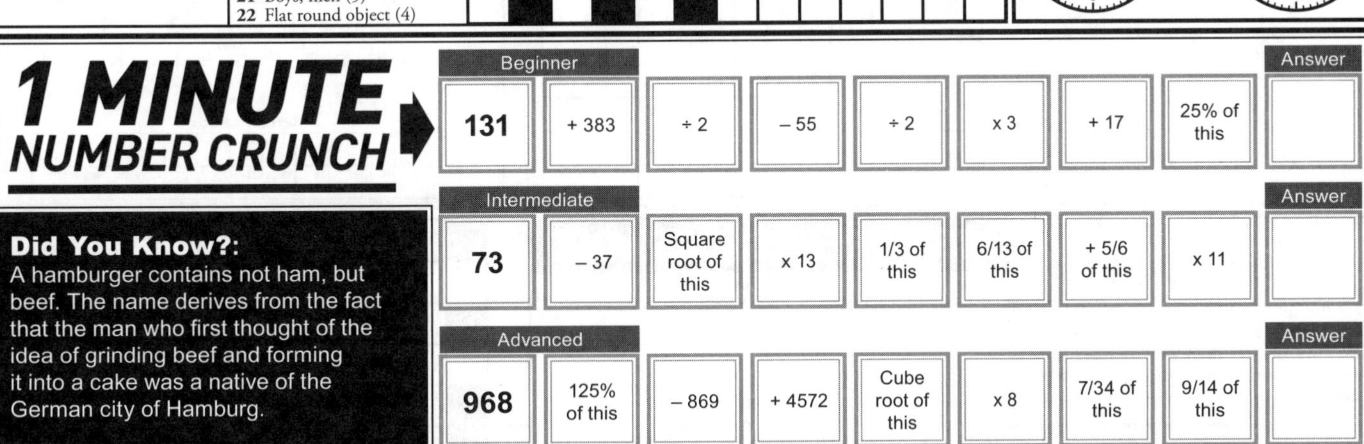

1 MINUTE NUMBER CRUNCH
Beginner
131 | + 383 | ÷ 2 | – 55 | ÷ 2 | x 3 | + 17 | 25% of this | Answer
Intermediate
73 | – 37 | Square root of this | x 13 | 1/3 of this | 6/13 of this | + 5/6 of this | x 11 | Answer
Advanced
968 | 125% of this | – 869 | + 4572 | Cube root of this | x 8 | 7/34 of this | 9/14 of this | Answer
Did You Know?:
A hamburger contains not ham, but beef. The name derives from the fact that the man who first thought of the idea of grinding beef and forming it into a cake was a native of the German city of Hamburg.

WORDSEARCH WORKOUT

```
Z D V C L E O P A T R A E
L Q O K F S I V E T H X U
G A G N G C O L A S E R Z
R T E G N O U J P O R O G
E L L N N V L D U H M S O
Y A S F I I I L P G I M Y
D S B R N R L F O L T L K
A B L S Q M J Y A P F A N
G L U I R A O S A R A N O
G U E F M I Y T E R U I T
E E A M F R N T H C G D G
R H O W H T T G J G A R R
M C E C F U I P L Y U A A
P Q M N B Z C P R E F C S
L A R I M D A D E R T G S
```

LEPIDOPTERA

APOLLO
ATLAS BLUE
BUFF TIP
BUTTERFLY
CARDINAL
CHRYSALIS
CLEOPATRA
COMMA
DRYAD
GHOST
GRAYLING
GREY DAGGER
HERMIT
KNOT GRASS
MOTH
PUPA
RED ADMIRAL
RINGLET
RIVULET
VOGELS BLUE

DOUBLE FUN SUDOKU

TASTY TEASER

2	6		9					7
4					3	5	8	
	7			1	6	3		
7	1	2	8	4				
	5						9	
				3	2	1	7	4
		9	6	8			5	
	4	8	2					3
6					5		4	1

BRAIN BUSTER

			9	2	4			
4	8		5		1		6	2
9				8				5
	4						5	
3								1
	2						9	
1				4				3
7	5		1		3		4	6
			8	7	6			

WHATEVER NEXT?

In the diagram below, which letter should replace the question mark?

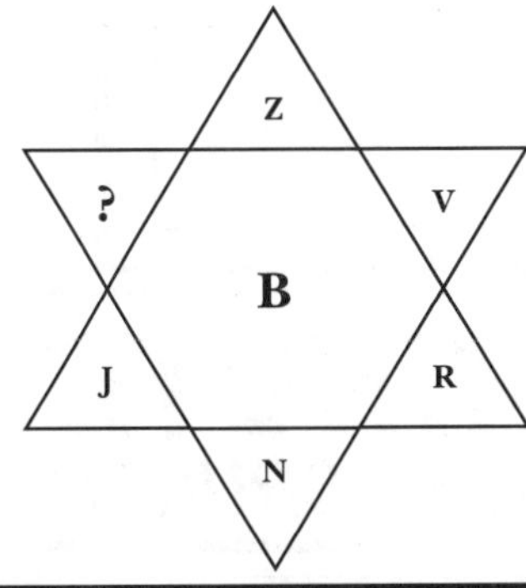

BRAIN TEASER

On a school outing, 81% of the boys had lost a shoe, 82% of the boys had lost a sock, 77% of the boys had lost a handkerchief and 68% of the boys had lost a hat.

What percentage at least must have lost all four items?

Mind Over Matter

Given that the letters are valued 1-26 according to their places in the alphabet, can you crack the mystery code to reveal the missing letter?

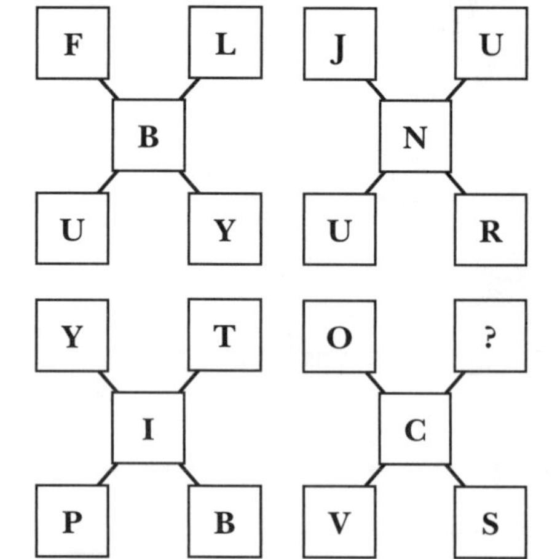

DOUBLE FUN SUDOKU

TASTY TEASER

	4			7		9		5
				1	3		6	7
	1	8				2		4
2					6	3		
	6	9	1		7	5	4	
		5	9					8
3		6				1	8	
4	9		3	8				
5		7		9			2	

BRAIN BUSTER

	5		9	8	3		2	
	8	2	1		7	5	3	
8	4		3		1		6	5
2								3
7	3		5		2		4	9
	2	6	7		5	4	9	
	7		8	3	9		5	

CODEWORD CONUNDRUM

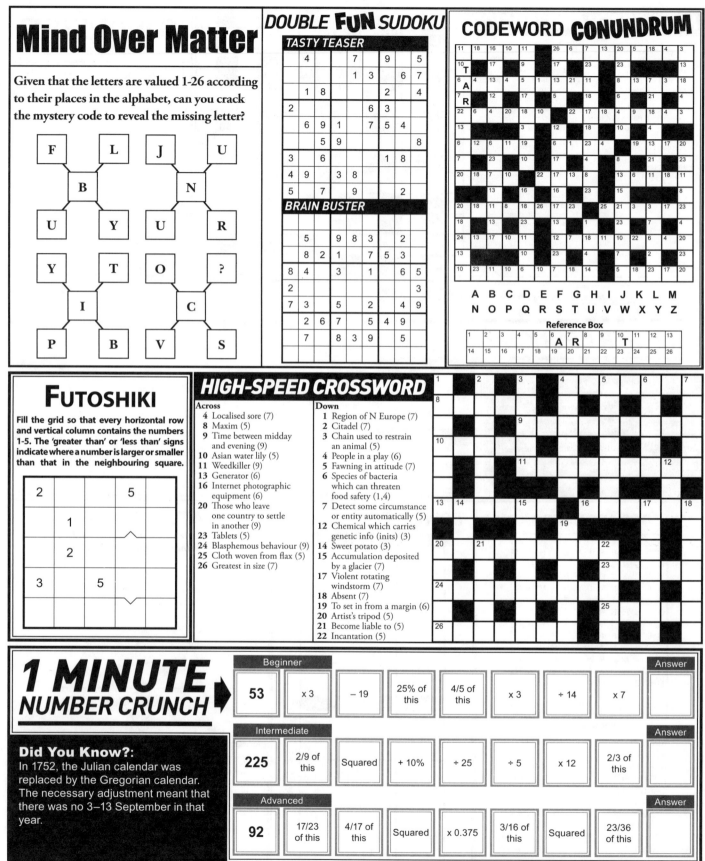

A B C D E F G H I J K L M

N O P Q R S T U V W X Y Z

Reference Box

1	2	3	4	5	6 A	7 R	8	9	10 T	11	12	13
14	15	16	17	18	19	20	21	22	23	24	25	26

FUTOSHIKI

Fill the grid so that every horizontal row and vertical column contains the numbers 1-5. The 'greater than' or 'less than' signs indicate where a number is larger or smaller than that in the neighbouring square.

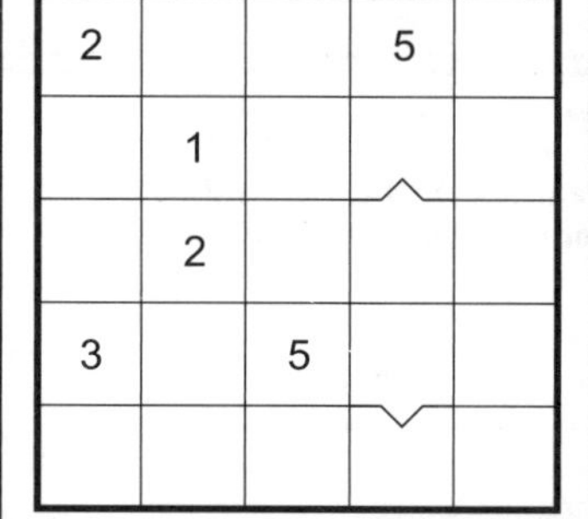

HIGH-SPEED CROSSWORD

Across

4 Localised sore (7)
8 Maxim (5)
9 Time between midday and evening (9)
10 Asian water lily (5)
11 Weedkiller (9)
13 Generator (6)
16 Internet photographic equipment (6)
20 Those who leave one country to settle in another (9)
23 Tablets (5)
24 Blasphemous behaviour (9)
25 Cloth woven from flax (5)
26 Greatest in size (7)

Down

1 Region of N Europe (7)
2 Citadel (7)
3 Chain used to restrain an animal (5)
4 People in a play (6)
5 Fawning in attitude (7)
6 Species of bacteria which can threaten food safety (1,4)
7 Detect some circumstance or entity automatically (5)
12 Chemical which carries genetic info (inits) (3)
14 Sweet potato (3)
15 Accumulation deposited by a glacier (7)
17 Violent rotating windstorm (7)
18 Absent (7)
19 To set in from a margin (6)
20 Artist's tripod (5)
21 Become liable to (5)
22 Incantation (5)

1 MINUTE NUMBER CRUNCH

Beginner

53	x 3	– 19	25% of this	4/5 of this	x 3	÷ 14	x 7	Answer

Intermediate

225	2/9 of this	Squared	+ 10%	÷ 25	÷ 5	x 12	2/3 of this	Answer

Advanced

92	17/23 of this	4/17 of this	Squared	x 0.375	3/16 of this	Squared	23/36 of this	Answer

Did You Know?:
In 1752, the Julian calendar was replaced by the Gregorian calendar. The necessary adjustment meant that there was no 3–13 September in that year.

BATTLESHIP BOUT

Can you place the vessels into the diagram? Some parts of vessels or sea squares have already been filled in. A number to the right or below a row or column refers to the number of occupied squares in that row or column.
Any vessel may be positioned horizontally or vertically, but no part of a vessel touches part of any other vessel, either horizontally, vertically or diagonally.

Empty Area of Sea: ≈
Aircraft Carrier:
Battleships:
Cruisers:
Submarines:

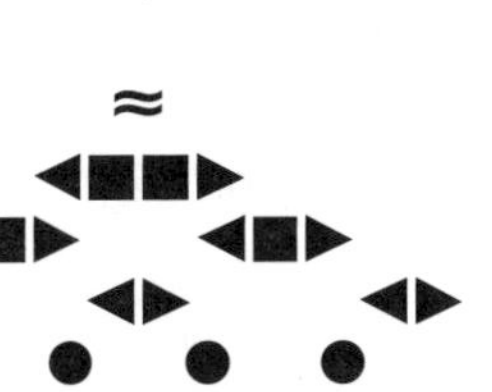

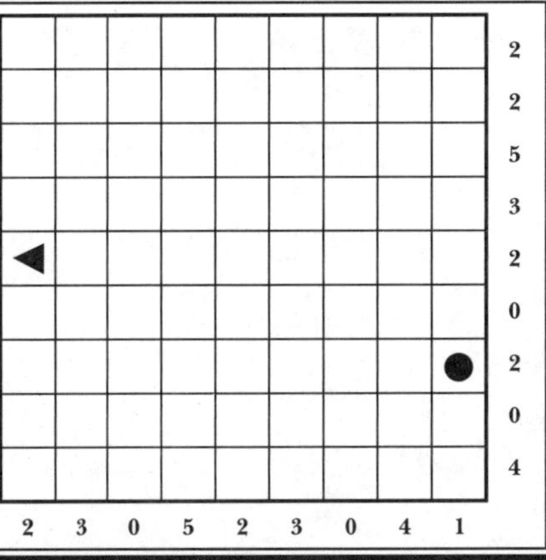

Did You Know?:
The Leaning Tower of Pisa is about seventeen and a half feet off-centre. On realising that the tower was beginning to lean, the original builders abandoned construction. In spite of this, work was resumed about a hundred years later.

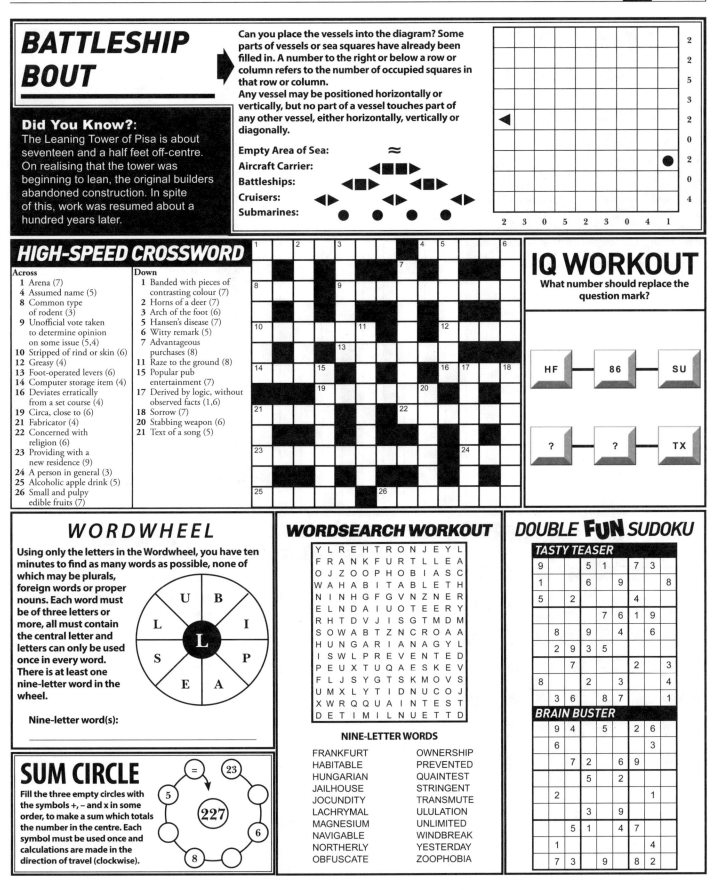

HIGH-SPEED CROSSWORD

Across
1 Arena (7)
4 Assumed name (5)
8 Common type of rodent (3)
9 Unofficial vote taken to determine opinion on some issue (5,4)
10 Stripped of rind or skin (6)
12 Greasy (4)
13 Foot-operated levers (6)
14 Computer storage item (4)
16 Deviates erratically from a set course (4)
19 Circa, close to (6)
21 Fabricator (4)
22 Concerned with religion (6)
23 Providing with a new residence (9)
24 A person in general (3)
25 Alcoholic apple drink (5)
26 Small and pulpy edible fruits (7)

Down
1 Banded with pieces of contrasting colour (7)
2 Horns of a deer (7)
3 Arch of the foot (6)
5 Hansen's disease (7)
6 Witty remark (5)
7 Advantageous purchases (8)
11 Raze to the ground (8)
15 Popular pub entertainment (7)
17 Derived by logic, without observed facts (1,6)
18 Sorrow (7)
20 Stabbing weapon (6)
21 Text of a song (5)

IQ WORKOUT

What number should replace the question mark?

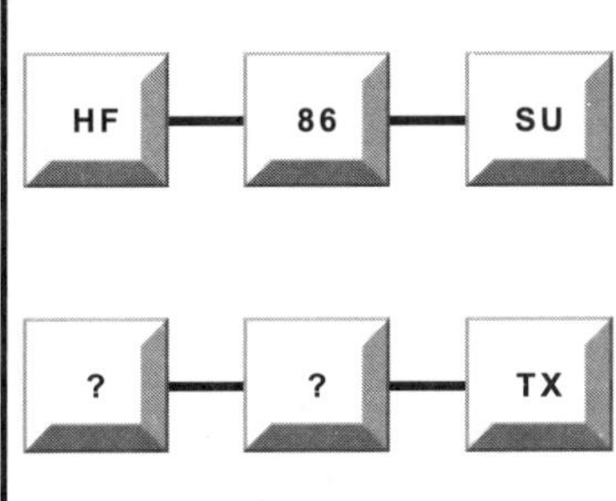

WORDWHEEL

Using only the letters in the Wordwheel, you have ten minutes to find as many words as possible, none of which may be plurals, foreign words or proper nouns. Each word must be of three letters or more, all must contain the central letter and letters can only be used once in every word. There is at least one nine-letter word in the wheel.

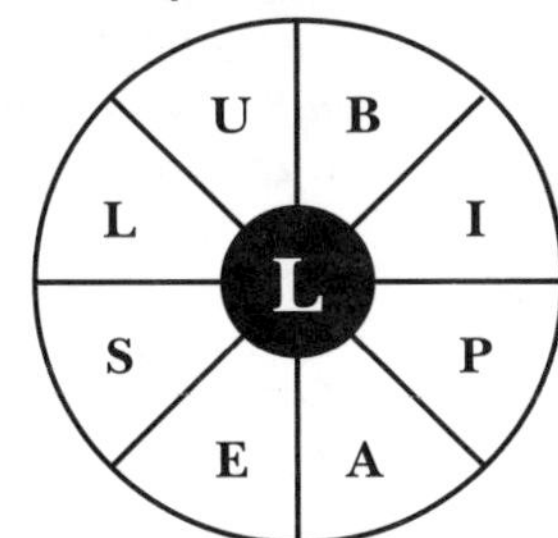

Nine-letter word(s): ____________________

SUM CIRCLE

Fill the three empty circles with the symbols +, – and x in some order, to make a sum which totals the number in the centre. Each symbol must be used once and calculations are made in the direction of travel (clockwise).

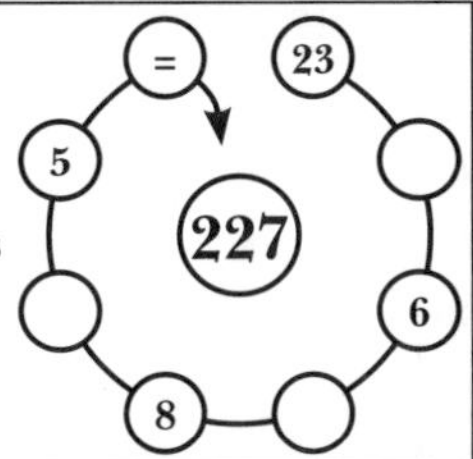

WORDSEARCH WORKOUT

Y	L	R	E	H	T	R	O	N	J	E	Y	L
F	R	A	N	K	F	U	R	T	L	L	E	A
O	J	Z	O	O	P	H	O	B	I	A	S	C
W	A	H	A	B	I	T	A	B	L	E	T	H
N	I	N	H	G	F	G	V	N	Z	N	E	R
E	L	N	D	A	I	U	O	T	E	E	R	Y
R	H	T	D	V	J	I	S	G	T	M	D	M
S	O	W	A	B	T	Z	N	C	R	O	A	A
H	U	N	G	A	R	I	A	N	A	G	Y	L
I	S	W	L	P	R	E	V	E	N	T	E	D
P	E	U	X	T	U	Q	A	E	S	K	E	V
F	L	J	S	Y	G	T	S	K	M	O	V	S
U	M	X	L	Y	T	I	D	N	U	C	O	J
X	W	R	Q	Q	U	A	I	N	T	E	S	T
D	E	T	I	M	I	L	N	U	E	T	T	D

NINE-LETTER WORDS

FRANKFURT
HABITABLE
HUNGARIAN
JAILHOUSE
JOCUNDITY
LACHRYMAL
MAGNESIUM
NAVIGABLE
NORTHERLY
OBFUSCATE
OWNERSHIP
PREVENTED
QUAINTEST
STRINGENT
TRANSMUTE
ULULATION
UNLIMITED
WINDBREAK
YESTERDAY
ZOOPHOBIA

DOUBLE FUN SUDOKU

TASTY TEASER

9			5	1		7	3	
1			6		9			8
5		2				4		
				7	6	1	9	
	8		9		4		6	
	2	9	3	5				
		7				2		3
8			2		3			4
	3	6		8	7			1

BRAIN BUSTER

	9	4		5		2	6	
	6						3	
		7	2		6	9		
			5		2			
	2						1	
			3		9			
		5	1		4	7		
	1						4	
	7	3		9		8	2	

1 MINUTE NUMBER CRUNCH

Beginner								Answer
64	÷ 8	x 5	1/10 of this	+ 19	– 8	1/5 of this	– 2	

Intermediate								Answer
627	÷ 3	+ 648	Add to its reverse	÷ 5	– 127	3/4 of this	+ 2/3 of this	

Advanced								Answer
142857	Double it	3/37 of this	5/11 of this	7/10 of this	5/9 of this	60% of this	5/9 of this	

Did You Know?:
In the 1640s, the English parliament banned the eating of mince pies on Christmas Day. They argued that as the recipe included herbs that were once related to pagan rituals, the pies were insufficiently puritan. Holly and ivy decorations were also banned.

HIGH-SPEED CROSSWORD

Across

1 Make moist (6)
3 French sweet blackcurrant liqueur (6)
7 Digitally encoded recording, smaller than a phonograph record (7,4)
10 Roman XIX (8)
11 Act presumptuously (4)
13 Finnish steam bath (5)
14 Provide food for an event (5)
18 At high volume (4)
19 Known for certain (8)
21 Transducer used to detect and measure light (8,3)
22 Sycophant (6)
23 Rook in the game of chess (6)

Down

1 Pour from a bottle into one more ornate (6)
2 Requiring precise accuracy (8)
4 Bloc (4)
5 Vendor (6)
6 Painful eyelid swellings (5)
8 Very small in scale (9)
9 Armistice, truce (9)
12 Early Christian church (8)
15 Flowered (6)
16 Minor or small-minded (5)
17 Cut or eliminate (6)
20 Measure (out) (4)

IQ WORKOUT

Which set of letters is the odd one out?

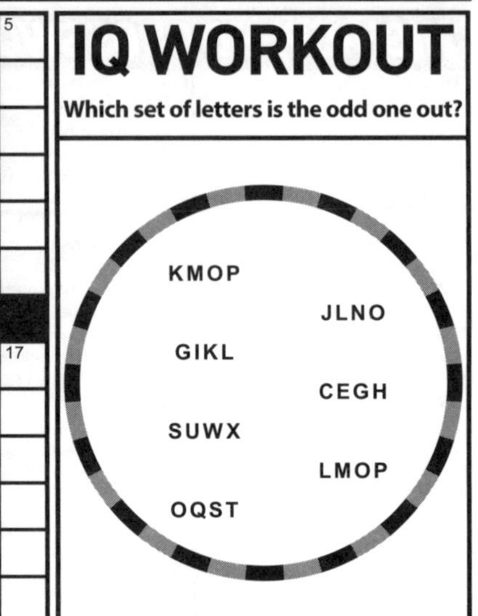

CODEWORD CONUNDRUM

A B C D E F G H I J K L M
N O P Q R S T U V W X Y Z

Reference Box

1	2	3 R	4	5	6	7	8	9	10	11	12	13
14	15	16 O	17	18	19	20	21	22 T	23	24	25	26

DOUBLE FUN SUDOKU

TASTY TEASER

2				3		1	7	5
4			2		1			
5			8	6	7			
		4	1		6		5	
1	6						3	9
	5		3		4	8		
			7	2	5			8
			9		8			3
8	7	9		4				2

BRAIN BUSTER

5								2
	6	8		9		4	3	
1			4		5			7
	2			5			7	
			9		1			
	3			8			2	
3			8		6			9
	7	6		1		5	4	
2								8

SPIDOKU

Each of the eight segments of the spider's web should be filled with a different number from 1 to 8, in such a way that every ring also contains a different number from 1 to 8.

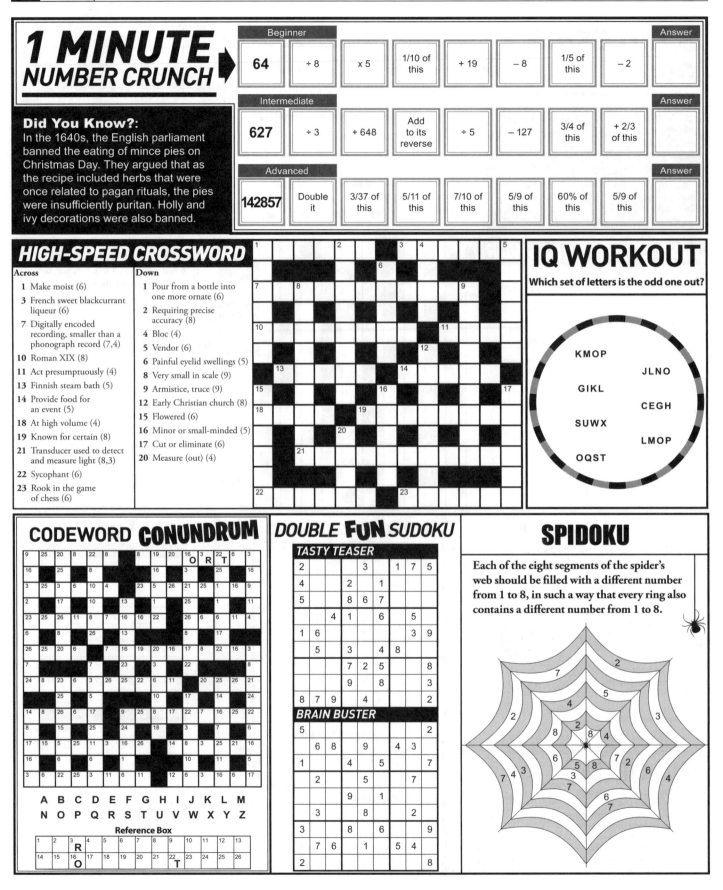

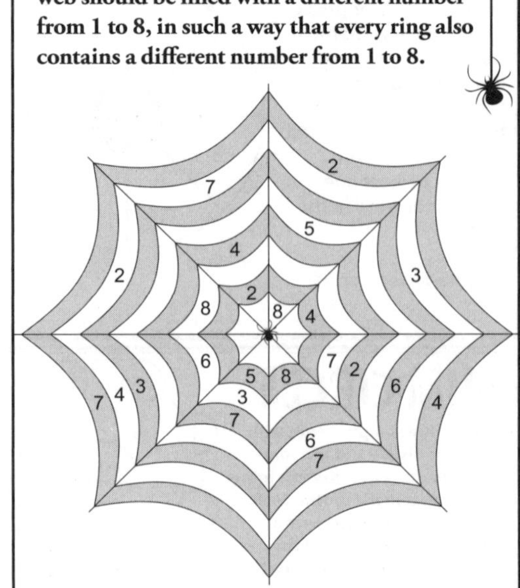

Logi-Six

Every row and column of this grid should contain one each of the letters A, B, C, D, E and F. Each of the six shapes (marked by thicker lines) should also contain one each of the letters A, B, C, D, E and F. Can you complete the grid?

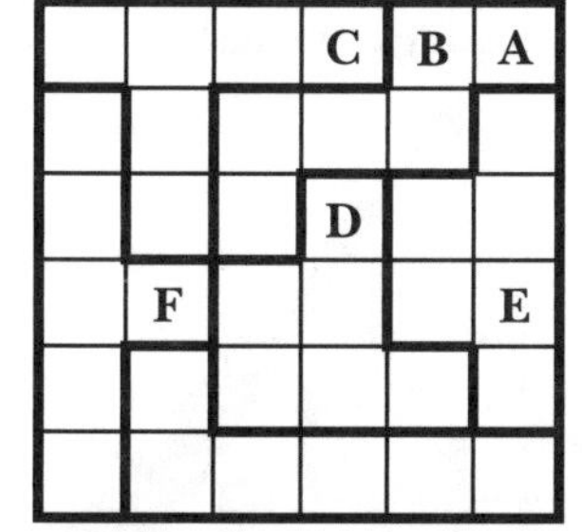

HIGH-SPEED CROSSWORD

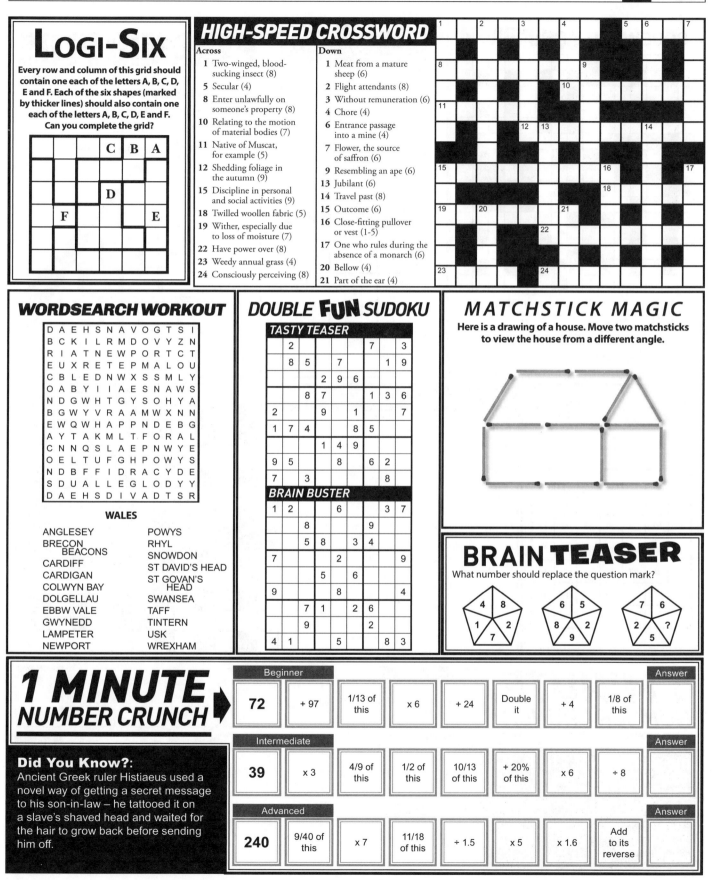

Across
1 Two-winged, blood-sucking insect (8)
5 Secular (4)
8 Enter unlawfully on someone's property (8)
10 Relating to the motion of material bodies (7)
11 Native of Muscat, for example (5)
12 Shedding foliage in the autumn (9)
15 Discipline in personal and social activities (9)
18 Twilled woollen fabric (5)
19 Wither, especially due to loss of moisture (7)
22 Have power over (8)
23 Weedy annual grass (4)
24 Consciously perceiving (8)

Down
1 Meat from a mature sheep (6)
2 Flight attendants (8)
3 Without remuneration (6)
4 Chore (4)
6 Entrance passage into a mine (4)
7 Flower, the source of saffron (6)
9 Resembling an ape (6)
13 Jubilant (6)
14 Travel past (8)
15 Outcome (6)
16 Close-fitting pullover or vest (1-5)
17 One who rules during the absence of a monarch (6)
20 Bellow (4)
21 Part of the ear (4)

WORDSEARCH WORKOUT

D	A	E	H	S	N	A	V	O	G	T	S	I
B	C	K	I	L	R	M	D	O	V	Y	Z	N
R	I	A	T	N	E	W	P	O	R	T	C	T
E	U	X	R	E	T	E	P	M	A	L	O	U
C	B	L	E	D	N	W	X	S	S	M	L	Y
O	A	B	Y	I	I	A	E	S	N	A	W	S
N	D	G	W	H	T	G	Y	S	O	H	Y	A
B	G	W	Y	V	R	A	A	M	W	X	N	N
E	W	Q	W	H	A	P	P	N	D	E	B	G
A	Y	T	A	K	M	L	T	F	O	R	A	L
C	N	N	Q	S	L	A	E	P	N	W	Y	E
O	E	L	T	U	F	G	H	P	O	W	Y	S
N	D	B	F	F	I	D	R	A	C	Y	D	E
S	D	U	A	L	L	E	G	L	O	D	Y	Y
D	A	E	H	S	D	I	V	A	D	T	S	R

WALES

ANGLESEY
BRECON BEACONS
CARDIFF
CARDIGAN
COLWYN BAY
DOLGELLAU
EBBW VALE
GWYNEDD
LAMPETER
NEWPORT
POWYS
RHYL
SNOWDON
ST DAVID'S HEAD
ST GOVAN'S HEAD
SWANSEA
TAFF
TINTERN
USK
WREXHAM

DOUBLE FUN SUDOKU

TASTY TEASER

	2					7		3
	8	5		7			1	9
			2	9	6			
		8	7			1	3	6
2			9		1			7
1	7	4			8	5		
			1	4	9			
9	5			8		6	2	
7		3					8	

BRAIN BUSTER

1	2			6			3	7
		8				9		
		5	8		3	4		
7				2				9
			5		6			
9				8				4
		7	1		2	6		
		9				2		
4	1			5			8	3

MATCHSTICK MAGIC

Here is a drawing of a house. Move two matchsticks to view the house from a different angle.

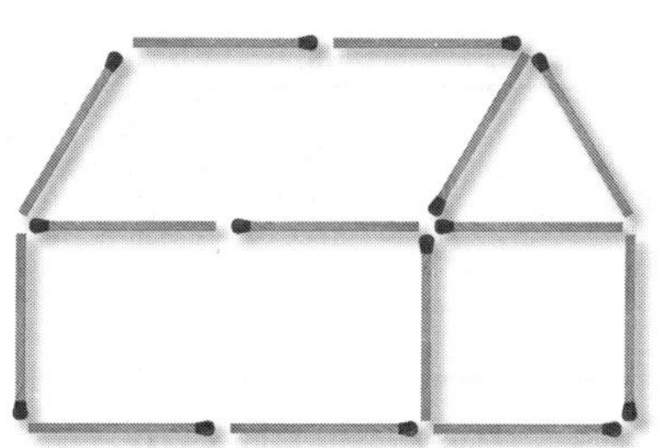

BRAIN TEASER

What number should replace the question mark?

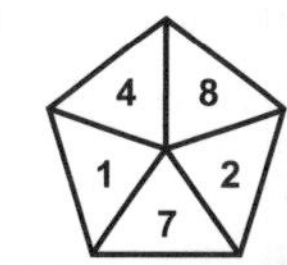

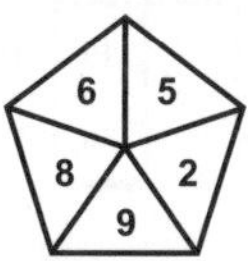

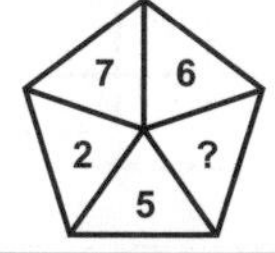

1 MINUTE NUMBER CRUNCH

Beginner								Answer
72	+ 97	1/13 of this	x 6	+ 24	Double it	+ 4	1/8 of this	

Intermediate								Answer
39	x 3	4/9 of this	1/2 of this	10/13 of this	+ 20% of this	x 6	÷ 8	

Advanced								Answer
240	9/40 of this	x 7	11/18 of this	÷ 1.5	x 5	x 1.6	Add to its reverse	

Did You Know?:
Ancient Greek ruler Histiaeus used a novel way of getting a secret message to his son-in-law – he tattooed it on a slave's shaved head and waited for the hair to grow back before sending him off.

CODEWORD CONUNDRUM

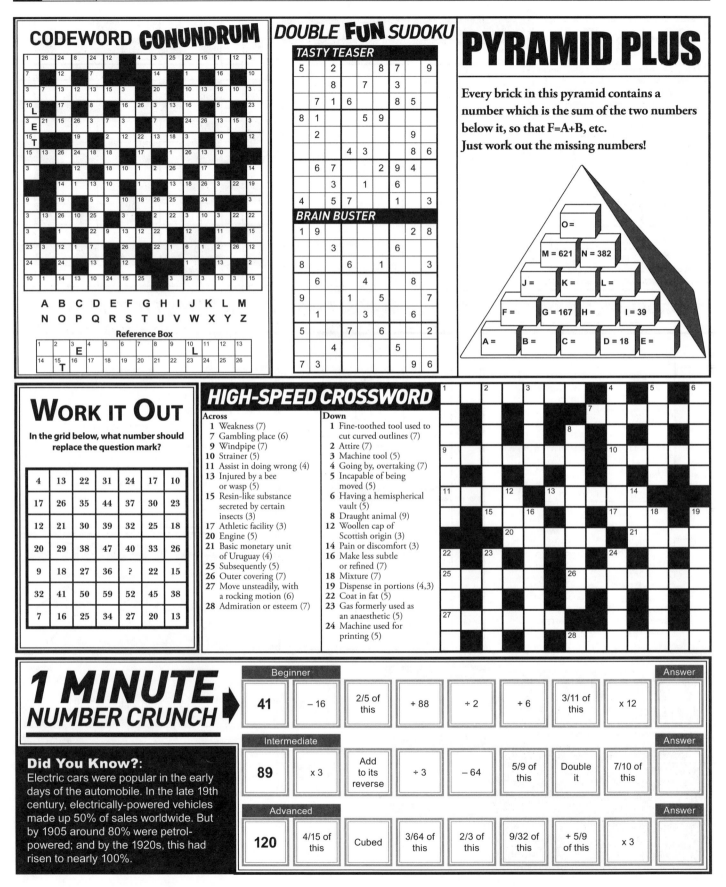

A B C D E F G H I J K L M

N O P Q R S T U V W X Y Z

Reference Box

1	2	3 E	4	5	6	7	8	9	10 L	11	12	13
14	15 T	16	17	18	19	20	21	22	23	24	25	26

DOUBLE FUN SUDOKU

TASTY TEASER

5		2			8	7		9
		8		7		3		
	7	1	6			8	5	
8	1			5	9			
	2						9	
			4	3			8	6
	6	7			2	9	4	
		3		1		6		
4		5	7			1		3

BRAIN BUSTER

1	9						2	8
		3				6		
8			6		1			3
	6			4			8	
9			1		5			7
	1			3			6	
5			7		6			2
		4				5		
7	3						9	6

PYRAMID PLUS

Every brick in this pyramid contains a number which is the sum of the two numbers below it, so that F=A+B, etc.
Just work out the missing numbers!

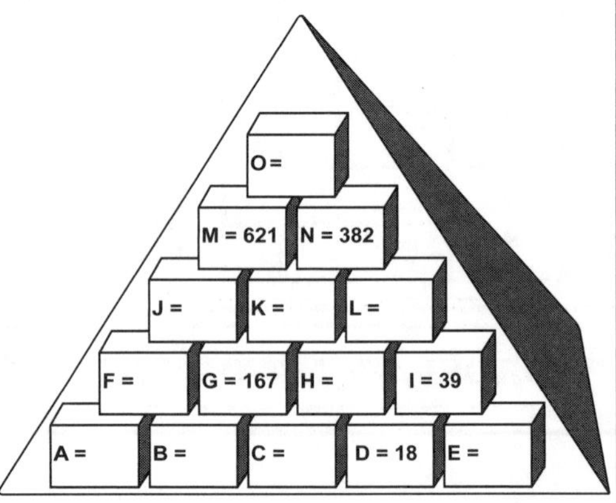

WORK IT OUT

In the grid below, what number should replace the question mark?

4	13	22	31	24	17	10
17	26	35	44	37	30	23
12	21	30	39	32	25	18
20	29	38	47	40	33	26
9	18	27	36	?	22	15
32	41	50	59	52	45	38
7	16	25	34	27	20	13

HIGH-SPEED CROSSWORD

Across

1 Weakness (7)
7 Gambling place (6)
9 Windpipe (7)
10 Strainer (5)
11 Assist in doing wrong (4)
13 Injured by a bee or wasp (5)
15 Resin-like substance secreted by certain insects (3)
17 Athletic facility (3)
20 Engine (5)
21 Basic monetary unit of Uruguay (4)
25 Subsequently (5)
26 Outer covering (7)
27 Move unsteadily, with a rocking motion (6)
28 Admiration or esteem (7)

Down

1 Fine-toothed tool used to cut curved outlines (7)
2 Attire (7)
3 Machine tool (5)
4 Going by, overtaking (7)
5 Incapable of being moved (5)
6 Having a hemispherical vault (5)
8 Draught animal (9)
12 Woollen cap of Scottish origin (3)
14 Pain or discomfort (3)
16 Make less subtle or refined (7)
18 Mixture (7)
19 Dispense in portions (4,3)
22 Coat in fat (5)
23 Gas formerly used as an anaesthetic (5)
24 Machine used for printing (5)

1 MINUTE NUMBER CRUNCH

Beginner

41	– 16	2/5 of this	+ 88	÷ 2	+ 6	3/11 of this	x 12	Answer

Intermediate

89	x 3	Add to its reverse	÷ 3	– 64	5/9 of this	Double it	7/10 of this	Answer

Advanced

120	4/15 of this	Cubed	3/64 of this	2/3 of this	9/32 of this	+ 5/9 of this	x 3	Answer

Did You Know?:
Electric cars were popular in the early days of the automobile. In the late 19th century, electrically-powered vehicles made up 50% of sales worldwide. But by 1905 around 80% were petrol-powered; and by the 1920s, this had risen to nearly 100%.

HIGH-SPEED CROSSWORD

Across
1 Assimilate or take in (6)
4 Jeopardy (6)
9 Official language of Tanzania (7)
10 Horse's bit (7)
11 Subtraction sign (5)
12 Black treacle (8)
15 Echo sounder (acronym) (5)
16 Located (8)
18 Smudge, daub (5)
19 Sudden attack (7)
21 Holding under a rental agreement (7)
22 Wrench, twist (6)
23 Act against an attack (6)

Down
1 Take for granted (6)
2 Not circulating or flowing (8)
3 Harnesses (5)
5 Spanish fortress or palace built by the Moors (7)
6 Barbed spear for landing large fish (4)
7 Cites (6)
8 In a corrupt and deceitful manner (11)
12 Vehicle test (inits) (3)
13 Chap (3)
14 Certain to be successful (4-4)
15 Japanese warrior (7)
16 Burns with steam (6)
17 Devoid of warmth and cordiality (6)
18 Oil-bearing laminated rock (5)
20 Commotion (4)

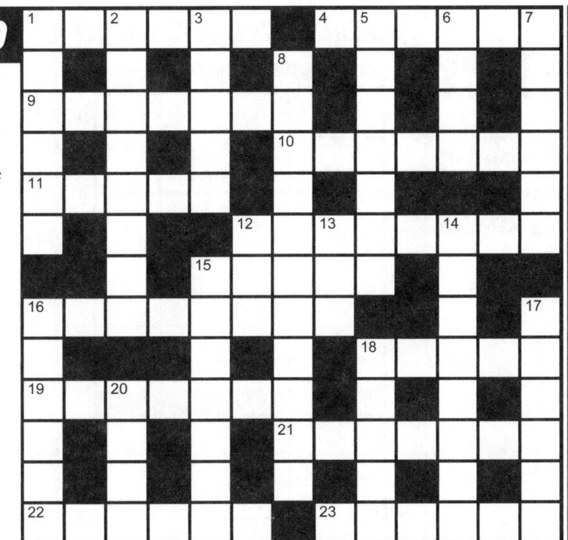

SUMMING UP

In the square below, change the positions of six numbers, one per horizontal row, vertical column and long diagonal line of six smaller squares, in such a way that the numbers in each row, column and long diagonal line total exactly 144. Any number may appear more than once in a row, column or line.

25	45	12	38	15	25
36	44	24	26	40	6
4	21	8	38	19	21
12	8	44	8	54	22
9	4	16	32	38	37
25	38	29	6	10	25

DOMINO PLACEMENT

A standard set of 28 dominoes has been laid out as shown. Can you draw in the edges of them all? The check-box is provided as an aid and the domino already placed will help.

Did You Know?:

More people die in floods than in other kinds of natural disasters. The deadliest known flood occurred on the Yellow River in 1931 – it claimed the lives of over one million people.

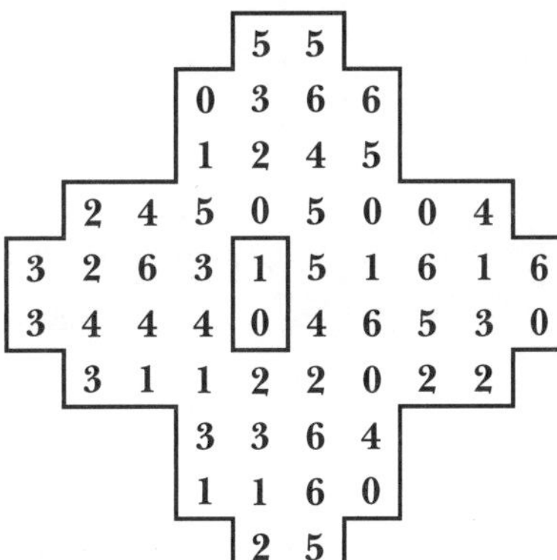

0-0	0-1	0-2	0-3	0-4	0-5	0-6
	✓					

1-1	1-2	1-3	1-4	1-5	1-6	2-2

2-3	2-4	2-5	2-6	3-3	3-4	3-5

3-6	4-4	4-5	4-6	5-5	5-6	6-6

WORDSEARCH WORKOUT

S	J	K	W	E	E	T	J	P	W	R	G	G
P	F	F	S	B	H	S	S	B	T	I	A	W
I	S	R	O	L	L	J	O	P	P	O	R	Y
H	V	J	K	A	A	P	B	B	R	N	D	U
C	N	C	O	C	O	M	W	H	E	E	L	J
Q	E	D	K	K	N	N	D	C	E	Y	A	U
D	D	P	E	J	D	J	H	K	A	B	Z	D
S	O	R	B	A	X	Z	A	Y	Y	R	P	N
T	D	F	A	C	Y	T	K	U	Q	O	D	Y
T	C	C	N	K	S	Z	Z	D	P	U	X	S
G	F	T	D	T	S	H	O	E	Y	G	K	T
C	A	S	I	N	O	N	E	A	R	E	K	C
L	U	U	T	M	Y	C	X	L	M	O	K	V
D	H	R	T	Y	I	B	V	E	B	P	N	E
U	M	A	B	D	A	L	X	R	T	H	D	E

CASINO

BANDIT
BLACKJACK
CARDS
CASINO
CHIPS
DEALER
DECK
DICE
JACKPOT
LIMIT
NOIR
ODDS
POKER
ROLL
ROUGE
SHOE
SPREAD
STAKE
WHEEL
ZERO

DOUBLE FUN SUDOKU

TASTY TEASER

5	8	7				4	3	6
		3	6			5		
	2		8	3			1	
	6		1			7		
7			5		2			4
		8			3		9	
	7			9	4		6	
		2			8	1		
8	4	9				2	7	5

BRAIN BUSTER

		1	5		2			
			4					5
				9			8	4
5		3	6					
7				5				9
					1	2		3
9	5			7				
4					6			
			8		5	6		

WHATEVER NEXT?

In the diagram below, which letter should replace the question mark?

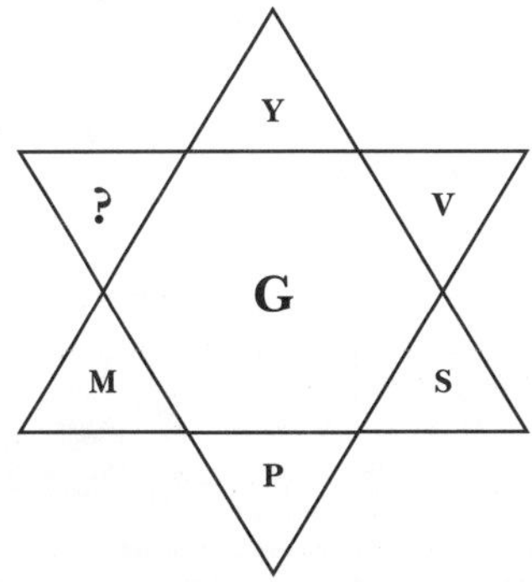

BRAIN TEASER

How many minutes is it before 12 noon if 132 minutes later it will be three times as many minutes before 3.00pm?

Mind Over Matter

Given that the letters are valued 1-26 according to their places in the alphabet, can you crack the mystery code to reveal the missing letter?

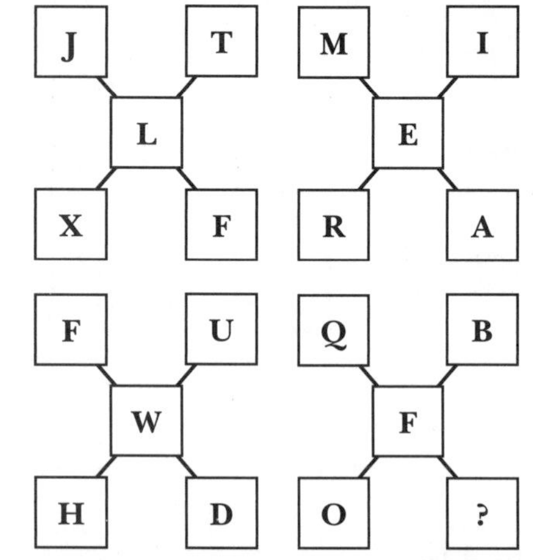

DOUBLE FUN SUDOKU

TASTY TEASER

		4		3			7	2
3	6		9	4				5
1	9	7			8			
				6	3	1		
	4	5				2	6	
		1	4	2				
			5			6	9	7
2				9	1		4	8
5	8			7		3		

BRAIN BUSTER

	8						6	
	4		8		1		9	
5		7		2		3		1
		3		5		6		
			4		2			
		6		8		9		
7		9		4		1		8
	3		7		5		2	
	6						5	

CODEWORD CONUNDRUM

4	19	7	10	4	20	■	10	11	6	10	8	19	4	16
16	■	16	■	19	■	2	■	15	■	5	■	14	■	10
18	15	7 T	19 O	24 N	■	15	24	3	19	15	8	15	24	26
11	■	10	■	5	19	24	■	16	■	16	■	9	■	11
15	19	24	■	16	■	8	19	24	9	14	26	10	7	16
16	■	14	■	10	■	■	8	■	19	■	4	■	4	■
5	15	13	12	14	15	16	7	■	15	13	19	6	10	4
■	17	■	14	■	26	■	10	■	24	■	25	■	8	■
4	10	5	15	10	11	■	3	15	7	10	11	15	7	20
■	26	■	8	■	19	■	16	■	■	6	■	7	■	10
25	19	4	21	23	19	4	13	16	■	13	■	8	19	13
23	■	10	■	16	■	19	■	10	22	7	■	23	■	23
15	24	3	15	5	15	19	14	13	■	10	1	15	19	17
17	■	16	■	26	■	13	■	20	■	15	■	16	■	10
13	16	4	18	16	24	7	13	■	10	24	19	4	10	21

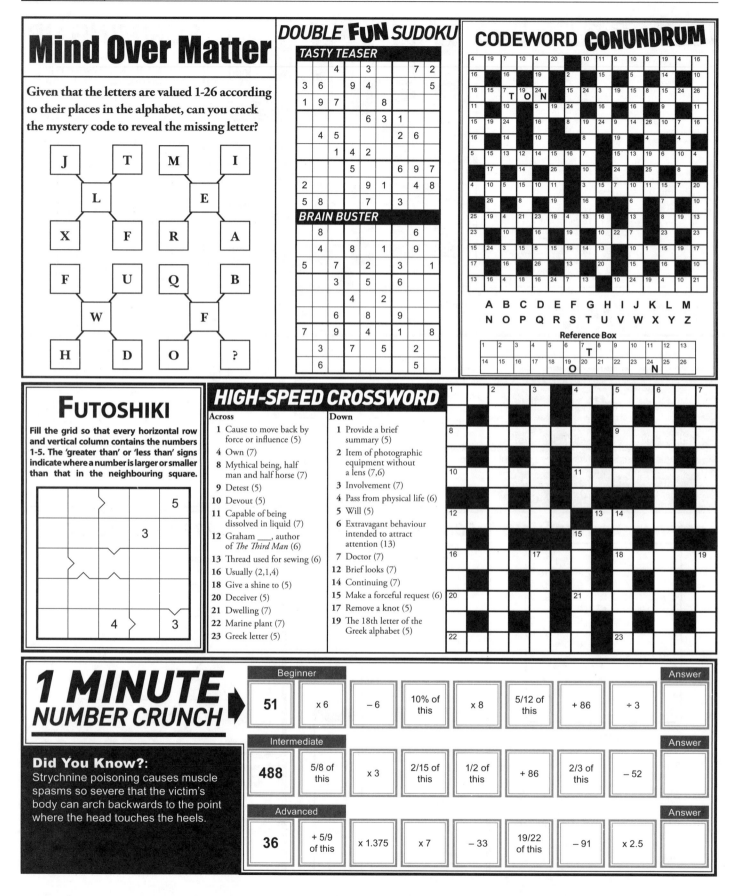

A B C D E F G H I J K L M

N O P Q R S T U V W X Y Z

Reference Box

1	2	3	4	5	6	7	8	9	10	11	12	13
						T						
14	**15**	**16**	**17**	**18**	**19**	**20**	**21**	**22**	**23**	**24**	**25**	**26**
					O					N		

FUTOSHIKI

Fill the grid so that every horizontal row and vertical column contains the numbers 1-5. The 'greater than' or 'less than' signs indicate where a number is larger or smaller than that in the neighbouring square.

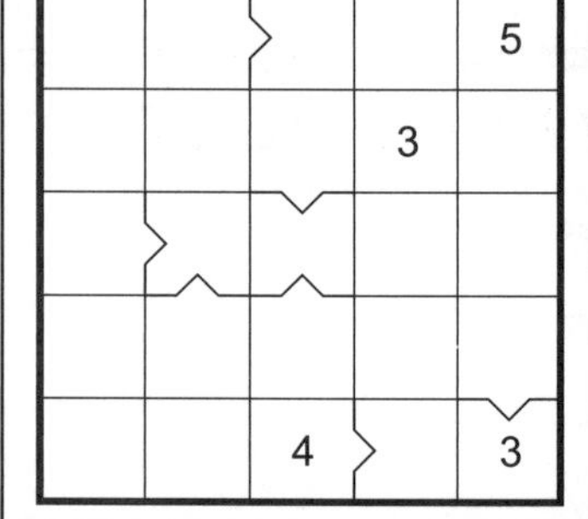

HIGH-SPEED CROSSWORD

Across

1 Cause to move back by force or influence (5)
4 Own (7)
8 Mythical being, half man and half horse (7)
9 Detest (5)
10 Devout (5)
11 Capable of being dissolved in liquid (7)
12 Graham ___, author of *The Third Man* (6)
13 Thread used for sewing (6)
16 Usually (2,1,4)
18 Give a shine to (5)
20 Deceiver (5)
21 Dwelling (7)
22 Marine plant (7)
23 Greek letter (5)

Down

1 Provide a brief summary (5)
2 Item of photographic equipment without a lens (7,6)
3 Involvement (7)
4 Pass from physical life (6)
5 Will (5)
6 Extravagant behaviour intended to attract attention (13)
7 Doctor (7)
12 Brief looks (7)
14 Continuing (7)
15 Make a forceful request (6)
17 Remove a knot (5)
19 The 18th letter of the Greek alphabet (5)

Beginner

51	x 6	– 6	10% of this	x 8	5/12 of this	+ 86	÷ 3	Answer

Intermediate

488	5/8 of this	x 3	2/15 of this	1/2 of this	+ 86	2/3 of this	– 52	Answer

Advanced

36	+ 5/9 of this	x 1.375	x 7	– 33	19/22 of this	– 91	x 2.5	Answer

Did You Know?:
Strychnine poisoning causes muscle spasms so severe that the victim's body can arch backwards to the point where the head touches the heels.

1 MINUTE NUMBER CRUNCH

Beginner								Answer
100	– 42	1/2 of this	+ 7	50% of this	+ 9	1/3 of this	x 5	

Intermediate								Answer
85	3/5 of this	x 8	÷ 17	Squared	÷ 9	5/8 of this	x 3.5	

Advanced								Answer
583	–77	4/11 of this	x 0.625	x 0.4	x 13	Double it	– 555	

Did You Know?:
A skydiver in free-fall will travel at a maximum of 120 miles per hour. This produces air-pressure sufficient to force oxygen into the body through the skin.

HIGH-SPEED CROSSWORD

Across
1 Gazebo (11)
9 First appearance (5)
10 Cardinal number (3)
11 Concise in manner (5)
12 Charged particle (3)
14 Grovel (5)
15 Undue partiality to one's relations and close friends (8)
17 Secret watcher (3)
18 Of a female (3)
20 Highest level of warning (3,5)
22 Abstract form of painting that produces dramatic visual effects (2,3)
25 Cut wood (3)
26 Spotted or calico horse (5)
27 High mountain (3)
28 Harden to (5)
29 Not absolutely essential (11)

Down
2 Removes the outer covering (7)
3 Freedom from vanity (7)
4 Hydrophobia (6)
5 Of the eye (5)
6 Gleamed (5)
7 On purpose (11)
8 Characterised by violent emotions (11)
13 Projecting bay window (5)
16 Drama set to music (5)
18 Impedes the progress of (7)
19 Go back in (2-5)
21 Put up with (6)
23 Poplar tree (5)
24 Lightweight cord (5)

PARTITIONS

Draw walls to partition the grid into areas (some are already drawn in). Each area must contain two circles, area sizes must match those numbers shown next to the grid and each '+' must be linked to at least two walls.

2, 4, 4, 4, 5, 6

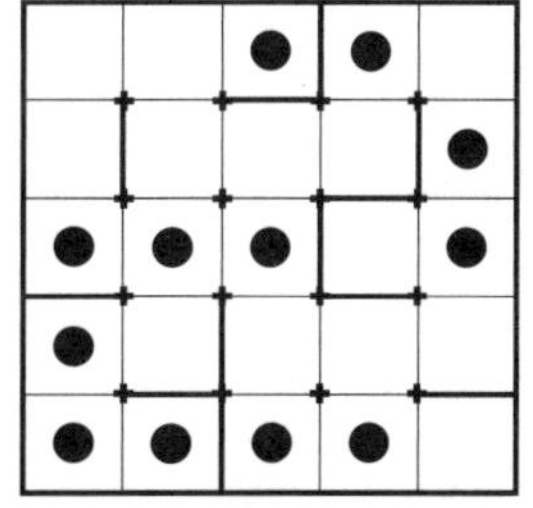

WORDWHEEL

Using only the letters in the Wordwheel, you have ten minutes to find as many words as possible, none of which may be plurals, foreign words or proper nouns. Each word must be of three letters or more, all must contain the central letter and letters can only be used once in every word. There is at least one nine-letter word in the wheel.

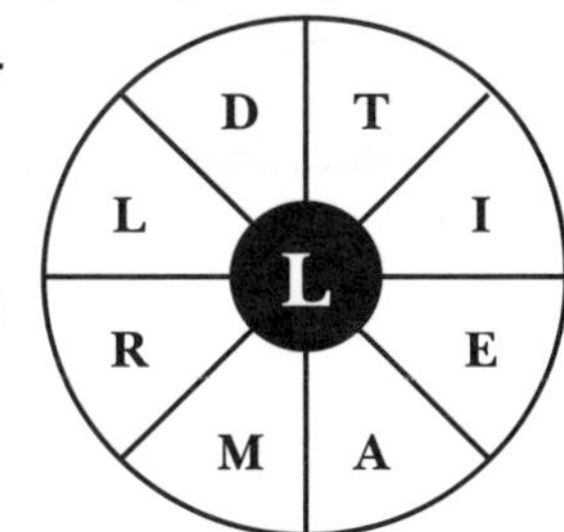

Nine-letter word(s):

WORDSEARCH WORKOUT

E L K U L T O C K E H S L
S E O B S J A K G C W H E
U T Q J K S M A R W L I X
O O S F T T T U N K T A W
H H N L V T H O S E U N W
N W E I O C I E K E M X Y
W K F C S S E R A E U T Q
O I K D N A A G P T I M E
T Y N A F M C A E S R G X
L H M D R E L U R L A E P
C I N E M A U E V R L M E
B K P D C I V Q A D O O B
V U I E O I L G S H S T C
S A U V N D F L N O M E K
Q W B U N G A L O W M L J

BUILDINGS

BUNGALOW
CASINO
CASTLE
CHURCH
CINEMA
COLLEGE
COTTAGE
GARAGE
HOTEL
MANSION
MOSQUE
MOTEL
MUSEUM
PALACE
SOLARIUM
SUPERMARKET
THEATRE
TOWNHOUSE
UNIVERSITY
WINDMILL

SUM CIRCLE

Fill the three empty circles with the symbols +, – and x in some order, to make a sum which totals the number in the centre. Each symbol must be used once and calculations are made in the direction of travel (clockwise).

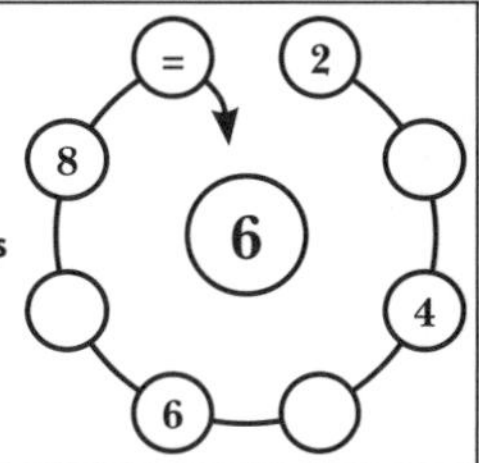

DOUBLE FUN SUDOKU

TASTY TEASER

9	6		2	5		8		
1		7	9					2
			1			6	7	
6			4			7	3	
	8		7		9		1	
	3	4			8			5
	5	8			4			
3					2	9		4
		9		6	1		2	3

BRAIN BUSTER

3								2
5		1				4		7
		7	8		4	6		
	3		9	5	2		7	
	6		1	3	8		4	
		9	7		6	5		
1		4				2		9
6								4

1 MINUTE NUMBER CRUNCH

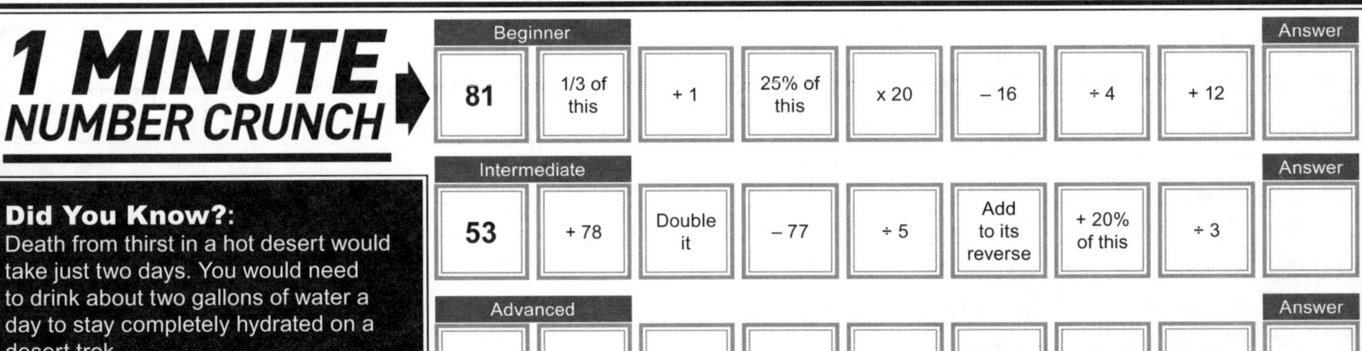

Beginner

81	1/3 of this	+ 1	25% of this	x 20	– 16	÷ 4	+ 12	Answer

Intermediate

53	+ 78	Double it	– 77	÷ 5	Add to its reverse	+ 20% of this	÷ 3	Answer

Advanced

112	5/14 of this	Cubed	x 0.375	– 8667	2/3 of this	1/2 of this	+ 965	Answer

Did You Know?:
Death from thirst in a hot desert would take just two days. You would need to drink about two gallons of water a day to stay completely hydrated on a desert trek.

HIGH-SPEED CROSSWORD

Across

1 Cravings (7)
6 Gaming cube (3)
8 Wear away (5)
9 Formed by forcing molten metal into a mould (3-4)
10 Brittle fragment (5)
11 Arrangements of thick and thin parallel lines printed onto a commodity (8)
13 Sharp piercing cry (6)
15 Dislike intensely (6)
18 Showing the wearing effects of overwork or suffering (8)
19 Become less in amount or intensity (3,2)
21 Slowly moving mass of ice (7)
22 Wash off soap (5)
23 Before, poetically (3)
24 Foot lever (7)

Down

2 Inscription on a tombstone (7)
3 Came to a conclusion (8)
4 Small sofa (6)
5 Spinning toys (4)
6 Fiasco (7)
7 Capable of being seen or noticed (7)
12 Lead a passive existence without using one's body or mind (8)
13 Isolate (7)
14 Reinstate (7)
16 Resembling a dream (7)
17 Objective (6)
20 Weak (4)

IQ WORKOUT

What number should replace the question mark?

CODEWORD CONUNDRUM

A B C D E F G H I J K L M
N O P Q R S T U V W X Y Z

Reference Box

1	2	3 C	4	5	6	7	8	9	10	11	12	13
14	15	16	17	18	19	20 Y	21 O	22	23	24	25	26

DOUBLE FUN SUDOKU

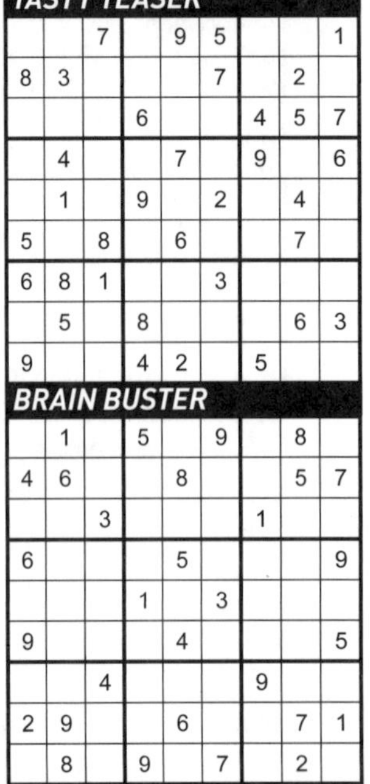

TASTY TEASER

		7		9	5			1
8	3				7		2	
			6			4	5	7
	4			7		9		6
	1		9		2		4	
5		8		6			7	
6	8	1			3			
	5		8				6	3
9			4	2		5		

BRAIN BUSTER

	1		5		9		8	
4	6			8			5	7
		3				1		
6				5				9
			1		3			
9				4				5
		4				9		
2	9			6			7	1
	8		9		7		2	

SPIDOKU

Each of the eight segments of the spider's web should be filled with a different number from 1 to 8, in such a way that every ring also contains a different number from 1 to 8.

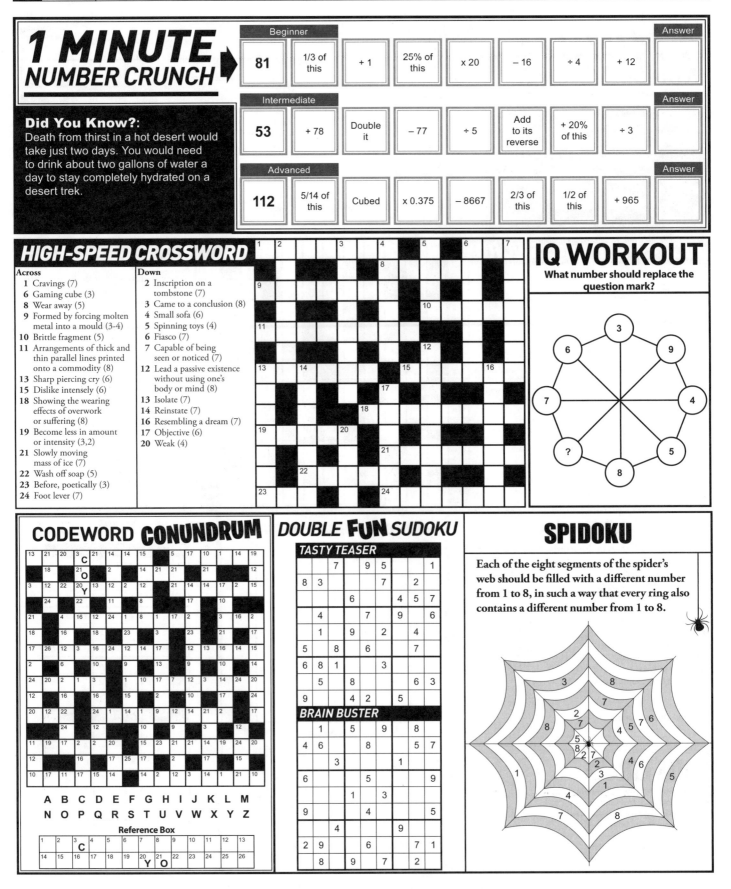

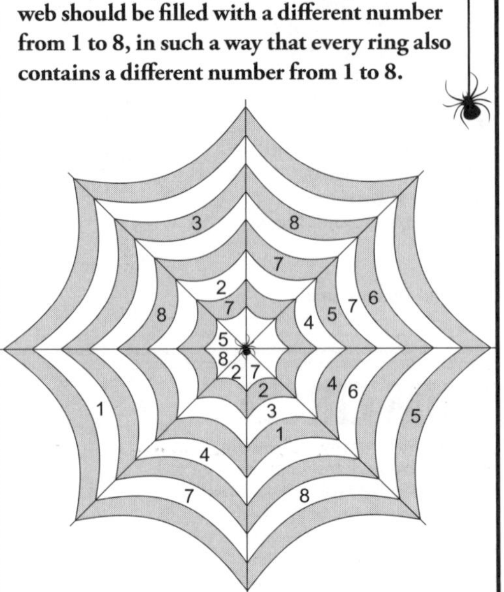

LOGI-SIX

Every row and column of this grid should contain one each of the letters A, B, C, D, E and F. Each of the six shapes (marked by thicker lines) should also contain one each of the letters A, B, C, D, E and F. Can you complete the grid?

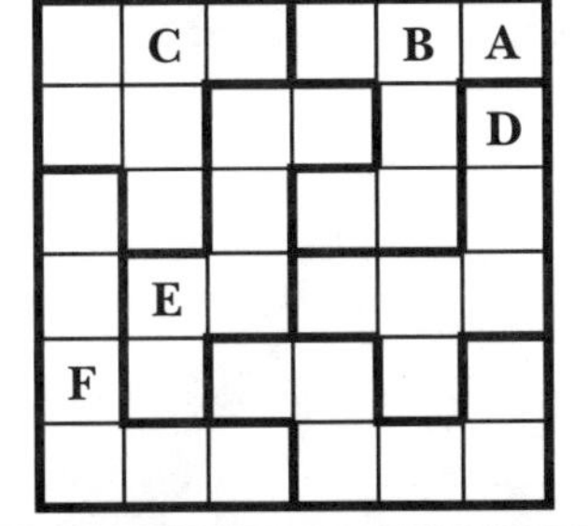

HIGH-SPEED CROSSWORD

Across

1 Soft fabric made from the wool of a goat (8)
5 Automobiles (4)
9 Curl of hair (7)
10 Narrow to a point (5)
11 Mischievous elf in Irish folklore (10)
14 Weighing machine (6)
15 Paper handkerchief (6)
17 Flavour sensation that remains after eating or drinking (10)
20 Vehicles used to travel over snow (5)
21 Bram Stoker's vampire (7)
22 Brief written record (4)
23 Reduce in rank (8)

Down

1 Birthday missive (4)
2 Fine grit (4)
3 Shape consisting of four arrowheads with their points towards the centre (7,5)
4 Give up work (6)
6 Assess (8)
7 More alien (8)
8 Equipment constantly used as part of a profession or occupation (5-2-5)
12 Hired murderer (8)
13 Most distant or remote (8)
16 Attendant who carries golf clubs for a player (6)
18 Distinctive quality (4)
19 Bundle of straw or hay (4)

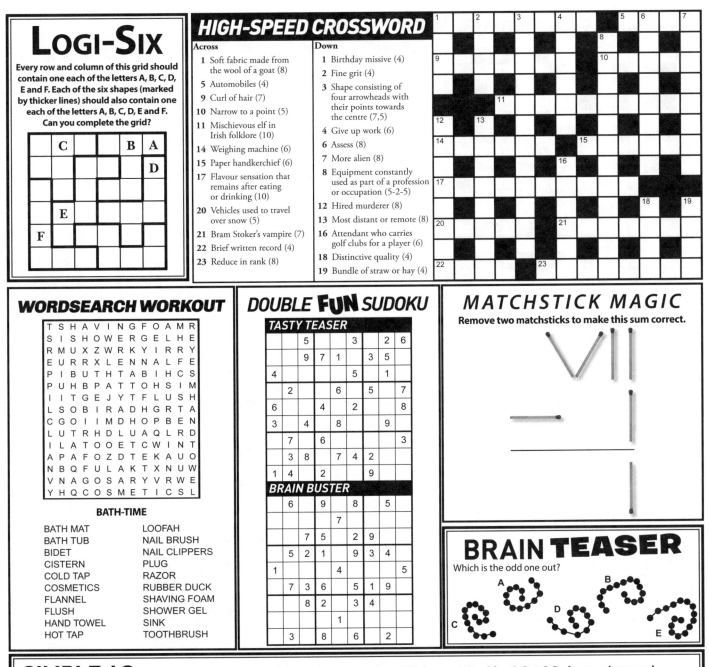

WORDSEARCH WORKOUT

T S H A V I N G F O A M R
S I S H O W E R G E L H E
R M U X Z W R K Y I R R Y
E U R R X L E N N A L F E
P I B U T H T A B I H C S
P U H B P A T T O H S I M
I I T G E J Y T F L U S H
L S O B I R A D H G R T A
C G O I I M D H O P B E N
L U T R H D L U A Q L R D
I L A T O O E T C W I N T
A P A F O Z D T E K A U O
N B Q F U L A K T X N U W
V N A G O S A R Y V R W E
Y H Q C O S M E T I C S L

BATH-TIME

BATH MAT
BATH TUB
BIDET
CISTERN
COLD TAP
COSMETICS
FLANNEL
FLUSH
HAND TOWEL
HOT TAP
LOOFAH
NAIL BRUSH
NAIL CLIPPERS
PLUG
RAZOR
RUBBER DUCK
SHAVING FOAM
SHOWER GEL
SINK
TOOTHBRUSH

DOUBLE FUN SUDOKU

TASTY TEASER

		5			3		2	6
		9	7	1		3	5	
4					5		1	
	2			6		5		7
6			4		2			8
3		4		8			9	
	7		6					3
	3	8		7	4	2		
1	4		2			9		

BRAIN BUSTER

	6		9		8		5	
				7				
		7	5		2	9		
	5	2	1		9	3	4	
1				4				5
	7	3	6		5	1	9	
		8	2		3	4		
				1				
	3		8		6		2	

MATCHSTICK MAGIC

Remove two matchsticks to make this sum correct.

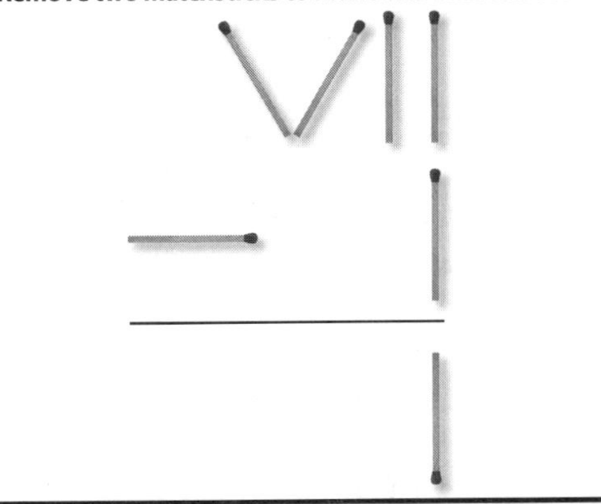

BRAIN TEASER

Which is the odd one out?

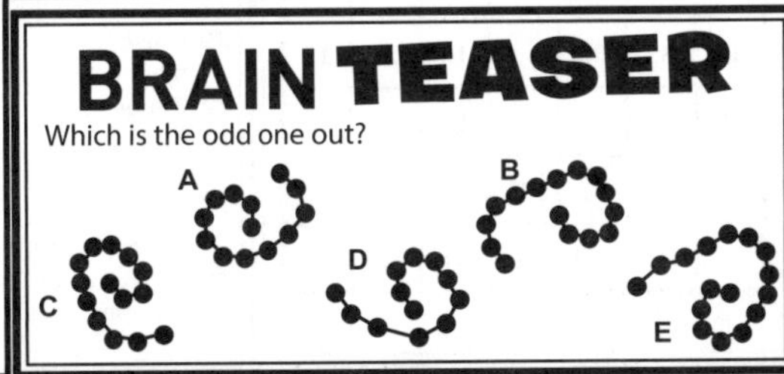

SIMPLE AS A, B, C ?

Each of the small squares in the grid below contains either A, B or C. Each row, column, and diagonal line of six squares has exactly two of each letter. Can you tell the letter in each square?

Across

1 The Cs are between the Bs
2 The Bs are between the As
3 No two letters the same are directly next to each other
4 No two letters the same are directly next to each other
5 The Cs are between the As
6 The Bs are between the Cs

Down

1 Each C is directly next to and below a B
2 No two letters the same are directly next to each other
3 The Cs are lower than the Bs
4 The Bs are lower than the Cs
5 Each C is directly next to and below a B
6 No two letters the same are directly next to each other

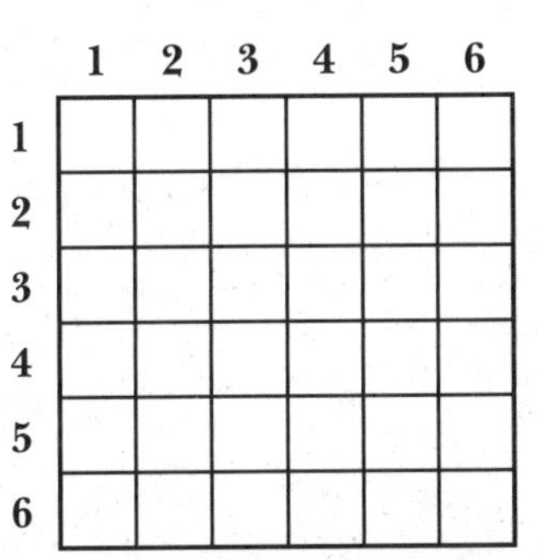

Did You Know?:

In ancient India, physicians used to use live ants to stitch wounds together. The ants would bite through the edges of the wound then doctors would remove their bodies, leaving their heads in place to hold the wound together.

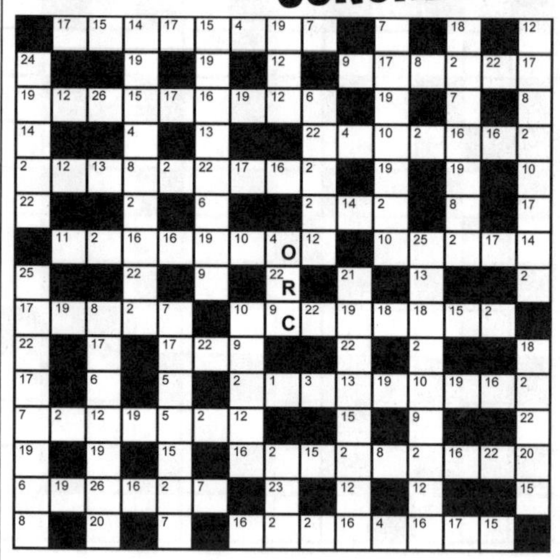

A B C D E F G H I J K L M

N O P Q R S T U V W X Y Z

Reference Box

1	2	3	4 O	5	6	7	8	9 C	10	11	12	13
14	15	16	17	18	19	20	21	22 R	23	24	25	26

DOUBLE FUN SUDOKU

TASTY TEASER

				3	8		2	5
3		1				6	9	
9				2		4	7	
	6				5	8		
5		4	3		2	7		9
		7	4				1	
	7	2		4				6
	8	5				3		1
4	9		8	1				

BRAIN BUSTER

	1			6			9	
			2	4	8			
	8	6	9		1	7	4	
		7				6		
	9						1	
		3				5		
	5	8	7		9	2	6	
			3	5	6			
	7			2			3	

PYRAMID PLUS

Every brick in this pyramid contains a number which is the sum of the two numbers below it, so that F=A+B, etc.
Just work out the missing numbers!

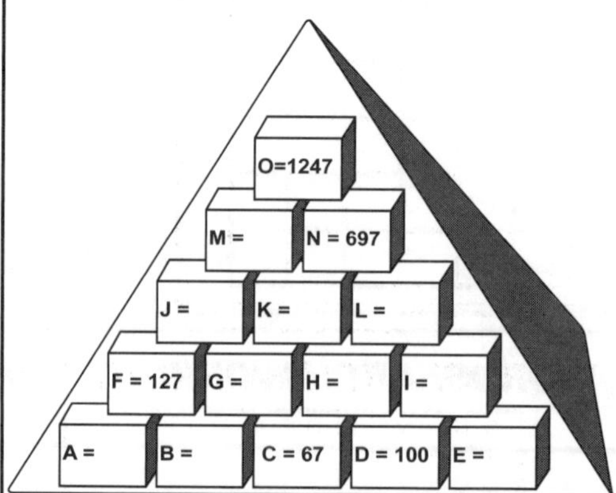

WORK IT OUT

In the grid below, what number should replace the question mark?

4	12	24	19	1	16	9
7	10	3	12	7	5	1
11	22	27	31	8	21	10
18	32	30	43	15	26	11
29	54	57	?	23	47	21
47	86	87	117	38	73	32
76	140	144	191	61	120	53

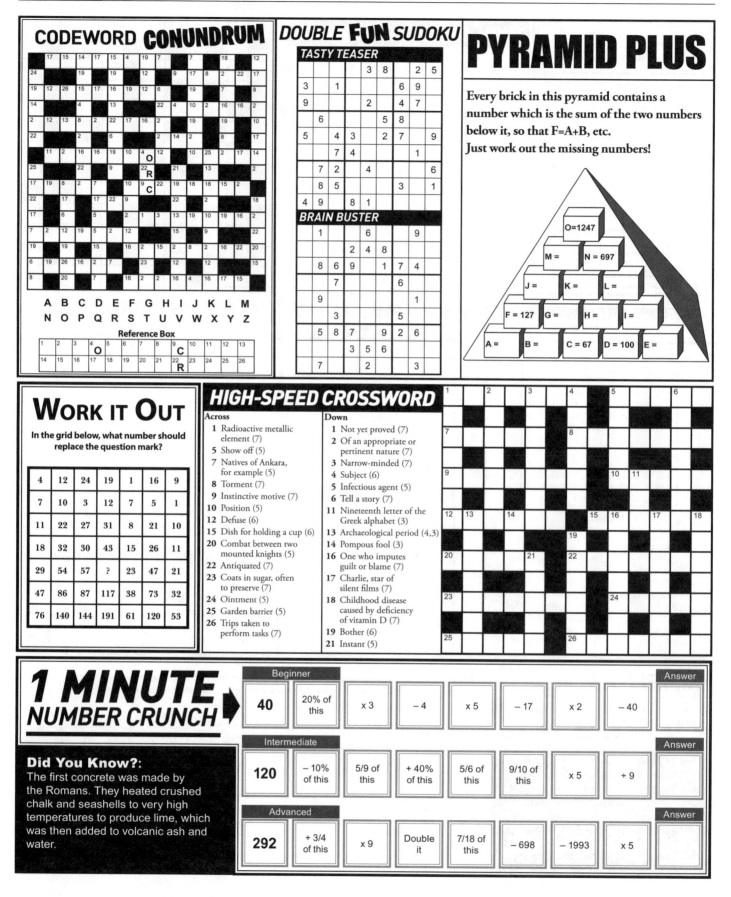

HIGH-SPEED CROSSWORD

Across

1 Radioactive metallic element (7)
5 Show off (5)
7 Natives of Ankara, for example (5)
8 Torment (7)
9 Instinctive motive (7)
10 Position (5)
12 Defuse (6)
15 Dish for holding a cup (6)
20 Combat between two mounted knights (5)
22 Antiquated (7)
23 Coats in sugar, often to preserve (7)
24 Ointment (5)
25 Garden barrier (5)
26 Trips taken to perform tasks (7)

Down

1 Not yet proved (7)
2 Of an appropriate or pertinent nature (7)
3 Narrow-minded (7)
4 Subject (6)
5 Infectious agent (5)
6 Tell a story (7)
11 Nineteenth letter of the Greek alphabet (3)
13 Archaeological period (4,3)
14 Pompous fool (3)
16 One who imputes guilt or blame (7)
17 Charlie, star of silent films (7)
18 Childhood disease caused by deficiency of vitamin D (7)
19 Bother (6)
21 Instant (5)

1 MINUTE NUMBER CRUNCH

Beginner

40	20% of this	x 3	– 4	x 5	– 17	x 2	– 40	Answer

Intermediate

120	– 10% of this	5/9 of this	+ 40% of this	5/6 of this	9/10 of this	x 5	÷ 9	Answer

Advanced

292	+ 3/4 of this	x 9	Double it	7/18 of this	– 698	– 1993	x 5	Answer

Did You Know?:
The first concrete was made by the Romans. They heated crushed chalk and seashells to very high temperatures to produce lime, which was then added to volcanic ash and water.

HIGH-SPEED CROSSWORD

Across

1 Ornamental plaster used to cover walls (6)
4 Tobacco user (6)
7 Decorative knot (3)
8 Parts of a river where the current is very fast (6)
9 Vulnerability to the elements (8)
13 Against (6)
15 Crescent-shaped yellow fruit (6)
16 Speak unfavourably about (6)
17 Dealer, seller (6)
19 Tall hat worn by some British soldiers (8)
23 Nap in the early afternoon (6)
24 H Rider Haggard novel (3)
25 Any leafy plants eaten as vegetables (6)
26 Substance that turns red in acid (6)

Down

1 Ride the waves of the sea on a board (4)
2 Emergency (6)
3 Be preoccupied with something (6)
4 Exchange (4)
5 Porridge ingredient (4)
6 Cereal thrown at weddings (4)
10 Transmitting live (2-3)
11 Hired (6)
12 Be on one's guard against (6)
14 Inner drives (5)
17 Threads of metal foil (6)
18 Miserable (6)
19 Sudden very loud noise (4)
20 Nark, chafe (4)
21 Expression of love (4)
22 Podium (4)

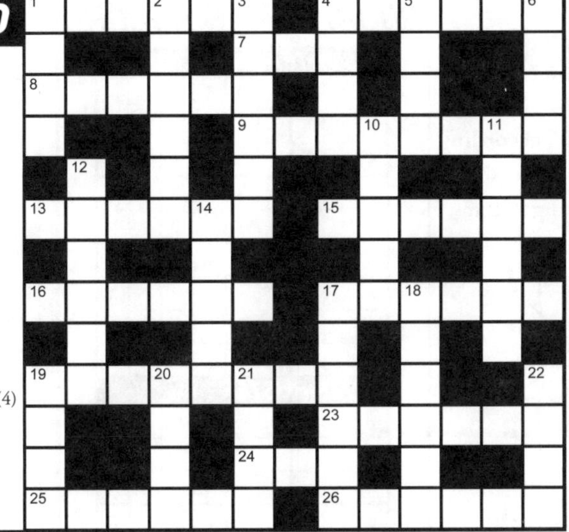

SUMMING UP

In the square below, change the positions of six numbers, one per horizontal row, vertical column and long diagonal line of six smaller squares, in such a way that the numbers in each row, column and long diagonal line total exactly 211. Any number may appear more than once in a row, column or line.

24	49	31	31	44	54
48	35	26	31	36	40
49	54	35	24	26	34
27	45	36	57	16	33
23	29	34	50	13	35
43	21	35	29	49	20

BATTLESHIP BOUT

Kodak introduced colour negative film in the 1930s, but in 2009 the company ceased production of their world-famous Kodachrome film, because of competition from digital photography.

Can you place the vessels into the diagram? Some parts of vessels or sea squares have already been filled in. A number to the right or below a row or column refers to the number of occupied squares in that row or column.
Any vessel may be positioned horizontally or vertically, but no part of a vessel touches part of any other vessel, either horizontally, vertically or diagonally.

Empty Area of Sea:
Aircraft Carrier:
Battleships:
Cruisers:
Submarines:

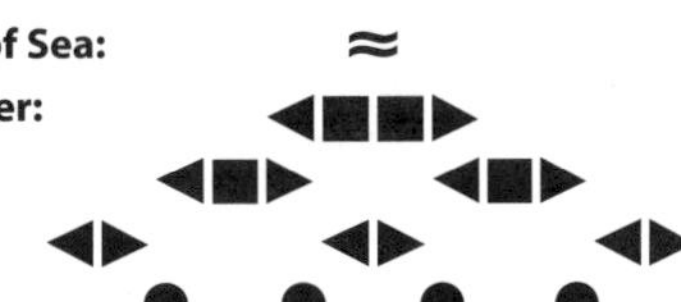

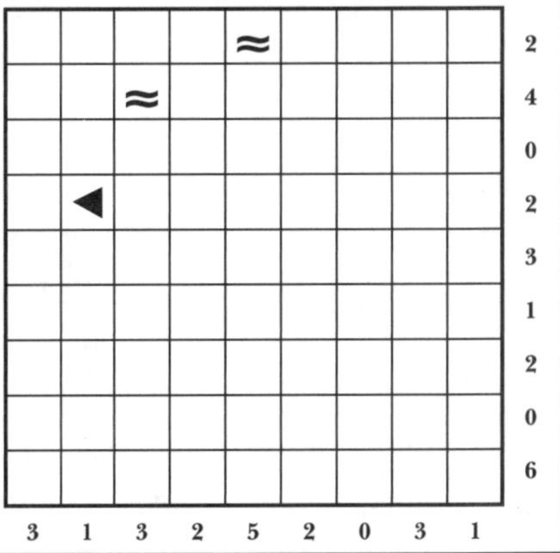

WORDSEARCH WORKOUT

L	L	A	B	T	O	O	F	S	S	E	H	C
L	A	C	R	O	S	S	E	L	W	B	Y	G
E	R	U	U	J	U	I	X	L	K	R	S	S
A	T	H	G	I	F	H	O	L	E	S	E	T
G	Y	S	B	A	T	O	N	H	M	Z	M	P
U	E	H	Y	N	P	C	C	Z	Z	F	B	L
E	K	M	E	Y	B	R	P	I	G	B	L	T
Q	C	F	A	D	A	D	U	Q	I	A	J	G
Z	O	C	S	H	G	Q	C	N	B	E	E	N
Y	H	B	P	B	A	L	G	Y	G	Z	W	I
T	U	R	O	V	T	O	E	C	Z	K	Z	T
V	R	W	R	S	E	L	F	I	L	N	Q	H
F	L	A	T	U	L	G	U	R	U	A	A	C
S	Z	T	C	O	L	Q	O	F	D	X	D	A
K	N	V	V	K	E	X	O	M	O	X	B	Y

SPORTS AND GAMES

ARCHERY
BAGATELLE
BATON
BINGO
BOWLS
CHESS
FIGHT
FOOTBALL
HOCKEY
HOLES
LACROSSE
LEAGUE
LUDO
POOL
QUIZZES
RUGBY
SPORT
TRACK
VOLLEYBALL
YACHTING

DOUBLE FUN SUDOKU

TASTY TEASER

			6	1	5			
		8					2	7
	9	4		8		3		6
	3		8			7	1	5
7			5		6			4
9	5	2			7		8	
6		5		7		8	3	
2	7					4		
			9	6	4			

BRAIN BUSTER

				2				
		9	5		3	6		
3			4		6			5
9		5	1		2	3		7
	7			9			2	
1		2	7		4	5		8
7			6		1			4
		1	3		7	8		
				8				

WHATEVER NEXT?

In the diagram below, which number should replace the question mark?

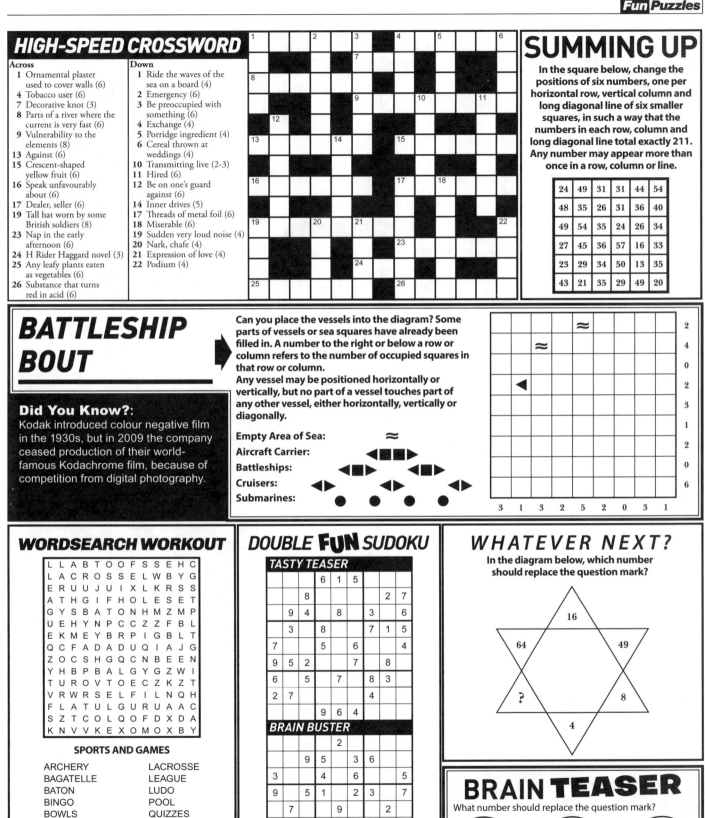

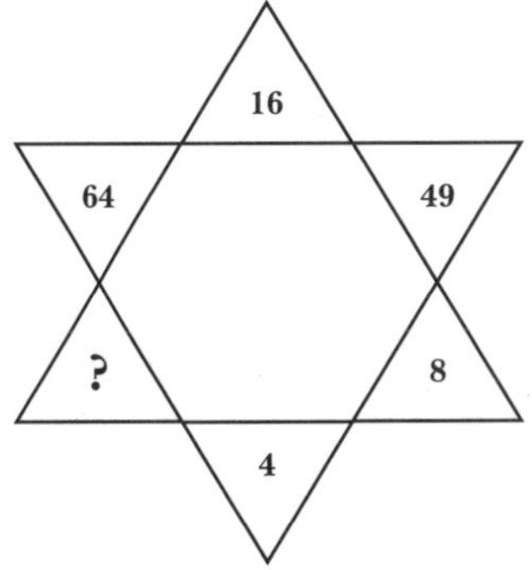

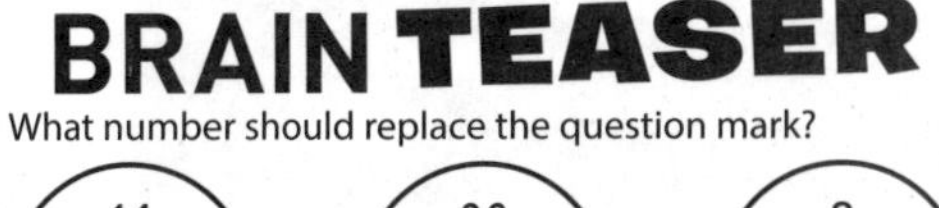

What number should replace the question mark?

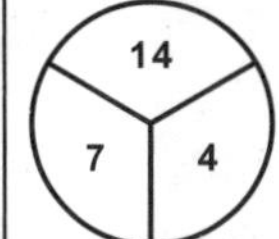

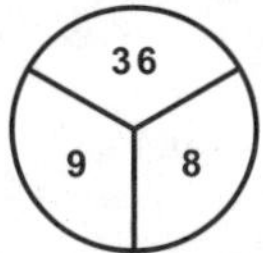

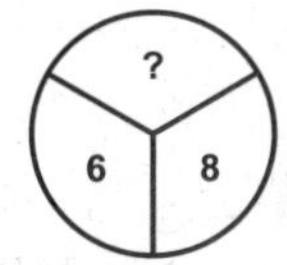

Mind Over Matter

Given that the letters are valued 1-26 according to their places in the alphabet, can you crack the mystery code to reveal the missing letter?

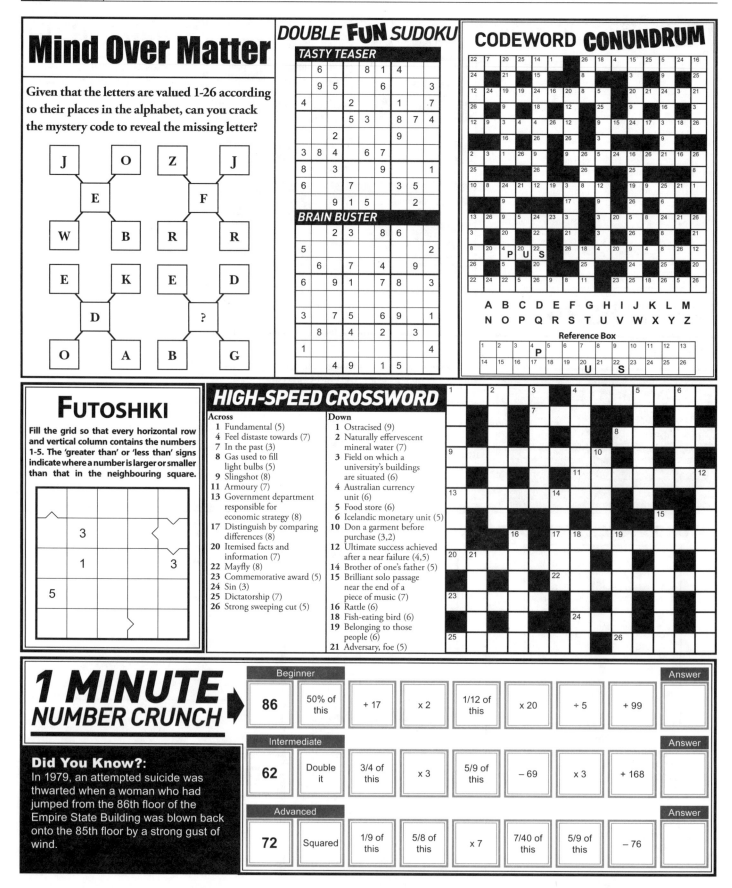

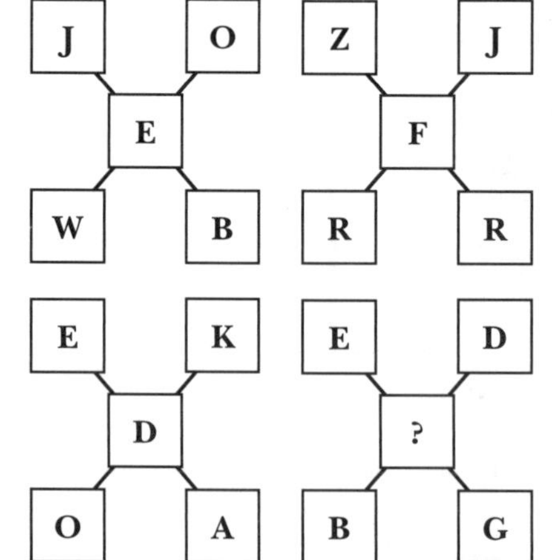

DOUBLE FUN SUDOKU

TASTY TEASER

	6			8	1	4		
	9	5			6			3
4			2			1		7
			5	3		8	7	4
		2				9		
3	8	4		6	7			
8		3			9			1
6			7			3	5	
		9	1	5			2	

BRAIN BUSTER

		2	3		8	6		
5								2
	6		7		4		9	
6		9	1		7	8		3
3		7	5		6	9		1
	8		4		2		3	
1								4
		4	9		1	5		

CODEWORD CONUNDRUM

22	7	20	25	14	1	■	26	18	4	15	25	5	24	16
24	■	21	■	15	■	■	8	■	■	3	■	9	■	25
12	24	19	19	24	16	20	8	5	■	20	21	24	3	21
26	■	9	■	18	■	12	■	25	■	9	■	16	■	3
12	9	3	4	4	26	12	■	9	15	24	17	3	18	26
■	■	16	■	26	■	26	■	3	■	■	■	9	■	■
2	3	1	26	9	■	9	26	5	24	16	26	21	16	26
25	■	■	■	26	■	■	26	■	■	25	■	■	■	8
10	8	24	21	12	19	3	8	12	■	19	9	25	21	1
■	■	9	■	■	■	17	■	9	■	26	■	6	■	■
13	26	9	5	24	23	3	■	3	20	5	8	24	21	26
3	■	20	■	22	■	21	■	3	■	26	■	8	■	21
8	20	4 P	20 U	22 S	■	26	18	4	20	9	4	8	26	12
26	■	5	■	20	■	■	25	■	■	24	■	25	■	20
22	24	22	5	26	9	8	11	■	23	25	18	26	5	26

A B C D E F G H I J K L M

N O P Q R S T U V W X Y Z

Reference Box

1	2	3	4 P	5	6	7	8	9	10	11	12	13
14	15	16	17	18	19	20 U	21	22 S	23	24	25	26

FUTOSHIKI

Fill the grid so that every horizontal row and vertical column contains the numbers 1-5. The 'greater than' or 'less than' signs indicate where a number is larger or smaller than that in the neighbouring square.

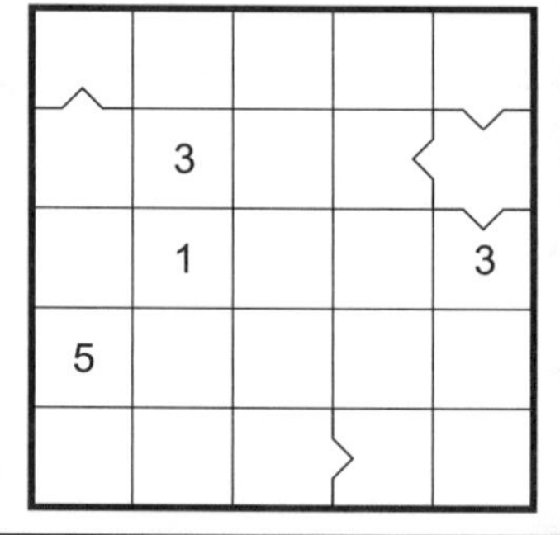

HIGH-SPEED CROSSWORD

Across

1 Fundamental (5)
4 Feel distaste towards (7)
7 In the past (3)
8 Gas used to fill light bulbs (5)
9 Slingshot (8)
11 Armoury (7)
13 Government department responsible for economic strategy (8)
17 Distinguish by comparing differences (8)
20 Itemised facts and information (7)
22 Mayfly (8)
23 Commemorative award (5)
24 Sin (3)
25 Dictatorship (7)
26 Strong sweeping cut (5)

Down

1 Ostracised (9)
2 Naturally effervescent mineral water (7)
3 Field on which a university's buildings are situated (6)
4 Australian currency unit (6)
5 Food store (6)
6 Icelandic monetary unit (5)
10 Don a garment before purchase (3,2)
12 Ultimate success achieved after a near failure (4,5)
14 Brother of one's father (5)
15 Brilliant solo passage near the end of a piece of music (7)
16 Rattle (6)
18 Fish-eating bird (6)
19 Belonging to those people (6)
21 Adversary, foe (5)

1 MINUTE NUMBER CRUNCH

Beginner

								Answer
86	50% of this	+ 17	x 2	1/12 of this	x 20	÷ 5	+ 99	

Intermediate

								Answer
62	Double it	3/4 of this	x 3	5/9 of this	– 69	x 3	+ 168	

Advanced

								Answer
72	Squared	1/9 of this	5/8 of this	x 7	7/40 of this	5/9 of this	– 76	

Did You Know?:
In 1979, an attempted suicide was thwarted when a woman who had jumped from the 86th floor of the Empire State Building was blown back onto the 85th floor by a strong gust of wind.

DOMINO PLACEMENT

A standard set of 28 dominoes has been laid out as shown. Can you draw in the edges of them all? The check-box is provided as an aid and the domino already placed will help.

				2	5				
			0	2	6	6			
			1	5	5	5			
	1	4	0	4	4	4	3	3	
1	3	2	2	3	5	3	0	4	2
4	5	1	6	3	6	1	2	0	0
	2	6	5	0	1	3	1	1	
			0	0	6	2			
			5	6	4	6			
				3	4				

0-0	0-1	0-2	0-3	0-4	0-5	0-6
						✓

1-1	1-2	1-3	1-4	1-5	1-6	2-2

2-3	2-4	2-5	2-6	3-3	3-4	3-5

3-6	4-4	4-5	4-6	5-5	5-6	6-6

Did You Know?:
Lions are colour-blind, which is why they can't distinguish between a zebra's black and white stripes and the green and yellow of surrounding vegetation.

HIGH-SPEED CROSSWORD

Across
1 Large crate in which goods are placed for shipment (7,4)
7 Causing great astonishment and consternation (8)
8 Gumbo (4)
9 Lay bare (6)
11 Bring to humbler state (6)
13 Informal term for a British policeman (5)
14 Fanatical (5)
17 Smear with ointment (6)
20 Playful like a lively kitten (6)
22 Diplomacy (4)
23 Candied plant stalks used to flavour cakes and trifles (8)
24 Have an argument or dispute (coll) (5,6)

Down
1 Artist's crayon (6)
2 Japanese form of fencing (5)
3 Artlessness (7)
4 Roll of tobacco (5)
5 Rebuke (5)
6 Stiff straw hat with a flat crown (6)
10 Picture recorded by a camera (5)
12 Divisions of quantity (5)
14 Safe places (7)
15 Any of various small breeds of fowl (6)
16 Get around, circumvent (6)
18 Lay to rest (5)
19 Salvers (5)
21 Ice house (5)

IQ WORKOUT

What number should replace the question mark?

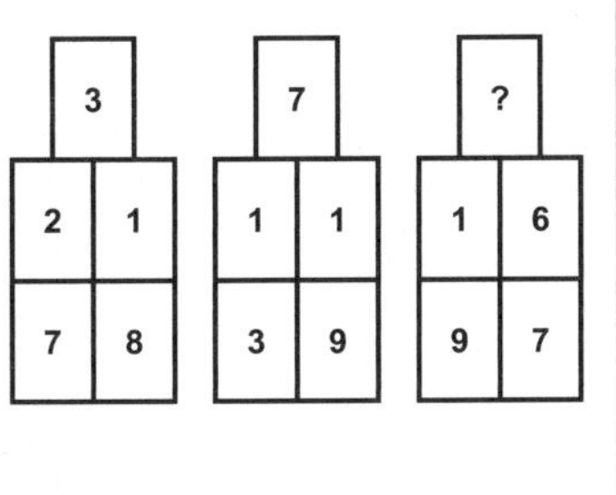

WORDWHEEL

Using only the letters in the Wordwheel, you have ten minutes to find as many words as possible, none of which may be plurals, foreign words or proper nouns. Each word must be of three letters or more, all must contain the central letter and letters can only be used once in every word. There is at least one nine-letter word in the wheel.

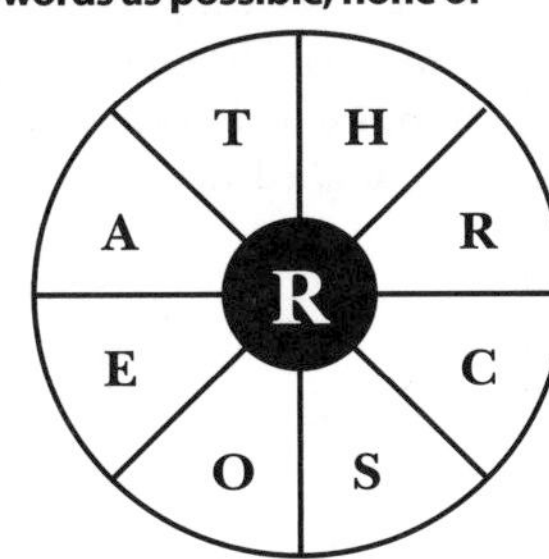

Nine-letter word(s):

SUM CIRCLE

Fill the three empty circles with the symbols +, – and x in some order, to make a sum which totals the number in the centre. Each symbol must be used once and calculations are made in the direction of travel (clockwise).

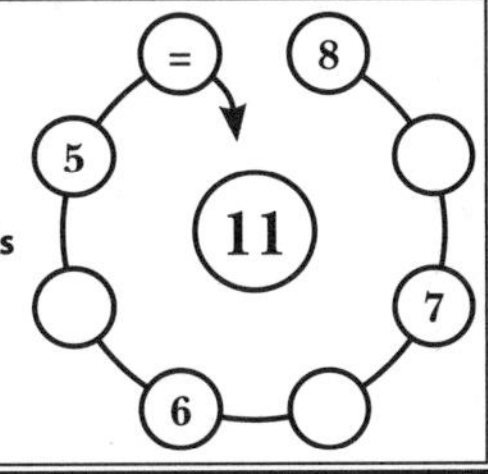

WORDSEARCH WORKOUT

G	H	T	C	C	Q	J	B	Y	C	N	P	L
R	S	O	E	V	T	W	K	U	W	A	U	W
A	I	P	R	A	M	E	K	I	N	P	C	O
T	D	A	E	O	T	U	A	T	X	E	A	B
E	N	E	A	T	L	E	J	P	S	C	E	P
R	I	T	L	G	D	L	A	Y	L	U	T	U
L	T	E	B	U	H	W	I	S	P	A	Z	O
A	A	V	O	L	O	K	W	N	P	S	T	S
L	R	D	W	H	I	S	K	G	G	O	C	E
U	G	P	L	C	O	F	F	E	E	P	O	T
T	N	Q	E	E	Y	P	I	P	Z	T	I	N
A	D	E	S	S	E	R	T	B	O	W	L	N
P	U	C	E	E	F	F	O	C	F	X	R	T
S	T	W	A	F	I	S	H	F	O	R	K	H
A	I	P	I	E	D	I	S	H	A	K	G	T

KITCHEN ITEMS

CEREAL BOWL
COFFEE CUP
COFFEE POT
DESSERT BOWL
FISH FORK
GRATER
GRATIN DISH
KETTLE
LADLE
PIE DISH
RAMEKIN
ROLLING PIN
SAUCEPAN
SOUP BOWL
SPATULA
TEA PLATE
TEACUP
TEAPOT
TEASPOON
WHISK

DOUBLE FUN SUDOKU

TASTY TEASER

		4	1	3	7			
		6		2		4	1	9
		5	9		6			
5			3		9		4	
	3	9				8	2	
	4		5		2			7
			7		8	2		
8	1	7		5		6		
			4	6	1	7		

BRAIN BUSTER

	5		2		3		6	
				8				
2			6		1			9
3	4		5		8		9	1
		2		7		8		
1	9		3		4		5	6
4			8		6			7
				3				
	3		4		7		1	

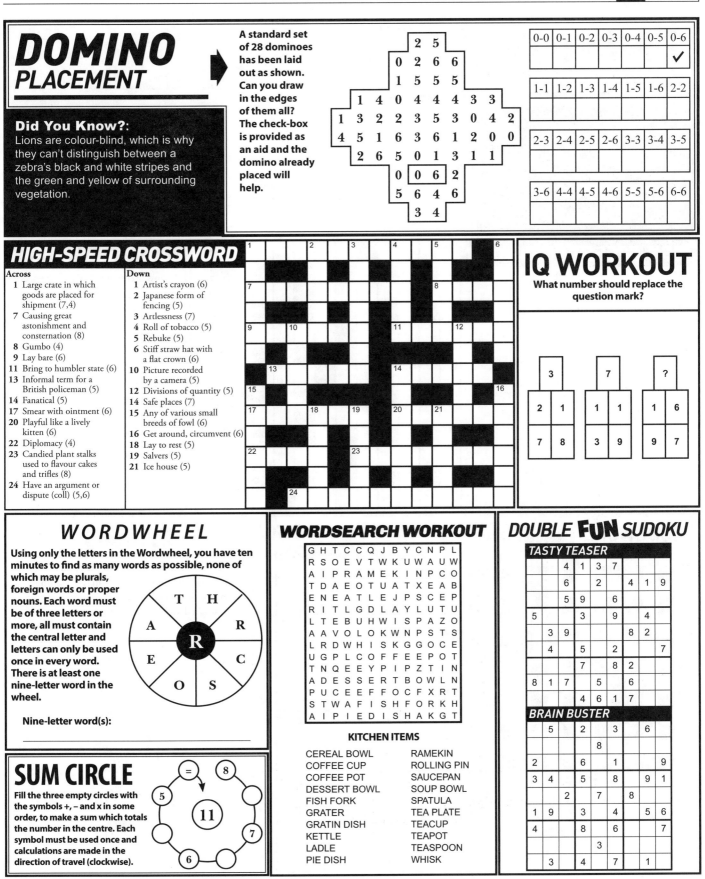

1 MINUTE NUMBER CRUNCH

Beginner								Answer
89	+ 47	1/4 of this	50% of this	x 6	– 15	÷ 3	+ 39	

Intermediate								Answer
261	x 2	÷ 9	250% of this	3/5 of this	÷ 3	x 7	– 45	

Advanced								Answer
247	3/13 of this	5/19 of this	x 35	5/21 of this	Cube root of this	x 1.4	x 45	

Did You Know?:
Joseph von Fraunhofer's fortunes improved after the building in which he worked as a 12-year-old apprentice collapsed around him. His rescuer was a Bavarian prince, who provided the boy with the means to become a great inventor in the field of optics.

HIGH-SPEED CROSSWORD

Across
1 Gait (4)
3 Secret (8)
9 Egocentric (7)
10 Wild rose (5)
11 In the centre of (5)
12 Large dark low cloud (7)
13 Shun (6)
15 Gathering of the minimal number of members of an organisation to conduct business (6)
17 Whirlwind (7)
18 Baking appliances (5)
20 In a softened tone (5)
21 Sea captain (7)
22 Machine for destroying documents (8)
23 Use a keyboard (4)

Down
1 Small adhesive tokens stuck on letters or packages (7,6)
2 Large stringed instrument (5)
4 Division of a group into opposing factions (6)
5 Bacterial infection of the lungs (12)
6 Engage in boisterous, drunken merrymaking (7)
7 Ornamented evergreen used as a seasonal decoration (9,4)
8 Unsupported by other people (6-6)
14 Custodian of a museum (7)
16 Foam used in hair styling (6)
19 Containing nothing (5)

IQ WORKOUT

In how many circles does a black dot appear?

CODEWORD CONUNDRUM

DOUBLE FUN SUDOKU

TASTY TEASER

	5	3	1		2		7	
6				4		8		
		7	3		9		6	
	8				7	3		2
	9			1			5	
5		4	6				1	
	6		5		8	2		
		5		9				7
	4		2		1	6	9	

BRAIN BUSTER

		1		8			3	
	2	9			4			6
5						9		4
					8		9	7
3	6		7					
4		3						9
2			6			5	7	
	7			2		1		

SPIDOKU

Each of the eight segments of the spider's web should be filled with a different number from 1 to 8, in such a way that every ring also contains a different number from 1 to 8.

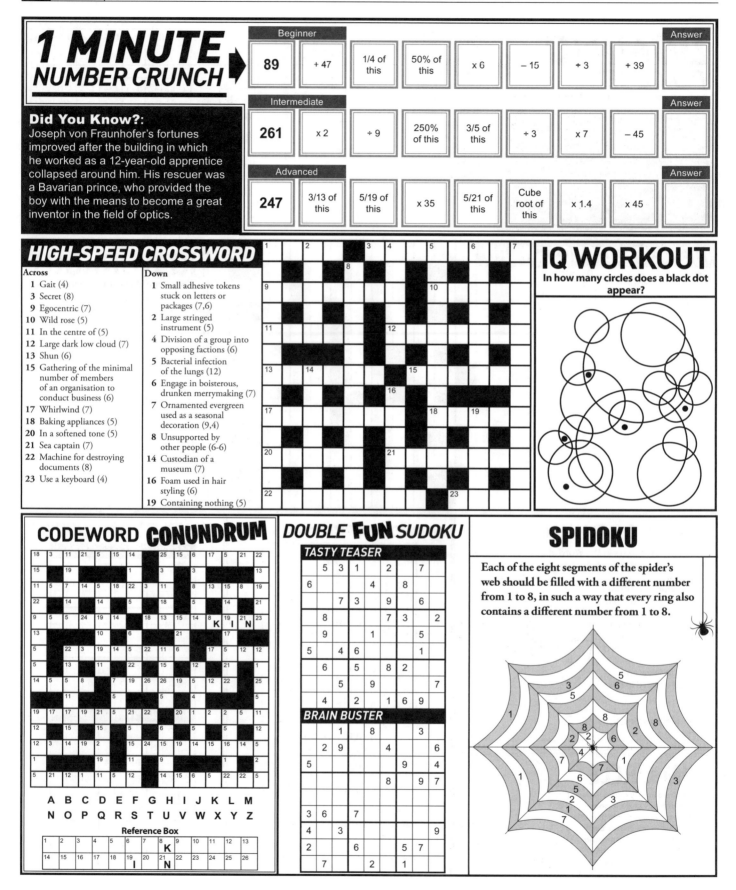

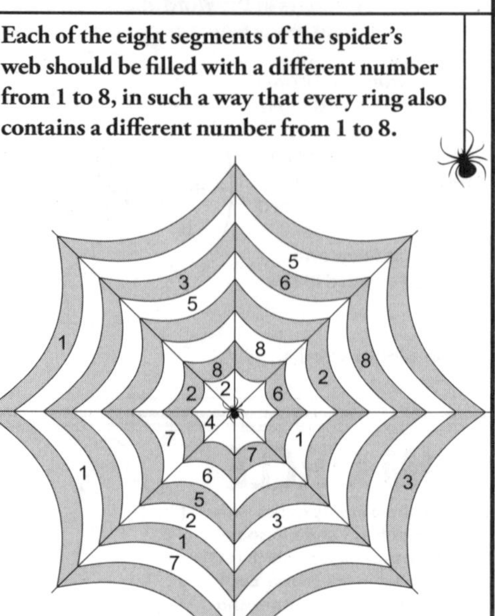

LOGI-SIX

Every row and column of this grid should contain one each of the letters A, B, C, D, E and F. Each of the six shapes (marked by thicker lines) should also contain one each of the letters A, B, C, D, E and F. Can you complete the grid?

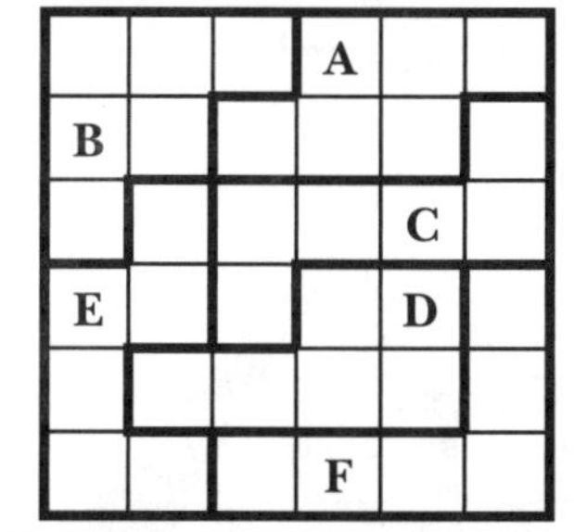

HIGH-SPEED CROSSWORD

Across

1 Fix together (6)
8 Fragrant (8)
9 Strip fixed to something to hold it firm (6)
10 Wagner's flying captain (8)
11 Breed of monkey (6)
12 Watcher (8)
16 Someone who deliberately causes wrecks (8)
18 Remove by cutting out (6)
21 Nuclear-powered submarine (8)
23 Frightened (6)
24 Coniferous plant (4,4)
25 Leave in the lurch (6)

Down

2 Garbage (5)
3 Poker stakes (5)
4 Good-looking (8)
5 Sea vessel (4)
6 Rubs soap all over (7)
7 Become wider (6)
11 Oil platforms (4)
13 Emphasised (8)
14 Hoarfrost (4)
15 Sell illicit products such as drugs or alcohol (7)
17 Middle-Eastern language (6)
19 Category (5)
20 Blaspheme (5)
22 Fat used in cooking (4)

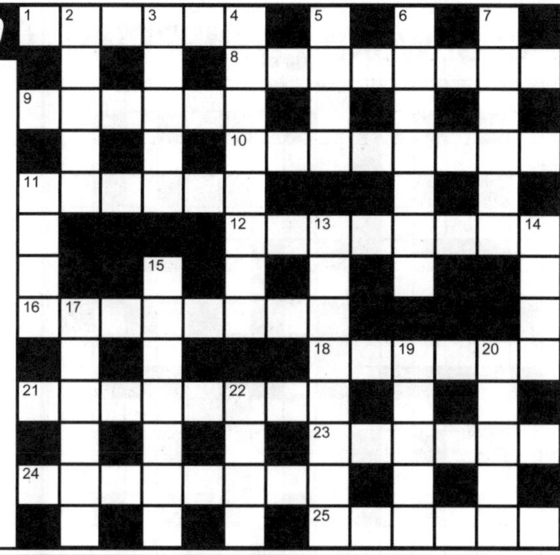

WORDSEARCH WORKOUT

```
D M S U O E G A R U O C L
U I G N I T C A X E P U A
N S G R Y P Y Y U S B C T
C R T I A K M T K J P R Q
O E F N R N Y B V C Z I T
M S T E Z X I T T H O U J
P O T A V E N T S N O R N
R L D U R A B L E T U G R
O U I E M U R E S S K M O
M T V A K O D B E U M P B
I E D T F L I N T Y G L B
S A F F N T L T I L H M U
I V Q P D N O M A I D P T
N K J F A U S T E R E B S
G H R I G O R O U S O J V
```

HARD WORDS

ADAMANT, AUSTERE, BRAVE, COURAGEOUS, DIAMOND, DURABLE, EXACTING, FLINTY, GRANITE, INDURATE, NUMB, RESOLUTE, RIGID, RIGOROUS, ROCKY, SEVERE, SOLID, STOUT, STUBBORN, UNCOMPROMISING

DOUBLE FUN SUDOKU

TASTY TEASER

	7	9					4	3
		3		5			2	6
			8	9		1		5
	6				2			7
	2	1	5		9	3	6	
4			1				8	
3		2		7	8			
6	5			2		4		
8	1					7	9	

BRAIN BUSTER

7			1		4			9
	8		2		6		3	
		5				6		
8		9	6		1	7		5
4		7	3		8	1		2
		2				4		
	7		8		2		9	
3			4		5			6

MATCHSTICK MAGIC

Move two matchsticks to make two squares.

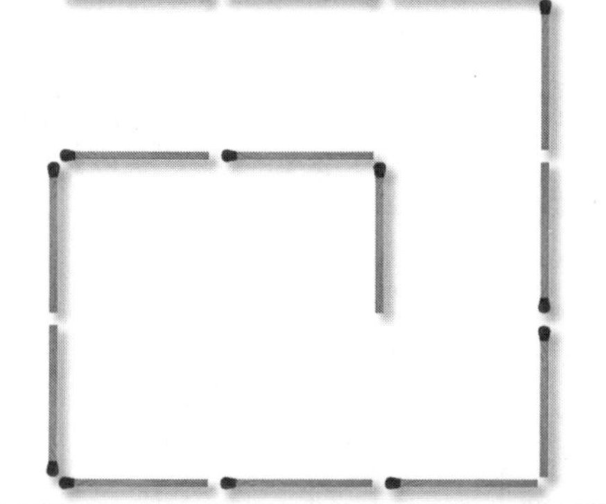

BRAIN TEASER

A B C D E F G H

What letter is two letters to the left of the letter immediately to the right of the letter three letters to the left of the letter three letters to the right of the letter C?

DOMINO PLACEMENT

A standard set of 28 dominoes has been laid out as shown. Can you draw in the edges of them all? The check-box is provided as an aid and the domino already placed will help.

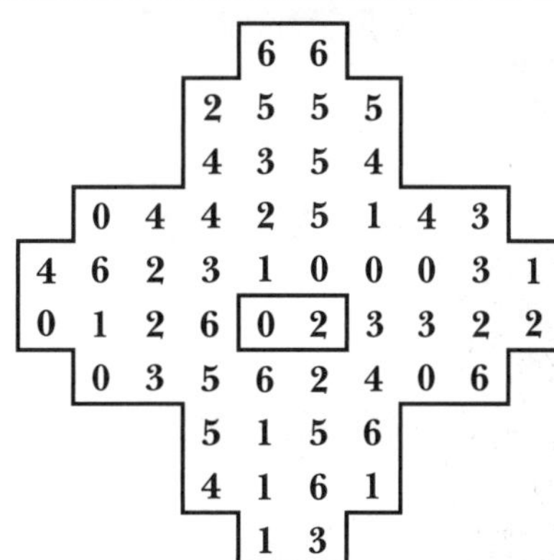

0-0	0-1	0-2	0-3	0-4	0-5	0-6
		✓				

1-1	1-2	1-3	1-4	1-5	1-6	2-2

2-3	2-4	2-5	2-6	3-3	3-4	3-5

3-6	4-4	4-5	4-6	5-5	5-6	6-6

Did You Know?:
More energy is used during the eating and digestion process involved in consuming a stick of celery than is gained from the nutritional value of the celery.

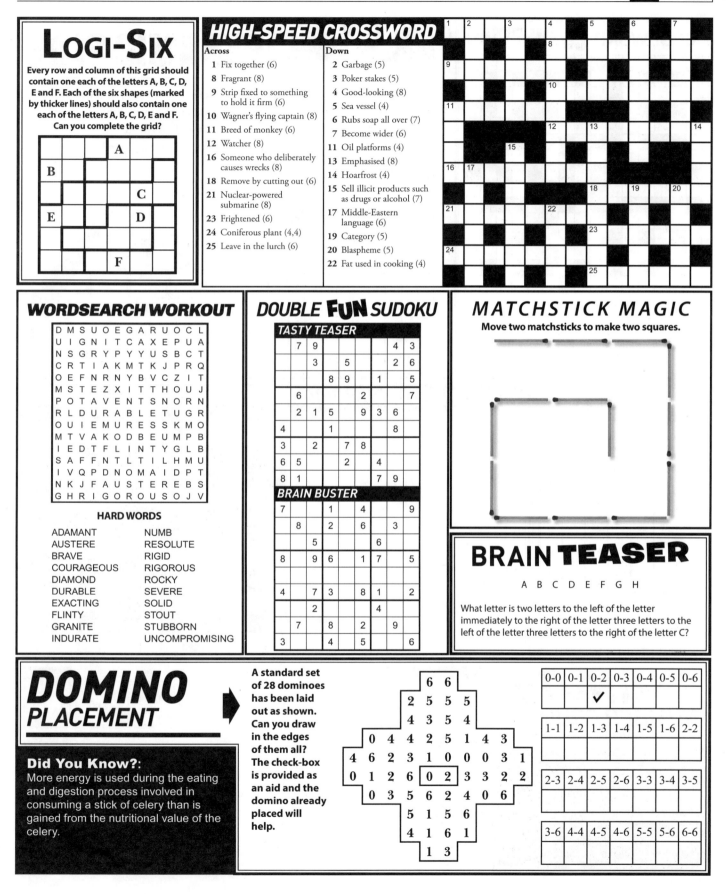

13	21	22	5	8	11		16	25	21	22	2	11	5	8
21		16		11		3		21		16 A		17		11
1	3	19	25	5		8	3	9	5	20 R	17	5	20	21
12		25		5	10	5		20		25 C		12		21
25	17	5	16	9		1	5	16	11	17	11	20	16	9
3				5			22		24				9	
13	16	4	21	20	12	11	2		5	15	15	21	20	11
	20		14		19		8		16		16		21	
23	21	1	12	16	25		12	19	26	8	11	16	19	1
	13				3		16			6				2
4	16	14	14	5	20	12	19	18		3	19	9	12	19
3		16		7		19		5	20	16		20		16
1	12	8	16	9	9	5	16	20		20	3	12	19	8
18		12		5		9		13		5		13		11
5	8	25	16	22	16	11	5		12	1	12	21	25	2

A B C D E F G H I J K L M

N O P Q R S T U V W X Y Z

Reference Box

1	2	3	4	5	6	7	8	9	10	11	12	13
14	15	16 A	17	18	19	20 R	21	22	23	24	25 C	26

DOUBLE FUN SUDOKU

TASTY TEASER

		2		4		1		
3		4	1			5		6
	6	1			7	9	4	
7	1			2	8			
	3						5	
			3	6			9	1
	8	3	5			4	7	
2		9			4	6		8
		7		9		2		

BRAIN BUSTER

				6		9	8	
5			1					
		6		5	8		2	
			4					7
	8			2			6	
3					5			
	7		9	4		1		
					3			4
	9	2		8				

PYRAMID PLUS

Every brick in this pyramid contains a number which is the sum of the two numbers below it, so that F=A+B, etc. Just work out the missing numbers!

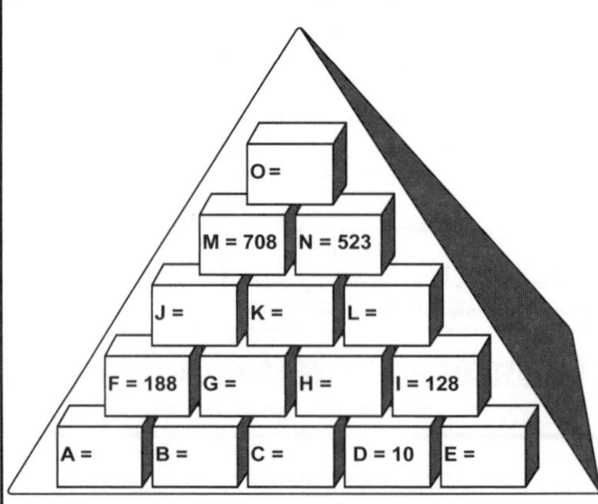

WORK IT OUT

In the grid below, what number should replace the question mark?

13	18	10	15	7	12	4
41	49	44	52	47	55	50
32	37	29	34	26	31	23
29	37	32	40	35	43	38
19	24	16	21	13	18	10
19	27	22	30	25	33	28
?	46	38	43	35	40	32

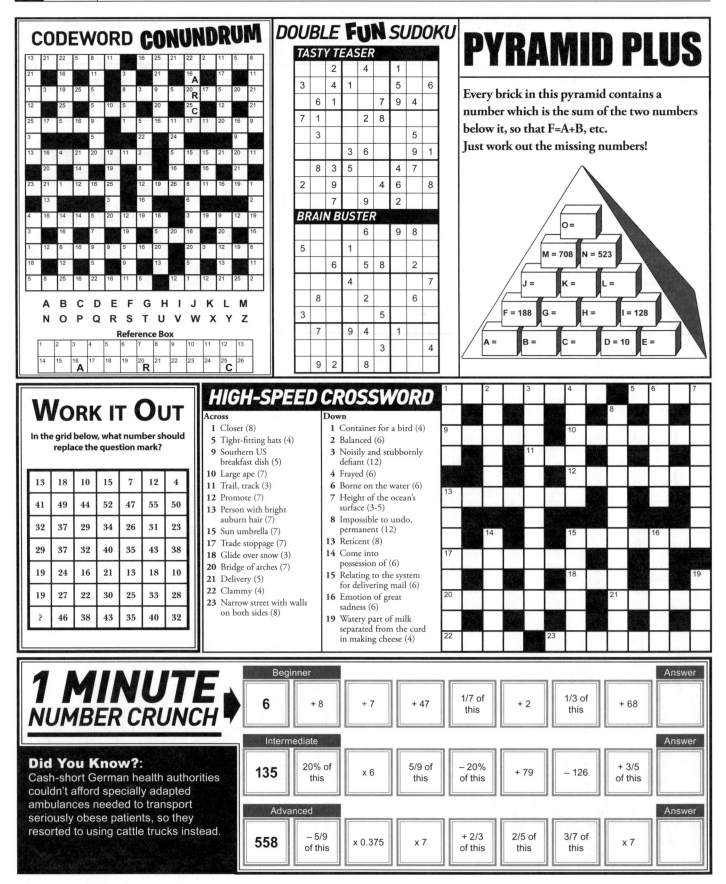

HIGH-SPEED CROSSWORD

Across

1 Closet (8)
5 Tight-fitting hats (4)
9 Southern US breakfast dish (5)
10 Large ape (7)
11 Trail, track (3)
12 Promote (7)
13 Person with bright auburn hair (7)
15 Sun umbrella (7)
17 Trade stoppage (7)
18 Glide over snow (3)
20 Bridge of arches (7)
21 Delivery (5)
22 Clammy (4)
23 Narrow street with walls on both sides (8)

Down

1 Container for a bird (4)
2 Balanced (6)
3 Noisily and stubbornly defiant (12)
4 Frayed (6)
6 Borne on the water (6)
7 Height of the ocean's surface (3-5)
8 Impossible to undo, permanent (12)
13 Reticent (8)
14 Come into possession of (6)
15 Relating to the system for delivering mail (6)
16 Emotion of great sadness (6)
19 Watery part of milk separated from the curd in making cheese (4)

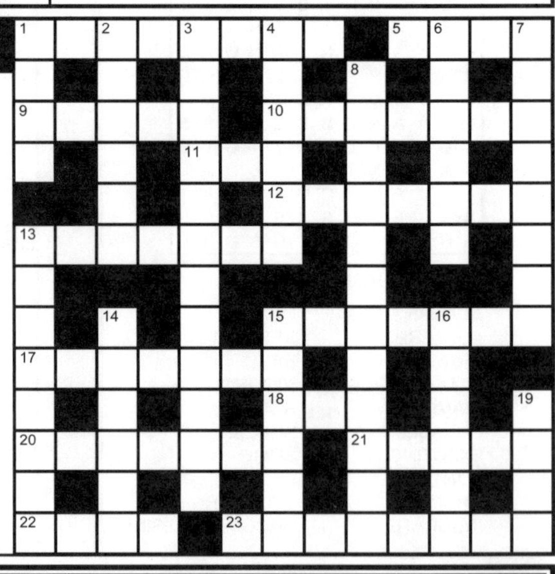

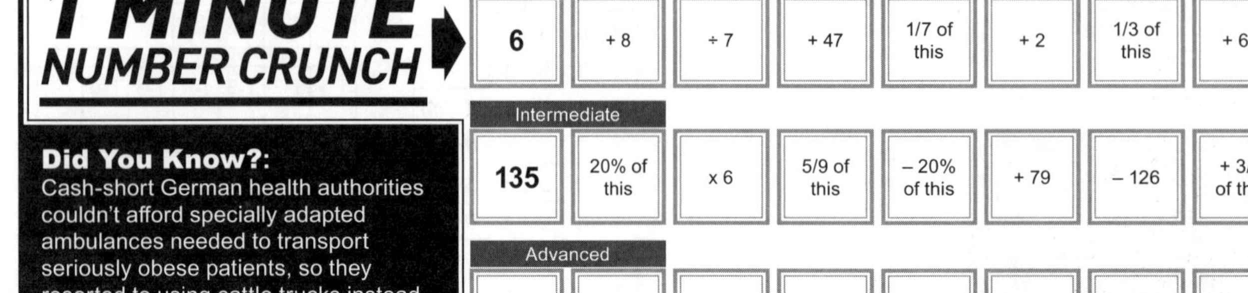

1 MINUTE NUMBER CRUNCH
Beginner
6
+ 8
÷ 7
+ 47
1/7 of this
+ 2
1/3 of this
+ 68
Answer
Intermediate
135
20% of this
x 6
5/9 of this
– 20% of this
+ 79
– 126
+ 3/5 of this
Answer
Advanced
558
– 5/9 of this
x 0.375
x 7
+ 2/3 of this
2/5 of this
3/7 of this
x 7
Answer

Did You Know?:
Cash-short German health authorities couldn't afford specially adapted ambulances needed to transport seriously obese patients, so they resorted to using cattle trucks instead.

HIGH-SPEED CROSSWORD

Across

4 Compositor (6)
6 Observe with care (4,4)
7 Roof in the form of a dome (6)
9 Blackthorn fruit (4)
10 Feverish cold (abbr) (3)
11 Britain's only native venomous snake (5)
12 Send out or emit (7)
15 Most desirable possible under a restriction (7)
17 Banter (5)
20 Auction item (3)
21 Hardwood (4)
22 Disarrange or rumple (6)
23 Drink made of wine mixed with sparkling water (8)
24 Cuts into two equal pieces (6)

Down

1 Posted, sent (6)
2 Harmful to living things (11)
3 Protective coverings of buildings (5)
4 Concerning those who are not members of the clergy (7)
5 Join the military (6)
8 Country that maintains repressive control over the people by means of secret forces (6,5)
11 Flurry (3)
13 Female sheep (3)
14 Pitiable (7)
16 Asian temple (6)
18 Electric razor (6)
19 Retail establishment (5)

IQ WORKOUT

Draw in the hands on the final clock.

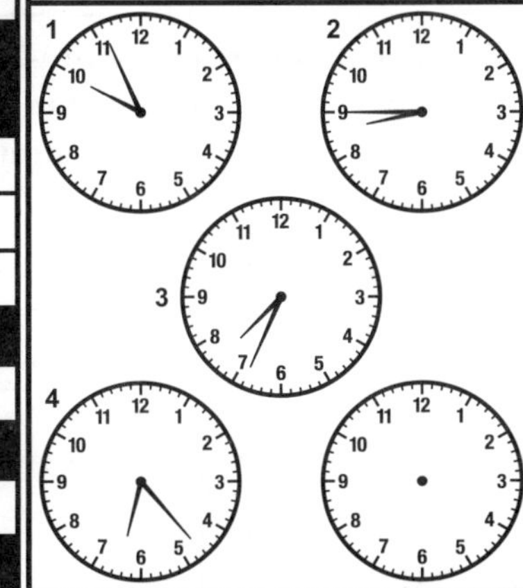

Beginner								**Answer**
15	x 3	1/9 of this	+ 49	1/9 of this	Squared	+ 20	1/4 of this	
Intermediate								**Answer**
26	x 8	3/4 of this	÷ 3	x 12	5/8 of this	3/10 of this	÷ 9	
Advanced								**Answer**
1369	Square root of this	x 11	+ 2047	1/2 of this	+ 2/3 of this	3/5 of this	÷ 3	

Did You Know?:
Pigeons will not perch on an item that contains the metal, gallium. Researchers are looking into spraying statues, etc, with a gallium-based solution to stop the birds fouling them.

WORDSEARCH WORKOUT

R	O	L	C	I	T	A	M	O	T	U	A	X
Q	T	A	N	A	L	O	G	U	E	E	E	X
D	I	G	I	T	A	L	I	J	P	V	B	J
D	H	Q	H	C	T	A	W	T	S	I	R	W
I	N	C	H	U	B	T	B	P	D	D	A	T
N	N	I	T	V	N	P	T	R	G	U	C	E
N	O	I	B	A	T	T	E	R	Y	Z	E	K
W	J	T	A	F	W	V	E	N	P	T	L	C
F	E	E	E	H	E	G	T	R	D	R	E	O
X	O	A	K	L	C	Q	N	J	O	A	T	P
R	W	B	V	X	E	Z	F	I	H	U	N	W
K	A	T	R	J	M	K	H	C	R	Q	T	T
K	I	N	E	T	I	C	S	E	S	R	U	N
C	H	R	O	N	O	G	R	A	P	H	P	R
Y	Q	R	E	P	E	A	T	I	N	G	A	A

WATCHES

ANALOGUE
AUTOMATIC
BATTERY
BRACELET
CHAIN
CHRONOGRAPH
DIGITAL
DIVE
FOB
HUNTER
KINETIC
LEVER
NURSE'S
PENDANT
POCKET
QUARTZ
REPEATING
RING WATCH
SKELETON
WRISTWATCH

DOUBLE FUN SUDOKU

TASTY TEASER

8	7	3				9	6	5
1			5	8				4
		6	7			8		
2					8	5		
	3		6		4		9	
		9	1					7
		1			5	4		
7				2	3			9
9	6	4				2	5	3

BRAIN BUSTER

	2	4	6			3		
		6					5	8
7			9				2	
	9		7					
2								1
					1		4	
	7				5			6
8	3					5		
		5			7	4	9	

WHATEVER NEXT?

In the diagram below, which number should replace the question mark?

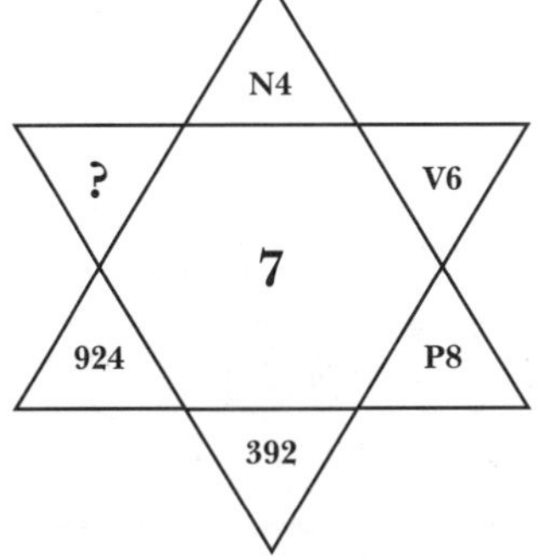

BRAIN TEASER

What number should replace the question mark?

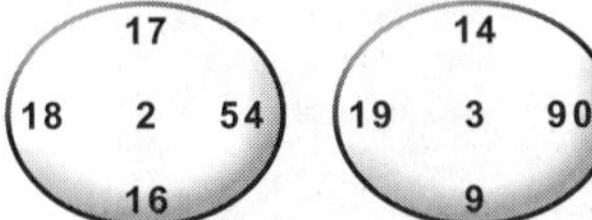

Mind Over Matter

Given that the letters are valued 1-26 according to their places in the alphabet, can you crack the mystery code to reveal the missing letter?

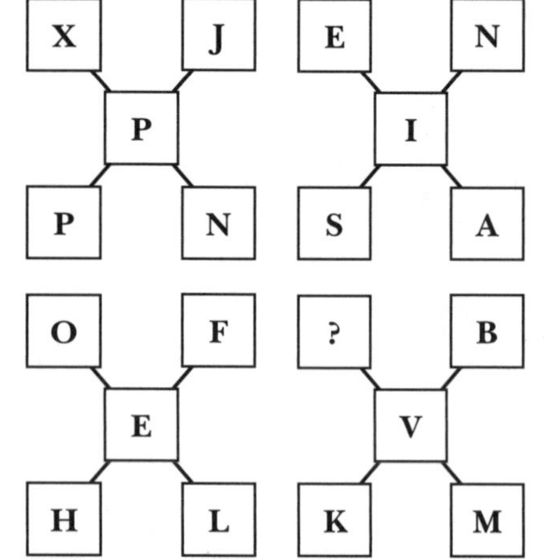

DOUBLE FUN SUDOKU

TASTY TEASER

7					2			
		4	9	5		3		1
	6	9		1		8	4	
	9		4			2	5	8
	1						3	
4	7	8			5		9	
	5	6		3		7	8	
9		2		8	7	6		
			1					5

BRAIN BUSTER

	1		8		5		7	
				4				
		8	7		1	3		
	9	1	5		2	4	6	
4				3				2
	2	7	4		6	1	3	
		9	2		7	6		
				9				
	5		6		8		2	

CODEWORD CONUNDRUM

14	26	20	20	15	13	■	15	18	13	4	19	6	21	1
25	■	■	1	■	11	■	■	25	■	15	■	25	■	11
21	26	6	26	21	18	17	16 S	14	■	5	■	6	■	14
25	■	■	24	■	20	■	26 A	20	20	18	26	25	16	15
16	18	19	6	■	1	25	10 G	■	■	15	■	■	■	10
■	15	■	11	■	19	■	11	24	17	8	■	12	■	4
16	6	26	14	19	24	26	■	11	■	19	14	26	10	11
26	■	22	■	24	■	3	26	4	■	9	■	7	■	23
5	18	25	2	15	■	15	■	14	25	15	7	7	19	24
15	■	26	■	5	15	6	26	■	24	■	15	■	4	■
10	■	■	■	5	■	■	18	19	6	■	11	26	2	16
25	20	1	15	26	9	26	18	■	4	■	18	■	■	19
26	■	19	■	3	■	18	17	4	19	21	19	16	6	16
4	■	16	■	18	■	11	■	■	15	■	6	■	■	26
13	19	16	1	15	9	15	18	■	13	19	15	16	15	18

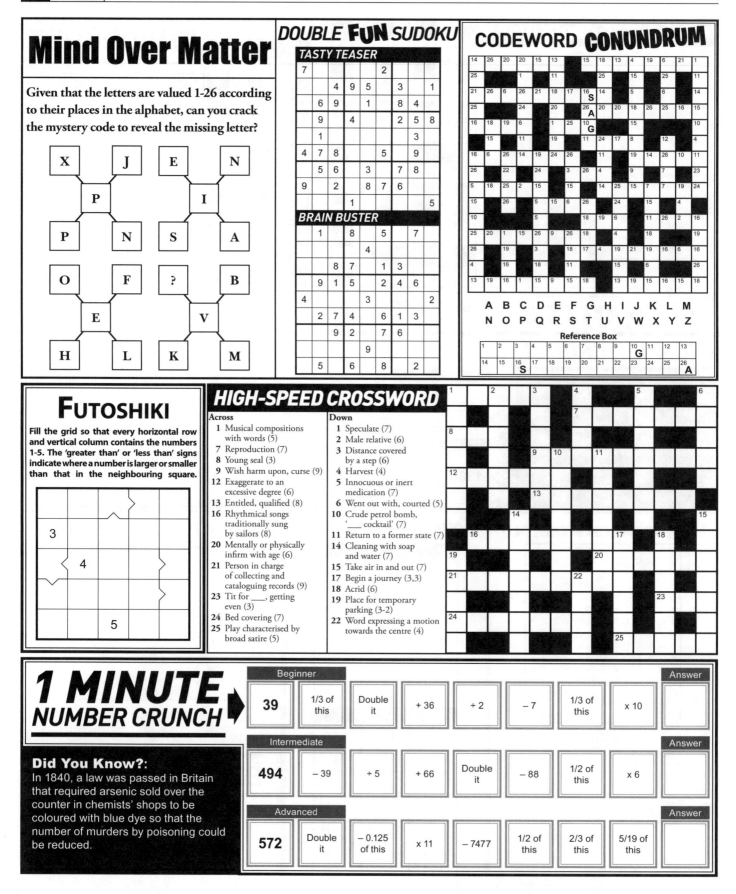

A B C D E F G H I J K L M

N O P Q R S T U V W X Y Z

Reference Box

1	2	3	4	5	6	7	8	9	10	11	12	13
									G			
14	**15**	**16**	**17**	**18**	**19**	**20**	**21**	**22**	**23**	**24**	**25**	**26**
		S										A

FUTOSHIKI

Fill the grid so that every horizontal row and vertical column contains the numbers 1-5. The 'greater than' or 'less than' signs indicate where a number is larger or smaller than that in the neighbouring square.

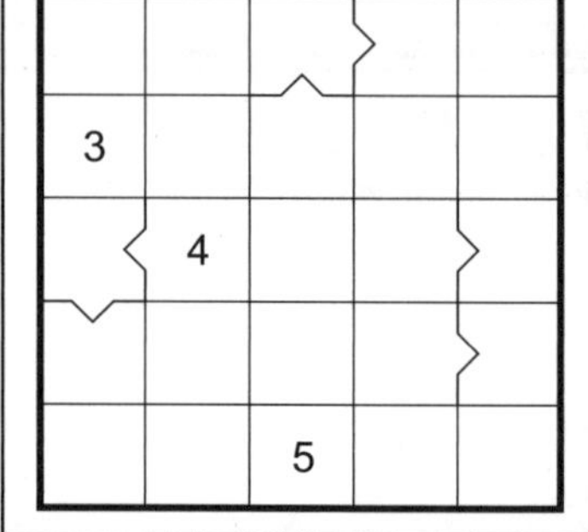

HIGH-SPEED CROSSWORD

Across

1 Musical compositions with words (5)
7 Reproduction (7)
8 Young seal (3)
9 Wish harm upon, curse (9)
12 Exaggerate to an excessive degree (6)
13 Entitled, qualified (8)
16 Rhythmical songs traditionally sung by sailors (8)
20 Mentally or physically infirm with age (6)
21 Person in charge of collecting and cataloguing records (9)
23 Tit for ___, getting even (3)
24 Bed covering (7)
25 Play characterised by broad satire (5)

Down

1 Speculate (7)
2 Male relative (6)
3 Distance covered by a step (6)
4 Harvest (4)
5 Innocuous or inert medication (7)
6 Went out with, courted (5)
10 Crude petrol bomb, '___ cocktail' (7)
11 Return to a former state (7)
14 Cleaning with soap and water (7)
15 Take air in and out (7)
17 Begin a journey (3,3)
18 Acrid (6)
19 Place for temporary parking (3-2)
22 Word expressing a motion towards the centre (4)

1 MINUTE NUMBER CRUNCH

									Answer
Beginner	39	1/3 of this	Double it	+ 36	÷ 2	– 7	1/3 of this	x 10	
Intermediate	494	– 39	÷ 5	+ 66	Double it	– 88	1/2 of this	x 6	
Advanced	572	Double it	– 0.125 of this	x 11	– 7477	1/2 of this	2/3 of this	5/19 of this	

Did You Know?:
In 1840, a law was passed in Britain that required arsenic sold over the counter in chemists' shops to be coloured with blue dye so that the number of murders by poisoning could be reduced.

BATTLESHIP BOUT

Did You Know?:
Almost half of the bones in the human body are contained in the hands and feet. One person in twenty has an extra pair of ribs: the superfluous bones may cause problems and can be removed by surgery.

Can you place the vessels into the diagram? Some parts of vessels or sea squares have already been filled in. A number to the right or below a row or column refers to the number of occupied squares in that row or column.
Any vessel may be positioned horizontally or vertically, but no part of a vessel touches part of any other vessel, either horizontally, vertically or diagonally.

Empty Area of Sea:
Aircraft Carrier:
Battleships:
Cruisers:
Submarines:

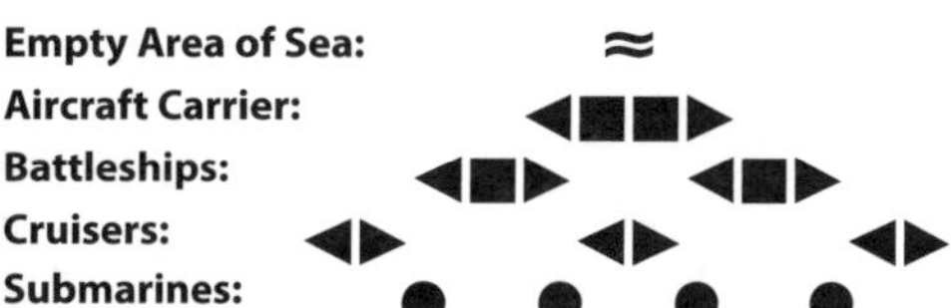

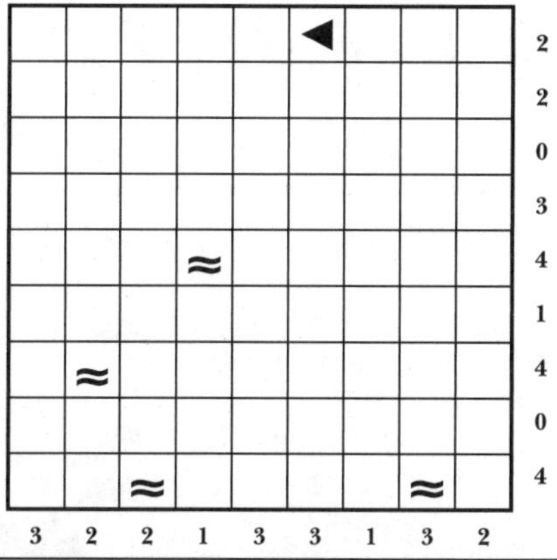

HIGH-SPEED CROSSWORD

Across
1 Person of exceptional importance and reputation (8)
7 Maddened (6)
8 Seventh letter of the Greek alphabet (3)
9 Disorderly fighting (6)
11 Diminish (6)
12 Burdened (5)
14 Confiscate (7)
17 Bride-to-be (7)
18 Gives a clue (5)
21 Colourful flowering plant (6)
23 Dry gully (6)
25 Animal doctor (3)
26 Tiny Japanese tree (6)
27 Upright (8)

Down
1 Consortium of companies formed to limit competition (6)
2 Prunes (4)
3 Clean with a broom (5)
4 Edible marine mollusc with a fan-shaped shell (7)
5 Divisions of a week (4)
6 ___ XVI, the Pope (8)
10 Coil of knitting wool (5)
13 Technician who produces moving cartoons (8)
15 Male member of a religious order (5)
16 City in western Israel (3,4)
19 Hand tool for lifting loose material (6)
20 Forest god (5)
22 Erotic desire (4)
24 Of or relating to the ear (4)

1		2			3		4	■	5	■	6	■
	■		■	■		■	7					
	■		■	■	8			■		■		■
9			10			■	11					
	■	■		■		■		■	■	■		■
12	13				■	14			15			
■		■		■	16	■		■		■		■
17							■	18				19
■		■	■	■		■	20	■		■	■	
21			22			■	23			24		
■		■		■	25			■	■		■	
26						■		■	■		■	
■		■		■	27							

IQ WORKOUT

What number should replace the question mark?

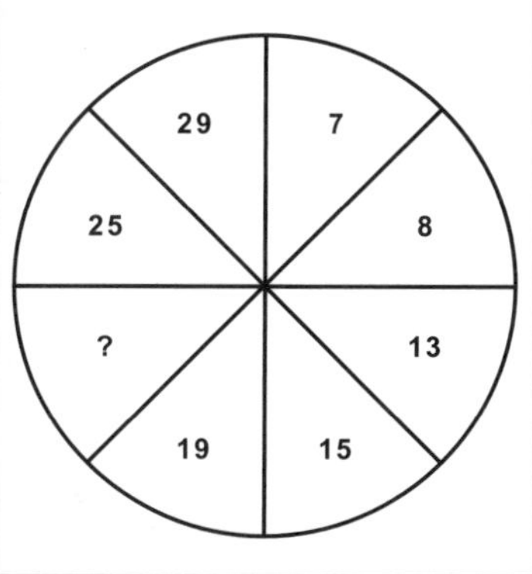

WORDWHEEL

Using only the letters in the Wordwheel, you have ten minutes to find as many words as possible, none of which may be plurals, foreign words or proper nouns. Each word must be of three letters or more, all must contain the central letter and letters can only be used once in every word. There is at least one nine-letter word in the wheel.

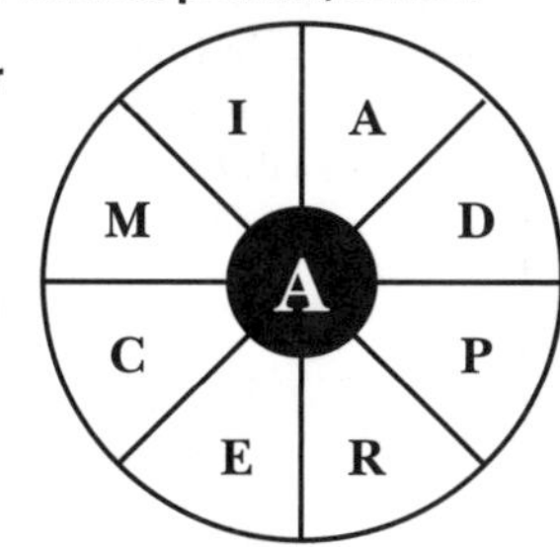

Nine-letter word(s):

SUM CIRCLE

Fill the three empty circles with the symbols +, – and x in some order, to make a sum which totals the number in the centre. Each symbol must be used once and calculations are made in the direction of travel (clockwise).

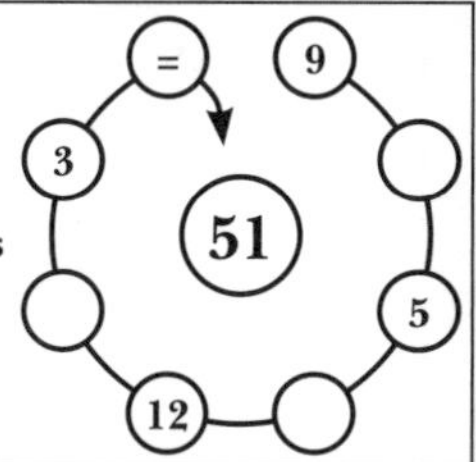

WORDSEARCH WORKOUT

N	E	V	R	K	Q	V	E	A	J	A	X	L
A	E	L	N	S	S	E	S	E	R	D	G	H
I	B	E	Z	T	D	N	R	E	E	D	J	B
I	B	E	T	W	E	E	N	R	E	R	M	A
S	I	T	R	H	L	E	G	F	S	E	F	T
D	W	N	F	D	G	R	P	E	R	S	O	T
E	G	E	D	Z	E	I	Z	R	E	S	R	E
P	E	G	D	E	C	E	E	A	V	E	E	N
R	E	E	N	B	V	J	N	C	O	E	S	D
E	E	E	E	L	E	G	A	T	E	E	E	E
S	R	D	R	L	P	S	E	T	T	E	E	E
S	F	C	E	G	E	M	E	B	K	U	C	C
E	J	Z	N	E	E	M	X	E	J	Y	S	A
D	V	K	Q	U	M	D	Q	Z	C	C	X	E
B	O	A	B	S	E	N	T	E	E	H	G	Y

THREE ES

ABERDEEN
ABSENTEE
ADDRESSEE
ATTENDEE
BESEECH
BETWEEN
CAREFREE
DEGREE
DEPRESSED
EERIE
EIGHTEEN
FORESEE
GENTEEL
GREENER
LEGATEE
MELEE
OVERSEER
REDEEM
SETTEE
VENEER

DOUBLE FUN SUDOKU

TASTY TEASER

5			2		9	3		
		3			6	2		8
6		1		8	4			
	4		6	1			8	
	9	2				6	1	
	1			4	2		7	
			7	6		1		5
2		8	5			4		
		7	4		3			6

BRAIN BUSTER

	5						2	
		7	2		6	5		
8			3		5			4
	8	4	9		2	6	1	
	2	6	1		7	9	8	
6			5		9			1
		1	4		8	3		
	3						7	

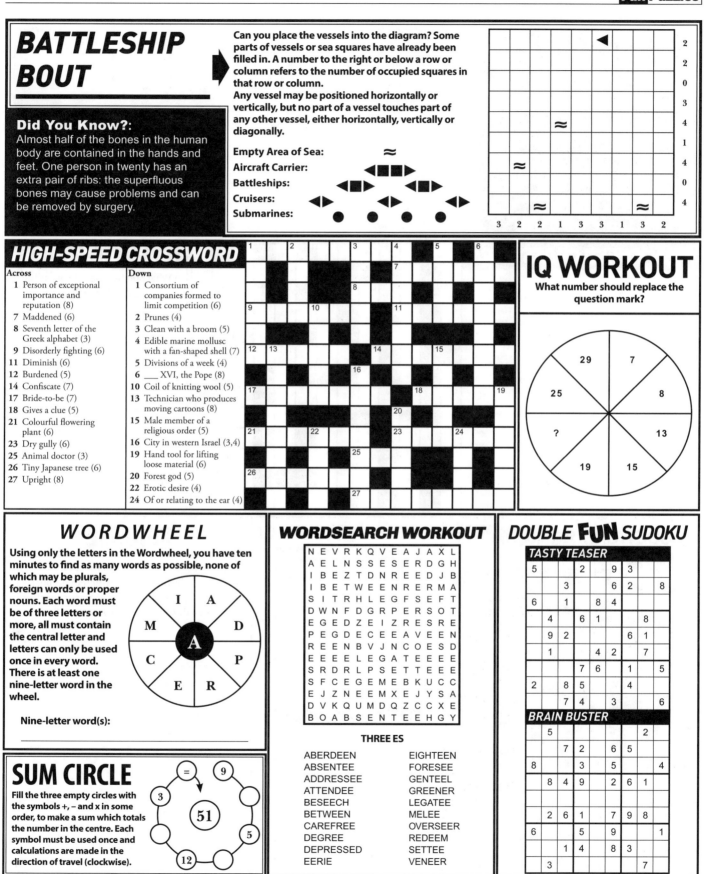

1 MINUTE NUMBER CRUNCH

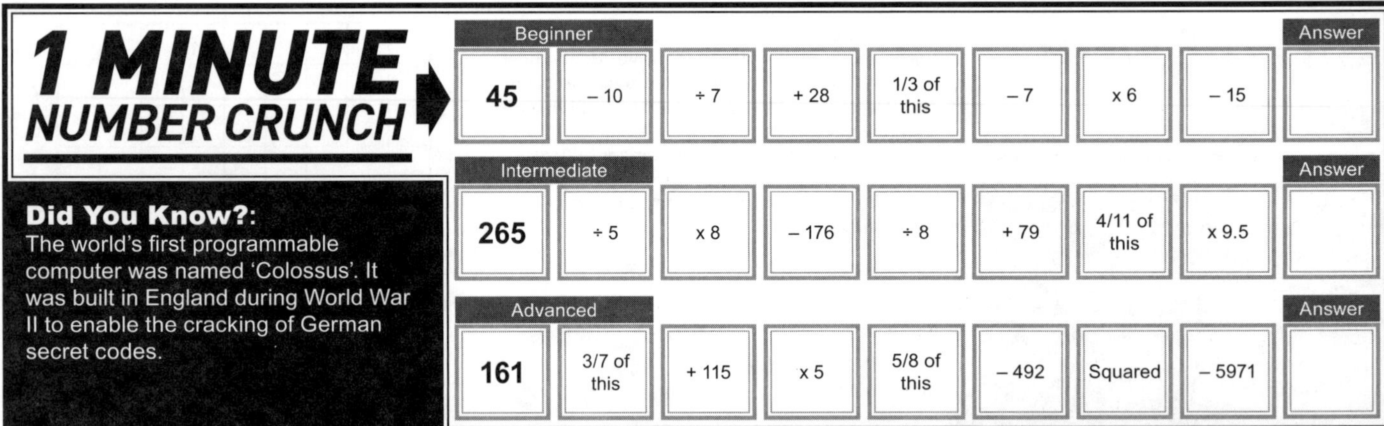

Beginner								Answer
45	– 10	÷ 7	+ 28	1/3 of this	– 7	x 6	– 15	

Intermediate								Answer
265	÷ 5	x 8	– 176	÷ 8	+ 79	4/11 of this	x 9.5	

Advanced								Answer
161	3/7 of this	+ 115	x 5	5/8 of this	– 492	Squared	– 5971	

Did You Know?: The world's first programmable computer was named 'Colossus'. It was built in England during World War II to enable the cracking of German secret codes.

HIGH-SPEED CROSSWORD

Across

1 Country, capital Minsk (7)
7 Stoppage (7)
8 Deep yellow colour (5)
10 Inspiring admiration or wonder (7)
12 Smile affectedly or derisively (5)
13 Chronic drinker (9)
17 Incite (9)
20 Civil and religious leader of a Muslim state (5)
22 Lockjaw (7)
25 With the extremity facing the observer (3,2)
26 Get over an illness (7)
27 Casual tops (1-6)

Down

1 Seizes with the teeth (5)
2 Natural inclinations (8)
3 Scratch (6)
4 Was dressed in (4)
5 Anise-flavoured Greek liqueur (4)
6 Official who is expected to ensure fair play (7)
9 Bathing costume (6)
11 ___ Lanka (3)
14 Stank (6)
15 Commercial passenger plane (8)
16 Marsh bird of the heron family (7)
18 Beverage (3)
19 Declare (6)
21 Notable achievements (5)
23 Equipment for a horse (4)
24 Body of a church (4)

IQ WORKOUT

What number should replace the question mark?

3
4 9 6
2 3 6 9 4
3 ? 4 9 6 3 2

CODEWORD CONUNDRUM

DOUBLE FUN SUDOKU

TASTY TEASER

8			4		2			3
		3		7		5		
	7	6		9		2	8	
	2	9	8		1	4	7	
1			7		5			2
	5	7	2		9	3	1	
	6	1		5		8	2	
		4		2		1		
7			1		4			6

BRAIN BUSTER

7	9				4		8	
2	8						5	
				5	7			2
3					5			
9		8				5		1
			4					8
6			2	7				
	5						7	4
	3		5				1	9

SPIDOKU

Each of the eight segments of the spider's web should be filled with a different number from 1 to 8, in such a way that every ring also contains a different number from 1 to 8.

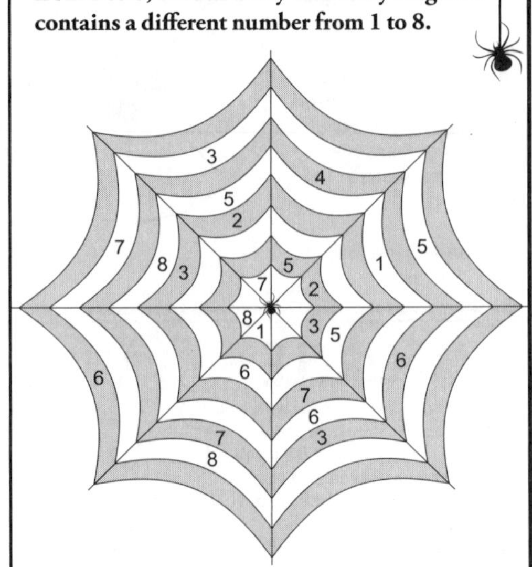

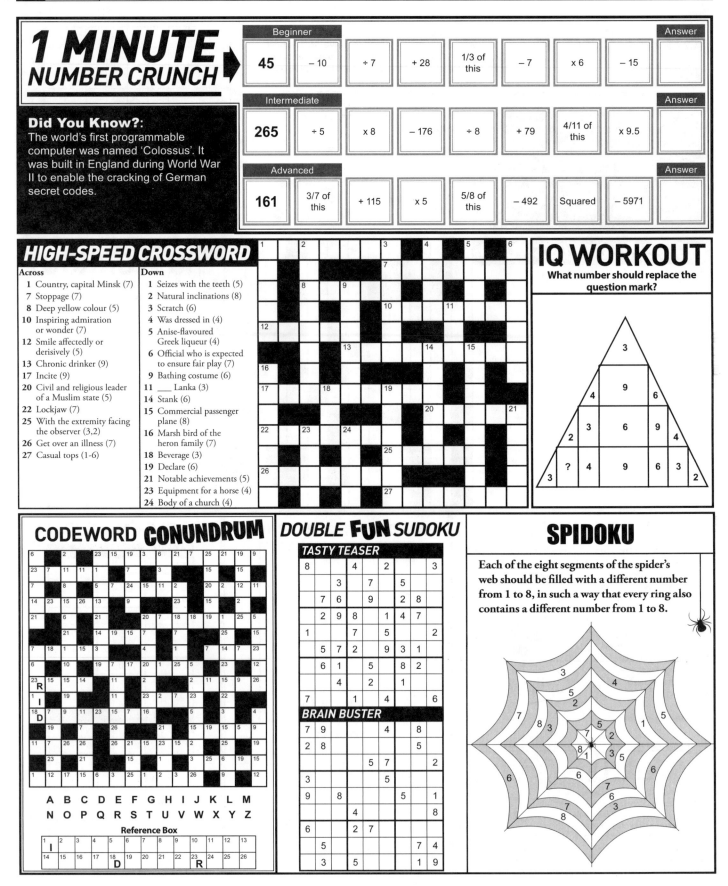

LOGI-SIX

Every row and column of this grid should contain one each of the letters A, B, C, D, E and F. Each of the six shapes (marked by thicker lines) should also contain one each of the letters A, B, C, D, E and F. Can you complete the grid?

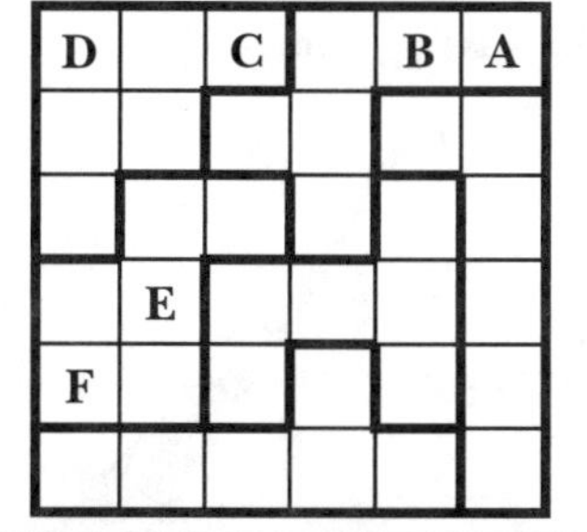

HIGH-SPEED CROSSWORD

Across

1 Spring that discharges hot water and steam (6)
5 Blueprint (6)
8 Part of the eye (6)
10 Building for housing horses (6)
11 Measure of gold's purity (5)
12 Higher in position (5)
14 Comfortable room in a pub (6,3)
17 Gradual increase in volume (9)
19 Legerdemain (5)
22 Strongboxes for valuables (5)
24 In operation (6)
25 Deer horn (6)
26 Pincers (6)
27 One who voluntarily suffers death (6)

Down

2 Outermost atmospheric layer (9)
3 From that time (5)
4 Back end (4)
5 Meant (8)
6 Surgeon's knife (7)
7 Christmas (4)
9 British nobleman (4)
13 Working parts of an engine (9)
15 In a foreign country (8)
16 Title of respect placed after a man's name (7)
18 Portent (4)
20 On the move (5)
21 Distort, buckle (4)
23 Cultivated land as a unit (4)

WORDSEARCH WORKOUT

```
T A M E C A L P K F S W T
C L J R L B K X E L O A C
N A N G E D O V T O U T F
D D R O R P A V C W P E X
E E I V O A P L H E B R C
S S W D I P V E U R O J O
S S I D S N S Y P S W U L
E E N Q S I G A B T L G A
R R E T A K B D E O H K Z
T T B U L P C R I T A A Y
P B O R G A B A U S G T S
L O T E E N I T P A H F U
A W T E N A R S C O O S S
T L L N I M D U P R N G A
E V E N W P H M K A Z Q N
```

SETTING A TABLE

BREAD
CARVING DISH
DESSERT BOWL
DESSERT PLATE
FLOWERS
FORK
GRAVY BOAT
KETCHUP
LADLE
LAZY SUSAN
MUSTARD
NAPKIN
PEPPER
PLACE MAT
SOUP BOWL
TEASPOON
TUREEN
WATER JUG
WINE BOTTLE
WINE GLASS

DOUBLE FUN SUDOKU

TASTY TEASER

4			3					6
		1	2	8		9		
6	5	9				2	3	8
9					4	1		
	2		6		5		9	
		8	7					3
2	1	7				3	5	9
		4		7	3	6		
5					1			7

BRAIN BUSTER

	1						3	
		2	9		1	8		
4			7		6			5
3	5		1		7		4	8
9	7		2		8		5	6
1			6		3			2
		4	8		9	5		
	6						9	

MATCHSTICK MAGIC

Move one matchstick to make this sum correct.

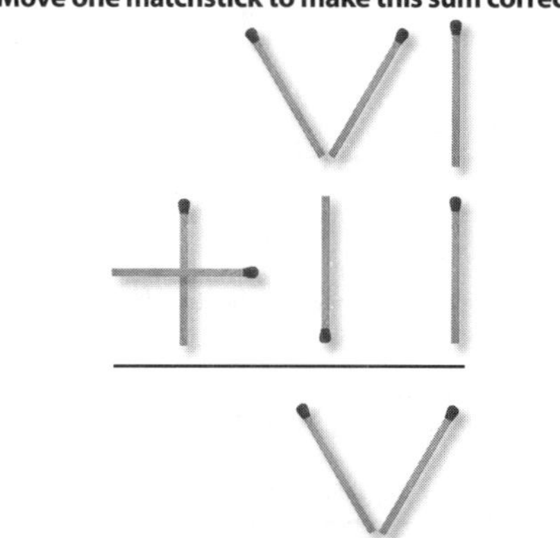

BRAIN TEASER

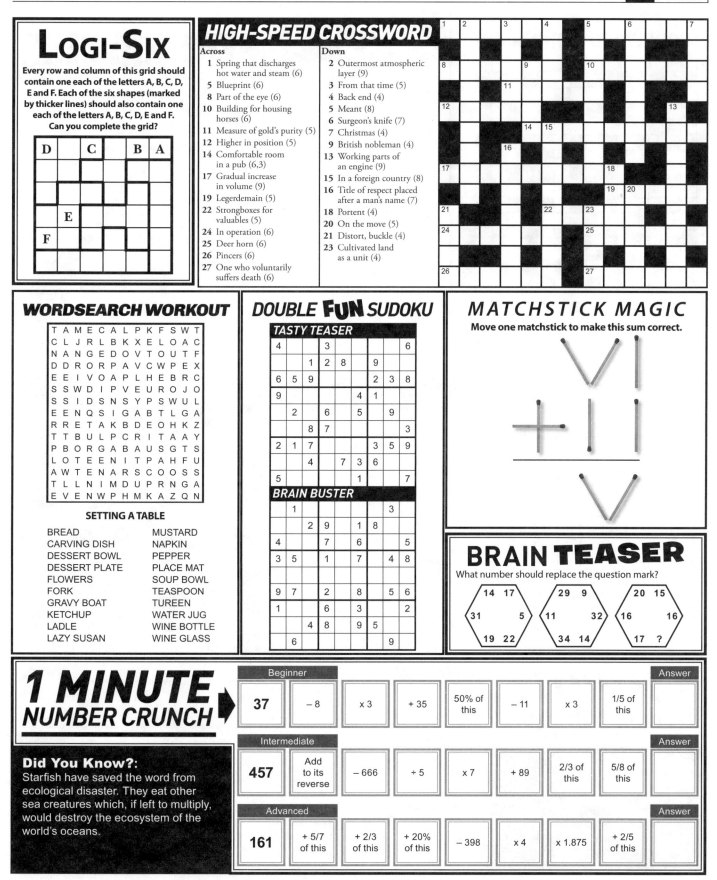

What number should replace the question mark?

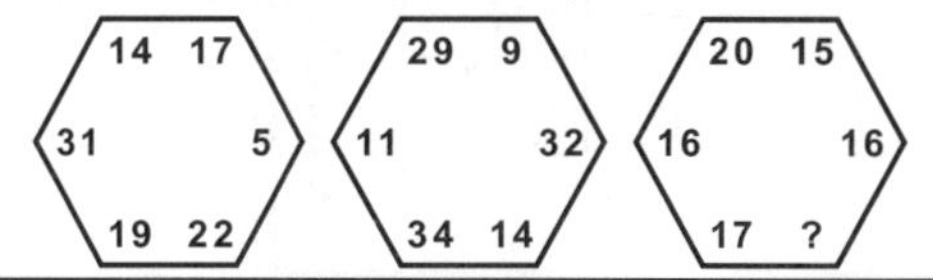

1 MINUTE NUMBER CRUNCH

Beginner								Answer
37	– 8	x 3	+ 35	50% of this	– 11	x 3	1/5 of this	

Intermediate								Answer
457	Add to its reverse	– 666	÷ 5	x 7	+ 89	2/3 of this	5/8 of this	

Advanced								Answer
161	+ 5/7 of this	+ 2/3 of this	+ 20% of this	– 398	x 4	x 1.875	+ 2/5 of this	

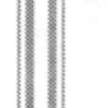

Did You Know?:
Starfish have saved the word from ecological disaster. They eat other sea creatures which, if left to multiply, would destroy the ecosystem of the world's oceans.

CODEWORD CONUNDRUM

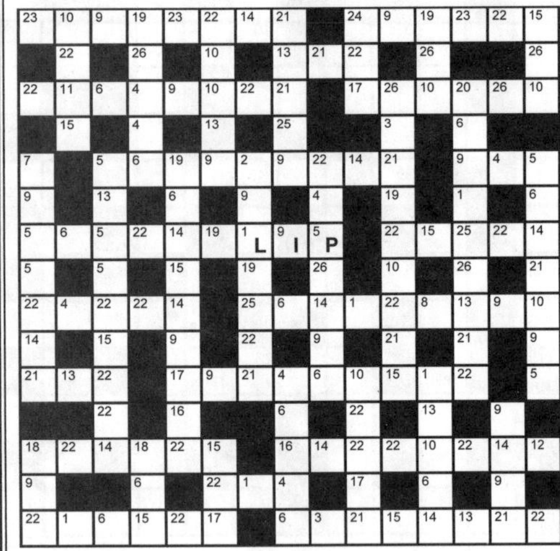

A B C D E F G H I J K L M
N O P Q R S T U V W X Y Z

Reference Box

1 L	2	3	4	5 P	6	7	8	9 I	10	11	12	13
14	15	16	17	18	19	20	21	22	23	24	25	26

DOUBLE FUN SUDOKU

TASTY TEASER

		3	9	6	2			
		5	7		8			
		8		4		3	9	7
	3		5		4			2
	6	7				1	4	
5			6		7		3	
1	9	2		5		8		
			2		1	4		
			3	8	9	2		

BRAIN BUSTER

					1			8
			7	2				3
3	1	9		6				4
	7					3		
5		6				2		1
		3					8	
4				8		9	5	7
7				4	3			
6			5					

PYRAMID PLUS

Every brick in this pyramid contains a number which is the sum of the two numbers below it, so that F=A+B, etc. Just work out the missing numbers!

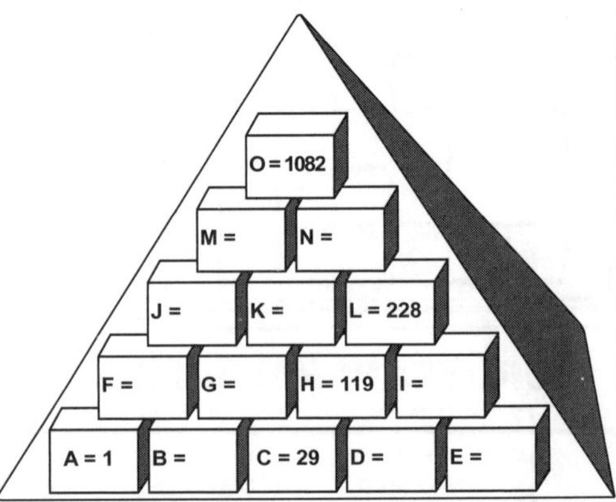

WORK IT OUT

In the grid below, what number should replace the question mark?

6	11	2	4	9	5	7
24	44	8	16	36	20	28
20	40	4	12	32	16	24
100	200	20	60	?	80	120
95	195	15	55	155	75	115
570	1170	90	330	930	450	690
564	1164	84	324	924	444	684

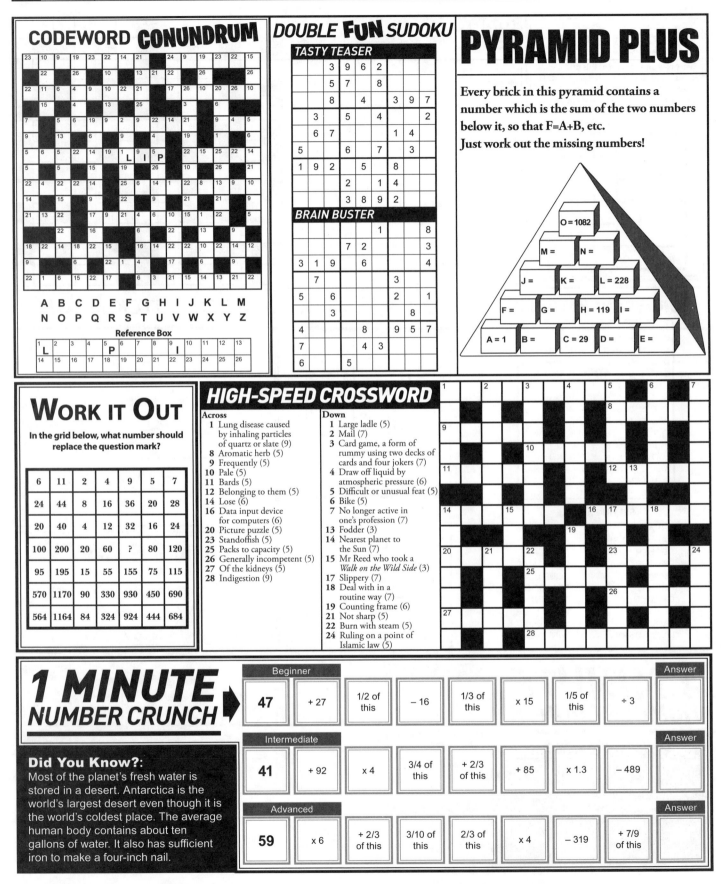

HIGH-SPEED CROSSWORD

Across

1 Lung disease caused by inhaling particles of quartz or slate (9)
8 Aromatic herb (5)
9 Frequently (5)
10 Pale (5)
11 Bards (5)
12 Belonging to them (5)
14 Lose (6)
16 Data input device for computers (6)
20 Picture puzzle (5)
23 Standoffish (5)
25 Packs to capacity (5)
26 Generally incompetent (5)
27 Of the kidneys (5)
28 Indigestion (9)

Down

1 Large ladle (5)
2 Mail (7)
3 Card game, a form of rummy using two decks of cards and four jokers (7)
4 Draw off liquid by atmospheric pressure (6)
5 Difficult or unusual feat (5)
6 Bike (5)
7 No longer active in one's profession (7)
13 Fodder (3)
14 Nearest planet to the Sun (7)
15 Mr Reed who took a *Walk on the Wild Side* (3)
17 Slippery (7)
18 Deal with in a routine way (7)
19 Counting frame (6)
21 Not sharp (5)
22 Burn with steam (5)
24 Ruling on a point of Islamic law (5)

1 MINUTE NUMBER CRUNCH

Beginner

47	+ 27	1/2 of this	– 16	1/3 of this	x 15	1/5 of this	÷ 3	Answer

Intermediate

41	+ 92	x 4	3/4 of this	+ 2/3 of this	+ 85	x 1.3	– 489	Answer

Advanced

59	x 6	+ 2/3 of this	3/10 of this	2/3 of this	x 4	– 319	+ 7/9 of this	Answer

Did You Know?:
Most of the planet's fresh water is stored in a desert. Antarctica is the world's largest desert even though it is the world's coldest place. The average human body contains about ten gallons of water. It also has sufficient iron to make a four-inch nail.

HIGH-SPEED CROSSWORD

Across
1 Child's magazine (5)
7 In the news (7)
8 Flight company (7)
10 Dog that can be trained to fetch game (9)
12 Areas where vehicles may be left temporarily (3,5)
14 Additional (4)
16 Deserve by one's efforts (4)
18 Annoying (8)
20 Crushed, persecuted (9)
23 Huge destructive wave (7)
24 Moderately slow tempo in music (7)
25 Resin used chiefly in strong adhesives (5)

Down
1 Collarbone (8)
2 Distinguishing symbol (6)
3 Fibre from the outer husk of a coconut (4)
4 Printing command to ignore a former deletion (4)
5 Lacking animation (8)
6 Surfaces of a cut gemstone (6)
9 Inflammation of a nerve accompanied by pain (8)
11 Puts aside, earmarks (8)
13 Gland located behind the stomach (8)
15 Infinite time (8)
17 Add on, supplement (6)
19 Size of a book (6)
21 Part of a flower (4)
22 Dandy (4)

SUMMING UP

In the square below, change the positions of six numbers, one per horizontal row, vertical column and long diagonal line of six smaller squares, in such a way that the numbers in each row, column and long diagonal line total exactly 228. Any number may appear more than once in a row, column or line.

58	38	23	32	62	40
51	38	30	26	46	45
37	59	38	44	20	38
41	55	38	29	18	44
19	38	53	43	38	13
30	25	32	51	52	24

DOMINO PLACEMENT

A standard set of 28 dominoes has been laid out as shown. Can you draw in the edges of them all? The check-box is provided as an aid and the domino already placed will help.

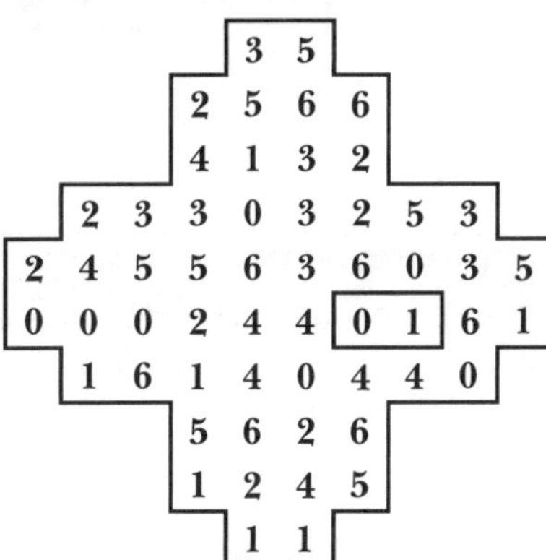

0-0	0-1	0-2	0-3	0-4	0-5	0-6
	✓					

1-1	1-2	1-3	1-4	1-5	1-6	2-2

2-3	2-4	2-5	2-6	3-3	3-4	3-5

3-6	4-4	4-5	4-6	5-5	5-6	6-6

Did You Know?:

The Swiss people hold the world record for eating the most chocolate. Each Swiss averages a consumption of ten kilos (22 pounds) per year. Surprisingly this is twice the amount that the average American consumes.

WORDSEARCH WORKOUT

N E P R V R K I T R D B W
A D L N E U I T N E I N M
M O V M R P X M R Y E O V
U E O L Y O H I N W W D A
R E R E G R H B R V T O L
A B N I R S R A W F H E E
S K R G A S D E N J L R X
C X T A A D O W M T A E A
G L R R N G O N A I E G R
A E O B I D G C L R H I A
U D L M E H Y E B X F O G
E Z L R F R B B J P J N O
G I F W O O G K U Y J R R
Q T U M L N O I K C C D N
Q M W B M A D S L P K D R

LORD OF THE RINGS

ARAGORN
ARWEN
BERGIL
BRANDYBUCK
DWARF
EDORAS
ELF
ELROND
EOMER
EOWYN
EREGION
GIMLI
LOBELIA
MERIADOC
MERRY
ORC
ROHAN
SARUMAN
SHIRE
TROLL

DOUBLE FUN SUDOKU

TASTY TEASER

6			3					9
	4		2	1			7	
1	2	3				8	4	6
	7				9			4
		4	6		8	2		
3			5				1	
4	3	8				7	5	2
	6			5	3		9	
5					7			8

BRAIN BUSTER

	6						8	5
	7				6		2	1
3				8	4			
7			6					
1		9				6		2
					5			9
			8	6				4
8	1		5				9	
4	9						6	

WHATEVER NEXT?

In the diagram below, which letter should replace the question mark?

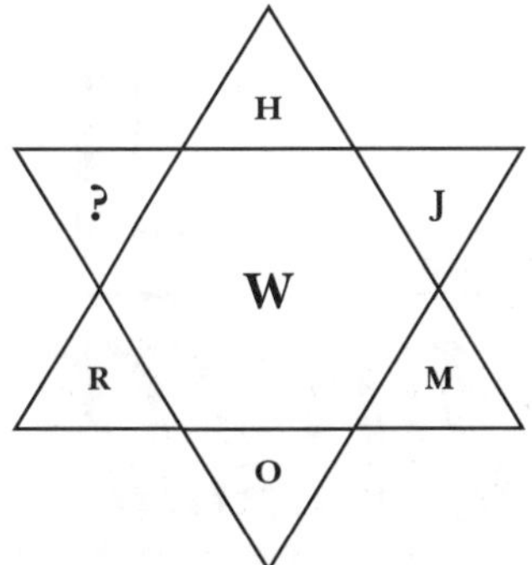

BRAIN TEASER

A B C D E F G H

What letter is two letters after the letter which is immediately after the letter four letters before the letter which is two letters after the letter E?

Mind Over Matter

Given that the letters are valued 1-26 according to their places in the alphabet, can you crack the mystery code to reveal the missing letter?

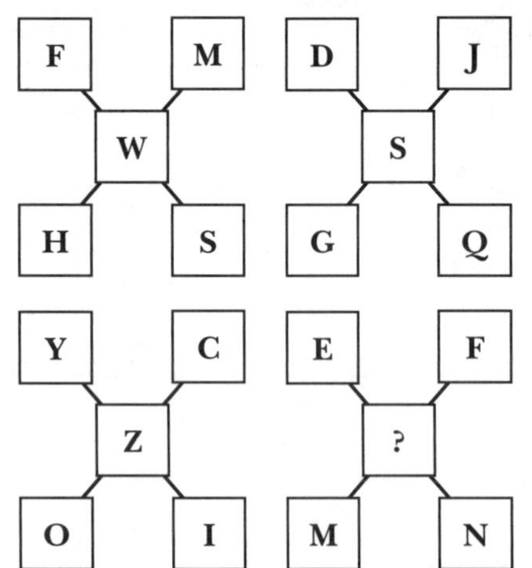

DOUBLE FUN SUDOKU

TASTY TEASER

		6		4		3		
1		5			7	4		6
	3	7	8			9	1	
				6	1		2	3
	8						9	
2	4		9	5				
	7	4			3	2	5	
5		8	2			7		9
		2		7		6		

BRAIN BUSTER

3				6		8		
	7						1	2
4		8			5		6	
	8	7	9					
					8	5	2	
	5		1			6		7
7	1						4	
		2		9				3

CODEWORD CONUNDRUM

A B C D E F G H I J K L M

N O P Q R S T U V W X Y Z

Reference Box

1	2	3	4	5	6	7	8	9	10	11	12	13
		A										

14	15	16	17	18	19	20	21	22	23	24	25	26
								B	F			

FUTOSHIKI

Fill the grid so that every horizontal row and vertical column contains the numbers 1-5. The 'greater than' or 'less than' signs indicate where a number is larger or smaller than that in the neighbouring square.

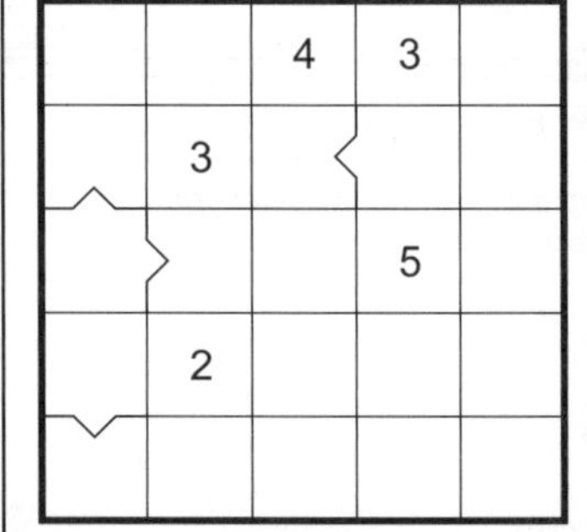

HIGH-SPEED CROSSWORD

Across
1 Lay to rest (6)
4 Medicated lozenge used to soothe the throat (6)
7 Leading caption of a newspaper article (8)
8 Restricts the number or amount of (4)
9 Cooks slowly and for a long time in liquid (5)
10 Manor-house with lands adjacent to it not let out to tenants (7)
12 Haphazardly, at random (6)
13 Voucher that can be redeemed as needed (6)
15 Perpetually young (7)
18 Pathfinder (5)
20 Estimate the value (4)
21 Conclusion (8)
22 Page border (6)
23 Dropsy (6)

Down
1 Attitude, beliefs (5)
2 Catastrophe (7)
3 Distance indicator at the side of a road (9)
4 Particular items (5)
5 Lads (5)
6 From the Orient (7)
11 Whisky made illegally (9)
12 Word of transposed letters (7)
14 Biographical sketch (7)
16 Enrol (5)
17 Chair used as a carriage (5)
19 Kingdom in the South Pacific (5)

1 MINUTE NUMBER CRUNCH

Beginner								Answer
12	1/6 of this	+ 20	Double it	– 30	÷ 7	+ 66	25% of this	

Intermediate								Answer
61	– 15	x 3	x 1.5	÷ 9	+ 57	7/10 of this	x 11	

Advanced								Answer
117	5/9 of this	8/13 of this	÷ 2.5	Squared	+ 0.625	5/16 of this	– 7/10 of this	

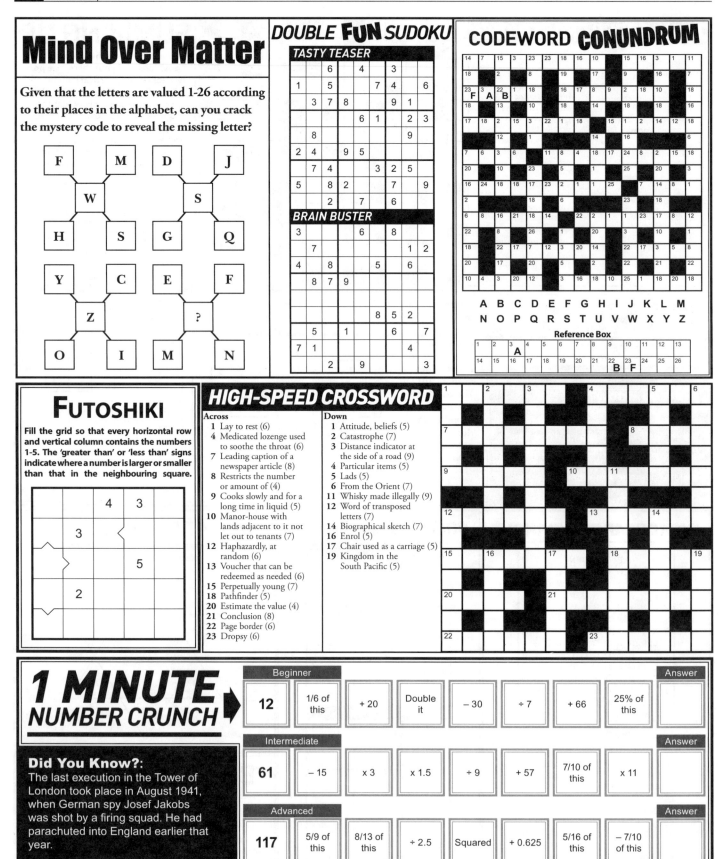

Did You Know?:
The last execution in the Tower of London took place in August 1941, when German spy Josef Jakobs was shot by a firing squad. He had parachuted into England earlier that year.

1 MINUTE NUMBER CRUNCH

Beginner								Answer
35	x 3	+ 81	÷ 6	x 9	– 42	+ 3	5/12 of this	

Intermediate								Answer
89	Add to its reverse	Double it	x 1.5	÷ 3	– 78	x 4	+ 47	

Advanced								Answer
11	x 33	– 1/3 of this	x 9	11/18 of this	Add its cube root to this	1/2 of this	x 4	

Did You Know?:
The eyelid muscle is the fastest in the human body. This tiny muscle enables the average person to blink at least 15,000 times a day.

HIGH-SPEED CROSSWORD

Across
1 Martial art (4,2)
4 Plant stalks used as roofing material (6)
7 Declare null or void (10)
8 Africa's longest river (4)
10 Island republic in the South Pacific Ocean (5)
12 Knitted or woven with a diamond-shaped pattern (6)
13 Characterised by romantic association (6)
15 Playing-card suit (6)
18 Maker of archery equipment (6)
20 Acquiesce (5)
21 Rubbish receptacles (4)
23 Pointing out or revealing clearly (10)
24 Evergreen shrub with dark green shiny leaves (6)
25 Cover for a corpse (6)

Down
1 Interlace yarn in a series of loops (4)
2 Mother of one's father or mother (6)
3 One of a kind (6)
4 Drinking vessel (6)
5 Wide street or thoroughfare (6)
6 One who extracts fuel from a pit (4,5)
9 Correct or appropriate behaviour (9)
11 Succulent plant (4)
14 Double-reed woodwind instrument (4)
16 Abstain from (6)
17 Bicycle seat (6)
18 Elastic straps that hold up trousers (6)
19 Confused multitude of things (6)
22 Group of cows (4)

PARTITIONS

Draw walls to partition the grid into areas (some are already drawn in). Each area must contain two circles, area sizes must match those numbers shown next to the grid and each '+' must be linked to at least two walls.

2, 3, 6, 7, 7

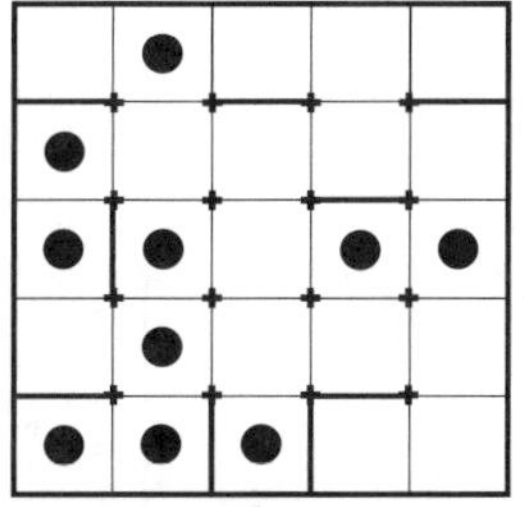

WORDWHEEL

Using only the letters in the Wordwheel, you have ten minutes to find as many words as possible, none of which may be plurals, foreign words or proper nouns. Each word must be of three letters or more, all must contain the central letter and letters can only be used once in every word. There is at least one nine-letter word in the wheel.

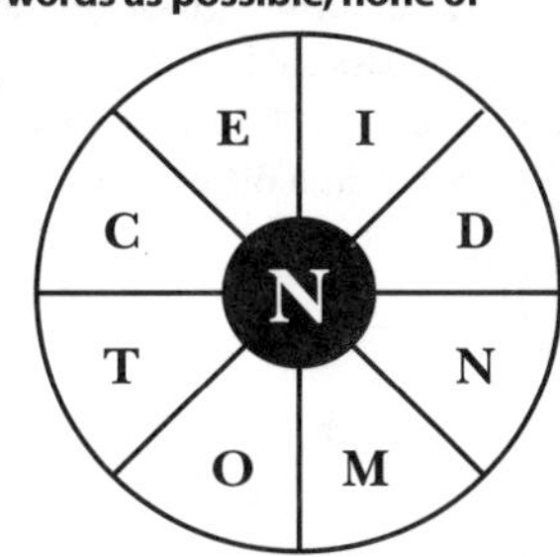

Nine-letter word(s):

SUM CIRCLE

Fill the three empty circles with the symbols +, – and x in some order, to make a sum which totals the number in the centre. Each symbol must be used once and calculations are made in the direction of travel (clockwise).

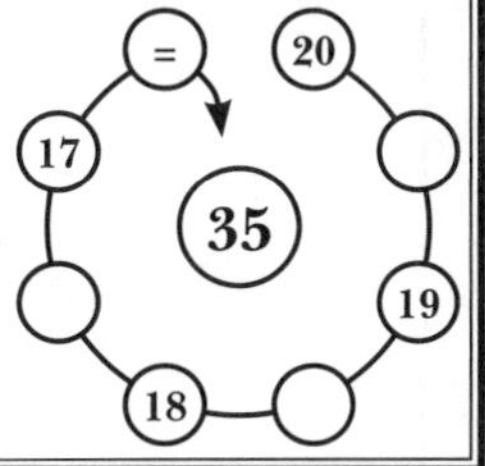

WORDSEARCH WORKOUT

U F O D I E Y P Z K W L J
T H E P A S T H X R I B P
Z Z E L A W S D W O R C Y
M Z Q T B A T H E W I F E
Y G N I K N I S W H G S L
N A S N E I L A T U N N O
F Y F A C M N T Y A I I M
G A C A U A E F K L N F E
N S H N Q L S E L Z O F A
I P A R P S D T K Y R O T
L M S E B N E I L Y I C I
I N E M E M O R I E S N N
A H S S W C K Z S H S W G
S S S H T H E F U T U R E
D A F O O T B A L L A G T

DREAMS

ALIENS
ANIMALS
CASTLES
CHASES
COFFINS
CROWDS
EATING
FANTASY
FLYING
FOOTBALL
IRONING
MEMORIES
NAKEDNESS
SAILING
SHEEP
SINKING
THE FUTURE
THE PAST
THE WIFE
WORK

DOUBLE FUN SUDOKU

TASTY TEASER

4		8			6	3		9
7				5				8
1	3		4				7	5
	2	5		1	9			
		6				9		
			3	7		2	8	
6	1				2		9	4
2				4				7
5		4	8			1		2

BRAIN BUSTER

		5				1		
7			5		4			2
	8		6		1		5	
	6	1	8		9	7	3	
	2	7	1		3	9	6	
	9		7		2		4	
6			3		5			9
		4				8		

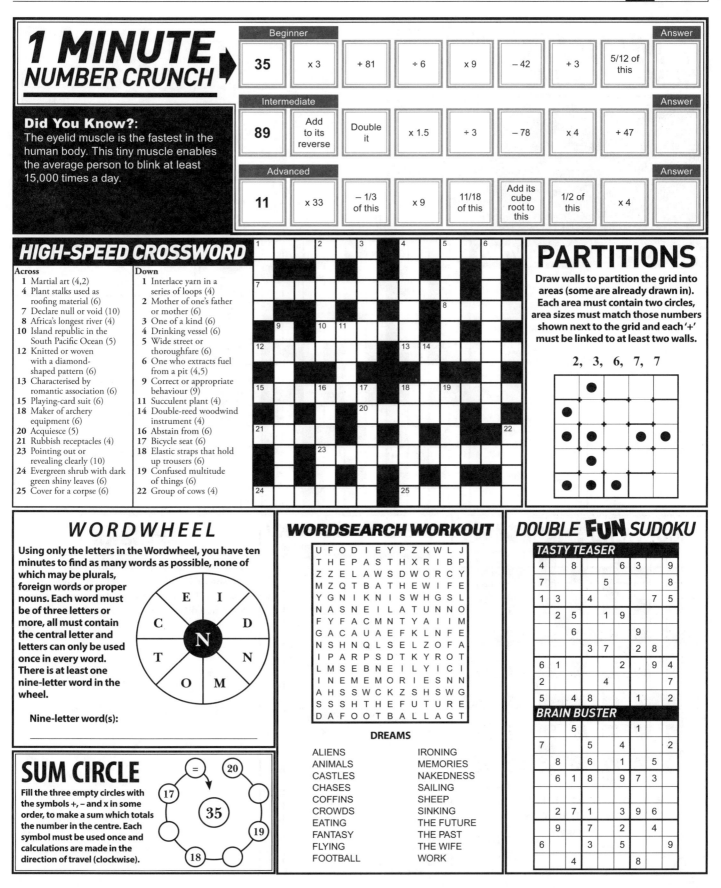

1 MINUTE NUMBER CRUNCH

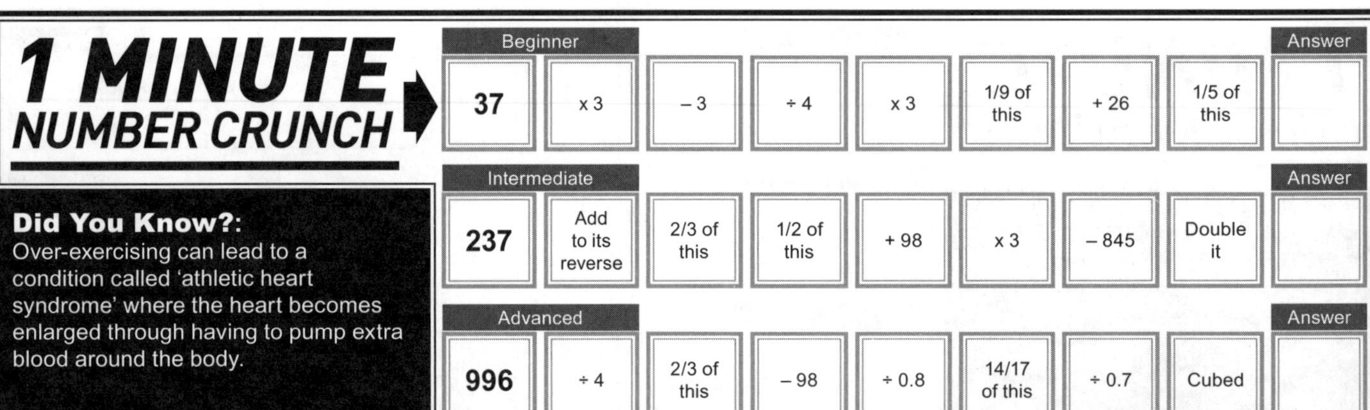

Beginner								Answer
37	x 3	– 3	÷ 4	x 3	1/9 of this	+ 26	1/5 of this	
Intermediate								**Answer**
237	Add to its reverse	2/3 of this	1/2 of this	+ 98	x 3	– 845	Double it	
Advanced								**Answer**
996	÷ 4	2/3 of this	– 98	÷ 0.8	14/17 of this	÷ 0.7	Cubed	

Did You Know?: Over-exercising can lead to a condition called 'athletic heart syndrome' where the heart becomes enlarged through having to pump extra blood around the body.

HIGH-SPEED CROSSWORD

Across

1 Former French coin (5)
4 Makes a more or less disguised reference to (7)
8 Practice (9)
9 Two-sixths (5)
10 Filled to repletion (9)
13 Spanish "tomorrow" (6)
14 Expels air from the lungs with a sudden sharp sound (6)
16 Take back ownership (9)
19 Mike ___, former heavyweight champion boxer (5)
20 Breed taking cuttings (of plants) (9)
22 Chest of drawers (7)
23 Evade (5)

Down

1 Floating wreckage of a ship (7)
2 Inclined to suffer mishaps (8-5)
3 Coagulated milk used to make cheese (5)
4 Burned remains (3)
5 Goes in front (5)
6 Conspicuous or noteworthy (13)
7 Firm (5)
11 Natives of Iraq or Jordan, for example (5)
12 Peruvian tribe at the time of the Spanish conquest (5)
15 Cheat (7)
16 Quick (5)
17 Clicks smartly (5)
18 Warhorse (5)
21 Atmosphere (3)

IQ WORKOUT

What number is missing?

74286
28674
67428
?
86742

CODEWORD CONUNDRUM

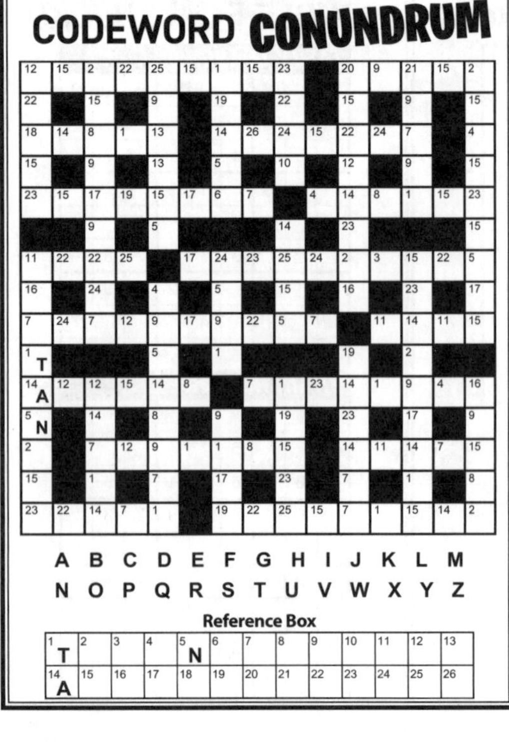

DOUBLE FUN SUDOKU

TASTY TEASER

	8					5		9
			3	6	8			
	7	2		5			1	6
1	5	4	7			2		
8			1		6			5
		7			5	1	9	3
6	2			7		3	8	
			6	4	1			
5		9					7	

BRAIN BUSTER

		3				2		
		2	9		8	1		
5	4						8	9
	6			7			3	
		7	5		3	4		
	5			4			2	
9	1						7	3
		8	1		9	6		
		6				5		

SPIDOKU

Each of the eight segments of the spider's web should be filled with a different number from 1 to 8, in such a way that every ring also contains a different number from 1 to 8.

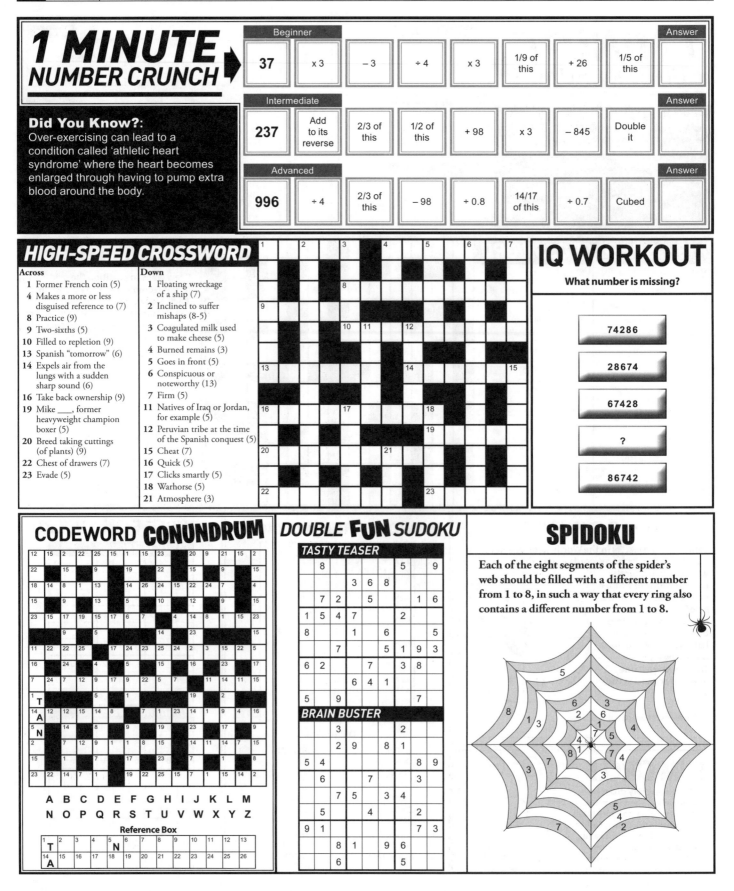

LOGI-SIX

Every row and column of this grid should contain one each of the letters A, B, C, D, E and F. Each of the six shapes (marked by thicker lines) should also contain one each of the letters A, B, C, D, E and F. Can you complete the grid?

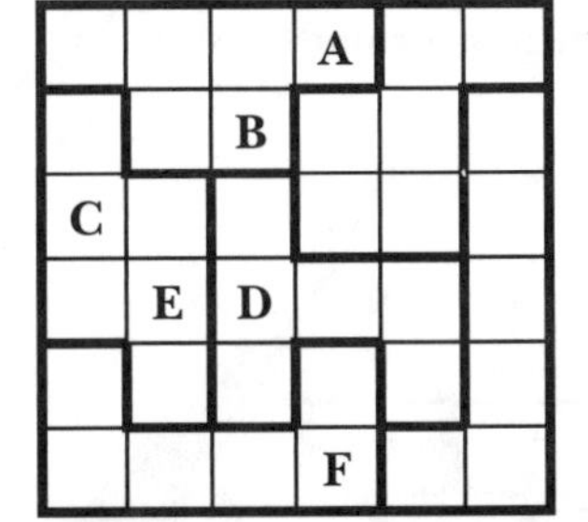

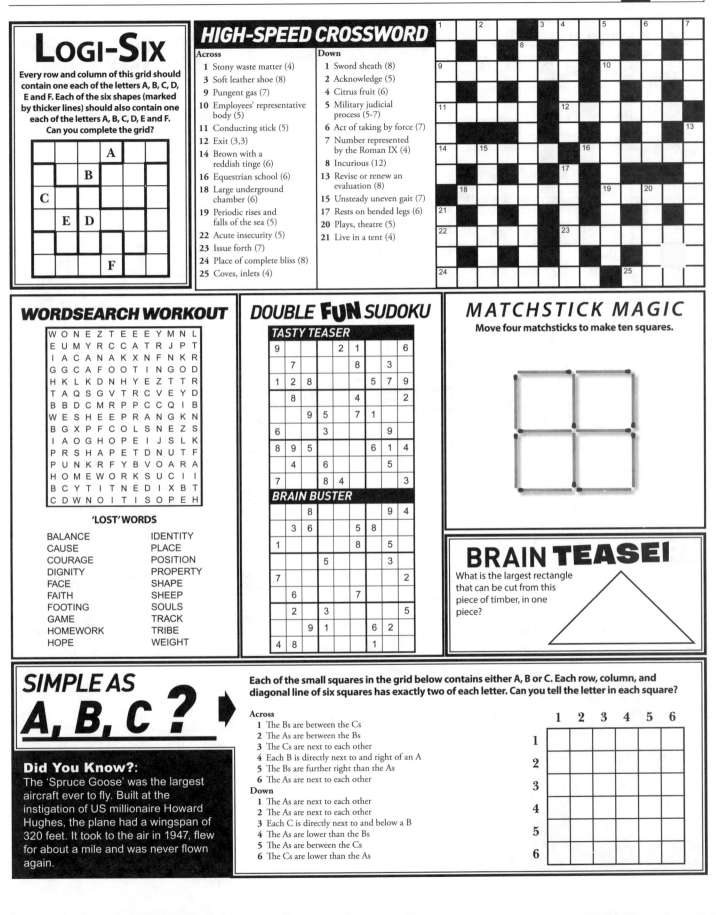

HIGH-SPEED CROSSWORD

Across

1 Stony waste matter (4)
3 Soft leather shoe (8)
9 Pungent gas (7)
10 Employees' representative body (5)
11 Conducting stick (5)
12 Exit (3,3)
14 Brown with a reddish tinge (6)
16 Equestrian school (6)
18 Large underground chamber (6)
19 Periodic rises and falls of the sea (5)
22 Acute insecurity (5)
23 Issue forth (7)
24 Place of complete bliss (8)
25 Coves, inlets (4)

Down

1 Sword sheath (8)
2 Acknowledge (5)
4 Citrus fruit (6)
5 Military judicial process (5-7)
6 Act of taking by force (7)
7 Number represented by the Roman IX (4)
8 Incurious (12)
13 Revise or renew an evaluation (8)
15 Unsteady uneven gait (7)
17 Rests on bended legs (6)
20 Plays, theatre (5)
21 Live in a tent (4)

WORDSEARCH WORKOUT

W	O	N	E	Z	T	E	E	E	Y	M	N	L
E	U	M	Y	R	C	C	A	T	R	J	P	T
I	A	C	A	N	A	K	X	N	F	N	K	R
G	G	C	A	F	O	O	T	I	N	G	O	D
H	K	L	K	D	N	H	Y	E	Z	T	T	R
T	A	Q	S	G	V	T	R	C	V	E	Y	D
B	B	D	C	M	R	P	P	C	C	Q	I	B
W	E	S	H	E	E	P	R	A	N	G	K	N
B	G	X	P	F	C	O	L	S	N	E	Z	S
I	A	O	G	H	O	P	E	I	J	S	L	K
P	R	S	H	A	P	E	T	D	N	U	T	F
P	U	N	K	R	F	Y	B	V	O	A	R	A
H	O	M	E	W	O	R	K	S	U	C	I	I
B	C	Y	T	I	T	N	E	D	I	X	B	T
C	D	W	N	O	I	T	I	S	O	P	E	H

'LOST' WORDS

BALANCE
CAUSE
COURAGE
DIGNITY
FACE
FAITH
FOOTING
GAME
HOMEWORK
HOPE
IDENTITY
PLACE
POSITION
PROPERTY
SHAPE
SHEEP
SOULS
TRACK
TRIBE
WEIGHT

DOUBLE FUN SUDOKU

TASTY TEASER

9				2	1			6
	7				8		3	
1	2	8				5	7	9
	8				4			2
		9	5		7	1		
6			3				9	
8	9	5				6	1	4
	4		6				5	
7			8	4				3

BRAIN BUSTER

		8					9	4
	3	6			5	8		
1					8		5	
			5				3	
7								2
	6				7			
	2		3					5
		9	1			6	2	
4	8					1		

MATCHSTICK MAGIC

Move four matchsticks to make ten squares.

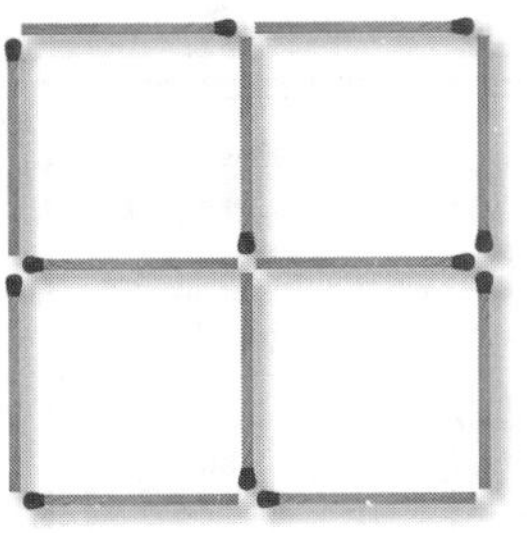

BRAIN TEASER

What is the largest rectangle that can be cut from this piece of timber, in one piece?

SIMPLE AS A, B, C ?

Each of the small squares in the grid below contains either A, B or C. Each row, column, and diagonal line of six squares has exactly two of each letter. Can you tell the letter in each square?

Across

1 The Bs are between the Cs
2 The As are between the Bs
3 The Cs are next to each other
4 Each B is directly next to and right of an A
5 The Bs are further right than the As
6 The As are next to each other

Down

1 The As are next to each other
2 The As are next to each other
3 Each C is directly next to and below a B
4 The As are lower than the Bs
5 The As are between the Cs
6 The Cs are lower than the As

	1	2	3	4	5	6
1						
2						
3						
4						
5						
6						

Did You Know?:
The 'Spruce Goose' was the largest aircraft ever to fly. Built at the instigation of US millionaire Howard Hughes, the plane had a wingspan of 320 feet. It took to the air in 1947, flew for about a mile and was never flown again.

CODEWORD CONUNDRUM

A B C D E F G H I J K L M

N O P Q R S T U V W X Y Z

Reference Box

1	2	3	4	5	6	7	8	9	10	11	12	13 A
14	15	16	17	18 R	19	20	21	22	23 T	24	25	26

DOUBLE FUN SUDOKU

TASTY TEASER

7	6		9		8			3
	9		4		5			6
		2		7			4	
8			6			4	3	
4				8				7
	1	9			2			5
	5			3		6		
6			1		7		2	
2			8		9		1	4

BRAIN BUSTER

1		5		7		8		3
	8	6				9	2	
	1		7		5		6	
		2				5		
	7		2		9		3	
	5	7				4	8	
9		1		3		7		6

PYRAMID PLUS

Every brick in this pyramid contains a number which is the sum of the two numbers below it, so that F=A+B, etc.
Just work out the missing numbers!

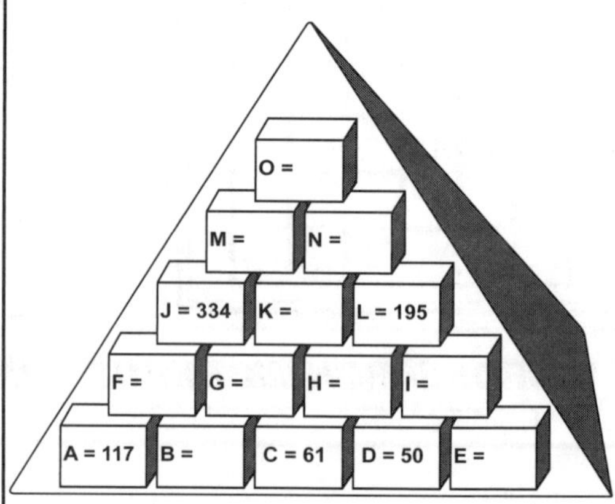

WORK IT OUT

In the grid below, what number should replace the question mark?

144	141	138	135	132	129	198
147	90	87	84	81	126	195
150	93	60	57	78	123	192
153	96	63	?	75	120	189
156	99	66	69	72	117	186
159	102	105	108	111	114	183
162	165	168	171	174	177	180

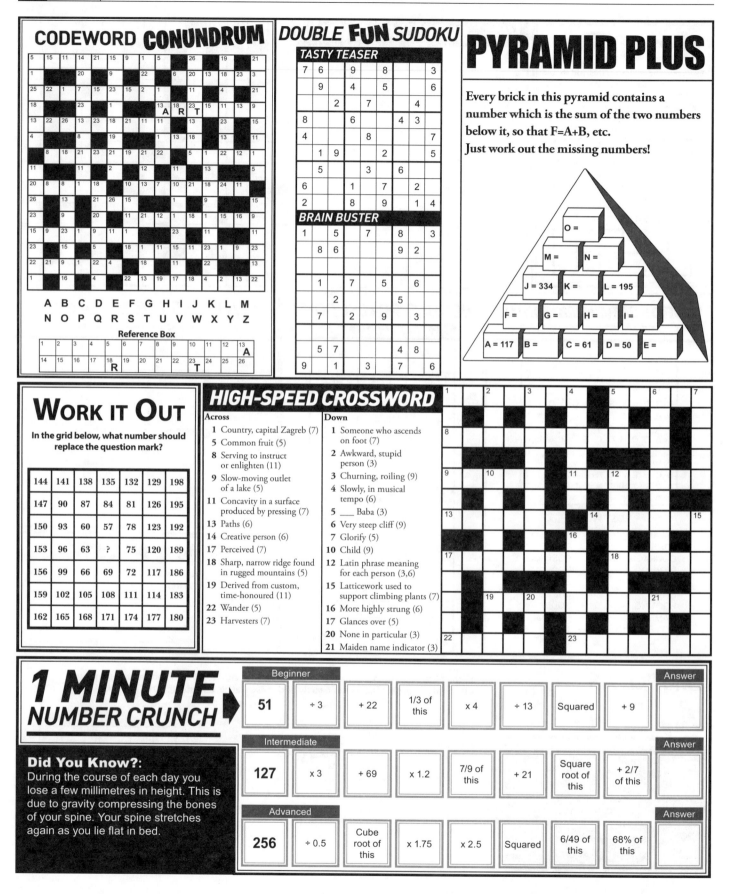

HIGH-SPEED CROSSWORD

Across

1 Country, capital Zagreb (7)
5 Common fruit (5)
8 Serving to instruct or enlighten (11)
9 Slow-moving outlet of a lake (5)
11 Concavity in a surface produced by pressing (7)
13 Paths (6)
14 Creative person (6)
17 Perceived (7)
18 Sharp, narrow ridge found in rugged mountains (5)
19 Derived from custom, time-honoured (11)
22 Wander (5)
23 Harvesters (7)

Down

1 Someone who ascends on foot (7)
2 Awkward, stupid person (3)
3 Churning, roiling (9)
4 Slowly, in musical tempo (6)
5 ___ Baba (3)
6 Very steep cliff (9)
7 Glorify (5)
10 Child (9)
12 Latin phrase meaning for each person (3,6)
15 Latticework used to support climbing plants (7)
16 More highly strung (6)
17 Glances over (5)
20 None in particular (3)
21 Maiden name indicator (3)

1 MINUTE NUMBER CRUNCH

Beginner

								Answer
51	÷ 3	+ 22	1/3 of this	x 4	÷ 13	Squared	+ 9	

Intermediate

								Answer
127	x 3	+ 69	x 1.2	7/9 of this	+ 21	Square root of this	+ 2/7 of this	

Advanced

								Answer
256	÷ 0.5	Cube root of this	x 1.75	x 2.5	Squared	6/49 of this	68% of this	

Did You Know?:
During the course of each day you lose a few millimetres in height. This is due to gravity compressing the bones of your spine. Your spine stretches again as you lie flat in bed.

HIGH-SPEED CROSSWORD

Across

1 All over the world (6)
5 Large box with a lid (5)
9 Spaceman (9)
10 Absolute (5)
11 In another location (9)
13 Curtains (6)
15 Courageous men (6)
19 Metal object sounded to warn of danger (5,4)
21 Deep opening in the earth's surface (5)
22 Mica (9)
24 End in a particular way (5)
25 Illness (6)

Down

2 Thin strips of wood, used in plastering, etc (5)
3 Hoot with derision (3)
4 Weighted down with weariness (6)
5 Reflective road stud (4-3)
6 Enthusiastic (5)
7 Vacuum container that preserves temperature of hot or cold drinks (7,5)
8 Complex pattern of constantly changing colours and shapes (12)
12 Clairvoyance (inits) (3)
14 Consider in detail (7)
16 Steal (3)
17 Whitish 'meal' drunk before an x-ray (6)
18 Financial institutions (5)
20 Large antelope (5)
23 Mousse (3)

■	1	2		3		4	■	5		6		7
8	■		■		■		■		■		■	
9									■		■	
	■		■	■	■		■	10				
11			12						■		■	
	■	■		■	■		■		■	■	■	
13				14		■	15		16			
	■	■	■		■	17	■	■		■	■	
	■	18	■	19						20		
21					■		■	■	■		■	
	■		■	22				23				
	■		■		■		■		■		■	
24					■	25						■

SUMMING UP

In the square below, change the positions of six numbers, one per horizontal row, vertical column and long diagonal line of six smaller squares, in such a way that the numbers in each row, column and long diagonal line total exactly 234. Any number may appear more than once in a row, column or line.

39	30	33	44	51	47
33	39	22	33	39	43
40	61	39	27	29	45
29	53	39	51	20	15
36	47	36	40	63	44
67	36	40	42	39	13

Beginner								Answer
47	+ 61	1/6 of this	+ 12	x 6	– 6	1/2 of this	1/3 of this	

Intermediate								Answer
42	+ 19	x 9	2/3 of this	÷ 3	+ 11	4/7 of this	x 4	

Advanced								Answer
62	÷ 0.5	x 8	11/16 of this	x 3	5/6 of this	80% of this	x 0.25	

Did You Know?:
The phrase 'Has the cat got your tongue?' comes from the days when the cat-o'-nine-tails was used to inflict punishment. The mere threat of the use of this device was said to render a victim mute with terror, hence the saying.

WORDSEARCH WORKOUT

T	Q	H	G	Y	I	C	D	Y	L	L	O	H
B	T	K	L	B	Y	L	A	A	S	A	G	E
W	R	I	K	V	S	C	F	N	V	N	U	I
T	L	Y	L	F	I	I	R	E	E	I	A	F
D	C	E	O	L	A	U	R	O	R	W	D	P
L	A	V	E	N	D	E	R	I	L	N	I	A
K	M	G	M	M	Y	F	Y	C	P	I	I	K
X	N	H	A	W	C	R	V	L	Z	G	V	H
A	Y	Y	Z	J	A	S	M	I	N	E	L	E
W	Y	E	B	M	M	K	X	C	O	L	P	G
S	P	F	E	U	H	V	I	Y	F	L	P	B
D	P	S	L	H	E	C	E	Z	M	A	A	U
J	O	S	C	T	E	V	J	L	C	J	W	U
R	P	O	G	L	G	N	G	O	C	Z	S	B
K	Q	V	Y	I	Z	I	V	Y	I	R	T	C

FLOWERY GIRLS' NAMES

ANGELICA
BRYONY
CICELY
DAISY
DAVIDA
FERN
HOLLY
IRIS
IVY
JASMINE
LAVENDER
LILY
MAY
NIGELLA
OLIVE
PANSY
POPPY
ROSEMARY
SAGE
VIOLA

DOUBLE FUN SUDOKU

TASTY TEASER

		6			5	8	4	
	2			9	7			6
1	8	5	4					
		7		3			8	2
		1	9		2	7		
5	6			8		3		
					8	6	3	7
3			6	2			1	
	5	4	3			9		

BRAIN BUSTER

	4	8		6		9	3	
		9				2		
	5		9		3		8	
			8		2			
		3				1		
			3		6			
	6		4		1		5	
		1				4		
	2	5		8		3	7	

WHATEVER NEXT?

In the diagram below, which number should replace the question mark?

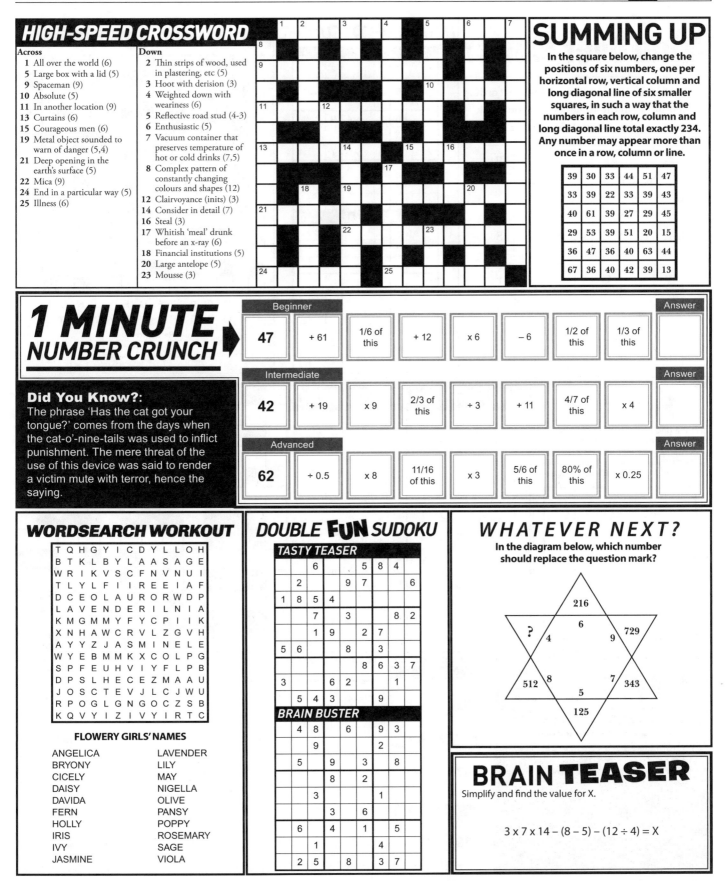

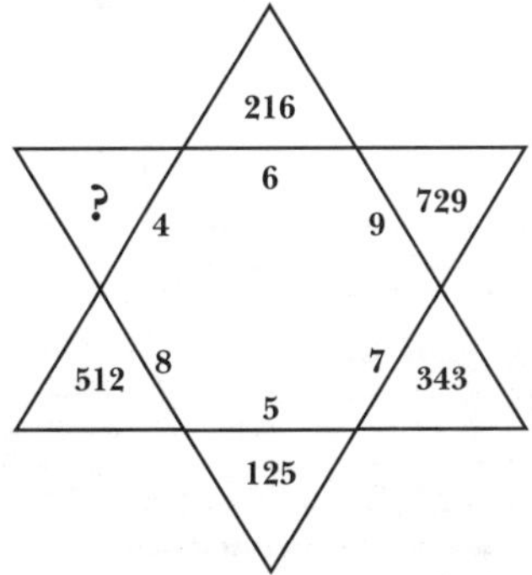

BRAIN TEASER

Simplify and find the value for X.

$$3 \times 7 \times 14 - (8 - 5) - (12 \div 4) = X$$

Mind Over Matter

Given that the letters are valued 1-26 according to their places in the alphabet, can you crack the mystery code to reveal the missing letter?

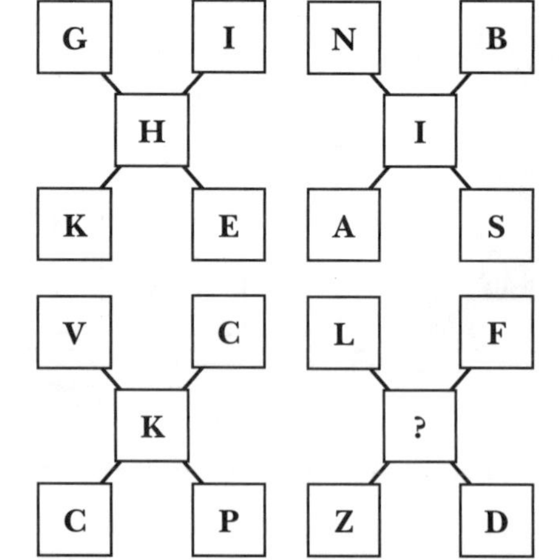

DOUBLE FUN SUDOKU

TASTY TEASER

6		4		1		2		3
		2		6		5		
	3		5		2		7	
7		5	2		4	9		6
	6		1		7		2	
2		8	9		6	7		1
	8		6		5		4	
		1		7		8		
4		6		9		3		7

BRAIN BUSTER

							8	
3		1	8	5		9		7
			9	1				
8				7			1	
7			2		1			4
	4			6				8
				9	6			
4		7		2	3	6		5
	2							

CODEWORD CONUNDRUM

20	■	26	■	16	11	13	12	4	24	14	13	14	20	17
5	9	16	24	8	■	24	■	■	11	■	16	■	7	■
14	■	9	■	8	24	16	7	3	8	11	24	13	20	24
8	16	3	14	24	■	19	■	■	8	■	17	■	26	■
14	■	14	■	4	■	20	26	6	14	24	14	19	16	2
19	■	17	16	7	3	■	16	■	16	■	■	4	■	20
16	17	12	■	13	■	■	24	■	7	■	22	11	14	7
13	■	7	■	17	4	8	13	20	17	13	■	7	■	18
14	25	20	1	■	11	■	14	■	■	24 R	■	13	11	13
4	■	17	■	■	13	■	7	■	21	16 A	6	20	■	12
7	4	17	13	16	2	18	14	16	■	7 N	■	7	■	20
■	11	■	9	■	23	■	■	26	■	17	6	16	9	7
14	7	5	14	10	14	5	11	16	13	20	■	7	■	14
■	19	■	24	■	7	■	■	15	■	6	20	19	16	7
25	20	2	2	14	18	20	24	20	7	13	■	20	■	18

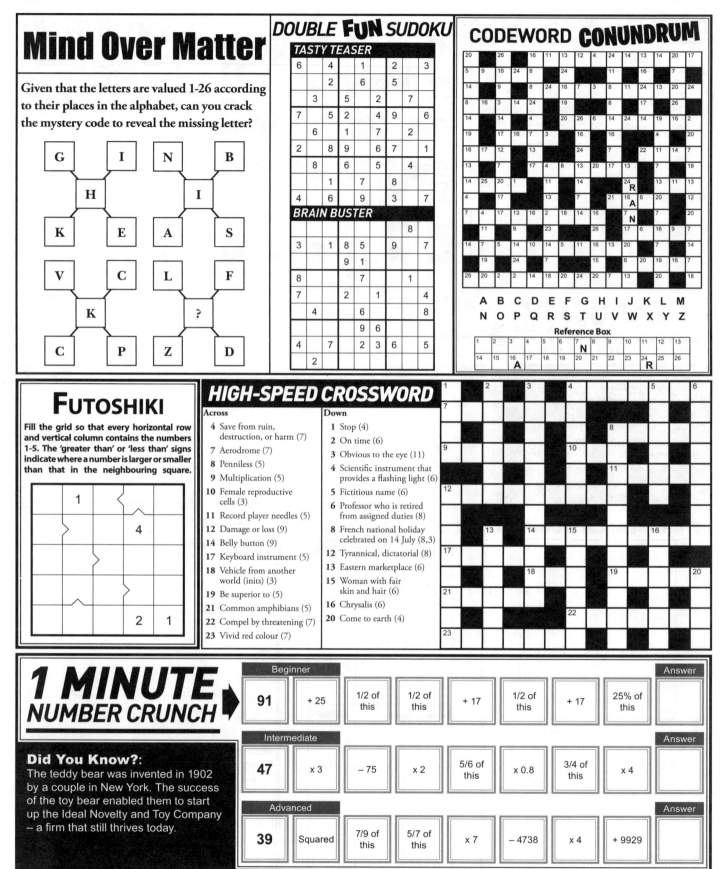

A B C D E F G H I J K L M

N O P Q R S T U V W X Y Z

Reference Box

1	2	3	4	5	6	7 N	8	9	10	11	12	13
14	15	16 A	17	18	19	20	21	22	23	24 R	25	26

FUTOSHIKI

Fill the grid so that every horizontal row and vertical column contains the numbers 1-5. The 'greater than' or 'less than' signs indicate where a number is larger or smaller than that in the neighbouring square.

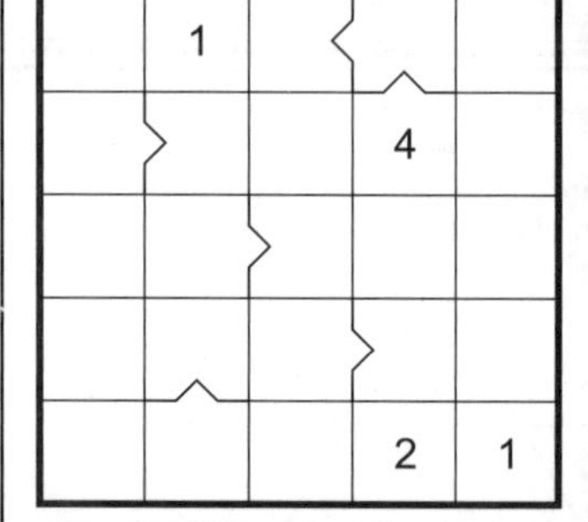

HIGH-SPEED CROSSWORD

Across

4 Save from ruin, destruction, or harm (7)
7 Aerodrome (7)
8 Penniless (5)
9 Multiplication (5)
10 Female reproductive cells (3)
11 Record player needles (5)
12 Damage or loss (9)
14 Belly button (9)
17 Keyboard instrument (5)
18 Vehicle from another world (inits) (3)
19 Be superior to (5)
21 Common amphibians (5)
22 Compel by threatening (7)
23 Vivid red colour (7)

Down

1 Stop (4)
2 On time (6)
3 Obvious to the eye (11)
4 Scientific instrument that provides a flashing light (6)
5 Fictitious name (6)
6 Professor who is retired from assigned duties (8)
8 French national holiday celebrated on 14 July (8,3)
12 Tyrannical, dictatorial (8)
13 Eastern marketplace (6)
15 Woman with fair skin and hair (6)
16 Chrysalis (6)
20 Come to earth (4)

Beginner								Answer
91	+ 25	1/2 of this	1/2 of this	+ 17	1/2 of this	+ 17	25% of this	

Intermediate								Answer
47	x 3	– 75	x 2	5/6 of this	x 0.8	3/4 of this	x 4	

Advanced								Answer
39	Squared	7/9 of this	5/7 of this	x 7	– 4738	x 4	+ 9929	

Did You Know?:

The teddy bear was invented in 1902 by a couple in New York. The success of the toy bear enabled them to start up the Ideal Novelty and Toy Company – a firm that still thrives today.

DOMINO PLACEMENT

A standard set of 28 dominoes has been laid out as shown. Can you draw in the edges of them all? The check-box is provided as an aid and the domino already placed will help.

				6	6				
			3	0	2	1			
			1	4	4	1			
	3	3	3	6	1	6	4	4	
2	1	5	3	5	5	4	2	3	6
2	0	2	6	3	0	0	3	4	0
	0	2	5	0	0	1	2	1	
			1	2	4	6			
			5	6	5	5			
				4	5				

0-0	0-1	0-2	0-3	0-4	0-5	0-6

1-1	1-2	1-3	1-4	1-5	1-6	2-2
			✓			

2-3	2-4	2-5	2-6	3-3	3-4	3-5

3-6	4-4	4-5	4-6	5-5	5-6	6-6

Did You Know?:
In World War II, British soldiers became known as 'Tommies', after an example name that was used to assist in the completion of the enlistment form. The example name was 'Thomas Atkins'.

HIGH-SPEED CROSSWORD

Across

1 Foretell or prophesy (13)
7 Interweave (4)
8 Sketchy summary of the main points of a theory (6)
9 Stairs (5)
10 Facilitate (4)
12 Pulling along behind (6)
13 Earnings (5)
15 One who drives cars at high speeds (5)
18 Wispy white cloud (6)
20 Pack (4)
21 Walk about in a stealthy manner (5)
22 Subtle difference in meaning (6)
23 Affirm (4)
24 Green mint-flavoured liqueur (5,2,6)

Down

1 Missile discharged from a firearm (6)
2 Domestic birds (5)
3 Lubricated (5)
4 Betting adviser (7)
5 Designer, creator of plans (9)
6 Naval flag (6)
11 Way of access (upward and downward) consisting of a set of steps (9)
14 Hang freely (7)
16 Relating to a person or thing regarded as a representative symbol (6)
17 Change direction abruptly (6)
19 Ancient city mentioned in conjunction with Gomorrah (5)
20 Murdered (5)

IQ WORKOUT

Which is the odd one out?

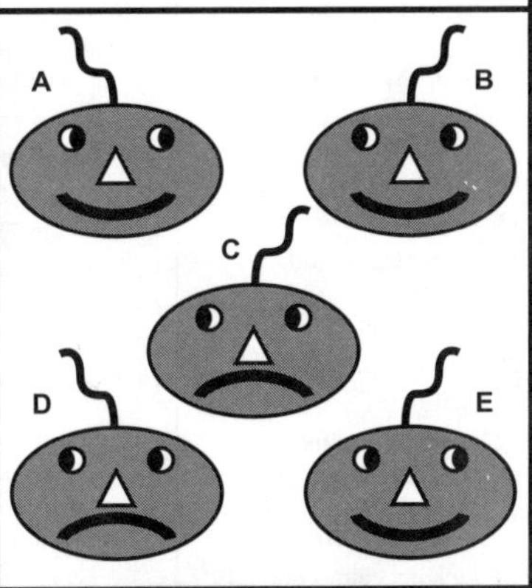

WORDWHEEL

Using only the letters in the Wordwheel, you have ten minutes to find as many words as possible, none of which may be plurals, foreign words or proper nouns. Each word must be of three letters or more, all must contain the central letter and letters can only be used once in every word. There is at least one nine-letter word in the wheel.

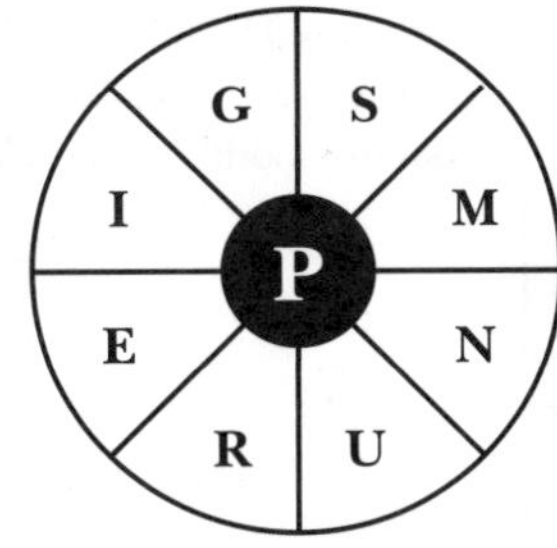

Nine-letter word(s):

SUM CIRCLE

Fill the three empty circles with the symbols +, – and x in some order, to make a sum which totals the number in the centre. Each symbol must be used once and calculations are made in the direction of travel (clockwise).

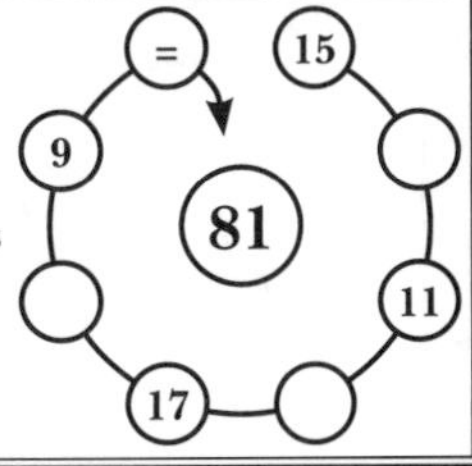

WORDSEARCH WORKOUT

```
E S E E G F G R O O M Q C
U G W N O H A P M Y R O L
I G Y M V G D Y S N C N Q
O L M R E G R P T R N M L
E U L G R T Y E N F O T M
W T W L N G G T E G G A G
G T Y A E A U K H D I U D
Z O G O S S O G G R Y F E
F N D P S K D G I D M Y T
E E I D C H A N S A M W N
P N Q E E I L G U I N J U
G D G U T S N O R O B T R
U R U G B X S G H D R A G
C E Y U C I B E Y B X G L
Z D T E G D A G S W K W R
```

G WORDS

GADGET
GAIT
GANTRY
GASPING
GECKO
GEESE
GERM
GIANT
GIFT
GLUE
GLUTTON
GODDESSES
GOVERNESS
GREEDY
GRIMY
GROOM
GROUNDSEL
GRUNTED
GURU
GYPSY

DOUBLE FUN SUDOKU

TASTY TEASER

1	6	4		5			3	
			1	8	2		6	
			4		3		7	
		2	7		5			6
5	9						4	8
6			8		4	7		
	5		2		9			
	2		6	3	1			
	3			7		9	2	1

BRAIN BUSTER

		5			1			
1			8	3				9
3								7
				5			2	8
5	2		3		4		7	6
9	4			7				
4								2
6				1	8			3
			7			8		

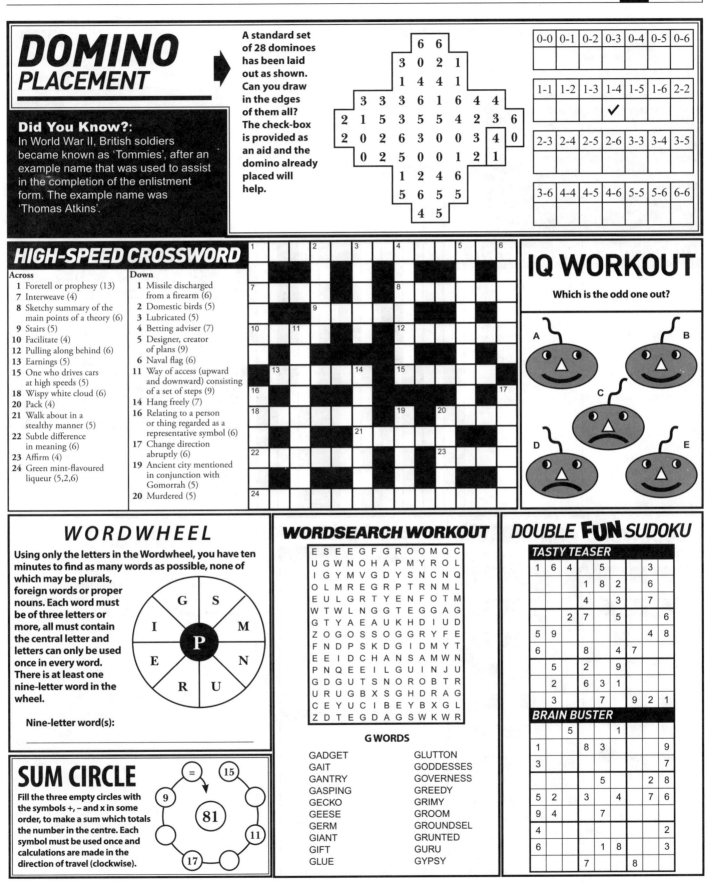

1 MINUTE NUMBER CRUNCH

Beginner								Answer
189	– 37	1/2 of this	+ 6	1/2 of this	+ 22	2/9 of this	x 3	

Intermediate								Answer
17	Squared	x 2	+ 125	x 3	– 1617	+ 1/3 of this	– 497	

Advanced								Answer
234	10/13 of this	Less the square of 13	Squared	+ 683	÷ 0.4	2/67 of this	÷ 1.25	

Did You Know?:
In Memphis, Tennessee, beggars must obtain a permit before they can pester tourists on the streets of the city. And in the US state of Arizona, it is illegal to refuse someone's request for a glass of water.

HIGH-SPEED CROSSWORD

Across
1 Grain stores (5)
5 Item of footwear (4)
7 Savoury appetiser (6)
8 Person who avoids the company of others (5)
9 Part of a limb farthest from the torso (9)
10 Young newt (3)
11 Herald (9)
15 Visitor from another country (9)
19 Had a meal (3)
20 Consciousness (9)
21 Dialect (5)
22 Screens out, sifts (6)
23 "Beware the ___ of March", advice given to Julius Caesar (4)
24 Link up, connect (3,2)

Down
1 Brine-cured (6)
2 Distance end to end (6)
3 Howl (6)
4 Ball game played with long-handled racquets (8)
5 Appearing to be (7)
6 Workers' dining hall (7)
12 Designer of machinery (8)
13 Send on (7)
14 Lower someone's spirits (7)
16 Stand firm (6)
17 Dog-like (6)
18 Discourse (6)

IQ WORKOUT

What numbers should replace the question marks?

21	23	22	25	27	26
34	35	33	30	31	29
37	39	38	?	43	42
50	51	49	?	47	45
53	55	54	57	59	58
66	67	65	62	63	61

CODEWORD CONUNDRUM

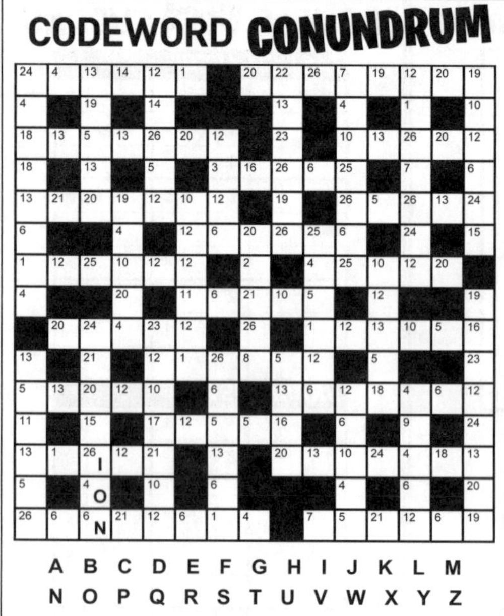

A B C D E F G H I J K L M
N O P Q R S T U V W X Y Z

Reference Box

1	2	3	4	5	6	7	8	9	10	11	12	13
			O		N							
14	15	16	17	18	19	20	21	22	23	24	25	26
												I

DOUBLE FUN SUDOKU

TASTY TEASER

		7	8			5		6
8	4	3					1	
			7	1				9
3	6		9	8			7	
4			3		5			1
	8			2	6		9	5
9				6	8			
	1					9	2	4
5		2			4	7		

BRAIN BUSTER

				8				
8			5		4			7
		6	7		2	5		
4		5	3		7	9		1
	3			9			5	
1		8	6		5	7		3
		1	2		6	4		
2			4		1			9
				3				

SPIDOKU

Each of the eight segments of the spider's web should be filled with a different number from 1 to 8, in such a way that every ring also contains a different number from 1 to 8.

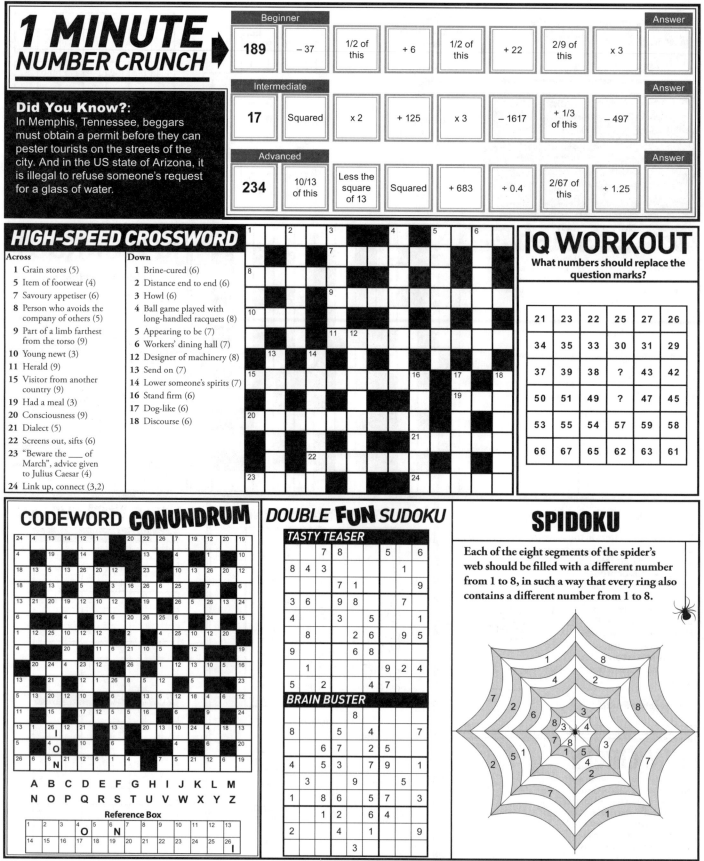

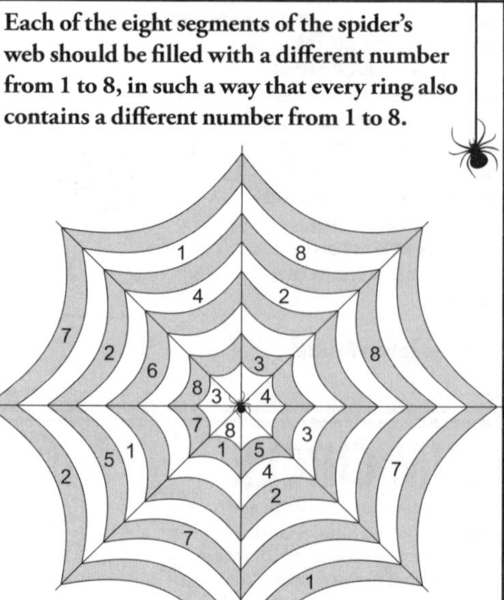

LOGI-SIX

Every row and column of this grid should contain one each of the letters A, B, C, D, E and F. Each of the six shapes (marked by thicker lines) should also contain one each of the letters A, B, C, D, E and F. Can you complete the grid?

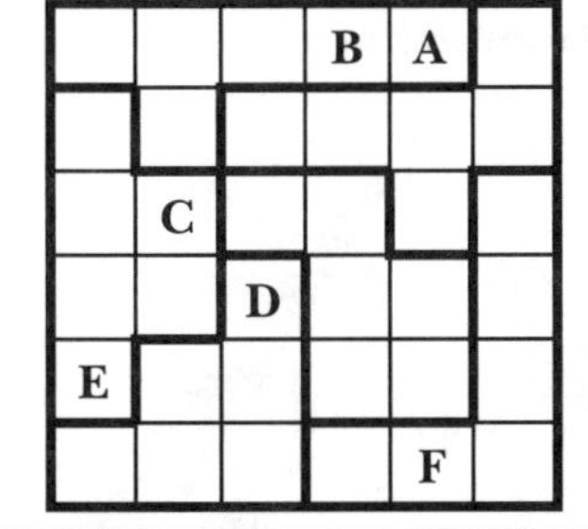

HIGH-SPEED CROSSWORD

Across

1 Dish out (5)
4 Icy covering of a mountain peak (7)
8 Circuit (3)
9 Structure consisting of a row of evenly spaced columns (9)
10 Rise as vapour (5)
11 Romanies (7)
13 Roman priestesses vowed to chastity (6,7)
15 Pocket, misappropriate (7)
17 Priory residents (5)
19 Performance of a musical composition (9)
21 Exclude (3)
22 Fund of money put by as a reserve (4,3)
23 In advance (5)

Down

1 Garments of a jockey (5)
2 Bottle up (7)
3 Include as part of something broader (9)
4 Autonomous, not controlled by outside forces (4-9)
5 Have (3)
6 American raccoon (5)
7 Gives delight (7)
12 Uncontrollable desire to set fire to things (9)
13 Old soldier (7)
14 Ungentle (7)
16 Squeals like a pig (5)
18 Cut finely (5)
20 Extreme anger (3)

WORDSEARCH WORKOUT

```
K A K A W A H I E M Y L H
S U U L A Y S A N R A I L
U H A Z K E Z O W O L F W
Q C C T L L I B E Z D A B
H A A O A Q G D N A W B U
A I O S R E Z A T L Y A S
W U L Y P U R L V Q N L H
A H A C T I A G J N S I W
I F I G A S A D N N W T R
I B K M B P Q N A J R I E
M O A E I U E P T V E G N
A Y A O A O R L O I N E K
M R P G X A A R I D G R G
O I G C T M J P E O O E G
O A L X M K Q E V Q N D R
```

EXTINCT ANIMALS

ADZEBILL
AKIALOA
ATLAS BEAR
AUROCHS
BALI TIGER
BUSH WREN
CAPE LION
CASPIAN TIGER
DODO
EZO WOLF
GREAT AUK
HAWAII MAMO
HUIA
KAKAWAHIE
LAYSAN RAIL
MOA
PIOPIO
QUAGGA
TARPAN
YALDWYN'S WREN

DOUBLE FUN SUDOKU

TASTY TEASER

					3	9	7	5
6	9			1		8		
2			7	8			4	1
			8	6		5		
	4	6				2	8	
		5		4	1			
3	8			7	5			6
		1		9			3	2
9	7	4	2					

BRAIN BUSTER

5	9		7		3		1	6
			1	9	6			
	6						7	
9	2		5		8		6	1
4								9
1	8		6		9		2	4
	5						3	
			2	5	4			
6	4		9		7		5	2

MATCHSTICK MAGIC

Move two matchsticks to make this sum correct.

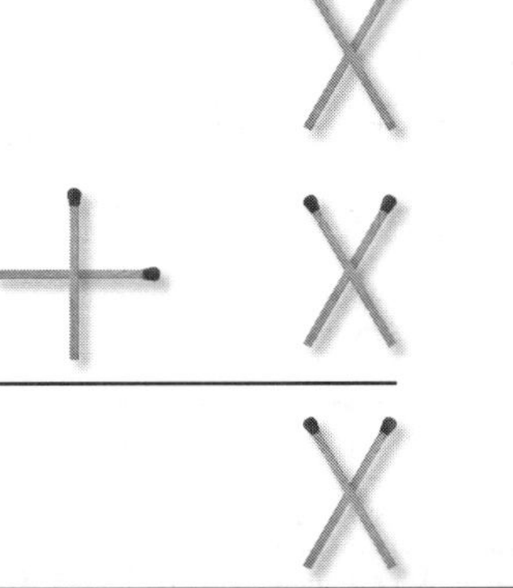

BRAIN TEASER

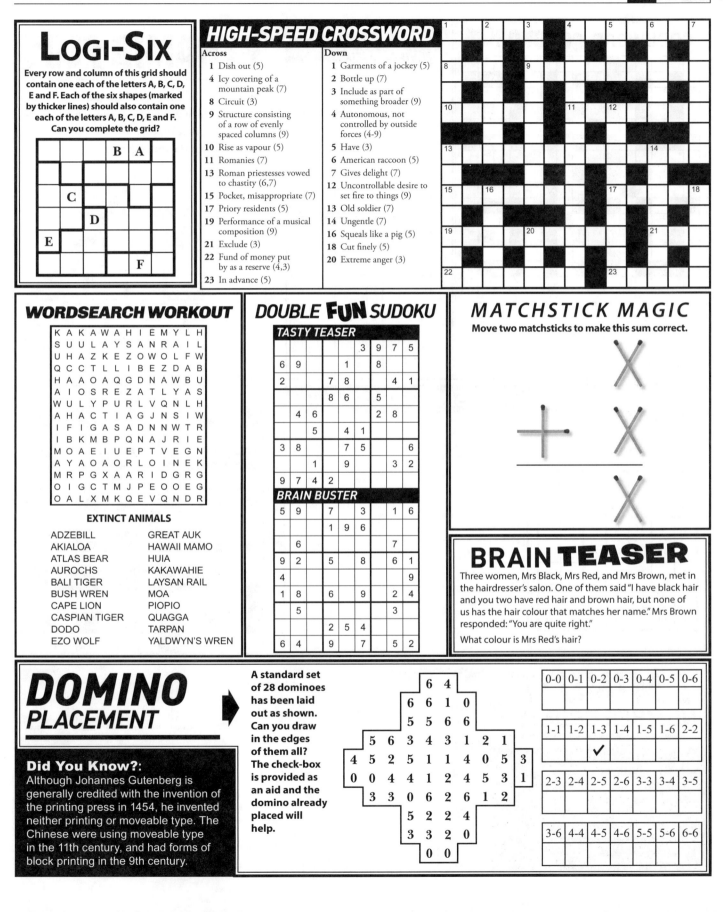

Three women, Mrs Black, Mrs Red, and Mrs Brown, met in the hairdresser's salon. One of them said "I have black hair and you two have red hair and brown hair, but none of us has the hair colour that matches her name." Mrs Brown responded: "You are quite right."

What colour is Mrs Red's hair?

DOMINO PLACEMENT

A standard set of 28 dominoes has been laid out as shown. Can you draw in the edges of them all? The check-box is provided as an aid and the domino already placed will help.

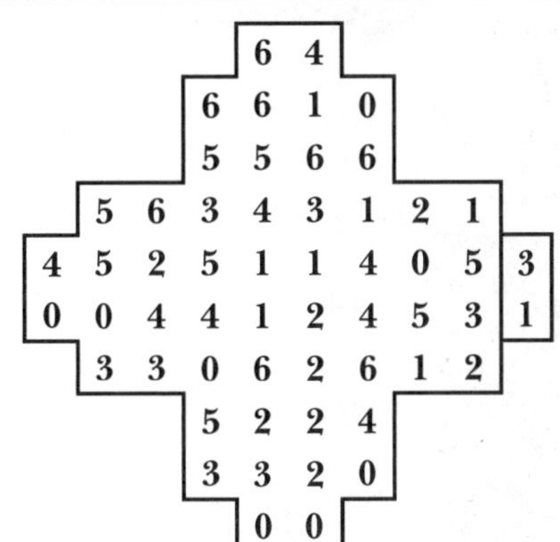

0-0	0-1	0-2	0-3	0-4	0-5	0-6

1-1	1-2	1-3	1-4	1-5	1-6	2-2
		✓				

2-3	2-4	2-5	2-6	3-3	3-4	3-5

3-6	4-4	4-5	4-6	5-5	5-6	6-6

Did You Know?:
Although Johannes Gutenberg is generally credited with the invention of the printing press in 1454, he invented neither printing or moveable type. The Chinese were using moveable type in the 11th century, and had forms of block printing in the 9th century.

CODEWORD CONUNDRUM

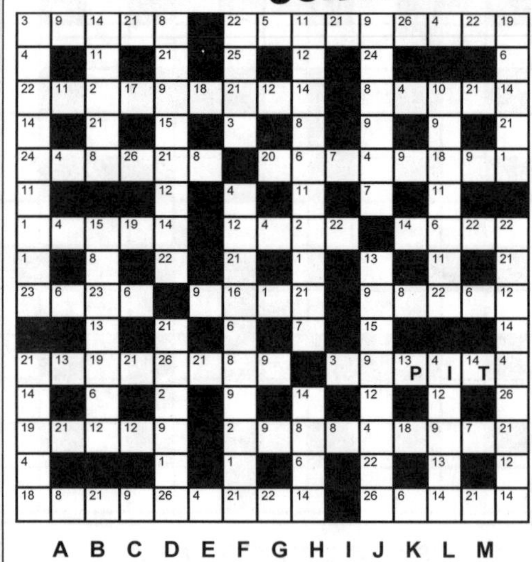

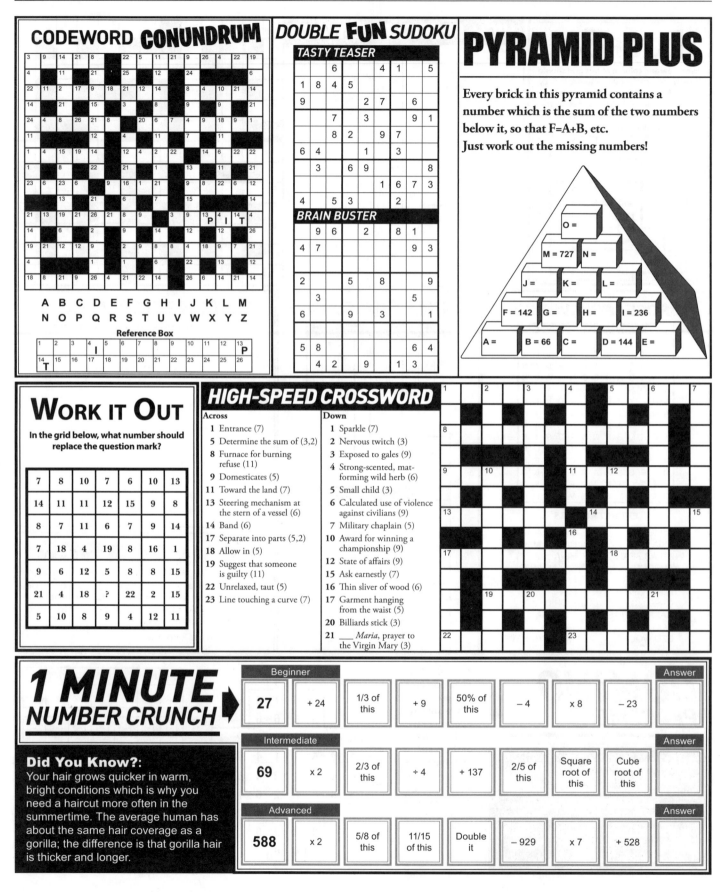

A B C D E F G H I J K L M

N O P Q R S T U V W X Y Z

Reference Box

1	2	3	4 I	5	6	7	8	9	10	11	12	13 P
14 T	15	16	17	18	19	20	21	22	23	24	25	26

DOUBLE FUN SUDOKU

TASTY TEASER

		6			4	1		5
1	8	4	5					
9				2	7		6	
		7		3			9	1
		8	2		9	7		
6	4			1		3		
	3		6	9				8
					1	6	7	3
4		5	3			2		

BRAIN BUSTER

	9	6		2		8	1	
4	7						9	3
2			5		8			9
	3						5	
6			9		3			1
5	8						6	4
	4	2		9		1	3	

PYRAMID PLUS

Every brick in this pyramid contains a number which is the sum of the two numbers below it, so that F=A+B, etc.
Just work out the missing numbers!

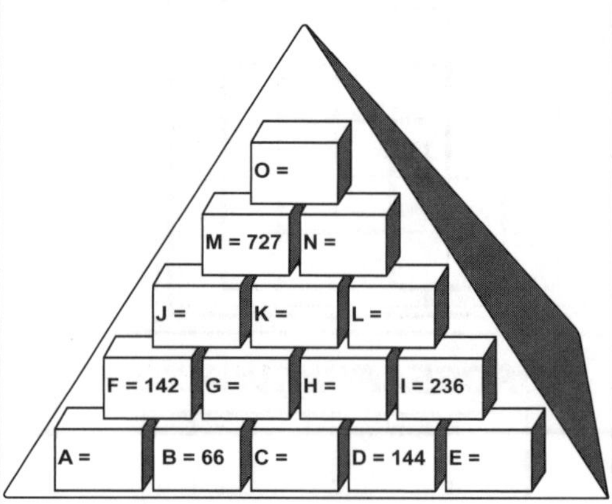

WORK IT OUT

In the grid below, what number should replace the question mark?

7	8	10	7	6	10	13
14	11	11	12	15	9	8
8	7	11	6	7	9	14
7	18	4	19	8	16	1
9	6	12	5	8	8	15
21	4	18	?	22	2	15
5	10	8	9	4	12	11

HIGH-SPEED CROSSWORD

Across

1 Entrance (7)
5 Determine the sum of (3,2)
8 Furnace for burning refuse (11)
9 Domesticates (5)
11 Toward the land (7)
13 Steering mechanism at the stern of a vessel (6)
14 Band (6)
17 Separate into parts (5,2)
18 Allow in (5)
19 Suggest that someone is guilty (11)
22 Unrelaxed, taut (5)
23 Line touching a curve (7)

Down

1 Sparkle (7)
2 Nervous twitch (3)
3 Exposed to gales (9)
4 Strong-scented, mat-forming wild herb (6)
5 Small child (3)
6 Calculated use of violence against civilians (9)
7 Military chaplain (5)
10 Award for winning a championship (9)
12 State of affairs (9)
15 Ask earnestly (7)
16 Thin sliver of wood (6)
17 Garment hanging from the waist (5)
20 Billiards stick (3)
21 ___ *Maria*, prayer to the Virgin Mary (3)

Beginner								Answer
27	+ 24	1/3 of this	+ 9	50% of this	– 4	x 8	– 23	

Intermediate								Answer
69	x 2	2/3 of this	÷ 4	+ 137	2/5 of this	Square root of this	Cube root of this	

Advanced								Answer
588	x 2	5/8 of this	11/15 of this	Double it	– 929	x 7	+ 528	

Did You Know?:
Your hair grows quicker in warm, bright conditions which is why you need a haircut more often in the summertime. The average human has about the same hair coverage as a gorilla; the difference is that gorilla hair is thicker and longer.

HIGH-SPEED CROSSWORD

Across
1 Aviator hired to fly experimental aeroplanes in designed manoeuvres (4,5)
5 Tap lightly (3)
7 Exist in large quantities (6)
8 Celebrated (6)
10 Spanish sparkling white wine (4)
11 Educational institution (7)
14 Capital of Ukraine (4)
16 Stake (3)
17 Units (1/6 inch) used in printing (3)
20 Attention (4)
23 Lawlessness (7)
25 Small hard fruit (4)
27 Frozen spike of water (6)
28 Coarse cloth (6)
29 Golfing device (3)
30 Unanimity (9)

Down
1 Unfreeze (4)
2 Motto (6)
3 Item eaten on Shrove Tuesday (7)
4 Use a dragnet (5)
5 Marked by suitability (6)
6 Having flavour (8)
9 One of four playing cards in a deck (3)
12 Above, beyond (4)
13 Devil worshipper (8)
15 Irritation (4)
18 Communiqué (7)
19 Overnight case (6)
21 Yes (3)
22 Failing in what duty requires (6)
24 Griping tummy ache (5)
26 Deprivation (4)

IQ WORKOUT

Draw in the hands on the final clock.

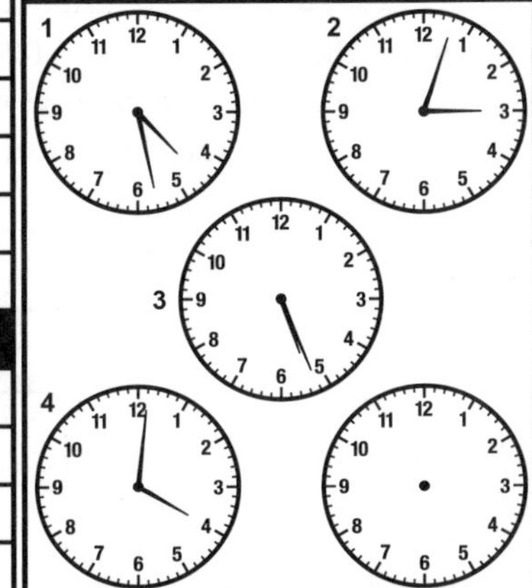

Beginner

25	+ 93	1/2 of this	+ 7	2/11 of this	1/3 of this	+ 28	x 4	Answer

Intermediate

452	÷ 4	+ 169	x 1.5	7/9 of this	Double it	– 479	x 3	Answer

Advanced

129	2/3 of this	x 13	Double it	– 25% of this	– 949	5/14 of this	– 2/5 of this	Answer

Did You Know?:
Although 2,600 years ago, mathematician Pythagoras said the Earth was a sphere, and astronomer Aristarchos, 2,300 years ago said the Earth revolved around the Sun, 1,600 years were to pass before they were believed.

WORDSEARCH WORKOUT

M F D R Z T X F O M Z C G
C A N X N X U T A D A J Q
O Q O D U W F N G Z N M Y
B B M V T G G A A A O S R
N L L E M O N R P E A R R
U Z A J E U K R P N P X E
T G Z C G Y D U E S N I B
X K L E K N L C C A N D E
P Q J O Z C B D A T M N L
S R H P D R U E N S X I K
B L U E B E R R Y U J R C
F D O N F K A X R M J A U
L Y C H E E H L F A D M H
O L I V E L I M E I N A C
B L C H E R R Y E Q G T V

FRUIT AND NUT

ALMOND
BLACKCURRANT
BLUEBERRY
CHERRY
COBNUT
FIG
HUCKLEBERRY
LEMON
LIME
LYCHEE
MANGO
NUTMEG
OLIVE
PEANUT
PEAR
PECAN
PRUNE
REDCURRANT
SATSUMA
TAMARIND

DOUBLE FUN SUDOKU

TASTY TEASER

		8	3	5			9	
4			7			1	5	
2		1			8			3
			5	1		2	7	6
		9				8		
1	2	6		4	7			
6			9			3		7
	8	5			4			1
	4			2	3	6		

BRAIN BUSTER

5				4				9
	2		6		9		5	
		4	3		7	2		
3		9				6		1
	8						9	
2		5				3		8
		6	1		4	5		
	1		5		8		7	
9				3				4

WHATEVER NEXT?

In the diagram below, which letter should replace the question mark?

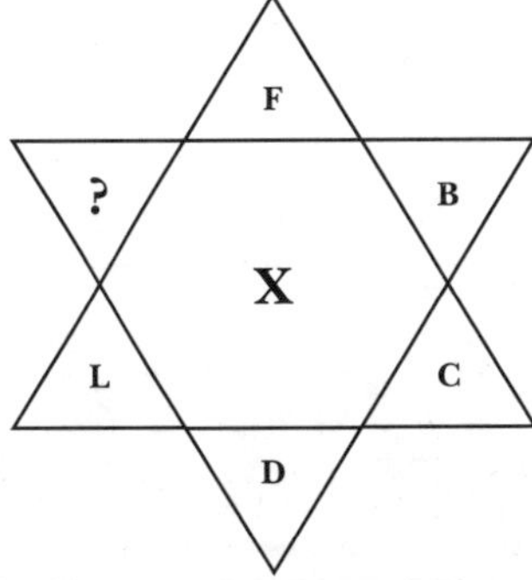

BRAIN TEASER

What should replace the question marks?

			A	5	D	11	G	17	J
									23
7									M
?	?	Y	47	V	41	S	35	P	29

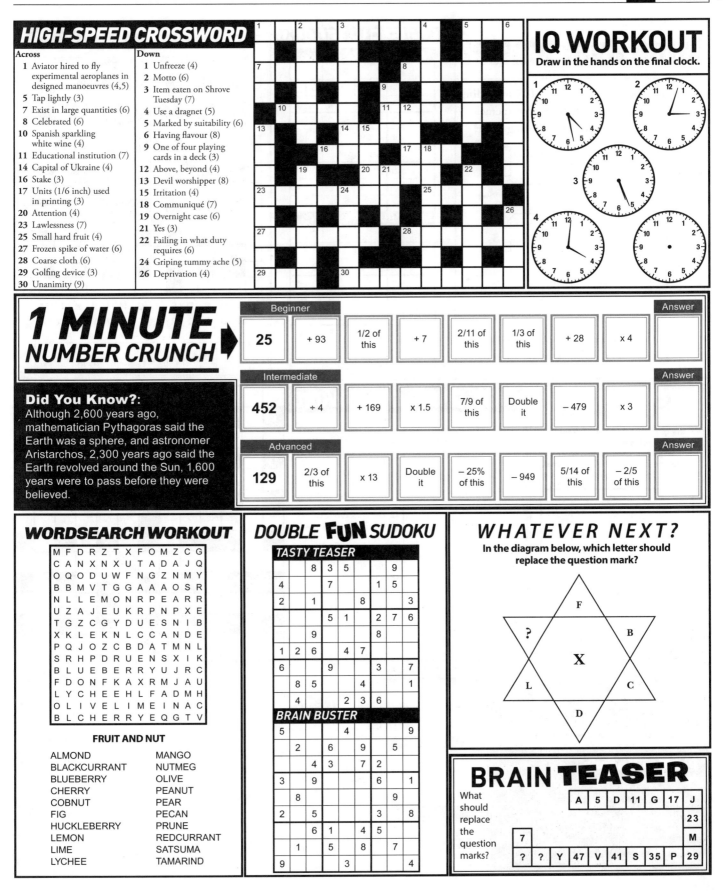

Mind Over Matter

Given that the letters are valued 1-26 according to their places in the alphabet, can you crack the mystery code to reveal the missing letter?

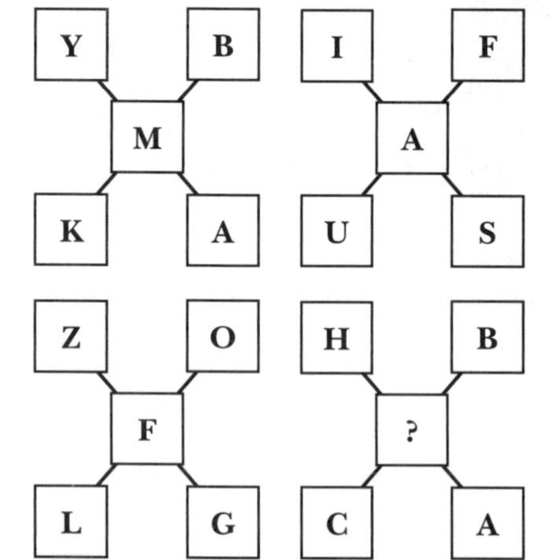

DOUBLE FUN SUDOKU

TASTY TEASER

		6	7		3			5
2				8			6	
		5	9		1	4		7
7	1				5	2		
		4		9		3		
		9	6				4	8
6		3	1		9	8		
	5			3				4
1			4		2	6		

BRAIN BUSTER

	8		1		2		6	
	9	1		5		3	8	
6	5						3	8
9		7				6		4
2	1						5	7
	6	2		3		5	4	
	7		6		9		1	

CODEWORD CONUNDRUM

3	15	23	21	20	22	6	16	18		16 L	20	20	17	10
19		13		2		15		10		23 A		16		25
23	14	14	20	24		23	9	23	15	3 D	10	3		19
16		19		16		19		15		18		10		5
17	19	21	22	23	16	16	18		6	16	23	22	21	10
		2		9				13		19				22
12	20	20	8		17	1	2	10	23	8	19	10	17	24
10		2		4		2		22		10		11		15
23	14	17	24	10	13	19	20	2	17		23	25	17	10
3				24		26				6		10		
14	10	15	23	24	10		23	24	24	20	15	22	10	18
20		20		19		16		12		10		17		20
23		5	23	17	5	23	3	10		24	12	19	22	8
15		8		20		17		24		2		7		10
3	20	18	10	22		24	15	23	22	17	5	10	22	3

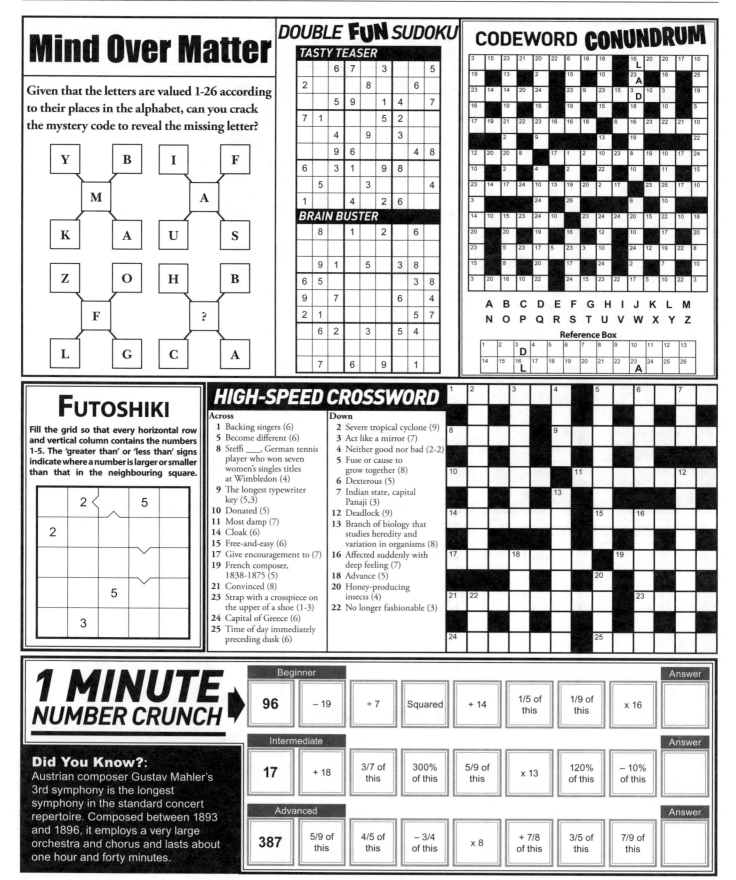

A B C D E F G H I J K L M

N O P Q R S T U V W X Y Z

Reference Box

1	2	3	4	5	6	7	8	9	10	11	12	13
		D										
14	**15**	**16**	**17**	**18**	**19**	**20**	**21**	**22**	**23**	**24**	**25**	**26**
		L							A			

FUTOSHIKI

Fill the grid so that every horizontal row and vertical column contains the numbers 1-5. The 'greater than' or 'less than' signs indicate where a number is larger or smaller than that in the neighbouring square.

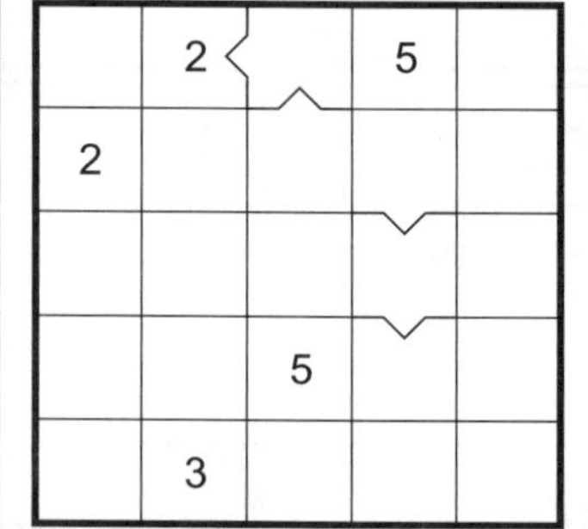

HIGH-SPEED CROSSWORD

Across

1 Backing singers (6)
5 Become different (6)
8 Steffi ___, German tennis player who won seven women's singles titles at Wimbledon (4)
9 The longest typewriter key (5,3)
10 Donated (5)
11 Most damp (7)
14 Cloak (6)
15 Free-and-easy (6)
17 Give encouragement to (7)
19 French composer, 1838-1875 (5)
21 Convinced (8)
23 Strap with a crosspiece on the upper of a shoe (1-3)
24 Capital of Greece (6)
25 Time of day immediately preceding dusk (6)

Down

2 Severe tropical cyclone (9)
3 Act like a mirror (7)
4 Neither good nor bad (2-2)
5 Fuse or cause to grow together (8)
6 Dexterous (5)
7 Indian state, capital Panaji (3)
12 Deadlock (9)
13 Branch of biology that studies heredity and variation in organisms (8)
16 Affected suddenly with deep feeling (7)
18 Advance (5)
20 Honey-producing insects (4)
22 No longer fashionable (3)

1 MINUTE NUMBER CRUNCH

Beginner								Answer
96	– 19	÷ 7	Squared	+ 14	1/5 of this	1/9 of this	x 16	

Intermediate								Answer
17	+ 18	3/7 of this	300% of this	5/9 of this	x 13	120% of this	– 10% of this	

Advanced								Answer
387	5/9 of this	4/5 of this	– 3/4 of this	x 8	+ 7/8 of this	3/5 of this	7/9 of this	

Did You Know?:
Austrian composer Gustav Mahler's 3rd symphony is the longest symphony in the standard concert repertoire. Composed between 1893 and 1896, it employs a very large orchestra and chorus and lasts about one hour and forty minutes.

Page 2

1 Minute Number Crunch

Beginner
75 x 2 = 150, 150 – 72 = 78, 78 ÷ 3 = 26, 26 + 18 = 44, 44 ÷ 4 x 3 = 33, 33 x 4 = 132, 132 ÷ 11 = 12

Intermediate
7^3 = 343, 343 + 7 = 350, 350 + 35 = 385, 385 x 0.4 = 154, 154 x 2 = 308, 308 x 0.75 = 231, 231 + 169 = 400

Advanced
784 ÷ 14 x 9 = 504, 504 + 196 (504 ÷ 18 x 7) = 700, 350% of 700 = 2450, 2450 – 1294 = 1156, 75% of 1156 = 867, 867 ÷ 3 x 8 = 2312, 2312 ÷ 1/4 = 9248

High-Speed Crossword

E	X	C	E	E	D	E	D		C		H	
L		A			I		R	E	A	S	O	N
O	U	T	S	E	T		U		N		M	
P			P		C	A	N	I	S	T	E	R
E			I		H		K				M	
S	T	A	R	E		H	E	A	R	S	A	Y
	O		A		P		N		A		D	
N	U	C	L	E	A	R		S	T	E	E	P
	R				P		S		H			E
H	I	S	T	O	R	I	C		E			S
	S		A		I		A	R	R	E	S	T
S	T	R	U	C	K		R			Y		L
	S		T		A	N	Y	W	H	E	R	E

IQ Workout

A – The figures at both ends move alternately, first the figure originally on the extreme left moves from left to right, then the figure originally on the extreme right moves from right to left.

Codeword Conundrum

M	A	G	I	C	A	L		C	A	P	A	B	L	E
A		A		L		O		R		E		R		D
M	A	T	R	I	M	O	N	Y		R		E		I
M		E		M		S		S	U	S	P	E	C	T
O		S	U	B	J	E	C	T		U		Z		O
T			G		E			A	M	A	T	E	U	R
H	O	W	L		R	E	A	L		D			N	
	P		Y	A	K		P		F	E	E		D	
	A			P		D	E	A	L		D	O	O	R
G	L	I	M	P	S	E			E		G			E
O		N		R		P	L	E	A	S	E	S		Q
S	A	V	I	O	U	R		X		P		P		U
S		E		A		E	X	P	L	O	S	I	V	E
I		R		C		S		E		O		C		S
P	I	T	C	H	E	S		L	E	N	I	E	N	T

Tasty Teaser

8	6	5	7	2	3	9	1	4
2	3	9	1	6	4	5	8	7
1	7	4	5	9	8	6	2	3
6	2	3	8	4	5	1	7	9
7	5	8	9	3	1	4	6	2
9	4	1	6	7	2	8	3	5
4	8	2	3	5	6	7	9	1
5	1	7	2	8	9	3	4	6
3	9	6	4	1	7	2	5	8

Brain Buster

8	1	4	9	2	5	6	3	7
3	9	6	8	7	4	2	1	5
7	5	2	1	6	3	4	8	9
9	7	8	4	1	2	3	5	6
2	3	1	6	5	9	8	7	4
6	4	5	7	3	8	9	2	1
5	8	9	3	4	7	1	6	2
4	6	7	2	8	1	5	9	3
1	2	3	5	9	6	7	4	8

Spidoku

Page 3

Logi-Six

C	E	D	F	B	A
A	B	C	D	F	E
D	A	E	B	C	F
E	F	B	A	D	C
F	D	A	C	E	B
B	C	F	E	A	D

High-Speed Crossword

C	A	R	E	E	R		S	C	A	R	A	B
	L		L		A		E		B			A
O	G	R	E		C		A	M	O	U	N	T
	E		G	U	E	S	S		L			H
O	B	E	Y				H		I	D	L	E
	R			A	C	R	O	S	S			R
W	A	Y	S		H		R		H	I	S	S
E			A	Z	A	L	E	A			E	
B	O	L	T		R				G	A	L	A
S			I		A	L	P	H	A		L	
I	N	W	A	R	D		A		R	E	E	D
T			T		E		S		B		R	
E	X	C	E	S	S		S	P	O	U	S	E

Wordsearch Workout

Double Fun Sudoku

Tasty Teaser

3	2	1	5	6	9	8	4	7
6	5	7	8	2	4	1	9	3
4	8	9	7	3	1	6	2	5
8	6	4	3	5	7	9	1	2
9	1	5	6	4	2	3	7	8
7	3	2	9	1	8	5	6	4
2	4	6	1	8	3	7	5	9
1	7	3	4	9	5	2	8	6
5	9	8	2	7	6	4	3	1

Brain Buster

4	2	8	6	9	1	3	5	7
1	5	3	8	7	2	4	9	6
9	6	7	5	4	3	2	1	8
3	9	5	2	6	4	7	8	1
6	4	2	1	8	7	5	3	9
8	7	1	3	5	9	6	4	2
5	8	9	7	3	6	1	2	4
2	3	6	4	1	8	9	7	5
7	1	4	9	2	5	8	6	3

Matchstick Magic

The matchsticks which have been moved are outlined.

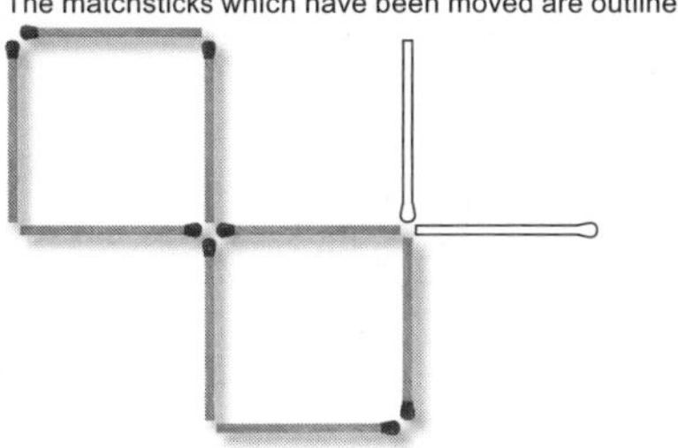

Brain Teaser

36 minutes

Domino Placement

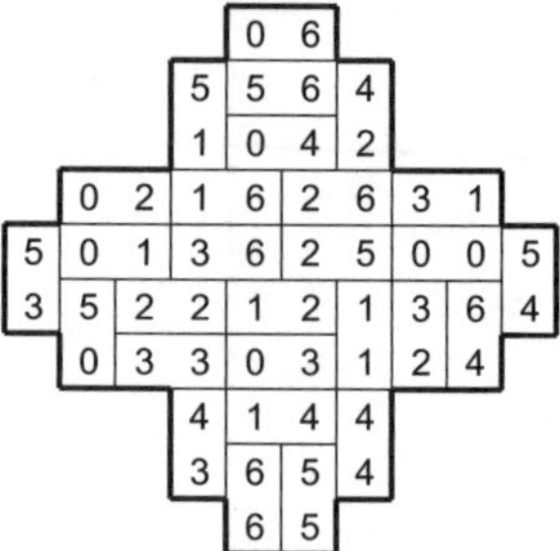

Page 4

Codeword Conundrum

J	O	S	T	L	E		F	A	N	D	A	N	G	O
U			R		D		R			O		E		U
M	A	G	A	Z	I	N	E		I	N	J	E	C	T
B			G		T		A	I	R			D		S
O	O	Z	E		I	N	K		A	D	R	I	F	T
	W		D		O		Y	E	T			N		A
E	N	V	Y	I	N	G		P	E	P	P	E	R	Y
X		I		L		A	W	E		E		S		E
Q	U	E	L	L	E	D		E	L	A	P	S	E	D
U		W			A	S	H		O		E		L	
I	M	P	A	I	R		A	N	Y		T	A	M	P
S		O			L	O	W		A		U			A
I	D	I	O	C	Y		S	I	L	E	N	C	E	R
T		N		A			E		T		I			T
E	X	T	E	R	I	O	R		Y	E	A	R	L	Y

Double Fun Sudoku

Tasty Teaser

7	9	8	3	4	5	2	1	6
4	3	5	2	6	1	9	7	8
2	6	1	7	9	8	5	4	3
9	7	2	1	8	4	3	6	5
8	4	6	5	3	7	1	9	2
5	1	3	9	2	6	4	8	7
1	2	7	6	5	9	8	3	4
6	5	4	8	1	3	7	2	9
3	8	9	4	7	2	6	5	1

Brain Buster

7	3	9	4	6	8	2	1	5
5	6	1	2	3	9	4	8	7
8	2	4	7	1	5	9	3	6
4	8	7	3	9	6	5	2	1
2	1	5	8	4	7	3	6	9
3	9	6	1	5	2	7	4	8
6	7	3	5	2	1	8	9	4
1	4	8	9	7	3	6	5	2
9	5	2	6	8	4	1	7	3

Pyramid Plus

A=74, B=138, C=55, D=134, E=56, F=212, G=193, H=189, I=190, J=405, K=382, L=379, M=787, N=761, O=1548.

Work it Out

22 – All of the numbers in any row across total 162.

High-Speed Crossword

1 Minute Number Crunch

Beginner
124 – 16 = 108, 108 ÷ 9 = 12, 12 x 7 = 84, 84 + 36 = 120, 120 x 3 = 360, 360 ÷ 20 = 18, 18 x 3 = 54

Intermediate
1973 – 982 = 991, 991 + 39 = 1030, 1030 + 148 = 1178, 1178 ÷ 19 = 62, 62 x 7 = 434, 434 – 48 = 386, 386 ÷ 2 = 193

Advanced
4 to the power of 4 = 256, 256 ÷ 16 x 9 = 144, 144 ÷ 12 x 11 = 132, 132 ÷ 22 x 9 = 54, 54 x 18 = 972, 972 – 677 = 295, 295 + 236 (295 ÷ 5 x 4) = 531

Page 5

High-Speed Crossword

C	A	T	C	H		P	L	U	M	M	E	T
O		R		O	V	A		R		E		E
M	E	A	N	S		R		B	L	A	D	E
P		M		T		I		A		S		M
O		P	L	E	A	S	A	N	T	L	Y	
S				S		H				E		S
E	L	A	P	S	E		C	L	O	S	E	T
R		V				C		E				A
	F	A	L	S	E	A	L	A	R	M		R
F		R		T		V		F		A		T
E	X	I	L	E		I		L	U	N	G	E
E		C		E		A	G	E		I		R
S	T	E	L	L	A	R		T	R	A	P	S

IQ Workout

Clocks gain 105 minutes, then 100 minutes, then 95 minutes and finally 90 minutes.

1 Minute Number Crunch

Beginner
9 x 8 = 72, 72 + 36 (72 ÷ 2) = 108, 108 – 56 = 52, 52 ÷ 4 = 13, 13 + 94 = 107, 107 – 11 = 96, 96 ÷ 6 = 16

Intermediate
87 + 56 = 143, 143 x 3 = 429, 429 x 2 = 858, 858 – 669 = 189, 189 ÷ 9 x 4 = 84, 84 ÷ 7 x 5 = 60, 220% of 60 = 132

Advanced
20^3 = 8000, 99% of 8000 = 7920, 7920 ÷ 5 x 3 = 4752, 4752 + 891 (4752 ÷ 16 x 3) = 5643, 5643 – 3979 = 1664, 1664 ÷ 32 x 9 = 468, 468 x 7 = 3276

Wordsearch Workout

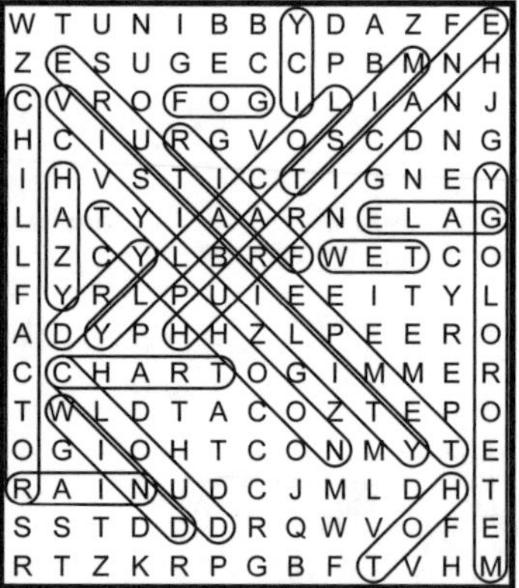

Double Fun Sudoku

Tasty Teaser

5	1	9	2	8	3	6	7	4
4	8	6	1	9	7	5	3	2
3	7	2	4	5	6	8	9	1
2	4	5	3	1	8	7	6	9
7	9	1	5	6	4	3	2	8
6	3	8	7	2	9	4	1	5
1	2	4	6	3	5	9	8	7
9	5	3	8	7	1	2	4	6
8	6	7	9	4	2	1	5	3

Brain Buster

4	8	3	5	6	2	1	9	7
7	9	2	8	3	1	4	6	5
1	5	6	7	9	4	8	3	2
3	7	5	4	2	6	9	8	1
9	4	8	1	7	5	3	2	6
6	2	1	3	8	9	5	7	4
2	1	7	9	5	3	6	4	8
5	6	9	2	4	8	7	1	3
8	3	4	6	1	7	2	5	9

Whatever Next?

369 – Starting at the top, 5–3=2x3=6, 6–3=3x3=9, 9–3=6x3=18, 18–3=15x3=45, 45–3=42x3=126, and 126–3=123x3=369.

Brain Teaser

3 – So that all lines across and down total 10.

Page 6

Mind Over Matter

The value of the letter in the central square is the sum total of the values of the letters in the other squares. Thus the missing value is 22, so the missing letter is V.

1 Minute Number Crunch

Beginner
99 + 18 (9 + 9) = 117, 117 ÷ 3 = 39, 39 + 13 (39 ÷ 3) = 52, 52 ÷ 2 = 26, 26 + 58 = 84, 84 ÷ 12 = 7, 7 x 5 = 35

Intermediate
829 – 555 = 274, 274 ÷ 2 = 137, 137 + 85 = 222, 222 ÷ 37 = 6, 6^3 = 216, 216 ÷ 9 x 3 = 72, 72 ÷ 8 x 3 = 27

Advanced
94 x 11 = 1034, 1034 ÷ 0.5 = 2068, 2068 + 1551 (2068 ÷ 4 x 3) = 3619, 3619 – 2917 = 702, 702 + 624 (702 ÷ 9 x 8) = 1326, 1326 + 663 (1326 ÷ 2) = 1989, 1989 ÷ 9 x 14 = 3094

Page 10

Codeword Conundrum

Double Fun Sudoku

Tasty Teaser

5	3	8	1	2	7	6	4	9
2	6	9	8	3	4	1	5	7
7	1	4	9	5	6	3	8	2
6	4	2	7	9	1	5	3	8
9	5	3	6	8	2	4	7	1
1	8	7	3	4	5	2	9	6
8	9	5	2	1	3	7	6	4
3	7	1	4	6	9	8	2	5
4	2	6	5	7	8	9	1	3

Brain Buster

6	7	4	2	9	1	3	8	5
2	1	8	3	5	6	4	9	7
5	3	9	7	4	8	6	2	1
9	8	6	5	1	4	2	7	3
1	5	7	9	2	3	8	6	4
4	2	3	8	6	7	5	1	9
7	6	2	1	3	5	9	4	8
8	4	5	6	7	9	1	3	2
3	9	1	4	8	2	7	5	6

Pyramid Plus

A=121, B=69, C=92, D=122, E=129, F=190, G=161, H=214, I=251, J=351, K=375, L=465, M=726, N=840, O=1566.

Work it Out

29 – The numbers in each horizontal row total 100.

High-Speed Crossword

1 Minute Number Crunch

Beginner
8^2 = 64, 64 - 49 = 15, 15 x 9 = 135, 135 ÷ 15 x 2 = 18, 18 + 67 = 85, 85 + 17 (85 ÷ 5) = 102, 102 ÷ 3 = 34

Intermediate
55 ÷ 11 x 4 = 20, 20 x 1.75 = 35, 35 ÷ 7 x 2 = 10, 400% of 10 = 40, 40 + 47 = 87, 87 ÷ 3 x 2 = 58, 58 ÷ 0.5 = 116

Advanced
459 ÷ 17 x 8 = 216, 216 ÷ 36 x 29 = 174, 174 ÷ 3 x 8 = 464, 62.5% of 464 = 290, 290 + 777 = 1067, 1067 x 4 = 4268, 4268 + 3201 (75% of 4268) = 7469

Page 11

High-Speed Crossword

R	O	S	E	B	U	D		A	D	L	I	B
E		T		I		A			R			O
E	K	E		A	N	T	I	P	A	S	T	O
L		A		S		E			W			T
E	N	D	U	E			S		E	E	L	S
C		F		D	I	S	T	U	R	B		
T	H	A	T		S		A		S	U	D	S
		S	E	A	L	E	G	S		L		W
S	I	T	E		E			P	O	L	K	A
T			N			B		H		I		G
A	D	V	A	N	T	A	G	E		E	L	M
I			G			G		R		N		A
R	I	P	E	N		S	W	E	E	T	E	N

Summing Up

31	6	11	31	47	**11**
22	22	35	**8**	27	23
23	**31**	22	24	14	23
18	39	27	20	9	24
21	26	16	34	**13**	27
22	13	**26**	20	27	29

Domino Placement

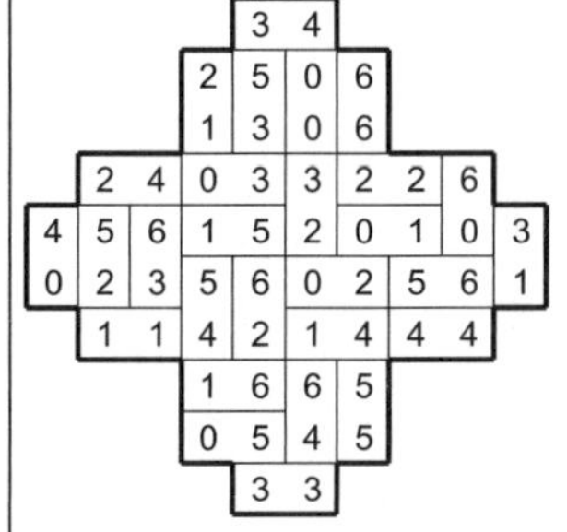

Wordsearch Workout

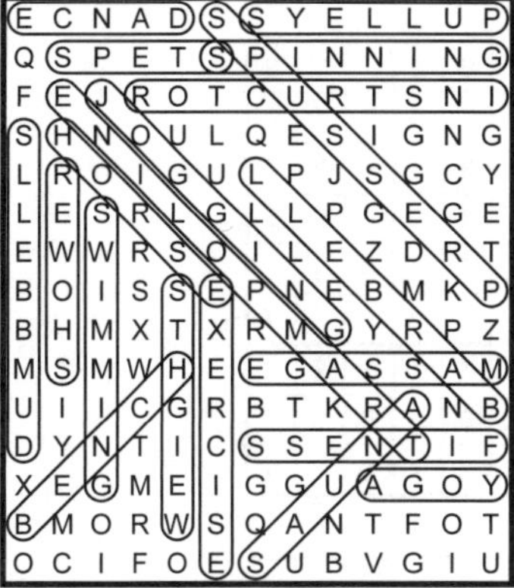

Double Fun Sudoku

Tasty Teaser

7	2	4	9	3	6	8	5	1
9	8	3	7	1	5	6	2	4
1	6	5	8	2	4	9	3	7
5	4	2	1	6	7	3	9	8
3	9	6	4	8	2	1	7	5
8	1	7	3	5	9	2	4	6
2	5	8	6	7	3	4	1	9
4	7	1	2	9	8	5	6	3
6	3	9	5	4	1	7	8	2

Brain Buster

6	3	1	4	7	2	9	8	5
9	5	2	8	6	1	7	4	3
4	8	7	3	5	9	1	6	2
5	1	6	2	4	3	8	7	9
8	4	3	1	9	7	5	2	6
2	7	9	5	8	6	4	3	1
7	6	5	9	3	8	2	1	4
3	2	4	7	1	5	6	9	8
1	9	8	6	2	4	3	5	7

Whatever Next?

G – Assign a number to each letter according to its place in the alphabet, so B=2, D=4, F=6, J=10 and L=12, making a total of 34. The total in the centre is 41, so the missing letter is G (=7).

Brain Teaser

16

Page 12

Mind Over Matter

The sum total of the values of the letters in the bottom squares is subtracted from the sum total of the values of the letters in the top squares. Thus the missing value is 19, so the missing letter is S.

Double Fun Sudoku

Tasty Teaser

4	5	9	7	6	2	1	3	8
6	2	3	4	1	8	7	5	9
1	8	7	9	3	5	4	2	6
7	3	4	1	8	6	2	9	5
2	9	6	5	7	4	8	1	3
5	1	8	3	2	9	6	4	7
3	6	5	8	4	1	9	7	2
8	7	1	2	9	3	5	6	4
9	4	2	6	5	7	3	8	1

Brain Buster

4	2	7	5	3	1	9	6	8
5	6	3	9	7	8	2	1	4
1	9	8	2	6	4	3	7	5
7	8	9	6	4	5	1	3	2
6	4	2	3	1	9	8	5	7
3	5	1	7	8	2	4	9	6
9	3	5	4	2	6	7	8	1
2	1	6	8	9	7	5	4	3
8	7	4	1	5	3	6	2	9

Codeword Conundrum

A	X	I	S		C	L	A	N	G		B	O	S	S
L			E	A	R		O		A			B		A
S	O	U	R		A	C	R	O	S	S		O	W	L
O			V		F		T			P	L	E	A	T
		S	O	F	T		A	G	U	E			L	
P	I	E		I		M		R		W	H	E	L	P
I		N		S	L	O	G	A	N			X		A
Q	U	I	L	T		S		V		Y	O	U	N	G
U		O			G	A	Z	E	B	O		D		E
E	G	R	E	T		I		L		K		E	N	D
	E			A	R	C	H		B	E	N	D		
A	N	T	I	C			Y		A		U			B
B	E	E		O	B	J	E	C	T		T	A	M	E
E		A			I		N		H	U	T			L
T	A	K	E		G	R	A	Z	E		Y	A	W	L

Futoshiki

4	1	3	2	5
3	4	2	5	1
2	3	5	1	4
1	5	4	3	2
5	2	1	4	3

High-Speed Crossword

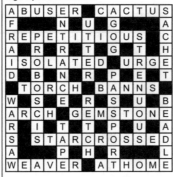

A	B	U	S	E	R		C	A	C	T	U	S
F				N		U		G				A
R	E	P	E	T	I	T	I	O	U	S		C
A		R		R		T		G		T		H
I	S	O	L	A	T	E	D		U	R	G	E
D		B		N		R		P		E		T
	T	O	R	C	H		B	A	N	N	S	
W		S		E		R		S		U		B
A	R	C	H		G	E	M	S	T	O	N	E
R		I		T		T		P		U		A
S		S	T	A	R	C	R	O	S	S	E	D
A				P		H		R				L
W	E	A	V	E	R		A	T	H	O	M	E

1 Minute Number Crunch

Beginner
22 x 7 = 154, 154 ÷ 2 = 77, 77 ÷ 11 x 4 = 28, 28 + 14 (50% of 28) = 42, 42 – 9 = 33, 33 x 4 = 132, 132 ÷ 11 x 7 = 84

Intermediate
27 x 3 = 81, 81 – 56 = 25, 80% of 25 = 20, 850% of 20 = 170, 170 ÷ 10 x 7 = 119, 119 x 2 = 238, 238 + 823 = 1061

Advanced
96 x 14 = 1344, 1344 + 1008 (1344 ÷ 4 x 3) = 2352, 2352 ÷ 6 x 5 = 1960, 35% of 1960 = 686, 686 + 155 = 841, square root of 841 = 29, 29 x 13 = 377

Page 13

1 Minute Number Crunch

Beginner
1234 x 2 = 2468, 2468 – 999 = 1469, 1469 + 31 = 1500, 90% of 1500 = 1350, 1350 ÷ 5 = 270, 270 ÷ 5 = 54, 54 x 3 = 162

Intermediate
99 ÷ 9 x 5 = 55, 55 ÷ 11 x 5 = 25, square root of 25 = 5, 5 + 1 = 6, 6 + 5 = 11, 11^2 = 121, 121 x 3 = 363

Advanced
96 x 4 = 384, 384 + 72 (384 ÷ 16 x 3) = 456, 456 ÷ 6 x 5 = 380, 380 – 342 (90% of 380) = 38, 38 + 795 = 833, 833 x 7 = 5831, 5831 – 2978 = 2853

High-Speed Crossword

B	O	L	I	V	I	A	N		P	L	E	A
O		A		E		R				E		C
T	A	N	T	R	U	M	S			A		C
A		T		S		S	T	E	E	P	L	E
N	I	E	C	E			E					S
Y		R		S	P	A	R	T	A	C	U	S
		N			A		E			O		
S	U	S	P	I	C	I	O	N		N		C
E					K			A	T	S	E	A
R	A	T	C	H	E	T		I		P		M
I		O			T	A	I	L	P	I	P	E
E		G				C		E		R		L
S	L	A	Y		G	O	O	D	N	E	S	S

Partitions

●		●		
●		●	●	
	●	●		
			●	
●		●		

Wordwheel

The nine-letter word is: DISTORTED

Wordsearch Workout

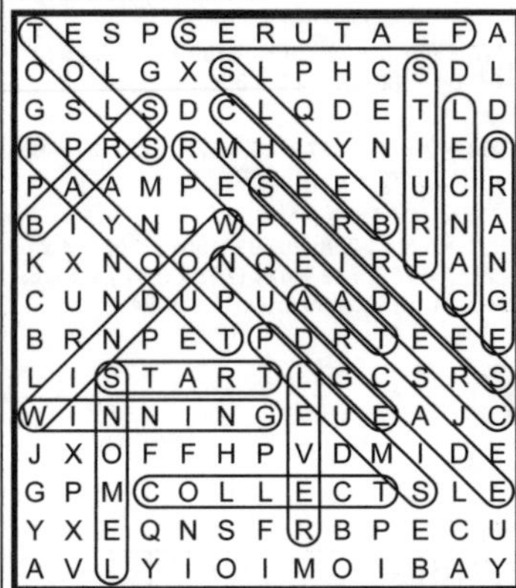

Double Fun Sudoku

Tasty Teaser

1	6	9	7	2	3	8	5	4
8	2	5	4	9	6	1	7	3
4	3	7	5	1	8	2	9	6
5	1	6	9	4	7	3	8	2
7	4	3	8	5	2	9	6	1
2	9	8	6	3	1	7	4	5
9	5	1	2	7	4	6	3	8
6	7	2	3	8	5	4	1	9
3	8	4	1	6	9	5	2	7

Brain Buster

4	6	5	3	8	2	9	1	7
7	2	8	4	1	9	3	5	6
9	3	1	6	7	5	2	4	8
2	7	4	8	9	1	5	6	3
5	8	3	7	6	4	1	2	9
1	9	6	2	5	3	8	7	4
8	1	2	9	4	6	7	3	5
3	4	9	5	2	7	6	8	1
6	5	7	1	3	8	4	9	2

Sum Circle

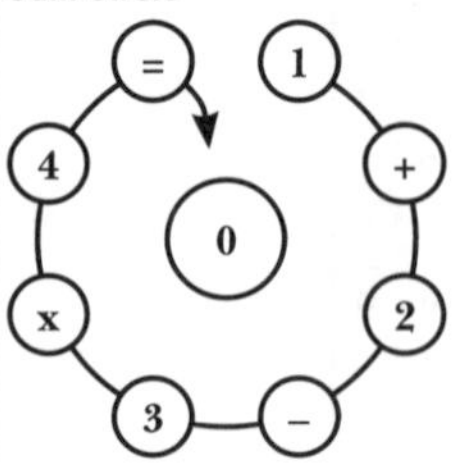

Page 14

1 Minute Number Crunch

Beginner
14 x 6 = 84, 84 ÷ 2 = 42, 42 ÷ 7 = 6, 6 x 2.5 = 15, 500% of 15 = 75, 75 x 3 = 225, 225 ÷ 15 = 15

Intermediate
424 – 128 = 296, 296 ÷ 2 = 148, 148 ÷ 4 = 37, 37 x 7 = 259, 259 + 955 = 1214, 1214 x 2 = 2428, 2428 – 1957 = 471

Advanced
558 + 372 (558 ÷ 3 x 2) = 930, 930 ÷ 10 x 7 = 651, 651 + 465 (651 ÷ 7 x 5) = 1116, 1116 – 248 (1116 ÷ 9 x 2) = 868, 868 – 277 = 591, 591 ÷ 3 x 8 = 1576, 1576 + 591 (1576 ÷ 8 x 3) = 2167

High-Speed Crossword

P	E	R	H	A	P	S		P		A		T
O		A		R			G	A	L	L	E	Y
P		D		R		R		R		T		P
C	O	I	N	A	G	E		S	P	A	R	E
O		A		Y		S		L		R		D
R	I	N	D		D	I	V	E	R			
N		T		H		D		Y		M		G
			L	A	T	E	R		S	E	R	E
B		B		M		N		C		D		N
R	O	O	T	S		C	H	A	L	I	C	E
A		G		T		E		P		A		S
S	W	E	D	E	N			E		T		I
S		Y		R		A	I	R	L	E	S	S

IQ Workout

A	B	C	D	E
C	D	E	A	B
E	A	B	C	D
B	C	D	E	A
D	E	A	B	C

Codeword Conundrum

S	U	P	E	R		M	A	J	O	R	E	T	T	E
E		Y		I		A		A		E				R
B	U	L	L	D	O	Z	E	R		V	I	S	T	A
A		O		D		E		D		E		L		S
C	A	N	V	A	S		F	I	X	A	T	I	V	E
E				N		S		N		L		C		
O	P	T	I	C		Q	U	I	P		D	I	S	C
U		W		E		U		E		B		N		A
S	K	I	D		H	A	I	R		O	U	G	H	T
		T		F		B		E		T				A
S	U	C	C	U	M	B	S		P	A	R	S	E	C
I		H		N		L		W		N		T		L
D	O	Y	E	N		I	M	A	G	I	N	A	R	Y
E				E		N		F		S		I		S
S	P	O	T	L	I	G	H	T		T	H	R	U	M

Tasty Teaser

8	7	2	5	6	3	9	1	4
6	9	1	8	7	4	3	2	5
4	3	5	9	1	2	6	7	8
3	5	7	2	9	1	4	8	6
1	8	9	7	4	6	2	5	3
2	6	4	3	5	8	7	9	1
9	2	8	6	3	5	1	4	7
7	1	6	4	8	9	5	3	2
5	4	3	1	2	7	8	6	9

Brain Buster

2	3	8	1	7	4	5	6	9
5	9	7	8	6	3	1	2	4
1	6	4	5	2	9	8	7	3
7	8	9	2	4	5	3	1	6
4	5	3	6	9	1	2	8	7
6	1	2	7	3	8	9	4	5
9	4	1	3	8	6	7	5	2
8	2	6	9	5	7	4	3	1
3	7	5	4	1	2	6	9	8

Spidoku

Page 15

Logi-Six

C	D	F	E	B	A
B	A	D	F	E	C
E	B	C	A	F	D
F	C	A	B	D	E
A	F	E	D	C	B
D	E	B	C	A	F

High-Speed Crossword

C	A	R	E	S	S		E	D	G	I	N	G
A		E		H		M		I		M		L
R	E	C	L	I	N	E		S		A		I
A		O		R		A	T	T	E	M	P	T
F	O	R	C	E	P	S		A				C
E		D				U		N	O	R	T	H
		E		S	T	R	U	T		E		
M	E	R	R	Y		E				S		L
O				R		M	O	U	N	T	I	E
R	E	S	P	I	T	E		L		R		A
A		L		N		N	E	T	T	I	N	G
S		U		G		T		R		C		U
S	T	R	E	E	T		R	A	T	T	L	E

Wordsearch Workout

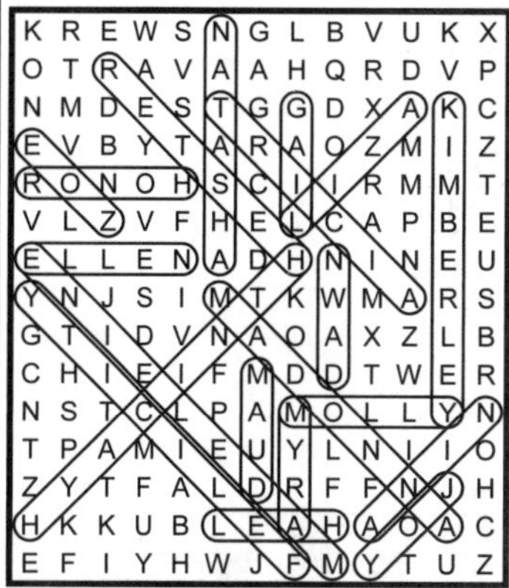

Double Fun Sudoku

Tasty Teaser

7	6	8	9	1	3	4	2	5
4	9	2	7	5	6	1	3	8
1	5	3	4	8	2	7	9	6
6	8	1	3	2	5	9	7	4
2	4	9	6	7	8	3	5	1
3	7	5	1	9	4	6	8	2
9	2	6	5	3	1	8	4	7
5	1	7	8	4	9	2	6	3
8	3	4	2	6	7	5	1	9

Brain Buster

3	2	6	7	4	9	8	1	5
5	9	7	1	3	8	4	2	6
4	8	1	6	5	2	9	3	7
1	7	9	2	6	3	5	4	8
2	4	3	8	7	5	1	6	9
8	6	5	9	1	4	3	7	2
6	1	8	3	9	7	2	5	4
7	5	2	4	8	1	6	9	3
9	3	4	5	2	6	7	8	1

Matchstick Magic

The matchsticks which have been removed are outlined.

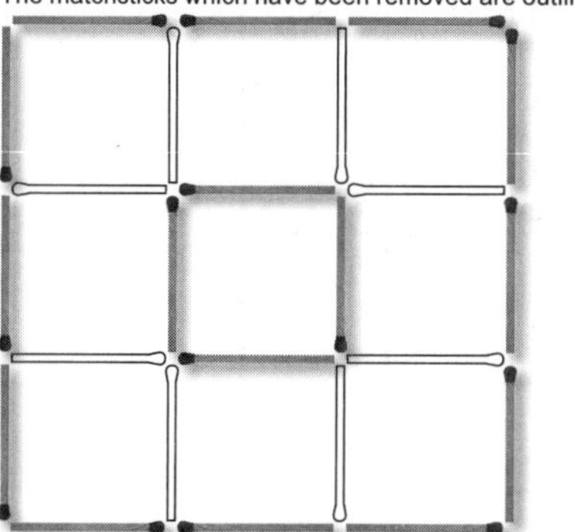

Brain Teaser

14

Simple as A, B, C

B	A	C	B	C	A
A	B	B	C	C	A
C	C	A	A	B	B
A	B	B	C	A	C
C	C	A	B	A	B
B	A	C	A	B	C

Page 16

Codeword Conundrum

J	E	A	L	O	U	S	L	Y		T	I	M	E	S
U		M		D		U		A		E		E		O
R	A	B	I	D		A	N	N	E	X	E	D		U
O		I		I		V		K		T		A		N
R	E	G	A	T	H	E	R		F	U	R	L	E	D
		U		Y				Z		R				N
T	O	O	L		D	E	L	I	B	E	R	A	T	E
U		U		T		K		N		D		P		S
R	E	S	U	R	G	E	N	C	E		O	P	U	S
B				A		D				M		L		
U	N	B	E	N	T		B	R	E	A	K	I	N	G
L		A		Q		E		O		D		C		I
E		L	A	U	N	D	R	Y		C	H	A	R	D
N		S		I		I		A		A		N		D
T	R	A	W	L		T	E	L	E	P	A	T	H	Y

Double Fun Sudoku

Tasty Teaser

2	6	1	8	9	4	5	3	7
9	7	8	6	3	5	4	1	2
4	3	5	1	2	7	6	9	8
3	1	4	5	7	6	2	8	9
5	8	2	3	4	9	1	7	6
6	9	7	2	8	1	3	5	4
7	2	9	4	1	3	8	6	5
1	4	6	9	5	8	7	2	3
8	5	3	7	6	2	9	4	1

Brain Buster

5	8	7	6	4	1	2	9	3
6	1	3	8	9	2	5	4	7
9	4	2	7	5	3	8	1	6
4	9	6	5	1	7	3	8	2
8	2	5	3	6	9	4	7	1
7	3	1	2	8	4	9	6	5
2	7	4	9	3	6	1	5	8
1	6	8	4	2	5	7	3	9
3	5	9	1	7	8	6	2	4

Pyramid Plus

A=24, B=124, C=68, D=35, E=60, F=148, G=192, H=103, I=95, J=340, K=295, L=198, M=635, N=493, O=1128.

Work it Out

17 – The totals of the numbers in the vertical columns increases by 6.

High-Speed Crossword

S	K	I	M	P		C	L	A	S	S	I	C
C		N		O		A		B		I		O
A	U	D	I	T	O	R		A	U	G	U	R
B		E		H		R		S		N		T
S	E	T	T	O		O	N	E	T	I	M	E
		E		L		T				F		G
S	C	R	E	E	N		A	D	M	I	R	E
T		M				E		I		C		
A	N	I	S	E	E	D		S	T	A	N	D
R		N		N		I		M		N		I
T	R	A	I	N		B	L	I	S	T	E	R
U		T		U		L		S		L		G
P	R	E	C	I	S	E		S	T	Y	L	E

1 Minute Number Crunch

Beginner
88 ÷ 4 x 3 = 66, 66 + 49 = 115, 115 ÷ 5 x 3 = 69, 69 – 42 = 27, 27 + 18 (27 ÷ 3 x 2) = 45, 45 x 4 = 180, 180 ÷ 10 x 3 = 54

Intermediate
394 ÷ 2 = 197, 197 + 88 = 285, 285 ÷ 3 = 95, 120% of 95 = 114, 114 – 77 = 37, 37 x 2 = 74, 74 x 5 = 370

Advanced
7 to the power of 4 = 2401, 2401 x 8 = 19208, 19208 – 6936 = 12272, 12272 ÷ 16 x 5 = 3835, 60% of 3835 = 2301, 2301 – 1534 (2301 ÷ 3 x 2) = 767, 767 x 14 = 10738

Page 17

High-Speed Crossword

	S	U	F	F	I	C	I	E	N	C	Y	
A		N		A		H		R		H		P
R		H		C	E	A	S	E		A	L	E
C	R	A	F	T		F		C		I		R
H		P		U		E		T	U	R	N	S
A	P	P	L	A	U	S	E					I
E		Y		L				M		R		S
O					A	R	G	U	M	E	N	T
L	I	G	H	T		A		S		G		E
O		E		E		N		S	P	A	I	N
G	O	T		N	A	C	R	E		T		C
Y		U		O		I		L		T		E
	A	P	H	R	O	D	I	S	I	A	C	

Summing Up

27	**3**	14	29	36	37
28	24	**35**	12	26	21
38	39	24	**12**	10	23
15	34	26	36	15	**20**
25	32	13	38	**14**	24
13	14	34	19	45	21

1 Minute Number Crunch

Beginner
78 + 15 = 93, 93 ÷ 3 = 31, 31 x 4 = 124, 124 + 20 = 144, 144 ÷ 12 = 12, 12 x 8 = 96, 96 ÷ 2 = 48

Intermediate
291 + 49 = 340, 20% of 340 = 68, 68 ÷ 4 = 17, 17 x 7 = 119, 119 x 2 = 238, 238 – 190 = 48, 48 + 32 = 80

Advanced
342 ÷ 19 x 5 = 90, 170% of 90 = 153, 153 + 119 (153 ÷ 9 x 7) = 272, 272 x 0.625 = 170, 170 ÷ 34 x 5 = 25, 25^3 = 15625, 15625 ÷ 5 x 4 = 12500

Wordsearch Workout

Double Fun Sudoku

Tasty Teaser

8	7	9	6	5	1	3	4	2
5	2	3	7	8	4	1	6	9
1	6	4	3	2	9	5	7	8
3	9	2	4	6	5	8	1	7
7	1	8	2	9	3	6	5	4
4	5	6	8	1	7	2	9	3
2	8	1	9	4	6	7	3	5
9	3	5	1	7	8	4	2	6
6	4	7	5	3	2	9	8	1

Brain Buster

4	6	3	9	7	8	1	2	5
7	5	1	4	2	3	9	6	8
9	8	2	1	6	5	4	7	3
2	1	8	7	3	9	5	4	6
3	9	5	6	8	4	7	1	2
6	4	7	2	5	1	8	3	9
1	7	6	8	9	2	3	5	4
5	2	9	3	4	7	6	8	1
8	3	4	5	1	6	2	9	7

Whatever Next?

12 – The central number is 60 and the lower numbers are 60% of the higher numbers on opposite points of the star.

Brain Teaser

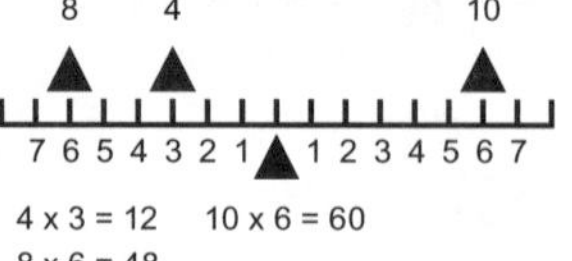

4 x 3 = 12   10 x 6 = 60
8 x 6 = 48
60

Page 18

Mind Over Matter

The sum total of the values in the top squares equals the value of the central square, as does the sum total of the values in the bottom squares. Thus the missing value is 3, so the missing letter is C.

Double Fun Sudoku

Tasty Teaser

8	1	4	6	9	5	7	2	3
9	5	3	1	7	2	8	6	4
6	7	2	3	8	4	9	1	5
4	9	1	5	6	3	2	8	7
5	6	7	9	2	8	4	3	1
3	2	8	4	1	7	6	5	9
1	4	9	8	5	6	3	7	2
7	3	6	2	4	1	5	9	8
2	8	5	7	3	9	1	4	6

Brain Buster

1	7	6	3	9	8	4	5	2
4	5	8	6	7	2	3	9	1
3	9	2	5	1	4	8	7	6
9	6	5	4	3	1	7	2	8
7	8	3	2	6	9	1	4	5
2	4	1	7	8	5	6	3	9
5	1	9	8	4	7	2	6	3
8	3	7	9	2	6	5	1	4
6	2	4	1	5	3	9	8	7

Codeword Conundrum

Q	U	I	R	K	Y		A		C		D	O	E	S
U		G		N		A	L	K	A	L	I			K
A	L	L	I	A	N	C	E		V		F	A	K	E
D		O		C		H		S	E	L	F			W
S	P	O	O	K	I	E	S	T			I	S	L	E
	E				N			A	P	E	D			R
C	A	M	O	U	F	L	A	G	E		E	B	B	S
	C		U		L		S		D		N		U	
J	E	S	T		U	P	H	O	L	S	T	E	R	Y
U			W	A	X	Y			A				N	
G	A	L	A			R	E	P	R	O	B	A	T	E
U			R	A	Z	E		A		L		L		V
L	O	A	D		E		C	I	V	I	L	I	S	E
A			L	E	S	I	O	N		V		A		R
R	U	B	Y		T		T		F	E	I	S	T	Y

Futoshiki

3	5	2	4	1
2	3	1	5	4
5	4 >	3	1 <	2
1	2	4	3	5
4	1	5	2 <	3

High-Speed Crossword

R	E	B	U	I	L	D		J		B	U	S
	D			L		A	R	O	S	E		E
S	I	M	I	L	A	R		E		C		X
	T			F		K		Y	E	A	S	T
M	I	S	T	A	K	E	N			U		A
	O			T		N		M		S		N
S	N	I	P	E	R		L	A	T	E	S	T
A		N		D		J		T			H	
T		N			D	E	C	E	A	S	E	D
S	A	I	N	T		S		R			A	
U		N		E		T	H	I	R	S	T	Y
M		G	R	A	Z	E		A			H	
A	S	S		T		R	E	L	A	X	E	D

1 Minute Number Crunch

Beginner
232 – 34 = 198, 198 ÷ 2 = 99, 99 ÷ 9 x 5 = 55, 55 ÷ 11 x 4 = 20, 20 + 19 = 39, 39 ÷ 3 x 2 = 26, 26 + 42 = 68

Intermediate
29 x 3 = 87, 87 + 78 = 165, 165 ÷ 11 = 15, 15 + 25 = 40, 40 ÷ 10 x 3 = 12, 12 x 7 = 84, 84 ÷ 3 = 28

Advanced
702 ÷ 39 x 7 = 126, 126 + 224 = 350, 350 ÷ 10 x 7 = 245, 245 ÷ 5 x 3 = 147, 147 ÷ 3 x 2 = 98, 98 x 7 = 686, 686 x 2.5 = 1715

Page 19

Domino Placement

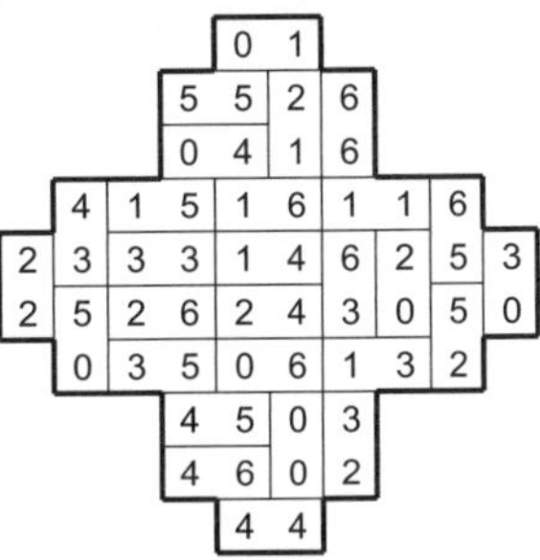

High-Speed Crossword

P	A	S	T	I	L	L	E		S	C	O	T
E		A		N		A		D		A		I
E	R	R	A	T	I	C		E	R	R	O	R
K		I		E		T		L		D		E
			A	R	T	I	F	I	C	I	A	L
G		I		M		C		C		N		E
R	A	N	G	E	R		H	A	R	A	S	S
A		V		D		S		T		L		S
P	R	I	V	I	L	E	G	E	D			
H		T		A		V		S		D		A
I	D	I	O	T		E	A	S	E	O	F	F
T		N		E		R		E		M		A
E	R	G	O		R	E	I	N	D	E	E	R

IQ Workout

3

Wordwheel

The nine-letter word is: OBJECTIVE

Wordsearch Workout

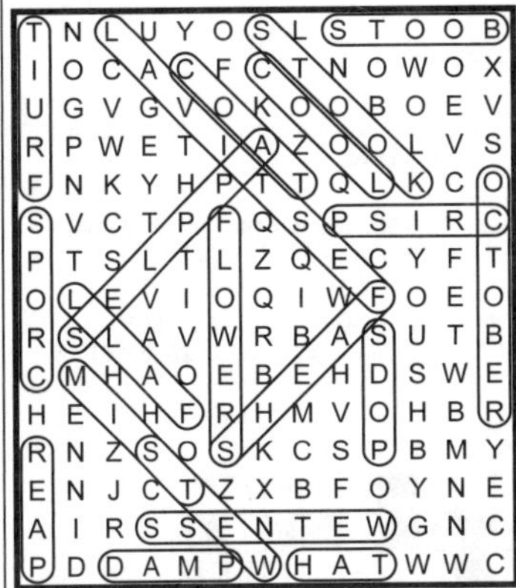

Double Fun Sudoku

Tasty Teaser

6	1	7	8	2	4	5	3	9
5	4	9	1	3	7	6	8	2
8	3	2	9	5	6	1	7	4
7	8	4	5	9	1	2	6	3
1	2	3	7	6	8	9	4	5
9	6	5	2	4	3	8	1	7
2	7	8	3	1	9	4	5	6
4	9	1	6	7	5	3	2	8
3	5	6	4	8	2	7	9	1

Brain Buster

4	2	7	6	8	9	3	5	1
1	9	3	5	7	2	6	4	8
5	6	8	4	1	3	2	7	9
3	8	9	2	4	1	5	6	7
6	7	4	3	5	8	9	1	2
2	1	5	9	6	7	4	8	3
8	3	6	7	9	5	1	2	4
7	5	2	1	3	4	8	9	6
9	4	1	8	2	6	7	3	5

Sum Circle

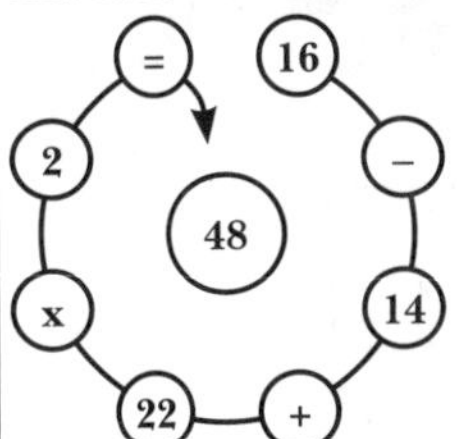

Page 20

1 Minute Number Crunch

Beginner

29 – 15 = 14, 14 ÷ 2 = 7, 7 + 86 = 93, 93 ÷ 3 = 31, 31 x 5 = 155, 155 – 122 = 33, 33 ÷ 11 = 3

Intermediate

9% of 700 = 63, 63 – 28 = 35, 35 x 4 = 140, 140 + 42 (140 ÷ 10 x 3) = 182, 182 ÷ 2 = 91, 91 – 17 = 74, 74 + 123 = 197

Advanced

22^2 = 484, 484 x 4 = 1936, 1936 ÷ 16 x 5 = 605, 605 ÷ 0.25 = 2420, 2420 – 987 = 1433, 1433 x 2 = 2866, 2866 + 777 = 3643

High-Speed Crossword

T	R	A	F	F	I	C		C	A	B	E	R
I		D		A		A		O			X	
G	N	A	T	S		S	L	A	C	K	E	N
R		P		H		H		T			C	
E	N	T	W	I	N	E		S	U	N	U	P
S		O		O		W					T	
S	E	R	E	N	E		A	S	L	E	E	P
	A					E		T		M		E
D	R	O	W	N		S	I	R	L	O	I	N
	L			E		T		I		T		A
C	O	M	P	E	T	E		D	R	I	L	L
	B			D		E		E		O		T
B	E	A	K	S		M	A	S	O	N	R	Y

IQ Workout

$18\frac{5}{8}$ – There are two series (+ $\frac{7}{8}$ and – $\frac{3}{4}$):

16, $16\frac{7}{8}$, $17\frac{3}{4}$, $18\frac{5}{8}$

21, $20\frac{1}{4}$, $19\frac{1}{2}$.

Codeword Conundrum

D	E	P	T	H		P	E	S	T	I	L	E	N	T
E		A		A		I		Y		R				A
P	H	R	E	N	E	T	I	C		R	I	S	E	R
A		T		D		H		O		U		W		D
R	O	Y	A	L	S		A	P	O	P	L	E	X	Y
T				E		D		H		T		E		
I	N	F	E	R		O	K	A	Y		E	P	I	C
N		E		S		W		N		A		E		U
G	R	I	P		K	N	O	T		C	A	R	O	B
		G		Z		L		S		C				B
K	I	N	K	A	J	O	U		Q	U	A	R	R	Y
A		E		N		A		A		S		E		H
R	A	D	I	I		D	E	S	P	E	R	A	D	O
M				E		E		H		R		V		L
A	S	S	U	R	E	D	L	Y		S	I	E	V	E

Tasty Teaser

7	8	6	9	5	1	3	2	4
5	2	1	3	4	6	8	9	7
4	3	9	8	2	7	1	5	6
9	6	4	5	1	3	2	7	8
8	7	2	6	9	4	5	1	3
3	1	5	7	8	2	4	6	9
6	4	3	2	7	5	9	8	1
2	9	7	1	3	8	6	4	5
1	5	8	4	6	9	7	3	2

Brain Buster

9	5	7	4	3	1	6	8	2
8	1	3	7	2	6	9	4	5
4	2	6	9	8	5	3	1	7
5	3	4	1	7	2	8	6	9
1	9	8	5	6	3	2	7	4
7	6	2	8	9	4	1	5	3
3	7	1	6	4	9	5	2	8
2	4	5	3	1	8	7	9	6
6	8	9	2	5	7	4	3	1

Spidoku

Wordsearch Workout

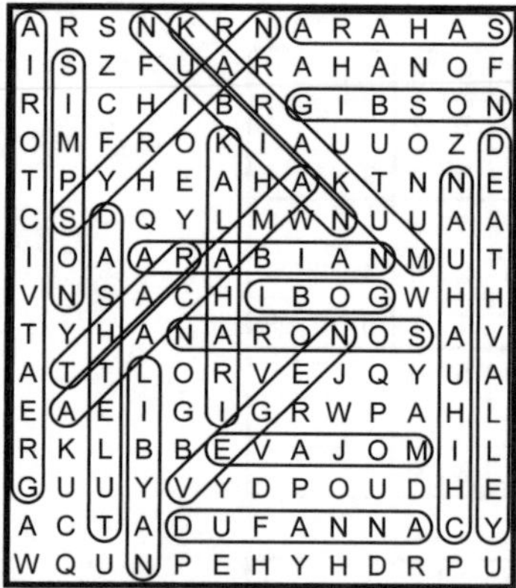

Double Fun Sudoku

Tasty Teaser

6	4	7	5	8	3	1	2	9
2	3	1	7	4	9	6	5	8
9	8	5	1	6	2	7	4	3
5	1	8	2	7	6	3	9	4
4	7	2	3	9	1	8	6	5
3	9	6	4	5	8	2	1	7
1	6	4	8	3	5	9	7	2
7	2	3	9	1	4	5	8	6
8	5	9	6	2	7	4	3	1

Brain Buster

9	4	1	2	5	8	3	7	6
3	8	5	6	7	9	1	4	2
7	6	2	4	1	3	9	5	8
5	3	4	7	8	2	6	9	1
1	2	6	5	9	4	8	3	7
8	9	7	1	3	6	4	2	5
6	1	3	9	2	7	5	8	4
2	5	8	3	4	1	7	6	9
4	7	9	8	6	5	2	1	3

Page 21

Logi-Six

D	E	F	C	B	A
A	B	C	F	D	E
C	A	E	D	F	B
F	D	B	A	E	C
E	C	D	B	A	F
B	F	A	E	C	D

High-Speed Crossword

C	H	E	E	R	S		S	P	L	I	N	T
H			Y		I		A		A			A
A	B	B	E	S	S		F		S			M
R			L		T	R	E	A	T	I	S	E
	B		I		E			L			M	
L	A	D	D	E	R		C	O	F	F	E	R
	O			X				H			L	
O	B	R	I	E	N		B	A	B	B	L	E
	A			R			U		E		Y	
A	B	A	T	T	O	I	R		H			F
V			A		R		S	T	I	G	M	A
I			P		G		A		N			N
D	R	E	S	S	Y		R	A	D	I	U	S

Matchstick Magic

The matchsticks which have been moved are outlined.

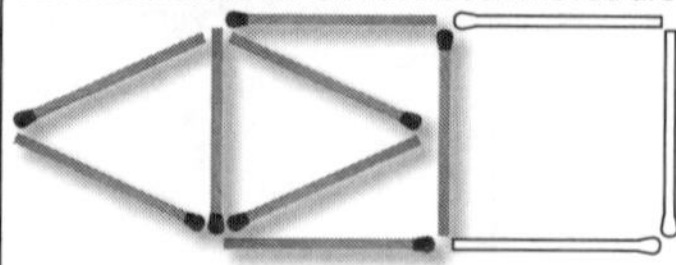

Brain Teaser

6859 – They are cube numbers:

16^3 = 4096

17^3 = 4913

18^3 = 5832

19^3 = 6859

Domino Placement

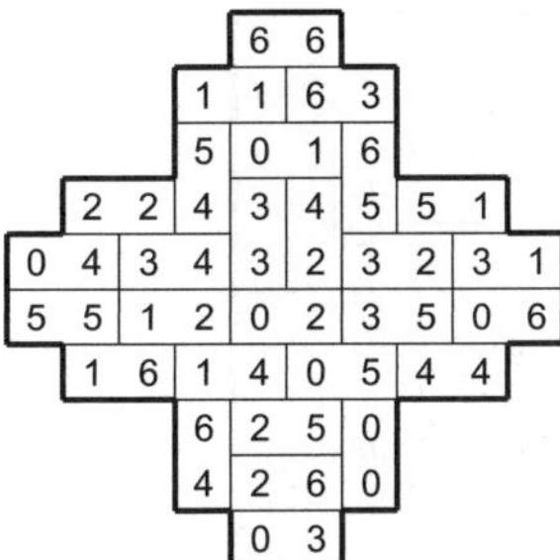

Page 22

Codeword Conundrum

W	A	S	H	B	A	S	I	N		T	A	P	E	R
A		N		L		H		E		A		I		E
G	U	A	N	O		A	V	A	R	I	C	E		P
E		K		N		L		T		L		C		U
S	T	E	A	D	I	L	Y		A	S	P	E	C	T
		B		E				A		P				E
S	H	I	N		A	C	Q	U	A	I	N	T	E	D
C		T		Z		A		N		N		E		L
A	M	E	L	I	O	R	A	T	E		A	R	M	Y
R				G		D				U		M		
E	F	F	I	G	Y		J	A	U	N	D	I	C	E
C		E		U		D		L		A		N		P
R		M	A	R	T	I	N	I		B	R	A	V	O
O		U		A		V		A		L		T		X
W	O	R	S	T		A	U	S	T	E	R	E	L	Y

Double Fun Sudoku

Tasty Teaser

1	3	6	8	9	4	5	7	2
4	5	7	2	3	1	6	8	9
9	2	8	5	7	6	3	4	1
3	8	2	7	4	9	1	6	5
6	4	5	1	8	3	2	9	7
7	1	9	6	5	2	4	3	8
2	7	1	3	6	8	9	5	4
5	9	3	4	1	7	8	2	6
8	6	4	9	2	5	7	1	3

Brain Buster

9	2	7	3	8	1	5	6	4
5	6	8	2	9	4	1	7	3
3	4	1	7	6	5	2	8	9
1	3	2	9	4	8	7	5	6
4	7	5	6	3	2	8	9	1
6	8	9	1	5	7	3	4	2
7	9	6	8	1	3	4	2	5
2	1	4	5	7	9	6	3	8
8	5	3	4	2	6	9	1	7

Pyramid Plus

A=22, B=58, C=99, D=75, E=119, F=80, G=157, H=174, I=194, J=237, K=331, L=368, M=568, N=699, O=1267.

Work it Out

30 – The numbers in each horizontal row, each vertical column and each of the two diagonal lines of seven smaller squares total 175.

High-Speed Crossword

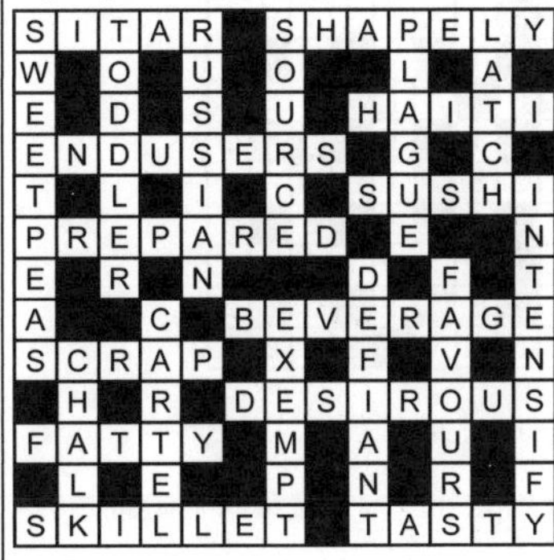

S	I	T	A	R		S	H	A	P	E	L	Y
W		O		U		O			L		A	
E		D		S		U		H	A	I	T	I
E	N	D	U	S	E	R	S		G		C	
T		L		I		C		S	U	S	H	I
P	R	E	P	A	R	E	D		E			N
E		R		N				D		F		T
A			C		B	E	V	E	R	A	G	E
S	C	R	A	P		X		F		V		N
	H		R		D	E	S	I	R	O	U	S
F	A	T	T	Y		M		A		U		I
	L		E			P		N		R		F
S	K	I	L	L	E	T		T	A	S	T	Y

1 Minute Number Crunch

Beginner

71 – 22 = 49, 49 x 2 = 98, 98 + 26 = 124, 50% of 124 = 62, 62 + 19 = 81, 81 ÷ 3 = 27, 27 x 2 = 54

Intermediate

59 x 3 = 177, 177 – 114 = 63, 63 + 21 (63 ÷ 3) = 84, 84 ÷ 12 x 5 = 35, 35 ÷ 7 x 3 = 15, 15 x 13 = 195, 195 + 85 = 280

Advanced

52 ÷ 13 x 7 = 28, 28 x 9 = 252, 252 ÷ 6 = 42, 42^2 = 1764, 1764 – 1323 (1764 ÷ 4 x 3) = 441, 441 ÷ 9 x 5 = 245, 245 + 147 (60% of 245) = 392

Page 23

High-Speed Crossword

M	A	D	E	I	R	A	C	A	K	E		A
E			X		E		Y		Y			M
E	L	L	I	P	S	I	S		L	A	M	A
K			S		T		T		I			Z
E	A	R	T	H	Y		S	L	E	E	V	E
R		O			L					V		D
	B	A	D	G	E		D	E	C	A	Y	
A		M					U			N		O
M	O	S	A	I	C		C	U	R	S	E	D
E			G		A		H		E			I
N	O	V	A		S	C	E	N	A	R	I	O
D			T		T		S		C			U
S		N	E	C	E	S	S	I	T	O	U	S

IQ Workout

The clock moves back 3 hours 9 minutes, forwards 9 hours 3 minutes, back 3 hours 9 minutes and forwards 9 hours 3 minutes.

1 Minute Number Crunch

Beginner

36 ÷ 12 = 3, 3 x 20 = 60, 60 + 3 = 63, 63 ÷ 21 = 3, 3 x 19 = 57, 57 + 18 = 75, 75 ÷ 3 = 25

Intermediate

13 x 9 = 117, 117 + 414 = 531, 531 ÷ 9 x 5 = 295, 295 ÷ 5 = 59, 59 + 63 = 122, 122 x 5 = 610, 610 ÷ 10 x 9 = 549

Advanced

26^3 = 17576, 17576 ÷ 8 x 3 = 6591, 6591 + 4394 (6591 ÷ 3 x 2) = 10985, 60% of 10985 = 6591, 6591 – 4607 = 1984, 1984 ÷ 16 x 5 = 620, 620 ÷ 5 x 3 = 372

Wordsearch Workout

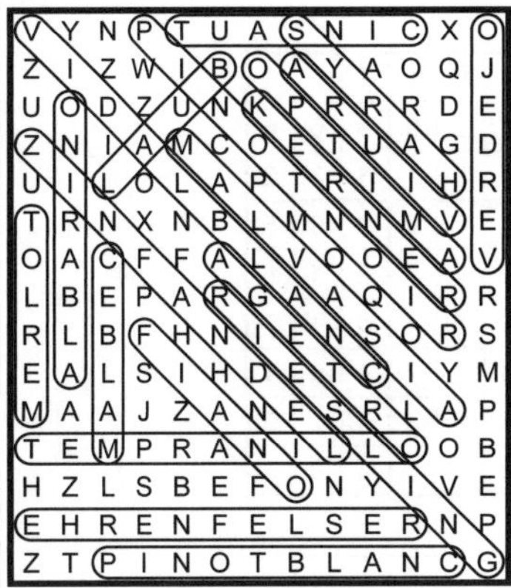

Double Fun Sudoku

Tasty Teaser

8	7	1	4	5	3	2	9	6
3	2	4	7	6	9	5	8	1
6	9	5	1	8	2	3	4	7
7	5	6	2	9	4	8	1	3
2	1	9	8	3	5	7	6	4
4	3	8	6	1	7	9	2	5
1	4	2	5	7	8	6	3	9
5	8	3	9	4	6	1	7	2
9	6	7	3	2	1	4	5	8

Brain Buster

7	2	3	8	4	5	9	1	6
1	9	5	3	6	2	4	7	8
4	8	6	7	1	9	3	2	5
2	3	4	9	8	6	1	5	7
9	6	8	5	7	1	2	3	4
5	1	7	2	3	4	6	8	9
3	4	1	6	5	7	8	9	2
6	7	9	1	2	8	5	4	3
8	5	2	4	9	3	7	6	1

Whatever Next?

P – Assign a number to each letter according to its place in the alphabet. Working clockwise from the top, add the two together, so A+B(1+2)=3, A+E(1+5)=6, C+F(3+6)=9, etc. E=5, so P(16) is needed to make the final figure to 21, and E+P=21.

Brain Teaser

133

Page 24

Mind Over Matter

The sum total of the values of the letters in each diagonal line of three are all equal. Thus the missing value is 16, so the missing letter is P.

Double Fun Sudoku

Tasty Teaser

9	2	8	3	6	5	1	7	4
1	3	7	4	2	8	9	5	6
5	4	6	7	9	1	8	3	2
6	8	4	1	7	2	3	9	5
7	1	5	6	3	9	2	4	8
2	9	3	8	5	4	6	1	7
3	5	2	9	8	7	4	6	1
8	6	1	5	4	3	7	2	9
4	7	9	2	1	6	5	8	3

Brain Buster

2	8	7	3	9	6	1	4	5
9	3	5	1	8	4	6	7	2
1	6	4	2	7	5	3	8	9
5	2	8	7	4	1	9	3	6
4	1	9	8	6	3	5	2	7
6	7	3	9	5	2	4	1	8
3	9	1	5	2	7	8	6	4
7	5	6	4	1	8	2	9	3
8	4	2	6	3	9	7	5	1

Codeword Conundrum

W	H	E	L	P		M	O	T	H	P	R	O	O	F
A		X		E		E		H		E				R
I	N	T	E	R	C	E	D	E		S	E	P	I	A
S		R		V		K		M		E		E		N
T	R	A	V	E	L		E	S	O	T	E	R	I	C
B				R		L		E		A		J		
A	T	O	M	S		U	G	L	Y		Q	U	A	D
N		R		E		X		V		D		R		A
D	I	G	S		P	U	R	E		E	M	E	R	Y
		A		B		R		S		C				L
A	M	N	I	O	T	I	C		G	E	M	I	N	I
P		Z		N		A		W		M		N		G
P	L	A	Y	S		N	A	I	L	B	R	U	S	H
L				A		C		T		E		R		T
E	M	P	T	I	N	E	S	S		R	E	E	D	S

Futoshiki

5	4	1 <	2	3
1	3 >	2	5 >	4
4	2 ∧	5	3 >	1
3	5	4	1	2
2 >	1	3	4	5

High-Speed Crossword

W	A	L	K		F	I	N	I	S	H	E	D
H		U		T		N		N		E		R
O	R	C	H	I	D	S		T	R	A	C	E
O		R		T		E		E		T		S
P	L	E	A	T		C	A	R	R	I	E	S
I				L		T		M		N		I
N	A	N	T	E	S		A	I	R	G	U	N
G		E		T		I		T				G
C	O	M	P	A	S	S		T	E	M	P	T
O		E		T		O		E		E		A
U	P	S	E	T		M	I	N	I	C	A	B
G		I		L		E		T		C		L
H	O	S	T	E	L	R	Y		B	A	B	E

1 Minute Number Crunch

Beginner

36 ÷ 6 = 6, 6 x 17 = 102, 102 – 86 = 16, 16 x 4 = 64, 64 ÷ 16 x 5 = 20, 20 + 48 = 68, 68 x 2 = 136

Intermediate

1215 ÷ 5 = 243, 243 ÷ 27 = 9, 9 + 5 (9 ÷ 9 x 5) = 14, 14 ÷ 7 x 3 = 6, 6 + 4 (6 ÷ 3 x 2) = 10, 950% of 10 = 95, 95 + 36 = 131

Advanced

13 x 24 = 312, 312 ÷ 12 x 5 = 130, 130 + 117 (130 ÷ 10 x 9) = 247, 247 ÷ 13 x 6 = 114, 114 + 76 (114 ÷ 3 x 2) = 190, 190 x 4 = 760, 760 ÷ 8 x 3 = 285

Page 25

Battleships

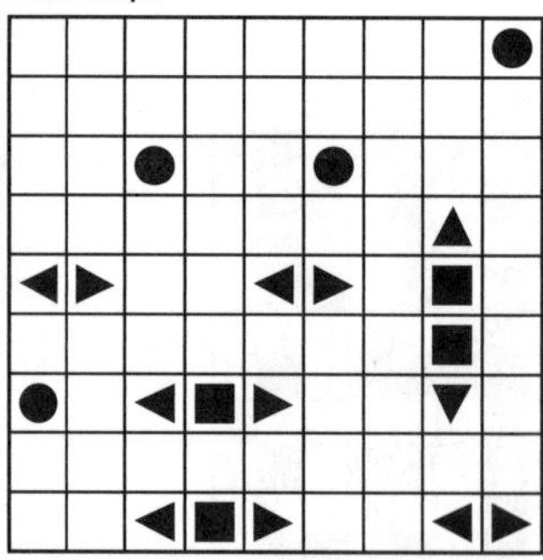

High-Speed Crossword

K	A	Y	A	K	S		D		H		B	
	B		T		O	N	E	S	I	D	E	D
P	U	T	O	F	F		L		T		C	
	S		M		T	R	I	L	L	I	O	N
F	E	A	S	T	S				I		M	
I					E	M	B	O	S	S	E	D
N			I		L		A		T			A
S	H	A	M	B	L	E	S					W
	E		I				E	N	S	I	G	N
G	R	A	T	E	F	U	L		K		O	
	N		A		R		E	D	I	S	O	N
D	I	S	T	R	E	S	S		E		S	
	A		E		E		S	E	R	V	E	R

IQ Workout

99 – Add alternately the first or second digit of the previous number to the next number in the sequence.

Wordwheel

The nine-letter word is: CURRENTLY

Wordsearch Workout

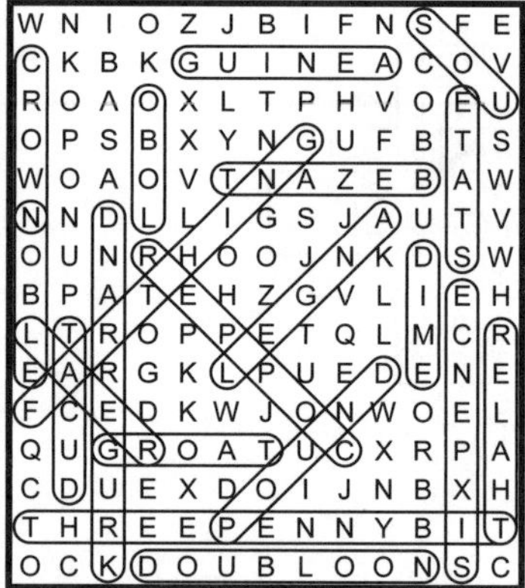

W	N	I	O	Z	J	B	I	F	N	S	F	E
C	K	B	K	G	U	I	N	E	A	C	O	V
R	O	A	O	X	L	T	P	H	V	O	E	U
O	P	S	B	X	Y	N	G	U	F	B	T	S
W	O	A	O	V	T	N	A	Z	E	B	A	W
N	N	D	L	L	I	G	S	J	A	U	T	V
O	U	N	R	H	O	O	J	N	K	D	S	W
B	P	A	T	E	H	Z	G	V	L	I	E	H
L	T	R	O	P	P	E	T	Q	L	M	C	R
E	A	R	G	K	L	P	U	E	D	E	N	E
F	C	E	D	K	W	J	O	N	W	O	E	L
Q	U	G	R	O	A	T	U	C	X	R	P	A
C	D	U	E	X	D	O	I	J	N	B	X	H
T	H	R	E	E	P	E	N	N	Y	B	I	T
O	C	K	D	O	U	B	L	O	O	N	S	C

Double Fun Sudoku

Tasty Teaser

9	6	2	3	1	8	7	5	4
1	3	7	5	2	4	9	8	6
4	8	5	7	9	6	2	3	1
6	5	1	4	7	3	8	2	9
3	2	4	9	8	5	1	6	7
8	7	9	2	6	1	5	4	3
7	9	3	6	5	2	4	1	8
2	4	8	1	3	7	6	9	5
5	1	6	8	4	9	3	7	2

Brain Buster

7	9	6	3	4	1	2	5	8
5	8	2	6	9	7	1	4	3
3	1	4	5	2	8	9	6	7
6	7	9	4	1	3	8	2	5
4	3	1	2	8	5	7	9	6
2	5	8	9	7	6	3	1	4
1	4	3	8	5	2	6	7	9
9	6	7	1	3	4	5	8	2
8	2	5	7	6	9	4	3	1

Sum Circle

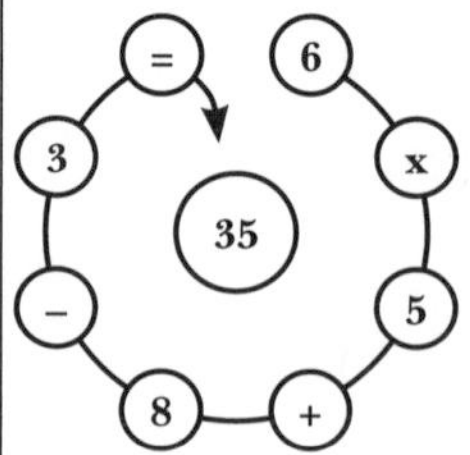

Page 26

1 Minute Number Crunch

Beginner
63 – 22 = 41, 41 x 2 = 82, 82 – 16 = 66, 66 ÷ 3 = 22, 22 + 10 = 32, 32 ÷ 4 = 8, 8 + 88 = 96

Intermediate
21 ÷ 7 x 3 = 9, 9 x 6 = 54, 54 ÷ 2 = 27, 27 x 7 = 189, 189 + 422 = 611, 611 x 2 = 1222, 1222 – 649 = 573

Advanced
61 ÷ 0.5 = 122, 122 x 12 = 1464, 1464 ÷ 0.6 = 2440, 2440 ÷ 8 x 3 = 915, 915 + 244 (915 ÷ 15 x 4) = 1159, 1159 x 2 = 2318, 2318 – 978 = 1340

High-Speed Crossword

M	I	S	T	A	K	E	N		A	S	K	S
E		N	A	P		D				H		I
A	R	E	N	A		I	C	E	L	A	N	D
T		E	G	R	E	T				M		E
		Z		T		O	I	L	W	E	L	L
W	H	E	T	H	E	R		I		D		I
I				E				S				N
Z		J		I		A	N	T	I	Q	U	E
A	B	A	N	D	O	N		E		U		
R		G				D	A	N	T	E		S
D	O	G	S	T	A	R		E	R	U	P	T
R		E				E		R	U	E		A
Y	A	R	N		P	A	S	S	E	D	B	Y

IQ Workout

G – Move five letters forward in the alphabet, then three back, alternately.

Codeword Conundrum

S	H	E	I	K	H		E	S	C	A	P	A	D	E
U		M		I		J		L		W		L		N
R	I	P	E	N		U	N	A	D	A	P	T	E	D
V		E		D	U	D		K		I		A		O
E	A	R		E		O	V	E	R	T	H	R	E	W
Y		O		S			O		O		O		N	
S	C	R	A	T	C	H	Y		D	A	R	I	N	G
	H		L		O		A		E		D		U	
L	A	Z	I	L	Y		G	E	O	D	E	S	I	C
	I		B		P		E			U		U		O
A	N	T	I	Q	U	A	R	Y		L		P	A	N
M		H		U		C		O	I	L		P		N
I	N	E	X	A	C	T	L	Y		A	B	O	D	E
S		I		F		O		O		R		S		C
S	U	R	E	F	I	R	E		A	D	V	E	N	T

Tasty Teaser

4	3	7	1	9	2	8	5	6
9	6	2	8	5	4	3	7	1
5	1	8	3	6	7	2	9	4
1	4	9	7	2	8	5	6	3
6	2	5	4	3	9	1	8	7
8	7	3	5	1	6	9	4	2
2	9	1	6	4	5	7	3	8
3	8	4	9	7	1	6	2	5
7	5	6	2	8	3	4	1	9

Brain Buster

7	1	3	4	6	5	2	9	8
9	2	4	1	8	7	6	3	5
5	8	6	2	3	9	4	7	1
2	3	9	5	7	4	1	8	6
8	6	7	3	2	1	9	5	4
1	4	5	8	9	6	3	2	7
6	9	8	7	1	2	5	4	3
3	5	2	6	4	8	7	1	9
4	7	1	9	5	3	8	6	2

Spidoku

Page 27

Logi-Six

E	F	D	C	B	A
B	A	C	F	E	D
F	B	A	E	D	C
D	E	B	A	C	F
A	C	E	D	F	B
C	D	F	B	A	E

High-Speed Crossword

	C		W		A		S	E	S	A	M	E
T	I	R	A	M	I	S	U				U	
	C		L		T		B	A	R	R	E	N
B	A	I	L		C	A	D				S	
	D		P		H		U		I		L	
S	A	L	A	D		M	E	R	M	A	I	D
A			P		D		D		P			A
C	R	E	E	P	E	R		M	A	D	A	M
	E		R		S		A		R		W	
	P				E	B	B		T	R	A	P
C	O	O	K	E	R		B		I		K	
	R				T	W	O	F	A	C	E	D
E	T	H	I	C	S		T		L		N	

Wordsearch Workout

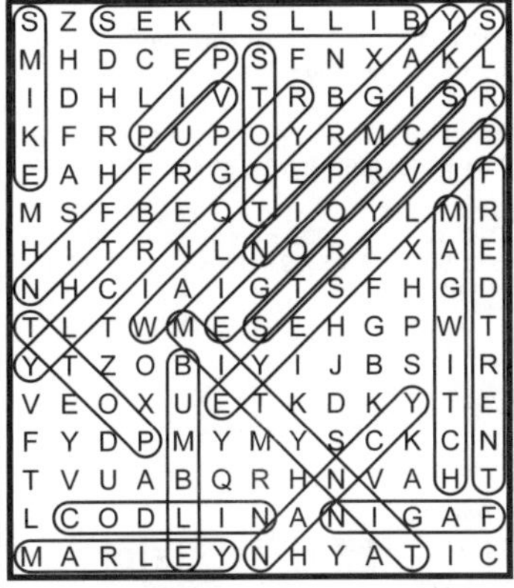

Double Fun Sudoku

Tasty Teaser

4	6	3	7	9	1	2	8	5
2	8	1	6	5	3	7	4	9
7	5	9	4	2	8	6	1	3
6	9	2	1	7	4	5	3	8
1	7	5	8	3	2	9	6	4
3	4	8	9	6	5	1	7	2
5	1	6	3	8	9	4	2	7
9	3	4	2	1	7	8	5	6
8	2	7	5	4	6	3	9	1

Brain Buster

2	4	1	5	6	3	7	9	8
8	3	7	9	1	4	5	2	6
9	6	5	2	7	8	3	4	1
5	9	2	6	3	1	4	8	7
1	8	4	7	2	5	9	6	3
3	7	6	8	4	9	2	1	5
7	1	8	4	5	2	6	3	9
4	5	9	3	8	6	1	7	2
6	2	3	1	9	7	8	5	4

Matchstick Magic

The matchsticks which have been moved are outlined.

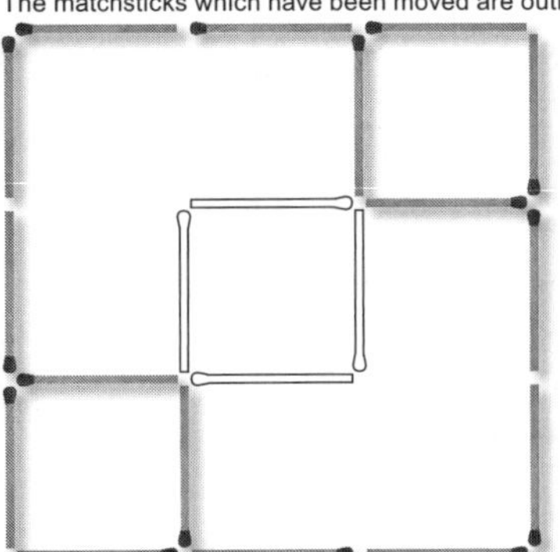

Brain Teaser

7% – Single per pair = €3.50
Pack per pair = €3.25
Saving per pair = €0.25

1 Minute Number Crunch

Beginner
104 + 17 = 121, 121 ÷ 11 x 2 = 22, 22 x 4 = 88, 88 – 16 = 72, 72 ÷ 6 x 5 = 60, 60 + 90 = 150, 150 ÷ 3 = 50

Intermediate
390 ÷ 10 x 7 = 273, 273 ÷ 3 x 2 = 182, 182 x 2 = 364, 75% of 364 = 273, 273 – 87 = 186, 186 ÷ 6 = 31, 31 x 12 = 372

Advanced
293 + 739 = 1032, 1032 – 645 (1032 ÷ 8 x 5) = 387, 387 ÷ 9 x 2 = 86, 86 x 7 = 602, 602 ÷ 14 x 5 = 215, 215 + 129 (215 ÷ 5 x 3) = 344, 275% of 344 = 946

Page 28

Codeword Conundrum

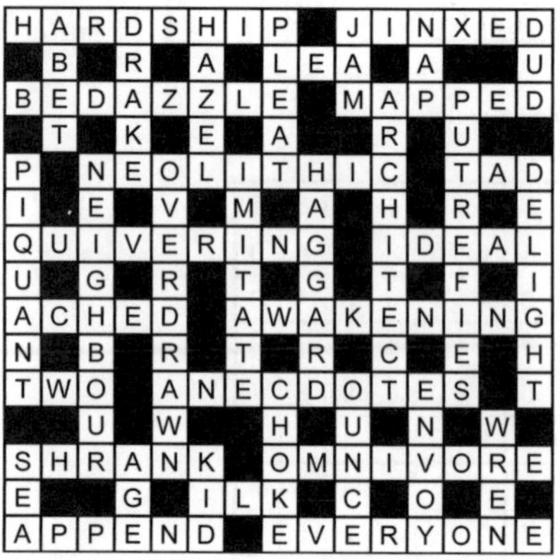

Double Fun Sudoku

Tasty Teaser

9	7	8	1	3	6	5	4	2
5	1	3	2	7	4	8	6	9
4	6	2	9	5	8	7	3	1
2	9	5	4	1	7	6	8	3
6	3	1	5	8	9	4	2	7
8	4	7	6	2	3	9	1	5
1	2	9	8	4	5	3	7	6
7	8	6	3	9	2	1	5	4
3	5	4	7	6	1	2	9	8

Brain Buster

8	1	2	7	6	5	9	4	3
4	5	9	2	3	1	8	7	6
3	7	6	8	9	4	2	5	1
2	4	5	3	8	9	6	1	7
9	8	7	5	1	6	3	2	4
1	6	3	4	7	2	5	9	8
5	2	8	6	4	7	1	3	9
7	3	1	9	5	8	4	6	2
6	9	4	1	2	3	7	8	5

Pyramid Plus

A=84, B=77, C=21, D=53, E=6, F=161, G=98, H=74, I=59, J=259, K=172, L=133, M=431, N=305, O=736.

Work it Out

85 – The numbers in the horizontal rows increase by 13, 14, 15, 16, 17, 18 and 19.

High-Speed Crossword

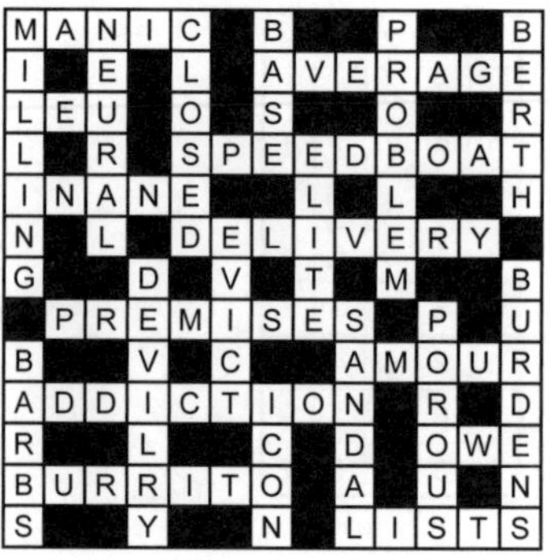

1 Minute Number Crunch

Beginner
234 – 6 = 228, 50% of 228 = 114, 114 – 96 = 18, 18 ÷ 9 x 4 = 8, 8^2 = 64, 64 ÷ 4 = 16, 16 x 2 = 32

Intermediate
49 x 2 = 98, 98 – 19 = 79, 79 x 3 = 237, 237 – 109 = 128, 128 ÷ 8 = 16, 16 x 1.5 = 24, 24 ÷ 8 x 5 = 15

Advanced
5 x 5 x 9 = 225, square root of 225 = 15, 15 x 39 = 585, 585 + 260 (585 ÷ 9 x 4) = 845, 845 ÷ 5 = 169, 169 – 77 = 92, 92 x 3.75 = 345

Page 29

High-Speed Crossword

S	H	E	A	R	S		H		A		C	
U		V			C	H	A	T	R	O	O	M
P		E			R		N		I		H	
P	U	R	S	U	E		D	R	A	W	E	R
L			T		W		L				R	
E	S	S	A	Y		S	E	E	S	R	E	D
	E		R		M		R		T		N	
B	A	T	T	L	E	S		P	A	N	T	S
	W				E		L		I			I
L	A	M	E	N	T		I	N	N	I	N	G
	T		S		I		V			N		N
R	E	S	P	O	N	S	E			C		E
	R		Y		G		S	U	N	H	A	T

Summing Up

44	17	24	30	38	**18**
32	28	31	**23**	31	26
15	40	28	50	15	23
35	**45**	31	6	15	39
26	22	19	42	**31**	31
19	19	**38**	20	41	34

Domino Placement

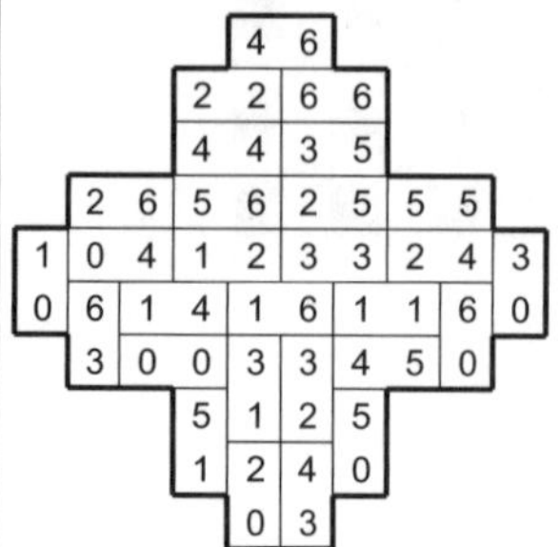

Wordsearch Workout

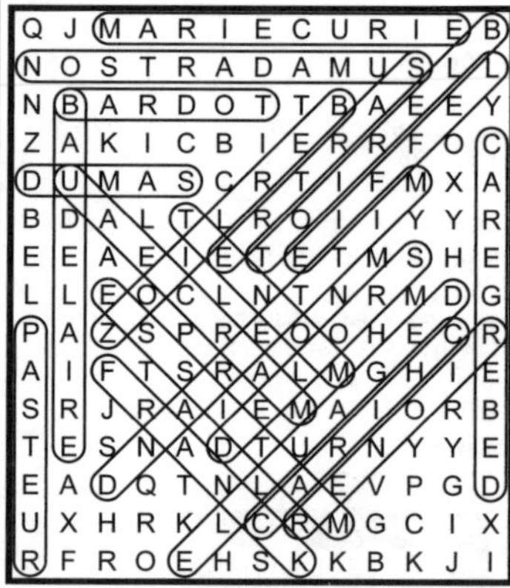

Double Fun Sudoku

Tasty Teaser

5	9	4	2	1	6	3	8	7
1	7	6	3	8	9	5	2	4
8	2	3	5	7	4	6	1	9
2	3	8	7	9	1	4	6	5
6	5	9	8	4	2	1	7	3
7	4	1	6	3	5	8	9	2
4	6	5	1	2	7	9	3	8
9	8	2	4	6	3	7	5	1
3	1	7	9	5	8	2	4	6

Brain Buster

1	6	7	4	5	3	8	9	2
8	4	3	6	2	9	7	1	5
5	9	2	1	7	8	3	6	4
4	2	5	3	9	1	6	7	8
7	8	9	2	4	6	5	3	1
3	1	6	7	8	5	2	4	9
6	3	8	9	1	2	4	5	7
2	7	1	5	3	4	9	8	6
9	5	4	8	6	7	1	2	3

Whatever Next?

B – Assign a number to each letter according to its place in the alphabet, so E=5, L=12, P=16, S=19 and Z=26. Then take the lowest number from the highest in the point directly opposite to give the centre total, so the missing letter is B (=2).

Brain Teaser

Tuesday

Page 30

Mind Over Matter

The sum total of the letters in all five boxes is 60. Thus the missing value is 14, so the missing letter is N.

Double Fun Sudoku

Tasty Teaser

3	6	8	4	2	5	7	9	1
5	4	2	1	9	7	3	6	8
7	1	9	6	3	8	4	5	2
6	8	4	2	5	9	1	3	7
1	2	3	7	8	6	9	4	5
9	5	7	3	1	4	2	8	6
8	9	1	5	7	3	6	2	4
4	7	5	9	6	2	8	1	3
2	3	6	8	4	1	5	7	9

Brain Buster

8	6	2	4	3	7	9	1	5
7	3	1	8	5	9	6	4	2
4	5	9	2	6	1	8	3	7
2	9	3	5	8	4	1	7	6
1	8	4	3	7	6	2	5	9
6	7	5	1	9	2	4	8	3
9	1	8	7	2	5	3	6	4
5	4	6	9	1	3	7	2	8
3	2	7	6	4	8	5	9	1

Codeword Conundrum

	O	V	E	R	W	O	R	K		H		I		C
Z			L		O		U		T	U	R	N	E	R
E	N	J	O	Y	M	E	N	T		M		S		E
B			Q		A			I	N	B	O	U	N	D
R	E	P	U	G	N	A	N	T		U		L		I
A			E		I			L	E	G		A		T
	H	A	N	D	S	O	M	E		S	P	R	E	E
T			C		E		E		S		R			D
A	N	G	E	L		S	T	I	C	K	I	N	G	
X		A		O	W	L			R		N			M
A		I		G		E	N	D	O	S	C	O	P	Y
T	E	N	S	I	L	E			U		I			R
I		F		C		K	I	D	N	A	P	P	E	R
O	C	U	L	A	R		L		G		L			H
N		L		L		B	L	U	E	B	E	L	L	

Futoshiki

3	2	4	1 <	5
1	4	2	5	3
4	1	5 >	3	2
2	5	3 <	4	1
5	3	1	2	4

High-Speed Crossword

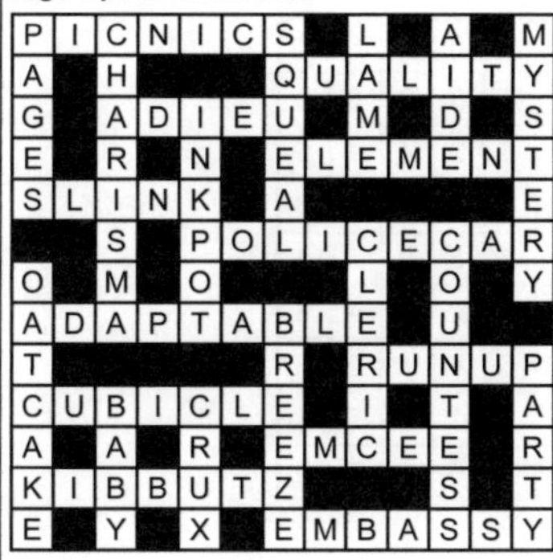

1 Minute Number Crunch

Beginner
38 + 212 = 250, 250 ÷ 10 = 25, 25 x 7 = 175, 175 ÷ 5 = 35, 35 x 2 = 70, 70 – 7 = 63, 63 ÷ 9 x 2 = 14

Intermediate
424 – 148 = 276, 276 ÷ 3 x 2 = 184, 184 x 3 = 552, 552 ÷ 4 x 3 = 414, 414 ÷ 9 x 8 = 368, 368 ÷ 2 = 184, 184 + 129 = 313

Advanced
29^3 = 24389, 24389 – 15497 = 8892, 8892 ÷ 4 x 3 = 6669, 6669 ÷ 9 x 5 = 3705, 3705 ÷ 15 x 7 = 1729, 1729 x 2 = 3458, 3458 – 2569 = 889

Page 31

1 Minute Number Crunch

Beginner
25% of 104 = 26, 26 x 2 = 52, 52 + 53 = 105, 105 ÷ 5 = 21, 21 + 19 = 40, 40 ÷ 4 = 10, 10 x 39 = 390

Intermediate
127 + 43 = 170, 170 + 34 (20% of 170) = 204, 204 ÷ 4 = 51, 51 ÷ 3 = 17, 17 + 283 = 300, 31% of 300 = 93, 93 – 67 = 26

Advanced
43 x 7 = 301, 301 + 199 = 500, 69% of 500 = 345, 345 ÷ 15 x 9 = 207, 207 ÷ 23 x 17 = 153, 153 ÷ 9 x 4 = 68, 68 x 7 = 476

High-Speed Crossword

Partitions

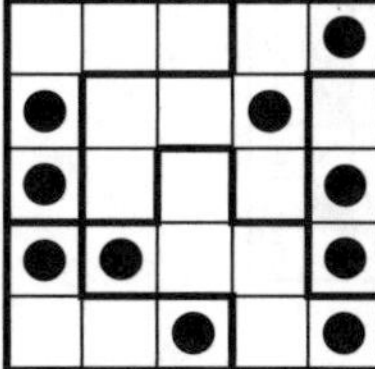

Wordwheel

The nine-letter word is: MINUSCULE

Wordsearch Workout

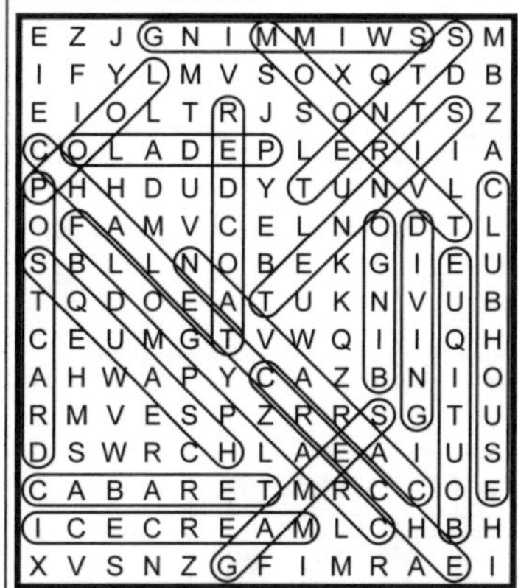

Double Fun Sudoku

Tasty Teaser

8	2	3	5	6	7	9	4	1
4	9	7	2	1	8	3	6	5
5	6	1	3	4	9	2	7	8
6	7	5	4	2	1	8	3	9
9	4	8	7	5	3	6	1	2
3	1	2	8	9	6	7	5	4
2	3	9	1	7	4	5	8	6
1	8	6	9	3	5	4	2	7
7	5	4	6	8	2	1	9	3

Brain Buster

4	8	7	3	2	5	9	1	6
1	6	2	4	7	9	5	3	8
3	5	9	1	8	6	7	2	4
5	2	3	9	1	4	6	8	7
8	7	1	6	5	2	3	4	9
6	9	4	7	3	8	2	5	1
2	4	5	8	9	7	1	6	3
9	1	6	2	4	3	8	7	5
7	3	8	5	6	1	4	9	2

Sum Circle

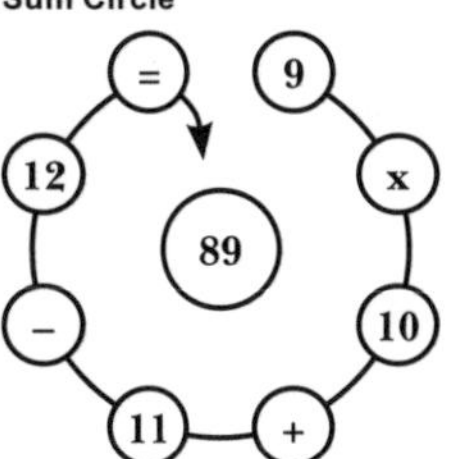

Page 32

1 Minute Number Crunch

Beginner

92 + 18 = 110, 110 ÷ 10 = 11, 11 + 38 = 49, 49 ÷ 7 = 7, 7 + 56 = 63, 63 ÷ 9 x 2 = 14, 14 + 88 = 102

Intermediate

32 x 5 = 160, 160 + 16 = 176, 176 ÷ 4 = 44, 44 ÷ 11 x 5 = 20, 20 x 4.5 = 90, 90 ÷ 5 = 18, 18 x 3 = 54

Advanced

221 x 6 = 1326, 1326 ÷17 x 6 = 468, 468 + 1427 = 1895, 1895 – 379 = 1516, 75% of 1516 = 1137, 1137 x 5 = 5685, 5685 + 2274 (40% of 5685) = 7959

High-Speed Crossword

B	A	R	R	I	S	T	E	R		B		B
O		E		N		A		A	R	O	M	A
G	L	A	S	S		K		V		N		S
U		D		U	N	I	T	E		U		K
S	T	E	E	R		N		L	I	S	L	E
		R		E		G			N			T
R	E	S	O	R	T		C	E	N	S	U	S
U			D			E		R		T		
B	E	S	E	T		R		O	R	A	T	E
B		I		R	O	A	D	S		M		A
I		R		I		S		I	C	I	N	G
S	C	E	N	E		E		O		N		L
H		N		S	H	R	I	N	K	A	G	E

IQ Workout

49.5 – Add 3, then multiply by 3, alternately.

Codeword Conundrum

C	R	A	Y	O	N		P	R	O	J	E	C	T	S
R		V		R			I			O		H		M
E	X	E	R	C	I	S	E	S		I	M	A	G	E
E		R		H		O		L		N		N		L
P	L	A	T	E	A	U		E	X	T	I	N	C	T
		G		S		T		E				E		
W	H	E	A	T		H	O	P	E	F	U	L	L	Y
A				R			W			R				E
S	U	B	M	A	R	I	N	E		E	X	I	S	T
		L				D		R		Q		N		
S	E	A	S	I	D	E		R	O	U	T	I	N	E
T		Z		N		A		O		E		T		D
A	L	I	E	N		S	H	R	I	N	K	I	N	G
I		N		E			A			C		A		E
R	E	G	A	R	D	E	D		C	Y	C	L	E	D

Tasty Teaser

9	7	5	2	3	8	1	6	4
6	4	2	7	9	1	3	8	5
3	1	8	4	6	5	9	7	2
7	6	4	8	2	9	5	1	3
2	5	3	6	1	7	8	4	9
8	9	1	5	4	3	7	2	6
5	2	7	9	8	4	6	3	1
4	3	9	1	7	6	2	5	8
1	8	6	3	5	2	4	9	7

Brain Buster

2	5	4	1	9	6	3	8	7
7	8	1	4	5	3	2	6	9
3	6	9	7	8	2	4	1	5
1	9	8	3	4	7	5	2	6
5	4	7	6	2	8	9	3	1
6	2	3	5	1	9	7	4	8
8	7	5	2	6	4	1	9	3
4	3	6	9	7	1	8	5	2
9	1	2	8	3	5	6	7	4

Spidoku

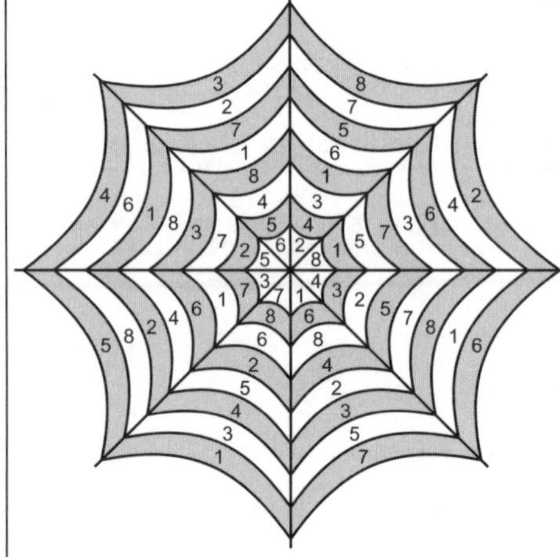

Page 33

Logi-Six

D	E	C	F	B	A
B	F	D	C	A	E
F	A	E	B	D	C
E	D	B	A	C	F
A	C	F	D	E	B
C	B	A	E	F	D

High-Speed Crossword

S	C	A	M	P		B			P		B	
E		F		A		A	C	C	L	A	I	M
R	E	F	I	N	E	R	Y		A		C	
G		O		E		S	L	I	T	H	E	R
E		R			D		I		Y		P	
A	D	D	I	T	I	O	N		P	U	S	S
N			D		S		D		U			E
T	H	E	E		P	H	E	A	S	A	N	T
	A		N		E		R			N		P
W	R	I	T	I	N	G		O		G		I
	D		I		S	A	P	P	H	I	R	E
S	E	T	T	L	E	S		U		N		C
	N		Y			H		S	C	A	L	E

Wordsearch Workout

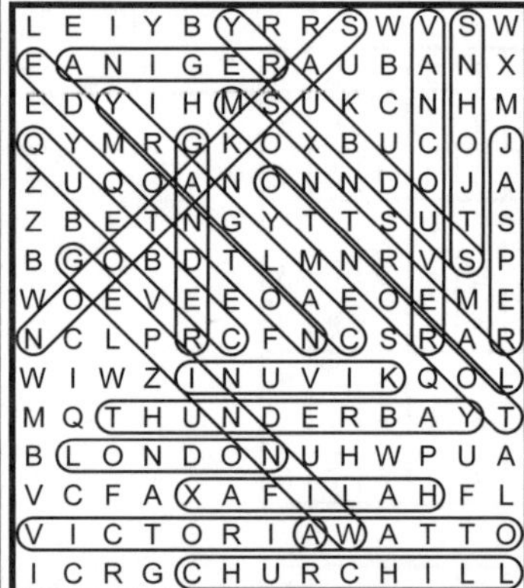

Double Fun Sudoku

Tasty Teaser

3	1	8	4	7	9	5	6	2
4	2	9	1	5	6	3	8	7
7	6	5	3	8	2	1	4	9
8	9	4	5	3	1	7	2	6
6	3	2	8	9	7	4	5	1
5	7	1	2	6	4	9	3	8
2	4	3	7	1	8	6	9	5
9	8	7	6	4	5	2	1	3
1	5	6	9	2	3	8	7	4

Brain Buster

7	1	9	6	2	5	3	4	8
5	8	3	4	9	7	2	6	1
4	2	6	8	1	3	5	9	7
8	3	2	9	6	1	4	7	5
1	9	4	7	5	2	6	8	3
6	5	7	3	4	8	9	1	2
9	7	8	2	3	6	1	5	4
3	4	5	1	8	9	7	2	6
2	6	1	5	7	4	8	3	9

Matchstick Magic

The matchsticks which have been moved are outlined.

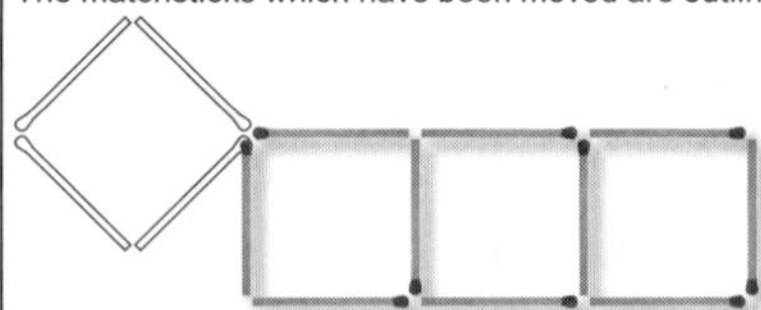

Brain Teaser

E = 36 – Multiply the number of sides by three.

Simple as A, B, C

B	C	A	B	A	C
C	B	B	C	A	A
C	C	A	A	B	B
A	A	C	C	B	B
A	B	B	A	C	C
B	A	C	B	C	A

Page 34

Codeword Conundrum

P	A	R	T	I	C	L	E		Q	U	A	R	T	O
	R		I		A		N		U		L			B
L	U	M	B	A	R		G	L	I	M	P	S	E	S
	M		I		A		U		Z		H			O
E		J	A	Y	W	A	L	K		N	A	S	A	L
X		U			A		F	O	X	Y		U		E
H	O	M	O	N	Y	M		A		M	I	N	U	S
I		B		A		A		L		P		B		C
L	I	L	A	C		R		A	C	H	I	E	V	E
A		E		R	E	S	T		E			A		N
R	I	D	G	E		H	O	O	D	L	U	M		T
A			U		O		I		I		R		A	
T	E	A	T	O	W	E	L		L	I	B	I	D	O
E			S		E		E		L		A		Z	
S	W	A	Y	E	D		T	R	A	I	N	E	E	S

Double Fun Sudoku

Tasty Teaser

7	5	9	2	4	6	3	8	1
3	6	2	7	8	1	5	9	4
1	4	8	9	5	3	6	7	2
6	1	4	3	9	7	8	2	5
2	7	5	1	6	8	4	3	9
9	8	3	5	2	4	1	6	7
5	3	6	4	7	2	9	1	8
8	9	7	6	1	5	2	4	3
4	2	1	8	3	9	7	5	6

Brain Buster

8	9	2	7	5	6	3	4	1
3	1	6	2	9	4	7	8	5
4	5	7	8	3	1	6	9	2
7	6	1	9	8	2	5	3	4
9	8	5	4	6	3	2	1	7
2	4	3	5	1	7	9	6	8
6	7	8	3	4	5	1	2	9
1	2	9	6	7	8	4	5	3
5	3	4	1	2	9	8	7	6

Pyramid Plus

A=121, B=25, C=96, D=67, E=126, F=146, G=121, H=163, I=193, J=267, K=284, L=356, M=551, N=640, O=1191.

Work it Out

28 – The numbers in each vertical column increase by 3, 5, 7, 8, 6 and 4.

High-Speed Crossword

L	O	A	T	H	E		P	L	A	S	M	A
I		C		Y			E			T		S
M	E	T	A	P	H	O	R		M	E	N	U
I		R		O		R	I	P		P		N
T	R	E	A	T		B	L	E	S	S	E	D
		S		H				J				E
S	Y	S	T	E	M		C	O	O	L	E	R
L				S				R		E		
I	N	S	P	I	R	E		A	G	O	R	A
P		O		S	O	L		T		N		T
P	A	N	S		O	F	F	I	C	I	A	L
E		I			M			V		N		A
R	E	C	U	R	S		D	E	T	E	R	S

1 Minute Number Crunch

Beginner
57 + 17 = 74, 74 ÷ 2 = 37, 37 + 19 = 56, 56 ÷ 4 = 14, 14 reversed = 41, 41 + 55 = 96, 25% of 96 = 24

Intermediate
23 x 11 = 253, 253 – 192 = 61, 61 x 4 = 244, 244 + 62 = 306, 306 ÷ 3 = 102, 102 ÷ 6 x 5 = 85, 85 + 97 = 182

Advanced
19 x 15 = 285, 285 x 3 = 855, 855 ÷ 19 x 5 = 225, 225 x 14 = 3150, 70% of 3150 = 2205, 2205 ÷ 5 x 3 = 1323, 1323 ÷ 9 x 7 = 1029

Page 35

High-Speed Crossword

S	T	A	M	P	S		B	A	S	A	L	T
N			A		E	G	O		T		I	
A	G	E	S		C		R		R		F	
G			T		O	P	E	N	E	Y	E	D
	C		E		N		A		S		S	
T	O	R	R	I	D		L	A	S	S	I	E
	H			C				D			Z	
T	E	A	S	E	T		C	O	S	S	E	T
	R		H		H		A		A		D	
P	E	T	I	T	I	O	N		I			C
	N		E		R		V		L	A	V	A
	C		L		T	E	A		O			N
D	E	A	D	L	Y		S	P	R	I	T	E

Summing Up

14	16	13	30	34	30
31	22	24	**9**	27	24
26	35	22	18	20	**16**
23	33	27	26	**5**	23
18	**10**	29	31	29	20
25	21	**22**	23	22	24

Battleships

					▲		●	
◀	■	▶			■			
					▼		◀	▶
		▲						
●		▼				◀	▶	
●							●	
		◀	■	■	▶			

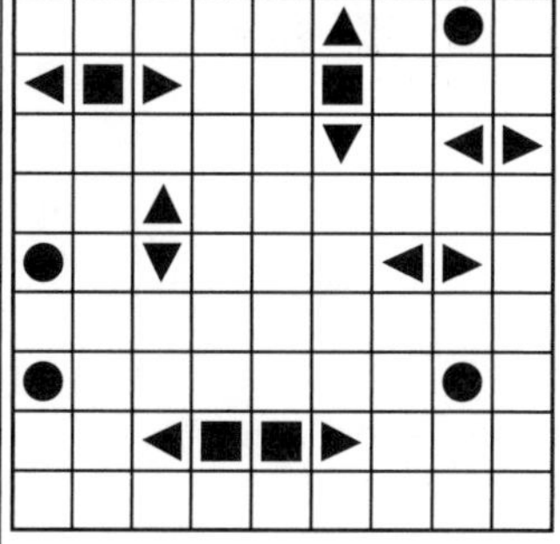

Wordsearch Workout

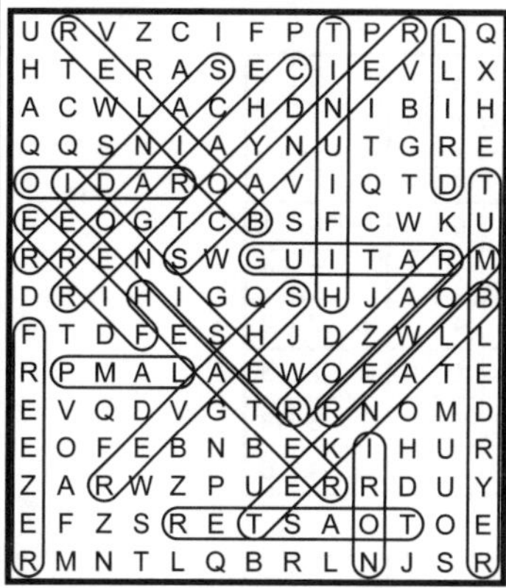

U	R	V	Z	C	I	F	P	T	P	R	L	Q
H	T	E	R	A	S	E	C	I	E	V	L	X
A	C	W	L	A	C	H	D	N	I	B	I	H
Q	Q	S	N	I	A	Y	N	U	T	G	R	E
O	I	D	A	R	O	A	V	I	Q	T	D	T
E	E	O	G	T	C	B	S	F	C	W	K	U
R	R	E	N	S	W	G	U	I	T	A	R	M
D	R	I	H	I	G	Q	S	H	J	A	O	B
F	T	D	F	E	S	H	J	D	Z	W	L	L
R	P	M	A	L	A	E	W	O	E	A	T	E
E	V	Q	D	V	G	T	R	R	N	O	M	D
E	O	F	E	B	N	B	E	K	I	H	U	R
Z	A	R	W	Z	P	U	E	R	R	D	U	Y
E	F	Z	S	R	E	T	S	A	O	T	O	E
R	M	N	T	L	Q	B	R	L	N	J	S	R

Double Fun Sudoku

Tasty Teaser

6	8	4	9	2	7	1	3	5
9	2	5	3	8	1	7	4	6
7	3	1	4	5	6	2	8	9
4	1	9	5	3	2	8	6	7
2	7	8	6	1	9	3	5	4
5	6	3	7	4	8	9	2	1
8	9	6	2	7	4	5	1	3
3	4	2	1	9	5	6	7	8
1	5	7	8	6	3	4	9	2

Brain Buster

8	5	1	4	6	7	3	9	2
9	2	3	5	1	8	7	6	4
7	6	4	3	9	2	5	1	8
6	8	2	9	4	5	1	3	7
1	7	5	2	3	6	8	4	9
4	3	9	8	7	1	6	2	5
5	4	7	1	2	3	9	8	6
2	1	6	7	8	9	4	5	3
3	9	8	6	5	4	2	7	1

Whatever Next?

7 – The numbers in the outer points of the star all add up to the central figure.

Brain Teaser

207 – 72 + 3^2, + 4^2, + 5^2, + 6^2, + 7^2

Page 36

Mind Over Matter

The value of the letter in the central square is the sum total of the values of the letters in the other squares. Thus the missing value is 24, so the missing letter is X.

Double Fun Sudoku

Tasty Teaser

8	6	7	9	1	4	2	5	3
3	2	9	7	5	8	1	6	4
4	1	5	3	2	6	8	9	7
7	3	8	2	9	5	6	4	1
2	5	4	6	7	1	3	8	9
1	9	6	8	4	3	5	7	2
6	7	3	1	8	9	4	2	5
9	4	1	5	6	2	7	3	8
5	8	2	4	3	7	9	1	6

Brain Buster

7	8	2	6	3	1	4	9	5
3	4	5	9	7	8	6	1	2
9	1	6	4	2	5	3	7	8
6	7	1	3	8	4	2	5	9
8	3	4	2	5	9	1	6	7
5	2	9	7	1	6	8	3	4
4	6	8	5	9	3	7	2	1
2	9	3	1	4	7	5	8	6
1	5	7	8	6	2	9	4	3

Codeword Conundrum

Z	E	A	L	O	T		A		H	I	J	A	C	K
O		L			H	O	N	E	Y		A		H	
N	O	B	O	D	Y		G		E		I		I	
A		I			M		S	E	N	I	L	I	T	Y
L		N		V	E	N	T		A			N		E
	Y	O	G	A		O		B		K	O	A	L	A
P				C	A	R	T	O	O	N		N		S
U	M	B	R	A		M		D		I	N	E	P	T
B		E		N	E	A	R	I	N	G				Y
L	I	G	H	T		L		C		H	U	S	K	
I		I			W		S	E	C	T		A		M
C	O	N	Q	U	E	S	T		R			F		E
	X		U		I		A		A	F	I	E	L	D
	E		I		R	E	N	E	W			S		A
U	N	I	T	E	D		K		L	E	N	T	I	L

Futoshiki

4	2	3	5	1
3	4	2	1	5
2	1	5	4	3
5	3	1	2	4
1	5	4	3	2

High-Speed Crossword

G	R	A	B	S		P	R	E	V	I	E	W
O		D		L		I		X		N		A
D		M		E	L	E	G	A	N	T	L	Y
S	E	I	N	E				M		R		N
E		N		T	O	M	B	S	T	O	N	E
N		I			U		L			S		
D	I	S	C	U	S		I	S	O	P	O	D
		T			T		N			E		E
S	A	R	C	A	S	T	I	C		C		F
N		A		D				R	O	T	O	R
A	T	T	R	I	B	U	T	E		I		A
R		O		O		S		S		O		U
E	U	R	A	S	I	A		S	Y	N	O	D

1 Minute Number Crunch

Beginner

131 – 28 = 103, 103 x 2 = 206, 206 + 39 = 245, 245 ÷ 5 = 49, 49 ÷ 7 x 2 = 14, 14 x 6 = 84, 50% of 84 = 42

Intermediate

1947 x 2 = 3894, 3894 – 1821 = 2073, 2073 ÷ 3 = 691, 691 + 104 = 795, 795 ÷ 15 = 53, 53 x 4 = 212, 212 – 79 = 133

Advanced

330 ÷ 15 x 4 = 88, 88 ÷ 11 x 10 = 80, 80 ÷ 8 x 5 = 50, 50 x 5.5 = 275, 275 ÷ 25 x 7 = 77, 77 + 33 = 110, 110 – 77 (110 ÷ 10 x 7) = 33

Page 37

Domino Placement

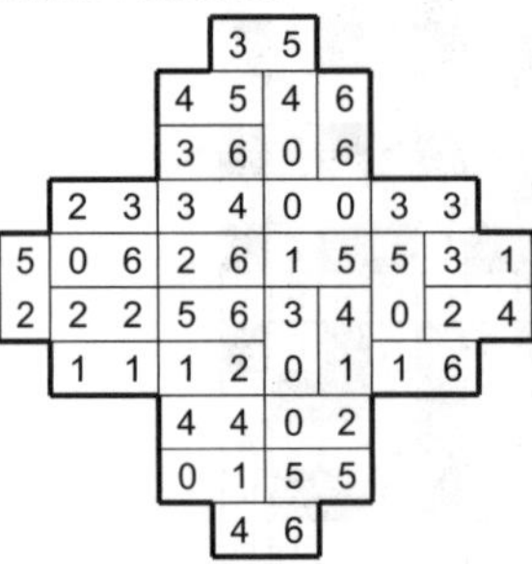

				3	5				
			4	5	4	6			
			3	6	0	6			
	2	3	3	4	0	0	3	3	
5	0	6	2	6	1	5	5	3	1
2	2	2	5	6	3	4	0	2	4
	1	1	1	2	0	1	1	6	
			4	4	0	2			
			0	1	5	5			
				4	6				

High-Speed Crossword

S	A	C	K		N	E	C	R	O	S	I	S
Y		A		F		G		I		P		L
C	A	R	R	I	E	R		O	M	E	G	A
A		D		R		E		D		C		T
M	O	S	E	S		S	N	E	A	K	Y	
O				T		S		J		L		C
R	E	C	O	R	D		C	A	M	E	R	A
E		U		E		C		N				L
	P	R	E	F	E	R		E	X	T	R	A
S		I		U		U		I		H		M
P	R	O	P	S		M	A	R	T	I	N	I
A		U		A		B		O		N		N
R	E	S	T	L	E	S	S		A	G	U	E

IQ Workout

20

(7 + 26 + 17) –

(8 + 12 + 10) = 20

Wordwheel

The nine-letter word is: ARBORETUM

Wordsearch Workout

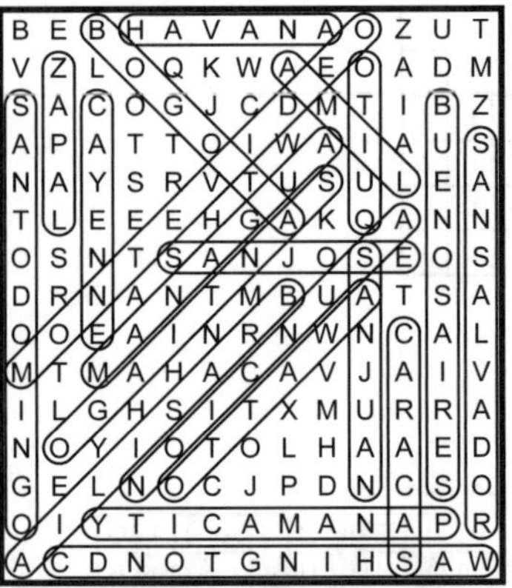

B	E	B	H	A	V	A	N	A	O	Z	U	T
V	Z	L	O	Q	K	W	A	E	O	A	D	M
S	A	C	O	G	J	C	D	M	T	I	B	Z
A	P	A	T	T	O	I	W	A	I	A	U	S
N	A	Y	S	R	V	T	U	S	U	L	E	A
T	L	E	E	E	H	G	A	K	Q	A	N	N
O	S	N	T	S	A	N	J	O	S	E	O	S
D	R	N	A	N	T	M	B	U	A	T	S	A
O	O	E	A	I	N	R	N	W	N	C	A	L
M	T	M	A	H	A	C	A	V	J	A	I	V
I	L	G	H	S	I	T	X	M	U	R	R	A
N	O	Y	I	O	T	O	L	H	A	A	E	D
G	E	L	N	O	C	J	P	D	N	C	S	O
O	I	Y	T	I	C	A	M	A	N	A	P	R
A	C	D	N	O	T	G	N	I	H	S	A	W

Double Fun Sudoku

Tasty Teaser

4	6	9	3	1	2	5	8	7
1	2	7	8	5	9	3	4	6
5	8	3	4	7	6	1	2	9
7	1	6	2	8	4	9	5	3
2	9	4	5	6	3	7	1	8
3	5	8	7	9	1	2	6	4
6	4	2	1	3	7	8	9	5
9	3	5	6	2	8	4	7	1
8	7	1	9	4	5	6	3	2

Brain Buster

1	5	4	3	6	9	8	7	2
7	8	9	4	1	2	3	6	5
2	3	6	7	5	8	1	9	4
9	7	5	2	8	1	6	4	3
6	2	3	9	4	5	7	8	1
8	4	1	6	3	7	2	5	9
4	9	2	8	7	3	5	1	6
3	1	7	5	9	6	4	2	8
5	6	8	1	2	4	9	3	7

Sum Circle

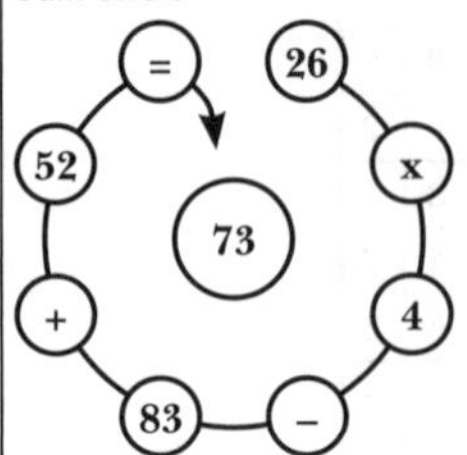

Page 38

1 Minute Number Crunch

Beginner
43 – 15 = 28, 28 ÷ 4 = 7, 7 x 3 = 21, 21 ÷ 7 = 3, 3² = 9, 9 + 16 = 25, 25 x 4 = 100

Intermediate
19 + 27 = 46, 46 x 3 = 138, 138 + 831 = 969, 969 ÷ 3 x 2 = 646, 646 – 259 = 387, 387 ÷ 9 x 5 = 215, 215 + 66 = 281

Advanced
425 ÷ 17 x 11 = 275, 275 ÷ 11 x 5 = 125, 125 x 0.4 = 50, 320% of 50 = 160, 160 ÷ 32 x 23 = 115, 115 ÷ 23 x 18 = 90, 90 ÷ 0.3 = 300

High-Speed Crossword

C	R	I	M	S	O	N		L	O	C	A	L
L		F		E		E		E		O		A
O	B	S	E	R	V	A	T	I	O	N		D
T				E		T				F		L
T	O	K	E	N		E	L	U	S	I	V	E
E		O		G		N		N		D		
D	E	A	D	E	N		S	C	R	A	W	L
		L		T		D		E		N		A
O	P	A	L	I	N	E		R	A	T	T	Y
A		B				C		T				E
S		E	X	T	R	A	V	A	G	A	N	T
I		A		O		M		I		B		T
S	P	R	I	G		P	A	N	A	C	H	E

IQ Workout

B – No 1 has 1 angle, No 2 has 3 angles, No 3 has 5 angles, No 4 has 7 angles, B has 9 angles.

Codeword Conundrum

W	I	S	E	C	R	A	C	K		S	Q	U	A	D
I		E		L		U		I		C		R		E
S	H	I	N	E		D	A	N	D	E	L	I	O	N
T		Z		F		I		K		N		N		S
E	J	E	C	T	I	O	N		R	E	V	E	R	E
R			O		R		E		E		A		A	
I			M		O	B	E	S	E		M		K	
A	C	U	M	E	N		D		N	E	P	H	E	W
	O		A		I	D	I	O	T		I			R
	M		N		N		E		R		S			E
L	A	P	D	O	G		R	H	Y	T	H	M	I	C
E		A		V		C		Y		A		A		K
A	P	P	R	E	H	E	N	D		S	E	N	N	A
V		E		R		D		R		T		I		G
E	G	R	E	T		E	X	O	N	E	R	A	T	E

Tasty Teaser

4	6	3	5	9	2	1	7	8
1	8	2	4	7	6	5	9	3
7	5	9	1	8	3	6	4	2
5	9	6	7	4	8	2	3	1
8	2	4	3	1	9	7	6	5
3	1	7	6	2	5	9	8	4
6	7	1	8	5	4	3	2	9
9	3	8	2	6	1	4	5	7
2	4	5	9	3	7	8	1	6

Brain Buster

5	9	8	4	3	6	2	7	1
3	2	7	9	1	5	4	6	8
6	1	4	2	8	7	9	5	3
4	8	5	1	7	9	6	3	2
9	7	6	3	5	2	1	8	4
2	3	1	8	6	4	5	9	7
8	6	9	7	2	1	3	4	5
7	5	2	6	4	3	8	1	9
1	4	3	5	9	8	7	2	6

Spidoku

Page 39

Logi-Six

B	C	F	E	D	A
E	A	C	D	F	B
D	B	A	C	E	F
C	F	D	B	A	E
A	D	E	F	B	C
F	E	B	A	C	D

High-Speed Crossword

	A	D	D	L	E	D		S	H	A	R	P
C		I		O		A		U		M		R
R	O	A	D	W	O	R	K	S		I		E
O		N				T		T	A	S	K	S
S	O	A	P	O	P	E	R	A		S		S
S			I			D		I				R
C	O	N	G	E	R		S	N	O	O	Z	E
O				Q		E			P			L
U		M		U	N	D	E	R	T	A	K	E
N	A	I	R	A		I				L		A
T		N		L	I	T	I	G	I	O	U	S
R		I		L		E		U		N		E
Y	U	M	M	Y		D	I	T	H	E	R	

Wordsearch Workout

Double Fun Sudoku

Tasty Teaser

3	9	2	6	5	8	4	7	1
5	8	7	4	1	3	6	9	2
4	1	6	2	9	7	8	3	5
2	6	4	9	7	1	5	8	3
1	5	8	3	6	2	9	4	7
9	7	3	5	8	4	1	2	6
8	3	9	1	2	5	7	6	4
6	4	1	7	3	9	2	5	8
7	2	5	8	4	6	3	1	9

Brain Buster

5	8	2	9	7	4	1	3	6
7	1	4	3	6	2	8	9	5
3	6	9	8	1	5	4	7	2
4	2	3	5	9	8	6	1	7
9	7	1	4	2	6	5	8	3
6	5	8	7	3	1	2	4	9
8	4	7	6	5	3	9	2	1
1	3	6	2	4	9	7	5	8
2	9	5	1	8	7	3	6	4

Matchstick Magic

The matchsticks which have been removed are outlined.

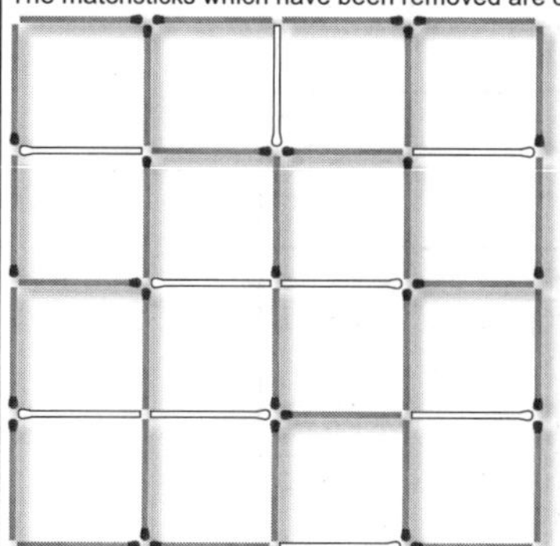

Brain Teaser

90°C

Domino Placement

				6	6				
			5	5	5	5			
			1	0	3	2			
	0	2	3	4	0	0	3	2	
3	6	5	1	4	2	6	0	1	3
2	4	3	4	4	6	5	0	6	3
	1	3	0	6	4	4	0	5	
			2	1	4	1			
			1	2	6	1			
				2	5				

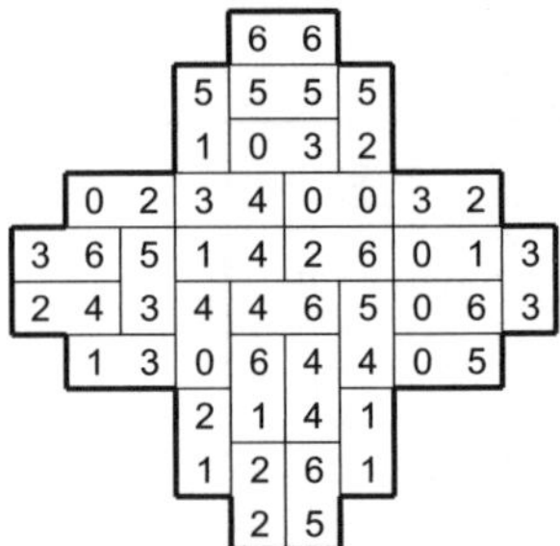

Page 40

Codeword Conundrum

S		C		A	S	P	H	Y	X	I	A	T	E	D
T	R	A	M	P		A		E			S		S	
I		N		P	I	V	O	T	S		P	I	T	H
F	E	N	C	E		E			E		I		E	
F		I		T			H	A	R	D	C	O	R	E
		B		I	S	L	E		V			F		E
E	X	A	L	T			R		E		A	F	A	R
W		L		E	Q	U	E	R	R	Y		I		I
E	P	I	C		U		T			U	N	C	L	E
R		S			A		I	D	O	L		I		
S	Y	M	B	O	L	I	C			E		A		K
	E		L		M			J		T	U	L	L	E
G	A	L	A		S	A	F	A	R	I		D		Y
	R		Z			I		M		D	R	O	V	E
U	N	D	E	S	I	R	A	B	L	E		M		D

Double Fun Sudoku

Tasty Teaser

8	9	3	6	5	1	7	2	4
7	2	6	9	8	4	5	3	1
1	5	4	2	7	3	9	8	6
5	7	9	1	6	8	3	4	2
3	6	1	5	4	2	8	7	9
4	8	2	3	9	7	6	1	5
9	3	8	4	1	5	2	6	7
6	1	7	8	2	9	4	5	3
2	4	5	7	3	6	1	9	8

Brain Buster

7	8	6	4	2	9	3	1	5
5	4	9	3	6	1	2	8	7
2	3	1	8	7	5	4	6	9
8	1	5	7	4	6	9	3	2
3	6	7	1	9	2	8	5	4
4	9	2	5	3	8	6	7	1
1	5	3	2	8	4	7	9	6
9	2	8	6	5	7	1	4	3
6	7	4	9	1	3	5	2	8

Pyramid Plus

A=45, B=57, C=143, D=36, E=4, F=102, G=200, H=179, I=40, J=302, K=379, L=219, M=681, N=598, O=1279.

Work it Out

29 – Reading down each column, take 4 from each preceding number until the central number, after which add 5 to each preceding number.

High-Speed Crossword

B		S		P		U	N	C	R	O	S	S
O	V	E	R	R	U	N				N		U
S		A		E		L		S	O	L	E	S
S	T	A	I	D		E	M	U		I		P
		I		E		S		B	I	N	G	E
W	O	R	M	C	A	S	T	S		E		N
O				E				T				S
N		R		S	U	B	M	A	R	I	N	E
D	E	E	D	S		U		N		T		
R		T		O	W	N		T	I	A	R	A
O	S	I	E	R		Y		I		L		C
U		N				I	M	A	G	I	N	E
S	H	A	K	E	U	P		L		C		R

1 Minute Number Crunch

Beginner

22 x 7 = 154, 154 ÷ 14 = 11, 11² = 121, 121 + 49 = 170, 170 ÷ 10 = 17, 17 – 8 = 9, 9 x 20 = 180

Intermediate

488 ÷ 8 = 61, 61 – 17 = 44, 44 + 20 (44 ÷ 11 x 5) = 64, cube root of 64 = 4, 4 x 26 = 104, 104 ÷ 4 x 3 = 78, 78 ÷ 3 = 26

Advanced

207 x 6 = 1242, 1242 ÷ 23 x 17 = 918, 918 ÷ 18 x 7 = 357, 357 + 238 (357 ÷ 3 x 2) = 595, 595 ÷ 5 x 4 = 476, 476 ÷ 1.75 = 272, 272 x 9 = 2448

Page 41

High-Speed Crossword

F	O	O	D	P	O	I	S	O	N	I	N	G
A			I		C		E			N		R
B	E	T	S		T		V	I	R	T	U	E
L			C	R	E	P	E			E		E
E	U	R	O		T		N	E	A	R	E	D
D		E					T			F		Y
	P	A	G	A	N		Y	E	M	E	N	
S		R			E					R		R
T	A	R	T	A	R		A		F	E	T	A
E		A			V	E	R	S	O			G
P	O	N	C	H	O		G		C	U	L	T
U		G			U		U		U			A
P	R	E	P	O	S	S	E	S	S	I	N	G

IQ Workout

The hour hand alternately loses 2 hours and 4 hours and the minute hand alternately gains 4 minutes and 2 minutes each time.

1 Minute Number Crunch

Beginner

73 + 17 = 90, 90 ÷ 9 x 5 = 50, 50 + 8 = 58, 58 ÷ 2 = 29, 29 reversed = 92, 50% of 92 = 46, 46 + 16 = 62

Intermediate

93 x 3 = 279, 279 ÷ 9 x 5 = 155, 155 – 47 = 108, 108 ÷ 12 x 7 = 63, 63 ÷ 7 = 9, 9 x 75 = 675, 675 + 97 = 772

Advanced

104 ÷ 13 x 8 = 64, square root of 64 = 8, 8 x 72 = 576, 175% of 576 = 1008, 1008 ÷ 12 x 5 = 420, 420 + 378 (420 ÷ 10 x 9) = 798, 798 + 897 = 1695

Wordsearch Workout

A	V	P	Q	G	B	E	D	T	I	A	K	Z
N	X	V	U	C	H	A	N	G	C	H	U	N
L	H	C	A	Y	A	N	G	Z	H	O	U	N
E	O	U	N	B	K	G	U	K	D	F	X	A
S	P	H	Z	Y	Y	O	A	A	I	O	D	N
H	G	C	H	L	H	Y	T	W	H	S	Q	J
A	N	N	O	Z	U	O	K	I	A	H	I	I
N	A	I	U	G	N	A	H	C	N	A	N	N
K	I	S	S	G	O	N	O	U	G	N	G	G
U	J	H	D	U	F	U	O	G	Z	Z	D	V
N	U	O	E	Q	U	H	E	S	H	J	A	C
M	I	N	H	S	Z	S	G	G	O	L	O	M
I	J	X	L	N	H	N	U	R	U	M	Q	I
N	D	C	A	N	O	A	G	Y	L	P	Q	Y
G	V	L	B	J	U	W	N	M	O	V	Y	X

Double Fun Sudoku

Tasty Teaser

5	3	2	9	7	1	6	4	8
6	9	8	5	2	4	3	7	1
4	1	7	6	8	3	9	2	5
8	6	5	1	9	2	7	3	4
3	7	9	8	4	5	2	1	6
2	4	1	3	6	7	8	5	9
9	5	3	2	1	6	4	8	7
7	2	6	4	5	8	1	9	3
1	8	4	7	3	9	5	6	2

Brain Buster

6	3	4	7	5	1	2	8	9
7	1	8	4	9	2	3	6	5
2	9	5	3	8	6	4	1	7
9	5	2	6	7	8	1	4	3
8	4	1	9	3	5	6	7	2
3	6	7	2	1	4	9	5	8
4	8	6	5	2	9	7	3	1
5	7	9	1	6	3	8	2	4
1	2	3	8	4	7	5	9	6

Whatever Next?

K – Assign a number to each letter according to its place in the alphabet, so A=1, B=2, C=3, etc. Adding together the values of the two letters in each point of the star results in the central figure, 17. F=6, so the missing letter is K(=11).

Brain Teaser

8

Left	Right
8 x 5 = 40	6 x 4 = 24
4 x 2 = 8	8 x 3 = 24
48	48

Page 42

Mind Over Matter

The sum total of the values of the letters in the two left squares minus the sum total of the values of the letters in the two right squares equals that of the central square. Thus the missing value is 9, so the missing letter is I.

Double Fun Sudoku

Tasty Teaser

3	2	9	8	7	5	1	4	6
5	7	4	6	9	1	2	3	8
6	1	8	3	4	2	9	7	5
9	6	2	1	3	4	5	8	7
4	3	5	2	8	7	6	1	9
1	8	7	5	6	9	3	2	4
7	5	6	4	2	3	8	9	1
8	4	3	9	1	6	7	5	2
2	9	1	7	5	8	4	6	3

Brain Buster

9	2	1	7	3	5	4	6	8
3	5	6	4	1	8	2	7	9
7	8	4	9	6	2	5	3	1
4	9	3	8	2	7	1	5	6
5	6	2	1	9	4	7	8	3
1	7	8	3	5	6	9	2	4
2	4	5	6	8	9	3	1	7
8	3	9	2	7	1	6	4	5
6	1	7	5	4	3	8	9	2

Codeword Conundrum

B	A	T	H	M	A	T	■	■	V	E	R	G	E	R
L	■	R	■	A	■	O	O	Z	E	■	I	■	■	O
E	P	O	X	Y	■	P	■	■	H	■	S	■	■	U
S	■	V	■	F	O	A	L	■	I	R	K	I	N	G
S	P	E	L	L	■	Z	I	N	C	■	■	N	■	H
■	O	■	■	O	■	■	M	■	L	■	■	D	■	N
S	T	R	A	W	■	O	B	J	E	C	T	I	V	E
Q	■	A	■	E	■	W	■	A	■	A	■	G	■	S
U	N	D	E	R	W	E	A	R	■	P	I	O	U	S
A	■	I	■	■	H	■	L	■	■	A	■	■	S	■
B	■	S	■	■	E	L	A	N	■	C	A	K	E	D
B	E	H	A	V	E	■	S	A	R	I	■	N	■	W
L	■	■	L	■	D	■	■	K	■	T	R	A	C	E
E	■	■	T	■	L	A	K	E	■	O	■	V	■	L
D	E	N	O	T	E	■	■	D	A	R	K	E	S	T

Futoshiki

2	3	1	4	5
4	2	5	3	1
3	1	4	5	2
5	4 >	2	1	3
1	5	3	2	4

High-Speed Crossword

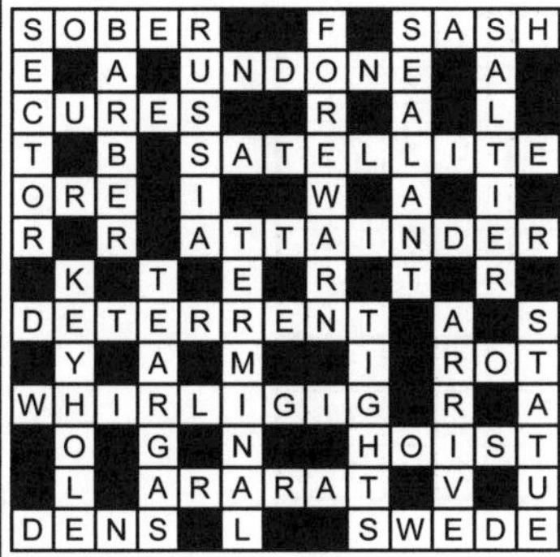

1 Minute Number Crunch

Beginner

33 – 4 = 29. 29 x 5 = 145, 145 – 15 = 130, 130 x 3 = 390, 390 – 90 = 300, 300 ÷ 6 x 5 = 250, 250 + 14 = 264

Intermediate

89 + 57 = 146, 146 – 29 = 117, 117 ÷ 9 x 5 = 65, 65 ÷ 5 x 4 = 52, 52 x 7 = 364, 364 x .75 = 273, 273 ÷ 3 = 91

Advanced

33 x 25 = 825, 825 ÷ 3 x 2 = 550, 550 ÷ 11 x 9 = 450, 28% of 450 = 126, 126 ÷ 14 x 5 = 45, 45 + 89 = 134, 134 ÷ 0.25 = 536

Page 43

Battleships

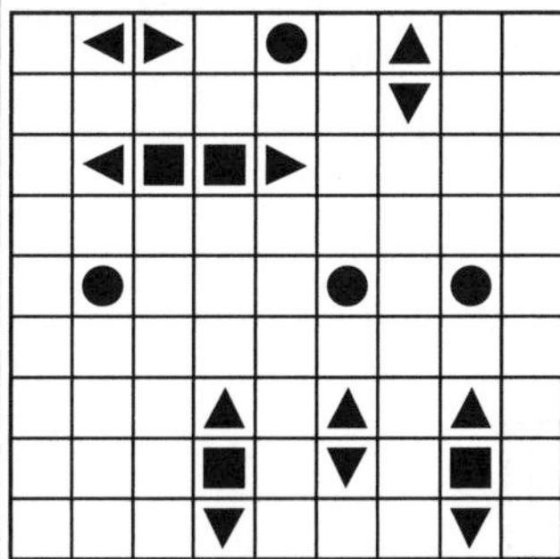

High-Speed Crossword

D	I	N	G	O	■	S	Q	U	E	A	K	Y
E	■	O	■	P	■	E	■	R	■	L	■	I
N	A	N	■	E	G	L	A	N	T	I	N	E
I	■	S	■	R	■	F	■	■	■	C	■	L
M	E	L	B	A	■	S	T	I	P	E	N	D
■	■	I	■	T	■	A	■	N	■	■	■	E
S	O	P	H	I	S	T	I	C	A	T	E	D
M	■	■	■	V	■	I	■	O	■	R	■	■
E	N	D	L	E	S	S	■	R	E	A	D	S
L	■	E	■	■	■	F	■	R	■	I	■	I
T	R	A	N	S	P	I	R	E	■	T	A	N
E	■	L	■	U	■	E	■	C	■	O	■	U
D	E	S	C	E	N	D	■	T	I	R	E	S

IQ Workout

48 – They are non-prime numbers 38 to 48.

Wordwheel

The nine-letter word is: TRUNCHEON

Wordsearch Workout

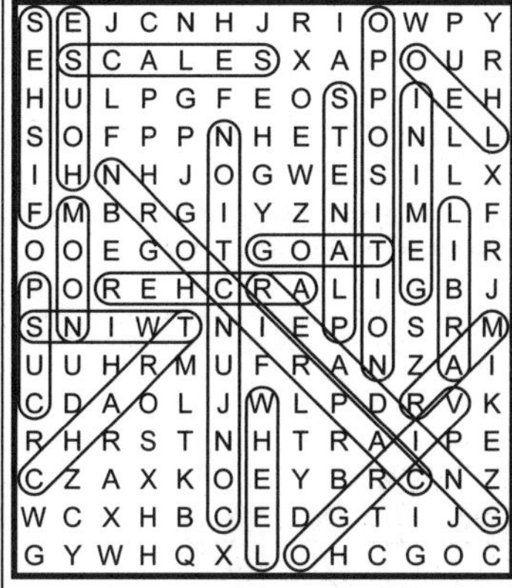

Double Fun Sudoku

Tasty Teaser

5	2	3	6	9	8	1	7	4
6	4	7	3	1	5	2	9	8
1	8	9	7	2	4	5	3	6
2	9	5	8	4	1	7	6	3
7	6	4	5	3	2	9	8	1
3	1	8	9	6	7	4	5	2
4	5	6	1	8	9	3	2	7
9	3	1	2	7	6	8	4	5
8	7	2	4	5	3	6	1	9

Brain Buster

3	5	8	7	1	4	2	6	9
1	7	2	3	6	9	8	5	4
9	4	6	5	2	8	3	1	7
6	1	5	9	3	2	4	7	8
2	8	7	4	5	6	9	3	1
4	9	3	1	8	7	6	2	5
5	2	9	8	7	3	1	4	6
7	6	4	2	9	1	5	8	3
8	3	1	6	4	5	7	9	2

Sum Circle

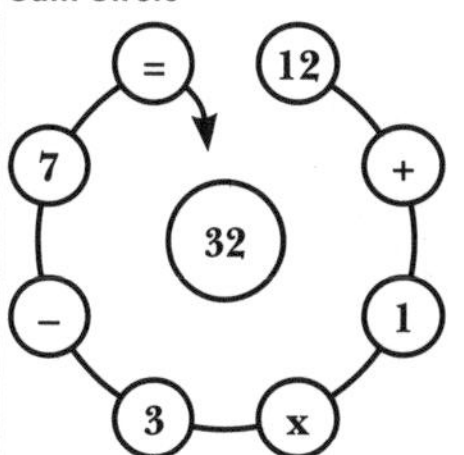

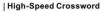

Page 44

1 Minute Number Crunch

Beginner
26 x 6 = 156, 156 ÷ 4 = 39, 39 x 2 = 78, 78 – 16 = 62, 62 ÷ 2 = 31, 31 + 19 = 50, 50 x 6 = 300

Intermediate
340 ÷ 17 = 20, 20 x 2.5 = 50, 50² = 2500, 20% of 2500 = 500, 15% of 500 = 75, 75 x 9 = 675, 675 ÷ 3 x 2 = 450

Advanced
55² = 3025, 80% of 3025 = 2420, 2420 ÷ 10 x 3 = 726, 726 + 484 (726 ÷ 3 x 2) = 1210, 1210 x 7 = 8470, 8470 – 982 = 7488, 7488 ÷ 18 x 7 = 2912

High-Speed Crossword

P	R	E	E	M	P	T		P	I	P	E	S
I		A		A		H		A		A		A
C	A	T	E	R	P	I	L	L	A	R		B
C				E		E				T		L
O	K	A	Y	S		V	A	M	P	I	R	E
L		D		N		E		E		T		
O	O	D	L	E	S		C	A	R	I	E	S
		R		S		G		N		O		H
B	E	E	F	T	E	A		W	I	N	D	Y
L		S				Z		H				N
I		S	T	O	N	E	C	I	R	C	L	E
S		E		A		B		L		O		S
S	W	E	A	T		O	N	E	R	O	U	S

IQ Workout

2 – Each side of the triangle contains the digits 1 to 9.

Codeword Conundrum

B	A	N	G	L	E		P	R	E	S	U	M	E	S
E			L		R		O			K		E		W
A	D	J	U	T	A	N	T		S	I	Z	Z	L	E
R			T		S		A	X	E			Z		E
D	E	F	T		E	A	T		R	E	C	A	N	T
	L		O		R		O	F	F			N		M
A	M	O	N	G	S	T		A	S	T	R	I	D	E
Q		P		N		I	N	K		I		N		A
U	N	E	Q	U	A	L		E	S	C	H	E	A	T
A		R			L	E	T		H		I		G	
P	E	A	N	U	T		H	O	E		R	H	E	A
L		T			A	Y	E		A		S			U
A	T	O	N	E	R		O	B	T	R	U	D	E	D
N		R		V			R		H		T			I
E	A	S	T	E	R	L	Y		E	X	E	M	P	T

Tasty Teaser

5	9	2	4	6	7	8	3	1
3	6	8	1	2	9	7	5	4
1	7	4	5	3	8	6	2	9
6	3	1	8	9	5	2	4	7
7	4	9	2	1	6	3	8	5
8	2	5	7	4	3	1	9	6
2	8	7	9	5	1	4	6	3
4	5	6	3	7	2	9	1	8
9	1	3	6	8	4	5	7	2

Brain Buster

2	5	7	6	4	1	3	9	8
6	9	3	5	7	8	2	4	1
4	1	8	2	3	9	6	7	5
5	6	4	1	2	3	9	8	7
3	8	1	9	6	7	5	2	4
7	2	9	8	5	4	1	6	3
1	3	2	4	8	6	7	5	9
9	4	6	7	1	5	8	3	2
8	7	5	3	9	2	4	1	6

Spidoku

Wordsearch Workout

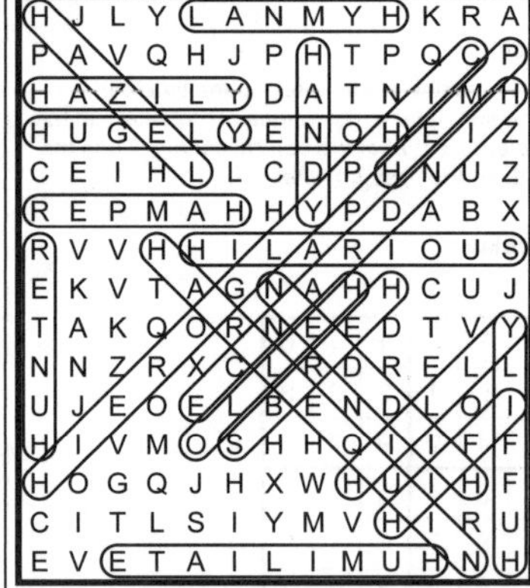

Double Fun Sudoku

Tasty Teaser

1	5	6	9	8	3	7	4	2
4	3	9	7	2	6	8	1	5
7	2	8	5	1	4	3	9	6
3	6	7	1	5	9	4	2	8
9	8	2	3	4	7	6	5	1
5	1	4	2	6	8	9	7	3
2	7	3	8	9	5	1	6	4
8	4	1	6	7	2	5	3	9
6	9	5	4	3	1	2	8	7

Brain Buster

9	6	1	7	3	4	5	8	2
3	5	2	8	6	1	4	9	7
7	8	4	5	9	2	3	1	6
4	1	3	6	2	8	7	5	9
5	2	9	4	7	3	8	6	1
8	7	6	9	1	5	2	4	3
1	3	5	2	4	6	9	7	8
2	4	7	1	8	9	6	3	5
6	9	8	3	5	7	1	2	4

Page 45

Logi-Six

D	E	F	C	B	A
C	A	B	E	D	F
A	D	C	F	E	B
B	F	D	A	C	E
F	B	E	D	A	C
E	C	A	B	F	D

High-Speed Crossword

M	E	T	R	O	N	O	M	E		S	E	E
A		E		V				L		T		V
D	A	N	C	E	R		P	A	R	A	D	E
E		N		R		G		T		V		R
	P	I	E	D		S	C	E	N	E	R	Y
C		S		U		T				S		O
R			D	E	T	R	A	C	T			N
O		J				I		O		L		E
S	T	E	P	S	O	N		N	E	A	P	
S		W		C		G		F		R		S
I	C	E	C	A	P		D	E	R	I	D	E
N		L		L				S		A		N
G	A	S		P	R	E	S	S	S	T	U	D

Matchstick Magic

The matchsticks have been placed as follows:

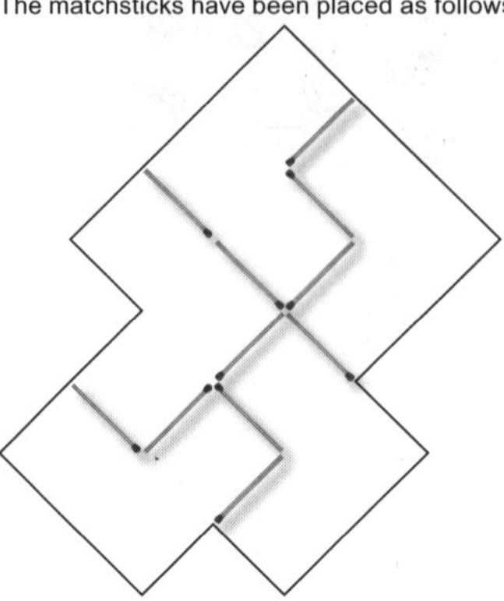

Brain Teaser

2415

Page 50

1 Minute Number Crunch

Beginner
10% of 150 = 15, 15 x 8 = 120, 50% of 120 = 60, 60 ÷ 12 x 3 = 15, 15 + 7 = 22, 22 ÷ 2 = 11, 11 x 10 = 110

Intermediate
269 + 47 = 316, 316 ÷ 4 = 79, 79 x 3 = 237, 237 – 88 = 149, 149 + 27 = 176, 176 ÷ 8 x 5 = 110, 110 + 11 = 121

Advanced
84 ÷ 7 x 5 = 60, 60^2 = 3600, 3600 ÷ 18 x 7 = 1400, 1400 – 578 = 822, 822 + 1096 = 1918, 1918 ÷ 2 = 959, 959 + 697 = 1656

High-Speed Crossword

B	R	I	E	F	S		B		K			G
	U			L		T	A	P	I	O	C	A
A	N	T	E	A	T	E	R		L			S
	I			T		N	E	G	L	E	C	T
E	N	M	A	S	S	E			E			R
C			S		O	T	T	E	R			I
O	D	E	S		D		I		B	A	I	T
N			I	R	A	T	E		E			I
O			S			A	R	R	E	A	R	S
M	Y	S	T	I	C	S		O			A	
I			A		H	E	D	O	N	I	S	M
C	O	U	N	T	E	R		S			P	
S			T		W		A	T	T	E	S	T

IQ Workout

B – A is the same as E with black/yellow reversal, and C is the same as D with black/yellow reversal.

Codeword Conundrum

O		M		O	P	A	L	E	S	C	E	N	C	E
B	R	I	E	F		V			E		X		A	
S		N		F	R	E	Q	U	E	N	T	I	N	G
T	R	E	S	S		R			D		R		A	
R		S		H		S	P	E	C	T	A	C	L	E
U		W	O	O	F		A		A			L		L
C	U	E		R			L		S		W	E	R	E
T		E		E	S	C	A	P	E	D		A		C
I	M	P	S		I		V			I		N	O	T
V		E			X		E		A	S	K	S		R
E	N	R	A	P	T	U	R	E		M		H		O
	O		Z		I			L		A	V	A	I	L
D	O	C	U	M	E	N	T	A	R	Y		V		Y
	S		R		T			N		E	J	E	C	T
L	E	V	E	L	H	E	A	D	E	D		N		E

Tasty Teaser

6	4	8	2	1	9	7	5	3
5	7	2	3	6	8	1	9	4
3	1	9	4	7	5	6	2	8
7	9	3	5	4	2	8	6	1
4	5	6	7	8	1	9	3	2
8	2	1	9	3	6	4	7	5
1	8	5	6	2	7	3	4	9
2	6	4	8	9	3	5	1	7
9	3	7	1	5	4	2	8	6

Brain Buster

8	5	3	2	7	9	6	1	4
4	7	2	1	6	5	8	3	9
6	1	9	3	4	8	5	7	2
3	4	8	7	5	1	2	9	6
1	6	5	4	9	2	7	8	3
2	9	7	6	8	3	4	5	1
7	2	1	8	3	4	9	6	5
9	8	4	5	1	6	3	2	7
5	3	6	9	2	7	1	4	8

Spidoku

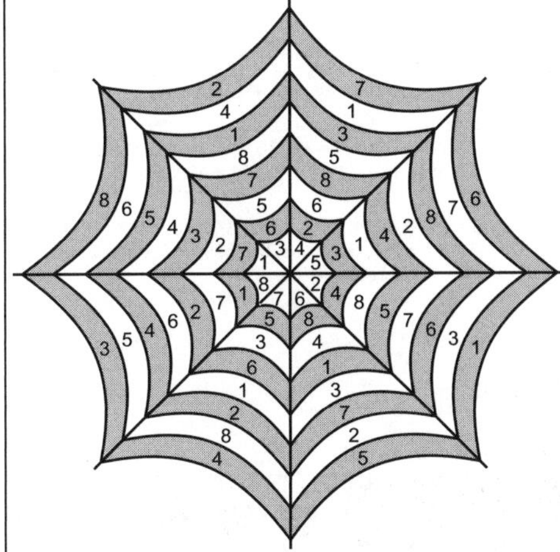

Page 51

Logi-Six

C	A	B	F	D	E
E	D	F	C	A	B
F	E	C	A	B	D
B	C	D	E	F	A
D	F	A	B	E	C
A	B	E	D	C	F

High-Speed Crossword

S	I	D	E	D	I	S	H		F	A	I	L
A		E		I		T			L			A
L		B		V		R	E	C	O	R	D	S
T	O	R	P	E	D	O			T			V
		I				P	R	A	I	R	I	E
M	U	S	E	U	M		I		L			G
O			N		O	R	B		L			A
V			T		S		S	L	A	C	K	S
E	N	G	R	O	S	S				A		
M			A			I	M	M	E	R	S	E
E	N	V	I	O	U	S		O		O		A
N			L			A		B		L		S
T	A	N	S		C	L	O	S	E	S	E	T

Wordsearch Workout

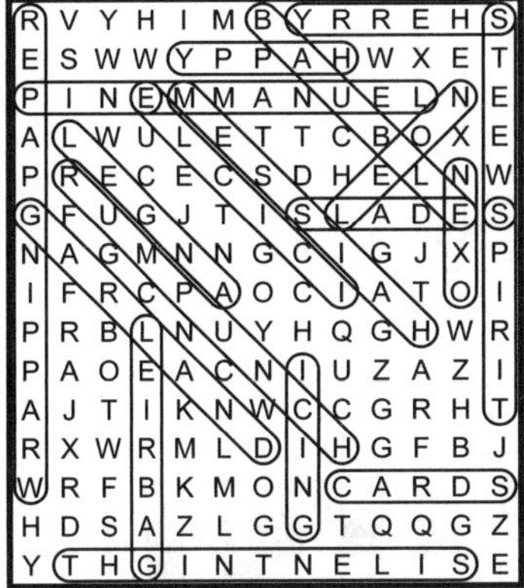

R	V	Y	H	I	M	B	Y	R	R	E	H	S
E	S	W	W	Y	P	P	A	H	W	X	E	T
P	I	N	E	M	M	A	N	U	E	L	N	E
A	L	W	U	L	E	T	T	C	B	O	X	E
P	R	E	C	E	C	S	D	H	E	L	N	W
G	F	U	G	J	T	I	S	L	A	D	E	S
N	A	G	M	N	N	G	C	I	G	J	X	P
I	F	R	C	P	A	O	C	I	A	T	O	I
P	R	B	L	N	U	Y	H	Q	G	H	W	R
P	A	O	E	A	C	N	I	U	Z	A	Z	I
A	J	T	I	K	N	W	C	C	G	R	H	T
R	X	W	R	M	L	D	I	H	G	F	B	J
W	R	F	B	K	M	O	N	C	A	R	D	S
H	D	S	A	Z	L	G	G	T	Q	Q	G	Z
Y	T	H	G	I	N	T	N	E	L	I	S	E

Double Fun Sudoku

Tasty Teaser

6	3	7	4	2	5	1	9	8
5	8	9	6	1	3	7	2	4
4	2	1	7	9	8	6	3	5
1	9	5	3	7	4	2	8	6
8	7	2	9	5	6	3	4	1
3	4	6	1	8	2	9	5	7
2	5	3	8	6	1	4	7	9
9	6	8	2	4	7	5	1	3
7	1	4	5	3	9	8	6	2

Brain Buster

4	9	8	2	1	7	6	3	5
3	5	6	4	8	9	2	7	1
1	2	7	3	6	5	8	9	4
5	8	9	6	4	3	7	1	2
2	3	4	7	9	1	5	8	6
7	6	1	8	5	2	9	4	3
6	4	3	9	2	8	1	5	7
9	7	5	1	3	6	4	2	8
8	1	2	5	7	4	3	6	9

Matchstick Magic

The matchsticks which have been moved are outlined.

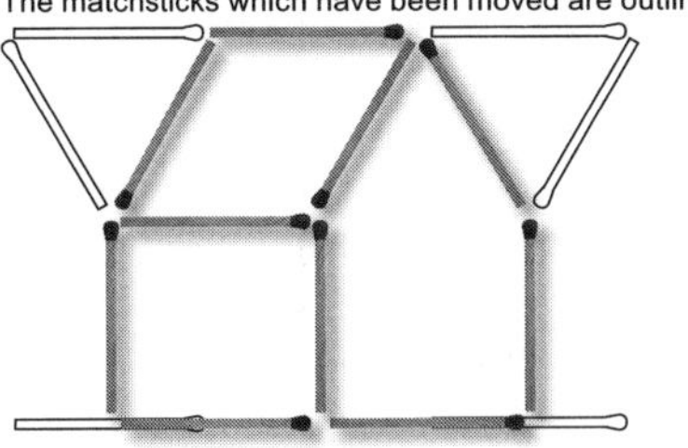

Brain Teaser

X – They are every 3rd letter in the alphabet with only straight lines.

A miss E, F
H miss I, K
L miss M, N
T miss V, W
X

Simple as A, B, C

B	B	A	C	C	A
A	C	C	B	B	A
B	B	A	A	C	C
C	A	B	C	A	B
A	C	B	B	A	C
C	A	C	A	B	B

Page 52

Codeword Conundrum

H	I	S	S		U	N	P	I	N		P	O	M	P
U			I	T	S		E		A			P		Y
F	L	A	X		A	V	E	N	G	E		U		R
F			T		G		V			C	A	S	T	E
		B	Y	T	E		E	T	C	H			W	
D	U	E		I		J		R		O	N	I	O	N
I		H		C	H	E	W	E	D			G		E
S	H	A	N	K		T		M		S	O	N	A	R
C		L			E	S	C	O	R	T		O		V
O	F	F	E	R		A		R		O		R	O	E
	L			I	A	M	B		C	A	S	E		
Q	U	A	I	L			R		L		P			P
U		R		E	R	R	A	T	A		R	A	T	E
I		I			A		W		S	E	A			A
Z	E	A	L		T	U	L	I	P		T	A	C	K

Double Fun Sudoku

Tasty Teaser

4	3	6	5	1	8	7	2	9
7	5	8	2	9	3	1	4	6
9	2	1	4	7	6	5	3	8
3	8	9	7	6	2	4	5	1
2	4	7	9	5	1	8	6	3
1	6	5	8	3	4	9	7	2
5	7	3	6	8	9	2	1	4
6	9	2	1	4	7	3	8	5
8	1	4	3	2	5	6	9	7

Brain Buster

7	4	9	6	8	2	5	1	3
1	5	6	7	9	3	4	2	8
2	3	8	1	4	5	6	9	7
8	1	5	4	3	7	9	6	2
4	9	7	8	2	6	3	5	1
3	6	2	5	1	9	7	8	4
5	2	1	9	7	4	8	3	6
9	8	4	3	6	1	2	7	5
6	7	3	2	5	8	1	4	9

Pyramid Plus

A=135, B=119, C=147, D=58, E=97, F=254, G=266, H=205, I=155, J=520, K=471, L=360, M=991, N=831, O=1822.

Work it Out

20 – Reading along each row from left to right, the sequence of numbers is the first number plus 2 equals the second number minus 3 equals the third number plus 4 equals the fourth number minus 5 equals the fifth number plus 6 equals the sixth number minus 7 equals the seventh number.

High-Speed Crossword

S	H	R	I	M	P		A		P		M	
H		A			U	P	S	T	R	E	A	M
A	S	P			R		H		I		N	
D		T	H	R	E	A	T		S	L	A	P
E		O			E		R		T		G	
S	C	R	E	E		C	A	B	I	N	E	T
			Y		S		Y		N			
C	O	V	E	R	E	D		H	E	R	B	S
	R		L		T		B			E		Y
H	I	F	I		S	I	E	N	N	A		N
	G		N		A		V			L	I	T
F	I	R	E	S	I	D	E			T		A
	N		R		L		L	A	R	Y	N	X

1 Minute Number Crunch

Beginner
77 ÷ 7 x 3 = 33, 33 x 4 = 132, 132 ÷ 12 x 3 = 33, 33 – 1 = 32, 50% of 32 = 16, 16 x 9 = 144, 144 ÷ 12 x 5 = 60

Intermediate
456 ÷ 3 x 2 = 304, 304 ÷ 4 = 76, 76 x 1.5 = 114, 114 x 3 = 342, 342 ÷ 9 x 5 = 190, 190 – 19 = 171, 171 ÷ 19 x 2 = 18

Advanced
599 ÷ 0.25 = 2396, 2396 x 2 = 4792, 375% of 4792 = 17970, 17970 ÷ 10 x 3 = 5391, 5391 – 2995 (5391 ÷ 9 x 5) = 2396, 2396 x 0.75 = 1797, 1797 – 878 = 919

Page 53

High-Speed Crossword

	D		M		B		M	A	T	U	R	E
C	O	L	O	R	A	D	O		H		O	
	N		R		B		N	E	A	T	L	Y
D	A	M	P	N	E	S	S		N		L	
	T		H		L		T		K		E	
L	E	A	S	E		L	E	I	S	U	R	E
I		R			R		R			G		A
E	S	C	A	P	E	E		U	S	H	E	R
	A		S		I		R		H		L	
	H		C		S	E	A	F	A	R	E	R
C	A	D	E	T	S		B		R		V	
	R		N		U	N	B	R	O	K	E	N
C	A	N	D	L	E		I		N		N	

Summing Up

54	8	**42**	20	59	36
38	36	29	**30**	39	47
32	65	36	34	**20**	32
33	45	39	38	17	47
29	**38**	45	43	31	33
33	27	28	54	53	**24**

1 Minute Number Crunch

Beginner
56 + 13 = 69, 69 ÷ 3 = 23, 23 reversed = 32, 32 – 4 = 28, 28 x 2 = 56, 56 + 4 = 60, 60 ÷ 15 = 4

Intermediate
49 ÷ 7 x 6 = 42, 42 ÷ 3 = 14, 14 x 5 = 70, 70 ÷ 0.2 = 350, 350 ÷ 5 x 4 = 280, 280 ÷ 70 = 4, 4^3 = 64

Advanced
578 ÷ 2 = 289, square root of 289 = 17, 17 + 68 = 85, 80% of 85 = 68, 68 x 1.75 = 119, 119 x 2 = 238, 238 – 109 = 129

Wordsearch Workout

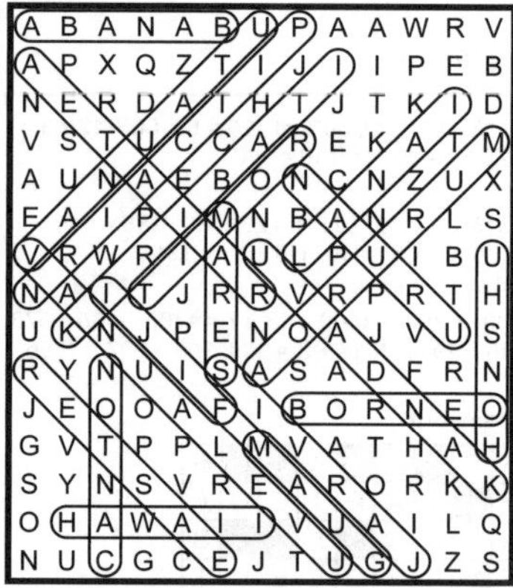

Double Fun Sudoku

Tasty Teaser

2	3	7	9	1	4	5	6	8
1	5	9	8	7	6	3	4	2
6	4	8	2	3	5	1	9	7
5	2	1	3	6	8	9	7	4
9	8	6	7	4	1	2	5	3
4	7	3	5	9	2	6	8	1
8	1	2	4	5	9	7	3	6
3	9	4	6	2	7	8	1	5
7	6	5	1	8	3	4	2	9

Brain Buster

7	9	5	4	3	8	1	2	6
4	3	6	2	5	1	9	8	7
8	2	1	6	9	7	5	4	3
2	5	9	3	1	4	6	7	8
3	6	7	8	2	9	4	1	5
1	4	8	7	6	5	2	3	9
6	1	2	5	7	3	8	9	4
9	8	3	1	4	6	7	5	2
5	7	4	9	8	2	3	6	1

Whatever Next?

N – Clockwise from the top, move 3 places forwards in the alphabet, then 2 back, 5 forwards, 2 back, 7 forwards (N), then 2 back, to L in the centre.

Brain Teaser

48
(6 + 7) x (5 – 2) = 39
(8 + 6) x (4 – 1) = 42
(10 + 2) x (6 – 2) = 48

Page 54

Mind Over Matter

The sum total of the values of the letters in the top squares and central square is equal to the sum total of the values in the bottom squares. Thus the missing value is 17, so the missing letter is Q.

Double Fun Sudoku

Tasty Teaser

4	7	3	2	5	8	6	1	9
8	2	1	6	7	9	3	4	5
5	9	6	1	4	3	7	2	8
2	3	9	4	8	7	1	5	6
1	5	4	3	2	6	9	8	7
6	8	7	5	9	1	2	3	4
7	1	2	8	6	5	4	9	3
3	6	5	9	1	4	8	7	2
9	4	8	7	3	2	5	6	1

Brain Buster

8	5	4	7	6	3	2	1	9
6	3	1	9	2	4	8	7	5
7	2	9	1	8	5	4	6	3
2	1	8	6	7	9	5	3	4
5	6	3	2	4	1	9	8	7
4	9	7	3	5	8	1	2	6
3	4	2	5	1	7	6	9	8
9	8	6	4	3	2	7	5	1
1	7	5	8	9	6	3	4	2

Codeword Conundrum

P	O	A	C	H		A	N	A	L	G	E	S	I	A
A		M		E		C		D		A				C
R	E	A	R	R	A	N	G	E		Z	I	L	C	H
A		S		O		E		Q		E		U		E
L	A	S	S	I	E		Q	U	I	B	B	L	E	D
Y				N		D		A		O		L		
T	H	E	M	E		E	A	T	S		D	A	I	S
I		R		S		J		E		E		B		T
C	H	O	P		W	E	L	L		F	O	Y	E	R
		T		B		C		Y		F				A
S	T	I	L	E	T	T	O		B	U	R	D	E	N
M		C		C		E		B		S		R		G
A	B	A	C	K		D	E	O	X	I	D	I	S	E
S				O		L		L		V		L		S
H	A	C	K	N	E	Y	E	D		E	C	L	A	T

Futoshiki

4	5	1	3	2
2 <	3	5	4	1
5	2 ∨	4	1 <	3
3	1	2	5	4
1 <	4	3	2	5

High-Speed Crossword

C	A	M	E		P	A	N	P	I	P	E	S
U		A		S		X		O		U		M
C	O	R	N	I	C	E		L	I	N	G	O
U		K		G				E		G		G
M	I	S	I	N	T	E	R	P	R	E	T	
B				I		Y		O		N		I
E	V	A		F	E	R	N	S		T	O	N
R		M		I		I		I				F
	U	N	A	C	C	E	P	T	A	B	L	E
M		E		A				I		U		R
A	R	S	O	N		G	N	O	C	C	H	I
S		I		C		A		N		K		O
S	C	A	V	E	N	G	E		T	S	A	R

1 Minute Number Crunch

Beginner

64 x 2 = 128, 128 + 6 = 134, 134 ÷ 2 = 67, 67 reversed = 76, 76 ÷ 2 = 38, 38 – 2 = 36, 36 ÷ 6 x 5 = 30

Intermediate

120 ÷ 15 x 2 = 16, 16 x 4 = 64, 64 x 2 = 128, 128 ÷ 8 x 5 = 80, 80 x 1.3 = 104, 104 ÷ 4 = 26, 26 x 7 = 182

Advanced

1997 + 666 = 2663, 2663 x 2 = 5326, 5326 – 958 = 4368, 4368 ÷ 3 x 2 = 2912, 2912 ÷ 16 x 5 = 910, 910 ÷ 5 x 3 = 546, 546 – 364 (546 ÷ 3 x 2) = 182

Page 55

Domino Placement

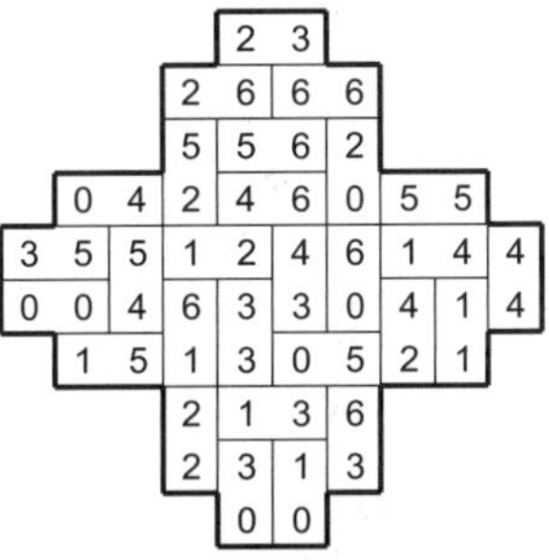

High-Speed Crossword

G	U	S	T	O		S	P	A	R	I	N	G
A		T		B	A	T		S		L		O
T	U	R	F	S		A		I	N	L	A	W
E		I		C		M		D		I		N
P		P	R	E	F	E	R	E	N	C	E	
O				N		N				I		N
S	U	C	K	E	D		S	C	Y	T	H	E
T		A				T		H				B
	I	N	C	A	P	A	C	I	T	Y		R
B		T		I		R		C		U		A
I	M	A	G	O		T		K	I	C	K	S
D		T		L		A	W	E		C		K
S	E	A	L	I	O	N		N	Y	A	L	A

IQ Workout

7

Left	Right
6 x 4 = 24	7 x 4 = 28
8 x 2 = <u>16</u>	6 x 2 = <u>12</u>
40	40

Wordwheel

The nine-letter word is: AESTHETIC

Wordsearch Workout

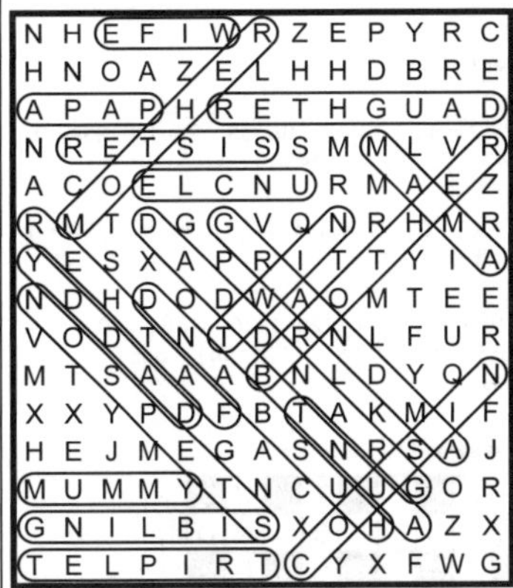

Double Fun Sudoku

Tasty Teaser

8	3	5	4	1	6	9	7	2
6	9	7	2	5	8	1	4	3
1	2	4	7	9	3	8	6	5
2	7	6	3	4	9	5	8	1
4	1	3	8	2	5	7	9	6
9	5	8	1	6	7	2	3	4
5	8	1	6	7	4	3	2	9
3	6	2	9	8	1	4	5	7
7	4	9	5	3	2	6	1	8

Brain Buster

5	8	6	3	1	7	9	4	2
1	2	3	4	9	8	6	5	7
4	7	9	2	5	6	8	3	1
9	3	1	7	8	4	5	2	6
6	5	2	9	3	1	7	8	4
7	4	8	5	6	2	3	1	9
3	1	5	6	2	9	4	7	8
2	6	7	8	4	5	1	9	3
8	9	4	1	7	3	2	6	5

Sum Circle

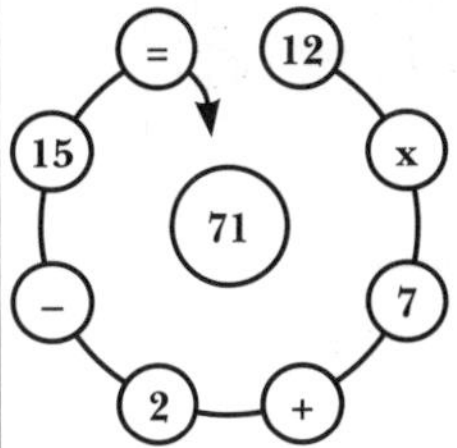

Page 56

1 Minute Number Crunch

Beginner
82 – 39 = 43, 43 x 2 = 86, 86 – 18 = 68, 68 x 2 = 136, 25% of 136 = 34, 34 – 14 = 20, 20 x 70 = 1400

Intermediate
21 ÷ 7 x 2 = 6, 6 + 15 = 21, 21^2 = 441, 441 ÷ 9 x 2 = 98, 98 + 4 = 102, 102 ÷ 17 = 6, 6^3 = 216

Advanced
366 x 5 = 1830, 1830 ÷ 3 x 2 = 1220, 1220 – 366 (1220 ÷ 10 x 3) = 854, 854 – 687 = 167, 167 x 3 = 501, 501 + 835 = 1336, 1336 ÷ 8 x 5 = 835

High-Speed Crossword

C	H	A	N	G	E		D		T		U	
L		J			S	U	R	R	O	U	N	D
E	X	A	M		T		Y		S		F	
M		R	A	C	E	M	E		S	E	A	R
A			T		R		Y				I	
T	A	R	R	Y		B	E	R	S	E	R	K
I			O		D	U	D		K			I
S	C	E	N	T	E	D		M	A	S	O	N
	O				A		E		T			D
I	R	I	S		D	I	A	D	E	M		N
	N		H		E		V		R	A	G	E
D	E	F	I	A	N	C	E			R		S
	R		N		D		S	I	N	E	W	S

IQ Workout

7 – Opposite numbers are multiplied and then the totals are added.

6 x 4 = 24, 3 x 7 = 21, 21 x 9 = 189, 24 + 21 + 189 = 234

11 x 9 = 99, 2 x 7 = 14, 8 x 8 = 64, 99 + 14 + 64 = 177

31 x 6 = 186, 5 x 14 = 70, 8 x 7 = 56, 186 + 70 + 56 = 312

Codeword Conundrum

F	A	S	C	I	N	A	T	E		W	A	S	T	E
E		U		R		S		B		H		Q		T
A	M	B	E	R		T	A	B	L	E	A	U		H
S		J		U		E		S		N		A		I
T	R	U	M	P	E	R	Y		H	E	C	T	I	C
		D		T				D		V				A
S	W	I	G		M	A	N	A	G	E	R	I	A	L
N		C		G		V		Z		R		N		L
O	V	E	R	L	O	O	K	E	D		S	E	X	Y
W				E		W				F		L		
F	O	R	M	A	L		A	S	P	I	R	A	N	T
L		A		M		S		E		N		S		H
A		B	L	I	N	K	E	R		I	N	T	E	R
K		B		N		I		V		S		I		E
E	K	I	N	G		T	O	O	T	H	A	C	H	E

Tasty Teaser

6	3	7	2	5	1	8	9	4
2	9	8	6	4	7	5	1	3
1	5	4	8	9	3	7	6	2
3	8	5	7	1	9	2	4	6
9	4	6	3	8	2	1	5	7
7	2	1	5	6	4	9	3	8
4	1	2	9	7	6	3	8	5
5	6	3	1	2	8	4	7	9
8	7	9	4	3	5	6	2	1

Brain Buster

2	6	8	4	7	3	1	5	9
9	1	3	6	5	8	2	7	4
5	4	7	1	2	9	8	3	6
1	3	2	5	4	7	9	6	8
6	5	4	9	8	2	7	1	3
7	8	9	3	6	1	5	4	2
8	7	1	2	3	6	4	9	5
4	9	6	8	1	5	3	2	7
3	2	5	7	9	4	6	8	1

Spidoku

Wordsearch Workout

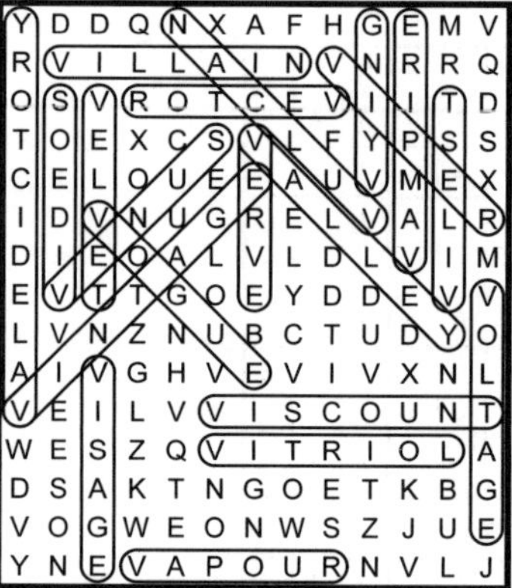

Double Fun Sudoku

Tasty Teaser

4	5	7	1	9	3	2	8	6
1	2	3	6	8	7	4	5	9
6	9	8	5	2	4	1	3	7
3	7	5	2	4	9	6	1	8
8	1	4	3	5	6	7	9	2
9	6	2	7	1	8	5	4	3
5	8	1	9	7	2	3	6	4
7	3	9	4	6	5	8	2	1
2	4	6	8	3	1	9	7	5

Brain Buster

5	6	9	1	8	3	7	4	2
4	7	8	9	6	2	3	5	1
3	1	2	4	7	5	8	9	6
9	3	6	5	1	4	2	7	8
7	5	1	2	3	8	9	6	4
8	2	4	6	9	7	5	1	3
1	8	3	7	5	6	4	2	9
2	9	5	8	4	1	6	3	7
6	4	7	3	2	9	1	8	5

Page 57

Logi-Six

F	C	E	D	B	A
E	A	D	B	C	F
C	B	A	E	F	D
A	D	F	C	E	B
B	F	C	A	D	E
D	E	B	F	A	C

High-Speed Crossword

	M	A	N	S	L	A	U	G	H	T	E	R
C		L		T		C		O		O		A
O	Z	O	N	E		C		A	P	R	O	N
S		O		R	O	E		T		S		G
M	U	F	T	I		D	E	S	P	I	S	E
O				L		E				O		
S	U	S	S	E	X		S	T	A	N	Z	A
		T				B		A				D
S	U	R	N	A	M	E		C	O	B	R	A
C		A		D		A	C	T		R		G
R	O	U	N	D		K		I	M	A	G	E
I		S		L		E		C		I		S
M	I	S	R	E	P	R	E	S	E	N	T	

Matchstick Magic

The matchsticks which have been removed are outlined: those remaining form the digit '9'.

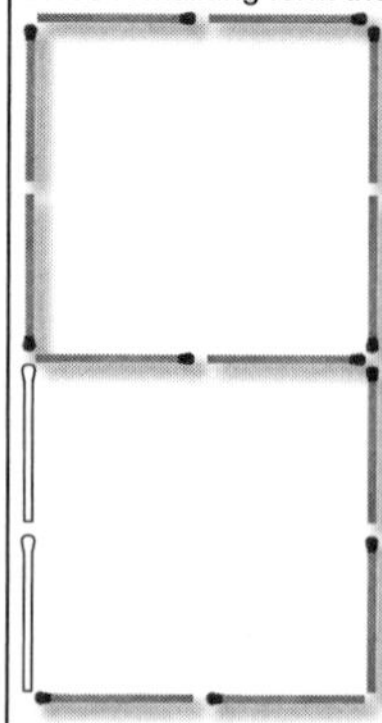

Brain Teaser

6/100 x 5/99 = 1/330

Domino Placement

				5	5				
			0	1	6	6			
			2	5	2	2			
	0	4	2	0	4	6	6	0	
0	3	3	1	0	3	6	3	4	1
0	5	1	1	5	2	4	5	2	1
	0	2	3	4	1	6	1	4	
			6	3	2	6			
			5	3	4	4			
				3	5				

Page 58

Codeword Conundrum

A	K	I	M	B	O		V		F		W	A	F	T
S		M		O		Z	E	N	I	T	H			A
S	M	A	L	L	P	O	X		V		E	M	I	R
E		G		U		N		J	E	S	T			T
T	R	O	U	S	S	E	A	U			S	O	F	A
	E				P			D	U	C	T			R
B	A	C	K	G	A	M	M	O	N		O	N	C	E
	C		N		R		O		I		N		H	
S	H	O	O		S	U	B	A	Q	U	E	O	U	S
Y			W	E	E	P			U				R	
R	E	E	L			O	B	S	E	R	V	A	N	T
I			E	A	R	N		E		I		B		A
N	E	E	D		A		D	A	I	N	T	I	E	R
G			G	A	R	T	E	R		D		D		O
E	P	E	E		E		N		A	S	P	E	C	T

Double Fun Sudoku

Tasty Teaser

6	4	1	3	8	9	5	7	2
9	2	5	4	7	6	8	3	1
8	3	7	5	1	2	6	9	4
1	7	3	9	4	8	2	6	5
2	8	4	6	5	3	7	1	9
5	6	9	1	2	7	4	8	3
4	5	8	7	9	1	3	2	6
3	1	2	8	6	4	9	5	7
7	9	6	2	3	5	1	4	8

Brain Buster

8	7	5	2	4	6	1	3	9
1	6	3	8	9	5	2	7	4
4	2	9	1	7	3	6	5	8
3	1	7	9	6	2	8	4	5
2	4	8	3	5	1	9	6	7
5	9	6	7	8	4	3	1	2
7	3	1	5	2	9	4	8	6
6	8	2	4	3	7	5	9	1
9	5	4	6	1	8	7	2	3

Pyramid Plus

A=138, B=17, C=148, D=13, E=131, F=155, G=165, H=161, I=144, J=320, K=326, L=305, M=646, N=631, O=1277.

Work it Out

145 and 148 – From the top left corner, follow a path around and spiral towards the centre, adding 3 to each number every time.

High-Speed Crossword

R	O	B	U	S	T		P	E	S	E	T	A
E		E		O			E		Q			H
P	L	A	Y	U	P		R		U			O
E		N			E	P	I	L	E	P	S	Y
L	A	S	S		A		T		A		U	
	G		O	A	R	L	O	C	K		L	
B	E	A	D		L		N		I	O	T	A
	N		A	N	Y	T	I	M	E		A	
	D		W		G		T		R	A	N	G
N	A	G	A	S	A	K	I			B		R
E			T		T		S	A	M	O	S	A
W			E		E			C		D		V
S	H	A	R	E	S		S	E	C	E	D	E

1 Minute Number Crunch

Beginner
61 x 3 = 183, 183 + 19 = 202, 202 ÷ 2 = 101, 101 – 66 = 35, 35 ÷ 5 = 7, 7 + 44 = 51, 51 ÷ 3 = 17

Intermediate
48 + 159 = 207, 207 ÷ 9 x 2 = 46, 46 x 2 = 92, 92 – 12 = 80, 25% of 80 = 20, 20^2 = 400, 75% of 400 = 300

Advanced
Cube root of 50653 = 37, 37 x 111 = 4107, 4107 ÷ 3 = 1369, 1369 – 987 = 382, 382 x 4 = 1528, 1528 – 573 (1528 x 0.375) = 955, 60% of 955 = 573

Page 59

High-Speed Crossword

P	L	A	S	T	I	C		O		S		B
R		M		R		R	I	S	O	T	T	O
O	C	A	R	I	N	A		C		R		W
P		T		P		M		A		A		L
E	Y	E	L	E	T		B	R	I	D	G	E
L		U			O		U					R
	G	R	O	U	N	D	G	L	A	S	S	
P					G		L			E		G
S	M	A	R	T	S		E	M	B	R	Y	O
Y		B		I		D		A		V		B
C		O		G		I	L	L	W	I	L	L
H	A	R	N	E	S	S		E		C		I
E		T		R		C	I	S	T	E	R	N

IQ Workout

Clocks lose 50 minutes, gain 60 minutes, lose 70 minutes and gain 80 minutes.

1 Minute Number Crunch

Beginner
131 + 383 = 514, 514 ÷ 2 = 257, 257 – 55 = 202, 202 ÷ 2 = 101, 101 x 3 = 303, 303 + 17 = 320, 25% of 320 = 80

Intermediate
73 – 37 = 36, square root of 36 = 6, 6 x 13 = 78, 78 ÷ 3 = 26, 26 ÷ 13 x 6 = 12, 12 + 10 (12 ÷ 6 x 5) = 22, 22 x 11 = 242

Advanced
125% of 968 = 1210, 1210 – 869 = 341, 341 + 4572 = 4913, cube root of 4913 = 17, 17 x 8 = 136, 136 ÷ 34 x 7 = 28, 28 ÷ 14 x 9 = 18

Wordsearch Workout

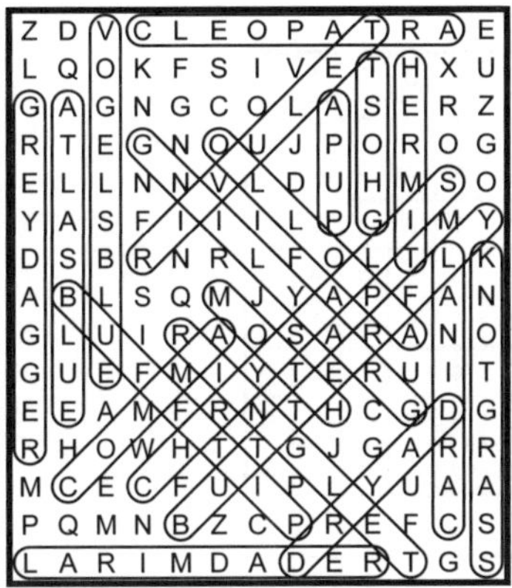

Z	D	V	C	L	E	O	P	A	T	R	A	E
L	Q	O	K	F	S	I	V	E	T	H	X	U
G	A	G	N	G	C	O	L	A	S	E	R	Z
R	T	E	G	N	O	U	J	P	O	R	O	G
E	L	L	N	N	V	L	D	U	H	M	S	O
Y	A	S	F	I	I	I	L	P	G	I	M	Y
D	S	B	R	N	R	L	F	O	L	T	L	K
A	B	L	S	Q	M	J	Y	A	P	F	A	N
G	L	U	I	R	A	O	S	A	R	A	N	O
G	U	E	F	M	I	Y	T	E	R	U	I	T
E	E	A	M	F	R	N	T	H	C	G	D	G
R	H	O	W	H	T	T	G	J	G	A	R	R
M	C	E	C	F	U	I	P	L	Y	U	A	A
P	Q	M	N	B	Z	C	P	R	E	F	C	S
L	A	R	I	M	D	A	D	E	R	T	G	S

Double Fun Sudoku

Tasty Teaser

2	6	3	9	5	8	4	1	7
4	9	1	7	2	3	5	8	6
8	7	5	4	1	6	3	2	9
7	1	2	8	4	9	6	3	5
3	5	4	1	6	7	2	9	8
9	8	6	5	3	2	1	7	4
1	3	9	6	8	4	7	5	2
5	4	8	2	7	1	9	6	3
6	2	7	3	9	5	8	4	1

Brain Buster

5	6	3	9	2	4	1	7	8
4	8	7	5	3	1	9	6	2
9	1	2	6	8	7	4	3	5
8	4	9	3	1	2	6	5	7
3	7	5	4	6	9	8	2	1
6	2	1	7	5	8	3	9	4
1	9	6	2	4	5	7	8	3
7	5	8	1	9	3	2	4	6
2	3	4	8	7	6	5	1	9

Whatever Next?

F – Start from the top and move clockwise, going back four letters in the alphabet each time, finally moving from J to F, then from F to B.

Brain Teaser

8%

81 + 82 + 77 + 68 = 308

Amongst 100 pupils, this gives 3 losses each, and 4 losses to 8 pupils.

Page 60

Mind Over Matter

The sum total of the values of the letters in the top left and bottom right squares is subtracted from the sum total of the values of the letters in the top right and bottom left squares, giving the value of the letter in the central square. Thus the missing value is 15, so the missing letter is O.

Double Fun Sudoku

Tasty Teaser

6	4	3	2	7	8	9	1	5
9	5	2	4	1	3	8	6	7
7	1	8	5	6	9	2	3	4
2	7	4	8	5	6	3	9	1
8	6	9	1	3	7	5	4	2
1	3	5	9	2	4	6	7	8
3	2	6	7	4	5	1	8	9
4	9	1	3	8	2	7	5	6
5	8	7	6	9	1	4	2	3

Brain Buster

4	1	3	2	5	6	9	8	7
6	5	7	9	8	3	1	2	4
9	8	2	1	4	7	5	3	6
8	4	9	3	7	1	2	6	5
2	6	5	4	9	8	7	1	3
7	3	1	5	6	2	8	4	9
3	2	6	7	1	5	4	9	8
1	7	4	8	3	9	6	5	2
5	9	8	6	2	4	3	7	1

Codeword Conundrum

S	I	F	T	S		P	A	R	O	D	Y	I	N	G
T		L		K		L		E		E				O
A	N	O	N	Y	M	O	U	S		C	O	R	G	I
R		W		L		Y		I		A		U		N
B	A	N	D	I	T		B	L	I	N	K	I	N	G
O				G		W		I		T		N		
A	W	A	S	H		A	M	E	N		H	O	L	D
R		E		T		L		N		C		U		E
D	I	R	T		B	L	O	C		O	A	S	I	S
		O		F		F		E		Q				C
D	I	S	C	I	P	L	E		J	U	G	G	L	E
I		O		E		O		M		E		R		N
V	O	L	T	S		W	R	I	S	T	B	A	N	D
O				T		E		N		R		Z		E
T	E	S	T	A	T	R	I	X		Y	I	E	L	D

Futoshiki

2	3	1	5	4
5	1	4	3	2
1	2	3	4	5
3	4	5	2	1
4	5	2	1	3

High-Speed Crossword

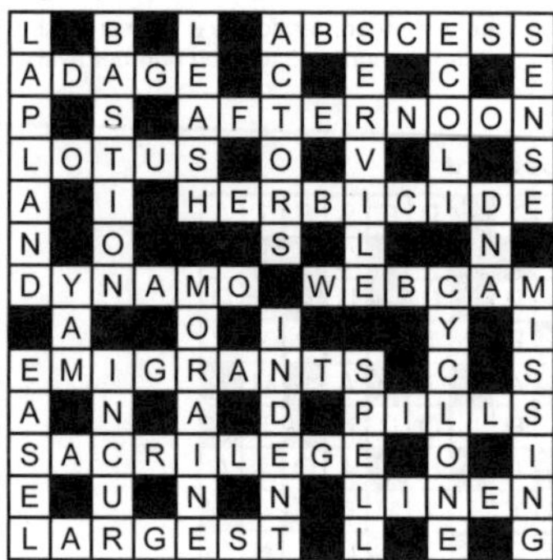

1 Minute Number Crunch

Beginner

53 x 3 = 159, 159 – 19 = 140, 25% of 140 = 35, 35 ÷ 5 x 4 = 28, 28 x 3 = 84, 84 ÷ 14 = 6, 6 x 7 = 42

Intermediate

225 ÷ 9 x 2 = 50, 50² = 2500, 2500 + 250 = 2750, 2750 ÷ 25 = 110, 110 ÷ 5 = 22, 22 x 12 = 264, 264 ÷ 3 x 2 = 176

Advanced

92 ÷ 23 x 17 = 68, 68 ÷ 17 x 4 = 16, 16² = 256, 256 x 0.375 = 96, 96 ÷ 16 x 3 = 18, 18² = 324, 324 ÷ 36 x 23 = 207

Page 61

Battleships

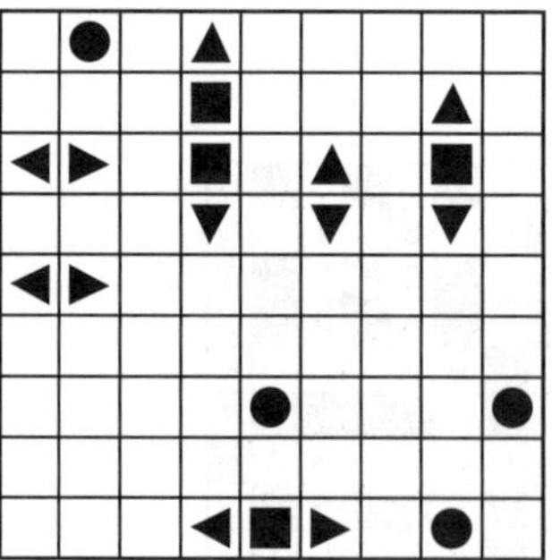

High-Speed Crossword

S	T	A	D	I	U	M		A	L	I	A	S
T		N		N			B		E			A
R	A	T		S	T	R	A	W	P	O	L	L
I		L		T			R		R			L
P	E	E	L	E	D		G		O	I	L	Y
E		R		P	E	D	A	L	S			
D	I	S	K		M		I		Y	A	W	S
			A	R	O	U	N	D		P		A
L	I	A	R		L		S	A	C	R	E	D
Y			A		I			G		I		N
R	E	H	O	U	S	I	N	G		O	N	E
I			K		H			E		R		S
C	I	D	E	R		B	E	R	R	I	E	S

IQ Workout

GC, 73

The numbers in the middle indicate the position of the letters on the left from the beginning of the alphabet (A to Z) and the position of the letters on the right from the end of the alphabet (Z to A).

Wordwheel

The nine-letter word is: PLAUSIBLE

Wordsearch Workout

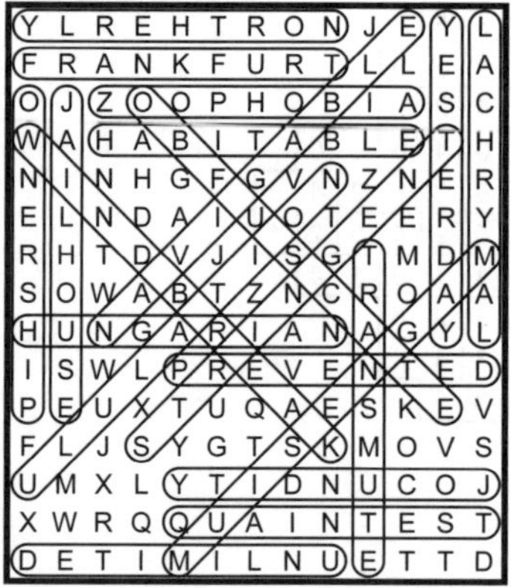

Double Fun Sudoku

Tasty Teaser

9	4	8	5	1	2	7	3	6
1	7	3	6	4	9	5	2	8
5	6	2	7	3	8	4	1	9
3	5	4	8	7	6	1	9	2
7	8	1	9	2	4	3	6	5
6	2	9	3	5	1	8	4	7
4	9	7	1	6	5	2	8	3
8	1	5	2	9	3	6	7	4
2	3	6	4	8	7	9	5	1

Brain Buster

3	9	4	8	5	1	2	6	7
8	6	2	9	4	7	1	3	5
1	5	7	2	3	6	9	8	4
9	3	1	5	6	2	4	7	8
5	2	6	4	7	8	3	1	9
7	4	8	3	1	9	6	5	2
6	8	5	1	2	4	7	9	3
2	1	9	7	8	3	5	4	6
4	7	3	6	9	5	8	2	1

Sum Circle

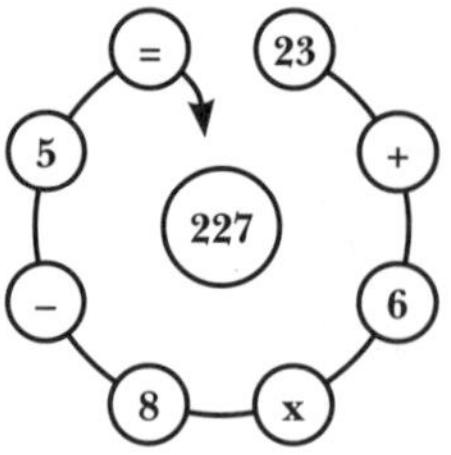

Page 62

1 Minute Number Crunch

Beginner
64 ÷ 8 = 8, 8 x 5 = 40, 40 ÷ 10 = 4, 4 + 19 = 23, 23 – 8 = 15, 15 ÷ 5 = 3, 3 – 2 = 1

Intermediate
627 ÷ 3 = 209, 209 + 648 = 857, 857 + 758 = 1615, 1615 ÷ 5 = 323, 323 – 127 = 196, 196 ÷ 4 x 3 = 147, 147 + 98 (147 ÷ 3 x 2) = 245

Advanced
142857 x 2 = 285714, 285714 ÷ 37 x 3 = 23166, 23166 ÷ 11 x 5 = 10530, 10530 ÷ 10 x 7 = 7371, 7371 ÷ 9 x 5 = 4095, 60% of 4095 = 2457, 2457 ÷ 9 x 5 = 1365

High-Speed Crossword

D	A	M	P	E	N		C	A	S	S	I	S
E				X		S		X				E
C	O	M	P	A	C	T	D	I	S	C		L
A		I		C		Y		S		E		L
N	I	N	E	T	E	E	N		D	A	R	E
T		I		I		S		B		S		R
	S	A	U	N	A		C	A	T	E	R	
F		T		G		P		S		F		D
L	O	U	D		D	E	F	I	N	I	T	E
O		R		M		T		L		R		L
R		E	L	E	C	T	R	I	C	E	Y	E
A				T		Y		C				T
L	A	C	K	E	Y		C	A	S	T	L	E

IQ Workout

LMOP – All the others progress in the sequence, for example, K (+1)M(+1)OP.

Codeword Conundrum

W	A	P	I	T	I		I	M	P	O	R	T	E	R
O		A		I				O		R		A		O
R	A	R	E	F	Y		B	U	N	G	A	L	O	W
K		S		F		J		L		A		L		D
B	A	N	D	I	C	O	O	T		N	E	E	D	Y
E		I		N		J				I		S		
N	A	P	E		C	O	M	P	O	S	I	T	O	R
C				C		B		R		T				I
H	I	B	E	R	N	A	T	E	D		P	A	N	G
		A		U				F		S		V		H
V	I	N	E	S		W	A	I	S	T	C	O	A	T
I		Q		A		H		X		R		C		E
S	Q	U	A	D	R	O	N		V	I	R	A	G	O
O		E		E		L				F		D		U
R	E	T	A	R	D	E	D		Z	E	R	O	E	S

Tasty Teaser

2	8	6	4	3	9	1	7	5
4	9	7	2	5	1	3	8	6
5	1	3	8	6	7	9	2	4
9	3	4	1	8	6	2	5	7
1	6	8	5	7	2	4	3	9
7	5	2	3	9	4	8	6	1
3	4	1	7	2	5	6	9	8
6	2	5	9	1	8	7	4	3
8	7	9	6	4	3	5	1	2

Brain Buster

5	4	3	7	6	8	1	9	2
7	6	8	1	9	2	4	3	5
1	9	2	4	3	5	6	8	7
9	2	1	3	5	4	8	7	6
6	8	7	9	2	1	3	5	4
4	3	5	6	8	7	9	2	1
3	5	4	8	7	6	2	1	9
8	7	6	2	1	9	5	4	3
2	1	9	5	4	3	7	6	8

Spidoku

Page 63

Logi-Six

F	D	E	C	B	A
B	A	D	E	C	F
E	B	F	D	A	C
A	F	C	B	D	E
D	C	A	F	E	B
C	E	B	A	F	D

High-Speed Crossword

M	O	S	Q	U	I	T	O		L	A	I	C
U		T		N		A				D		R
T	R	E	S	P	A	S	S			I		O
T		W		A		K	I	N	E	T	I	C
O	M	A	N	I			M					U
N		R		D	E	C	I	D	U	O	U	S
		D			L		A			V		
R	E	S	T	R	A	I	N	T		E		R
E					T			S	E	R	G	E
S	H	R	I	V	E	L		H		T		G
U		O			D	O	M	I	N	A	T	E
L		A				B		R		K		N
T	A	R	E		S	E	N	T	I	E	N	T

Wordsearch Workout

Double Fun Sudoku

Tasty Teaser

4	2	9	8	1	5	7	6	3
6	8	5	4	7	3	2	1	9
3	1	7	2	9	6	4	5	8
5	9	8	7	2	4	1	3	6
2	3	6	9	5	1	8	4	7
1	7	4	6	3	8	5	9	2
8	6	2	1	4	9	3	7	5
9	5	1	3	8	7	6	2	4
7	4	3	5	6	2	9	8	1

Brain Buster

1	2	4	9	6	5	8	3	7
3	7	8	2	1	4	9	5	6
6	9	5	8	7	3	4	1	2
7	8	3	4	2	1	5	6	9
2	4	1	5	9	6	3	7	8
9	5	6	3	8	7	1	2	4
8	3	7	1	4	2	6	9	5
5	6	9	7	3	8	2	4	1
4	1	2	6	5	9	7	8	3

Matchstick Magic

The matchsticks which have been moved are outlined.

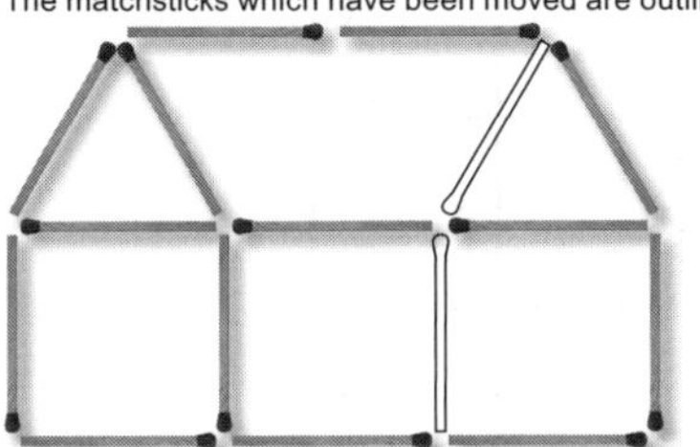

Brain Teaser

4 – The number in the top left sector plus the number in the bottom sector equals the sum of the numbers in the other three sectors.

1 Minute Number Crunch

Beginner
72 + 97 = 169, 169 ÷ 13 = 13, 13 x 6 = 78, 78 + 24 = 102, 102 x 2 = 204, 204 + 4 = 208, 208 ÷ 8 = 26

Intermediate
39 x 3 = 117, 117 ÷ 9 x 4 = 52, 52 ÷ 2 = 26, 26 ÷ 13 x 10 = 20, 20 + 4 (20% of 20) = 24, 24 x 6 = 144, 144 ÷ 8 = 18

Advanced
240 ÷ 40 x 9 = 54, 54 x 7 = 378, 378 ÷ 18 x 11 = 231, 231 ÷ 1.5 = 154, 154 x 5 = 770, 770 x 1.6 = 1232, 1232 + 2321 = 3553

Page 64

Codeword Conundrum

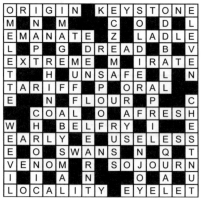

O	R	I	G	I	N		K	E	Y	S	T	O	N	E
M		N		M				C		O		D		L
E	M	A	N	A	T	E		Z		L	A	D	L	E
L		P		G		D	R	E	A	D		B		V
E	X	T	R	E	M	E		M		I	R	A	T	E
T			H		U	N	S	A	F	E		L		N
T	A	R	I	F	F		P		O	R	A	L		
E			N		F	L	O	U	R		P			C
		C	O	A	L		O		A	F	R	E	S	H
W		H		B	E	L	F	R	Y		I			E
E	A	R	L	Y		E		U	S	E	L	E	S	S
E		O		S	W	A	N	S		N		Q		T
V	E	N	O	M		R		S	O	J	O	U	R	N
I		I		A		N				O		A		U
L	O	C	A	L	I	T	Y		E	Y	E	L	E	T

Double Fun Sudoku

Tasty Teaser

5	3	2	1	4	8	7	6	9
6	4	8	9	7	5	3	1	2
9	7	1	6	2	3	8	5	4
8	1	6	2	5	9	4	3	7
3	2	4	8	6	7	5	9	1
7	5	9	4	3	1	2	8	6
1	6	7	3	8	2	9	4	5
2	9	3	5	1	4	6	7	8
4	8	5	7	9	6	1	2	3

Brain Buster

1	9	6	4	5	3	7	2	8
4	5	3	2	7	8	6	1	9
8	7	2	6	9	1	4	5	3
3	6	7	9	4	2	1	8	5
9	4	8	1	6	5	2	3	7
2	1	5	8	3	7	9	6	4
5	8	9	7	1	6	3	4	2
6	2	4	3	8	9	5	7	1
7	3	1	5	2	4	8	9	6

Pyramid Plus

A=102, B=97, C=70, D=18, E=21, F=199, G=167, H=88, I=39, J=366, K=255, L=127, M=621, N=382, O=1003.

Work it Out

29 – Reading along each row, add 9 to each preceding number until the central number, after which deduct 7 from each preceding number.

High-Speed Crossword

1 Minute Number Crunch

Beginner
41 – 16 = 25, 25 ÷ 5 x 2 = 10, 10 + 88 = 98, 98 ÷ 2 = 49, 49 + 6 = 55, 55 ÷ 11 x 3 = 15, 15 x 12 = 180

Intermediate
89 x 3 = 267, 267 + 762 = 1029, 1029 ÷ 3 = 343, 343 – 64 = 279, 279 ÷ 9 x 5 = 155, 155 x 2 = 310, 310 ÷ 10 x 7 = 217

Advanced
120 ÷ 15 x 4 = 32, 32³ = 32768, 32768 ÷ 64 x 3 = 1536, 1536 ÷ 3 x 2 = 1024, 1024 ÷ 32 x 9 = 288, 288 + 160 (288 ÷ 9 x 5) = 448, 448 x 3 = 1344

Page 65

High-Speed Crossword

A	B	S	O	R	B		D	A	N	G	E	R
S		T		E		D		L		A		E
S	W	A	H	I	L	I		C		F		F
U		G		N		S	N	A	F	F	L	E
M	I	N	U	S		H		Z				R
E		A			M	O	L	A	S	S	E	S
		N		S	O	N	A	R		U		
S	I	T	U	A	T	E	D			R		F
C				M		S		S	M	E	A	R
A	S	S	A	U	L	T		H		F		I
L		T		R		L	E	A	S	I	N	G
D		I		A		Y		L		R		I
S	P	R	A	I	N		D	E	F	E	N	D

Summing Up

25	**29**	12	38	15	25
36	44	24	26	**8**	6
37	21	8	38	19	21
12	8	44	**4**	54	22
9	4	16	32	38	**45**
25	38	**40**	6	10	25

Domino Placement

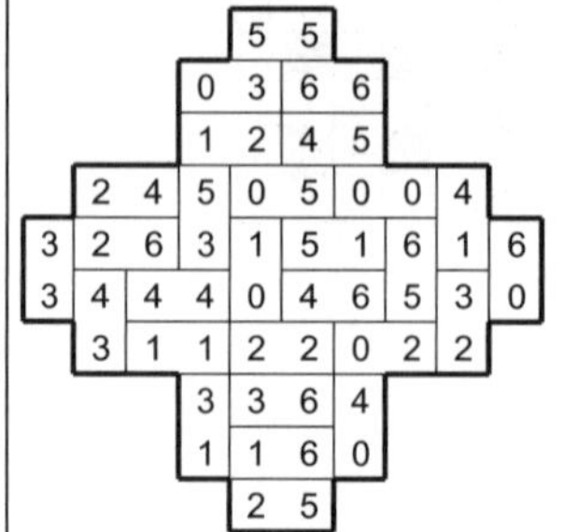

Wordsearch Workout

Double Fun Sudoku

Tasty Teaser

5	8	7	9	2	1	4	3	6
9	1	3	6	4	7	5	2	8
4	2	6	8	3	5	9	1	7
3	6	4	1	8	9	7	5	2
7	9	1	5	6	2	3	8	4
2	5	8	4	7	3	6	9	1
1	7	5	2	9	4	8	6	3
6	3	2	7	5	8	1	4	9
8	4	9	3	1	6	2	7	5

Brain Buster

8	4	1	5	3	2	9	7	6
3	7	9	4	6	8	1	2	5
2	6	5	1	9	7	3	8	4
5	8	3	6	2	9	7	4	1
7	1	2	3	5	4	8	6	9
6	9	4	7	8	1	2	5	3
9	5	6	2	7	3	4	1	8
4	2	8	9	1	6	5	3	7
1	3	7	8	4	5	6	9	2

Whatever Next?

J – Start from the top and move clockwise, going back three letters in the alphabet each time, finally moving from M to J, then from J to G.

Brain Teaser
24 minutes

Page 66

Mind Over Matter

The value of the letter in the bottom right is subtracted from the value in the bottom left; this total is subtracted from the sum total of the values in the two top squares, to give the value in the central square. Thus the missing value is 2, so the missing letter is B.

Double Fun Sudoku

Tasty Teaser

8	5	4	1	3	6	9	7	2
3	6	2	9	4	7	8	1	5
1	9	7	2	5	8	4	3	6
9	2	8	7	6	3	1	5	4
7	4	5	8	1	9	2	6	3
6	3	1	4	2	5	7	8	9
4	1	3	5	8	2	6	9	7
2	7	6	3	9	1	5	4	8
5	8	9	6	7	4	3	2	1

Brain Buster

3	8	1	5	7	9	2	6	4
6	4	2	8	3	1	5	9	7
5	9	7	6	2	4	3	8	1
8	1	3	9	5	7	6	4	2
9	7	5	4	6	2	8	1	3
4	2	6	1	8	3	9	7	5
7	5	9	2	4	6	1	3	8
1	3	8	7	9	5	4	2	6
2	6	4	3	1	8	7	5	9

Codeword Conundrum

R	O	T	A	R	Y		A	L	B	A	C	O	R	E
E		E		O		Z		I		D		U		A
P	I	T	O	N		I	N	V	O	I	C	I	N	G
L		A		D	O	N		E		E		J		L
I	O	N		E		C	O	N	J	U	G	A	T	E
E		U		A			C		O		R		R	
D	I	S	Q	U	I	E	T		I	S	O	B	A	R
	M		U		G		A		N		W		C	
R	A	D	I	A	L		V	I	T	A	L	I	T	Y
	G		C		O		E			B		T		A
W	O	R	K	H	O	R	S	E		S		C	O	S
H		A		E		O		A	F	T		H		H
I	N	V	I	D	I	O	U	S		A	X	I	O	M
M		E		G		S		Y		I		E		A
S	E	R	P	E	N	T	S		A	N	O	R	A	K

Futoshiki

3	2	1	4	5
1	4	5	3	2
4	3	2	5	1
2	5	3	1	4
5	1	4	2	3

High-Speed Crossword

R	E	P	E	L		P	O	S	S	E	S	S
E		I		I		E		H		X		U
C	E	N	T	A	U	R		A	B	H	O	R
A		H		I		I		L		I		G
P	I	O	U	S		S	O	L	U	B	L	E
		L		O		H				I		O
G	R	E	E	N	E		C	O	T	T	O	N
L		C				D		N		I		
A	S	A	R	U	L	E		G	L	O	S	S
N		M		N		M		O		N		I
C	H	E	A	T		A	B	I	D	I	N	G
E		R		I		N		N		S		M
S	E	A	W	E	E	D		G	A	M	M	A

1 Minute Number Crunch

Beginner

51 x 6 = 306, 306 – 6 = 300, 10% of 300 = 30, 30 x 8 = 240, 240 ÷ 12 x 5 = 100, 100 + 86 = 186, 186 ÷ 3 = 62

Intermediate

488 ÷ 8 x 5 = 305, 305 x 3 = 915, 915 ÷ 15 x 2 = 122, 122 ÷ 2 = 61, 61 + 86 = 147, 147 ÷ 3 x 2 = 98, 98 – 52 = 46

Advanced

36 + 20 (36 ÷ 9 x 5) = 56, 56 x 1.375 = 77, 77 x 7 = 539, 539 – 33 = 506, 506 ÷ 22 x 19 = 437, 437 – 91 = 346, 346 x 2.5 = 865

Page 67

1 Minute Number Crunch

Beginner

100 – 42 = 58, 58 ÷ 2 = 29, 29 + 7 = 36, 50% of 36 = 18, 18 + 9 = 27, 27 ÷ 3 = 9, 9 x 5 = 45

Intermediate

85 ÷ 5 x 3 = 51, 51 x 8 = 408, 408 ÷ 17 = 24, 24^2 = 576, 576 ÷ 9 = 64, 64 ÷ 8 x 5 = 40, 40 x 3.5 = 140

Advanced

583 – 77 = 506, 506 ÷ 11 x 4 = 184, 184 x 0.625 = 115, 115 x 0.4 = 46, 46 x 13 = 598, 598 x 2 = 1196, 1196 – 555 = 641

High-Speed Crossword

	S	U	M	M	E	R	H	O	U	S	E	
I		N		O		A		P		H		T
N		W		D	E	B	U	T		O	N	E
T	E	R	S	E		I		I	O	N		M
E		A		S		E		C	R	E	E	P
N	E	P	O	T	I	S	M		I			E
T		S	P	Y				H	E	R		S
I			E		R	E	D	A	L	E	R	T
O	P	A	R	T		N		M		E		U
N		S	A	W		D		P	I	N	T	O
A	L	P		I	N	U	R	E		T		U
L		E		N		R		R		E		S
	U	N	N	E	C	E	S	S	A	R	Y	

Partitions

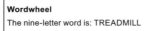

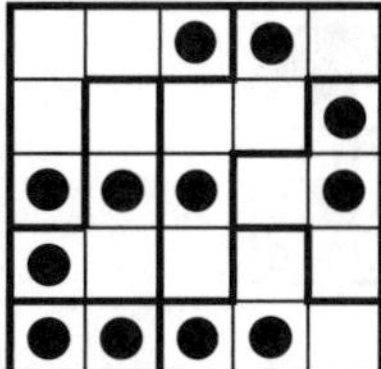

Wordwheel

The nine-letter word is: TREADMILL

Wordsearch Workout

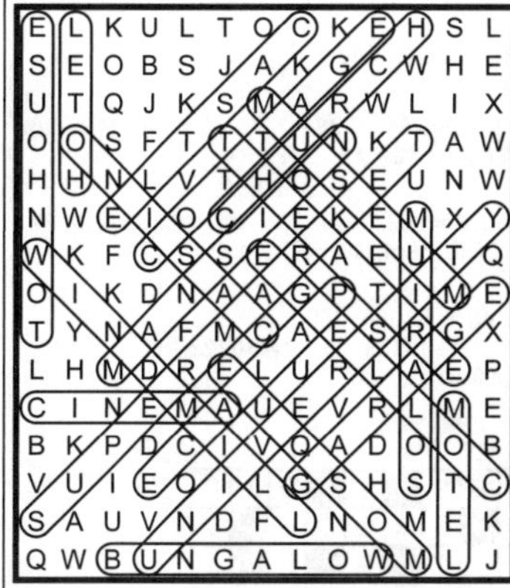

E	L	K	U	L	T	O	C	K	E	H	S	L
S	E	O	B	S	J	A	K	G	C	W	H	E
U	T	Q	J	K	S	M	A	R	W	L	I	X
O	O	S	F	T	T	T	U	N	K	T	A	W
H	H	N	L	V	T	H	O	S	E	U	N	W
N	W	E	I	O	C	I	E	K	E	M	X	Y
W	K	F	C	S	S	E	R	A	E	U	T	Q
O	I	K	D	N	A	A	G	P	T	I	M	E
T	Y	N	A	F	M	C	A	E	S	R	G	X
L	H	M	D	R	E	L	U	R	L	A	E	P
C	I	N	E	M	A	U	E	V	R	L	M	E
B	K	P	D	C	I	V	Q	A	D	O	O	B
V	U	I	E	O	I	L	G	S	H	S	T	C
S	A	U	V	N	D	F	L	N	O	M	E	K
Q	W	B	U	N	G	A	L	O	W	M	L	J

Double Fun Sudoku

Tasty Teaser

9	6	3	2	5	7	8	4	1
1	4	7	9	8	6	3	5	2
8	2	5	1	4	3	6	7	9
6	9	1	4	2	5	7	3	8
5	8	2	7	3	9	4	1	6
7	3	4	6	1	8	2	9	5
2	5	8	3	9	4	1	6	7
3	1	6	5	7	2	9	8	4
4	7	9	8	6	1	5	2	3

Brain Buster

3	4	6	5	7	9	8	1	2
5	8	1	6	2	3	4	9	7
2	9	7	8	1	4	6	5	3
4	3	8	9	5	2	1	7	6
9	1	5	4	6	7	3	2	8
7	6	2	1	3	8	9	4	5
8	2	9	7	4	6	5	3	1
1	7	4	3	8	5	2	6	9
6	5	3	2	9	1	7	8	4

Sum Circle

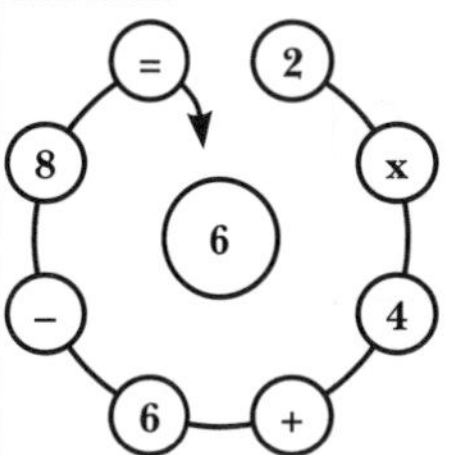

Page 68

1 Minute Number Crunch

Beginner
81 ÷ 3 = 27, 27 + 1 = 28, 25% of 28 = 7, 7 x 20 = 140, 140 – 16 = 124, 124 ÷ 4 = 31, 31 + 12 = 43

Intermediate
53 + 78 = 131, 131 x 2 = 262, 262 – 77 = 185, 185 ÷ 5 = 37, 37 + 73 = 110, 110 + 22 (20% of 110) = 132, 132 ÷ 3 = 44

Advanced
112 ÷ 14 x 5 = 40, 40^3 = 64000, 64000 x 0.375 = 24000, 24000 – 8667 = 15333, 15333 ÷ 3 x 2 = 10222, 10222 ÷ 2 = 5111, 5111 + 965 = 6076

High-Speed Crossword

D	E	S	I	R	E	S		T		D	I	E
	P			E		E	R	O	D	E		V
D	I	E	C	A	S	T		P		B		I
	T			S		T		S	H	A	R	D
B	A	R	C	O	D	E	S			C		E
	P			N		E		V		L		N
S	H	R	I	E	K		D	E	T	E	S	T
E		E		D		T		G			U	
C		S			C	A	R	E	W	O	R	N
L	E	T	U	P		R		T			R	
U		O		U		G	L	A	C	I	E	R
D		R	I	N	S	E		T			A	
E	R	E		Y		T	R	E	A	D	L	E

IQ Workout

2 – Opposite numbers total 11.

Codeword Conundrum

B	O	Y	C	O	T	T	S		Z	E	N	I	T	H
	V		O		R		T	O	O		O			A
C	A	P	Y	B	A	R	A		O	T	T	E	R	S
	L		P		W		F			E		N		
O		Q	U	A	L	I	F	I	E	R		C	U	R
V		U		V		M		C		M		O		E
E	J	A	C	U	L	A	T	E		A	B	U	T	S
R		D		N		G		B		G		N		T
L	Y	R	I	C		I	N	E	X	A	C	T	L	Y
A		U		U		S		R		N		E		L
Y	A	P		L	I	T	I	G	A	T	O	R		E
		L		A			N		G		C		A	
W	H	E	R	R	Y		S	M	O	O	T	H	L	Y
A			U		E	K	E		R		E		S	
N	E	W	E	S	T		T	R	A	C	T	I	O	N

Tasty Teaser

4	6	7	2	9	5	8	3	1
8	3	5	1	4	7	6	2	9
1	2	9	6	3	8	4	5	7
3	4	2	5	7	1	9	8	6
7	1	6	9	8	2	3	4	5
5	9	8	3	6	4	1	7	2
6	8	1	7	5	3	2	9	4
2	5	4	8	1	9	7	6	3
9	7	3	4	2	6	5	1	8

Brain Buster

7	1	2	5	3	9	4	8	6
4	6	9	2	8	1	3	5	7
8	5	3	4	7	6	1	9	2
6	4	1	7	5	8	2	3	9
5	2	7	1	9	3	6	4	8
9	3	8	6	4	2	7	1	5
1	7	4	8	2	5	9	6	3
2	9	5	3	6	4	8	7	1
3	8	6	9	1	7	5	2	4

Spidoku

Page 69

Logi-Six

E	C	D	F	B	A
B	A	F	C	E	D
A	F	B	D	C	E
D	E	A	B	F	C
F	D	C	E	A	B
C	B	E	A	D	F

High-Speed Crossword

C	A	S	H	M	E	R	E		C	A	R	S
A		A		A		E		S		P		T
R	I	N	G	L	E	T		T	A	P	E	R
D		D		T		I		O		R		A
			L	E	P	R	E	C	H	A	U	N
A		F		S		E		K		I		G
S	C	A	L	E	S		T	I	S	S	U	E
S		R		C		C		N		E		R
A	F	T	E	R	T	A	S	T	E			
S		H		O		D		R		A		B
S	L	E	D	S		D	R	A	C	U	L	A
I		S		S		I		D		R		L
N	O	T	E		R	E	L	E	G	A	T	E

Wordsearch Workout

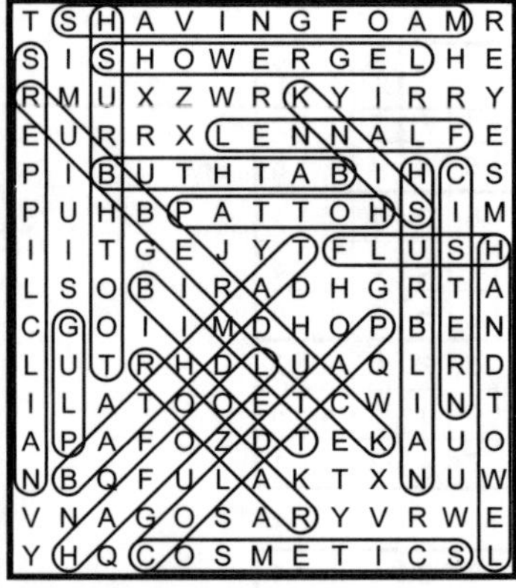

Double Fun Sudoku

Tasty Teaser

7	1	5	9	4	3	8	2	6
2	8	9	7	1	6	3	5	4
4	6	3	8	2	5	7	1	9
8	2	1	3	6	9	5	4	7
6	9	7	4	5	2	1	3	8
3	5	4	1	8	7	6	9	2
5	7	2	6	9	1	4	8	3
9	3	8	5	7	4	2	6	1
1	4	6	2	3	8	9	7	5

Brain Buster

2	6	1	9	3	8	7	5	4
3	9	5	4	7	1	6	8	2
8	4	7	5	6	2	9	1	3
6	5	2	1	8	9	3	4	7
1	8	9	3	4	7	2	6	5
4	7	3	6	2	5	1	9	8
9	1	8	2	5	3	4	7	6
5	2	6	7	1	4	8	3	9
7	3	4	8	9	6	5	2	1

Matchstick Magic

The matchsticks which have been removed are outlined.

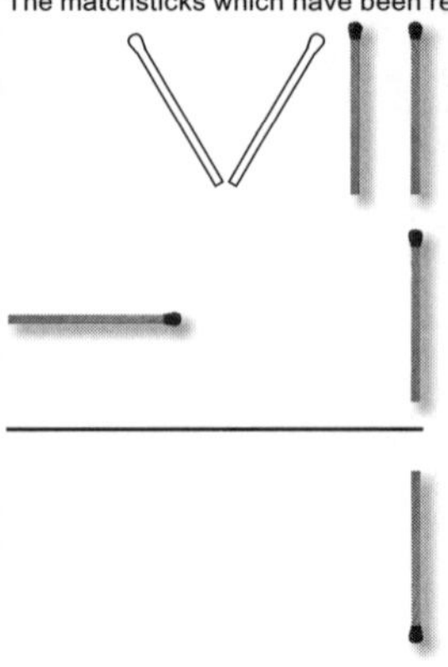

Brain Teaser

D – It goes anti-clockwise from outer to inner, the others going clockwise from outer to inner.

Simple as A, B, C

B	C	A	C	A	B
C	A	B	C	B	A
A	C	B	A	C	B
A	B	C	A	B	C
B	A	C	B	C	A
C	B	A	B	A	C

Page 70

Codeword Conundrum

	A	L	K	A	L	O	I	D		D		B		N
H			I		I		N		C	A	M	E	R	A
I	N	F	L	A	T	I	N	G		I		D		M
K			O		U			R	O	S	E	T	T	E
E	N	U	M	E	R	A	T	E		I		I		S
R			E		G			E	K	E		M		A
	J	E	T	T	I	S	O	N		S	P	E	A	K
P			R		C		R		V		U			E
A	I	M	E	D		S	C	R	I	B	B	L	E	
R		A		A	R	C			R		E			B
A		G		Z		E	X	Q	U	I	S	I	T	E
D	E	N	I	Z	E	N			L		C			R
I		I		L		T	E	L	E	M	E	T	R	Y
G	I	F	T	E	D		W		N		N			L
M		Y		D		T	E	E	T	O	T	A	L	

Double Fun Sudoku

Tasty Teaser

7	4	6	9	3	8	1	2	5
3	2	1	7	5	4	6	9	8
9	5	8	6	2	1	4	7	3
2	6	9	1	7	5	8	3	4
5	1	4	3	8	2	7	6	9
8	3	7	4	6	9	5	1	2
1	7	2	5	4	3	9	8	6
6	8	5	2	9	7	3	4	1
4	9	3	8	1	6	2	5	7

Brain Buster

4	1	2	5	6	7	3	9	8
7	3	9	2	4	8	1	5	6
5	8	6	9	3	1	7	4	2
8	4	7	1	9	5	6	2	3
2	9	5	6	8	3	4	1	7
1	6	3	4	7	2	5	8	9
3	5	8	7	1	9	2	6	4
9	2	4	3	5	6	8	7	1
6	7	1	8	2	4	9	3	5

Pyramid Plus

A=66, B=61, C=67, D=100, E=135, F=127, G=128, H=167, I=235, J=255, K=295, L=402, M=550, N=697, O=1247.

Work it Out

74 – Reading down each column, add each number to the preceding number.

High-Speed Crossword

U	R	A	N	I	U	M		V	A	U	N	T
N		P		N		A		I			A	
T	U	R	K	S		T	O	R	T	U	R	E
R		O		U		T		U			R	
I	M	P	U	L	S	E		S	T	E	A	D
E		O		A		R			A		T	
D	I	S	A	R	M		S	A	U	C	E	R
	R		S			H		C		H		I
J	O	U	S	T		A	R	C	H	A	I	C
	N			R		S		U		P		K
C	A	N	D	I	E	S		S	A	L	V	E
	G			C		L		E		I		T
F	E	N	C	E		E	R	R	A	N	D	S

1 Minute Number Crunch

Beginner
20% of 40 = 8, 8 x 3 = 24, 24 – 4 = 20, 20 x 5 = 100, 100 – 17 = 83, 83 x 2 = 166, 166 – 40 = 126

Intermediate
120 – 12 (10% of 120) = 108, 108 ÷ 9 x 5 = 60, 60 + 24 (40% of 60) = 84, 84 ÷ 6 x 5 = 70, 70 ÷ 10 x 9 = 63, 63 x 5 = 315, 315 ÷ 9 = 35

Advanced
292 + 219 (292 ÷ 4 x 3) = 511, 511 x 9 = 4599, 4599 x 2 = 9198, 9198 ÷ 18 x 7 = 3577, 3577 – 698 = 2879, 2879 – 1993 = 886, 886 x 5 = 4430

Page 71

High-Speed Crossword

S	T	U	C	C	O		S	M	O	K	E	R
U			R		B	O	W		A			I
R	A	P	I	D	S		A		T			C
F			S		E	X	P	O	S	U	R	E
	B		I		S			N			E	
V	E	R	S	U	S		B	A	N	A	N	A
	W			R				I			T	
M	A	L	I	G	N		T	R	A	D	E	R
	R			E			I		B		D	
B	E	A	R	S	K	I	N		J			D
A			I		I		S	I	E	S	T	A
N			L		S	H	E		C			I
G	R	E	E	N	S		L	I	T	M	U	S

Summing Up

24	**27**	31	31	44	54
48	35	26	31	36	**35**
49	54	35	**13**	26	34
24	45	36	57	16	33
23	29	34	50	**40**	35
43	21	**49**	29	49	20

Battleships

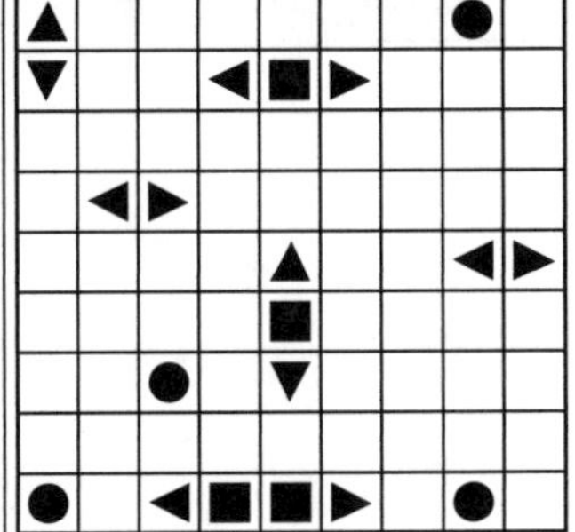

Wordsearch Workout

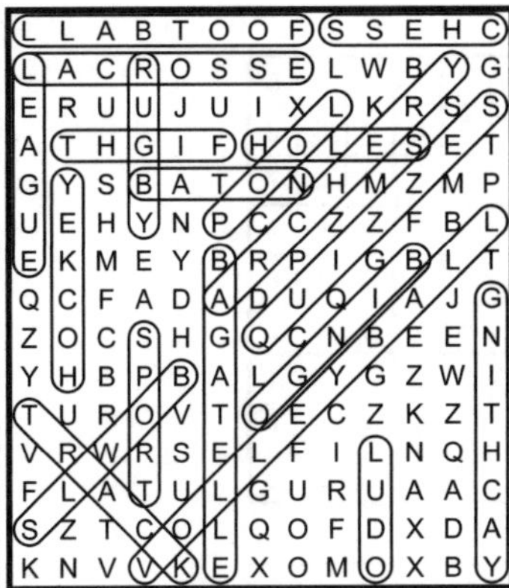

L	L	A	B	T	O	O	F	S	S	E	H	C
L	A	C	R	O	S	S	E	L	W	B	Y	G
E	R	U	U	J	U	I	X	L	K	R	S	S
A	T	H	G	I	F	H	O	L	E	S	E	T
G	Y	S	B	A	T	O	N	H	M	Z	M	P
U	E	H	Y	N	P	C	C	Z	Z	F	B	L
E	K	M	E	Y	B	R	P	I	G	B	L	T
Q	C	F	A	D	A	D	U	Q	I	A	J	G
Z	O	C	S	H	G	Q	C	N	B	E	E	N
Y	H	B	P	B	A	L	G	Y	G	Z	W	I
T	U	R	O	V	T	Q	E	C	Z	K	Z	T
V	R	W	R	S	E	L	F	I	L	N	Q	H
F	L	A	T	U	L	G	U	R	U	A	A	C
S	Z	T	C	O	L	Q	O	F	D	X	D	A
K	N	V	V	K	E	X	O	M	O	X	B	Y

Double Fun Sudoku

Tasty Teaser

3	2	7	6	1	5	9	4	8
5	6	8	4	9	3	1	2	7
1	9	4	7	8	2	3	5	6
4	3	6	8	2	9	7	1	5
7	8	1	5	3	6	2	9	4
9	5	2	1	4	7	6	8	3
6	4	5	2	7	1	8	3	9
2	7	9	3	5	8	4	6	1
8	1	3	9	6	4	5	7	2

Brain Buster

5	1	6	9	2	8	4	7	3
8	4	9	5	7	3	6	1	2
3	2	7	4	1	6	9	8	5
9	8	5	1	6	2	3	4	7
4	7	3	8	9	5	1	2	6
1	6	2	7	3	4	5	9	8
7	9	8	6	5	1	2	3	4
2	5	1	3	4	7	8	6	9
6	3	4	2	8	9	7	5	1

Whatever Next?

7 – Each of the lower numbers is the square root of the higher number in the opposite point of the star.

Brain Teaser

24

6 x 8 = 48/2

Page 72

Mind Over Matter

The sum total of the values of the top two squares is equal to the square of the value of the central square, as is the sum total of the values of the bottom two squares. Thus the missing value is 3, so the missing letter is C.

Double Fun Sudoku

Tasty Teaser

2	6	7	3	8	1	4	9	5
1	9	5	4	7	6	2	8	3
4	3	8	2	9	5	1	6	7
9	1	6	5	3	2	8	7	4
5	7	2	8	1	4	9	3	6
3	8	4	9	6	7	5	1	2
8	5	3	6	2	9	7	4	1
6	2	1	7	4	8	3	5	9
7	4	9	1	5	3	6	2	8

Brain Buster

9	4	2	3	5	8	6	1	7
5	7	3	6	1	9	4	8	2
8	6	1	7	2	4	3	9	5
6	5	9	1	4	7	8	2	3
4	1	8	2	9	3	7	5	6
3	2	7	5	8	6	9	4	1
7	8	5	4	6	2	1	3	9
1	9	6	8	3	5	2	7	4
2	3	4	9	7	1	5	6	8

Codeword Conundrum

S	Q	U	A	W	K	■	E	M	P	H	A	T	I	C
I	■	N	■	H	■	■	L	■	■	O	■	R	■	A
D	I	F	F	I	C	U	L	T	■	U	N	I	O	N
E	■	R	■	M	■	D	■	A	■	R	■	C	■	O
D	R	O	P	P	E	D	■	R	H	I	Z	O	M	E
■	■	C	■	E	■	E	■	O	■	■	■	R	■	■
J	O	K	E	R	■	R	E	T	I	C	E	N	C	E
A	■	■	■	E	■	■	E	■	■	A	■	■	■	L
B	L	I	N	D	F	O	L	D	■	F	R	A	N	K
■	■	R	■	■	■	Z	■	R	■	E	■	X	■	■
V	E	R	T	I	G	O	■	O	U	T	L	I	N	E
O	■	U	■	S	■	N	■	O	■	E	■	L	■	N
L	U	P	U	S	■	E	M	P	U	R	P	L	E	D
E	■	T	■	U	■	■	A	■	■	I	■	A	■	U
S	I	S	T	E	R	L	Y	■	G	A	M	E	T	E

Futoshiki

1	2	3	4	5
2	3	5	1	4
4	1	2	5	3
5	4	1	3	2
3	5	4	2	1

High-Speed Crossword

B	A	S	I	C	■	D	I	S	L	I	K	E
O	■	E	■	A	G	O	■	■	A	■	R	■
Y	■	L	■	M	■	L	■	A	R	G	O	N
C	A	T	A	P	U	L	T	■	D	■	N	■
O	■	Z	■	U	■	A	R	S	E	N	A	L
T	R	E	A	S	U	R	Y	■	R	■	■	A
T	■	R	■	■	N	■	O	■	■	C	■	S
E	■	■	M	■	C	O	N	T	R	A	S	T
D	E	T	A	I	L	S	■	H	■	D	■	L
■	N	■	R	■	E	P	H	E	M	E	R	A
M	E	D	A	L	■	R	■	I	■	N	■	U
■	M	■	C	■	■	E	R	R	■	Z	■	G
T	Y	R	A	N	N	Y	■	S	L	A	S	H

1 Minute Number Crunch

Beginner

50% of 86 = 43, 43 + 17 = 60, 60 x 2 = 120, 120 ÷ 12 = 10, 10 x 20 = 200, 200 ÷ 5 = 40, 40 + 99 = 139

Intermediate

62 x 2 = 124, 124 ÷ 4 x 3 = 93, 93 x 3 = 279, 279 ÷ 9 x 5 = 155, 155 – 69 = 86, 86 x 3 = 258, 258 + 168 = 426

Advanced

72^2 = 5184, 5184 ÷ 9 = 576, 576 ÷ 8 x 5 = 360, 360 x 7 = 2520, 2520 ÷ 40 x 7 = 441, 441 ÷ 9 x 5 = 245, 245 – 76 = 169

Page 73

Domino Placement

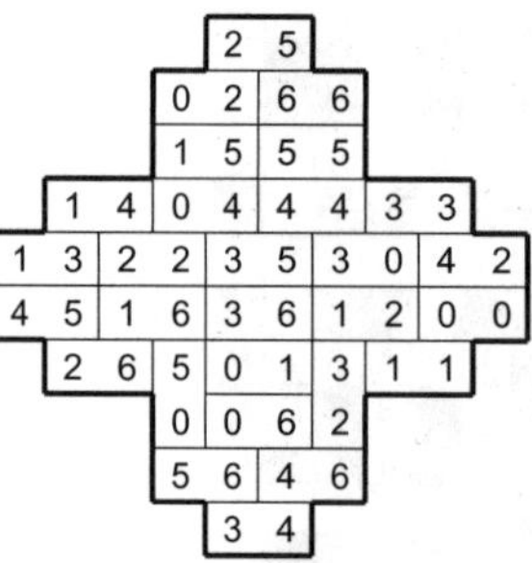

				2	5				
			0	2	6	6			
			1	5	5	5			
	1	4	0	4	4	4	3	3	
1	3	2	2	3	5	3	0	4	2
4	5	1	6	3	6	1	2	0	0
	2	6	5	0	1	3	1	1	
			0	0	6	2			
			5	6	4	6			
				3	4				

High-Speed Crossword

P	A	C	K	I	N	G	C	A	S	E	■	B
A	■	■	E	■	A	■	I	■	C	■	■	O
S	T	U	N	N	I	N	G	■	O	K	R	A
T	■	■	D	■	V	■	A	■	L	■	■	T
E	X	P	O	S	E	■	R	E	D	U	C	E
L	■	H	■	■	T	■	■	■	■	N	■	R
■	B	O	B	B	Y	■	R	A	B	I	D	■
B	■	T	■	■	■	■	E	■	■	T	■	B
A	N	O	I	N	T	■	F	R	I	S	K	Y
N	■	■	N	■	R	■	U	■	G	■	■	P
T	A	C	T	■	A	N	G	E	L	I	C	A
A	■	■	E	■	Y	■	E	■	O	■	■	S
M	■	C	R	O	S	S	S	W	O	R	D	S

IQ Workout

4

4 x 19 = 76

Wordwheel

The nine-letter word is: ORCHESTRA

Wordsearch Workout

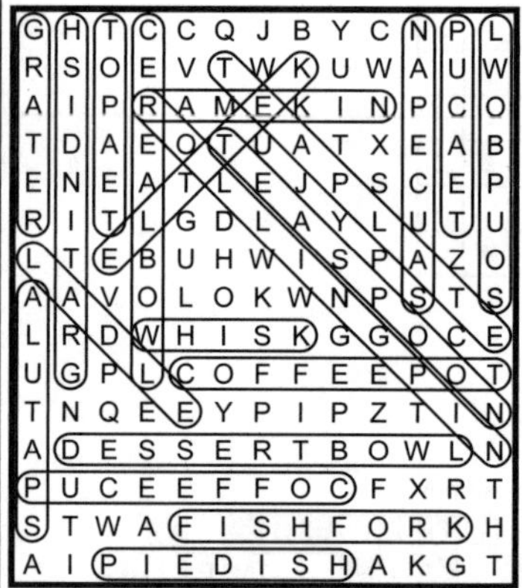

G	H	T	C	C	Q	J	B	Y	C	N	P	L
R	S	O	E	V	T	W	K	U	W	A	U	W
A	I	P	R	A	M	E	K	I	N	P	C	O
T	D	A	E	O	T	U	A	T	X	E	A	B
E	N	E	A	T	L	E	J	P	S	C	E	P
R	I	T	L	G	D	L	A	Y	L	U	T	U
L	T	E	B	U	H	W	I	S	P	A	Z	O
A	A	V	O	L	O	K	W	N	P	S	T	S
L	R	D	W	H	I	S	K	G	G	O	C	E
U	G	P	L	C	O	F	F	E	E	P	O	T
T	N	Q	E	E	Y	P	I	P	Z	T	I	N
A	D	E	S	S	E	R	T	B	O	W	L	N
P	U	C	E	E	F	F	O	C	F	X	R	T
S	T	W	A	F	I	S	H	F	O	R	K	H
A	I	P	I	E	D	I	S	H	A	K	G	T

Double Fun Sudoku

Tasty Teaser

2	9	4	1	3	7	5	6	8
3	7	6	8	2	5	4	1	9
1	8	5	9	4	6	3	7	2
5	2	8	3	7	9	1	4	6
7	3	9	6	1	4	8	2	5
6	4	1	5	8	2	9	3	7
4	6	3	7	9	8	2	5	1
8	1	7	2	5	3	6	9	4
9	5	2	4	6	1	7	8	3

Brain Buster

7	5	4	2	9	3	1	6	8
9	1	6	7	8	5	3	2	4
2	8	3	6	4	1	5	7	9
3	4	7	5	6	8	2	9	1
5	6	2	1	7	9	8	4	3
1	9	8	3	2	4	7	5	6
4	2	5	8	1	6	9	3	7
6	7	1	9	3	2	4	8	5
8	3	9	4	5	7	6	1	2

Sum Circle

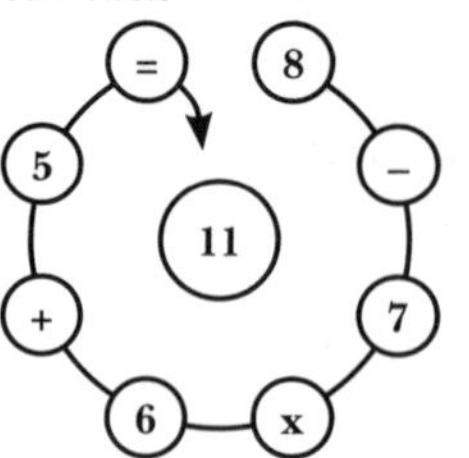

Page 74

1 Minute Number Crunch

Beginner
89 + 47 = 136, 136 ÷ 4 = 34, 50% of 34 = 17, 17 x 6 = 102, 102 – 15 = 87, 87 ÷ 3 = 29, 29 + 39 = 68

Intermediate
261 x 2 = 522, 522 ÷ 9 = 58, 250% of 58 = 145, 145 ÷ 5 x 3 = 87, 87 ÷ 3 = 29, 29 x 7 = 203, 203 – 45 = 158

Advanced
247 ÷ 13 x 3 = 57, 57 ÷ 19 x 5 = 15, 15 x 35 = 525, 525 ÷ 21 x 5 = 125, cube root of 125 = 5, 5 x 1.4 = 7, 7 x 45 = 315

High-Speed Crossword

P	A	C	E		E	S	O	T	E	R	I	C
O		E		S		C		U		O		H
S	E	L	F	I	S	H		B	R	I	A	R
T		L		N		I		E		S		I
A	M	O	N	G		S	T	R	A	T	U	S
G				L		M		C		E		T
E	S	C	H	E	W		Q	U	O	R	U	M
S		U		H		M		L				A
T	O	R	N	A	D	O		O	V	E	N	S
A		A		N		U		S		M		T
M	U	T	E	D		S	K	I	P	P	E	R
P		O		E		S		S		T		E
S	H	R	E	D	D	E	R		T	Y	P	E

IQ Workout

9

Codeword Conundrum

C	O	R	N	E	A	L		P	A	Y	M	E	N	T
A		I				U		O		O				H
R	E	F	L	E	C	T	O	R		K	H	A	K	I
T		L		L		E		C		E		L		N
W	E	E	V	I	L		C	H	A	L	K	I	N	G
H				X		Y			N			M		
E		T	O	I	L	E	T	R	Y		M	E	S	S
E		H		R		T		A		S		N		U
L	E	E	K		F	I	Z	Z	I	E	S	T		P
		R			E			E		Q				E
I	M	M	I	N	E	N	T		J	U	D	D	E	R
S		A		A		E		Y		E		E		S
S	O	L	I	D		A	V	A	I	L	A	B	L	E
U				I		R		W				U		D
E	N	S	U	R	E	S		L	A	Y	E	T	T	E

Tasty Teaser

8	5	3	1	6	2	4	7	9
6	1	9	7	4	5	8	2	3
4	2	7	3	8	9	5	6	1
1	8	6	9	5	7	3	4	2
3	9	2	8	1	4	7	5	6
5	7	4	6	2	3	9	1	8
9	6	1	5	7	8	2	3	4
2	3	5	4	9	6	1	8	7
7	4	8	2	3	1	6	9	5

Brain Buster

7	4	1	9	8	6	2	3	5
8	2	9	5	3	4	7	1	6
5	3	6	2	1	7	9	8	4
1	5	2	4	6	8	3	9	7
9	8	7	1	5	3	4	6	2
3	6	4	7	9	2	8	5	1
4	1	3	8	7	5	6	2	9
2	9	8	6	4	1	5	7	3
6	7	5	3	2	9	1	4	8

Spidoku

Page 75

Logi-Six

C	D	E	A	F	B
B	A	C	D	E	F
F	B	A	E	C	D
E	F	B	C	D	A
D	E	F	B	A	C
A	C	D	F	B	E

High-Speed Crossword

A	T	T	A	C	H		B		L		D	
	R		N		A	R	O	M	A	T	I	C
B	A	T	T	E	N		A		T		L	
	S		E		D	U	T	C	H	M	A	N
R	H	E	S	U	S				E		T	
I					O	B	S	E	R	V	E	R
G			B		M		T		S			I
S	A	B	O	T	E	U	R					M
	R		O				E	X	C	I	S	E
N	A	U	T	I	L	U	S		L		W	
	B		L		A		S	C	A	R	E	D
P	I	N	E	T	R	E	E		S		A	
	C		G		D		D	E	S	E	R	T

Wordsearch Workout

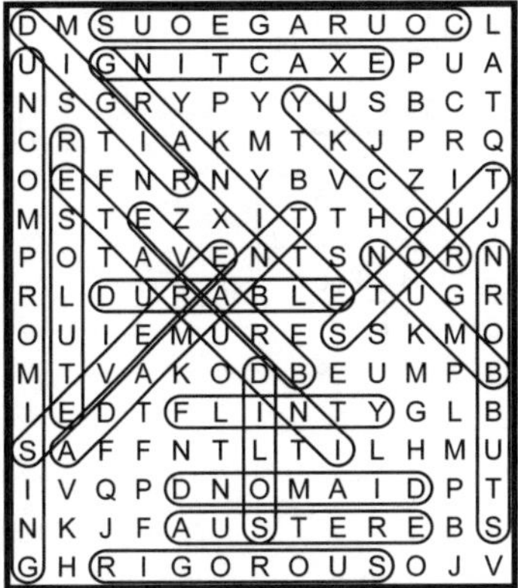

Double Fun Sudoku

Tasty Teaser

5	7	9	2	1	6	8	4	3
1	8	3	7	5	4	9	2	6
2	4	6	8	9	3	1	7	5
9	6	8	3	4	2	5	1	7
7	2	1	5	8	9	3	6	4
4	3	5	1	6	7	2	8	9
3	9	2	4	7	8	6	5	1
6	5	7	9	2	1	4	3	8
8	1	4	6	3	5	7	9	2

Brain Buster

7	6	3	1	5	4	8	2	9
9	8	1	2	7	6	5	3	4
2	4	5	9	8	3	6	1	7
8	3	9	6	2	1	7	4	5
1	2	6	5	4	7	9	8	3
4	5	7	3	9	8	1	6	2
6	1	2	7	3	9	4	5	8
5	7	4	8	6	2	3	9	1
3	9	8	4	1	5	2	7	6

Matchstick Magic

The matchsticks which have been moved are outlined.

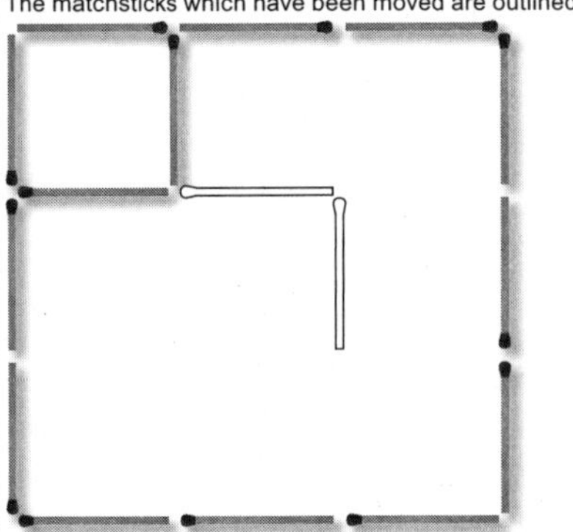

Brain Teaser

B

Domino Placement

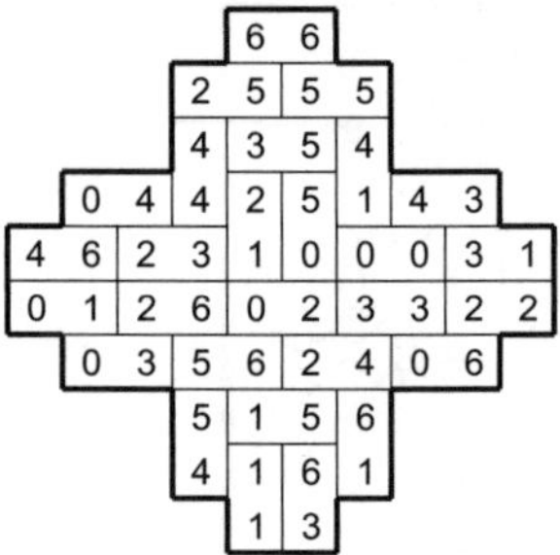

Page 76

Codeword Conundrum

M	O	L	E	S	T		A	C	O	L	Y	T	E	S
O		A		T		U		O		A		H		T
D	U	N	C	E		S	U	P	E	R	H	E	R	O
I		C		E	V	E		R		C		I		O
C	H	E	A	P		D	E	A	T	H	T	R	A	P
U				E			L		W				P	
M	A	J	O	R	I	T	Y		E	F	F	O	R	T
	R		B		N		S		A		A		O	
Z	O	D	I	A	C		I	N	K	S	T	A	N	D
	M				U		A			Q				Y
J	A	B	B	E	R	I	N	G		U	N	P	I	N
U		A		X		N		E	R	A		R		A
D	I	S	A	P	P	E	A	R		R	U	I	N	S
G		I		E		P		M		E		M		T
E	S	C	A	L	A	T	E		I	D	I	O	C	Y

Double Fun Sudoku

Tasty Teaser

5	9	2	6	4	3	1	8	7
3	7	4	1	8	9	5	2	6
8	6	1	2	5	7	9	4	3
7	1	5	9	2	8	3	6	4
9	3	6	4	7	1	8	5	2
4	2	8	3	6	5	7	9	1
6	8	3	5	1	2	4	7	9
2	5	9	7	3	4	6	1	8
1	4	7	8	9	6	2	3	5

Brain Buster

7	3	1	2	6	4	9	8	5
5	2	8	1	3	9	7	4	6
9	4	6	7	5	8	3	2	1
2	5	9	4	1	6	8	3	7
1	8	4	3	2	7	5	6	9
3	6	7	8	9	5	4	1	2
6	7	3	9	4	2	1	5	8
8	1	5	6	7	3	2	9	4
4	9	2	5	8	1	6	7	3

Pyramid Plus

A=53, B=135, C=80, D=10, E=118, F=188, G=215, H=90, I=128, J=403, K=305, L=218, M=708, N=523, O=1231.

Work it Out

41 – In the first row, add 5 to the first number, subtract 8 from the second, add 5 to the third, etc; in the second row, add 8 to the first number, subtract 5 from the second, etc; then repeat this process for the remaining rows, adding and subtracting 5 and/or 8 alternately.

High-Speed Crossword

C	U	P	B	O	A	R	D		C	A	P	S
A		O		B		A		I		F		E
G	R	I	T	S		G	O	R	I	L	L	A
E		S		T	A	G		R		O		L
		E		R		E	L	E	V	A	T	E
R	E	D	H	E	A	D		V		T		V
E				P				E				E
S		O		E		P	A	R	A	S	O	L
E	M	B	A	R	G	O		S		O		
R		T		O		S	K	I		R		W
V	I	A	D	U	C	T		B	I	R	T	H
E		I		S		A		L		O		E
D	A	N	K		A	L	L	E	Y	W	A	Y

1 Minute Number Crunch

Beginner
6 + 8 = 14, 14 ÷ 7 = 2, 2 + 47 = 49, 49 ÷ 7 = 7, 7 + 2 = 9, 9 ÷ 3 = 3, 3 + 68 = 71

Intermediate
20% of 135 = 27, 27 x 6 = 162, 162 ÷ 9 x 5 = 90, 90 – 18 (20% of 90) = 72, 72 + 79 = 151, 151 – 126 = 25, 25 + 15 (25 ÷ 5 x 3) = 40

Advanced
558 – 310 (558 ÷ 9 x 5) = 248, 248 x 0.375 = 93, 93 x 7 = 651, 651 + 434 (651 ÷ 3 x 2) = 1085, 1085 ÷ 5 x 2 = 434, 434 ÷ 7 x 3 = 186, 186 x 7 = 1302

Page 77

High-Speed Crossword

	M		D		R		S	E	T	T	E	R
T	A	K	E	N	O	T	E				N	
	I		L		O		C	U	P	O	L	A
S	L	O	E		F	L	U		O		I	
	E		T		S		L		L		S	
A	D	D	E	R		R	A	D	I	A	T	E
D			R		H		R		C			W
O	P	T	I	M	A	L		T	E	A	S	E
	A		O		P		S		S		H	
	G		U		L	O	T		T	E	A	K
T	O	U	S	L	E		O		A		V	
	D				S	P	R	I	T	Z	E	R
H	A	L	V	E	S		E		E		R	

IQ Workout

Clocks lose 1 hour 11 minutes each time.

1 Minute Number Crunch

Beginner
15 x 3 = 45, 45 ÷ 9 = 5, 5 + 49 = 54, 54 ÷ 9 = 6, 6^2 = 36, 36 + 20 = 56, 56 ÷ 4 = 14

Intermediate
26 x 8 = 208, 208 ÷ 4 x 3 = 156, 156 ÷ 3 = 52, 52 x 12 = 624, 624 ÷ 8 x 5 = 390, 390 ÷ 10 x 3 = 117, 117 ÷ 9 = 13

Advanced
Square root of 1369 = 37, 37 x 11 = 407, 407 + 2047 = 2454, 2454 ÷ 2 = 1227, 1227 + 818 (1227 ÷ 3 x 2) = 2045, 2045 ÷ 5 x 3 = 1227, 1227 ÷ 3 = 409

Wordsearch Workout

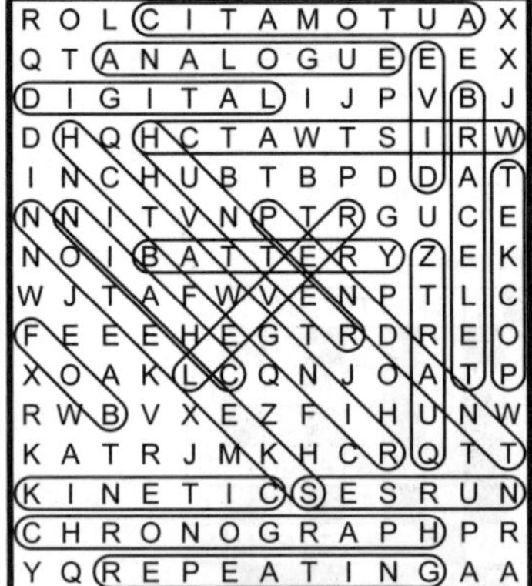

R	O	L	C	I	T	A	M	O	T	U	A	X
Q	T	A	N	A	L	O	G	U	E	E	E	X
D	I	G	I	T	A	L	I	J	P	V	B	J
D	H	Q	H	C	T	A	W	T	S	I	R	W
I	N	C	H	U	B	T	B	P	D	D	A	T
N	N	I	T	V	N	P	T	R	G	U	C	E
N	O	I	B	A	T	T	E	R	Y	Z	E	K
W	J	T	A	F	W	V	E	N	P	T	L	C
F	E	E	E	H	E	G	T	R	D	R	E	O
X	O	A	K	L	C	Q	N	J	O	A	T	P
R	W	B	V	X	E	Z	F	I	H	U	N	W
K	A	T	R	J	M	K	H	C	R	Q	T	T
K	I	N	E	T	I	C	S	E	S	R	U	N
C	H	R	O	N	O	G	R	A	P	H	P	R
Y	Q	R	E	P	E	A	T	I	N	G	A	A

Double Fun Sudoku

Tasty Teaser

8	7	3	2	4	1	9	6	5
1	9	2	5	8	6	7	3	4
4	5	6	7	3	9	8	2	1
2	1	7	3	9	8	5	4	6
5	3	8	6	7	4	1	9	2
6	4	9	1	5	2	3	8	7
3	2	1	9	6	5	4	7	8
7	8	5	4	2	3	6	1	9
9	6	4	8	1	7	2	5	3

Brain Buster

9	2	4	6	5	8	3	1	7
3	1	6	4	7	2	9	5	8
7	5	8	9	1	3	6	2	4
6	9	1	7	8	4	2	3	5
2	4	7	5	3	9	8	6	1
5	8	3	2	6	1	7	4	9
4	7	2	3	9	5	1	8	6
8	3	9	1	4	6	5	7	2
1	6	5	8	2	7	4	9	3

Whatever Next?

896 – Assign a number to each letter according to its place in the alphabet, so A=1, B=2, C=3, etc. Multiply this by the number in the same point of the star and then by the central figure, to give the number in the opposite point of the star. P(16)x8=128x7=896.

Brain Teaser

2

54+16=70÷(18+17)=2 90+9=99÷(19+14)=3
55+35=90÷(26+19)=2

Page 78

Mind Over Matter

The sum total of the values of the letter in the right squares is subtracted from the sum total of the values of the letters in the left squares to give the value of the letter in the central square. Thus the missing value is 26, so the missing letter is Z.

Double Fun Sudoku

Tasty Teaser

7	3	1	8	4	2	5	6	9
8	2	4	9	5	6	3	7	1
5	6	9	7	1	3	8	4	2
6	9	3	4	7	1	2	5	8
2	1	5	6	9	8	4	3	7
4	7	8	3	2	5	1	9	6
1	5	6	2	3	9	7	8	4
9	4	2	5	8	7	6	1	3
3	8	7	1	6	4	9	2	5

Brain Buster

9	1	3	8	6	5	2	7	4
2	7	5	9	4	3	8	1	6
6	4	8	7	2	1	3	9	5
3	9	1	5	7	2	4	6	8
4	8	6	1	3	9	7	5	2
5	2	7	4	8	6	1	3	9
8	3	9	2	5	7	6	4	1
1	6	2	3	9	4	5	8	7
7	5	4	6	1	8	9	2	3

Codeword Conundrum

M	A	P	P	E	D		E	L	D	R	I	T	C	H
U			H		O			U		E		U		O
C	A	T	A	C	L	Y	S	M		F		T		M
U			N		P		A	P	P	L	A	U	S	E
S	L	I	T		H	U	G			E				G
	E		O		I		O	N	Y	X		J		R
S	T	A	M	I	N	A		O		I	M	A	G	O
A		Q		N		B	A	R		V		Z		W
F	L	U	K	E		E		M	U	E	Z	Z	I	N
E		A		F	E	T	A		N		E		R	
G				F			L	I	T		O	A	K	S
U	P	H	E	A	V	A	L		R		L			I
A		I		B		L	Y	R	I	C	I	S	T	S
R		S		L		O			E		T			A
D	I	S	H	E	V	E	L		D	I	E	S	E	L

Futoshiki

5	3	2 >	1	4
3	1	4	2	5
2 <	4	1	5 >	3
1	5	3	4 >	2
4	2	5	3	1

High-Speed Crossword

S	O	N	G	S		C			P			D
U		E		T		R	E	P	L	I	C	A
P	U	P		R		O			A			T
P		H		I	M	P	R	E	C	A	T	E
O	V	E	R	D	O		E		E			D
S		W		E	L	I	G	I	B	L	E	
E			W		O		R		O			B
	S	H	A	N	T	I	E	S		B		R
L			S		O		S	E	N	I	L	E
A	R	C	H	I	V	I	S	T		T		A
Y			I			N		O		T	A	T
B	L	A	N	K	E	T		F		E		H
Y			G			O		F	A	R	C	E

1 Minute Number Crunch

Beginner
39 ÷ 3 = 13, 13 x 2 = 26, 26 + 36 = 62, 62 ÷ 2 = 31, 31 – 7 = 24, 24 ÷ 3 = 8, 8 x 10 = 80

Intermediate
494 – 39 = 455, 455 ÷ 5 = 91, 91 + 66 = 157, 157 x 2 = 314, 314 – 88 = 226, 226 ÷ 2 = 113, 113 x 6 = 678

Advanced
572 x 2 = 1144, 1144 – 143 (1144 x 0.125) = 1001, 1001 x 11 = 11011, 11011 – 7477 = 3534, 3534 ÷ 2 = 1767, 1767 ÷ 3 x 2 = 1178, 1178 ÷ 19 x 5 = 310

Page 79

Battleships

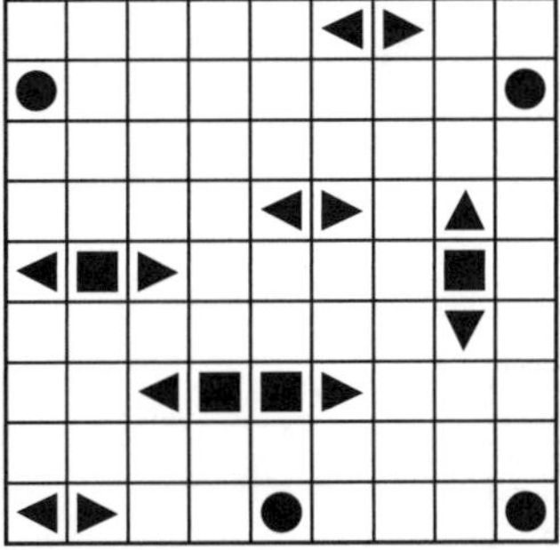

High-Speed Crossword

C	O	L	O	S	S	U	S		D		B	
A		O			W		C	R	A	Z	E	D
R		P			E	T	A		Y		N	
T	U	S	S	L	E		L	E	S	S	E	N
E			K		P		L				D	
L	A	D	E	N		F	O	R	F	E	I	T
	N		I		T		P		R		C	
F	I	A	N	C	E	E		H	I	N	T	S
	M				L		S		A			H
D	A	H	L	I	A		A	R	R	O	Y	O
	T		U		V	E	T			T		V
B	O	N	S	A	I		Y			I		E
	R		T		V	E	R	T	I	C	A	L

IQ Workout

22 – There are two series
(+6) 7-13-19-25
(+7) 8-15-22-29

Wordwheel

The nine-letter word is: PARAMEDIC

Wordsearch Workout

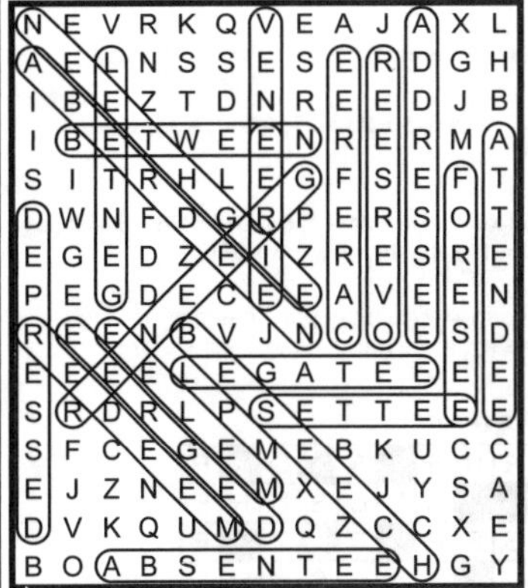

N	E	V	R	K	Q	V	E	A	J	A	X	L
A	E	L	N	S	S	E	S	E	R	D	G	H
I	B	E	Z	T	D	N	R	E	E	D	J	B
I	B	E	T	W	E	E	N	R	E	R	M	A
S	I	T	R	H	L	E	G	F	S	E	F	T
D	W	N	F	D	G	R	P	E	R	S	O	T
E	G	E	D	Z	E	I	Z	R	E	S	R	E
P	E	G	D	E	C	E	E	A	V	E	E	N
R	E	E	N	B	V	J	N	C	O	E	S	D
E	E	E	E	L	E	G	A	T	E	E	E	E
S	R	D	R	L	P	S	E	T	T	E	E	E
S	F	C	E	G	E	M	E	B	K	U	C	C
E	J	Z	N	E	E	M	X	E	J	Y	S	A
D	V	K	Q	U	M	D	Q	Z	C	C	X	E
B	O	A	B	S	E	N	T	E	E	H	G	Y

Double Fun Sudoku

Tasty Teaser

5	8	4	2	7	9	3	6	1
9	7	3	1	5	6	2	4	8
6	2	1	3	8	4	7	5	9
3	4	5	6	1	7	9	8	2
7	9	2	8	3	5	6	1	4
8	1	6	9	4	2	5	7	3
4	3	9	7	6	8	1	2	5
2	6	8	5	9	1	4	3	7
1	5	7	4	2	3	8	9	6

Brain Buster

9	5	3	7	8	4	1	2	6
1	4	7	2	9	6	5	3	8
8	6	2	3	1	5	7	9	4
3	8	4	9	5	2	6	1	7
7	1	9	8	6	3	4	5	2
5	2	6	1	4	7	9	8	3
6	7	8	5	3	9	2	4	1
2	9	1	4	7	8	3	6	5
4	3	5	6	2	1	8	7	9

Sum Circle

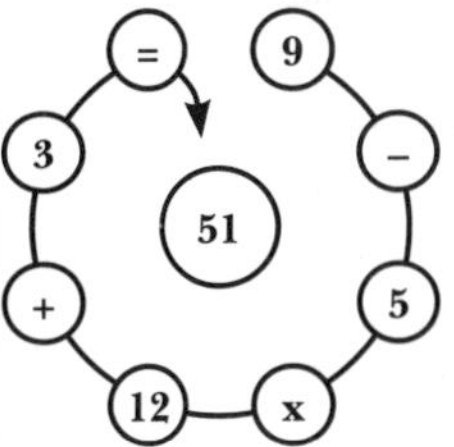

Page 80

1 Minute Number Crunch

Beginner
45 – 10 = 35, 35 ÷ 7 = 5, 5 + 28 = 33, 33 ÷ 3 = 11, 11 – 7 = 4, 4 x 6 = 24, 24 – 15 = 9

Intermediate
265 ÷ 5 = 53, 53 x 8 = 424, 424 – 176 = 248, 248 ÷ 8 = 31, 31 + 79 = 110, 110 ÷ 11 x 4 = 40, 40 x 9.5 = 380

Advanced
161 ÷ 7 x 3 = 69, 69 + 115 = 184, 184 x 5 = 920, 920 ÷ 8 x 5 = 575, 575 – 492 = 83, 83^2 = 6889, 6889 – 5971 = 918

High-Speed Crossword

B	E	L	A	R	U	S		W		O		R
I		E				C	L	O	S	U	R	E
T		A	M	B	E	R		R		Z		F
E		N		I		A	W	E	S	O	M	E
S	M	I	R	K		P			R			R
		N		I	N	E	B	R	I	A	T	E
B		G		N				E		I		E
I	N	S	T	I	G	A	T	E		R		
T			E			S		K	A	L	I	F
T	E	T	A	N	U	S		E		I		E
E		A		A		E	N	D	O	N		A
R	E	C	O	V	E	R				E		T
N		K		E		T	S	H	I	R	T	S

IQ Workout

2 – Start at the top and then move right to left along the second row, then back left to right along the third row etc, repeating the numbers 36942.

Codeword Conundrum

C		O		R	E	L	U	C	T	A	N	T	L	Y
R	A	B	B	I		A		U			E		E	
A		J		G	A	Z	E	B	O		W	O	M	B
F	R	E	S	H		Y			R		E		O	
T		C		T			W	A	D	D	L	I	N	G
		T		F	L	E	A		A			N		E
A	D	I	E	U			X		I		A	F	A	R
C		V		L	A	P	W	I	N	G		R		M
R	E	E	F		B		O			O	B	E	Y	S
I		L			B		R	O	A	R		Q		
D	A	Y	B	R	E	A	K			G		U		X
	L		A		S			T		E	L	E	G	Y
B	A	S	S		S	T	E	R	E	O		N		L
	R		T			E		I		U	N	C	L	E
I	M	P	E	C	U	N	I	O	U	S		Y		M

Tasty Teaser

8	9	5	4	1	2	7	6	3
2	1	3	6	7	8	5	4	9
4	7	6	5	9	3	2	8	1
3	2	9	8	6	1	4	7	5
1	4	8	7	3	5	6	9	2
6	5	7	2	4	9	3	1	8
9	6	1	3	5	7	8	2	4
5	8	4	9	2	6	1	3	7
7	3	2	1	8	4	9	5	6

Brain Buster

7	9	5	6	2	4	1	8	3
2	8	6	9	1	3	4	5	7
4	1	3	8	5	7	9	6	2
3	2	4	1	8	5	7	9	6
9	6	8	7	3	2	5	4	1
5	7	1	4	6	9	3	2	8
6	4	9	2	7	1	8	3	5
1	5	2	3	9	8	6	7	4
8	3	7	5	4	6	2	1	9

Spidoku

Page 81

Logi-Six

D	F	C	E	B	A
E	B	D	F	A	C
A	D	B	C	F	E
C	E	A	B	D	F
F	A	E	D	C	B
B	C	F	A	E	D

High-Speed Crossword

G	E	Y	S	E	R		D	E	S	I	G	N
	X		I		E		E		C			O
C	O	R	N	E	A		S	T	A	B	L	E
	S		C	A	R	A	T		L			L
U	P	P	E	R			I		P		M	
	H			L	O	U	N	G	E	B	A	R
	E		E		V		E		L		C	
C	R	E	S	C	E	N	D	O			H	
	E		Q		R			M	A	G	I	C
W			U		S	A	F	E	S		N	
A	C	T	I	V	E		A	N	T	L	E	R
R			R		A		R		I		R	
P	L	I	E	R	S		M	A	R	T	Y	R

Wordsearch Workout

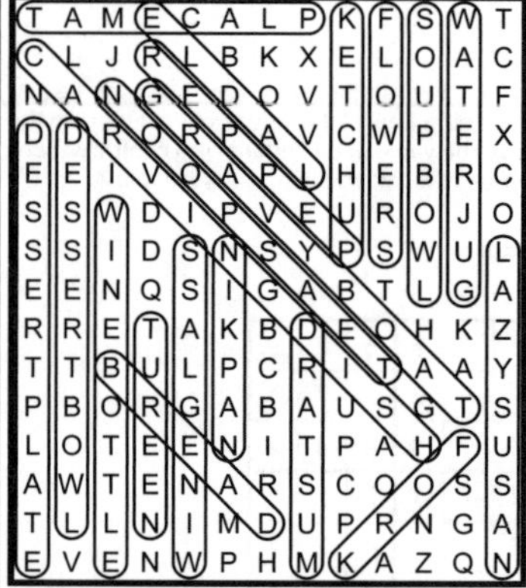

Double Fun Sudoku

Tasty Teaser

4	8	2	3	5	9	7	1	6
3	7	1	2	8	6	9	4	5
6	5	9	1	4	7	2	3	8
9	6	5	8	3	4	1	7	2
7	2	3	6	1	5	8	9	4
1	4	8	7	9	2	5	6	3
2	1	7	4	6	8	3	5	9
8	9	4	5	7	3	6	2	1
5	3	6	9	2	1	4	8	7

Brain Buster

5	1	7	4	8	2	6	3	9
6	3	2	9	5	1	8	7	4
4	8	9	7	3	6	1	2	5
3	5	6	1	9	7	2	4	8
2	4	8	3	6	5	9	1	7
9	7	1	2	4	8	3	5	6
1	9	5	6	7	3	4	8	2
7	2	4	8	1	9	5	6	3
8	6	3	5	2	4	7	9	1

Matchstick Magic

The matchsticks which have been moved are outlined.

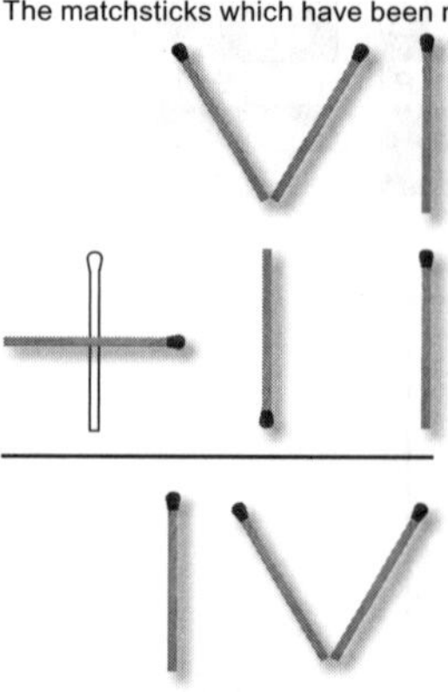

Brain Teaser

12 – In the 1st hexagon opposite numbers add up to 36. In the 2nd hexagon opposite numbers add up to 43. In the 3rd hexagon opposite numbers add up to 32.

1 Minute Number Crunch

Beginner
37 – 8 = 29, 29 x 3 = 87, 87 + 35 = 122, 50% of 122 = 61, 61 – 11 = 50, 50 x 3 = 150, 150 ÷ 5 = 30

Intermediate
457 + 754 = 1211, 1211 – 666 = 545, 545 ÷ 5 = 109, 109 x 7 = 763, 763 + 89 = 852, 852 ÷ 3 x 2 = 568, 568 ÷ 8 x 5 = 355

Advanced
161 + 115 (161 ÷ 7 x 5) = 276, 276 + 184 (276 ÷ 3 x 2) = 460, 460 + 92 (20% of 460) = 552, 552 – 398 = 154, 154 x 4 = 616, 616 x 1.875 = 1155, 1155 + 462 (1155 ÷ 5 x 2) = 1617

Page 82

Codeword Conundrum

Double Fun Sudoku

Tasty Teaser

4	7	3	9	6	2	5	8	1
9	1	5	7	3	8	6	2	4
6	2	8	1	4	5	3	9	7
8	3	9	5	1	4	7	6	2
2	6	7	8	9	3	1	4	5
5	4	1	6	2	7	9	3	8
1	9	2	4	5	6	8	7	3
3	8	6	2	7	1	4	5	9
7	5	4	3	8	9	2	1	6

Brain Buster

2	6	7	4	3	1	5	9	8
8	5	4	7	2	9	1	6	3
3	1	9	8	6	5	7	2	4
1	7	2	6	5	8	3	4	9
5	8	6	3	9	4	2	7	1
9	4	3	1	7	2	6	8	5
4	3	1	2	8	6	9	5	7
7	2	5	9	4	3	8	1	6
6	9	8	5	1	7	4	3	2

Pyramid Plus

A=1, B=132, C=29, D=90, E=19, F=133, G=161, H=119, I=109, J=294, K=280, L=228, M=574, N=508, O=1082.

Work it Out

160 – Reading down each column, multiply the first number by 4, then deduct 4, then multiply by 5, then deduct 5, then multiply by 6, then deduct 6.

High-Speed Crossword

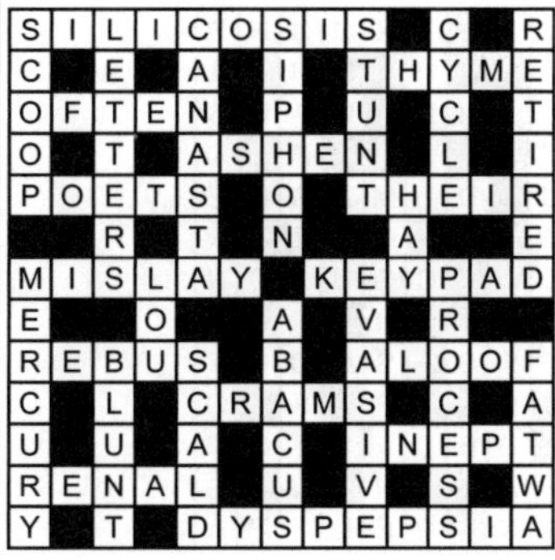

1 Minute Number Crunch

Beginner
47 + 27 = 74, 74 ÷ 2 = 37, 37 – 16 = 21, 21 ÷ 3 = 7, 7 x 15 = 105, 105 ÷ 5 = 21, 21 ÷ 3 = 7

Intermediate
41 + 92 = 133, 133 x 4 = 532, 532 ÷ 4 x 3 = 399, 399 + 266 (399 ÷ 3 x 2) = 665, 665 + 85 = 750, 750 x 1.3 = 975, 975 – 489 = 486

Advanced
59 x 6 = 354, 354 + 236 (354 ÷ 3 x 2) = 590, 590 ÷ 10 x 3 = 177, 177 ÷ 3 x 2 = 118, 118 x 4 = 472, 472 – 319 = 153, 153 + 119 (153 ÷ 9 x 7) = 272

Page 83

High-Speed Crossword

C	O	M	I	C		S			L		F	
L		A		O		T	O	P	I	C	A	L
A	I	R	L	I	N	E			F		C	
V		K		R	E	T	R	I	E	V	E	R
I		E			U		E		L		T	
C	A	R	P	A	R	K	S		E	L	S	E
L			A		I		E		S			T
E	A	R	N		T	I	R	E	S	O	M	E
	P		C		I		V			C		R
O	P	P	R	E	S	S	E	D		T		N
	E		E			T	S	U	N	A	M	I
A	N	D	A	N	T	E		D		V		T
	D		S			M		E	P	O	X	Y

Summing Up

58	**13**	23	32	62	40
51	38	30	26	**38**	45
29	59	38	44	20	38
41	55	38	**32**	18	44
19	38	53	43	38	**37**
30	25	**46**	51	52	24

Domino Placement

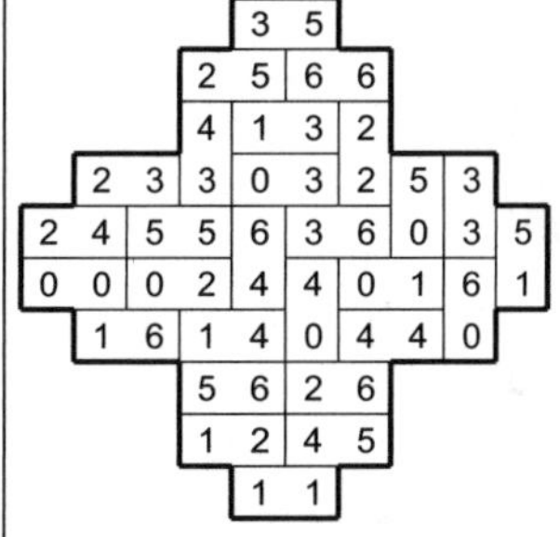

Wordsearch Workout

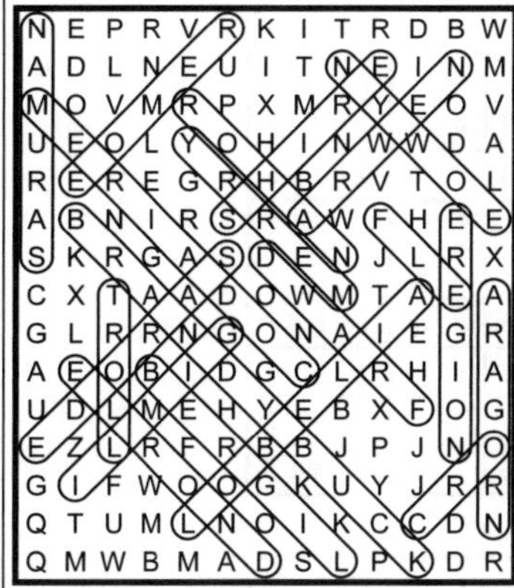

Double Fun Sudoku

Tasty Teaser

6	5	7	3	8	4	1	2	9
8	4	9	2	1	6	5	7	3
1	2	3	7	9	5	8	4	6
2	7	5	1	3	9	6	8	4
9	1	4	6	7	8	2	3	5
3	8	6	5	4	2	9	1	7
4	3	8	9	6	1	7	5	2
7	6	2	8	5	3	4	9	1
5	9	1	4	2	7	3	6	8

Brain Buster

2	6	4	9	1	7	3	8	5
9	7	8	3	5	6	4	2	1
3	5	1	2	8	4	9	7	6
7	4	5	6	9	2	8	1	3
1	3	9	4	7	8	6	5	2
6	8	2	1	3	5	7	4	9
5	2	7	8	6	9	1	3	4
8	1	6	5	4	3	2	9	7
4	9	3	7	2	1	5	6	8

Whatever Next?

T – Start at the top and move forwards in the alphabet first 2 places, then 3, then 2, then 3, then 2 (to T), then 3 to W.

Brain Teaser

F

Page 84

Mind Over Matter

The value of the letter in the central square is half that of the sum total of the values of the letters in the other squares. Thus the missing value is 19, so the missing letter is S.

Double Fun Sudoku

Tasty Teaser

8	9	6	1	4	5	3	7	2
1	2	5	3	9	7	4	8	6
4	3	7	8	2	6	9	1	5
7	5	9	4	6	1	8	2	3
6	8	1	7	3	2	5	9	4
2	4	3	9	5	8	1	6	7
9	7	4	6	8	3	2	5	1
5	6	8	2	1	4	7	3	9
3	1	2	5	7	9	6	4	8

Brain Buster

3	9	1	7	6	2	8	5	4
5	7	6	4	8	9	3	1	2
4	2	8	3	1	5	7	6	9
2	8	7	9	5	1	4	3	6
1	6	5	2	4	3	9	7	8
9	3	4	6	7	8	5	2	1
8	5	3	1	2	4	6	9	7
7	1	9	8	3	6	2	4	5
6	4	2	5	9	7	1	8	3

Codeword Conundrum

D	I	S	A	F	F	E	C	T		S	C	A	L	P
E		U		O		X		R		Q		C		I
F	A	B	L	E		C	R	O	Q	U	E	T		E
E		J		T		E		D		E		E		C
R	E	U	S	A	B	L	E		S	L	U	D	G	E
		G		L				D		C				M
I	M	A	M		P	O	W	E	R	H	O	U	S	E
N		T		F		V		L		Y		N		A
C	H	E	E	R	F	U	L	L	Y		I	D	O	L
U				E		M				F		E		
M	O	C	K	E	D		B	U	L	L	F	R	O	G
B		O		Z		L		N		A		T		L
E		B	R	I	G	A	N	D		B	R	A	V	O
N		R		N		V		U		B		K		B
T	W	A	N	G		A	C	E	T	Y	L	E	N	E

Futoshiki

1	5	4	3	2
2	3	1 <	4	5
4 >	1	2	5	3
5	2	3	1	4
3	4	5	2	1

High-Speed Crossword

E	N	T	O	M	B		T	R	O	C	H	E
T		R		I			H			H		A
H	E	A	D	L	I	N	E		C	A	P	S
O		G		E			S			P		T
S	T	E	W	S		D	E	M	E	S	N	E
		D		T				O				R
A	N	Y	H	O	W		C	O	U	P	O	N
N				N				N		R		
A	G	E	L	E	S	S		S	C	O	U	T
G		N			E			H		F		O
R	A	T	E		D	E	C	I	S	I	O	N
A		E			A			N		L		G
M	A	R	G	I	N		O	E	D	E	M	A

1 Minute Number Crunch

Beginner

12 ÷ 6 = 2, 2 + 20 = 22, 22 x 2 = 44, 44 – 30 = 14, 14 ÷ 7 = 2, 2 + 66 = 68, 25% of 68 = 17

Intermediate

61 – 15 = 46, 46 x 3 = 138, 138 x 1.5 = 207, 207 ÷ 9 = 23, 23 + 57 = 80, 80 ÷ 10 x 7 = 56, 56 x 11 = 616

Advanced

117 ÷ 9 x 5 = 65, 65 ÷ 13 x 8 = 40, 40 ÷ 2.5 = 16, 16² = 256, 256 + 160 (256 x 0.625) = 416, 416 ÷ 16 x 5 = 130, 130 – 91 (130 ÷ 10 x 7) = 39

Wordsearch Workout

Page 85

1 Minute Number Crunch

Beginner

35 x 3 = 105, 105 + 81 = 186, 186 ÷ 6 = 31, 31 x 9 = 279, 279 – 42 = 237, 237 + 3 = 240, 240 ÷ 12 x 5 = 100

Intermediate

89 + 98 = 187, 187 x 2 = 374, 374 x 1.5 = 561, 561 ÷ 3 = 187, 187 – 78 = 109, 109 x 4 = 436, 436 + 47 = 483

Advanced

11 x 33 = 363, 363 – 121 (363 ÷ 3) = 242, 242 x 9 = 2178, 2178 ÷ 18 x 11 = 1331, 1331 + 11 (cube root of 1331) = 1342, 1342 ÷ 2 = 671, 671 x 4 = 2684

High-Speed Crossword

K	U	N	G	F	U		T	H	A	T	C	H
N			R		N		E		V		O	
I	N	V	A	L	I	D	A	T	E		A	
T			N		Q		C		N	I	L	E
	P		N	A	U	R	U		U		M	
A	R	G	Y	L	E		P	O	E	T	I	C
	O			O				B			N	
S	P	A	D	E	S		B	O	W	Y	E	R
	R		E		A	G	R	E	E		R	
B	I	N	S		D		A		L			H
	E		I	N	D	I	C	A	T	I	V	E
	T		S		L		E		E			R
M	Y	R	T	L	E		S	H	R	O	U	D

Partitions

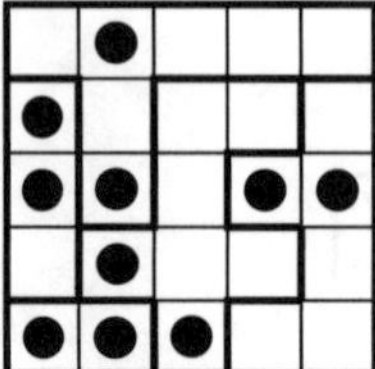

Wordwheel

The nine-letter word is: CONDIMENT

Double Fun Sudoku

Tasty Teaser

4	5	8	7	2	6	3	1	9
7	6	9	1	5	3	4	2	8
1	3	2	4	9	8	6	7	5
8	2	5	6	1	9	7	4	3
3	7	6	2	8	4	9	5	1
9	4	1	3	7	5	2	8	6
6	1	7	5	3	2	8	9	4
2	8	3	9	4	1	5	6	7
5	9	4	8	6	7	1	3	2

Brain Buster

3	4	5	2	7	8	1	9	6
7	1	6	5	9	4	3	8	2
9	8	2	6	3	1	4	5	7
5	6	1	8	2	9	7	3	4
8	3	9	4	6	7	5	2	1
4	2	7	1	5	3	9	6	8
1	9	3	7	8	2	6	4	5
6	7	8	3	4	5	2	1	9
2	5	4	9	1	6	8	7	3

Sum Circle

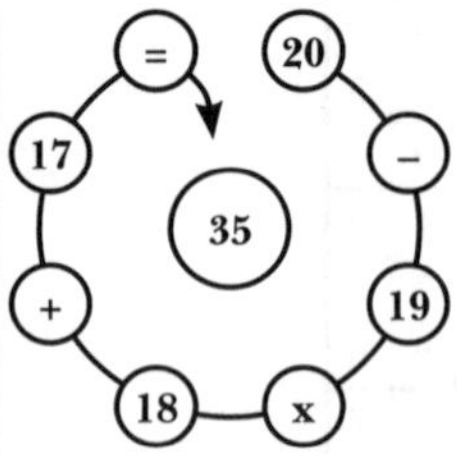

Page 86

1 Minute Number Crunch

Beginner
37 x 3 = 111, 111 – 3 = 108, 108 ÷ 4 = 27, 27 x 3 = 81, 81 ÷ 9 = 9, 9 + 26 = 35, 35 ÷ 5 = 7

Intermediate
237 + 732 = 969, 969 ÷ 3 x 2 = 646, 646 ÷ 2 = 323, 323 + 98 = 421, 421 x 3 = 1263, 1263 – 845 = 418, 418 x 2 = 836

Advanced
996 ÷ 4 = 249, 249 ÷ 3 x 2 = 166, 166 – 98 = 68, 68 ÷ 0.8 = 85, 85 ÷ 17 x 14 = 70, 70 ÷ 0.7 = 100, 100^3 = 1000000

High-Speed Crossword

F	R	A	N	C		A	L	L	U	D	E	S
L		C		U		S		E		I		O
O		C		R	E	H	E	A	R	S	A	L
T	H	I	R	D				D		T		I
S		D		S	A	T	I	S	F	I	E	D
A		E			R		N			N		
M	A	N	A	N	A		C	O	U	G	H	S
		T			B		A			U		W
R	E	P	O	S	S	E	S	S		I		I
A		R		N				T	Y	S	O	N
P	R	O	P	A	G	A	T	E		H		D
I		N		P		I		E		E		L
D	R	E	S	S	E	R		D	O	D	G	E

IQ Workout

42867 – Each number is the last three digits of the number above followed by the first two digits.

Codeword Conundrum

P	E	D	O	M	E	T	E	R		J	I	V	E	D
O		E		I		H		O		E		I		E
W	A	L	T	Z		A	Q	U	E	O	U	S		F
E		I		Z		N		X		P		I		E
R	E	C	H	E	C	K	S		F	A	L	T	E	R
		I		N				A		R				E
B	O	O	M		C	U	R	M	U	D	G	E	O	N
Y		U		F		N		E		Y		R		C
S	U	S	P	I	C	I	O	N	S		B	A	B	E
T				N		T				H		D		
A	P	P	E	A	L		S	T	R	A	T	I	F	Y
N		A		L		I		H		R		C		I
D		S	P	I	T	T	L	E		A	B	A	S	E
E		T		S		C		R		S		T		L
R	O	A	S	T		H	O	M	E	S	T	E	A	D

Tasty Teaser

4	8	6	2	1	7	5	3	9
9	1	5	3	6	8	4	2	7
3	7	2	9	5	4	8	1	6
1	5	4	7	9	3	2	6	8
8	9	3	1	2	6	7	4	5
2	6	7	4	8	5	1	9	3
6	2	1	5	7	9	3	8	4
7	3	8	6	4	1	9	5	2
5	4	9	8	3	2	6	7	1

Brain Buster

8	9	3	4	1	5	2	6	7
6	7	2	9	3	8	1	5	4
5	4	1	7	2	6	3	8	9
1	6	4	8	7	2	9	3	5
2	8	7	5	9	3	4	1	6
3	5	9	6	4	1	7	2	8
9	1	5	2	6	4	8	7	3
7	3	8	1	5	9	6	4	2
4	2	6	3	8	7	5	9	1

Spidoku

Page 87

Logi-Six

E	D	C	A	F	B
D	F	B	C	A	E
C	B	A	E	D	F
F	E	D	B	C	A
B	A	F	D	E	C
A	C	E	F	B	D

High-Speed Crossword

S	L	A	G		M	O	C	C	A	S	I	N
C		D		U		R		O		E		I
A	M	M	O	N	I	A		U	N	I	O	N
B		I		I		N		R		Z		E
B	A	T	O	N		G	E	T	O	U	T	
A				T		E		M		R		R
R	U	S	S	E	T		M	A	N	E	G	E
D		T		R		K		R				A
	C	A	V	E	R	N		T	I	D	E	S
C		G		S		E		I		R		S
A	N	G	S	T		E	M	A	N	A	T	E
M		E		E		L		L		M		S
P	A	R	A	D	I	S	E		B	A	Y	S

Wordsearch Workout

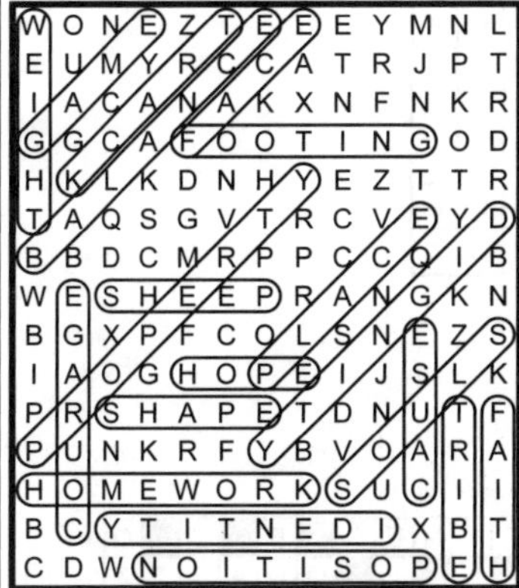

Double Fun Sudoku

Tasty Teaser

9	5	3	7	2	1	4	8	6
4	7	6	9	5	8	2	3	1
1	2	8	4	3	6	5	7	9
5	8	7	1	9	4	3	6	2
2	3	9	5	6	7	1	4	8
6	1	4	3	8	2	7	9	5
8	9	5	2	7	3	6	1	4
3	4	2	6	1	9	8	5	7
7	6	1	8	4	5	9	2	3

Brain Buster

2	5	8	7	6	1	3	9	4
9	3	6	4	2	5	8	1	7
1	4	7	9	3	8	2	5	6
8	9	2	5	4	6	7	3	1
7	1	4	8	9	3	5	6	2
3	6	5	2	1	7	9	4	8
6	2	1	3	7	9	4	8	5
5	7	9	1	8	4	6	2	3
4	8	3	6	5	2	1	7	9

Matchstick Magic

The matchsticks which have been moved are outlined.

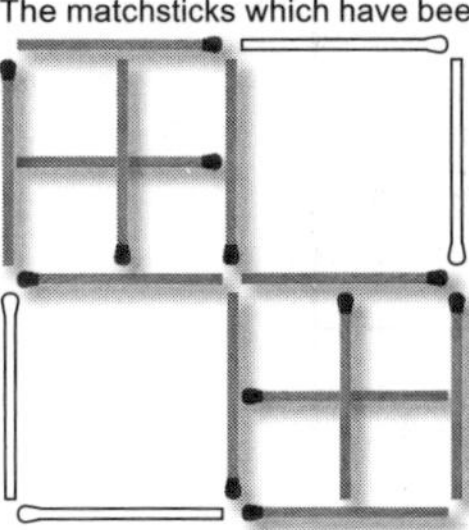

Brain Teaser

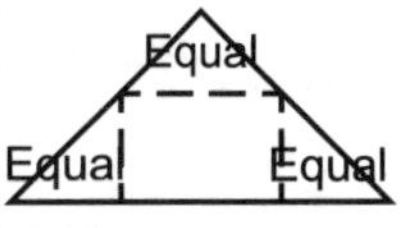

Simple as A, B, C

C	A	B	B	C	A
B	A	C	C	A	B
C	C	B	B	A	A
A	B	C	A	B	C
A	C	A	C	B	B
B	B	A	A	C	C

Page 88

Codeword Conundrum

D	I	S	J	O	I	N	E	D		B		C		O
E			U		N		L		Q	U	A	R	T	Z
F	L	E	X	I	T	I	M	E		S		Y		O
R			T		E			A	R	T	I	S	A	N
A	L	B	A	T	R	O	S	S		A		T		I
Y			P		C			E	A	R		A		S
	P	R	O	T	O	C	O	L		D	E	L	V	E
S			S		M		V		S		A			D
U	P	P	E	R		W	A	X	W	O	R	K	S	
B		A		O	B	I			E		N			I
T		N		U		S	O	V	E	R	E	I	G	N
I	N	T	E	N	S	E			T		S			S
T		I		D		R	E	S	I	S	T	E	N	T
L	O	N	E	L	Y		R		S		L			A
E		G		Y		L	A	C	H	R	Y	M	A	L

Double Fun Sudoku

Tasty Teaser

7	6	4	9	1	8	2	5	3
1	9	3	4	2	5	7	8	6
5	8	2	3	7	6	9	4	1
8	7	5	6	9	1	4	3	2
4	2	6	5	8	3	1	9	7
3	1	9	7	4	2	8	6	5
9	5	1	2	3	4	6	7	8
6	4	8	1	5	7	3	2	9
2	3	7	8	6	9	5	1	4

Brain Buster

1	2	5	9	7	6	8	4	3
7	8	6	3	1	4	9	2	5
4	3	9	5	2	8	6	1	7
8	1	3	7	4	5	2	6	9
6	9	2	1	8	3	5	7	4
5	7	4	2	6	9	1	3	8
2	6	8	4	5	7	3	9	1
3	5	7	6	9	1	4	8	2
9	4	1	8	3	2	7	5	6

Pyramid Plus

A=117, B=78, C=61, D=50, E=34, F=195, G=139, H=111, I=84, J=334, K=250, L=195, M=584, N=445, O=1029.

Work it Out

54 – From the top right corner, follow a clockwise path around and spiral towards the centre, deducting 3 from each number every time.

High-Speed Crossword

C	R	O	A	T	I	A		A	P	P	L	E
L		A		U		D		L		R		X
I	N	F	O	R	M	A	T	I	V	E		A
M				B		G				C		L
B	A	Y	O	U		I	M	P	R	I	N	T
E		O		L		O		E		P		
R	O	U	T	E	S		A	R	T	I	S	T
		N		N		E		C		C		R
S	I	G	H	T	E	D		A	R	E	T	E
C		S				G		P				L
A		T	R	A	D	I	T	I	O	N	A	L
N		E		N		E		T		E		I
S	T	R	A	Y		R	E	A	P	E	R	S

1 Minute Number Crunch

Beginner

51 ÷ 3 = 17, 17 + 22 = 39, 39 ÷ 3 = 13, 13 x 4 = 52, 52 ÷ 13 = 4, 4^2 = 16, 16 + 9 = 25

Intermediate

127 x 3 = 381, 381 + 69 = 450, 450 x 1.2 = 540, 540 ÷ 9 x 7 = 420, 420 + 21 = 441, square root of 441 = 21, 21 + 6 (21 ÷ 7 x 2) = 27

Advanced

256 ÷ 0.5 = 512, cube root of 512 = 8, 8 x 1.75 = 14, 14 x 2.5 = 35, 35^2 = 1225, 1225 ÷ 49 x 6 = 150, 68% of 150 = 102

Page 89

High-Speed Crossword

	G	L	O	B	A	L		C	H	E	S	T
K		A		O		E		A		A		H
A	S	T	R	O	N	A	U	T		G		E
L		H				D		S	H	E	E	R
E	L	S	E	W	H	E	R	E		R		M
I			S			N		Y				O
D	R	A	P	E	S		H	E	R	O	E	S
O				X		B			O			F
S		B		A	L	A	R	M	B	E	L	L
C	H	A	S	M		R				L		A
O		N		I	S	I	N	G	L	A	S	S
P		K		N		U		E		N		K
E	N	S	U	E		M	A	L	A	D	Y	

Summing Up

29	30	33	44	51	47
33	39	**47**	33	39	43
40	61	39	27	**22**	45
29	53	39	51	20	**42**
36	**15**	36	40	63	44
67	36	40	**39**	39	13

1 Minute Number Crunch

Beginner

47 + 61 = 108, 108 ÷ 6 = 18, 18 + 12 = 30, 30 x 6 = 180, 180 – 6 = 174, 174 ÷ 2 = 87, 87 ÷ 3 = 29

Intermediate

42 + 19 = 61, 61 x 9 = 549, 549 ÷ 3 x 2 = 366, 366 ÷ 3 = 122, 122 + 11 = 133, 133 ÷ 7 x 4 = 76, 76 x 4 = 304

Advanced

62 ÷ 0.5 = 124, 124 x 8 = 992, 992 ÷ 16 x 11 = 682, 682 x 3 = 2046, 2046 ÷ 6 x 5 = 1705, 80% of 1705 = 1364, 1364 x 0.25 = 341

Wordsearch Workout

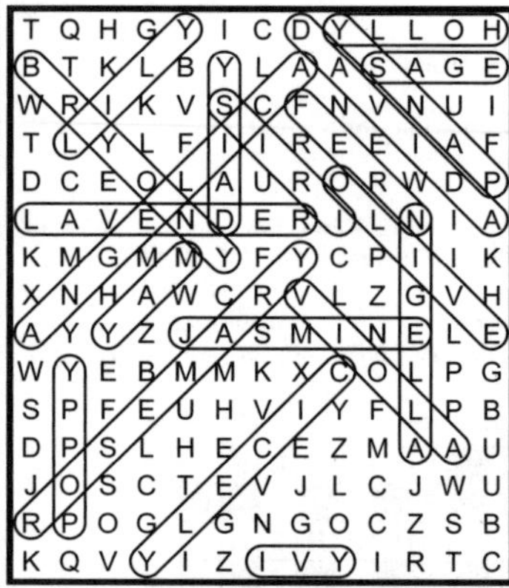

Double Fun Sudoku

Tasty Teaser

7	9	6	2	1	5	8	4	3
4	2	3	8	9	7	1	5	6
1	8	5	4	6	3	2	7	9
9	4	7	1	3	6	5	8	2
8	3	1	9	5	2	7	6	4
5	6	2	7	8	4	3	9	1
2	1	9	5	4	8	6	3	7
3	7	8	6	2	9	4	1	5
6	5	4	3	7	1	9	2	8

Brain Buster

2	4	8	1	6	7	9	3	5
7	3	9	5	4	8	2	1	6
1	5	6	9	2	3	7	8	4
5	7	4	8	1	2	6	9	3
6	9	3	7	5	4	1	2	8
8	1	2	3	9	6	5	4	7
9	6	7	4	3	1	8	5	2
3	8	1	2	7	5	4	6	9
4	2	5	6	8	9	3	7	1

Whatever Next?

64 – The numbers in the outer points of the star are the cubes of the adjacent numbers in the central hexagon.

Brain Teaser

(21 x 14) – 3 – 3 = 288

Page 90

Mind Over Matter

The value of the letter in the central square is one quarter of the sum total of the value of the letters in the outer four squares. Thus the missing value is 12, so the missing letter is L.

Double Fun Sudoku

Tasty Teaser

6	5	4	7	1	8	2	9	3
8	7	2	3	6	9	5	1	4
1	3	9	5	4	2	6	7	8
7	1	5	2	3	4	9	8	6
9	6	3	1	8	7	4	2	5
2	4	8	9	5	6	7	3	1
3	8	7	6	2	5	1	4	9
5	9	1	4	7	3	8	6	2
4	2	6	8	9	1	3	5	7

Brain Buster

9	7	4	6	3	2	5	8	1
3	6	1	8	5	4	9	2	7
2	5	8	9	1	7	4	3	6
8	3	6	4	7	5	2	1	9
7	9	5	2	8	1	3	6	4
1	4	2	3	6	9	7	5	8
5	1	3	7	9	6	8	4	2
4	8	7	1	2	3	6	9	5
6	2	9	5	4	8	1	7	3

Codeword Conundrum

E		M		A	U	T	H	O	R	I	T	I	E	S
D	W	A	R	F		R			U		A		N	
I		W		F	R	A	N	K	F	U	R	T	E	R
F	A	K	I	R		C			F		S		M	
I		I		O		E	M	P	I	R	I	C	A	L
C		S	A	N	K		A		A			O		E
A	S	H		T			R		N		Q	U	I	N
T		N		S	O	F	T	E	S	T		N		G
I	B	E	X		U		I			R		T	U	T
O		S			T		N		J	A	P	E		H
N	O	S	T	A	L	G	I	A		N		N		E
	U		W		Y			M		S	P	A	W	N
I	N	D	I	V	I	D	U	A	T	E		N		I
	C		R		N			Z		P	E	C	A	N
B	E	L	L	I	G	E	R	E	N	T		E		G

Futoshiki

4	1	2 <	3	5
5 >	2	1	4	3
1	4 >	3	5	2
2	3	5 >	1	4
3	5	4	2	1

High-Speed Crossword

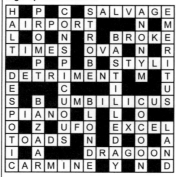

H		P		C		S	A	L	V	A	G	E
A	I	R	P	O	R	T				N		M
L		O		N		R		B	R	O	K	E
T	I	M	E	S		O	V	A		N		R
		P		P		B		S	T	Y	L	I
D	E	T	R	I	M	E	N	T		M		T
E				C				I				U
S		B		U	M	B	I	L	I	C	U	S
P	I	A	N	O		L		L		O		
O		Z		U	F	O		E	X	C	E	L
T	O	A	D	S		N		D		O		A
I		A				D	R	A	G	O	O	N
C	A	R	M	I	N	E		Y		N		D

1 Minute Number Crunch

Beginner

91 + 25 = 116, 116 ÷ 2 = 58, 58 ÷ 2 = 29, 29 + 17 = 46, 46 ÷ 2 = 23, 23 + 17 = 40, 25% of 40 = 10

Intermediate

47 x 3 = 141, 141 – 75 = 66, 66 x 2 = 132, 132 ÷ 6 x 5 = 110, 110 x 0.8 = 88, 88 ÷ 4 x 3 = 66, 66 x 4 = 264

Advanced

39^2 = 1521, 1521 ÷ 9 x 7 = 1183, 1183 ÷ 7 x 5 = 845, 845 x 7 = 5915, 5915 – 4738 = 1177, 1177 x 4 = 4708, 4708 + 9929 = 14637

Page 91

Domino Placement

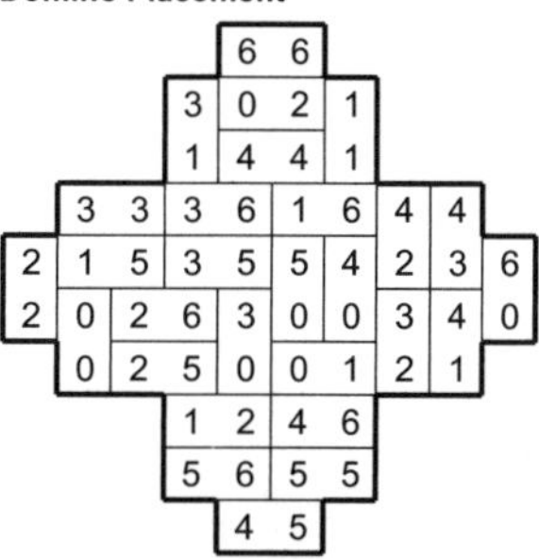

High-Speed Crossword

P	R	O	G	N	O	S	T	I	C	A	T	E
E			E		I		I			R		N
L	A	C	E		L		P	R	E	C	I	S
L			S	T	E	P	S			H		I
E	A	S	E		D		T	O	W	I	N	G
T		T					E			T		N
	W	A	G	E	S		R	A	C	E	R	
I		I			U					C		S
C	I	R	R	U	S		S		S	T	O	W
O		C			P	R	O	W	L			E
N	U	A	N	C	E		D		A	V	E	R
I		S			N		O		I			V
C	R	E	M	E	D	E	M	E	N	T	H	E

IQ Workout

B

A is a mirror image of C, but with the mouths turned in opposite directions;

D is a mirror image of E, but with the mouths turned in opposite directions;

B has no match.

Wordwheel

The nine-letter word is: PRESUMING

Wordsearch Workout

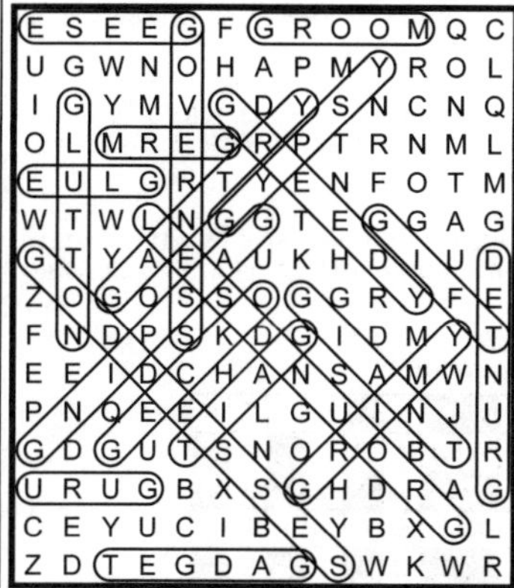

Double Fun Sudoku

Tasty Teaser

1	6	4	9	5	7	8	3	2
3	7	9	1	8	2	5	6	4
2	8	5	4	6	3	1	7	9
8	4	2	7	9	5	3	1	6
5	9	7	3	1	6	2	4	8
6	1	3	8	2	4	7	9	5
7	5	1	2	4	9	6	8	3
9	2	8	6	3	1	4	5	7
4	3	6	5	7	8	9	2	1

Brain Buster

8	7	5	9	2	1	3	6	4
1	6	4	8	3	7	2	5	9
3	9	2	4	6	5	1	8	7
7	3	6	1	5	9	4	2	8
5	2	1	3	8	4	9	7	6
9	4	8	6	7	2	5	3	1
4	8	7	5	9	3	6	1	2
6	5	9	2	1	8	7	4	3
2	1	3	7	4	6	8	9	5

Sum Circle

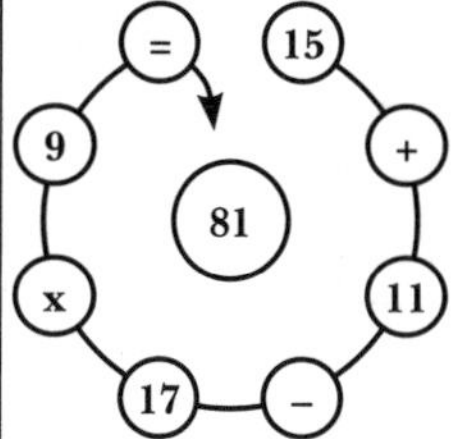

Page 92

1 Minute Number Crunch

Beginner
189 – 37 = 152, 152 ÷ 2 = 76, 76 + 6 = 82, 82 ÷ 2 = 41, 41 + 22 = 63, 63 ÷ 9 x 2 = 14, 14 x 3 = 42

Intermediate
17^2 = 289, 289 x 2 = 578, 578 + 125 = 703, 703 x 3 = 2109, 2109 – 1617 = 492, 492 + 164 (492 ÷ 3) = 656, 656 – 497 = 159

Advanced
234 ÷ 13 x 10 = 180, 180 – 169 (square of 13) = 11, 11^2 = 121, 121 + 683 = 804, 804 ÷ 0.4 = 2010, 2010 ÷ 67 x 2 = 60, 60 ÷ 1.25 = 48

High-Speed Crossword

S	I	L	O	S	■	■	L	■	S	O	C	K
A		E		C	A	N	A	P	E	■	A	■
L	O	N	E	R	■	■	C	■	E	■	N	■
T		G	■	E	X	T	R	E	M	I	T	Y
E	F	T	■	A	■	■	O	■	I	■	E	■
D		H	■	M	E	S	S	E	N	G	E	R
	F		D	■	N	■	S	■	G	■	N	■
F	O	R	E	I	G	N	E	R	■	C	■	S
	R		P	■	I	■	■	E	■	A	T	E
A	W	A	R	E	N	E	S	S	■	N	■	R
■	A	■	E	■	E	■	■	I	D	I	O	M
■	R	■	S	I	E	V	E	S	■	N	■	O
I	D	E	S	■	R	■	■	T	I	E	I	N

IQ Workout

41

46

Start top left and move along the top row, then back along the second etc, in the sequence +2, –1, +3, etc.

Codeword Conundrum

C	O	A	X	E	D	■	S	W	I	F	T	E	S	T
O		T		X	■	■	■	A	■	O	■	D	■	R
M	A	L	A	I	S	E	■	P	■	R	A	I	S	E
M		A	■	L	■	V	Y	I	N	G	■	F	■	N
A	U	S	T	E	R	E	■	T	■	I	L	I	A	C
N	■	■	O	■	E	N	S	I	G	N	■	C	■	H
D	E	G	R	E	E	■	Q	■	O	G	R	E	S	■
O	■	■	S	■	K	N	U	R	L	■	E	■	■	T
	S	C	O	P	E	■	I	■	D	E	A	R	L	Y
A		U	■	E	D	I	B	L	E	■	L	■	■	P
L	A	S	E	R	■	N	■	A	N	E	M	O	N	E
K		H	■	J	E	L	L	Y	■	N	■	Z	■	C
A	D	I	E	U	■	A	■	S	A	R	C	O	M	A
L		O	■	R	■	N	■	■	■	O	■	N	■	S
I	N	N	U	E	N	D	O	■	F	L	U	E	N	T

Tasty Teaser

1	9	7	8	4	2	5	3	6
8	4	3	6	5	9	2	1	7
2	5	6	7	1	3	8	4	9
3	6	5	9	8	1	4	7	2
4	2	9	3	7	5	6	8	1
7	8	1	4	2	6	3	9	5
9	7	4	2	6	8	1	5	3
6	1	8	5	3	7	9	2	4
5	3	2	1	9	4	7	6	8

Brain Buster

5	1	7	9	8	3	2	4	6
8	2	9	5	6	4	3	1	7
3	4	6	7	1	2	5	9	8
4	6	5	3	2	7	9	8	1
7	3	2	1	9	8	6	5	4
1	9	8	6	4	5	7	2	3
9	8	1	2	7	6	4	3	5
2	7	3	4	5	1	8	6	9
6	5	4	8	3	9	1	7	2

Spidoku

Page 93

Logi-Six

C	D	E	B	A	F
D	F	B	C	E	A
F	C	A	E	D	B
A	B	D	F	C	E
E	A	F	D	B	C
B	E	C	A	F	D

High-Speed Crossword

S	E	R	V	E	■	S	N	O	W	C	A	P
I	■	E	■	N	■	E	■	W	■	O	■	L
L	A	P	■	C	O	L	O	N	N	A	D	E
K	■	R	■	O	■	F	■	■	■	T	■	A
S	T	E	A	M	■	G	Y	P	S	I	E	S
■	■	S	■	P	■	O	■	Y	■	■	■	E
V	E	S	T	A	L	V	I	R	G	I	N	S
E	■	■	■	S	■	E	■	O	■	G	■	■
T	R	O	U	S	E	R	■	M	O	N	K	S
E	■	I	■	■	■	N	■	A	■	O	■	H
R	E	N	D	I	T	I	O	N	■	B	A	R
A	■	K	■	R	■	N	■	I	■	L	■	E
N	E	S	T	E	G	G	■	A	H	E	A	D

Wordsearch Workout

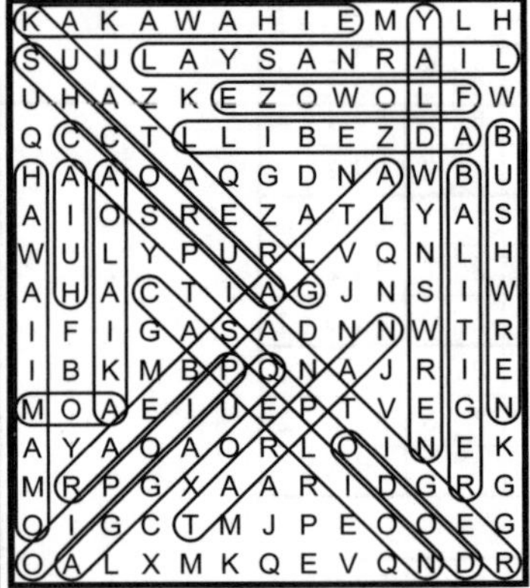

Double Fun Sudoku

Tasty Teaser

4	1	8	6	2	3	9	7	5
6	9	7	5	1	4	8	2	3
2	5	3	7	8	9	6	4	1
7	3	9	8	6	2	5	1	4
1	4	6	3	5	7	2	8	9
8	2	5	9	4	1	3	6	7
3	8	2	1	7	5	4	9	6
5	6	1	4	9	8	7	3	2
9	7	4	2	3	6	1	5	8

Brain Buster

5	9	4	7	8	3	2	1	6
7	3	2	1	9	6	8	4	5
8	6	1	4	2	5	9	7	3
9	2	3	5	4	8	7	6	1
4	7	6	3	1	2	5	8	9
1	8	5	6	7	9	3	2	4
2	5	9	8	6	1	4	3	7
3	1	7	2	5	4	6	9	8
6	4	8	9	3	7	1	5	2

Matchstick Magic

The matchsticks which have been moved are outlined.

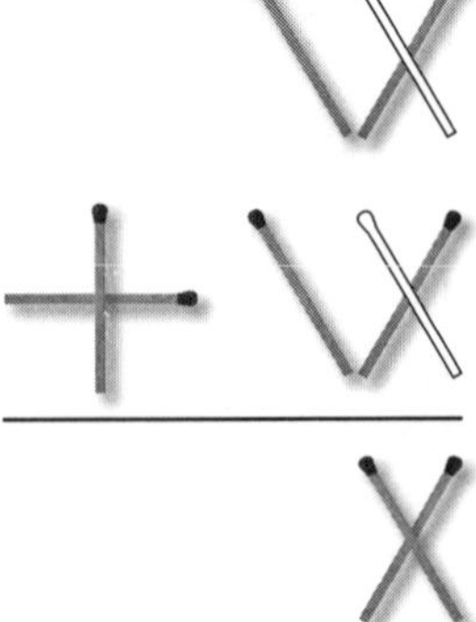

Brain Teaser

Black

Domino Placement

					6	4			
				6	6	1	0		
				5	5	6	6		
	5	6	3	4	3	1	2	1	
4	5	2	5	1	1	4	0	5	3
0	0	4	4	1	2	4	5	3	1
	3	3	0	6	2	6	1	2	
				5	2	2	4		
				3	3	2	0		
					0	0			

Page 94

Codeword Conundrum

W	A	T	E	R		S	Q	U	E	A	M	I	S	H
I		U		E		K		N		F				O
S	U	B	J	A	C	E	N	T		R	I	V	E	T
T		E		G		W		R		A		A		E
F	I	R	M	E	R		Z	O	D	I	A	C	A	L
U				N		I		U		D		U		
L	I	G	H	T		N	I	B	S		T	O	S	S
L		R		S		E		L		P		U		E
Y	O	Y	O		A	X	L	E		A	R	S	O	N
		P		E		O		D		G				T
E	P	H	E	M	E	R	A		W	A	P	I	T	I
T		O		B		A		T		N		N		M
H	E	N	N	A		B	A	R	R	I	C	A	D	E
I				L		L		O		S		P		N
C	R	E	A	M	I	E	S	T		M	O	T	E	T

Double Fun Sudoku

Tasty Teaser

2	7	6	9	8	4	1	3	5
1	8	4	5	6	3	9	2	7
9	5	3	1	2	7	8	6	4
5	2	7	8	3	6	4	9	1
3	1	8	2	4	9	7	5	6
6	4	9	7	1	5	3	8	2
7	3	1	6	9	2	5	4	8
8	9	2	4	5	1	6	7	3
4	6	5	3	7	8	2	1	9

Brain Buster

3	9	6	4	2	5	8	1	7
4	7	5	6	8	1	2	9	3
8	2	1	7	3	9	5	4	6
2	1	4	5	6	8	3	7	9
9	3	7	1	4	2	6	5	8
6	5	8	9	7	3	4	2	1
1	6	9	3	5	4	7	8	2
5	8	3	2	1	7	9	6	4
7	4	2	8	9	6	1	3	5

Pyramid Plus

A=76, B=66, C=103, D=144, E=92, F=142, G=169, H=247, I=236, J=311, K=416, L=483, M=727, N=899, O=1626.

Work it Out

5 – Any 2x2 block of four squares contains numbers which total 40, thus:

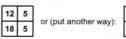

12	5
18	5

or (put another way):

5	22
9	4

High-Speed Crossword

1 Minute Number Crunch

Beginner
27 + 24 = 51, 51 ÷ 3 = 17, 17 + 9 = 26, 50% of 26 = 13, 13 – 4 = 9, 9 x 8 = 72, 72 – 23 = 49

Intermediate
69 x 2 = 138, 138 ÷ 3 x 2 = 92, 92 ÷ 4 = 23, 23 + 137 = 160, 160 ÷ 5 x 2 = 64, square root of 64 = 8, cube root of 8 = 2

Advanced
588 x 2 = 1176, 1176 ÷ 8 x 5 = 735, 735 ÷ 15 x 11 = 539, 539 x 2 = 1078, 1078 – 929 = 149, 149 x 7 = 1043, 1043 + 528 = 1571

Page 95

High-Speed Crossword

T	E	S	T	P	I	L	O	T		P	A	T
H		L		A				R		R		A
A	B	O	U	N	D		F	A	M	O	U	S
W		G		C		A		W		P		T
	C	A	V	A		C	O	L	L	E	G	E
S		N		K	I	E	V			R		F
A			B	E	T		E	M	S			U
T		V			C	A	R	E		R		L
A	N	A	R	C	H	Y		S	E	E	D	
N		L		O		E		S		M		L
I	C	I	C	L	E		C	A	L	I	C	O
S		S		I				G		S		S
T	E	E		C	O	N	S	E	N	S	U	S

IQ Workout

Clocks alternately lose 85 minutes and gain 143 minutes each time.

1 Minute Number Crunch

Beginner
25 + 93 = 118, 118 ÷ 2 = 59, 59 + 7 = 66, 66 ÷ 11 x 2 = 12, 12 ÷ 3 = 4, 4 + 28 = 32, 32 x 4 = 128

Intermediate
452 ÷ 4 = 113, 113 + 169 = 282, 282 x 1.5 = 423, 423 ÷ 9 x 7 = 329, 329 x 2 = 658, 658 – 479 = 179, 179 x 3 = 537

Advanced
129 ÷ 3 x 2 = 86, 86 x 13 = 1118, 1118 x 2 = 2236, 2236 – 559 (25% of 2236) = 1677, 1677 – 949 = 728, 728 ÷ 14 x 5 = 260, 260 – 104 (260 ÷ 5 x 2) = 156

Wordsearch Workout

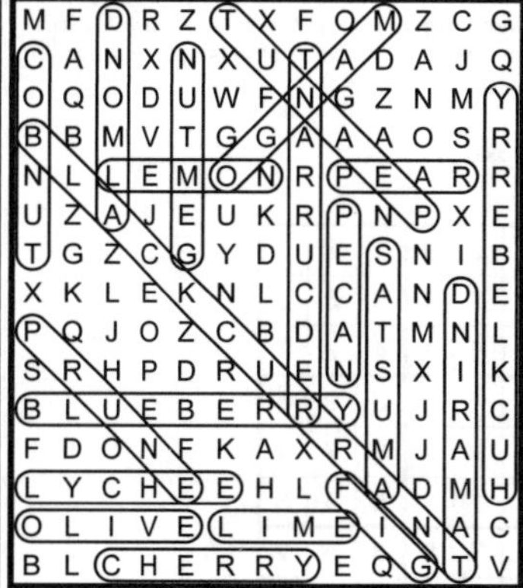

Double Fun Sudoku

Tasty Teaser

7	6	8	3	5	1	4	9	2
4	9	3	7	6	2	1	5	8
2	5	1	4	9	8	7	6	3
8	3	4	5	1	9	2	7	6
5	7	9	2	3	6	8	1	4
1	2	6	8	4	7	5	3	9
6	1	2	9	8	5	3	4	7
3	8	5	6	7	4	9	2	1
9	4	7	1	2	3	6	8	5

Brain Buster

5	6	7	2	4	1	8	3	9
1	2	3	6	8	9	4	5	7
8	9	4	3	5	7	2	1	6
3	4	9	8	7	5	6	2	1
6	8	1	4	2	3	7	9	5
2	7	5	9	1	6	3	4	8
7	3	6	1	9	4	5	8	2
4	1	2	5	6	8	9	7	3
9	5	8	7	3	2	1	6	4

Whatever Next?

H – Assign a number to each letter according to its place in the alphabet, then multiply the numbers in opposite points to give the central number.

Brain Teaser

B 27 – Starting top left, the letters progress through the alphabet, omitting two letters each time. The numbers represent the sum of the positions in the alphabet of the missing letters. When the end of the alphabet is reached return to A as if the letters were written in a circle.

Page 96

Mind Over Matter

The value of the letter in the top right is deducted from that in the top left, and the value of the letter in the bottom right is deducted from that in the bottom left, then the result of the bottom sum is taken from that of the top to give the value in the central square. Thus the missing value is 4, so the missing letter is D.

Double Fun Sudoku

Tasty Teaser

4	9	6	7	2	3	1	8	5
2	7	1	5	8	4	9	6	3
8	3	5	9	6	1	4	2	7
7	1	8	3	4	5	2	9	6
5	6	4	2	9	8	3	7	1
3	2	9	6	1	7	5	4	8
6	4	3	1	7	9	8	5	2
9	5	2	8	3	6	7	1	4
1	8	7	4	5	2	6	3	9

Brain Buster

4	8	3	1	9	2	7	6	5
5	2	6	8	7	3	4	9	1
7	9	1	4	5	6	3	8	2
6	5	4	9	2	7	1	3	8
9	3	7	5	8	1	6	2	4
2	1	8	3	6	4	9	5	7
1	6	2	7	3	8	5	4	9
3	4	9	2	1	5	8	7	6
8	7	5	6	4	9	2	1	3

Codeword Conundrum

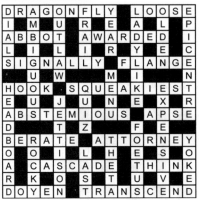

D	R	A	G	O	N	F	L	Y		L	O	O	S	E
I		M		U		R		E		A		L		P
A	B	B	O	T		A	W	A	R	D	E	D		I
L		I		L		I		R		Y		E		C
S	I	G	N	A	L	L	Y		F	L	A	N	G	E
		U		W				M		I				N
H	O	O	K		S	Q	U	E	A	K	I	E	S	T
E		U		J		U		N		E		X		R
A	B	S	T	E	M	I	O	U	S		A	P	S	E
D				T		Z				F		E		
B	E	R	A	T	E		A	T	T	O	R	N	E	Y
O		O		I		L		H		E		S		O
A		C	A	S	C	A	D	E		T	H	I	N	K
R		K		O		S		T		U		V		E
D	O	Y	E	N		T	R	A	N	S	C	E	N	D

Futoshiki

1	2	3	5	4
2	1	4	3	5
4	5	1	2	3
3	4	5	1	2
5	3	2	4	1

High-Speed Crossword

C	H	O	R	U	S		C	H	A	N	G	E
	U		E		O		O		D		O	
G	R	A	F		S	P	A	C	E	B	A	R
	R		L		O		L		P			
G	I	V	E	N		W	E	T	T	E	S	T
	C		C		G		S				T	
M	A	N	T	L	E		C	A	S	U	A	L
	N				N		E		M		L	
H	E	A	R	T	E	N		B	I	Z	E	T
			A		T		B		T		M	
P	O	S	I	T	I	V	E		T	B	A	R
	U		S		C		E		E		T	
A	T	H	E	N	S		S	U	N	S	E	T

1 Minute Number Crunch

Beginner

96 – 19 = 77, 77 ÷ 7 = 11, 11^2 = 121, 121 + 14 = 135, 135 ÷ 5 = 27, 27 ÷ 9 = 3, 3 x 16 = 48

Intermediate

17 + 18 = 35, 35 ÷ 7 x 3 = 15, 300% of 15 = 45, 45 ÷ 9 x 5 = 25, 25 x 13 = 325, 120% of 325 = 390, 390 – 39 (10% of 390) = 351

Advanced

387 ÷ 9 x 5 = 215, 215 ÷ 5 x 4 = 172, 172 – 129 (172 ÷ 4 x 3) = 43, 43 x 8 = 344, 344 + 301 (344 ÷ 8 x 7) = 645, 645 ÷ 5 x 3 = 387, 387 ÷ 9 x 7 = 301

ARCTURUS
This edition published in 2013 by Arcturus Publishing Limited
26/27 Bickels Yard, 151–153 Bermondsey Street,
London SE1 3HA

ISBN: 978-1-78212-126-8
AD002715EN

Printed in Malaysia